The Innate Mind

The Innate Mind

Structure and Contents

Edited by
Peter Carruthers
Stephen Laurence
Stephen Stich

UNIVERSITY PRESS
2005

OXFORD
UNIVERSITY PRESS

Oxford University Press, Inc., publishes works that further
Oxford University's objective of excellence
in research, scholarship, and education.

Oxford   New York
Auckland   Cape Town   Dar es Salaam   Hong Kong   Karachi
Kuala Lumpur   Madrid   Melbourne   Mexico City   Nairobi
New Delhi   Shanghai   Taipei   Toronto

With offices in
Argentina   Austria   Brazil   Chile   Czech Republic   France   Greece
Guatemala   Hungary   Italy   Japan   Poland   Portugal   Singapore
South Korea   Switzerland   Thailand   Turkey   Ukraine   Vietnam

Copyright © 2005 by Oxford University Press, Inc.

Published by Oxford University Press, Inc.
198 Madison Avenue, New York, New York 10016
www.oup.com

Oxford is a registered trademark of Oxford University Press

All rights reserved. No part of this publication may be reproduced,
stored in a retrieval system, or transmitted, in any form or by any means,
electronic, mechanical, photocopying, recording, or otherwise,
without the prior permission of Oxford University Press.

Library of Congress Cataloging-in-Publication Data

The innate mind : structure and contents / edited by
Peter Carruthers, Stephen Laurence, Stephen Stich.
p. cm.
Includes bibliographical references and index.
ISBN-13 978-0-19-517967-5; 978-0-19-517999-6 (pbk.)
ISBN 0-19-517967-6; ISBN 0-19-517999-4 (pbk.)
1. Cognitive science.   2. Philosophy of mind.   3. Nativism (Psychology)
I. Carruthers, Peter, 1952–   II. Laurence, Stephen.   III. Stich, Stephen P.
BD418.3.I56 2005
153—dc22   2004056813

2 4 6 8 9 7 5 3 1
Printed in the United States of America
on acid-free paper

Preface

This is the first book of a projected three volumes to be born out of the three-year interdisciplinary *Innateness and the Structure of the Mind* project. The project is primarily funded by a grant from the UK's Arts and Humanities Research Board, awarded to Stephen Laurence. The overall aim of the project is to undertake a comprehensive assessment of where nativist theorizing stands now and determine what directions future research should take. Accordingly we have tried to bring together many of the top researchers across the cognitive sciences working within a broadly nativist perspective. We hope that these volumes will illustrate the scope and power of contemporary nativism, and help point the way for future research in cognitive science. This volume discusses the likely overall architecture and some of the probable features of the innate human mind. Subsequent volumes will examine the interactions between innate minds and culture, and will consider a range of foundational issues concerning innateness. They will also attempt to sketch some future directions for nativist inspired research in cognitive science. (For further information, see the project's website at: http://www.shef.ac.uk/~phil/AHRB-Project).

The topic of nativism lends itself well to cross-disclipinary research—indeed, many of the significant questions in this area can only be adequately addressed through interdisciplinary research. Accordingly, the project has brought together a distinguished international team of more than 75 researchers from across the cognitive sciences to examine a range of themes and issues from a broadly nativist perspective. Participants were brought together in a series of small workshops over the course of a year to exchange ideas and try out new lines of thought, before presenting their draft volume papers at a concluding public conference. In the 2001–2 academic year four workshops were held, one in New Jersey, one in Maryland, and two in Sheffield, with the concluding conference being held in Sheffield in July 2002.

The editors have selected the best, most focused papers from the concluding conference, as well as commissioning some other chapters from those scientists and scholars whose relevant research became known to us in the course of the project. These chapters were displayed in draft on a closed website for the other participants to read and take account of, and were rewritten in the light of feedback provided by the editors and the referees. The result, we believe, is an integrated volume of cutting-edge essays, pushing forward the boundaries of nativist inspired research in cognitive science.

Many people have helped to make this a better volume. We would like to thank everyone who attended the workshops and conference for their contributions through comments and discussions. We would especially like to express our gratitude to all those who presented a talk or a commentary at the conference or one of the workshops, but who for a variety of reasons don't have a chapter in the present volume (some of this work will be included in later volumes). In this regard we would like to thank: Paul Bloom, Robert Boyd, Stanislas Dehaene, Randy Gallistel, Rochel Gelman, Lila Gleitman, Juan-Carlos Gomez, Marc Hauser, Joe Henrich, Norbert Hornstein, David Lightfoot, Richard Nisbett, David Papineau, Steven Pinker, Denis Walsh, and Fei Xu. Their efforts surely helped to make the project a success.

We also acknowledge the generous funding for this project provided by the UK's Arts and Humanities Research Board, as well as financial support from the Hang Seng Centre for Cognitive Studies (founded in 1992 through the generosity and far-sightedness of Sir Q. W. Lee), the Evolution and Higher Cognition Research Group at Rutgers, and the Cognitive Studies Group at Maryland. Thanks to Simon Fitzpatrick for constructing the index. Finally, we should like to thank Tom Simpson, the project's Research Associate, for all his assistance—particularly in helping to ensure that the Sheffield workshops and the end of the year conference ran smoothly, and for his work in preparing the volume for press.

Contents

List of Contributors   xi

1   Introduction: Nativism Past and Present   3
     Tom Simpson, Peter Carruthers, Stephen Laurence, and Stephen Stich

PART ONE   ARCHITECTURE

2   What Developmental Biology Can Tell Us about Innateness   23
     Gary F. Marcus

3   Innateness and (Bayesian) Visual Perception: Reconciling Nativism and Development   34
     Brian J. Scholl

4   Modularity and Relevance: How Can a Massively Modular Mind Be Flexible and Context-Sensitive?   53
     Dan Sperber

5   Distinctively Human Thinking: Modular Precursors and Components   69
     Peter Carruthers

6   Language and the Development of Spatial Reasoning   89
     Anna Shusterman and Elizabeth Spelke

7   The Complexity of Cognition: Tractability Arguments for Massive Modularity   107
     Richard Samuels

8 Toward a Reasonable Nativism   122
   Tom Simpson

PART TWO   LANGUAGE AND CONCEPTS

9 Strong versus Weak Adaptationism in Cognition and Language   141
   Scott Atran

10 The Innate Endowment for Language: Underspecified
   or Overspecified?   156
   Mark C. Baker

11 Brass Tacks in Linguistic Theory: Innate Grammatical Principles   175
   Stephen Crain, Andrea Gualmini, and Paul Pietroski

12 Two Insights about Naming in the Preschool Child   198
   Susan A. Gelman

13 Number and Natural Language   216
   Stephen Laurence and Eric Margolis

PART THREE   THEORY OF MIND

14 Parent-Offspring Conflict and the Development of
   Social Understanding   239
   Daniel J. Povinelli, Christopher G. Prince, and Todd M. Preuss

15 Reasoning about Intentionality in Preverbal Infants   254
   Susan C. Johnson

16 What Neurodevelopmental Disorders Can Reveal about Cognitive
   Architecture: The Example of Theory of Mind   272
   Helen Tager-Flusberg

PART FOUR   MOTIVATION

17 The Plausibility of Adaptations for Homicide   291
   Joshua D. Duntley and David M. Buss

18 Resolving the Debate on Innate Ideas: Learnability Constraints and the
   Evolved Interpenetration of Motivational and Conceptual Functions   305
   John Tooby, Leda Cosmides, and H. Clark Barrett

19 Cognitive Neuroscience and the Structure of the Moral Mind   338
   Joshua Greene

20 Innateness and Moral Psychology   353
    Shaun Nichols

References   371

Index   417

List of Contributors

Scott Atran, Centre National de la Recherche Scientifique, Paris, and Department of Psychology, University of Michigan

Mark C. Baker, Department of Linguistics, Rutgers University

Clark Barrett, Department of Anthropology, University of California, Los Angeles

David M. Buss, Department of Psychology, University of Texas at Austin

Peter Carruthers, Department of Philosophy, University of Maryland

Leda Cosmides, Department of Psychology, University of California, Santa Barbara

Stephen Crain, Macquarie Center for Cognitive Science, Macquarie University

Joshua D. Duntley, Department of Psychology, University of Texas, Austin

Susan A. Gelman, Department of Psychology, University of Michigan

Joshua Greene, Department of Psychology, Princeton University

Andrea Gualmini, Department of Linguistics, University of Maryland

Susan C. Johnson, Department of Psychology, Stanford University

Stephen Laurence, Department of Philosophy, University of Sheffield

Gary F. Marcus, Department of Psychology, New York University

Eric Margolis, Department of Philosophy, Rice University

Shaun Nichols, Department of Philosophy, College of Charlston

Paul Pietroski, Departments of Linguistics and Philosophy, University of Maryland

Daniel J. Povinelli, New Iberia Research Center, University of Louisiana, Lafayette

Todd M. Preuss, New Iberia Research Center, University of Louisiana, Lafayette

Christopher G. Prince, Department of Psychology, University of Minnesota, Duluth

Richard Samuels, Department of Philosophy, King's College, London

Brian J. Scholl, Department of Psychology, Yale University

Anna Shusterman, Department of Psychology, Harvard University

Tom Simpson, Department of Philosophy, University of Sheffield

Elizabeth Spelke, Department of Psychology, Harvard University

Dan Sperber, Centre National de la Recherche Scientifique, Paris

Stephen Stich, Department of Philosophy, Rutgers University

Helen Tager-Flusberg, Department of Psychology, Boston University

John Tooby, Department of Anthropology, University of California, Santa Barbara

The Innate Mind

TOM SIMPSON, PETER CARRUTHERS,
STEPHEN LAURENCE, & STEPHEN STICH

Introduction
Nativism Past and Present

Nativist theorizing is thriving. Present in the works of Plato, although much neglected since, nativism is once more at the forefront of contemporary developmental and cognitive theory. This resurgence owes much to the pioneering arguments of Noam Chomsky, which provided a much-needed counterbalance to the excesses of empiricism, and stimulated a huge amount of productive work in linguistics and cognitive psychology over the past half century. But nativist theorizing has also received a powerful impetus from work in genetics and evolutionary biology, as biological thinking has begun to permeate psychology and philosophy of mind. Consequently, a broad range of research across the cognitive sciences over the past 20 years or more has been inspired by nativist theorizing. There have also been some revolutionary results.

This book is the first of three volumes that present some of these results and discuss their implications. These volumes will draw together research and arguments from philosophers, psychologists, linguists, anthropologists, primatologists, and other cognitive scientists to provide an integrated and detailed picture of where nativist theory currently stands and of what its future holds. Taken together, these volumes present a detailed and wide-ranging study of the current state and the possible future development of twenty-first-century nativism. In so doing, they also provide unparalleled insight into what we, as humans, are.

This first volume focuses on the fundamental architecture of the mind, and on some of its innate contents. The essays contained herein investigate such questions as: What capacities, processes, representations, biases, and connections are innate? What role do these innate elements play in the development of our mature cognitive capacities? Which of these elements are shared with other members of the animal kingdom? What, in short, is the structure of the innate mind? A summary of these investigations, and of the answers that they provide, can be found in the final section of this introduction. First, however, we will briefly review some of the recent (and not so recent) debates in philosophy, psychology, anthropology, evolutionary theory, and other cognitive sciences that provide a background for the topics with which this volume is concerned.

1 A Brief History of Nativism

Philosophical consideration of the innate structure of the mind has a long and complex history.[1] Plato was one of the earliest—and most extreme—nativists. In the *Phaedo* and the *Meno* Plato argued that, since we have knowledge and abilities for which experience is insufficient, these things must not have been taught to us but rather must have been present in us at birth. Plato's extreme, and highly implausible, form of nativism essentially took *all* knowledge to be innate. For Plato all genuine knowledge is something that we "recollect" from what we already know.

Philosophers of the Enlightenment also examined the questions that Plato had addressed. This time, however, discussion concerned not only why certain things may be innate and what in particular these things may be but also what we should take the very term "innate" to mean. In his *Essay Concerning Human Understanding* John Locke argued that there can be "no innate principles in the mind" because, among other things, no useful sense can be given to the notion of innateness itself. Locke argued that if innateness literally means "in the mind at birth," then innate principles must play *from birth* the same kinds of role that such principles play in our minds later in life. But this, Locke claimed, is clearly not the case, since many supposedly innate principles play no role in the mental lives of infants and "idiots." However, Locke continued, if the innateness of certain principles is to be read merely as the claim that such principles are somehow potentially or *dispositionally* in our minds at birth, then we require some criteria by which we may distinguish those principles that are innate from those that are not. According to Locke, such criteria cannot be found. Locke concluded that there is therefore no reasonable way in which the notion of innateness can be deployed, and thus no way to be a nativist about the origins of the principles in question.

Few have found this particular argument of Locke's convincing. Presence at birth is merely *evidence* for innateness,[2] it is not criterial. There are many physical features of our bodies that are plainly innate, of course, but that aren't present at birth. Facial hair in men would be one example. There is no reason to think that innate features of our minds should be any different. This is fortunate for Locke, for he too will need at least some basic innate machinery to get things off the ground—truly *blank* slates cannot learn anything.

This means that the burden of characterizing what it is for something to be innate is as much a problem for empiricists as it is for nativists. How much of a burden this is, however, is not entirely clear. Scientific progress in investigating a kind does not generally depend on having an airtight characterization of that kind.

---

1. A clear and informative summary of the history of this debate can be found in Stich (1975b).
2. Likewise for a variety of other characteristics often linked to innateness, such as universality. And just as universality is only a defeasible guide to innateness (belief that the sky is blue may well be universal, but it is not innate), so presence at birth is only a defeasible guide to innateness—some learning appears to happen in the womb. This explains, for example, newborns' preference for stories repeatedly read to them in the final trimester of pregnancy (DeCasper & Spence, 1986).

Just as we can investigate the phenomena of locomotion, memory, chemical interaction, or planetary movement without fully explicit characterizations of the kinds involved, so too with innateness. If one is wanted, a first-pass characterization of innateness might take a cognitive mechanism, representation, bias, or connection to be innate to the extent that it emerges at some point in the course of normal development but is not a product of learning. In any case, the nativism/empiricism dispute is not about what innateness is. Rather, it is about what, and what sorts of things, we should take to be innate.

"Nativism" and "empiricism" are, of course, labels for broad families of views, and there is no such thing as "the nativist position" or "the empiricist position." Moreover, a theorist might be more or less nativist with respect to one domain or type of structure, but not another. As a result, there is a great deal of healthy disagreement among those who would take themselves to be broadly sympathetic to nativism—as will be evident in this volume. We can nonetheless characterize, in general terms, the ways in which nativist views tend to differ from empiricist views. Nativists are inclined to see the mind as the product of a relatively large number of innately specified, relatively complex, domain-specific structures and processes. Their empiricist counterparts incline toward the view that much less of the content of the mind exists prior to worldly experience, and that the processes that operate upon this experience are of a much more domain-general nature. In other words, empiricists favor an initial cognitive architecture that is largely content free, and in which general-purpose learning mechanisms operate on the input from the senses so as to build up the contents of the mind from the cognizer's experience of the world. Nativists, in contrast, favor an architecture that is both more detailed and more content laden, containing, for example, faculties or principles of inference that are specifically designed for the acquisition and performance of particular cognitive tasks. *This* is what the nativist/empiricist debate is really about.

We now come (via a somewhat lengthy stride) to the work of twentieth-century theorists. As Chomsky notes, contemporary nativists and empiricists agree that "the question is not whether innate structure is a prerequisite for learning, but rather what it is" (1980, p. 310). Where they differ is over the existence, richness, and complexity of the prespecified contents, structures, and processes of the mind. What is perhaps most significant and characteristic of the contemporary debate is that empirical data is now being brought to bear on the debate in a systematic way. This is strikingly evident in Chomsky's own work, and is undoubtedly at the heart of the resurgence of nativism. Unlike some nativists of the past who were more inclined to argue on broadly aprioristic grounds for nativism, contemporary nativists embracing broadly empirical arguments for innateness recognize that there is no incompatibility between empirical argumentation and nativist conclusions. Moreover, we now have, for the first time in this debate, a large body of data gained from decades of systematic, sustained, empirical research that bears on the questions at hand. While this research is solidly empirical in nature, the results that it has supplied have brought increasing discomfort to theorists of an empiricist persuasion. So let us now undertake a brief tour of some of its more salient aspects.

2 The Poverty of the Stimulus

Historically, the most important domain in the contemporary debate surrounding nativism is natural language. In the face of widespread empiricist conviction that children acquired language through instruction or conditioning and that the mechanisms of acquisition were both simple and entirely domain general, Chomsky argued that language acquisition is strongly innately guided—so much so that language acquisition would be better described as involving a process of maturation rather than one of learning or instruction (1957, 1965, 1967). Though Chomsky offered many arguments to support this view, perhaps the most important type of argument he offered was a version of the poverty of the stimulus argument (1967, 1975, 1981).

The central idea behind poverty of the stimulus arguments is that the knowledge[3] that cognizers acquire, to underpin certain cognitive abilities, is radically underdetermined by the input available to the cognizer in her developmental environment. In other words, arguments from the poverty of the stimulus claim, roughly, that the information available to a cognizer is too impoverished to provide her with the knowledge that the performance of certain cognitive abilities requires. Nativists conclude from such arguments that the required knowledge must thus originate elsewhere. If the information is not in the environment, then it is plausible to suppose that it is somehow innate. In particular, it is plausible to assume that a richer innate endowment than that posited by the empiricist is required to interact with the environmental information. Empiricists, in contrast, conclude that such arguments must be unsound. They argue, for example, that there is more information in the environment than the nativist allows, or that the child is a better learner than the nativist supposes.

In the case of language, a powerful version of the poverty of the stimulus Argument can be constructed against the background of contemporary linguistic theory.[4] The history of contemporary linguistic theory is, in part, one of discovering an enormous number of subtle regularities in our linguistic behavior—regularities that prior to contemporary linguistic theory simply were not noticed.[5] In attempting to come to grips with this huge (and growing) body of data, linguists have put forward many different theories concerning the structure of language. This immediately suggests that the environmental input is extremely unlikely to lead children equipped only with the empiricist's simple, domain-general learning

---

3. In most of what follows, the term "knowledge" should be interpreted loosely, to mean whatever faculties, capacities, representations, beliefs, etc. are appropriate to the cognitive task at hand. It should *not* be interpreted in the strict sense of justified true beliefs, unless explicitly stated.
4. For more a detailed version of this argument, see Laurence and Margolis (2001). See also Baker (2001), Crain and Thornton (1998), and Pinker (1994).
5. A similar point could be made concerning the study of vision, which has also been intensively investigated in the past 50 years. Indeed, the complexity of vision shows that even empiricist models, which assume the existence of "only" perceptual systems and general-purpose learning mechanisms, are committed to a great deal of innate machinery.

strategies to the correct hypothesis. There are too many tempting alternative hypotheses.

Indeed, if we truly suppose that children are empiricist learners, then it is not at all obvious how they would come to even some of the most basic assumptions about language: that it is a system of communication, that meanings are associated with words as opposed to individual sounds, that strings of sounds can be assigned more than one meaning and more than one syntactic structure, and so on. There are also theoretical decisions that need to be made, which linguists themselves have struggled with for years: are rules construction specific (e.g., is there a rule for forming a yes/no question from a declarative sentence) or is sentence structure dictated by a number of nonconstruction-specific rules interacting? Are rules optional or mandatory? Do rules apply in a fixed order, or are they unordered? And so on. Faced with all these possibilities, it would be a miracle if children were able to reliably arrive at the correct grammar using only the empiricist's few, simple, domain-general learning mechanisms.

Moreover, these considerations are supported by a variety of further arguments. To take just one example, one would naturally suppose that if children were empiricist learners, then collectively they would try out a huge number of different grammars, and that the types of mistakes they would make would be highly variable. In fact, though, the sorts of errors children make are highly circumscribed (Pinker, 1994; chapter 11 here). This provides further evidence that there is a rich innate endowment underwriting language acquisition.

If empiricist learners can't be expected to reliably arrive at the correct hypothesis concerning the structure of their language, the natural thing to assume is that children have a richer innate endowment than empiricists have assumed. And in fact, the real debate about language acquisition is not about *whether* a nativist model is correct but rather about *which sort* of nativist model is correct. Language is acquired on the basis of a rich, and significantly domain-specific, set of cognitive capacities, representations, or biases. Further research will help us to determine exactly which such cognitive structures are involved and just how rich and domain specific they are.

In spite of the strength and influence of Chomsky's poverty of the stimulus argument, such arguments are not the only ones for nativism. Indeed, it is important to recognize that nativism in a given domain is perfectly compatible with there being *ample* environmental evidence concerning that domain. So, for example, mallard ducks seem to have innate knowledge of the typical courtship behavior of their species—in spite of the fact that one can easily imagine a domain-general mechanism for acquiring this behavior from the many exemplars that the ducks are exposed to under normal circumstances. Our evidence for this is based on a type of poverty of the stimulus argument. Female mallard ducks that are raised exclusively with pintail ducks and have never seen the species-typical courtship behavior characteristic of female mallards, spontaneously display this behavior when they encounter a male mallard duck for the first time (Lorenz, 1957; Ariew, 1999). But though our evidence for this trait being innate comes through a poverty of the stimulus argument, under normal circumstances the stimuli are not at all impoverished—without the experimenters' intervention, female mallards would see many other female mallards engaging in their species-typical courtship behavior. There is no incompatibility between a trait being innate and there being ample environmental evidence for the trait to be acquired through learning.

It is sometimes suggested that empiricism is the default position concerning cognitive development, and that we should only be nativists as a last resort—or that nativists are somehow lazy, taking the easy way out and avoiding the hard job of spelling out how a cognitive structure could be acquired. There is, however, no reason to accept either of these charges. For any given domain, the question is simply what the best model of acquisition is, all things considered. There is no more reason to suppose that such models should proceed, if at all possible, only on the basis of some set of simple domain-general processes identified by the empiricist than there is to suppose that in building a television or a car engine we should only be allowed nuts and bolts and no other materials. Nativist theorizing isn't lazy; it's just that nativists prefer to work without their hands tied by arbitrary strictures on what sorts of materials they should work with. The methodological principle at work here is one all theorists should embrace: build the best model you can using whatever materials you need, in order to best accommodate all the known data (including developmental trajectory, evolutionary history, developmental dissociations, and so on).

While language is an important case for nativism, it is by no means the only area where nativist research has proved fruitful. We will now briefly consider some relevant results from developmental psychology and the other cognitive sciences, and some of the other sources of evidence that provide the backdrop to this volume.

3   Psychology and Anthropology

Perhaps the most striking aspect of human cognition is also the one that is easiest to miss: namely, its widespread uniformity and predictability. In our daily lives we tend to focus on the differences *between* individuals, and these differences can be the source of huge reward or suffering in both our personal and professional lives. However, if we take a step back from this high-resolution image, the similarities between all the members of our species become clear (Brown, 1991; Botterill & Caruthers, 1999; Chomsky, 1975). So too, indeed, do the similarities between humans and many other species of animal on our planet (Byrne, 1995; Gould & Gould, 1994; Tomasello & Call, 1997). Moreover, a century of work in the cognitive sciences has shown just how widespread and fundamental these similarities actually are.

Detailed empirical evidence that normal human cognitive development follows a largely uniform and structured pattern has been present since the work of Piaget (e.g., Piaget, 1936, 1937, 1959; Piaget & Inhelder, 1941, 1948, 1966). Piaget proposed a model of children's cognitive development that involved steady, across-the-board improvement in an individual's cognitive abilities, where this improvement was driven partly by the action of environmental stimuli, and partly by the unfolding in development of a suite of domain-general learning mechanisms.

However, work since, and in response to, Piaget has shown that development is in fact a much less unified affair *within* an individual, even though uniformity *across* individuals remains the norm. In other words, we now know that each individual's cognitive development follows a domain-specific trajectory for each cognitive domain (see for example, Baillargeon, 1994; Carey, 1985; Karmiloff-Smith, 1992; Spelke, 2003; Stromswold, 2000; Wellman, 1990). However, we also know that *within* each domain there exists a well-ordered pattern of development, and that this pattern is uniform for all normal members of our species (again, see for example, Baillargeon, 1994; Carey, 1985; Karmiloff-Smith, 1992; Spelke, 2003; Stromswold, 2000; Wellman, 1990).

Moreover, there has been a striking trend in the developmental psychology of the past 25 years or so, finding that very young infants are much more like adults, cognitively, than was supposed by Piaget. With more sophisticated experimental techniques, cognitive capacities have been shown to exist at a much younger age than was previously thought. In some cases, these experiments seem to demonstrate a poverty of the stimulus, with infants showing capacities and preferences literally from birth. Johnson and Morton (1991), for example, have shown that infants only hours old have a preferential interest in face-like shapes, and Meltzoff and Moore (1995), working with infants as young as 42 *minutes* old, have shown that newborns have the ability to imitate facial gestures.

In other cases, capacities have been demonstrated at much younger ages than Piaget hypothesized but where in principle infants may have gleaned the information from the environment. For example, Elizabeth Spelke and her colleagues have demonstrated that four-month-old babies have expectations and make inferences about the unity, solidity, and normal movements of objects (Baillargeon, 1994; Spelke et al., 1994). In one such experiment, Baillargeon and colleagues (1985) habituated five-and-a-half-month-old infants to a screen rotating back 180 degrees away from them on a flat surface. Following this, infants were tested under two conditions. One condition involved the same 180-degree movement of the screen but where an object that was occluded as the screen rotated back was in the path of the rotating screen. Since the object should have blocked the screen's rotation, this condition is an "impossible event condition." The other condition involved a novel movement of the screen to less than 180 degrees, where it encountered the blocking object. This condition is a "possible event condition" (see fig. 1.1).

Piaget took infants of this age to not represent the existence, or properties, of occluded objects. Thus, he should expect the infants to dishabituate more to the "possible event," which involves a novel movement of the screen. In fact, infants as young as five and a half months old dishabituate more to the "impossible event," suggesting that they do in fact represent the existence of the occluded object. Later experiments found similar results for four-and-a-half-month-olds, and at least some infants as young as three and a half months (see Baillargeon, 1987).

There is also now strong evidence that such domain-specific patterning occurs even when environmental input during the developmental process is highly restricted. For example, children develop normal linguistic abilities and at the normal rate even in cultures that address little if any speech either directly or indirectly to developing infants (Marcus, 1993; Pinker, 1994; Pye, 1992). Similarly, blind children acquire language at much the same pace and with a very similar

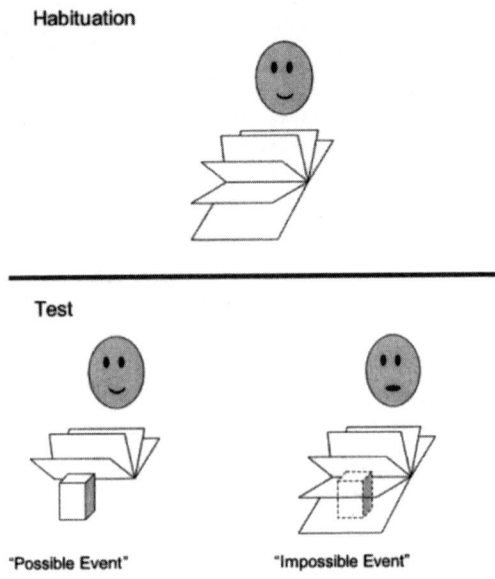

FIGURE 1.1 Adapted from Baillargeon, 1993.

developmental pattern to other children (Landau & Gleitman, 1985). This kind of evidence points strongly toward the existence of a uniform, species-wide, innate cognitive endowment that consists (at least in part) of various domain-specific faculties. Developmental psychology has thus filled in some of the details of the uniform pattern Piaget observed, but in a way radically different from what he would have expected.

In addition to the evidence for cognitive uniformity from developmental psychology, there is increasing evidence in similar vein from anthropological investigation (Atran, 1990, 2002; Boyer, 1994; Brown, 1991; Sperber, 1996). For example, Scott Atran argues that comparative data from studies of Maya Indians and rural North Americans support the existence of an innate, common cognitive system specific to our folk biology—our understanding of the taxonomy of the natural world and of the interrelations of life-forms within it (Atran, 2002). Similarly, Pascal Boyer has shown that while religious concepts and practice may appear to be both culturally diverse and individually idiosyncratic, such concepts and practices are in fact strongly constrained by universally shared systems for folk psychology, naive physics, folk biology, and understandings of artifacts, each of which is plausibly strongly innately constrained (Boyer, 1994, 2000).

What we find, therefore, is that a great deal of interesting work in both anthropology and developmental psychology is converging on a model of the innate mind involving the sorts of rich, domain-specific cognitive faculties that were originally appealed to by linguists following Chomsky. Moreover, there is increasing reason to believe that this convergence is not simply fortuitous.

4 Evolution

Evolutionary biology has proved an overwhelmingly successful twentieth-century descendant of Darwin's (1859, 1871, 1872) nineteenth-century work. Consequently, the latter half of the twentieth century has seen two significant attempts to apply the theory and methodology of evolutionary biology to human behavior and cognition. The first of these was sociobiology (Alexander, 1974; Wilson, 1975, 1978), which in turn gave rise to what is now called "behavioral ecology." Advocates of sociobiology argue that much of human behavior is as it is because it exhibits "adaptive function." That is, it has been beneficial to humans over evolutionary time and has therefore evolved and been retained due to natural selection. Understanding human behavior in this way has led to plausible explanations of many individual and group-level behavioral phenomena, including conflict resolution, mate choice, parental investment, and foraging strategies (Barrett et al., 2002; Dunbar, 1999; Smith & Winterhalder, 1992). Initially, many sociobiologists explicitly restricted themselves to explanations of behavior at the *functional* level. That is, they focused exclusively on the purpose that any given behavior serves in the life-history of an individual organism, and made no claims about the underlying causes of the adaptive behaviors thus observed. At the time sociobiology was first developed, even this limited application of evolutionary theory to human behavior was controversial enough. However, as work in behavioral ecology has progressed, claims concerning possible underlying causes of this behavior have been made, and there has been much fruitful—if still controversial—work in this regard (see, e.g., Krebs & Davies, 1984, 1991, 1997).

The extension of ideas from sociobiology and behavioral ecology to the likely causes of observed behavior also resulted in the development of what is now termed "evolutionary psychology" (Barkow et al., 1992; Pinker, 1997a, 2002; Tooby & Cosmides, 1992). Here again the focus is not on human behavior per se but on the cognitive mechanisms that underwrite it. Evolutionary psychologists argue that natural selection has equipped us with numerous evolved, domain-specific cognitive adaptations, and that these adaptations enable us as individuals to rapidly produce a variety of behaviors, which are more or less appropriate to whatever our current situation requires. Under this interpretation, what have been selected for over evolutionary time are cognitive mechanisms whose interactions can reliably generate behaviors that are positively correlated with our evolutionary fitness. And while these cognitive mechanisms evolved as a result of selective pressures in our distant past, they can nonetheless generate behaviors appropriate to more contemporary environments. In other words, evolution has provided us with certain innate, domain-specific faculties and mechanisms that then interact with our current beliefs in local conditions to cause our behavior. Human behavior and cognition are thus both *enabled and constrained* by our evolutionary history and the selective pressures that this involved.

One consequence of the evolutionary psychology perspective is that the evolved cognitive mechanisms that it proposes may generate behaviors that, while they were adaptive at one time in our evolutionary history, are now nonadaptive due to novel factors in our current circumstances. This is the cognitive equivalent of the fact that our evolutionary drive to consume and store fats and sugars whenever possible now underwrites the high levels of obesity in the modern world resulting from the easy availability of fat and sugar–rich diets (Galef, 1996). We have, to put it simply, "stone-age minds in a space-aged environment" (Dunbar, 1999, p. 784), and consequently there is the potential for a mismatch between our cognitive capabilities and our environmental circumstances. However, this potential mismatch has positive research implications, since empirical evidence of such a disparity will offer support for the claims of evolutionary psychologists.

Critics often argue that the claims of evolutionary psychologists are in fact little more than post hoc or "just-so" story-telling (Gould, 1997b; Rose & Rose, 2000). Such critics claim that reconstructions of our past environments are inherently speculative, and it is therefore a mistake to use the imagined properties of these environments as the basis for psychological theorizing. However, while our knowledge of past environments is indeed rather sparse in comparison to our knowledge of more contemporary circumstances, archaeologists are now providing increasing evidence of both the nature of these environments and of the kinds of cognitive behavior that (proto)humans engaged in within them (e.g., Mithen, 1996, 2000; Wynn, 1991, 2000).

Moreover, despite the current sparseness of the archaeological record, there are very many properties of our human ancestors and their environments of which we can be (almost) certain. For example: they had two sexes; they chose mates; they lived in a world where self-propelled motion reliably predicted that an entity was an animal and where objects conformed to the principles of kinematic geometry; they had faces; they had color vision; they interacted with conspecifics; they were predated upon; and so on (Tooby & Cosmides, 1992). All of these properties can be used to generate novel hypotheses concerning the cognitive mechanisms we may now possess, and there is no a priori reason to think that these hypotheses will be any less productive than those that are evolutionarily agnostic. There may well be no reason to think that hypotheses driven by evolutionary considerations are likely to be any *more* productive than agnostic ones (though we doubt this), but this is at best an argument for pursuing research programs driven by both kinds of consideration, rather than for ignoring or rejecting the proposals of evolutionary psychologists.

By and large, therefore, there is broad agreement that evolutionary pressures have played some role in determining the content of our innate cognitive endowment. There is also much healthy disagreement over the exact nature of the innate faculties and mechanisms that have evolved (Carruthers & Chamberlain, 2000; Heyes & Huber, 2000). Suffice it to say that all the authors in this volume, and indeed most other nativists, endorse some degree of evolutionary explanation of the contents and structure of our innate cognitive endowment. And, while there exist significant and important differences in just *how much* of this content and structure can or should be thus explained, there is also a universally shared belief that it is work of precisely the kind that this volume presents that will enable us to resolve these differences.

5 Modularity

Throughout the preceding sections we have spoken of domain-specific cognition, and of the domain-specific faculties, mechanisms, and structures that underwrite our cognitive abilities. We will now say a little more about this, and about the increasingly vexed issue of *cognitive modularity*.

That normal adult cognition consists, to some extent, in domain-specific faculties, mechanisms, and structures is beyond any doubt. The sheer volume of data to this effect, derived from studies into the cognitive abilities of normal subjects, subjects who have suffered brain lesions or other trauma, and subjects with abnormal developmental profiles, can admit of no other explanation. However, the extent to which this domain specificity is indicative of cognitive *modularity* is much more contentious.

Fodor (1983) provides the modern origins of modular models of cognition. Fodor argues that our "peripheral" cognitive systems—those involved in our senses and our language ability—are modular. What Fodor means is that these systems are innate, mandatory, fast, domain-specific, subject to characteristic patterns of development and breakdown, have proprietary inputs and shallow outputs, and, most importantly for Fodor, are informationally encapsulated: their internal processes are impervious to influence from other parts of cognition. The rest of our cognition, Fodor argues, is amodular, a fact easily demonstrated by the holistic or domain-general, that is, *unencapsulated*, nature of our conceptual processing. Since this original definition, he has softened his requirements a little, but for Fodor a module remains "a computational system with a proprietary database... [where] this device operates to map its characteristic inputs onto its characteristic outputs... [and] in the course of doing so, its informational resources are restricted to what is in the proprietary database" (2000, p. 63). For Fodor, then, modular cognitive systems exhibit encapsulation, and central cognition remains resolutely a-modular.

Other researchers have increasingly argued otherwise (Carruthers, 2003a, c; Pinker, 1997a; Scholl & Leslie, 1999b; Tooby & Cosmides, 1992). However, in so doing they have been required to adjust the definition of a module somewhat. Samuels (2000) provides an examination of such adjustments and of the most prominent and successful current notions of cognitive modularity. So too do many of the essays in this volume. We will therefore restrict ourselves here to a summary of the most salient aspects of this issue.

It is clear that cognitive faculties can theoretically exhibit domain-specificity or encapsulation with regard to both the *information* that they draw on when processing and the *computational processes* by which such processing is implemented. This, therefore, allows us to distinguish between *representational modules* and *computational modules*, respectively. To a first approximation, representational modules are domain-specific bodies of data (organized and integrated in the right kind of way); computational modules are domain-specific processing devices. Thus, for instance, "a parser might be conceived of as a computational module that deploys the contents of a [representational] module devoted to linguistic information in order to generate syntactic and semantic representations of physical sentence forms" (Samuels, 2000, p. 19). Similar points could be made for other cognitive domains.

However, we can also see that while these two kinds of module may (often) occur together in some given cognitive domain, it isn't *necessary* that they do so.

Domain-specific cognitive abilities could in theory depend upon representational modules to provide domain-specific information, which is then manipulated by various domain-*general* processes (that is, processes that don't have the domain specificity required for them to be considered as computational modules). Conversely, one could imagine that for some domain there exists a computational module designed to take as input the output from other modules so as to *generate* the representational module for that particular domain. The point to remember, therefore, is that representational modules and computational modules are modules of significantly different kinds, and a given cognitive domain might well involve one sort of module but not the other.

One consequence of this distinction is that for any given domain, the contents of either or both kinds of module may be innate. Thus it behooves both nativists and their opponents to be clear about which kind or kinds of module their claims concern. One purpose of this volume, and of the project of which it is a part, is to provide precisely the clarity required in this regard. Discussions and explanations of the extent to which cognitive *development* is modular must also take care to observe the representational/computational distinction, and to be equally clear on what precisely is being claimed. Again, many of the essays in this volume have this as an implicit aim.

Further adjustments to the post-Fodorian notion of modularity concern the properties required for a cognitive structure to be modular. In order for the domain-specific faculties found in *central cognition* to be modular, it is clearly the case that *input* to these faculties must be (at least partly) conceptual and that their *output* may be much deeper than that of peripheral systems. In addition, such faculties may be more open to influence from other faculties (i.e., to be less encapsulated) than peripheral modules appear to be. However, most of Fodor's other criteria, —for example, that such faculties are mandatory, fast (relative to other systems), domain specific, and subject to characteristic patterns of development and breakdown—remain. So, too, does the claim that at least some of these modules are innate. Thus central cognition can exhibit modularity in a meaningful and powerful sense, even if such modularity is not identical to that which Fodor initially proposed.

There remains, however, a question over *just how modular* central cognition is. Some theorists defend what is referred to as the "massive modularity hypothesis"— the claim that the human mind consists (almost) entirely of cognitive modules (Sperber, 1994; Tooby & Cosmides, 1992). Others argue for a "less massive" picture. On this view, certain cognitive abilities are indeed implemented by modular central systems, for example, our theory of mind (Baron-Cohen, 1995; Leslie, 1994). However, there is also no explicit denial of (and indeed some explicit defense of) the existence of some kind of "central executive" or otherwise "integrative" cognitive mechanism that is domain general, and perhaps initially largely content free, and that operates on the outputs of these cognitive modules. Finally, there are those who follow Fodor in steadfastly maintaining that only our peripheral systems are modular, and that the rest of our cognition is entirely amodular.

Why do certain theorists, and particularly Fodor, resist the pull of the "more massive" accounts? What underwrites Fodor's skepticism is what he terms the

"Abduction Problem" (Fodor, 2000). And, in fact, this problem is an instance of the more general question of how an explanation of human cognition in terms of domain-specific cognitive modules can be squared with the apparently domain-general flexibility of human cognition. This "Flexibility Problem" lies, in various disguises, at the heart of a number of worries, suggestions, and theories of many theorists who are nonetheless inclined to different degrees of "more massive" hypotheses. Moreover, it is clearly a problem that needs to be solved if anything more than a moderately modular conception of cognition is correct. However, since some of the chapters in this book deal explicitly with this question (Sperber, chapter 4 here; Carruthers, chapter 5 here; Samuels, chapter 7 here), further discussion can be put to one side. Suffice it to say that many of the authors in this volume endorse some degree of central systems modularity, while nonetheless healthily disagreeing over the extent to which such modularity will ultimately provide the whole story.

Research in philosophy, psychology, anthropology, and evolutionary theory thus all offers support for nativist theorizing. However, while we have emphasized the connections and similarities between the results from these disciplines, it is important to remember that such connections aren't necessary ones. That is, one can be a nativist but also reject (many) evolutionary explanations of the innate structures we possess. Similarly, one can accept varying degrees and definitions of cognitive modularity while remaining well within the nativist camp. Cognitive science is a multidisciplinary enterprise, and the results of each part of this enterprise are important and defensible independently of the whole. However, as with all scientific inquiry, when evidence from disparate sources converges, one should be inclined to see this as offering increasing support for the convergent view. We believe that this volume provides evidence of just such a convergence, and what we hope is that previously skeptical readers will become as inclined as we are to support the resultant convergent view: that nativist theorizing offers the best understanding of our cognitive abilities, and thus of our place in the natural world.

6 A Guide through This Volume

In the latter half of the twentieth century, then, nativism has gained increasing support from theoretical and empirical work in philosophy, psychology, linguistics, anthropology, evolutionary theory, and other cognitive sciences. This work provides the background for the essays in this volume, and for the larger project of which all three volumes are a part. We will now say a few words about each of the chapters constituting this first volume, highlighting various recurring themes and issues.

6.1 Architecture

The essays in Part I all focus on architectural issues, with many of them discussing the question of massive modularity and the problems that the latter view has in accounting for cognitive flexibility.

Marcus (chapter 2) examines an apparent tension created by recent research on neurological development and genetics on the one hand and cognitive development on the other. Work on brain development shows it to be surprisingly flexible, and the human genome appears far too small to specify brain structure to any fine degree of detail. On the other hand, work on cognitive development shows that many aspects of cognition are partly or largely prespecified (see secs.s 1–4 heretofore). Marcus reviews a number of ways the apparent tension between these facts can be resolved. He also presents several models and computer simulations of the ways genes code for neural development, showing how such a resolution can be achieved in practice.

Scholl (chapter 3), too, discusses and resolves an apparent tension: this time between innate prespecification and learning. He focuses on aspects of the human visual system as his key example, showing how the processes involved can be understood in terms of a form of Baysian inference, in which some aspects are innate and some set by experience, or in which innate "default settings" can be modified by experience. He suggests that this sort of result may generalize to central cognitive systems.

Our first discussion of the flexibility problem for massive modularity is provided by Sperber (chapter 4). He builds on his earlier work on relevance theory in linguistics (Sperber & Wilson, 1986, 1995) and argues here that massively modular architectures exhibit flexibility largely as a result of context-sensitive competition between modules for the allocation of cognitive resources. It is thus the cognitive system as a whole that exhibits flexibility, rather than any particular subsystem within it.

Carruthers (chapter 5), too, addresses the flexibility problem, sketching an account in which various cognitive modules combine to provide (the appearance of) domain-general thinking. In particular, he argues that various specific properties of a modular language faculty, in combination with the capacity for imagination and for the generation of cycles of cognitive activity, can enable humans to integrate information across cognitive domains without the need for a distinct, domain-general, central processor.

Shusterman and Spelke (chapter 6), too, defend the view that it is the language faculty that permits information from different modular domains to be combined. They focus on the integration of geometric and object-property information in particular. Building on previous experimental results, they discuss their recent language training study, which appears to demonstrate a causal role for language in enabling the integration of information across these two domains.

Samuels (chapter 7) provides a critical examination of one set of arguments that are thought to support massive modularity, which turn on the claim that modular mental organization is required for cognitive processes to be *computationally tractable*. While insisting that much in cognition must be innately specified, he doubts whether this particular claim (hence the massively modular version of nativism that it supports) can be adequately defended.

Simpson (chapter 8) attempts to sketch the outlines of what a reasonable form of nativism might look like. He is particularly concerned that the sort of view he develops shouldn't be confused with the set of more extreme nativist claims that are often attributed to nativists by their opponents.

6.2 Language and Concepts

The essays in Part II focus on a variety of nativist claims relating to language and concept acquisition.

Atran (chapter 9) draws a distinction between two kinds of adaptationist methodology. *Strong* adaptationism holds that complex design is best explained by task-specific adaptations to particular ancestral environments; whereas *weak* adaptationism claims that we should *not* assume that complex design is the result of such narrowly determined task- or niche-specific evolutionary pressures in the absence of substantial corroborating evidence. Atran argues that in certain cognitive domains, particularly folk biology, strong adaptationism has proved extremely useful for advancing research. But in other domains, particularly language, weak adaptationism has proved the better strategy.

Baker (chapter 10) focuses on two different views of *universal grammar* (one innately endowed component of the language faculty). Most linguists assume that universal grammar is *underspecified*—providing us with an incomplete grammar to be elaborated by learning. But the alternative (defended by Chomsky) is that it is *overspecified*—providing us with a full range of possible grammars from which we select one on the basis of environmental input. Underspecification is now the dominant view in the developmental sciences, and is often treated as the null hypothesis on grounds of greater possibility, parsimony, and simplicity. Baker takes issue with each of these grounds and concludes that we have in fact no reason to prefer underspecification to overspecification in the context of linguistic development.

Crain, Gualmini, and Pietroski (chapter 11) present detailed empirical work on several aspects of children's linguistic performance, focusing in particular on evidence that even two-year-old children understand that the meanings of determiners are "conservative," that the meaning of natural language disjunction is "inclusive-or," and that the structural notion of "c-command" governs a range of linguistic phenomena. They employ this and other work to defend three related versions of the argument from the poverty of the stimulus, each of which strongly supports the existence of an innate language faculty.

Associationist models of cognitive development come under fire from Gelman (chapter 12). She focuses on the development of *naming* in young children—the process by which young children learn or otherwise construct the meanings of words and concepts. She presents empirical evidence that by the age of 30 months, children have an "insight" into both *essentialism* and the *generic/nongeneric distinction*, and that these insights are neither directly taught during development nor reducible to information in the child's developmental environment.

Laurence and Margolis (chapter 13) take up the issue of the acquisition of number concepts, focusing on the innate mechanisms underlying our concepts for the positive integers. Some developmental psychologists hold that the positive integers are acquired on the basis of a domain-specific innate endowment that is transformed through the use of language. Laurence and Margolis argue that the best accounts of this sort have major shortcomings and are far from showing that language has this transforming power.

6.3 Theory of Mind

The essays in Part III focus on innateness claims relating to our ability to attribute mental states to one another, which generally goes under the name "theory of mind."

Povinelli, Prince, and Preuss (chapter 14) argue that the evolution of theory of mind in humans opened up much wider opportunities for parent–offspring conflict than had previously been available. In particular, they argue that human infants might have become increasingly skilled at exploiting adults' capacity for theory of mind, even when the infants themselves have yet to develop such a capacity. By being innately disposed to exhibit certain social behaviors like smiling, pointing, and gaze following, which increase adult caregivers' *erroneous* attributions of higher level or adult-like cognitive abilities to the infant, infants could induce caregivers to provide more or better care than they would otherwise have done.

Johnson (chapter 15) provides evidence that very young infants (c. 12–14 months) distinguish agents on the basis of a number of cues, including conversation-like patterns of interaction with other agents. She also provides evidence that infants conceive of agents as possessing mental states like desire. *Inter alia*, she takes up Povinelli and colleagues' challenge, arguing that the data support her own interpretation better than the claimed existence of a set of "releasers" for innate but "uncomprehending" social behaviors.

Tager-Flusberg (chapter 16) considers the role played by subjects with *neurodevelopmental disorders* in our investigations of cognitive development. She begins by presenting an overview of the methodological reasons for and against using subjects with certain neuro-developmental disorders (e.g., autism and Williams syndrome) to inform debates about normal and abnormal cognitive architecture. She then argues that studies of subjects with these kinds of disorders do indeed have much to offer, and that in fact many useful results have been obtained from previous studies, especially pertaining to the innate basis of theory of mind.

6.4 Motivation

The essays in Part IV all focus on claims about the innate basis of human motivational systems.

Buss and Duntley (chapter 17) apply evolutionary theorizing to the domain of homicide. To provide a comprehensive explanation of homicide, they propose the existence of suite of *evolved homicide mechanisms* (many of which are motivational or emotional in nature). These are cognitive mechanisms shaped over evolutionary time by selective pressures across a range of adaptive problems to which homicide might often enough have provided the solution. The especially high homicide rates in hunter-gatherer societies suggests that there would have been powerful selective pressures in this domain.

Tooby, Cosmides, and Barrett (chapter 18) ask why it is that, despite the power of poverty of stimulus arguments, many cognitive and behavioral scientists have still not been forced to recognize the truth of nativism. They suggest that this is primarily because the domains in which these arguments have hitherto been applied, for example, language or naive physics, are all ones in which the knowledge that children acquire is objectively present in their environment. So the possibility always remains open that children could somehow be acquiring this knowledge from the environment through general learning. In the case of motivation, however, this last bastion of resistance is unavailable, since desires don't serve to represent information that is already present in the environment. (The point of desire is to change the world, not to represent it.) The closest thing to a knockdown argument for nativism can therefore be developed in respect of innate motivational systems, Tooby, Cosmides, and Barrett argue.

Greene (chapter 19) and Nichols (chapter 20) both turn to consider what might be innate in the human capacity for moral thinking and feeling. Greene reviews a variety of sources of evidence for an innate moral faculty, before presenting brain-imaging data in support of the same conclusion. In his view, our moral thought is the product of an interaction between some "gut-reaction" moral emotions (many of which might be shared with our primate cousins) and our capacity for abstract reflection. Nichols focuses on the question of what marks off moral norms from rules of other kinds, such as those of etiquette. He argues that what is distinctive of morality is the attachment to a norm of certain sorts of innate emotional reaction (including disgust).

7 Conclusion

These are exciting times for the study of cognition. An unprecedented volume of work is being undertaken, and an unparalleled degree of interdisciplinary discourse is taking place. And as these efforts continue, support for nativist theorizing is rapidly increasing. This volume shows how widespread this support now is, with many philosophers, psychologists, linguists, anthropologists, primatologists, archaeologists, and other cognitive scientists all converging on nativist models of cognition and cognitive development. However, this volume also shows how much more work is still to be done, and points to a number of new directions for future research. We believe, therefore, that this book provides a substantial contribution to our understanding of cognition and of the nature of ourselves.

PART I

ARCHITECTURE

GARY F. MARCUS

What Developmental Biology Can Tell Us about Innateness

> [H]uman cognitive systems, when seriously investigated, prove to be no less marvelous and intricate than the physical structures that develop in the life of the organism. Why, then, should we not study the acquisition of a cognitive structure such as language more or less as we study some complex bodily organ?
>
> Noam Chomsky, *Reflections on Language*

1 An Apparent Paradox

In the last several years, our understanding of the genesis of the human mind has undergone radical revision. Babies were once thought to be blank slates, infinitely malleable. But dozens of recent experiments have shown that babies come to the world able to think and reason. As soon as they are born, babies can imitate facial gestures (Meltzoff & Moore, 1977), discriminate Dutch from Japanese (Nazzi et al., 1998), and distinguish a picture of a scrambled face and a picture of a normal face (Johnson et al., 1991). Within a few months they can anticipate sequences of events (Haith et al., 1988), keep track of objects that they cannot see (Spelke & Kestenbaum, 1986; Wynn, 1992), and discern abstract patterns in artificial languages (Gomez & Gerken, 1999; Marcus et al., 1999). Nativists like Steven Pinker (1994) and Stanislas Dehaene (1997) have suggested that infants are born with a "language instinct" and a "number sense." Elizabeth Spelke (1994, p. 438) has argued that infants are "endowed with abilities to perceive objects, persons, sets, and places." Since the function of our minds comes from the structure of our brains, these findings suggest that the microcircuitry of the brain is innate, largely wired up before birth.

But where does the structure of our brains come from? If instincts for mental capacities such as language, number, and intuitive physics are (partly) inborn,

---

I thank Athena Vouloumanos for comments and the NIH and HFSP for supporting the research.

rather than built up entirely in response to experience, the plans for building them must in some way be contained in the genome. But nobody has ever shown how a genome could build mind or brain.

Critics have said it cannot be done. Some have suggested that the number of genes is just too paltry in comparison to the number of neurons. There are 100 billion neural cells in a newborn's brain, yet only about 30,000 genes in a human genome (Edelman, 1988; International Human Genome Sequencing Consortium, 2001; Venter et al., 2001). There simply cannot be a gene for every neuron, or even for every cluster of a thousand neurons. Others have suggested that nothing as rigid as a genome could capture something as flexible as brain development. The left hemisphere, for example, usually plays host to our language faculty—yet some children who have lost their left hemisphere have been known to speak normally, shifting language from the left half of the brain to the right (Vicari et al., 2000); hardly, the critics suggest, what you would expect if the genome contained a blueprint for building the brain. Other studies have shown that the brain can be "rewired" (Sur & Leamey, 2001). Brain cells that would ordinarily become somatosensory cells can be transplanted into the visual cortex, sometimes taking on the identity of visual cells (O'Leary & Stanfield, 1989).

Quartz and Sejnowski (1997) have argued that this evidence for neural flexibility or plasticity poses "severe difficulties" for "the view that strong, domain-specific knowledge is built into cortical structures." They argued that "although the cortex is not a *tabula rasa*...it is largely equipotential at early stages," concluding that "nativist theories appear implausible" (p. 552, 555). Evidence for neural flexibility also figures prominently in Elman, Bates, Johnson, Karmiloff-Smith, Parisi, and Plunkett's (1996, p. 108) argument against what they dubbed "representational innateness." Instead, these authors take neural flexibility as evidence for a position in which "representation-specific predispositions" [are] "specified [only] at the subcortical level," "as little more than attention grabbers" that ensure that an organism will receive "massive experience of certain inputs."

But is such a retreat from nativism really necessary? Certainly, whenever we learn something the brain changes, but the converse need not be true—some changes in the brain occur even in the absence of learning. Taking Chomsky's notion of cognitive "organs" as a claim about development, we might expect cognitive organs to develop like other organs. Seen in that light, the findings of developmental flexibility are no longer quite so astonishing. Flexibility in brain development could be viewed as just a small part of a larger capacity of developing mammalian embryos to cope with the unexpected. Mammals invest hugely in the gestation of their offspring, and it behooves them to have mechanisms for coping with accidents during development (Gehring, 1998). As Cruz (1997, p. 484) has put it, "in a rapidly growing embryo consisting of cells caught in a dynamic flurry of proliferation, migration, and differentiation, it would be desirable for any given cell to retain some measure of developmental flexibility for as long as possible."

For example, when a cell that is ordinarily fated to be an eye cell (a "presumptive eye cell") is transplanted to the stomach, it becomes a stomach cell. In such a case, it makes little sense to speak of learning. The presumptive eye cell becomes a stomach cell because it gets a signal that tells it to follow the genetic instructions relevant to becoming a stomach cell. In a similar fashion, genes—rather than learning—may be what guides a presumptive somatosensory cell to become a visual cell.

Nobody has yet done the critical experiments—explorations of recovery from damage under conditions of informational deprivation—but a variety of recent studies suggest input from the external environment is not necessary for initial brain organization. For example, "knockout" mice that lack a gene (*Munc-18*) that is necessary for synaptic transmission show surprisingly normal brain development until birth, including "formation of layered structures, fiber pathways, and morphologically defined synapses" (Verhage, 2000, p. 864). Monkeys develop ocular dominance columns in the darkness of the womb (Horton & Hocking, 1996), and ferrets develop normal ocular dominance columns even when their retinas are removed (Crowley & Katz, 1999). None of these examples contradicts the eventual importance of neural activity in shaping neural circuitry, but, as Katz and colleagues put it in a recent review (2000, p. 199), "the current emphasis on correlation-based models, which may be appropriate for later plastic changes, could be obscuring the role of intrinsic signals that guide the initial establishment of functional architecture."

2 Intrinsic Signals

The rest of this chapter is a meditation on what it might mean for intrinsic signals to guide the initial establishment of functional architecture. What I will argue is that an understanding of the mechanisms by which the *body* develops can inform our understanding of the mechanisms by which the brain develops. As the developmental neurobiologists Fukuchi-Shimogori and Grove (2001, p. 1074) noted recently, more and more results point to a view in which the "patterning of the part of the brain responsible for our higher functions is coordinated by the same basic mechanisms and signaling protein families used to generate patterning in other embryonic organs." What's good enough for the body, I will suggest, is good enough for the brain.

2.1 The Toolkit of Developmental Biology

Two basic mechanisms are crucial to an embryo's self-assembly (Alberts et al., 1994; Gilbert, 2000; Wolpert, 1998). The first is *gene expression*. Genes can either be "expressed" or "repressed." What governs whether a particular gene is on or off is (among other things) the presence or absence of specific *regulatory* proteins that serve as enhancers or repressors for that gene (Jacob & Monod, 1961). When a gene is on, it sets into motion a transcription process that ultimately leads to the assembly of a particular protein. Among the many kinds of proteins the body can build are *regulatory* proteins, proteins that control the expression of another gene or even several other genes, each of which in turn might trigger several others, and so forth. These "cascades," also known as *regulatory networks* or *gene hierarchies*, are the second critical component of embryonic development, because they provide a way for a complex coordinated actions to emerge. For example, the fruit fly gene *Pax-6* triggers eye formation, and can be made to do so artificially in the fruit fly's leg or antenna, by triggering three (or perhaps more) other genes, each of which in turn launches the action of still more genes, ultimately snowballing into a powerful avalanche of about 2,500 (Gehring, 1998; Halder et al., 1995; Halder et al., 1998).

The second basic mechanism is *signaling*, communication within and between cells. Cells are chatterboxes that constantly communicate about their metabolic needs, the state of the organism in which they live, and so forth. One of the most important kinds of signals in embryogenesis is the *positional signal*, a signal that gives a developing cell information about its location within a growing embryo. Many of these signals come in the form of *gradients*, molecules that differ in their concentration according to location. In early stages of fruit fly development, for instance, the protein bicoid is most heavily concentrated toward the front (anterior) of the organism, and least heavily concentrated toward the back (posterior). Combinations of gradients yield precise three-dimensional information. For example, the gene that governs the region in a growing fruit fly embryo known as *even-skipped stripe 2* is triggered by high levels of the protein Hunchback in conjunction with low levels of the proteins Giant and Krüppel. Taken together, genes, cascades, signals, and gradients provide developing embryos with powerful tools for auto-assembly.

2.2 Genes and Gradients in Body and Mind

Evolution conserves. Each of these tools plays an equally critical role in vertebrate development. For instance, in the vertebrate limb bud (from which appendages such as fingers and toes sprout), a gradient of the protein Sonic Hedgehog runs from the posterior end (high concentration) to the anterior end (low). When that gradient is altered, the pattern of digit formation alters accordingly. For example, when experimenters inject the anterior end of a growing limb bud with a bead containing Sonic Hedgehog, thereby artificially increasing the concentration of Sonic Hedgehog expression, resulting embryos have two sets of mirror-reversed digits (Pearse & Tabin, 1998).

Recent experimental evidence suggests that gradients are just as important in brain development. One recent study looked at the gradient established by the gene *Emx-2*, within the neocortical ventricular zone (Bishop et al., 2000), the birthplace from which most cortical neurons emerge. Under normal conditions, *Emx-2* is expressed most heavily in caudal portions of the neocortical ventricular zone, less heavily in rostral regions. This gradient (along with a gradient of pax-6, which follows the reverse pattern) appears to play an important role in establishing the position of basic sensory areas such as V1 and A1. "Knockout mice" that have been engineered to lack *Emx-2* show a wide variety of changes. Downstream molecules that are ordinarily expressed only rostrally are expressed further caudally. Neurons in the occipital cortex that would ordinarily take on visual identity instead take on a somatosensory role, with visual regions correspondingly compressed—exactly what you would expect if neurons take on their identities in accordance with the positional cues that they get. Such studies provide powerful evidence that the overall system of development by positional specification has been conserved from body to brain.

2.3 Toward a More Comprehensive Theory

Studies like these suggest that the brain, much like the body, is initially sculpted by intrinsic signaling systems. But we are still a long way from a comprehensive understanding of how a brain develops. One problem is that current experimental techniques are extremely labor intensive. It can take a year or more to produce a single knockout strain (e.g., a breed of mice that lacks a particular gene), and there are several important limits on what can be learned from any given knockout experiment. For example, knockout animals can often compensate for missing genes using alternative (partly redundant) mechanisms. Moreover, the fact that only one or two genes can be typically knocked out in a given mouse makes it difficult to look at the mechanisms by which genes interact—a serious problem, given that most, if not all, behaviors (and correlated neural substrates) are influenced by many genes.[1]

No comprehensive theory allows us to address, even in principle, such questions as: what can a single gene do? what can a cascade of genes do?—or our fundamental question: could genes really drive the initial organization of the mind/brain, given that the genome is compact, and given that brain development is so resilient? Or must activity caused by external experience play a fundamental role, even in the brain's initial organization?

To better answer these questions, I aim to develop computational models of how genes—alone and in combination—work to build complex structure. In a nutshell, my strategy is to marry neural networks with genetics.

Traditional neural networks would not be adequate for this task. For one thing, most neural networks are, by design, largely unstructured prior to learning; the "connection weights" that run between nodes are typically initially set to random values, with every node in a given layer connecting to every node in the next layer. In the language of physics, such networks are high in entropy and correspondingly low in initial information (Loewenstein, 1999). In such models, the question of innateness scarcely arises; where there is no initial structure, there is no innateness. (There is also little biologically plausibility. As Nobel laureate David Hubel put it, "those who speak of random networks in the nervous system [appear not to be] constrained by any previous exposure to neuroanatomy.") Fortunately, more highly structured (if less well-publicized) models do exist and can offer a starting point for our investigations. For example (as illustrated in fig. 2.1) Hummel and Biederman (1992) have proposed a detailed, highly articulated network model of vision, replete

---

1. In any case, knockouts (and their naturally occurring counterpart, single-gene disorders) often tell us more about what disrupts a system than how that system works under normal circumstances. Just as removing a car's distributor wire would cause the car to stop without clarifying why the wire is important, knockouts sometimes tell us only that a particular gene is important to some particular pathway, without explaining what the role of that gene is in the larger system.

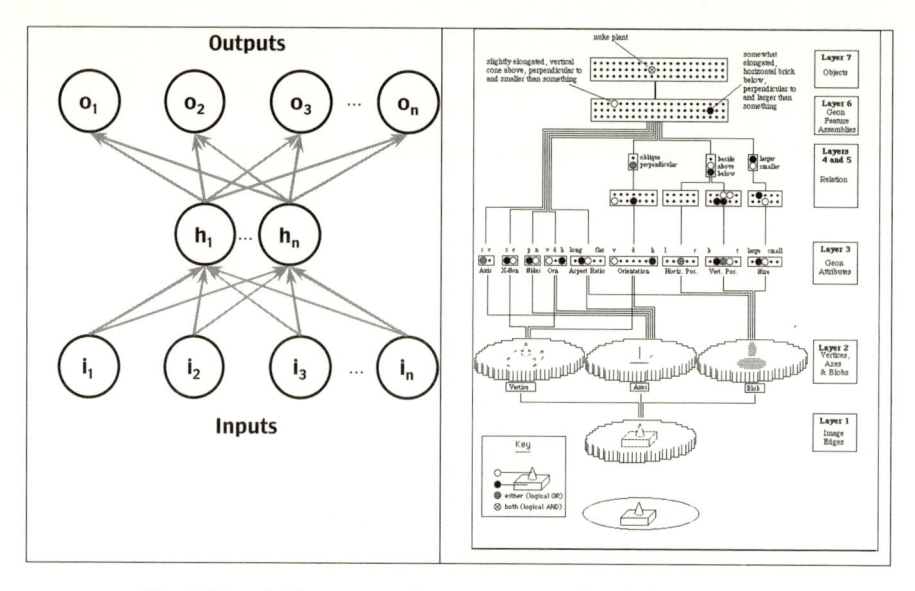

FIGURE 2.1 The left-hand illustrates a three-layer network, of the type most commonly found in cognitive science. The right-hand panel illustrates Hummel and Biederman's much more structured model of vision.

with the kind of informational encapsulation one might expect in a system with a substantial innate basis.

Hummel and Biederman (who were not concerned with developmental issues) simply stipulated the structure; in their actual model, the structure was hand-wired by the programmer. But one could instead take the model to be a provisional hypothesis about the initial structure of the visual system and ask, how might that structure *grow*? Intriguingly, the model would then serve as an example of innately guided learning. Much of its structure—machinery for recognizing primitives such as three-dimensional solids through combinations of edges, vertices, and the like—would by hypothesis be innate. But the final connections—representations of real-world objects in terms of component three-dimensional primitives—would be tuned on the basis of experience. How might the "innate" components of such a system arise?

2.4 A Neurogenetic Simulator (Prolegomena to a Future Understanding of Innateness)

Existing neural network models do not allow us to address this sort of question. In most models, there are only two options—either connections are learned on the basis of experience (hard to imagine in the case of a model as complex as Hummel and Biederman's) or they are simply stipulated, hard-wired in advance by a programmer. The question of how the initial connections themselves are formed is not entertained. What's missing is a system of genes, a way of allowing wiring to develop according to a genome.[2] Enhanced with such mechanisms, simulations could tell us something about the mechanisms by which real innate microcircuitry could in principle be built, especially if those simulations could be constrained by the exploding literature on the role genes play in neural development.

What would it take to build computer simulations of how genes could underwrite the development of the unlearned portion of a Hummel-Biederman-style structured network? Although I have not yet implemented a system so complex, I have taken a few steps toward this goal.

The first (time-consuming) step has been purely technical—it was necessary to build a "neurogenetic" simulator: a piece of software that takes as its input a genome and produces as its output *a neural network that unfolds over time*. This simulator incorporates genes, cascades, and gradients, plus all the usual components you might find in any neural network (nodes, connections, activation values, and the like). Corresponding to the distinction between the regulatory and coding parts of a gene, simulated genes are if-thens that control when cells migrate, and when they stop migrating, when axons form, what cues axons follow, where gradients are established, and when cells die. As in biology, genes are not specific to specific cells; rather, any given gene can participate in the growth of many cells. The system also includes virtual analogues of a molecular biologist's workbench, tools for staining cells according to which genes are expressed, tools for ablating cells, tools for "knocking out" genes, and so forth—what I have elsewhere described as "painless experimental genetics."

In the next section, I report a preliminary exploration that this simulator (still just a prototype) has made possible, as an early step toward an account of the biological processes that support innateness.

3 Topographic Maps: A Case Study

Topographic maps are ordered sets of connections between brain regions that preserve ordering. Such ordered connections offer an adaptive solution to the brain's task of computing in parallel (Barlow, 1981; Kaas, 1997), and are found throughout the brain (Kaas, 1997). For example, in the visual system, there are systematic connections between particular parts of the retina and particular parts of the tectum (in birds, fish, and reptiles) or between the retina and the superior colliculus (in mammals). Points that are adjacent on the retina correspond to points that are adjacent on the tectum (or superior colliculus).

---

2. A few existing neural networks (e.g., Nolfi & Parisi, 1995) include entities that are described as "genes," but the genes contained therein aren't really developmental entities. Rather than yielding instructions for growing a neural network over time, they simply specify the exact properties of the "neonate's" neural network, generally allocating one or more genes to each neuron. Such models are not consistent with the fact that in mammals the number of neurons massively outnumbers the number of genes, and, because they do not describe a true developmental process, they do not allow for explorations of plasticity (e.g., of what happens if a cell is transplanted or lesioned).

The most famous possible explanation for this systematicity comes from Sperry (1963, p. 707), who proposed the chemoaffinity hypothesis:

> an orderly cytochemical mapping in terms of two or more gradients of embryonic differentiation that spread across and through each other with their axes roughly perpendicular. These separate gradients successively superimposed on the retinal and tectal fields and surroundings would stamp each cell with its appropriate latitude and longitude expressed in a kind of chemical code with matching values between the retinal and tectal maps.

Sperry's prediction, initially not accepted because of work showing how flexible the development of the retinotectal projection could be, has been vindicated (albeit with a twist that I will describe in a moment) by recent molecular work. This work has finally laid bare (at least some of) the chemical code—a set of molecules known as ephrin ligands and Eph receptors—by which axons growing from the retina find their way to particular parts of the tectum. Two chemical gradients are established, one in the retinal ganglion cells, the other in the target area of the tectum. In the tectum, levels of ephrin-A (A2 and A5) signaling molecules vary from lowest in the rostral tectum to highest in the caudal tectum (Feldheim et al., 2000; Frisen et al., 1998; Hornberger et al., 1999). Retinal ganglion cells vary from low levels of corresponding Eph receptors in the nasal retina (which projects to the caudal tectum) to high levels of Eph receptors in the temporal retina (which projects to the rostral tectum). Mouse knockouts that lack ephrins A2 or A5 (or both) show disordered development of topographic maps (Feldheim et al., 2000; Frisen et al., 1998; Hornberger et al., 1999). As Sperry anticipated, gradients are critical to the proper formation of topographic maps.

But an ingenious recent experiment shows that the story is not quite as simple as the one Sperry sketched. What would happen, asked Brown and colleagues (2000), if levels of Eph receptors were artificially increased? Sperry's theory of "matching values" implies that each retinal cell carries a specific tag that corresponds to a matching tag in the tectum. On Sperry's view (as illustrated in fig. 2.2), we might expect that retinal cells with artificially inflated levels of Eph receptors would find new partners (or fail altogether to partner if no tectal cells had comparably high levels of ephrins)[3] while the remaining cells would connect as usual. Alternatively, as suggested by Brown and colleagues (2000) and depicted in the righthand panel of figure 2.2, retinal ganglion cells might wire themselves according to *relative* rather than absolute levels of Eph receptor expression. On that view, the normal retinal cells would shift to the "left" to make room "on the right" for the cells with artificially inflated levels of Eph receptor expression. To test this, Brown and colleagues (2000) created a transgenic mouse that had artificially elevated levels of Eph receptors in a random subset of its retinal ganglion cells; consistent with the hypothesis that retinal axons sort themselves in accordance to the levels of Eph receptor that they bear, rather than by a system of absolute tags,

---

3. Ephrins actually repel rather than attract Eph receptors, but to make the figure simpler, I pretend that it exerted an attraction.

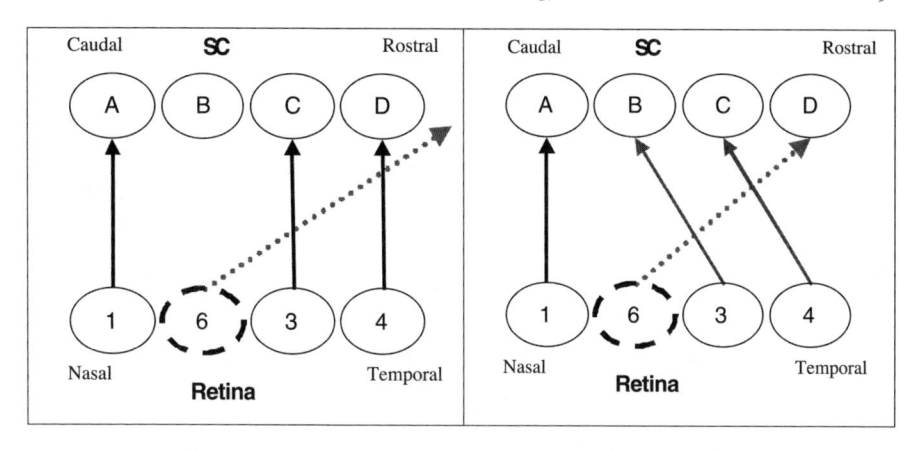

FIGURE 2.2 Predictions for what would happen if levels of Eph receptors in retina ganglion cell with dashed lines were artificially increased, from normal level of 2 units to 6. Left-hand illustrates "absolute tag" hypothesis; right-hand panel illustrates "relative" cue hypothesis.

cells with artificially high levels of Eph receptors formed a distinct map connecting further rostrally in the target colliculus. What matters is not the absolute number of Eph receptors borne by a particular retinal ganglion cell but rather the relative number.

Although topographic maps have long been the subject of intensive computational inquiry (Fraser & Perkel, 1990; Gierer, 1983; Hope et al., 1976; Miller et al., 1989; Prestige & Willshaw, 1975; Price & Willshaw, 2000; Swindale, 1996; von der Malsburg & Willshaw, 1977; Whitelaw & Cowan, 1981; Willshaw & von der Malsburg, 1976, 1979), no models of these results yet exist. More generally, none of the prior models makes use of genes, and so they have no natural way to incorporate the results from recent knockout experiments. Results like Brown and colleagues' are, however, easily captured within the framework of genes-and-gradients simulator that I am developing.

Within that framework, a set of approximately 20 genes suffices to give the "genetic instructions" necessary for building a topographic network. One set of genes governs the construction of two layers of cells, which can be thought of as retina and tectum. Another set of genes establishes gradients, including a gradient that runs from tectum to retina. A third set of genes guides axonal development, cueing "retinal ganglion cells" to build axons when the cell bodies have reached their final positions, and cueing them to seek the tectum. Genes consist of if-then rules, with the *if* part of a gene representing the regulatory region of a gene, and the *then* representing what happens if that gene is expressed (for simplicity, genes guide actions, such as migration or further gene expression, rather than protein synthesis). A typical example is a gene that says that IF *a cell is migrating AND it is a region that has less than a certain number of parts per million of the retinal-tectal gradient, THEN it should stop migrating.* Another gene says that IF *a cell is of a certain type AND it is NOT migrating, THEN it should send out an axon toward the regions that expresses the tectal cue.* Central to the model is an assumption—motivated by the

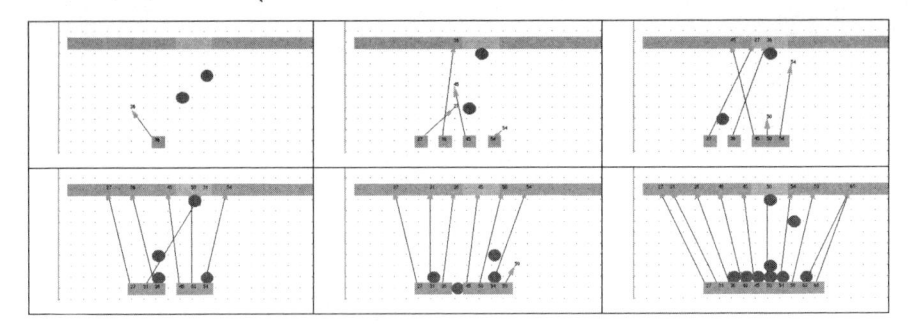

FIGURE 2.3 Stages in the simulated development of a topographic map. Dark circles depict migrating neurons, arrows depict axons. Grey rectangles indicate non-migrating neurons.

Brown results and a recent study that shows that retinal axons contain mRNA and affiliated translational machinery (Campbell & Holt, 2001)—that retinal axons can respond to cues (presumed to be levels of Eph receptors) from neighboring axons. This allows axons to "sort" themselves out, much like a group of schoolchildren ordering themselves by height. Figure 2.3 shows a series of stages in the development of a topographic network.[4]

Once the basic architecture is in place, knockin and knockout studies are easily simulated. Figure 2.4 shows a snapshot from a simulation of the Brown results; dark cells have artificially increased levels of Eph receptors (shown by the numbers near the arrowheads) and correspondingly shift to the right.

These results show how important recent findings can be readily captured by neurogenetic simulation. Because evolution conserves developmental mechanisms, the importance of understanding the interactions of ephrins and Eph receptors extends well beyond the retinotectal map. Ephrin-A ligands are implicated not just in the visual portions of the thalamus but also in topographic maps in auditory thalamus (Lyckman et al., 2001), in the somatosensory, auditory, and motor areas of the cortex (Vanderhaeghen et al., 2000), in the hippocampus (Brownlee et al., 2000), and in the topographic maps that motor axons form on muscles (Feng et al., 2000).

Still more generally, these simulations show how complex structure can arise in the absence of external experience, and they show how a small number of genes can guide the growth of many cells. (The basic set of genes can guide topographic connections between arbitrarily sized layers—once a developmental "recipe" is in place, it can be massively replicated.) Furthermore, they show that signaling should not be equated with experience—between-cell (and between-axon) signals are critical here, but those signals are generated entirely endogenously. Contra Elman and colleagues' implication that "interactions all the way down" (1996, p. 319) implies difficulty for nativism, these results show how endogenously generated cellular interactions can be the very stuff of nativism.

---

4. A movie of this is available online at: www.psych.nyu.edu/gary/bio/topo.mov.

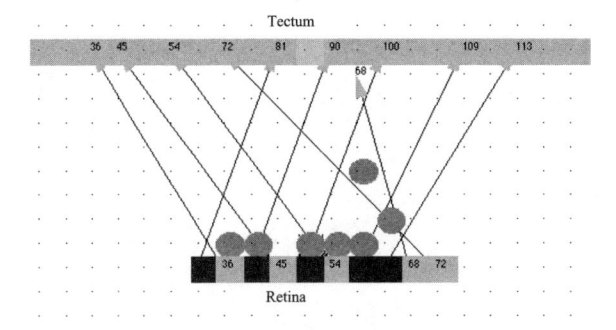

FIGURE 2.4 Simulation of experiment in which random subset of retinal cells has artificially elevated levels of Eph receptor expression.

4 Discussion

A major challenge for nativists has been to spell out how developmental flexibility and nativism can be reconciled. A major challenge for connectionists has been to spell out how innate constraints can be incorporated in neural network models. The models shown here show how synthesizing developmental biology and neural networks could help solve both problems, ultimately leading to an account of how some aspects of complex organization can arise in the absence of experience, in a system that is developmentally robust. Such demonstrations do not in any way obviate the importance of experience, but they do show that it is in principle quite feasible to build neural structure in the absence of experience. The extent to which particular cognitive processes are the product of genes—either independently of or in conjunction with experience—remains open, but the very possibility of biologically guided innate structure should no longer be in doubt.

The neurogenetic simulations introduced here show how the mechanisms that can build the body (e.g., gradients and gene expression) could build the brain; they also show how small numbers of genes could lead to large numbers of well-organized neurons by massive replication of simple circuits. Moreover, the systems here have a degree of developmental resilience; because, for example, systems rely on relative cues, individual cells can be lesioned with relatively little impact. While there is a long way to go, such demonstrations could represent valuable first steps toward a more complete account of how biological mechanisms can guide the construction of inborn neural architecture. In future work, such neurogenetic simulations could also be used as a tool to explore a related question, vital for understanding the evolution of language and cognition: how could small modifications to sets of developmental genes lead to new neural structure and new neural function?

3

BRIAN J. SCHOLL

Innateness and (Bayesian) Visual Perception

Reconciling Nativism and Development

1 A Research Strategy

Because innateness is such a complex and controversial issue when applied to higher level cognition, it can be useful to explore how nature and nurture interact in simpler, less controversial contexts. One such context is the study of certain aspects of visual perception—where rigorous models are possible, and where it is less controversial to claim that certain aspects of the visual system are in part innately specified. The hope is that scrutiny of these simpler contexts might yield lessons that can then be applied to debates about the possible innateness of other aspects of the mind. This chapter will explore a particular way in which visual processing may involve innate constraints and will attempt to show how such processing overcomes one enduring challenge to nativism. In particular, many challenges to nativist theories in other areas of cognitive psychology (e.g., "theory of mind," infant cognition) have focused on the later development of such abilities, and have argued that such development is in conflict with innate origins (since those origins would have to be somehow changed or overwritten). Innateness, in these contexts, is seen as antidevelopmental, associated instead with static processes and principles. In contrast, certain perceptual models demonstrate how the very same mental processes can both be innately specified and yet develop richly in response to experience with the environment. In fact, this process is entirely unmysterious, as is made clear in certain formal theories of visual perception, including those that appeal to spontaneous endogenous stimulation, and those based on Bayesian inference.

For helpful conversation and comments on earlier drafts, I thank Paul Bloom, Peter Carruthers, Erik Cheries, Frank Keil, Koleen McCrink, and Steve Mitroff. The preparation of this chapter was supported by National Institute of Mental Health grant number R03-MH63808-01 and National Science Foundation grant number BCS-0132444.

1.1 Innateness in Cognitive Science

One of the most persistent and important themes in cognitive science is the issue of whether and how various cognitive mechanisms, processes, abilities, and concepts may in some sense be innate. This debate is far older than cognitive science or even the modern incarnation of psychology (see Diamond, 1974; Samet, 1999), and (as the other essays in this volume attest) it remains a lively research topic today. In a sense, the continuing debate about innateness has been incredibly unifying, if only because it draws together researchers from so many different disciplines, who study so many distinct aspects of the mind. (An online search of the *MIT Encyclopedia of Cognitive Science* turns up discussions of innateness in almost every imaginable corner, in fields ranging from psychology and linguistics to ethology and neuroscience, and in specific topics ranging from imitation and ethics to numeracy and phantom limbs.)

Of course, questions of innateness have also long been among the most divisive and controversial issues in cognitive science. Indeed, one can hardly mention the yin of nativism without the yang of empiricism, and the combative tension between these two traditions is alive and well in all of the aforementionedareas of cognitive science. The suggestion of a possible nativist origin for part of almost any cognitive process always seems to evoke an academic quarrel, and such debates have sometimes polarized entire fields. Such debates will often even spill over into the popular press and the general public—especially when questions of innateness are raised about issues such as the nature of our emotions, or our mate-choice preferences (see Pinker, 2002).

1.2 "Barely Worth Mentioning"

Because issues surrounding innateness are liable to become so complex and controversial when applied to human cognition, some researchers have suggested that a useful strategy is to study how such issues play out in simpler and possibly less controversial contexts. Gallistel (2000), for instance, has attempted to study nativism (along with other issues such as computation and modularity) in circumscribed domains encountered by simpler organisms. As a case study, he has studied the nature of certain forms of wayfinding in insects. Bees, for example, are able to communicate the direction and distance of food to their hivemates, using the location of the sun in the sky as a reference angle. Their ability to do this year-round and even on cloudy days, moreover, indicates that they represent the solar ephemeris function: they know where the sun is in the sky as a function of the time of day and the day of the year—a function that varies depending on where the bees live. Studies of this process have gradually revealed a detailed picture of how innate and learned components contribute to this ability (e.g., Dyer & Dickinson, 1996). Even without ever experiencing the sun, bees still in some sense assume that it exists, and that it rises in the east and sets in the west—the one thing that is true of the ephemeris function anytime and anywhere—and they initially assume that it traverses this path with a discrete jump around noon. The shape and timing of this path are then gradually tuned by early visual experiences, in ways that are beginning to be understood, to match the actual ephemeris function for the sun at that location (Dyer & Dickinson, 1994). In few areas of human cognition are we able to obtain such a detailed and rigorous picture of how nature and nurture interact.

Gallistel (2000) stresses several specific lessons of this research for cognitive science, but perhaps the most important lesson is methodological: It is possible to gain insight into the ways nature and nurture cooperate by studying simpler cases that are more amenable to rigorous study and critical experiments, and at the same time are far less controversial. Indeed, Gallistel has stressed that claims of innate specialized structure are "barely worth mentioning" in certain parts of biology, in that they are assumed to be the norm. In this way, then, it is possible to study innateness in simpler contexts than higher level human cognition, and perhaps learn some important things about how nature and nurture interact in situations that are divorced from the abstractness, concern, and controversy that normally attends such projects. This chapter explores a similar strategy, but with a focus on what are perhaps simpler cognitive processes rather than simpler organisms. In particular, the aim of this chapter is to make a few specific points about how nature and nurture can interact in the context of certain theories of visual perception.

The study of vision is certainly one of the most successful projects of cognitive science: it has arguably enjoyed the most rigorous theories, the most developed computer models, and perhaps the tightest coupling so far of psychology and neuroscience. Some have argued that this is no accident. Neuroscientists have stressed that more than half of cortex is devoted to vision (at least in monkeys), and Fodor (1983) has famously argued that the relatively modular and encapsulated structure of "input systems" such as vision is bound to translate into greater empirical tractability. Innateness has certainly been a persistent theme in the study of visual perception, and in parts of vision research (e.g., face perception) it is just as controversial as in the study of higher level cognition (e.g., Gauthier & Nelson, 2001; Kanwisher & Moscovitch, 2000). However, whereas many scientists are hesitant to grant the existence of significant innate components for large swaths of human cognition, it is essentially uncontroversial among vision scientists that at least some portions of (early) visual perception are (in part) innately specified.[1]

The hope is that by studying the interaction of nature and nurture in visual perception, we might gain some useful insights that can then be applied to debates about nativism in other areas of cognitive science. This chapter is one small part of this project, and it attempts to dissolve apparent conflicts between innate structure and later development by focusing on how the very same visual processes can both

---

1. For the rest of this chapter, I will often drop caveats such as "in part." I take it as given that no mental process—perceptual or otherwise—is *entirely* innately specified, any more than any such process is entirely learned. The question of innateness is taken here to be whether any significant parts of the mind can develop without bona fide *learning* (see Pylyshyn, 1985, for careful definition and discussion of this distinction), taking for granted (1) that other mental abilities are largely learned via experience with the environment, and (2) that environmental interaction is also always likely to play a critical role in revealing innate structure.

be innately structured and yet themselves develop richly in response to experience with the environment.

2 Is Nativism Antidevelopmental?

Most researchers today recognize that the mind must develop as a result of some mixture of innateness and learning, but it is not always clear how this cooperation is to be forged. While some writers emphasize that even innate structure itself is designed to learn (e.g., Marler, 1991; Pinker, 1997a), others seem to assume that there is some inherent tension between the two: some processes may be (mostly) innate and others may be (mostly) learned, but there is a hesitancy to explore processes that are both innately determined and then themselves continue to develop via learning. Some of this tension is only sociological, in that nativist research programs are seen to somehow squelch the study of development: "Calling some skill or behavior innate tends to stop analysis of how it develops" (Fischer & Stewart, 1999, p. 150). In many contexts, however, it seems popular to assume that there is a deeper and more inherent conflict between nativism and development (e.g., Elman et al., 1996; Fischer & Bidell, 1991; Karmiloff-Smith, 1992; Quartz & Sejnowski, 1997; Thelen & Smith, 1994; for discussions of neuroscientific versions of such arguments, see Marcus, chapter 2 here). According to these views, innateness is seen as inherently "anti-developmental" (Gopnik, 1996, p. 174), and at root nativist research programs are seen as attempts at "minimizing change during development" (Quartz & Sejnowski, 1997, p. 537). Recent examples of this conflict are readily seen in two of the most active areas of cognitive developmental psychology: "initial knowledge" in infancy and "theory of mind."

2.1 *Examples from "Object Cognition" in Infancy*

One area of active nativist debate in cognitive development is the study of what young infants know about the physical world. Using looking-time measures to study the infant's object concept, developmental psychologists have demonstrated that infants even a few months old have a substantial amount of "initial knowledge" about objects, in domains such as physics and arithmetic (for reviews see Baillargeon, 2002; Spelke et al., 1995a; Wynn, 1998). This research has shown, for example, that infants have some appreciation of the fact that objects must trace spatiotemporally continuous paths through space (Spelke et al., 1995a); that objects will fall if unsupported (Needham & Baillargeon, 1993); that one plus one yields two, and other simple arithmetical facts (Feigenson et al., 2002; Wynn, 1992); that objects cannot pass through one another (Baillargeon et al., 1985; Spelke et al., 1992); that the mechanical interactions of objects will obey certain causal laws (Leslie & Keeble, 1987); and so on.

Some of the theorizing that has accompanied this research has had a strong nativist flavor, often phrased in terms of "core knowledge" (e.g., Spelke, 2000, 2003; Shusterman & Spelke, chapter 6 here). Under these proposals, the appreciation of physical and numerical laws revealed in looking-time experiments reflects the operation of innate principles of some form—albeit principles built into highly task- and domain-specific processes that are largely independent and encapsulated from each other and from other aspects of the mind.[2] These principles form the core of our knowledge of the world and provide the critical representations needed for bootstrapping by later learning. Many types of evidence have been adduced to support nativist theories of such abilities, including familiar arguments based on precocity, learnability, universality, and continuity with other branches of the phylogenetic tree (e.g., Spelke, 1988, 1998).

These nativist proposals have proven highly controversial. Indeed, debates that center on nativism have been featured prominently every few years at major infant cognition conferences and have resulted in a number of recent vigorous exchanges in the literature (e.g., Cohen & Marks, 2002, v. Wynn, 2002; Haith, 1998, v. Spelke, 1998; Smith, 1999, v. Baillargeon, 1999). The proponents of empiricist viewpoints have been just as lively as their nativist counterparts—suggesting for example that "claims that types of knowledge are innate [constitute] misdemeanors, if not outright psychological felonies" (Haith, 1998, p. 168)—and the arguments used to fuel such views have often made strong appeals to the perceived inability of nativist theories to accommodate later development (e.g., Bogartz et al., 1997; Cohen & Cashon, 2003; Fischer & Biddell, 1991; Johnson, 2003; Smith, 1999). Nativist theories are seen to "shut down attempts at process explanations and developmental analyses" and to be inherently "nondevelopmental" (Haith, 1998, pp. 176, 172). The biggest problem for nativist views is alleged to be simply that "development *happens*" (Johnson, 2003, p. 103). Theories of causality, for example, that rely on "an innate module" are taken to imply that "there is no room...for causality perception to develop in stages....Causality, according to Leslie and other nativists...is not something to study developmentally: it is a nonsequitur to study the development of something that doesn't change" (Cohen et al., 1998, pp. 172–3). And some writers have even argued explicitly that our eventual ability to overrule the dictates of innate principles (e.g., to understand Star Trek transporter beams, which violate laws of spatiotemporal continuity) falsify nativist claims based on "core knowledge" (Gopnik & Meltzoff, 1997).

2.2 *Examples from "Theory of Mind"*

Strikingly similar arguments are found in other areas of developmental research, such as "theory of mind." Many human behaviors are the result of internal mental states such as *beliefs* and *desires*. Such representations not only cause our behaviors but also form much of the currency of our mental lives: even young children perceive, interpret, predict, and explain the behavior of others in terms of their underlying mental states. The acquisition of such abilities—collectively referred to as a "theory of mind" (ToM)—is early, universal (except in certain clinical populations), seemingly effortless, and largely dissociable from more general intellectual

---

2. Even among theorists who are sympathetic to aspects of nativism, there is still much debate as to the exact format of these principles, and the degree to which they represent cognitive as opposed to perceptual (or attentional?) processing (e.g., Carey & Xu, 2001; Scholl & Leslie, 1999a).

development. In adults, the exercise of such abilities is often irresistible and seemingly instantaneous. Such facts—along with worries about learnability for concepts such as *belief*, whose referents cannot be directly seen, heard, or felt—have helped to inspire theories that take the core of ToM (though obviously not its mature competence) to be innate (e.g., Baron-Cohen, 1995; Leslie, 1994; Scholl & Leslie, 1999b, 2001)—"part of our genetic endowment triggered by appropriate environmental factors, much as, say, puberty is" (Scholl & Leslie, 2001, p. 697).

Again, nearly all of the arguments against such views tend to turn on the role of development (see Scholl & Leslie, 1999b, for extensive discussion). Several authors have said explicitly that certain nativist views are "nondevelopmental" or "antidevelopmental" and that only developmental evidence can decide whether certain nativist views of ToM are correct (e.g., Gopnik & Meltzoff, 1997; Gopnik & Wellman, 1994). Others argue that the mere fact of observed development in ToM—paradigmatically, the fact that children become able to pass the "false belief task" around the age of four—argues against theories based on "modularity nativism" (Wellman et al., 2001).[3] Theories of ToM based on an innate modular core are seen as incapable of accounting for change, without appeal to "the maturation of another innate structure, a later module coming on line.... It is... difficult, however, to see why evolution would have designed a sequence of incorrect modules, each maturing only to be replaced by another" (Gopnik & Meltzoff, 1997, pp. 54–5). This type of ridicule seems rooted in the idea that an encapsulated process with an innate basis is somehow unable to develop via contact with the environment. Even authors who are sympathetic to nativist and modular views of ToM seem uncomfortable with the idea that the innate processes can themselves change and develop. Rather, such theorists appeal to notions such as parameterization, derived from studies of linguistic nativism (e.g., Segal, 1996; Stich & Nichols, 1998). On such views, development is explained not by robust learning via interaction with the environment but by an executive "switching" mechanism that simply chooses at various times among preset options, all of which are still innately determined. Thus even nativist theorists are drawn to views that seem implausible (see Scholl & Leslie, 1999b, for discussion), on the basis of developmentally motivated concerns.

---

3. As with 'core knowledge' views of infants' object-cognition abilities, nativist theories of ToM have also often claimed that the innate processes are highly domain specific, informationally encapsulated, and possibly embodied in cognitive modules (e.g., Scholl & Leslie, 1999b, 2001). In general, of course, innateness and modularity are entirely dissociable concepts: "The claim of innateness is obviously not required of the modularity view" (Scholl & Leslie, 1999b, p. 134). However, we have sometimes treated innateness as a critical part of how modularity applies to the case of ToM, as have others who refer to "modularity nativism." This has sometimes lead to confusion (see Nichols & Stich, 2003), but it seems clear that most developmentally motivated arguments against the 'modularity nativism' view of ToM are in fact aimed at a certain conception of nativism, rather than anything intrinsic to modularity. For example, Gopnik and Meltzoff (1997) take themselves to be arguing against the following: "According to modularity theories, representations of the world are not constructed from evidence in the course of development. Instead, representations are produced by innate structures, modules, or constraints that have been constructed in the course of evolution" (p. 50).

2.3 Nativism and Flexibility

In the foregoing examples, arguments against innateness have been fueled by concerns that nativist origins preclude developmental flexibility. This view is not entirely unmotivated, of course. Such views are suggested by characterizations of the innate endowment as a set of *constraints* on development (e.g., Elman et al., 1996; Keil, 1991), a view that even some resolute nativist researchers take to be unfortunate: such constraint-based characterizations "imply that innate knowledge prevents people from learning" (Spelke, 1998, p. 194). Perhaps the strongest motivation for such views, however, is the simple fact that nativist theories rarely contain specific proposals for *how* later development would work, beyond peripheral ideas of triggering and maturation. Theories of core knowledge in infant object-cognition, for example, have been vague about just how later bootstrapping processes would harness the innate core representations, or just how it is possible for "hardwired" principles to later be unwired or rewired. Rather, such theories have appealed to "overriding" to explain radical change (see Stich & Nichols, 1998), wherein entirely new systems (perhaps with little or no innate basis) can eventually come online and overrule core knowledge. This issue also arises in the theory-of-mind literature, in suggestions that the innate contribution affects only "early ToM" (by analogy to "early vision"; e.g., Scholl & Leslie, 2001) — the implication being that development results from higher level processes that are not claimed to be innate. In sum, all of these views suggest that the actual innate processes themselves do not develop; rather, development occurs in a context beyond the innate content, which is still seen as static and unchanging.

3 Bayesian Visual Perception

The previous section sketched only a few examples of a wider perceived conflict between innateness and development. But is such a conflict really necessary? Some theories of visual perception, at least, suggest a negative answer: it may be possible for the *very same process* to be both innately determined and yet to later change (even radically) in response to interaction with the environment. This section sketches out one general framework, based on Bayesian inference, in which this is possible. After this brief introduction to Bayesian perception, section 4 explores how both Bayesian models and models based on spontaneous endogenous stimulation can incorporate both nativism and learning in the same processes.

3.1 The Impossibility of Visual Perception

Visual perception is the process of recovering useful information about the structure of the world, based the shifting patterns of light that enter the eyes. Perhaps the most fundamental fact about visual perception is that this task is, strictly speaking, impossible. That is, the shifting patterns of light that enter the eyes are insufficient by themselves to fix the structure of the external world from which that light was reflected or emitted (Marr, 1982) because there are always a multitude of possible structures in the world that could have given rise to those same patterns of

Innateness and (Bayesian) Visual Perception 41

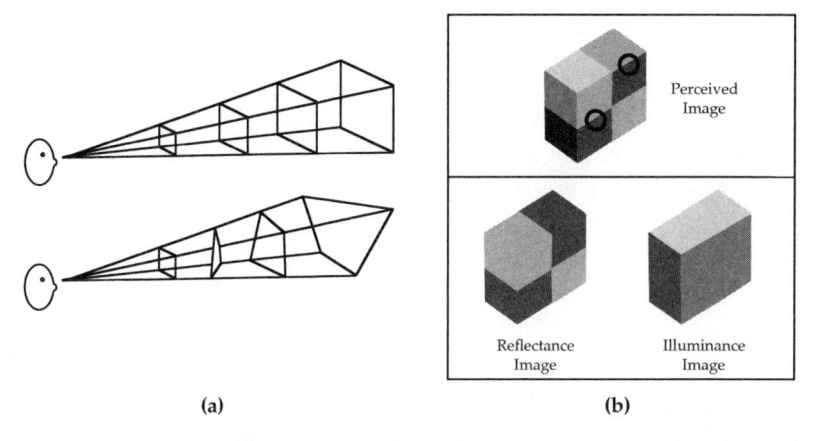

(a)   (b)

FIGURE 3.1 Two examples of underdetermination problems in visual perception. (a) A given 2D retinal shape could be caused by a real 3D object in the world of almost any size and shape (adapted from Feldman, 1999). (b) The light reaching the eyes is a product of the illumination from a light source and the reflectance of the 'paint', and it isn't strictly possible to recover only one of these operands (the reflectance, which we would like to see as constant regardless of the lighting) without 'unmultiplying'. Note that the two circled patches contain the same objective luminance edge, despite the fact that we see one caused by lighting and one caused by 'paint' (adapted from Adelson, 2000).

light. In this sense the visual system must solve an "inverse problem," which is technically not possible via deductive inference.

This underdetermination is most commonly appreciated in the case of depth and three-dimensional shape. A given patch of retinal stimulation, for example, could correspond to an object in the world of almost any size (since a small nearby object will create the same retinal image as a larger object further away) and almost any shape (see fig. 3.1a). Furthermore, objects in the world could in principle be changing constantly among these possibilities yet always continue to project the same retinal stimulation. Such dilemmas of underdetermination are in no way specific to depth perception but hold for almost every aspect of visual processing. Another example is the perception of surface lightness, where in everyday experience we commonly perceive the reflectance of a surface as constant in the face of changing illumination, despite the fact that the same luminance edge can be produced by either a change in lighting or a change in reflectance (fig. 3.1b). This is also technically impossible to achieve, since the actual number of photons that reach the eyes after reflecting off a surface will always be the product of the illumination from the light source (which we want to discount) and the reflectance of the surface (the "paint," which we want to know about). Separating these sources is not strictly possible, since it would essentially require the visual system to "unmultiply," for example, solving for R in the equation $R \times L = 12$ (see Adelson, 2000).

In each of these cases (and many others), accurate perception based only on the incoming visual information is impossible, due to an underdetermination problem. As a result, successful perception is possible only via the application of internal processing constraints, and the focus of much research in perception has been to determine the nature of these constraints (e.g., Marr, 1982; Rock, 1983). So what is their nature? At first blush, it seems unlikely that there would be any global answer to this question, simply because perception is generally thought to consist of many specialized and independent subprocesses (Marr, 1982; Palmer, 1999). For example, the processes that compute depth from disparity information are thought to be functionally (and sometimes neuroanatomically) distinct from those that determine phenomenal colors based on distributions of different cone outputs, those that compute the correspondences between items undergoing apparent motion, or those responsible for recognizing faces. The outputs of such processes may in some cases serve as inputs to others, and they may all eventually feed into more central mechanisms, but in general the processes that subserve each such individual task are likely to be specialized and functionally independent—making it unlikely on the face of it that there would be any single "nature" of perception. Despite this degree of specialization in the visual system, however, researchers have identified a few general principles that seem to run through all manners of visual processing. Perhaps the most powerful such principle is what might be called "coincidence avoidance."

3.2 Coincidence Avoidance and Perception as Unconscious Inference

The visual system, it appears, abhors a coincidence. One of the earliest and most forceful proponents of this view was Helmholtz, who popularized the idea in his principle of "unconscious inference" (1867/1925):[4]

Helmholtz's Principle of "Unconscious Inference"

What is perceived are essentially those objects and events that under normal conditions *would be most likely* to produce the received sensory stimulation.

The idea isn't that the visual system makes actual inferences by reasoning just as we do but rather that it operates *in accord with* such a principle, since doing so has proven selectively advantageous in the course of the visual system's phylogenetic development. This type of principle proves extremely adept at accounting for a wide variety of perceptual phenomena.

One can readily appreciate the operation of such a principle by considering some of the simple shapes in figure 3.2. You see figure 3.2a as a straight line rather than a line that curves in the plane parallel to your line of sight (which would project the same retinal stimulation). Why not perceive this latter possibility? The visual system discounts the curved-line interpretation because, while possible, it would require an "accidental" viewpoint: of all possible viewpoints of a

---

4. Recent scholarship in the history of vision science has uncovered examples of this principle—and of an astounding number of other supposedly recent insights—in the work of the Islamic scholar Al-hazen (965–1039). For fascinating discussion, see Howard (1996) and Sabra (1978).

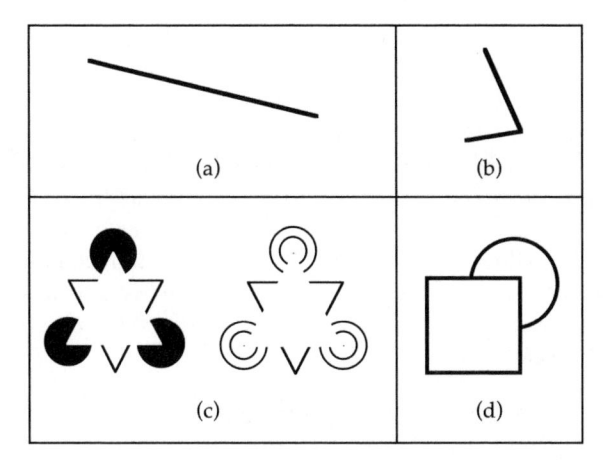

FIGURE 3.2 Four simple examples of the principle of unconscious inference in action. See text details.

curved three-dimensional wire, only a small number would produce a straight-line two-dimensional percept. (This is where the notion of likelihood enters Helmholtz's principle: if you chose a viewpoint randomly, it would be extremely *unlikely* to produce a single linear two-dimensional percept of a curved three-dimensional wire.) As such, the visual system assumes that a straight contour in an image corresponds to a straight contour in the world. Similarly, you see an "L" shape in figure 3.2b (rather than two independent segments which lie at different depths) because it would be unlikely for two independent contours to coterminate in the image if they weren't really connected somehow (e.g., if you randomly threw down matchsticks onto the floor, very few would end up aligned in this way). Slightly more complicated cases of illusory contours (fig. 3.2c) and amodal completion (fig. 3.2d) can also be interpreted in this way: you see illusory triangles in figure 3.2c because the other obvious possibility (involving a lucky perfect configuration of independent black shapes and contours) would be a coincidence and is judged to be unlikely; you see a partly occluded circle in figure 3.2d because the other obvious possibility (a pac-man perfectly abutting a square) would also require a coincidental and unlikely arrangement. Beyond these simple examples, similar judgments of probability and coincidence can explain many (or even most) other well-known aspects of visual processing (for extended discussion, see Hoffman, 1998; for specific discussions of "generic viewpoint" assumptions in vision, see Biederman, 1987; Freeman, 1996).

3.3 *Visual Perception as Bayesian Inference*

The idea of vision as unconscious inference has been adopted in recent years by more formal probabilistic theories of visual perception (Rao et al., 2002), especially models based on Bayesian inference. Bayesian inference is a method of optimal reasoning under uncertainty, and specifies how to choose rationally from among a set of mutually exclusive hypotheses (Hs) based on a given pattern of data (D).

Bayes' theorem requires you to first specify the "likelihood function," which models the probability of obtaining the observed data if you assume each hypothesis to be true—for each hypothesis H, $p(D|H)$, "the probability of the data given the hypothesis." This distribution (one resulting value for each H) is then convolved with a second distribution that models the probability of each hypothesis independent of the current data—$p(H)$, "the probability of the hypothesis." This is called the Bayesian "prior" and models the degree of "prior belief" in the conclusion. The product of the prior and the likelihood function is then divided by the probability of the data irrespective of the hypothesis, and this quotient constitutes the "posterior distribution," which specifies the relative degree of resulting belief for each hypothesis:

$$p(H|D) = \frac{p(D|H)\,p(H)}{p(D)}$$

In the context of Bayesian perception, however, the probability distribution of the data can be safely ignored as a normalizing constant, leaving us with:

$$p(H|D) = p(D|H)\,p(H)$$

Bayes' theorem simply tells you to choose the hypothesis that maximizes this value.[5]

Bayes' theorem constitutes optimal reasoning under uncertainty, but people do not always find such reasoning to be intuitive. Thus a common result in the psychology of decision-making has been to find that people ignore the prior distribution—even in situations such as medical diagnosis, where such errors can be disastrous (e.g., Kahneman & Tversky, 1972; for a review see Koehler, 1996). As a result, a common applied project in this literature has been to develop tools that teach laypeople to reason according to Bayes' theorem (e.g., Sedlmeier & Gigerenzer, 2001). However, despite the fact that people do not find Bayesian reasoning to be intuitive in conscious decision-making, a wealth of recent evidence suggests that the visual system does engage in "unconscious inference" in accord with Bayes' theorem (for reviews see Kersten et al., 2004; Kersten & Yuille, 2003; Knill & Richards, 1996; Mamassian et al., 2002).[6]

In the context of visual perception, the data consist of the visual image that arrives at the retina, and the hypotheses under consideration are the possible scenes

---

[5]. Or, if the cost of making certain kinds of errors is higher than others, the resulting posterior distribution might be convolved again with a cost function, and the maximum value in the resulting distribution may not always correspond to the maximum of the posterior distribution itself. More generally, one can also analyze the shape of the posterior distribution to analyze the reliability of the information: sharply peaked distributions indicate high reliability, while broad gradual distributions reflect relatively lower reliability.

[6]. In fact, some aspects of higher level cognition also seem to implicate implicit Bayesian processing—including categorization (e.g., Tenenbaum, 1999), causal reasoning (e.g., Tenenbaum & Griffiths, 2001), and word-learning (e.g., Tenenbaum & Xu, 2000)—but such ideas have been most successful and popular in vision science, to the extent that it is perhaps not hyperbole to claim that "Bayesian concepts are transforming perception research" (Geisler & Kersten, 2002, p. 508).

in the world that may have given rise to the image. Because, as noted above, this problem is underdetermined in many ways, the visual system must engage in probabilistic decision-making to choose which scene to assign as the conscious percept corresponding to the incoming image—and in many cases it does this by maximizing the posterior distribution in accord with Bayes's theorem:

$$p(\text{Scene} \mid \text{Image}) = p(\text{Image} \mid \text{Scene})\, p(\text{Scene})$$

In this context, ideas about "unconscious inference" in visual perception can be rigorously modeled and psychophysically tested. The likelihood function—p(Image | Scene)—models aspects of optics and projection that have been increasingly well understood (especially in the context of computer graphics), and the prior—p(Scene)—models the prior assumptions (sometimes called "natural constraints") that the visual system has about the structure of the world, and that are necessary in order to cope with underdetermination. When such models are constructed and tested against psychophysical data, the fit is often extremely close—suggesting (in the absence of other models that would yield similar predictions) that the visual system is actually reasoning in accord with Bayesian inference.[7]

One example of an assumption about the world that has been modeled in this way is the assumption that there is a single light source that comes from overhead (Rittenhouse, 1786). This is a particularly useful case, given that this "natural constraint" has typically been phrased as a vague proposition (just like many principles in infant cognition and theory of mind), yet it turns out to be explicable in Bayesian terms—and moreover, it turns out to be plausibly innate. Because of underdetermination problems, the visual system must use several heuristic cues to three-dimensional shape, and one such cue consists of luminance gradients on surfaces. In certain contexts, the visual system assumes that top-to-bottom lightness gradients in an image that are lighter at the top and darker at the bottom signal the presence of a convex surface—a "bump." In contrast, a top-to-bottom image gradient that is darker at the top and lighter near the bottom is seen to signal the presence of a concave surface—a "dent." As with most such notions, the results are easier to see than to read, and as such most observers will readily see the lower-middle disc in the "egg carton" in figure 3.3 as a concave dent, and the others as convex bumps (Ramachandran, 1988). In contrast, if you turn the page upside down, you'll see the opposite the pattern. Note that this phenomenon does not depend on artificial images: you can observe the same phenomenon in the real world, and in actual photographs such as the moon craters in figure 3.4. This phenomenon makes some

---

7. The assumed absence of other models that would yield similar good fits is critical, though a detailed discussion of this issue is beyond the scope of this chapter. In general, most cognitive modeling efforts have suffered not from an inability to fit data but from an ability (driven by an overabundance of free parameters) to fit *any* possible pattern of data. In such situations, the good fit of a model confers no support whatsoever for the psychological reality of that model, since other models with very different assumptions could fit the data just as well. For discussion of this critical issue see Roberts and Pashler (2000).

46 Architecture

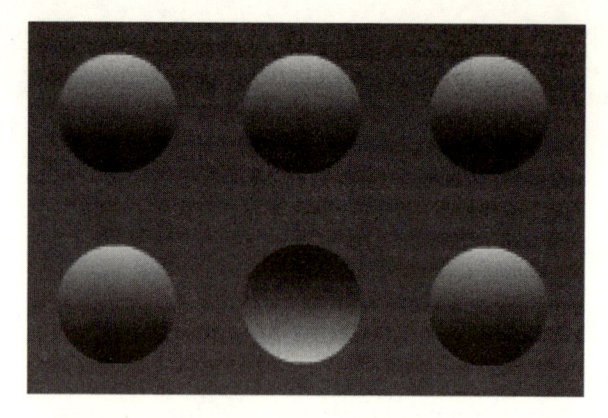

FIGURE 3.3 An example of the perceptual results of the visual system's assumption that light comes from overhead. The lower middle disc in the 'egg carton' can be resdily seen as a concave hole, while the other discs appear as convex bumps. Turning the picture upside down reverses this pattern. See text for discussion (adapted from Hoffman, 1998, and Ramachandran, 1988).

intuitive sense: when facing a surface that is itself facing the sun at an oblique angle, bumps on the surface will in fact be lighter toward their tops, while dents will be lighter toward their bottoms—due simply to the differential shadows produced in each case.

The critical thing to note about this phenomenon, however, is that the inference from shading to shape is only reliable given two assumptions. The first assumption is that there is only a single light source (since all of the discs in fig. 3.3 could be bumps if you assume that the lower-middle disc is simply lit by a separate light source—an assumption your visual system is not willing to make). Second, this inference is only valid if you assume that the light source is overhead (e.g., Berbaum et al., 1983; Rittenhouse, 1786)! This appears to be another of the assumptions that the visual system uses as a heuristic cue when computing shape from shading, in an attempt to combat underdetermination.[8] Where does this assumption come from—is it innate or is it learned from experience with the sun overhead? At least in some species, there is good evidence to suggest that this assumption is innately determined. Hershberger (1970), for example, raised chickens from egghood in an

---

8. Here are two other interesting facts about this bias: first, note that the assumption is of a bias from *overhead* rather than from *above*. The reason for this is that the light-source assumption appears to operate in a head-centered reference frame rather than a world-centered reference frame (Howard et al., 1990)—a fact that you can see for yourself by studying figures 3.3 and 3.4 while standing on your head. Second, more contemporary studies have actually demonstrated that most observers also assume that the single light source comes from a bit to the left of center, in addition to being overhead (Mamassian & Goutcher, 2001; Sun & Perona, 1998)! While good explanations of this are hard to come by, it may be related to the fact that we consistently orient our bodies relative to light sources when manipulating objects with our hands, combined with the fact that most people are righthanded (Sun & Perona, 1998).

FIGURE 3.4 An example of the "overhead illumination" assumption in a real photograph of moon craters. Turning the picture upside-down reverses convex and concave.

environment that was always lit from below, and trained them to discriminate bumps from dents. When the chickens were later tested (in isotropic lighting conditions) using stimuli such as the discs in figure 3.3, their behavior indicated that their visual systems still assumed that the light source came from overhead—directly contradicting all of their visual experience! As a result, he concluded that "there appears to be an innate perceptual parameter corresponding to an 'overhead source of illumination'" (p. 407).

Recent Bayesian modeling work has successfully cast this assumption as a Bayesian prior (Mamassian & Goutcher, 2001; Mamassian et al., 2002). Though the details of this model are beyond the scope of this chapter, it is worth noting that such a modeling effort has several advantages over simply talking in a vague but interesting way of an "assumption" about overhead illumination that is wired into the visual system. First, a Bayesian model shows how such a "principle" can exist in a more general visual architecture that also incorporates various other assumptions and priors. Second, such a model allows for a detailed study of how the "overhead illumination" prior interacts with other specific priors (such as the assumption of an overhead *viewpoint*; Mamassian & Landy, 1998), and how priors can interact and compete. Third, Bayesian models embody optimal reasoning under uncertainty, and as such they allow for an objective assessment of how good human performance is relative to an "ideal observer." Fourth, and perhaps most important, the model allows for a detailed investigation of the reliability of the prior: while human performance may always assume that the illumination comes from a particular angle, the model's illumination-location prior can be set to multiple values, and the resulting impact on discrimination can be rigorously studied. In this way the Bayesian model serves as both a *tool* (for really understanding what an overhead-illumination "assumption" could mean, and why and how it might have an impact on perception) and a *theory* (of how the human visual system actually employs the assumption). In this way, Bayesian models have allowed for "natural constraints" to be translated from vague statements into rigorous testable theories—"a psychophysics of constraints" (Knill et al., 1996).

Of course, this is just one example, but a Bayesian approach has also been successfully employed in similar ways to model phenomena in many other domains of visual perception—including the perception of color (Brainerd & Freeman, 1997), motion (Weiss et al., 2002), shape (Feldman, 2000), surfaces (Nakayama & Shimojo, 1992), and higher level aspects of perception such as object recognition (Liu et al., 1995) and perceptual grouping (Feldman, 2001). Of course there are many limitations to Bayesian modeling in perception (see note 7): for example, the Bayesian approach tends to work well for modeling specific functions, but non-Bayesian theories must account for the modular nature of perception itself (Knill et al., 1996) and are in many cases responsible for uncovering particular priors. Still, the Bayesian approach fits human performance exceedingly well in several contexts, and it allows for a detailed scientific understanding of how "principles" may be wired into the visual system. Moreover, because the Bayesian approach is in some sense optimal (a fact that motivates the increasingly common study of "ideal observers" in perception research), it is perhaps the most successful contemporary realization of David Marr's famous advice that the mind should be studied first from the computational level, when possible, so that we understand the nature of the information-processing problems themselves that the mind faces.

4 Reconciling Nativism and Development: Clues from Vision Science

This section aims to make a very simple point: there is no mystery in many theories of visual perception about how nature and nurture can interact. More specifically, both theories of Bayesian perception (sec. 4.1) and theories that appeal to spontaneous endogenous input (sec. 4.2) make it entirely unmysterious how the very same process can both be innately determined and yet later develop robustly via interaction with the environment.

4.1 Nature and Nurture Are Easily Combined in Bayesian Perception

As discussed in section 2, much of the controversy about nativist theories of higher level cognition has focused on the perceived conflict between innateness and development. Often nativism is simply written off as antidevelopmental, but even careful researchers tend to relegate development to processes outside the actual nativist components of their theories—to maturation, triggering, overriding, or simply other non-innate aspects of the mind. In contrast, Bayesian theories of visual perception constitute a case study of how such a separation is unnecessary. This simple point falls directly out of the general structure of the Bayesian framework. Innate assumptions and principles, in this framework, are realized as priors. And the underlying structure of these priors are simply distributions of values of variables—"p(Hypothesis)" for each hypothesis (scene) under consideration. Thus an innate principle—for example, the assumption of a single overhead light source discussed in section 3.3—is architecturally realized as the default value or "factory setting" of the relevant variable. But in no sense is that principle then written in stone, since its value can later be updated and tuned via interaction with the environment. This point has never really been stressed by Bayesian theorists in vision science, perhaps because they tend not to traffic in debates about nativism in their day-to-day research.

Many priors may be innate. This has been empirically demonstrated in some cases (e.g., the overhead-illumination principle; Hershberger, 1970) and is widely assumed in many others—including the visual system's prior assumptions that objects are rigid (Ullman, 1979), that objects are convex (e.g., Hoffman & Richards, 1984), and that motion is relatively slow (Weiss et al., 2002). In general theorizing beyond the scope of particular priors, moreover, most Bayesian theorists are happy to accept the possibility that "the priors are in the genes" (Kersten et al., 2004, p. 285). Other priors are probably formed by combining innate constraints with learning, however: "undoubtedly, the prior probability and likelihood distributions incorporated implicitly into the visual system arise through a combination of evolution and perceptual learning" (Geisler & Kersten, 2002, p. 509). Some specific priors, such as the bias for assuming that certain ambiguous image angles correspond to right angles in the actual scenes (e.g., Halper, 1997), may even have little or no innate component. In general, recent studies have shown that human perceptual systems—even those of young infants—are surprisingly good at picking out even subtle static and temporal statistical regularities in the environment (Chun, 2000; Fiser & Aslin, 2001, 2002a, b). Other theories of "opportunistic" learning suggest that some priors might be learned at only particular times when the visual system recognizes that relatively rare conditions of low ambiguity obtain (see Brady & Kersten, 2003; Kersten et al., 2004).

More generally, the Bayesian framework makes plain how priors can be *both* innate and later tuned via interaction with the environment: it is as simple as initializing a variable to a default value, and later updating the value of that variable (where each variable is really a distribution of values).[9] Indeed, it seems likely that this is the most common situation, since perceptual systems should take advantage of both nature and nurture as much as possible: "The Bayesian approach allows one to understand precisely how the reliability of different sources of information, including prior knowledge, should be combined by a perceptual system. Different sources of information do not always keep the same relative reliability, and hence a rational perceptual system should adjust the weights that it assigns to different information sources contingent upon their current relative reliabilities" (Geisler & Kersten, 2002, p. 509).

This updating could take place in several ways: by updating the actual distribution of a prior, by changing the relative weightings of various priors, by

---

9. Though many neuroscientists do not often talk about variables being stored in neural tissue, we know that they must exist, even in much simpler creatures such as ants (see Gallistel, 2000, for discussion).

adjusting the likelihood function, or even by adding (or removing) priors altogether. The critical point here is that it isn't the least bit mysterious how any of these forms of environmental tuning is possible, and several types of learning would occur not outside of the nativist framework but to *the very information that is itself thought to be innate*. Moreover, this type of updating could encompass bona fide *learning* (Pylyshyn, 1985). Unlike triggering, maturation, and strong parameterization, this form of development is not limited to highly constrained environmental cues but can in principle encompass entirely new and unexpected forms of information. Thus it needn't be true in a nativist theory that "the constraints remain unchanged through life" (Gopnik, 2003, p. 239). Rather, the priors in such architectures may simply characterize the *initial* state of the system, and may come to be updated or supplanted later. Moreover, some of the nativist content in a Bayesian framework may even be particular innate strategies for later learning: "it is largely an open question of how the human visual system learns the appropriate statistical priors, but some priors *as well as strategies for learning priors* are likely to be rooted in our genes" (Kersten & Yuille, 2003, p. 151, emphasis added).[10] In all of these ways, Bayesian theories of perception constitute a case study of an architecture in which innateness and development do not inherently conflict, and can richly interact.

4.2 A Second Example: Reconciling Nativism and Plasticity in Vision via Spontaneous Endogenous Activity

In fact, several types of theories of visual perception—not only those based on statistical inference—invoke both innateness and development, and make clear how these processes can comfortably coexist in the very same visual mechanisms. In this section I will mention one other general strategy for reconciling nativism and plasticity in vision science, which invokes spontaneous endogenous activity in perceptual systems, and has its roots in visual neurophysiology.

When most cognitive psychologists think about the role of environmental influences on the design of the visual system, they are likely to recall the textbook cases of the effects of deprivation on the development of ocular dominance columns. These famous studies by Hubel and Wiesel (1965, 1970; Wiesel & Hubel, 1965a, b) involved raising cats in conditions of either complete monocular deprivation or severely attenuated binocular input (via imposed strabismus) and showing that these early experiences severely impaired the development of normal structure in visual cortex and also the resulting binocular visual function. Similar work has shown that exposing animals to contours of only certain orientations during rearing leads to a predominance of cells that select for those orientations,

---

10. Detailed theories of how the visual system should go about learning priors and tuning innate priors have yet to be developed with the same rigor that characterizes most Bayesian theories, but landmarks for this project do exist. In particular, detailed models have recently been proposed for how natural selection itself can be modeled in Bayesian terms (Geisler & Diehl, 2002), and it seems likely that such models will apply to both phylogenetic and ontogenetic updating.

and a relative paucity of selective cells for those orientations the animals have never seen (e.g., Blakemore & Cooper, 1970; Sengpiel et al., 1999).

This well-known research tradition, however, is not the full story. More contemporary work in neurophysiology has demonstrated that the development of ocular dominance columns, for instance, occurs in two stages: the initial formation of the structures and subsequent environmental tuning. Effects of deprivation tend to affect the second stage, whereas the basic structure of cortical circuits forms even without any visual experience (for a review see Katz et al., 2000). Moreover, we have some idea of the mechanism by which this is possible: spontaneous internally generated cortical signals (e.g., O'Donovan, 1999; Shatz, 1996). That is, innate structure is formed via the very same mechanism that drives later environmental tuning; the difference concerns only whether the signals are generated internally or externally. For the development of ocular dominance columns, this strategy is particularly effective: since the two eyes are unconnected, spontaneous early visual activity in the retina creates statistically independent oscillating signals from each eye, which can be used in the developing cortex to determine that the activity arises from two separate loci (see Katz et al., 2000). In the context of orientation tuning a similar story holds, and the disruption of this spontaneous activity correspondingly impairs orientation selectivity (Weliky & Katz, 1997).

This type of situation—wherein nature and nurture operate on the very same mechanisms via internal versus external signals—may apply much more generally to the development of perceptual abilities, including higher level perceptual skills. For example, face recognition is an area of perception research that has also seen the type of conflict between innateness and development that is characteristic of debates about higher level cognition (see Pascalis & Slater, 2003), and many popular models of face perception assume that innate factors and subsequent learning occur in completely separate brain systems (e.g., CONLERN v. CONSPEC, in Morton & Johnson, 1991). Again, however, this separation between nature and nurture may not be necessary. More recent models of face perception, for instance, suggest that the very same processes may be innately structured via spontaneous endogenous activity, and then later develop via external input (e.g., Bednar, 2003). Only the initial endogenous pattern generators are assumed to be innate. (Note that such generators may involve bona fide innate structure, not just innate signals, as in the case of uncorrelated input from the two retinas.) The rest of the machinery involved in face perception simply acts on that input in the very same way that it acts on environmental input, and such processing needn't even "know" whether its input consists of innately driven spontaneous signals or faces in the external world. Moreover, as with Bayesian theories, detailed computational models of this process exist, demonstrating that there is nothing mysterious about this clever marriage of innateness and development (Bednar & Miikkulainen, 2003).

4.3 Conclusions: From Principles to Priors?

The same ultimate lesson can be drawn from work on both Bayesian models of perception and models of spontaneous endogenous activity in early visual development: the widespread perception of an inherent conflict between innateness and development is illusory. Innateness and development can act together in several ways, and can even act on the very same underlying processes. Innately specified structure can *itself* develop, and there is nothing mysterious about this process.

A goal for future work will be to adapt these types of architectures to the cases of higher level cognition in which innateness and development have not fit so well together. In both of the domains highlighted in section 2—infant object-cognition and theory of mind—nativist theories have tended to be phrased in terms of static-sounding principles and concepts, and such characterizations have tended to fuel the perception that such innate structure is incapable of significant change. But note that the priors of Bayesian perception sound equally static and inflexible when phrased in terms of abstract principles and assumptions ("Illumination comes from overhead"). Rigorous models have demonstrated how such abstract principles can be implemented in ways that are malleable, however, and it will be worth exploring such options (along with the possibility of spontaneous endogenous signals) in cases of higher level cognition. Some of the development in these domains may in fact involve more extrinsic or peripheral developmental processes such as triggering, maturation, overriding, parameterization, and so on, but these needn't be the whole story. Innate structure can in principle develop richly in response to environmental stimulation, and this development can bring about radical changes even in the initially innate structure itself.

The fact that nativist theories in higher level cognition also often appeal to modularity is no reason to doubt that such strategies can work. In practice, aspects of visual perception—including the foci of most low-level Bayesian modeling—are thought to be far more modular than higher level cognition (though see Carruthers, chapter 5 here; Sperber, chapter 4 here), and this has in no way frustrated the development of successful models that blend nature and nurture. In addition, there is no inherent conflict in principle between modularity and development (Scholl & Leslie, 1999b). Modules are often characterized primarily in terms of informational encapsulation, such that they can only act on a restricted range of possible inputs (Fodor, 1983, 2000). But this in no way stops modules from developing internally—and even altering their own input restrictions—on the basis of the information they do receive. Innate modules can also develop, in straightforward ways. Constructing theories such as those based on Bayesian inference or spontaneous endogenous input may be more challenging in the context of higher level cognition, but the work from visual perception can serve as a useful guide for such a project and demonstrates in rigorous case studies that there is at least no inherent conflict between innateness and development.

Even these future directions, however, are only a small piece of a much larger project. Researchers who are exploring foundational issues such as innateness, modularity, computation, evolution, and representation—all foci for intense controversy in the study of higher level cognition—might do well to explore how such notions are treated not only in simpler organisms (Gallistel, 2000) but also in simpler, less controversial, and more rigorously understood cognitive processes, such as visual perception. This is one specific context in which we see the hope of cognitive science: that scholars from superficially different research areas may still find common connections and useful insights that apply broadly to the organization of the mind.

4

DAN SPERBER

Modularity and Relevance
How Can a Massively Modular Mind Be Flexible and Context-Sensitive?

Let me start with a quotation from Randy Gallistel (1999, p. 1179, echoing Chomsky, 1975):

> Adaptive specialization of mechanisms is so ubiquitous and so obvious in biology, at every level of analysis, and for every kind of function, that no one thinks it necessary to call attention to it as a general principle about biological mechanisms. In this light, it is odd but true that most past and present contemporary theorizing about learning does not assume that learning mechanisms are adaptively specialized for the solution of particular kinds of problems. Most theorizing assumes that there is a general-purpose learning process in the brain, a process adapted only to solving the problem of learning.... From a biological perspective, this assumption is equivalent to assuming that there is a general-purpose sensory organ that solves the problem of sensing.

Gallistel's remark can be extended to cognition in general. It is odd but true that most past and present contemporary theorizing *about cognition* does not assume that cognitive mechanisms are adaptively specialized for the solution of particular kinds of problems. There is indeed a great divide today between a minority of cognitive scientists for whom mind-brains are best viewed as articulations of specialized modules and a majority for whom at least the *human* mind-brain is largely nonmodular. I belong to the minority and have argued the case for

---

Earlier versions of this chapter were presented at the Conference on the Innate Mind in Sheffield, England, in July 2003 and at the Rutgers Colloquium in Cognitive Science in February 2004. I thank the participants, and in particular Stephen Stich, as well as Gloria Origgi and Deirdre Wilson, for their comments and criticisms. The issues discussed in this chapter have been addressed in fruitful ways in particular in Carruthers (chapter 5 here), Samuels (chapter 7 here), Sterelny (2003), and, with novel insights, Barrett (forthcoming). I cannot here discuss the points of convergence and divergence between their views and mine, but I gratefully acknowledge their help in sharpening my own ideas.

massive modularity elsewhere.[1] What I want to do here is answer two questions: How can a massively modular mind be flexible? And: How can a massively modular mind be context-sensitive? The two questions are related: the context of cognitive processes is changing every fraction of a second, if only because it is modified by these very processes. In verbal comprehension, for instance, the interpretation of every utterance modifies the context in which the next utterance is interpreted. Context-sensitivity is the ability to take this ever-changing context into account. "Flexibility" (or "plasticity") is a metaphor that is best unpacked as meaning context-sensitivity in the longer run. An individual cognitive system is flexible if it can modify itself on the basis of experience. When humans in general are described as a particularly flexible species, it is even longer term context-sensitivity that is involved: over historical time, humans have adapted to very diverse natural and humanmade environments and have, for this, developed novel cognitive competencies. Clearly, a system that is flexible is in a better position to exhibit context-sensitivity in the short run.

1 Cognitive Modules Are a Type of Biological Module

Given that discussions of cognitive modularity often get bogged down in tedious terminological arguments, I might have been tempted to avoid the term "module" altogether if it were not that that there is much recent relevant work on biological modularity (e.g., Schlosser & Wagner, 2004), of which cognitive modularity is best seen, I want to argue, as a special case. It is hardly controversial that complex organisms are systems made up of many distinct subsystems—including but not limited to classical "organs," now often called "modules"—that may differ from one another functionally, structurally, ontogenetically, and phylogenetically. A modular organization is an effect of biological evolution, which responds in a piecemeal fashion to challenges presented by the environment. Arguably, modularity is also a condition of evolvability (Wagner & Altenberg, 1996). Because they are opportunistic responses to a great variety of problems and opportunities, it is in the nature of modules to be quite diverse in form, size, and function. Hence, one cannot both appreciate the role of modularity in biological systems and ask for a precise and rich definition of what a module is, or insist that a genuine module should resemble some prototype. Let me repeat, if you insist that a module should be defined in a narrow and rigid way, you are ignoring the evolutionary dimension of modularity.

Biological modules can be articulated in a variety of ways and can, in particular, contain submodules. For instance, the vertebrate digestive system is itself a complex module and contains as submodules various portions of the digestive tract such as the pharynx, the stomach, or the large intestine, glands such as the salivary glands or

---

1. See Sperber (1994), revised and expanded in Sperber (1996, 2001). It was under the influence of Chomsky that I was first led to argue that the human mind should be viewed as an articulation of autonomous domain-specific device (Sperber, 1974). Later, the work of Cosmides and Tooby (1992, 1994) convinced me that an evolutionary perspective, which I had taken as mere background, was crucial to developing such a view. Much of my thinking on the issue has, of course, been shaped by Fodor (1983), even when I disagree with him.

the liver, chemical modules such as hormones and enzymes produced by the glands, and so on. Inherited modules can evolve and both turn into and generate new modules in the lifetime of the organism. For instance, B lymphocytes are inherited cell-sized modules that evolve within the organism and generate antibodies, that is, new protein-sized modules the function of which is to bind to, and thereby neutralize, specific antigens. It may not be obvious at first to think of modules the size and character of freely moving short-lived cells and proteins, but, again, the point about a modular organization is that it may contain as modules any autonomously functioning device with a phylogenetic or ontogenetic history of its own.

If cognitive modules are real components of the cognitive system and not mere boxes in a nominalist flow-chart model, then they are a subtype of biological modules. They are characterized in particular by specific input conditions and by proprietary resources used to process inputs that meet these conditions. The inputs that happen to meet the input conditions of a given module constitute what I have called its *actual domain* (Sperber, 1994). In most cases, these input conditions are an imperfect but effective way of picking out items that belong to some objective category or domain of items in the environment. This objective domain then is the *proper domain* of the module. The function of the module is to inform the organism about items in its proper domain. It is with reference to such a proper domain that a module can be said to be domain specific. A module might, for instance, accept as inputs sounds exhibiting specific structural patterns, when, in the environment where this module operates, such sound patterns almost always correspond to speech in a given natural language. Then the proper domain of this module would be speech in that language (even if it might be activated by some nongenuinely linguistic sound pattern à la "Jabberwocky").

A cognitive module has its own procedures and may also have a database of its own. A face recognition module, for instance, has both data about the faces it is capable of recognizing and dedicated procedures to match perceptual inputs to these data. The fact that a module can draw only on a limited database, if any, to process its inputs is what Fodor (1983, 2000) calls "informational encapsulation," one of several criteria for modularity in his *Modularity of Mind* (1983) and the only one that plays a significant role in his book *The Mind Doesn't Work That Way* (2000). Because an informationally encapsulated device only has access to limited information, excluding some information that might in principle be pertinent to its producing the right outputs and that might be available elsewhere in the organism, it fails to exhibit the context-sensitivity that is characteristic of human cognition as a whole. Paradigm examples are provided by perceptual illusions: *I* (that is, a whole person) have the information that the two lines in the Müller-Lyer illusion are equal (say, I have measured them), but my visual perceptual device has no access to this information and keeps "seeing" them as unequal. Cognitive reflexes are, in this respect, extreme cases of encapsulation: given the proper input, they immediately deliver their characteristic output, whatever its appropriateness in the context.

It is important to distinguish *domain-specificity* from *encapsulation*. A device is *domain specific* if its function is to process only inputs belonging to some specific empirical domain (even if its input conditions do not perfectly pick out all and only items in this domain, so that there is a degree of mismatch between its proper and its actual domain). For instance, a face recognition device has as its function to process faces (even if its operation can also be triggered by merely face-like stimuli, e.g., masks). An *encapsulated* device is one that uses a limited database to process its inputs. A word recognition device, for instance, takes as characteristic inputs phonetic representations of speech and uses as a database a dictionary. It is plausible that there are domain-general mental devices. Working memory, for instance, might be seen as a domain-general device that processes inputs whatever their contents, and manages their level of activation for the benefit of other, inferential devices. I cannot think, on the other hand, of a plausible example of a nonencapsulated mental device, that is, of a device that would use the whole mental encyclopedia as its database. Nonencapsulation is, tautologically, a property of the mind as a whole, but it does not seem to be a property of any autonomous subcomponent of it.[2]

What a cognitive module does at a given time (if it does anything at all) is determined by the inputs it is processing, by its procedures, and by its database, if any. It is not *directly* governed by what other modules of the cognitive system are doing, and does not *directly* draw on the informational resources available to these other components. I stress "directly" because there are, of course, indirect ways in which modules affect one another. Apart from sensory organs, all components of the cognitive system get their inputs from other components: roughly speaking, face recognition gets its input from visual perception, pragmatic interpretation of utterances gets part of its input from linguistic decoding, and so on. So a module's operations are typically triggered by being fed as input the output of some other module. Moreover, the triggering input typically has been informed by the procedures and data of the feeder module. Still, once it is performing its function, a module works on its own and is unable to take advantage of information that might be present in the system as a whole but that is found neither in the input nor in the proprietary database of the module.

Isn't there a risk, though, when allowing for a great variety of modules networked in complex ways, of trivializing the notion of modularity to the point of confusing modules with the boxes used in diagrams representing the flow of

---

2. Fodor, it is true, gives as an example of nonencapsulation the case of modus ponens inference, that is, an inference that takes as input any pair of beliefs of the form {P, [If P then Q]} and produces as output the belief that Q. Modus ponens, Fodor argues (2000, pp. 60–62), applies to pairs of premises in virtue of their logical form and is otherwise indifferent to their informational content. An organism with a modus ponens device can use it across the board. Compare this with, say, a bridled modus ponens device that would apply to reasoning about number but not about food, people, or plants, in fact about nothing other than numbers. According to Fodor, this latter device would be encapsulated. However, the difference between the wholly general and the number-specific modus ponens devices is one of inputs, and therefore of domain specificity, not one of database, and therefore not of encapsulation. Both the general and the bridled modus ponens inferences apply a procedure to pairs of premises and do so without using any data. In particular, they ignore data that might cause a rational agent to refrain from performing the modus ponens inference and to question one or other of the premises instead (Harman, 1986). If there is a modus ponens inference procedure in the human mind, it is better viewed, I would argue, as cognitive reflex (Sperber, 2001).

information in cognitive processes? The risk is avoided, I maintain, by the modularist's commitment to biologically realistic interpretation of the boxes. A boxological flow chart can be interpreted as a mere algorithmic representation of a complex cognitive process showing how, in principle, the process could be materially realized but carrying no commitment regarding its actual implementation in mind-brains. The true modularist is interested in "boxes" that correspond to neurologically distinct devices. A neurologically distinct device, or module, need not occupy a single and continuous brain location all by itself—its boundaries need not be sharp—but still, it must be distinguishable not just functionally but also neurologically. This presupposes that a module has a distinct history in the development of the individual brain, and this in turn presupposes some genetic and evolutionary story about the conditions that make such an individual development possible.

The issue now is whether such an articulation of biologically real cognitive modules could exhibit the flexibility and context-sensitivity exhibited by the human mind as a whole.

2 Modularity and Flexibility

Modules are "rigid." The human mind, on the other hand, is "flexible." Since both "rigid" and "flexible" are metaphors, this raises not so much a serious objection to a modularist view of the human mind as an interesting question: How could flexibility be achieved in such a modular system? The answer is that most innate[3] cognitive modules are domain-specific *learning* mechanisms ("learning instincts," Marler, 1991, or "module templates," Sperber, 1994) that generate the working modules of acquired cognitive competence.

Even though the existence and many characteristics of mental modules are explained by biological evolution, this does not imply that modules are simply phenotypic expressions of genes, or that the development of each and every module is strongly canalized. On the contrary, it would be in the nature of modules to differ vastly from one another in this as in other respects. For some of the problems cognitive modules handle, "prewiring" may be appropriate. For other problems, an effective modular solution may involve adding data to the proprietary database of an otherwise predetermined module. In other cases still, the development of a module may involve drawing on information picked up from the environment not just to enrich the database but also to shape procedures.

There is, in fact, a full range of cases from innately specified modules to brain tissues that are merely ready to modularize competencies of a specific type. Here are five examples across this range:

- *Avoidance of vertical drops*: Human infants (and other baby animals also) perceive and avoid vertical drops in terrain, even if they have had no experience of falling before, as was demonstrated by means of the well-known "visual cliff" experiments initiated by Gibson and Walk

---

3. "Innate" in the sense of Samuels (2002).

(1960). This is an obvious modular adaptation to a serious hazard facing animals moving on the ground. To be efficient, this particular module had better not depend on learning. It is as good an example of an innate cognitive module as one may ever hope to find.
- *The Garcia effect* (Garcia & Koelling, 1966): Rats and other animals are innately equipped to develop an aversion to whatever type of food seems to have made them sick. This is a highly specialized one-pass-learning module. The outcome of such learning is a novel capacity, that of re-acting with aversion to a specific kind of food. If the rat develops, say, three such aversions, then it has three distinct abilities. It could be that the learning process and each specific aversive reaction are all carried out by the same module: learning consisting in adding to the initially empty proprietary database of the module data about specific foods to be avoided. Or it could be that the learning process results each time in the setting up of a new module or submodule dedicated to a specific aversive food. So which is it—one general food-aversion module with a growing database, or a learning module producing as many micro-modules as there are aversions? This is an empirical issue that might be decided by answering questions such as the following: Do aversive reactions to different foods employ different detection procedures (as opposed to the same procedure using different data)? Does a new aversion recruit distinct brain tissues? Can the more general ability to generate new aversions and each of the more specific aversions be selectively impaired? Positive answers to such questions would suggest that to each new aversion corresponds a new mini (sub) module.
- *Face recognition*: I assume that face recognition is modular (which is controversial, but see Kanwisher & Moscovitch, 2000). If so, we are dealing, as in the case of the Garcia effect, with two types of modular abilities: a *general* learning ability to form *specific* abilities to detect specific faces. Is there a general face recognition module that performs both functions or are individual-face-detectors developed as autonomous mini (sub) modules? This is an empirical question to which we do not have an answer. As in the case of the Garcia effect, these are nevertheless genuinely distinct possibilities involving subtle differences in the way these abilities may be carried out and impaired.
- *Language faculty and linguistic competences*: The language faculty is a complex learning module that, given proper linguistic and contextual inputs, yields one or, in the case of plurilinguals, several mental grammars. Each of these grammars is itself a complex module subserving both verbal coding and decoding in a given language. Each mental grammar has a distinct developmental story, and can selectively decay or be impaired. It is plausible that, say, the two mental grammars of a bilingual individual are submodules of a more general mental universal grammar and, as such, share some resources (Dehaene et al., 1997; Kim et al., 1997).
- *Reading*: Reading is too recent a cultural skill for a specialized innate module to have evolved. Yet reading systematically involves the same

brain site located in the left occipito-temporal sulcus and sometimes described as the "visual word form area." Dehaene speculates that "the human brain can learn to read because part of the primate visual ventral object recognition system spontaneously accomplishes operations closely similar to those required in word recognition, and possesses sufficient plasticity to adapt itself to new shapes, including those of letters and words. During the acquisition of reading, part of this system becomes highly specialized for the visual operations underlying location- and case-invariant word recognition.... Thus, reading acquisition proceeds by selection and local adaptation of a preexisting neural region, rather than by *de novo* imposition of novel properties onto that region" (Dehaene, forthcoming). Reading skill can be viewed as resulting from a process of ad hoc modularization of already specialized brain tissues.

With many innate modules being learning modules generating further modules, with brain areas ready to modularize, one may envisage that the human mind is characterized not only by massive modularity but also by *teeming modularity*. A great many highly specialized procedures—the size, say, of a specific concept or even of a particular inference rule—may be modular in the intended sense. That is, there may be a plethora of distinct biological devices emerging on some innate basis in the course of cognitive development, and functioning with a certain degree of autonomy in cognitive activity (a similar view, based on an analogy between cognitive modules and enzymes, is developed by Clark Barrett, forthcoming). I hope these remarks help one clarify how a massively modular mind may indeed be flexible, even if the detailed ways in which such flexibility is achieved are obviously a matter for empirical research.

3 How Can a Massively Modular Mind Be Context-Sensitive?

According to Fodor, in human cognition, only peripheral input systems are modular. One of the distinctive properties of modular input systems, he argues, is that their operations are mandatory. Supporters of the idea of massive modularity, not just at the input level but at all levels of cognitive activity, shouldn't lightly accept the idea that mandatoriness characterizes modular operations. If all the modules of a massively modular mind mandatorily processed any input available to them (including the outputs of other modules that meet their input conditions) there would be a computational explosion. Even if such a system could work at all, it is hard to see how it could exhibit the kind of context-sensitivity that is characteristic of human cognition. Every input would be processed in the same way in every situation. Of course, some limited context-sensitivity could still be built into such a system. The output of a given module could inhibit the operations of another module: the standard violent response to an apparently aggressive movement, for instance, can be inhibited by the perception of signs of playfulness. A danger detection module, acting as an "*and*-gate," may accept only complex inputs such as pairs of more elementary inputs, for instance a sound *and* a visual signal. In such cases, there is an in-built context-dependency, but it remains quite local, unlike the context-dependency displayed by ordinary human cognition in, for example, verbal comprehension.

If one takes for granted that modularity implies mandatoriness, then one should reject the massive modularity hypothesis. My strategy will be to examine and question the idea that the operation of modules must be mandatory—even in the case of Fodorian input modules. I will then argue that the system as a whole exhibits context-sensitivity through the allocation of energy among modules.

There are two senses in which a cognitive procedure might be said to be mandatory. In a first sense—the only one in which I will use the term—a procedure is mandatory if, given the appropriate input, it will follow its course and produce its output whatever the rest of the mind-brain is doing (except in cases of pathological or accidental impairments). In other words, the procedure is mandatory in the sense that an appropriate input is sufficient to trigger it in such a manner that it will run its course (and not just to give it some initial activation). In a second sense, a procedure is "mandatory" if it cannot be voluntarily willed or blocked (except in an indirect way, for instance by acting on the availability of the inputs rather than on the procedure itself)—for this I will only use "involuntary." When Fodor argues that the operations of mental modules are "mandatory," he seems to have both senses in mind. It is self-evident that a procedure that is mandatory in the first sense, that is, automatically stimulus triggered, would be "mandatory" in the second sense, that is, involuntary. There are procedures that are indeed both mandatory (in the first sense) and involuntary. For instance, perceiving an object as colored is automatically triggered by the stimulus and cannot be willed or blocked. Similarly, being presented with a pair of numbers such as 50 and 100 automatically triggers (in a person familiar with numbers) a comparison of their size, before any decision could be taken to perform or not to perform such a comparison. Still, the two properties, that of being mandatory, that is, input triggered, and that of being involuntary are far from being coextensive. There are many cognitive procedures over which the individual has no voluntary control and that, in the course of ordinary cognitive activity, may be inhibited or enhanced both by mind-internal factors such as expectations and by mind-external factors such as distracting stimuli. These procedures are neither voluntary nor mandatory.

If I see just in front of me, in broad daylight, the face of my Paris dentist, Monsieur Durand, I cannot help but recognize him. My face recognition module (or my Monsieur-Durand-detection submodule) does its job. But suppose I am lecturing in London. Some 30 faces in front of me are each clearly visible. I look cursorily at all of them and I recognize some colleagues. Even though I have looked at his face as much as at those of the people I immediately recognized, it is only toward the end of the lecture that I suddenly recognize, sitting there in the second row, Monsieur Durand, whom I would never have expected to see in such a place.

The operations of input modules seem mandatory when you consider only cases where the stimulus is, and stays long enough, at fixation, and the perceiver is not actively tracking some other stimulus. Striking experimental demonstration of this is provided by work on "inattentional blindness." For instance, Simons and Chabris (1999) found that about 50 percent of participants asked to monitor a basketball passing event on a screen failed to notice a gorilla that walked across the screen in full view, stopped in the middle of the players as the action continued all around it, turned to face the camera, thumped its chest, and then resumed walking. There are many, more banal cases, concerning most if not all input modules, where a stimulus is well within the field of perception but either is not in a focal position or is not sufficiently attended to, where the resources of the mind are invested in processing other competing stimuli, or inner thoughts, and where the module fails to process the stimulus (or at least fails to process it sufficiently): the familiar face is not recognized, the sentence structure is not parsed, the gorilla walks unnoticed. Let me insist, I am talking about cases where the psychophysical perceptual conditions for the operation of the module are satisfied and where, with less competition from other stimuli or other thoughts, or with appropriate expectations facilitating the process, the stimulus would have been processed. At least some of the procedures involved in perceiving the gorilla are not mandatory. There may well be an initial activation of the relevant procedures, but, when an individual's attention is focused on something else, they may not run their full course. I take it that the idea that visual perception is modular is not put in jeopardy by such data. Then, however, mandatoriness cannot be a defining trait of modules. (By the way, I am not trying to make a terminological but a substantive point. If these perceptual procedures that fail to deliver their expected output in the inattentional blindness experiments mentioned earlier are still "mandatory" by your definition, so be it. What matters here is that the availability of an appropriate input is not sufficient to cause these procedures to run their full course. The interesting issue then becomes: what other factors determine which procedures follow their course?)

The general point I am stressing here is this: mental modules in humans compete for energetic resources. Not all of them can operate simultaneously. This is true at all levels: perceptual, conceptual, and psychomotor. Contrast humans with simpler cognitive systems in this respect. Take a frog (or at least the idealized frog of philosophers—I am not making zoological claims). Here it sits, waiting for a fly moving within reach. There is no fly movement, no cognitive process other than the low-level monitoring of the visual field necessary to activate the get-the-fly module when appropriate. Is this a case of a wholly stimulus-driven module with mandatory operations? Almost, but not quite. Presumably the frog is also monitoring for possible predators and other dangers, and if a fly and a predator are sighted simultaneously, the operations of the get-the-fly module are preempted by those of the escape-the-predator module. This priority of the escape-the-predator module over all others (feeding and also mating modules) is clearly adaptive and is presumably built in. So the operations of the escape-the-predator module are fully mandatory, and those of the get-the-fly module are mandatory unless preempted. Frogs may well have a few more cognitive modules. Even so, it is plausible that the operations of each of them are mandatory except in the case of preemption, and that the order in which modules may preempt one another is fixed in the frog's nervous system. Moreover, cases of actual modular preemption are likely to be relatively rare (it is not very often that a frog is simultaneously presented with a possible prey, a possible predator, and a possible mate). The human predicament is quite different. If, as I have suggested, the human mind is teeming with modules, then, at all times, a number of modules have inputs available and must be competing for brain power to process them. Rather than a fixed and global preemption order, which would not be adaptive in this case, some flexible, context-sensitive energy allocation procedure must be at work.

What should this energy allocation procedure be doing, that is, how might it contribute to the efficiency of the human cognitive system as a whole? Again, contrast with (philosophers') frogs. Presumably there are just a few categories of stimuli, such as flies, that frogs can discriminate, and only in restricted conditions. They monitor their environment to check whether any of these categories happen to be instantiated and then produce the prewired behavioral response. Humans can discriminate tens of thousands of categories in their environment, very few of which trigger automatic behavioral responses. At any one moment, humans are monitoring their environment through all their senses and establish perceptual contact with a great many potential inputs for further processing. Frogs have no memory to speak of. Humans have vast amounts of information stored in memory. When processing a new input, humans bring some of this stored information to bear on it. Attending to a given stimulus, activating memorized information, bringing the two together, and drawing inferences are effort-demanding mental activities. Effort is a cost that should be incurred only in the expectation of a benefit. Different trains of thought involve quite different evolving allocations of efforts and may produce quite different cognitive benefits.

What are the benefits of cognitive activity? The reply that comes most readily to mind is that cognition helps the organism recognize and react to opportunities and problems present in its environment; a more precise answer would consist in describing in much greater detail the various kinds of opportunities and problems that cognition helps the organism cope with. In the human case, a massive investment is made in cognition, and much knowledge is gathered, updated, and corrected without any specific practical goal. Presumably, what looks like—and often is—the pursuit of knowledge for its own sake helps prepare for an open range of future contingencies. Of course, knowledge is not equally pursued in all directions. Humans develop interests that guide their cognitive investments. Again, it seems, spelling out the benefit of cognition for humans would amount to describing in detail these diverse interests and possibly to explaining what makes their pursuit worth the effort. So, whereas it is natural to think of mental energy or effort in quantitative terms, one tends to approach cognitive benefit in qualitative terms. A philosopher might want to leave the matter there, but a psychologist cannot. The brain can be expected to allocate its energetic resources, not in a random but in a beneficial way. To achieve this, it does not have to be able to attribute an absolute value to the expected cognitive benefit of the processing of all available inputs, but it must be able to select, among the inputs and procedures actually competing for energy, some with relatively higher expected benefits.

Cognitive efficiency is a matter of investing effort in processing the right inputs. What are the right inputs? Do they have a characteristic property that the mind-brain can use in order to select them? Deirdre Wilson and I have argued that they do, and that this property is relevance, in a precise sense that we have tried to define and that I will briefly outline here (Sperber & Wilson, 1995; Wilson & Sperber, 2004).

Relevance is a property of inputs to cognitive processes. At a fairly abstract level, relevance can be defined *relative to an inferential procedure and a context*: a piece of information is relevant in a context for a given inferential procedure, if processing the piece of information and the context together yields different conclusions from those that would be obtained by processing them separately. A bit more technically, a piece of information is relevant in a context for a given inferential procedure, just in case the set of conclusions that the inferential procedure derives from the union of this piece of information and the context, taken together as a single set of premises, is different from the union of the two sets of conclusions the inferential procedure would derive separately from the piece of information on the one hand and from the context on the other. For instance, if the procedure instantiates the elimination rules of propositional calculus, then (a) but not (b) is relevant in context (c):

(a) *p and r*

(b) *q and r*

(c) {*if p then s, if s then t*}

As can be easily verified, (a) in the context of (c) yields the two conclusions *s* and *t*, which are derivable neither from (a) alone nor from (c) alone, whereas (b) in the context of (c) yields no conclusions other than those derivable from (b) alone and from (c) alone.

This abstract definition is useful as a step toward defining relevance in a psychologically more pertinent way. A piece of information is relevant *to an individual at a time* only if there is a procedure and a context available to the individual at that time, relative to which the piece of information is relevant in the sense just proposed (this is just a necessary condition—for a fuller definition, see Sperber & Wilson, 1995, ch. 3).

Relevance is a property easily achieved: virtually any new piece of information that connects, however weakly, with what the individual already knows will be relevant by our definition. Relevance, however, is a matter of degree. Cognitive efficiency is not just a matter of processing relevant inputs; it is a matter of processing the most relevant inputs available. Everything else being equal, the greater the cognitive benefit yielded by the processing of an input, the greater its relevance. In addition—and this is quite specific to the approach taken by relevance theory— everything else being equal, the greater the cost of processing an input, the lesser its relevance. Here is a short artificial illustration. Being told by the doctor "You have flu" is likely to carry more cognitive effects, and therefore be more relevant, than being told "you are ill." Being told "you have flu" is also likely to be more relevant than being told "you have a disease spelled with the sixth, twelfth, and twenty-first letters of the alphabet," because the first of these two statements would yield the same cognitive effects as the second, but for less processing effort.

Cognitive efficiency, then, is a matter of maximizing the relevance of the inputs processed. There may well not be a unique way to maximize relevance and therefore to optimize cognitive efficiency. One input may be preferable to another in terms of benefits, the other in term of costs, and, in the absence of a common metric, there is no obvious way to decide between the two. Still, as long as some inputs are clearly more relevant and therefore preferable to others, it should be possible to enhance cognitive efficiency through input selection. In other words, we should not expect the system to do more than tend to optimize. But how can even this be achieved? To try and answer, I will look first at costs, and then at benefits and then will put the two together.

How can the brain optimally allocate energy? The solution could, in principle, be a cognitive one. That is, the brain could represent its own energy consumption, compute the expected cost of various procedures, and use this as a criterion in deciding how much to invest in each procedure. In other words, the brain might automatically be taking, every fraction of a second, decisions similar to those we consciously take once in a while when, for instance, we choose to save our effort by using a pocket calculator rather than perform a mental calculation. Note, however, that this cognitive way of minimizing the energetic costs of cognitive processes would involve a significant cost of its own, which might make it self-defeating.

Are there noncognitive ways of minimizing effort in mental processes? Consider the comparable problem of minimizing energy consumption in muscular movement. Muscles get their energy from chemical reactions. This energy can be converted into work or into heat. The efficiency of the process (except when the function of the movement is to provide heat, as when shivering) depends on letting as little energy as possible degrade into heat. These local chemical reactions depend on a supply of oxygen and nutrients from blood vessels, a supply that has its own energy costs and that can be insufficient or excessive for optimal efficiency. Blood vessels also have the function of removing carbon dioxide and waste products such as lactate. The removal of lactate from the muscle is slower than its production, causing, in case of prolonged use of the muscle, a perception of fatigue. Only above this threshold is muscular effort *represented* in the cognitive system—and even then in a very coarse manner—often inducing intentional reallocation of muscular effort. The regulation of effort—the production of the right quantity of energy in muscle tissue, the adjustment of blood flow, and so on—is otherwise achieved not through computations over representations but through noncognitive physiological procedures that, one may assume, are to a very large extent genetically specified. I suggest that the regulation of effort in cognitive processes is likewise achieved, for the most part, through noncognitive brain processes that are also largely genetically specified.

That the flow of energy in the brain is guided by noncognitive mechanisms may seem easy enough to accept. Isn't it just an aspect of the neurological implementation of cognitive processes? How could this be relevant to an understanding of cognition at a computational or algorithmic level, to use Marr's popular distinction? Well, I will argue that the regulation of this energy flow has cognitive, even epistemic, consequences.

Understanding how the brain is sensitive to the cost of various procedures may be difficult. Even more difficult is understanding how the brain could be sensitive to the size of the cognitive benefits resulting from the processing of various inputs.

To begin with, how can the brain distinguish, among all the cognitive changes that might be brought about by cognitive operations, those that are beneficial and those that are not, and which may even be costly (for instance, mistaken inferences)? Well, the brain has no other choice than to trust itself and be, so to speak, optimistic about its own procedures. That is, it should behave in a way consistent with the presumption that, in general, its perceptions are veridical and its inferences rational. In normal conditions, the processing of new inputs yields positive cognitive effects, that is, it results in an improvement of the individual's knowledge of her world, be it by adding new pieces of knowledge, updating or revising old ones, updating degrees of subjective probability in a way sensitive to new evidence, or merely reorganizing existing knowledge so as to facilitate future use. There are many exceptions, of course—cases where less processing would have resulted in better knowledge— but procedures that have tended to produce more negative than positive cognitive effects are likely to have been selected out. The relevance of this is that the brain would be roughly right in treating any and every cognitive effect as a positive effect, in other words, as a cognitive benefit.

But then what? Supposing it treats all cognitive effects as cognitive benefits, how could the brain then calculate the size of these cognitive effects? Should it count the number of conclusions arrived at? Should it treat the value of each conclusion as depending on its complexity? Should it multiply the value of each conclusion by its subjective probability? Should it give greater value (and how much greater?) to conclusions that have practical consequences, or relate to standing interests? How should it evaluate revisions of previous beliefs? And so on. Or are these even the right questions? Actually, it is not at all obvious that the brain should *calculate* the size of cognitive effects. There may be physiological indicators of the size of cognitive effects in the form of patterns of chemical or electrical activity at specific locations in the brain. A module receives some degree of activation from other modules with which it is connected. It is activated by upstream feeder modules that present it with inputs. It may be activated by downstream client modules that are already mobilized and that would benefit from receiving new or further inputs from it. Suppose that these physiological indicators locally determine the ongoing allocation of brain energy to the processing of specific inputs. These indicators may be coarse. Nevertheless, they may be sufficient to cause energy to flow toward those processes that are likely to generate relatively greater cognitive effects at a given time. In other words, just as effort need not be computed, cognitive effect need not be computed either, and both effort and effect factors may steer the train of our thoughts without themselves being thought about at all.

Someone might object: suppose there are physiological indicators of effort and effect. All they can indicate are past or current effort and effect, whereas what should guide the allocation of brain resources is *expected* effort and effect.[4] Answer: It is not true that indicators can only indicate past and present states of affairs. Dark clouds may indicate that rain is probable. The current level of lactate concentration in a muscle may indicate that the muscle cannot continue to perform the same amount of work for long. The differences in the patterns of activity of two competing cognitive processes may indicate which has the highest expected cognitive utility. Suppose the processing of inputs A and B are both currently producing the same

---

4. As with "expected utility" in expected utility theory, I am speaking of "expected relevance" without presupposing a cognitive process involving the formation of mentally represented expectations. In fact, I am arguing that people tend to maximize expected relevance without, in most cases, representing it.

level of effect, but the processing of A is producing these effects with greater effort. Or suppose the processing of inputs A and B are both currently requiring the same level of effort, but the processing of B is resulting in greater effect. Of course, it is impossible to be sure how things would evolve, but in both cases, a greater cognitive utility should be expected from the continued processing of B rather than A. A better indication still may be given by the direction in which levels of effect and effort are moving. If the processing of inputs A and B are producing the same amount of effect for the same amount of effort, but the amount of effect produced by the processing of A is on the decrease, whereas that of B is constant or on the increase, or if the amount of effort required by the processing of A is on the increase and that of B constant or on the decrease, then, again, greater cognitive utility should be expected from the continued processing of B rather than A.

If we look at the issue in an evolutionary perspective, what does all this mean? Imagine a species investing more and more in cognition, monitoring in a more and more fine-grained way more and more aspects of the environment, constructing an ever richer memory, and achieving this by use of an ever greater variety of perceptual and conceptual modules. The result would be a kind of attentional bottleneck: only very few of the available inputs could be treated attentionally, and only very limited background information could be brought to bear on the treatment of these inputs. This bottleneck would in turn create a strong and constant selective pressure for optimizing the choice of inputs to be processed, which, in the picture I am presenting, is equivalent to optimizing the allocation of energy to modules. Such a selective pressure should result in the evolution of a variety of traits contributing to an optimal allocation. I am not excluding the possibility that, among these traits, there may be mental devices directly involved in internal administration of resources, but I find it implausible, both for evolutionary and efficiency reasons, to imagine that this allocation of resources might be wholly or even mostly controlled by some central specialized device. For the same kind of reasons that, whether we like it or not, market economies work better than centrally managed ones, competition for resources among modules seems more likely to yield good results than centrally controlled allocation.

There are a wide variety of small changes in the functioning and articulation of modules that may each have contributed to improving the allocation of resources over evolutionary time, or that may contribute to it in cognitive development. These include, as I have already suggested, the use of simple and approximate indicators of the ongoing and expected expenditure of energy, and of the ongoing and expected cognitive impact of specific procedures.

Different modules may be more or less easily mobilized in a way that reflects their general contribution to relevance. Modules that are specialized in processing inputs with high cognitive impact in the history of the species (and in particular with high practical impact) should be given a greater initial claim on brain resources, with the possibility of preempting other procedures in a bottom-up fashion (as the literature on attention shows us is typically the case with, for instance, potential danger signals). (Incidentally, given that the human environment changes much faster than the human genome, this may occasionally have counteradaptive results. For instance, people living in an urban environment are uselessly startled by all-too-frequent sudden loud noises that would have deserved immediate attention in an ancestral environment.)

Inputs pertaining to an area of stable interest developed by the individual benefit from richer intramodular databases and from richer intermodular connections (the two ways in which richer background information is realized in a modular system). Modules processing such inputs should therefore be given a greater claim on energetic resources and mobilise more easily.

Inputs pertaining to ongoing cognitive processes also benefit, *ceteris paribus*, from a greater claim on resources, this time because of quantitative factors on the effort side: the devices and data needed to process these inputs are already mobilized, and therefore their processing is less costly than the processing of inputs for which inactive or less active devices must be given energy. Thus relevance to current cognitive activity is, *ceteris paribus*, greater relevance.

More generally, there are many different ways, some obvious, others still to be discovered, in which a massively modular system might improve the allocation of its energetic resources among its modules, doing so much better than random allocation. Some of the traits of human cognitive organization that tend to optimize relevance have emerged in the evolution of the species. Others emerge in cognitive development and throughout the cognitive life of the individual. These lifetime improvements are themselves made possible by the flexibility of the evolved modular system of human cognition. This flexibility, therefore, should not be seen as a mere ability to adjust cognitive capacities to the demands and opportunities of different environments. It also helps maximize the relevance achieved by ongoing cognitive processes. Flexibility, that is, long-term context-sensitivity, makes a critical contribution to short-term context-sensitivity.

4 Conclusion

The claim that the human cognitive system tends to allocate resources to the processing of available inputs according to their expected relevance is at the basis of relevance theory (where it constitutes the first, cognitive principle of relevance).[5] The main thesis of this chapter has been that this allocation can be achieved without

---

5. The cognitive principle of relevance has experimentally testable consequences, some of which are reviewed in Van der Henst & Sperber (2004). We have shown, for instance, with experiments on relational reasoning, that by manipulating contextual factors, people can be made either to derive logical implications from a given set of premises or to say that nothing follows from it (Van der Henst, Sperber, & Politzer, 2002). What the context does in this case, we claim, is raise or lower expectations of relevance that attach to the premises presented, thus triggering or, on the contrary, inhibiting, an inferential procedure. With experiments on the Wason selection task, we have shown that, by manipulating contextual factors, people can be made to apply one or other of several possible inferential procedures involved in the interpretation of conditionals and therefore to reach different conclusions from the same set of conditional premises (Sperber et al., 1995a; Girotto et al., 2001). What the context does in this case, we claim, is raise or lower expectations of relevance that attach to each of these procedures in their application to the premises. These experiments illustrate the main thesis of this chapter.

computing expected relevance. When an input meets the input condition of a given modular procedure, this gives this procedure some initial level of activation. Input-activated procedures are in competition for the energy resources that would allow them to follow their full course. What determines which of the procedures in competition get sufficient resources to trigger their full operation is the dynamics of their activation. These dynamics depend both on the prior degree of mobilization of a modular procedure and on the activation that propagates from other active modules. It is also quite conceivable that the mobilization of some procedures has inhibitory effects on some other procedures. The relevance-theoretic claim is that, at every instant, these dynamics of activation provide rough physiological indicators of expected relevance. The flow of energy in the system is locally regulated by these indicators. As a result, those input-procedure combinations that have the greatest expected relevance are the more likely ones to receive sufficient energy to follow their course. This is just a tendency, but it is strong enough to yield the kind of context-sensitivity that humans actually exhibit in their individual cognitive processes.[6]

I am well aware of the vague and speculative nature of the view outlined in this chapter. It calls both for greater empirical anchoring and for formal modeling. I nevertheless feel justified in putting forward this view, as it is supported by, paradoxically, an argument of Fodor himself. He writes:

> Turing's idea that mental processes are computations...together with Chomsky's idea that poverty of the stimulus arguments set a lower bound to the information a mind must have innately, are half of the New Synthesis. The rest is the "massive modularity" thesis and the claim that cognitive architecture is a Darwinian adaptation.... There are some very deep problems with viewing cognition as computational, but...these problems emerge primarily in respect to mental problems that *aren't* modular. The real appeal of the massive modularity thesis is that, if it is true, we can either solve these problems, or at least contrive to deny them center stage *pro tem*. (Fodor 2000, p. 23)

This should be a strong vindication of the massive modularity thesis. Fodor, however, goes on to say: "The bad news is that, since massive modularity thesis pretty clearly *isn't* true, we're sooner or later going to have to face up to the dire inadequacies of the only remotely plausible theory of the cognitive mind that we've got so far" (p. 23). His main reason for claiming that the thesis is not true is the alleged inability of a massively modular system to exhibit context-sensitivity. This is why it seemed worth explaining, however tentatively, how such a system might be context-sensitive, contrary to Fodor's claim. Since the massive modularity thesis *might* be true, we can keep exploring "the only remotely plausible theory of the cognitive mind that we've got so far," and that, surely, is good news.

---

6. In collective intellectual endeavors that are pursued over generations, and in science in particular, greater context sensitivity and greater relevance can be achieved, but these achievements cannot be explained just by individual cognitive psychology, and, contrary to what Fodor tends to do, should not be taken as a benchmark to assess models of human cognition (Sperber & Wilson, 1996). Rather, the explanation of these achievements calls for a kind of epidemiology of representations that looks at the effect of the causal chaining of individual cognitive processes across populations (Sperber, 1996).

PETER CARRUTHERS

Distinctively Human Thinking
Modular Precursors and Components

This chapter takes up, and sketches an answer to, the main challenge facing massively modular theories of the architecture of the human mind. This is to account for the distinctively flexible, non-domain-specific character of much human thinking. I shall show how the appearance of a modular language faculty within an evolving modular architecture might have led to these distinctive features of human thinking with only minor further additions and non-domain-specific adaptations.

1 On Modularity

To what extent is it possible to see the human mind as built up out of modular components? Before this question can be addressed, something first needs to be said about what a module is, in this context; and also about why the issue matters.

1.1 Fodorian Modularity

In the beginning of our story was Fodor (1983). Against the prevailing empiricist model of the mind as a general-purpose computer, Fodor argued that the mind contains a variety of specialized input and output systems, or *modules*, as well as a general-purpose central arena in which beliefs get fixed, decisions taken, and so on. Input systems might include a variety of visual systems (including face recognition),

---

Early versions of this chapter were delivered at a preparatory workshop during the first year of the AHRB Innateness and the Structure of the Mind project, held in Newark 12–14 October 2001, and at the "Innateness and the Structure of the Mind" conference that concluded the year, held in Sheffield 3–6 July 2002. I am grateful to those who participated in those discussions for valuable feedback, with special thanks to Mark Baker, Robert Boyd, Richard Samuels, Gabriel Segal, Dan Sperber, Stephen Stich, and John Tooby for comments and suggestions.

auditory systems, taste, touch, and so on; but they also include a language-faculty (which contains, simultaneously, an output/production system, or else divides into input and output subsystems).

In the course of his argument, Fodor provided us with an analysis (really a stipulative definition) of the notion of a module. Modules are said to be processing systems that (1) have proprietary transducers, (2) have shallow outputs, (3) are fast in relation to other systems, (4) are mandatory in their operation, (5) are encapsulated from the remainder of cognition, including the subject's background beliefs, (6) have internal processes that are inaccessible to the rest of cognition, (7) are innate or innately channeled to some significant degree, (8) are liable to specific patterns of breakdown, both in development and through adult pathology, and (9) develop according to a paced and distinctively-arranged sequence of growth. At the heart of Fodor's account is the notion of *encapsulation*, which has the potential to explain at least some of the other strands. Thus, it may be because modules are encapsulated from the subject's beliefs and other processes going on elsewhere in the mind that their operations can be fast and mandatory, for example. And it is because modules are encapsulated that we stand some chance of understanding their operations in computational terms. For, by being dedicated to a particular task and drawing on only a restricted range of information, their internal processes can be *computationally tractable*.

According to Fodor (1983, 2000), however, central/conceptual cognitive processes of belief-formation, reasoning, and decision-making are definitely *amodular* or holistic in character. Crucially, central processes are unencapsulated — beliefs in one domain can have an impact on belief-formation in other, apparently quite distinct, domains. And in consequence, central processes are *not* computationally tractable. On the contrary, they must somehow be so set up that any one of the subject's beliefs can be brought to bear in the solution to a problem. Since we have no idea how to build a computational system with these properties (Fodor has other reasons for thinking that connectionist approaches won't work), we have no idea how to begin modeling central cognition computationally. And this aspect of the mind is therefore likely to remain mysterious for the foreseeable future.

1.2 Central Modularity

In contrast to Fodor, many other writers have attempted to extend the notion of modularity to at least some central processes, arguing that there are modular central/conceptual systems as well as modular input and output systems (Atran, 2002; Baron-Cohen, 1995; Botterill & Carruthers, 1999; Carey, 1985; Carey & Spelke, 1994; Gallistel, 1990; Hauser & Carey, 1998; Hermer-Vazquez et al., 1999; Leslie, 1994; Smith & Tsimpli, 1995; Spelke, 1994). Those who adopt such a position are required to modify the notion of a module somewhat. Since central modules are supposed to be capable of taking conceptual inputs, such modules are unlikely to have proprietary transducers; and since they are charged with generating conceptualized outputs (e.g., beliefs or desires), their outputs cannot be shallow. Moreover, since central modules are supposed to operate on beliefs to generate other beliefs, for example, it seems unlikely that they can be fully encapsulated—at least *some* of the subject's existing beliefs can be accessed during processing by a central module. But the notion of a "module" is not thereby wholly denuded of content. For modules can still be (1) domain specific, taking only domain-specific inputs, or inputs containing concepts proprietary to the module in question, (2) fast in relation to other systems, (3) mandatory in their operation, (4) relatively encapsulated, drawing on a restricted domain-specific database; as well as (5) having internal processes or algorithms that are inaccessible to the rest of cognition, (6) being innate or innately channeled to some significant degree, (7) being liable to specific patterns of breakdown, and (8) displaying a distinctively ordered and paced pattern of growth.

I shall not here review the evidence—of a variety of different kinds—that is supposed to support the existence of central/conceptual modules that possess many of the foregoing properties (see Carruthers, 2003b, for a review). I propose simply to assume, first, that the notion of central-process modularity is a legitimate one; and second, that the case for central modularity is powerful and should be accepted in the absence of potent considerations to the contrary.

1.3 *Massive Modularity*

Others in the cognitive science community—especially those often referred to as "evolutionary psychologists"—have gone much further in claiming that the mind is wholly, or at least *massively*, modular in nature (Cosmides & Tooby, 1992, 1994; Gallistel, 2000; Pinker, 1997a; Sperber, 1994, 1996; Tooby & Cosmides, 1992). Again, a variety of different arguments are offered; these I shall briefly review, since they have a bearing on later discussion. But for the most part in what follows I shall simply assume that some form of massive modularity thesis is plausible, and is worth defending.

(Those who don't wish to grant the foregoing assumptions should still read on, however. For one of the main goals of this chapter is to consider whether there exists any powerful argument *against* massive modularity, premised upon the non-domain-specific character of central cognitive processes. If I succeed in showing that there is not, then that will at least demonstrate that any grounds for rejecting the assumption of massive modularity will have to come from elsewhere.)

One argument for massive modularity appeals to considerations deriving from evolutionary biology in general. The way that evolution of new systems or structures characteristically operates is by "bolting on" new special-purpose items to the existing repertoire. First, there will be a specific evolutionary pressure—some task or problem that recurs regularly enough and that, if a system can be developed that can solve it and solve it quickly, will confer fitness advantages on those possessing that system. Second, some system that is targeted specifically on that task or problem will emerge and become universal in the population. Often, admittedly, these domain-specific systems may emerge by utilizing, coopting, and linking together resources that were antecedently available; hence they may appear quite inelegant when seen in engineering terms. But they will still have been designed for a specific purpose, and are therefore likely to display all or many of the properties of central modules, outlined earlier.

A different—though closely related—consideration is negative, arguing that a general-purpose problem-solver *couldn't evolve*, and would always by out-competed by a suite of special-purpose conceptual modules. One point here is that a general-purpose problem-solver would be very slow and unwieldy in relation to any set of domain-specific competitors, facing, as it does, the problem of combinatorial explosion as it tries to search through the maze of information and options available to it. Another point relates more specifically to the mechanisms charged with generating desires. It is that many of the factors that promote long-term fitness are too subtle to be noticed or learned within the lifetime of an individual; in which case there couldn't be a general-purpose problem-solver with the general goal "promote fitness" or anything of the kind. On the contrary, a whole suite of fitness-promoting goals will have to be provided for, which will then require a corresponding set of desire-generating computational systems (Tooby, Cosmides, & Barrett, chapter 18 here).

The most important argument in support of massive modularity for my purposes, however, simply reverses the direction of Fodor's (1983, 2000) argument for pessimism concerning the prospects for computational psychology. It goes like this: the mind is computationally realized; amodular, or holistic, processes are computationally intractable; so the mind must consist wholly or largely of modular systems. Now, in a way Fodor doesn't deny either of the premises in this argument; nor does he deny that the conclusion follows. Rather, he believes that we have independent reasons to think that the conclusion is false; and he believes that we cannot even *begin* to see how amodular processes could be computationally realized. So he thinks that we had better give up attempting to do computational psychology (with respect to central cognition) for the foreseeable future. What is at issue in this debate, therefore, is not just the correct account of the structure of the mind but also whether certain scientific approaches to understanding the mind are worth pursuing.

Not all of Fodor's arguments for the holistic character of central processes are good ones. (In particular, it is a mistake to model individual cognition too closely on the practice of science, as Fodor does. See Carruthers, 2003a). But the point underlying them is importantly correct. And it is this that is apt to evince an incredulous stare from many people when faced with the more extreme modularist claims made by evolutionary psychologists. For we *know* that human beings are capable of linking together in thought items of information from widely disparate domains; indeed, this may be *distinctive* of human thinking (I shall argue that it is). We have no difficulty in thinking thoughts that link together information across modular barriers. How is this possible, if the arguments for massive modularity, and against domain-general cognitive processes, are sound?

1.4 A Look Ahead—The Role of Language

We are now in position to give rather more precise expression to the question with which this chapter began; and also to see its significance. Can we finesse the impasse between Fodor and the evolutionary psychologists by showing how non-domain-specific human thinking can be built up out of modular components?

If so, then we can retain the advantages of a massively modular conception of the mind—including the prospects for computational psychology—while at the same time doing justice to the distinctive flexibility and non-domain-specific character of some human thought processes.

This is the task that I propose to take up in this chapter. I shall approach the development of my model in stages, corresponding roughly to the order of its evolution. This is because it is important that the model should be consistent with what is known of the psychology of other animals, and also with what can be inferred about the cognition of our ancestors from the evidence of the fossil record.

I should explain at the outset, however, that according to my model, it is the language faculty that serves as the organ of intermodular communication, making it possible for us to combine contents across modular domains. One advantage of this view is that almost everyone now agrees (1) that the language faculty is a distinct input and output module of the mind, and (2) that the language faculty would need to have access to the outputs of any other central/conceptual belief or desire forming modules, in order that those contents should be expressible in speech. So in these respects language seems ideally placed to be the module that connects together other modules, if this idea can somehow be made good sense of.

Another major point in favor of the proposal is that there is now direct (albeit limited) empirical evidence in its support. Hermer-Vazquez and colleagues (1999) have proposed and tested the thesis that it is language that enables geometric and object-property information to be combined into a single thought, with dramatic results. This evidence is reviewed and extended in Shusterman and Spelke (chapter 6 here) and so does not need to be elaborated upon here.

2   Animal Minds

What cognitive resources were antecedently available, before the great-ape lineage began to evolve?

2.1   The Model

Taking the ubiquitous laboratory rat as a representative example, I shall assume that all mammals, at least, are capable of thought—in the sense that they engage in computations that deliver structured (propositional) belief-like states and desire-like states (Dickinson, 1994; Dickinson & Balleine, 2000). I shall also assume that these computations are largely carried out within modular systems of one sort or another (Gallistel, 1990, 2000). For after all, if the project here is to show how non-domain-specific thinking in humans can emerge out of modular components, then we had better assume that the initial starting-state (before the evolution of our species began) was a modular one. I shall assume, however, that mammals possess some sort of simple non-domain-specific practical reasoning system, which can take beliefs and desires as input, and then figure out what to do (I shall return to this in a moment). Simplifying greatly, one might represent the cognitive organization of mammals as depicted in figure 5.1 (I shall return to the simplifications shortly).

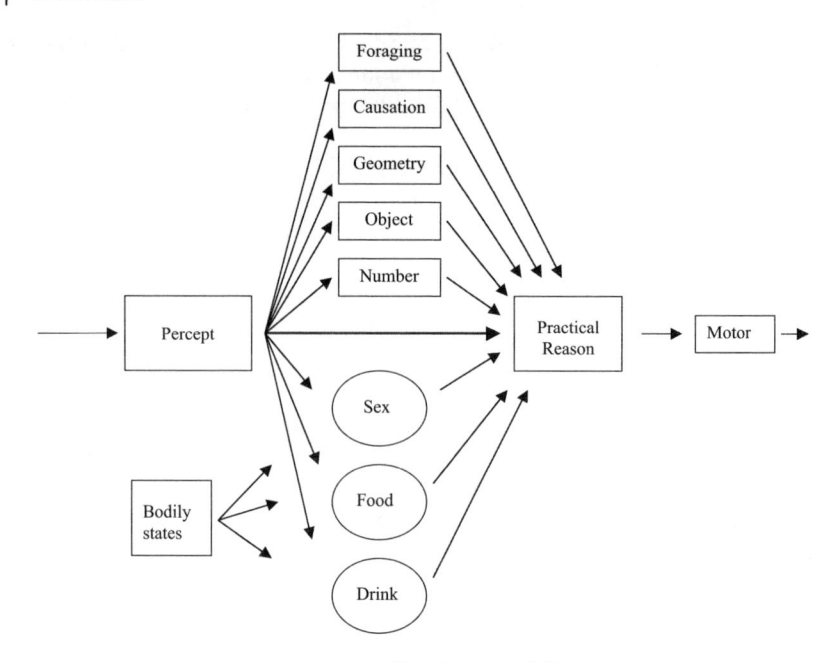

FIGURE 5.1 Rats (mammals?).

Here I am imagining a variety of input modules collapsed together under the heading "percept" for purposes of simplicity. (Of course I don't think that vision, audition, and so on are all really one big module; it is just that the differences between them don't matter for present purposes, and so don't need to be represented.) What *are* represented separately on the input side, however, are a set of systems for monitoring bodily states, which play an important role in the generation of desires (hunger, thirst, and so on). Then at the output end, I imagine a variety of motor-control systems collapsed together for our purposes under the heading "motor." And in between these two, I imagine a variety of belief- and desire-generating central modules, together with a practical reasoning system that receives its inputs from them (as well as from perception).

I assume that the practical reasoning system in animals (and probably also in us) is a relatively simple and limited-channel one. Perhaps it receives as input the currently strongest desire and searches among the outputs of the various belief-generating modules for something that can be done in relation to the perceived environment that will satisfy that desire. So its inputs have the form DESIRE [Y] and BELIEF [IF X THEN Y], where X should be something for which an existing action-schema exists. I assume that the practical reasoning system is *not* capable of engaging in other forms of inference (generating new beliefs from old), or of combining together beliefs from different modules; though perhaps it *is* capable of chaining together conditionals to generate a simple plan—for example, BELIEF [IF W THEN X], BELIEF [IF X THEN Y] → BELIEF [IF W THEN Y].

As for the modules that appear in the diagram, there is pretty robust evidence for each of them—at least, qua *system* if not qua *modular* system.[1] Thus there is plenty of evidence that rats (and many other animals and birds) can represent approximate numerosity (Gallistel, 1990); and there is evidence from monkeys, at least, that simple exact additions and subtractions can be computed for numbers up to about 3 (Dehaene, 1997; Hauser, 2000). Moreover, there is the evidence provided by Cheng (1986) that rats have a geometrical module, which is specialized for computing the geometrical relationships between the fixed surfaces in an environment (Gouteux & Spelke, 2001), and which they use especially when disoriented. In addition, there is the evidence collected by Dickinson and Shanks (1995) that rats make judgments of causality that closely mirror our own (including, apparently, essentially the same dispositions toward *illusions* of causality, in certain circumstances).

My guess is that many of the beliefs and desires generated by the central modules will have partially indexical contents. Thus a desire produced as output by the sex module might have the form "I want to mate with *that* female," and a belief produced by the causal-reasoning module might have the form "*That* caused *that*." So if the practical reasoning system is to be able to do anything with such contents, then it, too, would need to have access to the outputs of perception, to provide anchoring for the various indexicals—hence the bold arrow in figure 5.1 directly from percept to practical reason. The outputs of the practical reasoning system are likely to be indexical too, such as an intention of the form "I'll go *that* way."

2.2 Adding Complexity to the Model

One way figure 5.1 is oversimplified is that it probably radically underestimates the number of belief- and desire-forming modules that there are. This is especially true on the desire side, where of course all animals will have systems for generating pains/desires to avoid current noxious stimuli; and all animals will have systems for generating various emotions, such as anger (normally involving a desire to attack), fear (normally involving a desire to retreat), and so on. In addition, among social animals there will be systems for generating desires for such things as status. Similarly on the belief side, there will often be systems for kin-recognition and for computing degrees of relatedness, systems for recognizing an animal's position in a dominance hierarchy, and so on.

Another way figure 5.1 is probably oversimplified is that there may well exist informational relationships among the various belief-forming modules, in particular.[2] Thus one of the main functions of the numerosity module is to provide

---

1. The only case in which there is direct robust evidence of modularity that I know of concerns the geometric system, which does appear to be isolated in the right kind of way from the rest of cognition. See Cheng (1986) and Hermer and Spelke (1994).
2. Note that this means that the thesis of this chapter isn't that *no* integration of central-modular outputs takes place without language. Rather, the claim is that the mind's capacity to combine together central-modular contents will have been limited, prior to the evolution of language, and that the appearance of language makes such cross-modular integration well-nigh ubiquitous.

inputs to the foraging system, helping to calculate rates of return from various sources of food (Gallistel, 1990). I have not attempted to represent these in the diagram, partly for simplicity, partly because I have no fixed views on what the relevant informational relationships among modules actually are.

Another source of complexity that goes unrepresented in figure 5.1 is that each modular system presumably has some sort of domain-specific memory function attached. For central/conceptual modules don't just generate information "online," of course, for use in current practical reasoning. They are also going to be implicated in learning, and in generating new standing-state beliefs. So a more accurate version of figure 5.1 should probably show each central module as dividing into two components—a processing subsystem for generating domain-specific information and a domain-specific memory store for recording (some of) that information. Presumably, too, the processing subsystem should be able to access its proprietary memory store in the course of its computations, hence providing a constraint on the degree to which it is informationally encapsulated.

The final sort of oversimplification I want to mention is that there should probably also be links between (some of) the belief modules and (some of) the desire modules. For example, one would expect that information about degrees of relatedness (generated by the kin module) should be available as input to the module charged with generating sexual desire, suppressing the processes that would normally produce such desires in appropriate cases. And one might expect that information about rich or unusual sources of food (generated by the foraging module) might be taken as input by the hunger-generating module, sometimes causing a desire for food where there was none antecedently. And so on. In addition, one might expect that the content of whatever happens to be the currently strongest desire should have an impact upon the belief-generating modules, directing them to search for information that might help to satisfy that desire.

Although figure 5.1 is pretty simple, therefore, I don't really want to say that animal minds are that simple. The relevant claim to take away from the discussion is just that in all mammals (and so, *a fortiori*, in those mammals that were the immediate ancestors of the great ape lineage) there is probably a complex layer of belief- and desire-generating modules located between the various perceptual systems and some sort of limited-channel practical reasoning system.

3 Earlier Species of *Homo*

What changes began to occur in the basic mammalian cognitive architecture, during the evolution of the great apes and the transition to modern *Homo sapiens*?

3.1 Deepening Modules

At some point in the evolution of the great-ape lineage—whether in the common ancestor of ourselves and the chimpanzees or perhaps later, during the development of *Homo*—changes would have begun to occur. These were not initially changes of an architectural sort, I suggest. Rather, some of the existing suite of modules were deepened and enlarged, rendering their processing much more sophisticated; and perhaps some new modules were added, such as the social-exchange/cheater-detection module investigated by Cosmides and Tooby (1992; Fiddick et al., 2000). Thus some sort of social relationships module gradually developed into the beginnings of a mind-reading module; the foraging module became increasingly sophisticated, developing into a system of naive biology; the causal reasoning system developed into a form of naive physics; the object-property system expanded greatly to allow for many more object categorizations; and so on. The result is represented in figure 5.2.

I don't mean to claim that all of these changes occurred at the same time or for the same reason, of course. There is a complex story eventually to be unraveled here about the differing pressures—and no doubt their complex interactions—that led to the gradual deepening of different modules at various points in our ancestry. And for any given such change, it is still highly controversial at what evolutionary stage it first occurred.[3] Nor do I wish to claim that *all* modules have undergone a similar sort of transformation. On the contrary, it may well be that we still operate with essentially the same system for calculating approximate numerosities that is present in rats, for example.

By the time of *Homo ergaster* some quarter of a million years ago, all of the relevant changes would surely have taken place. Members of this group of species were plainly much smarter than present-day chimpanzees. They were able to move out of Africa into a wide variety of environments throughout Asia and Europe, including extremely harsh subtundra habitats. They had sophisticated stone-tool technologies. They were capable of adapting quickly to, and extracting relevant information concerning, wide variations in flora and fauna (Mithen, 1990). And all the evidence points to highly social creatures, capable of sustaining the complex social and personal relationships necessary for survival in such harsh environments, for the rearing of children with increasingly long periods of maternal dependency, and so on. (See Mithen, 1996, for a review of the evidence.)

Some of the data suggest, however, that members of *Homo ergaster* were *not* capable of the main elements of distinctively human thinking (Mithen, 1996).[4] Specifically, they weren't capable of creative thinking, or of generating radically new ideas. On the contrary, their stone-tool industries, for example, displayed long periods of stasis, with no significant changes of design over tens of thousands of years. And they don't appear to have been capable, as we are, of conjoining together ideas across modular boundaries. There is no sign that ideas concerning naive physics and ideas from naive biology could be combined to lead to the

---

3. See, e.g., Povinelli (2000), for evidence concerning the relative shallowness of the mind-reading and naive physics modules possessed by our nearest cousins, the chimpanzees.
4. Others have argued that distinctively human thinking emerged much earlier than the first arrival of *Homo sapiens sapiens* 100,000 years ago (McBrearty & Brooks, 2001), claiming that appearances to the contrary are an artifact of small sample sizes. If these views should prove to be correct, then they would only make my task that much easier, since they would allow greater time for the elements of distinctively human thinking to evolve together with language. I prefer to work with the more demanding assumption of late emergence.

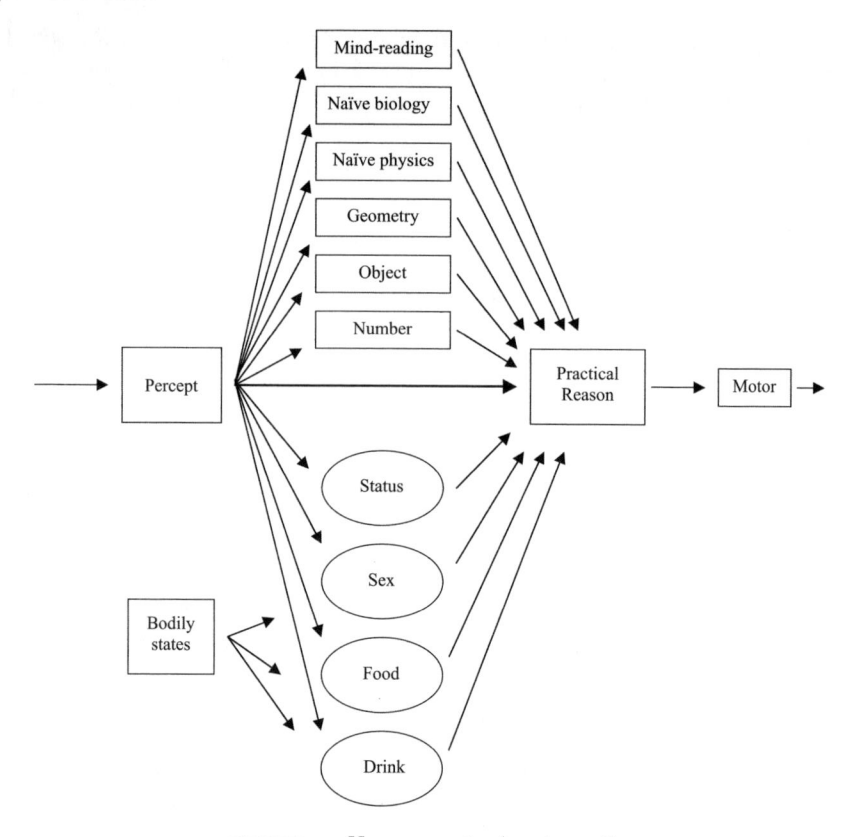

FIGURE 5.2 Homo ergaster (great apes?).

development of specialist stone hunting tools, such as we find in connection with *Homo sapiens sapiens*. Nor is there any evidence of analogical linkages between animal and social domains, such as we find in modern totemism, in the famous lion-man figurine from Hohlenstein-Stadel in Germany, and so on. It is for these reasons that I say the basic mammalian cognitive architecture was unchanged in members of *Homo ergaster* and before.

3.2 Developing Imagination

There is one further point I want to pick up on, resulting from the deepening of modules. This is that the extensive development and enriching of the object-property system would have made possible simple forms of sensory imagination. For the evidence is that imagery deploys the same top-down neural pathways in our perceptual systems that are deployed in normal perception for purposes of object-recognition (Kosslyn, 1994). As the number and range of object-categorizations available to our ancestors greatly increased (as it plainly did), so increasing pressure would have been put on the mechanisms concerned with object-recognition, leading to further strengthening of the top-down pathways used to "ask questions" of degraded, incomplete, or ambiguous input. It seems quite likely, then, that *Homo ergaster* would have been capable of generating visual and other images, even if this capacity was rarely used outside of the demands of object-recognition.

In fact, however, there is evidence of the use of rotated visual images by members of *Homo ergaster* some 400,000 years ago. This comes from the fine symmetries that they were able to impose upon their stone tools, while using a reductive technology that requires the planning of strikes some moves ahead. For Wynn (2000) makes out a powerful case that this can only be done if the stone-knapper is able to hold in mind an image of the desired shape that the stone would have when seen from the other side, rotating it mentally in such a way as to compare it with the shape of the stone now confronting him.

Then, given that members of *Homo ergaster* were capable of forming and manipulating mental images outside of the context of object-recognition, it may well be the case that they also used such images for purposes of *mental rehearsal* more generally. If they could form an image of an action they were about to perform, for example, then that image would be processed by the input systems in the usual way, and made available to the suite of central modules, some of which might then generate further predictions of the consequences of that action, and so forth. At any rate, this sort of mental rehearsal looms large in the cognition of our own species, as I will show hereafter; so it is interesting to note that it may well have been available to some of our more immediate ancestors as well.

4 The Emergence of Language

Most people think that language was probably a late-emerging capacity in the hominid lineage. Some people go so far as to put the emergence of language at the time of the "creative explosion" of the upper Paleolithic period, just 40,000 years ago and well after the appearance of anatomically modern humans some 60,000 years earlier (Noble & Davidson, 1996). Others wonder cautiously whether the Neanderthals might have had language (McBrearty & Brooks, 2001). But most are inclined to put the emergence of grammatical, syntax-involving, natural language with the first appearance of our species—*Homo sapiens sapiens*—about 100,000 to 120,000 years ago, in southern Africa (Bickerton, 1990, 1995; Stringer & Gamble, 1993; Mithen, 1996).

It does seem quite likely that some later species of *Homo ergaster* (including the Neanderthals) may have spoken a form of what Bickerton (1990, 1995) calls "protolanguage," similar to pidgin languages and the languages spoken by two-year-old children. This would be a system of spoken signs, with some distinction between nouns and verbs, perhaps, but with little other grammatical structure. Such "languages" have considerable utility (there is quite a lot that you can communicate using a pidgin language, for example), but they place considerable demands on the interpretational—mind-reading—skills of their hearers. This is because utterances that consist only of strings of nouns and verbs tend to be multiply ambiguous. Indeed, it may well be that the increasing use of protolanguage was one of the major pressures leading to the evolution of a full-blown sophisticated mind-reading capacity as we now know it (Goméz, 1998).

4.1 A Language-Involving Architecture

It seems likely, then, that at some point around the cusp of the first appearance of *Homo sapiens sapiens*, a system for processing and producing full-blown grammatical language began to emerge. I assume, as is now conventional, that this system divides into a core knowledge-base of grammatical and phonological knowledge, subserving separate production and comprehension systems. The result is depicted in figure 5.3, with all of the previous belief- and desire-generating modules now collapsed together for simplicity (and now with a double arrow between them to accommodate the fact, acknowledged earlier, that some belief modules deliver their outputs as input to some desire modules, and so forth).

At the protolanguage stage, I presume that the messages to be communicated were either the domain-specific outputs of one or other of the conceptual modules or the results of practical reasoning (such as an intention to act). So the causal sequence would go like this: first there exists a domain-specific propositional thought, generated by a central module, which the agent wants to communicate.[5] The agent then marshals a learned vocabulary and the resources of the mind-reading system to produce an utterance that is likely to convey that thought to a hearer, given the context. And in order for the hearer to be able to do anything with that thought, it has to be made available to the various belief- and desire-generating central systems. (At this stage, agents have no other inferential resources available to them, I am supposing.)

Similarly, with the emergence of the modern language-faculty, at least initially: each spoken sentence would be an encoding into grammatical language of a thought that is the output of a central module (or of the practical reasoning system); and each comprehended sentence would be made available to the full suite of central modules. The language faculty, then, is a unique kind of module, producing a radical new architecture to cognition. This isn't just because it is simultaneously both an input and an output module (though that is part of the

---

5. Does the desire to communicate these domain-specific thoughts presuppose that there is some system—presumably the mind-reading system—that has access to the outputs of all the others? If so, then it might be said there was *already* a system capable of linking together the outputs of all modules prior to the evolution of a language faculty, namely, the mind-reading system. However, that a system can take any contents as input doesn't mean that it is capable of combining those contents together into new thoughts, or of deriving arbitrary inferences from those inputs. Moreover, at least two other mechanisms to underpin these early forms of communication can be envisaged that are much more modest in their requirements. One is that people should be disposed to express in language information that is highly *salient*. The other is that they might operate via a form of subvocal *rehearsal*, of the sort that arguably becomes ubiquitous in contemporary humans (see hereafter). That is, people might rehearse potential utterances in imagination, selecting those that have the greatest number of relevant *effects* (upon themselves). It is far from obvious that either of these proposals should require intermodular communication to be taking place already at this early stage.

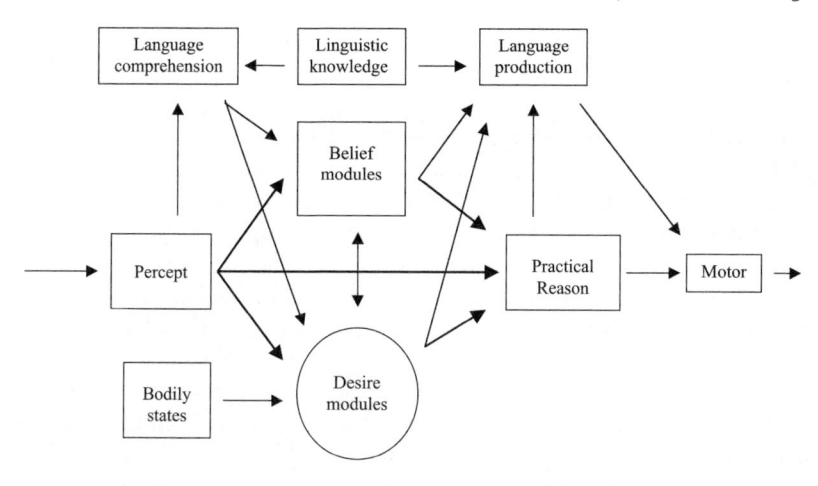

FIGURE 5.3 Archaic homo sapiens?

explanation). It is also because it is a module that—uniquely—feeds into, and draws outputs from, all of the central modular systems. This makes it a kind of "supermodule." It also means that there is a sense in which it isn't domain specific, since it can draw inputs relating to any domain. But in another sense it *is* domain specific. For the language faculty isn't interested in the *contents* of the thoughts it receives per se. Its job isn't to draw inferences from a belief as input to generate other beliefs, for example. Rather, its job is just to formulate that thought into a syntactically acceptable sentence. Since the function of the language faculty is to produce and decode linguistic utterances, *that* is its proper domain.

4.2 Interfacing Language and Other Modules

What kind of interface would need to have been built to enable the language faculty to communicate with the central modules? On the production side, this is (initially) relatively straightforward, at least in the sense of meshing with classical accounts of sentence production (e.g., Levelt, 1989). For each of the central modules would already have been charged with producing propositional outputs. The task for the language faculty is just that of mapping these outputs onto a sentential structure.[6]

---

6. In fact this task seems likely to be somewhat more complex than is often supposed. For although the geometric module will deliver outputs that are propositional—in the sense of having combinatorial structure of some sort—it seems unlikely that those outputs will already be such as to contain concepts like "left" and "right." (This may be the reason why such words are so difficult for children to learn. See Shusterman & Spelke, chapter 6 here.) So those outputs will need to be transformed into the appropriate conceptual structures before the process of encoding into language can take place.

But how does comprehension work? How does the comprehension subsystem of the language faculty provide inputs for the central modules? *Some* of these modules would already be set up to accept propositional inputs from *some* other central modules. But this wouldn't by any means provide for global availability of propositional contents. Nor would this provide any obvious way for the comprehension subsystem to take a sentence with a content that crosses modular boundaries (once that becomes possible—see hereafter) and to "carve it up" into appropriate chunks for consumption by the relevant domain-specific central modules.

There are perhaps a number of different ways this problem could have been solved, in principle. But I suspect that the way it was *actually* solved was via the construction of mental models. There is quite a bit of evidence of the role of mental models in discourse comprehension (see Harris, 2000, for reviews). And a mental model, being an analog quasi-perceptual structure, has the right format to be taken as input by a suite of central modules that were already geared up to receive perceptual inputs. So I suspect that the process goes something like this: upon receipt of a sentence as input, the comprehension system sets about constructing an analog model of its content, accessing semantic knowledge, and perhaps also relevant background beliefs. The resulting structure is then presented to all central modular systems as input. (These structures might also be stored in existing perceptual memory systems, in effect creating a virtual non-domain-specific memory system. See sec. 5.)

4.3 Combining Contents in Language

Returning now to the question of how domain-specific thoughts are encoded by the production subsystem of the language faculty—how can such thoughts be combined into a single non-domain-specific sentence? Some aspects of this are relatively easy to get a handle on. Suppose that the output of the geometric module is the thought THE FOOD IS IN THE CORNER WITH THE LONG WALL ON THE LEFT, while the output of the object-property system is the thought THE FOOD IS BY THE BLUE WALL.[7] Our problem is to understand how these two thoughts can be combined together to produce the single non-domain-specific sentence "The food is in the corner with the long blue wall on the left." Given that we are supposing that there is already a system for encoding thoughts into language, this reduces to the problem of understanding how this sentence might be generated from the two sentences "The food is in the corner with the long wall on the left" and "The food is by the blue wall."

Two points are suggestive of how this might be done. One is that natural language syntax allows for multiple embedding of adjectives and phrases. Thus one can have "The food is in the corner with the *long* wall on the left," "The food is in the corner with the *long straight* wall on the left," and so on. So there are already

---

7. I here follow the usual convention of using capitals to designate sentences of Mentalese, reserving quotation marks to designate sentences of English.

"slots" into which additional adjectives—such as "blue"—can be inserted. The second point is that the reference of terms like "the wall," "the food," and so on will need to be secured by some sort of indexing to the contents of current perception or recent memory—in which case it looks like it would not be too complex a matter for the language production system to take two sentences sharing a number of references like this, and to combine them into one by inserting adjectives from one into open adjective-slots in the other. And there would surely have been evolutionary pressure from the demands of swift and efficient communication for the language faculty to evolve just such a capacity.

5 Distinctively Human Thinking

We are already in a position to see how the addition of a language module to the preexisting modular architecture might provide *one* of the distinctive elements of human thought, namely, its capacity to combine together contents freely across modular domains. But we have, as yet, said nothing to suggest why tokens of natural language sentences should qualify as *thoughts*. From the fact that we can express, in speech, contents that cross modular domains, it doesn't yet follow that we can *reason with* or otherwise make use of those contents in any of the ways distinctive of thinking.

5.1 Using Language in Thought

As a first step toward seeing how the language faculty might underpin distinctively human thinking, recall a point made earlier, that modular input and output systems have substantial back-projecting neural pathways that make possible different forms of sensory and motor imagery; and that such images are processed by perceptual input-systems in the usual way, just as if they were percepts. Assuming that the same is true for language, then sentences formulated by the production subsystem could be displayed in auditory or motor imagination, hence become available to the comprehension subsystem that feeds off perceptual inputs and, via that, to all of the various central-process modules.

Cycles of activity would thus become possible, as follows. In response to perceptual or linguistic input, the central modules generate a variety of domain-specific outputs. These are made available to the language faculty, which combines some of them into a sentence that is displayed in imagination, processed by the comprehension subsystem, and made available to the central modules once again. The latter process the resulting input, generating new domain-specific output, which is again made available to the production subsystem of the language faculty, which formulates some of it into a new sentence; and so on. While there is no reason to think that this could be the *whole* of human thinking, it does suggest a way in which—given sufficient cycles of domain-specific activity—new non-domain-specific ideas and beliefs might be generated, which could go well beyond anything manifest in the initial input.

What, then, are the other main elements of distinctively human thinking that need to be explained? One, surely, is *creativity*. Humans are capable of creating new ideas that don't just *go beyond* the input but appear to be wholly unrelated to it. Humans engage in fantasy and pretence in which they create imaginary worlds quite

84 *Architecture*

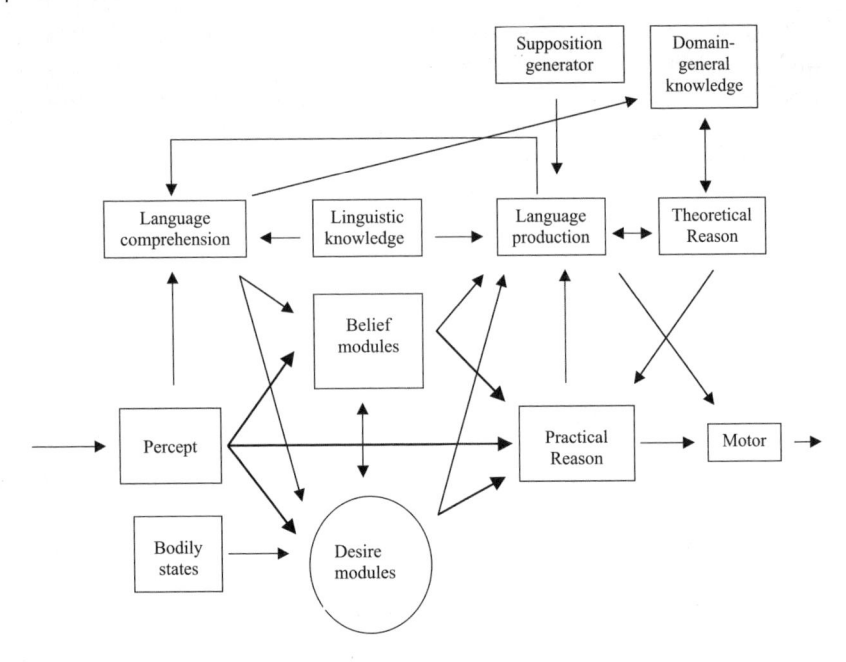

FIGURE 5.4 Homo sapiens sapiens.

unlike the real world. And humans are capable of forms of insight in which new ideas or new theories are produced that radically extend anything previously available. These capacities are not yet accounted for on the foregoing model.

Another main element in distinctively human thinking, however, concerns what humans *do* with new ideas once they are produced. Plainly, they can be remembered; so we need some sort of non-domain-specific memory system. But they can also be *evaluated*. We can take a new idea and decide whether or not it is a good one. Or we can consider two competing hypotheses and judge which of them is the better, and so on. When these functions are added to the architecture of figure 5.3, we get something like that depicted in figure 5.4.

Here four main elements have been added to the previous language-involving architecture. First, an arrow has been added backward from language production to language comprehension, enabling cycles of linguistic and domain-specific cognitive activity to occur in "inner speech." Second, a box for non-domain-specific memory has been added, taking input both from language comprehension (so that people can believe and remember what they are told) and from theoretical reason (see hereafter). Third, a supposition generator has been added, providing input to the language production system. Its function is to generate new sentences whose contents aren't produced from the outputs of the various central modules. Fourth, a box for theoretical reason has been added, which takes inputs from language production and domain-general memory, and which provides outputs to both domain-general memory and to practical reason, so that decisions on which sentences to accept can be both recalled and acted upon.

How radical would these departures be from the previous modular architecture, as represented in figure 5.3? And how plausible is it that these new functions could make their appearance within a relatively short time-span subsequent to (or coincident with) the evolution of the language faculty? Providing for the first two functions should have been relatively simple, as I have already shown. Thus there is every reason to think that the language faculty, like other input and output systems, would have been set up in such a way as to make it possible to display output-sentences in imagination, so that they can then be consumed by the input comprehension subsystem; hence making possible cycles of modular activity of the sort envisaged earlier. Moreover, if the comprehension subsystem operates by constructing analog mental models, as suggested earlier, then the results could be stored in existing perceptual memory systems—thus de facto creating a system of domain-general knowledge, given that the sentences comprehended can have non-domain-specific contents. But what of the supposer? And what of a faculty of theoretical reason? Is it plausible that such domain-general functions could have been built within the time-frame available, and that their operations should be computationally tractable?

5.2 Supposing and Pretending

In the case of the supposer, there is some reason to think that a simple initial disposition to generate new sentences for consideration—either at random or drawing on similarities and analogies suggested by perceptual or other input—might be sufficient. I have argued elsewhere (Carruthers, 2002b) that it is just such a disposition that gives rise to the ubiquitous and distinctive phenomenon of *pretend play* in human children; and that the function of such play may be to practice and hone a capacity for relevant and fruitful creative thinking. Here I shall be brief.

Consider the case of a young child pretending that a banana is a telephone. The overall similarity in shape between the banana and a telephone handset may be sufficient to activate the representation *telephone,* albeit weakly. If the child has an initial disposition to generate an appropriate sentence from such activations, she will then construct and entertain the sentence "That is a telephone." This is then comprehended and processed, accessing the knowledge that telephones can be used to call people, and that Grandma is someone who has been called in the past. If Grandma is someone whom the child *likes* talking to, then this may be sufficient to initiate an episode of pretend play. By representing herself *as* making a phone call to Grandma (using the banana), the child can gain some of the motivational rewards of talking to her. The whole sequence (including the initial generation of the supposition "That is a telephone") is then reinforced, making it more likely that the child will think creatively again in the future.

From such simple beginnings one can imagine that children gradually build up a set of heuristics for generating fruitful suppositions—relying on perceptual and other similarities, analogies that have proved profitable in the past, and so on. And with such a suppositional faculty up and running, the generative powers of the cognitive system represented in figure 5.4 would become radically transformed, becoming much less dependent upon perceptual and spoken input for its operations, and arguably displaying just the kinds of creativity in thought and behavior that we humans evince.

5.3 Inference to the Best Explanation

As for the faculty of theoretical reason, we need first to consider what such a faculty should contain. As I envisage it, a theoretical reasoning faculty is basically a faculty of inference to the best explanation, of the sort employed in science. While no one any longer thinks that it is possible to codify the principles involved, it is generally agreed that the good-making features of an explanation include such features as: *accuracy* (predicting all or most of the data to be explained, and explaining away the rest); *simplicity* (being expressible as economically as possible, with the fewest commitments to distinct kinds of fact and process); *consistency* (internal to the theory or model); *coherence* (with surrounding beliefs and theories, meshing together with those surroundings, or at least being consistent with them); *fruitfulness* (making new predictions and suggesting new lines of inquiry); and *explanatory scope* (unifying together a diverse range of data). Such principles are routinely employed in everyday life as well as science, of course, in thinking about a wide range of subject matters. And it is arguable that hunter-gatherers concerned with tracking prey will employ just such principles in the course of a hunt (Carruthers, 2002a; Liebenberg, 1990). So such a faculty very probably has a considerable ancestry, and would have been of vital adaptive significance.

There is some reason to think that a good proportion of these principles would come to us "for free" with the language faculty, however. (This point is argued more fully in Carruthers, 2003c.) For a strong case can be made for the vital role of considerations of *relevance* in the production and comprehension of speech (Sperber & Wilson, 1986, 1995). And there are two basic determinants of relevance, on such an account. First, utterances are relevant to the extent that they minimize the processing effort required to generate new information from them. Second, utterances are relevant to the extent that they issue in large amounts of new information. One would therefore expect that, when these principles are turned inwards, coopted for use in deciding whether or not to *accept* (believe) an internally generated sentence, they would lead to a preference for *simple but fecund* theories. That is, we should prefer statements that yield as much information as possible (unifying or predicting the maximum possible extent of data) but do so economically.

The other main strands in inference to the best explanation are then consistency and coherence with surrounding theories. There is no reason to think that this should require the introduction of anything radically new into the cognitive system, I think. Consistency with other beliefs can be checked by running the sentence that is up for acceptance back through the comprehension system, building a model of its content that can be compared with those already stored in non-domain-specific memory, and making its content available to the various domain-specific modules and their associated memory systems. Coherence can be checked by forming a conjunction of the sentence in question and any other theoretical belief, subjecting that conjunction to the processes just described.

If this account is along the right lines, then it is somewhat misleading to talk about a "faculty" of inference to the best explanation, and to represent it with a box in figure 5.4. For it doesn't have to be a functionally separate system, with a distinct neural realization. Rather, it is a sort of "virtual" faculty, built out of the operations of other systems. For there would already have had to be in place some system for deciding whether or not to believe a sentence received as input—that is, for deciding whether or not to accept the testimony of another person. And the relevance-theoretic preference for simple but fecund statements would already have been built into the language-interpretation system. What you get when imaged sentences of natural language are created by the supposition generator and cycled through the system would thus be a functional equivalent of a faculty of inference to the best explanation.

It appears, then, that none of the additions and changes necessary to transform the figure 5.3 architecture into the figure 5.4 architecture is especially demanding; nor is it implausible that those changes might have taken place within the relatively short time-frame available—either coincident with, or within a few tens of thousands of years of, the evolution of a language faculty. In which case it would seem that the main elements of distinctively human thinking can be secured from domain-specific modular components with a minimum of additional non-domain-specific apparatus. All that is needed, in effect, is a non-domain-specific memory system supervening on existing perceptual memory systems, and a disposition to generate new suppositions/sentences for consideration. The remainder of the new elements in the figure 5.4 architecture can be secured by coopting resources already available.

5.4 Outstanding Problems

Of course it would be foolish of me to pretend that all of the problems involved in understanding distinctively human cognition have now been addressed, let alone solved. For one thing, there remains the question of how some central-modular outputs rather than others get selected for encoding into language. Would this require the existence of some sort of general problem-solving executive system, overseeing the operations of all the other systems? If so, then the prospects for modeling human cognition in computational terms would not be looking too bright. For another thing, there remains the question of how the practical reasoning system can direct or moderate the activity of the central modules and the supposer, in such a way that those systems are directed toward the generation of contents that might prove useful in satisfying existing goals.

There is some reason to hope that the former problem can be understood in terms of the *salience* of different modular contents, where this might be modeled in terms of intermodular competition for scarce cognitive resources (Sperber, chapter 4 here). And one might expect that the latter problem could be addressed in terms of the operations of a variety of *attentional* systems, which either direct the various modules to work on some aspects of perceptual input rather than others, or cue those modules to be interested in certain sorts of contents rather than others, or both.

Perhaps a more serious problem, for my account, is to explain how domain-general knowledge can become *practical*. For all that I have really done so far is to explain how domain-general *sentences* might be generated and accepted. But how do these sentences then get to have an impact upon practical reasoning, and upon action? One option would be to say that there is a distinct parser/interface for the practical reasoning system that can take a natural language sentence as input and produce a representation in the right format to be processed in practical reasoning.

But this isn't a very attractive option for me, since it multiplies the number of computationally serious mechanisms that would need to be postulated in explaining how language comes to be the medium of intramodular integration. But it is still a possible option. After all, pressures of efficiency in communication alone might have been enough to explain the increasing use of language to combine the outputs of a number of different modules. And then there might have been selective advantages if the practical reasoning system could evolve a language interface so that it could take these crossmodular inputs directly, using them as a basis for action.

The more attractive option, for me, is to use a combination of three ideas: (1) cycles of linguistic activity in inner speech, (2) the use of mental models in speech comprehension, and (3) the access of the practical reasoning faculty to perceptual inputs. Here, then, is how the story might go. The crossdomain sentence "The toy is in the corner with a long blue wall on the left" is constructed and displayed in auditory imagination, thereby being taken as input by the language comprehension subsystem. That system sets to work to build a mental model of its content, where such a model is an analog quasi-perceptual representation. This model is then in the right format to be taken as input by the practical reasoning faculty, which must always have had access to perceptual outputs to underpin highly indexical planning in relation to the perceived environment. ("I'll take *that* one," "I'll go *that* way," "I'll fit *that* through *there* and then move it just *so*.") Then the practical reasoning faculty has access to both of the items of information that it needs (*long wall on left*, and *blue wall*) in order to achieve the goal of retrieving the toy, embedded within a single representation.

Admittedly, this story does emphasize that the role of mental models in my account is something of a hostage to fortune. Might it require the existence of some sort of General Problem Solver to construct a mental model from a given sentence as input? I hope not; and I don't see why it should; but I can't here demonstrate that it doesn't. However, investigation of these and other issues must await some future occasion. All that I can claim to have done here is to sketch a modular architecture that holds out the *promise* of understanding human cognition in modular and computationally tractable terms.

6 Conclusion

I have argued that it is both possible and plausible that distinctively human thinking should be constituted out of modular components, specifically components that implicate natural language. If this is the case, then those who argue against the thesis of massive modularity on the grounds that it cannot account for the non-domain-specific character of much human thought will have to find other reasons for their continued opposition. In fact, it looks like one can have one's massive modularity *and* one's non-domain-specific thinking and reasoning too. In addition, those who are already committed to believing in some form of massive modularity hypothesis now have an architectural proposal to investigate further.

ANNA SHUSTERMAN & ELIZABETH SPELKE

Language and the Development of Spatial Reasoning

Human adult thought appears to transcend animal and infant capabilities greatly. In this chapter, we explore the possibility that language learning provides a path to mature cognition, focusing on the domain of spatial reasoning to probe questions about innate structure and conceptual change. We first summarize evidence that aspects of early spatial cognition rely on modular systems that exhibit characteristic limits in infants and animals. We then discuss how language could serve to overcome these limits.

Do human and animal minds consist of a collection of domain- and task-specific, encapsulated systems, or do they center on a single, central capacity for coordinating information and planning actions? In either case, are human cognitive capacities relatively constant over ontogeny, or do they change qualitatively with development and learning? Finally, are humans' cognitive systems shared by other animals, particularly nonhuman primates, or are certain systems unique to us?

This chapter has two faces. On the one hand, we argue that human and animal minds indeed depend on a collection of domain-specific, task-specific, and encapsulated cognitive systems: on a set of cognitive "modules" in Fodor's (1983) sense. These systems are largely constant over human development: they emerge in human infancy and undergo little qualitative change thereafter. Such core knowledge systems underlie many aspects of human cognition, from attentive tracking of objects (Carey & Xu, 2001) to estimation of numerosity (Dehaene, 1997) to representation of agency and intentionality (Johnson, 2000). Moreover, these systems are largely shared by humans and a variety of nonhuman animals, suggesting that they evolved before the differentiation of the human species. They link the

---

We thank Sang Ah Lee for assistance in running the experiments and Susan Carey, Sang Ah Lee, Kristin Shutts, and Laura Wagner for comments on earlier versions of this chapter.

sophisticated cognitive achievements of human adults to those of humbler creatures lacking language, culture, or education.

On the other hand, we argue that human and animal minds are endowed with domain-general, central systems that orchestrate the information delivered by core knowledge systems. One such system, associative learning, is common to human adults, infants, and nonhuman animals; it allows organisms to adapt their behavior to long-term regularities in the environment. A second system, however, is unique to human children and adults: the language faculty and the specific natural languages whose acquisition the language faculty supports. The latter system provides a medium that human children and adults use to combine information rapidly and flexibly, both within and across core domains.

Natural language has two properties that make it a good candidate mechanism for supporting interaction across conceptual domains. First, natural language has the flexibility to name concepts in any domain: "think" or "want" in theory of mind, "left" or "long" in the domain of space, "cup" or "on" in the domain of object mechanics. Second, natural language has the combinatorial structure to enable concepts from separate domains to be conjoined in phrases and sentences, for example, "I think he wants the cup that's to the left of the newspaper." Uniquely human combinatorial capacities that bind together information common to humans and other animals have previously been proposed to account for various aspects of cognition, including knowledge of the physical world (Carey & Spelke, 1994), knowledge of number (Spelke & Tsivkin, 2001), and theory of mind (de Villiers & de Villiers, 2003). Here we focus on the domain of spatial cognition, specifically the case of spatial reorientation (Cheng, 1986; Margules & Gallistel, 1988). We present evidence that language provides a mechanism by which children overcome limits to their core mechanisms for spatial representation. The hypothesis that language learning supports the development of spatial cognition has been spelled out previously (Spelke, 2003); the research presented here both tests this position and probes the mechanisms by which language might give rise to uniquely human representations of the spatial layout of the environment.

This chapter is divided into three parts. First, we review the literature on spatial reorientation in animals and in young children, arguing that spatial reorientation bears the hallmarks of core knowledge and of modularity. Second, we review studies of older children and adults, arguing that human spatial representations change qualitatively over development and show capacities not found in any other species. Third, we present two new experiments investigating the role of emerging spatial language in uniquely human navigation performance.

1   The Case of Spatial Reorientation

Many navigating animals can represent their own changing locations by integrating information about position, direction, and speed (e.g., Mittelstaedt & Mittelstaedt, 1980; Müller & Wehner, 1988). Because these computations are subject to cumulative errors, animals need to correct their sense of position and orientation by drawing on environmental representations in memory (Gallistel, 1990). The process of error correction, or *reorientation*, has been documented in a wide range of animals and serves to reveal what aspects of space animals and humans encode, remember, and use to regain their bearings.

1.1 Comparative Studies on Reorientation

In the earliest reorientation studies, food-deprived rats were shown the location of a food reward near a corner of a rectangular room with numerous visual and olfactory cues (Cheng, 1986; Margules & Gallistel, 1988). The rats were removed from the room, disoriented, and then returned to the room and allowed to search for the food. Rats searched equally at the target corner and at the corner located at a 180-degree rotation from the target, a location that had the same *geometric* relationship to the shape of the environment as the target location (fig. 6.1). Surprisingly, the rats did not use any of the nongeometric cues, such as the distinctive odors, brightnesses, scents, or textures in different regions of the environment, to distinguish between the two geometrically equivalent choices.

Importantly, rats failed to reorient by nongeometric information even though they detected the information, remembered it, and used it in other ways to guide their navigation. For example, Cheng and Gallistel noted that oriented rats readily learn to forage at a location marked by a panel of a distinctive brightness, pattern, or odor (e.g., Suzuki et al., 1980). They speculated that nongeometrically defined landmarks serve as direct cues to significant environmental locations, but not as cues to reorientation. In a preliminary test of this hypothesis, Cheng (1986) trained rats to forage at a position marked by a landmark. After disorientation in a rectangular room, the rats searched for food primarily at the correct, trained location. Cheng speculated that their search was guided by two independent processes: a reorientation process based exclusively on the shape of the room, and a landmark process based on a learned association between the nongeometric cue and the goal location.

Subsequent research has replicated Cheng's training effect in a variety of species: disoriented rhesus monkeys (Gouteux et al., 2001), rats (Dudchenko et al.,

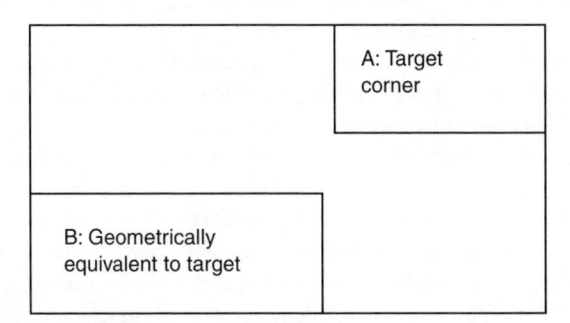

FIGURE 6.1 Schematic of the geometric effect in reorientation in a rectangular room. An object is hidden in the target corner (Corner A) while the subject watches. Following the disorientation procedure, there is no way to distinguish between Corner A and Corner B since they are located at rotationally symmetrical points (both are to the left of a short wall).

1997), and fish (Sovrano et al., 2002, 2003) have all been found, after training, to locate food in accordance both with the shape of the room and the position of a direct, nongeometrically defined landmark. Further evidence suggests that escape tasks engage landmark-based navigation processes more than otherwise identical foraging tasks. For example, Dudchenko and colleagues (1997) found that rats trained in a water maze (an aversive escape paradigm) learned to use landmark cues to find an underwater platform, even though they failed to do so in a foraging task equated for complexity, apparatus size, and amount of training.

Some investigators have argued that these data undermine Cheng and Gallistel's claim for a modular reorientation process (Gouteux et al., 2001; Dudchenko et al., 1997), but recent studies with fish, using an escape task, dramatically support the argument for two distinct processes (Sovrano et al., 2003). Disoriented fish were trained to find the escape door to a tank that, like the chamber Cheng used with rats, was rectangular in shape and was furnished with distinctive landmarks at each corner. After training, fish found the door effectively, using the landmarks. To determine how this information was used, the authors ran further tests in which they removed one or more landmarks. When all landmarks were removed, fish searched primarily and equally at the two geometrically appropriate doors, providing evidence that they used the shape of the environment to reorient themselves. But how does the presence of landmarks enhance performance further, distinguishing the correct door from its opposite? If landmarks were used for reorientation, the authors reasoned, then landmarks should enhance performance regardless of their spatial relation to the goal. In contrast, if landmarks were used to mark the goal position directly, only landmarks near the goal should enhance performance. Consistent with the second prediction, fish searched correctly when the landmarks far from the escape door were removed, leaving only the landmark near the escape door. However, they searched exclusively based on geometry when the landmark nearest the escape door was removed, leaving only the indirect, distal landmark. These findings and similar findings with monkeys (Gouteux et al., 2001) provide strong support for Cheng's original hypothesis: navigation depends both on a reorientation mechanism that is sensitive to the shape of the environment and on associative learning mechanisms that link significant locations with nearby landmarks.

In sum, there is strong evidence for a reorientation mechanism with clear signature limits: it is sensitive to the shape of the extended surface layout but not to other detectable kinds of environmental information. Two types of situations allow disoriented animals to navigate by nongeometric information: training tasks and aversive escape tasks. The weight of the evidence suggests, however, that the same reorientation mechanism, focusing on geometric cues, operates in these situations, and that its signature limits are bypassed by associative learning of direct links between a goal location and a nearby landmark. Many animals, therefore, can represent both the shape of the surface layout and significant locations in the layout, and each type of representation guides a distinct navigation process. But can these distinct processes be flexibly combined into a single, unitary representation? In many studies to date, rats, monkeys, and fish have shown little ability to combine geometric with nongeometric features of the environment.

1.2 Developmental Studies of Reorientation in Humans

Children, like rats, reorient using the geometric features of the environment while ignoring salient nongeometric landmarks (Gouteux & Spelke, 2001; Hermer & Spelke, 1994, 1996; Wang et al., 1999). Borrowing from the paradigm of Cheng and Gallistel, Hermer and Spelke (1994) tested adults and 18- to 24-month-old children in a rectangular room with either all white walls or three white walls and one blue wall. Subjects watched a toy being hidden in one of the corners of the room. They were disoriented by being spun around with their eyes closed and were then asked to find the hidden toy. In the all-white-wall condition, where there were only geometric cues available for reorientation, subjects searched equally in the correct and in the geometrically equivalent corners. In the blue-wall condition, adults readily used the blue wall as a landmark to search only in the correct corner. Children, however, performed like rats: they searched equally in both geometrically correct corners, failing to use the presence of the blue wall to restrict their search to the correct corner.

A series of controls ensured that children's failure occurred specifically when the navigation task required that they use nongeometric features to *reorient*. Like rats, children succeeded in attending to, remembering, and using such features when they served as a direct cue to a significant location. In one set of studies, for example, children played a game in which a xylophone would play each time they hit a distinctively colored wall. Some children were brought in for multiple visits to make the colored wall especially familiar. When children were disoriented and encouraged to make the music, they moved directly to the colored wall, indicating that they attended to it, remembered it, and used it to guide their spatial behavior. When, however, the children were asked to retrieve the hidden object, their search was not affected by the location of this wall. Like rats, children used a nongeometric landmark as a direct cue to a significant location but not as a cue for reorientation (Wang et al., 1999).

Another set of experiments established that this behavioral reliance on geometric cues was specific to the reorientation task. Two containers, each with a unique pattern and color scheme, were located in two corners along one wall of the rectangular room. Children watched a toy being hidden in one of the containers and then closed their eyes as the containers were quietly moved. Children who were disoriented while their eyes were closed searched for the toy in the container with the geometrically congruent location but incorrect visual features. Children who remained oriented while the containers were moved chose the geometrically wrong but visually correct container. When children were taken outside of the rectangular room to make their choice, both oriented and disoriented children chose the visually correct container more often. These results indicate that all of the children had encoded the visual patterns of the correct container but that these cues were unavailable to the cognitive system responsible for reorienting in the rectangular room (Hermer & Spelke, 1996).

Taken together, the studies on rats, children, and adults suggest that humans possess a mechanism for reorientation that is shared with other mammals and that uses geometric information about an environment while ignoring salient nongeometric cues. One incidental finding from the studies of adults suggests that the knowledge delivered by this system is not explicitly accessible: asked how they chose where to search for the hidden object, adults readily referred to the nongeometric landmark when it was available but rarely referred to the shape of the room. Indeed, some adults, after searching exclusively at the two geometrically appropriate corners, maintained that they had searched the four corners at random, simply following a "hunch" about where the hidden object might be. These incidental findings are consistent with Cheng's hypothesis that reorientation depends on an encapsulated system of representation.

1.3 A Geometric Module?

Although an abundance of evidence suggests that reorientation depends on an encapsulated process, some evidence from children suggests that geometry is not the critical property that determines what information is, and is not, accessible to that system. Learmonth, Nadel, and Newcombe (2002) replicated Hermer and Spelke's original finding with four-year-old children, providing evidence that children fail to use nongeometric information in the reorientation task in a small room, but demonstrated that the same children succeed in a room four times as large. However, room size in this experiment was confounded with at least two other factors, landmark distance and landmark size; the landmark in the large room was both larger and farther away from the reorienting child. A recent study demonstrated that the factor of landmark distance may explain the room size effect. Two-year-old children clearly were shown to use a distant nongeometric cue—a light source outside the small room—as a cue for reorientation (Dibble et al., 2003). Therefore, information about the shape of the environment is not always necessary for reorientation, because a distant light source can serve the same function.

Further experiments provide evidence that geometric information is not always sufficient for reorientation. Gouteux and Spelke (2001) tested four-year-old children in a large circular chamber with four indistinguishable landmarks placed in the same locations as the four corners of Hermer and Spelke's original rectangular room. Although the geometric configuration was the same as in past studies, children failed to reorient by this configuration of landmarks. Across a series of studies testing children in a rectangular configuration, children reoriented in accord with the shape of extended surfaces in the layout but not in accord with the shape of an array of objects.

A recent study qualifies the claim of a geometric module still further. Hupbach and Nadel (2003) tested two- to four-year-old children in a rhombus-shaped room: its four walls were equal in length but met at obtuse and acute angles. Although the major and minor axes of this room differed as dramatically as those in Hermer's original studies, the younger children failed to reorient by this difference. After observing an object hidden in an acute-angled corner, for example, they were equally likely to search at the corners with obtuse and acute angles. Although children's reorientation is affected by the differing lengths of the walls of a chamber, it evidently is not affected by the differing angles at which those walls meet.

Taken together, these findings suggest a reconceptualization of the "geometric module" as an encapsulated and task-specific mechanism that analyzes large, stable, three-dimensional features of the surface layout. Many researchers have argued that these features are the most dependable for navigating animals in natural environments (e.g., Biegler & Morris, 1993; Gallistel, 1990; Hermer & Spelke, 1996; Learmonth et al., 2002). Hills and oak trees are likely to maintain their size and geometric configuration over time, whereas the positions of snow patches, colors of the leaves, and location of small rocks do not. Although the findings suggest a different picture of how and why geometry is privileged in reorientation, they do not damage the notion that the reorientation process is modular or lessen the gap between the reorientation performance of animals and young children on the one hand and adults on the other. After all, a human adult *can* navigate using visual cues of any size and nature, spontaneously and on the first try. This ability is likely to depend on mechanisms that allow the spatial representations available to the reorientation module to interact with other conceptual domains. (See Carruthers, chapter 5 here).

In sum, many aspects of reorientation across a number of species, including young humans, bear the hallmarks of modular processing, such as a task-specific reliance on geometry and an encapsulated imperviousness to many kinds of sensory cues. This conclusion raises a question: Why do human adults perform so differently in reorientation tasks?

1.4 The Language Hypothesis in the Development of Spatial Representations and Reorientation

The studies just outlined provide a starting point for considering which capacities for spatial representation are present in human adults but not in children and rats. Cheng and Gallistel's rats, as well as Hermer and Spelke's 18- to 24-month-old children, demonstrated an ability to represent and use a concept like *left of the long wall* in locating objects. Using a geometric notion like *left of the long wall* to reorient would yield two answers in a rectangular room with two long walls. However, rats and children failed to encode a concept like *left of the red wall*, a concept that unambiguously selects the correct location but requires the use of the nongeometric feature *red*. Thus, it seems that both children and rats can represent concepts like *red wall* and geometrically defined locations like *left of the short wall*, but they cannot encode combined concepts like *left of the red wall*.

One of us has hypothesized that the acquisition of a specific, natural language allows humans to combine distinct conceptual domains of core knowledge (Spelke, 2003). On this view, the reorientation module is an innately specified, domain-specific cognitive system shared among humans and other animals. Because children and rats distinguish between the corners with a short wall on the *left* and the corners with a short wall on the *right*, this module is sensitive to sense relations (i.e., the difference between *left* and *right*) and thus contains the concepts *left* and *right*. A different system, perhaps an object-processing system, might represent the presence of a red wall and thus contain the concepts *red* and *wall* or even *red wall*. Without language, however, the only domain-general system available to combine these diverse concepts is the system of associative learning. Associative learning processes would allow an animal or child to learn gradually to search *both left of a long wall and at a red wall*. In the absence of extended learning, however, there is no way to bridge the separate concepts *left* and *red wall*; only language provides the syntactic structure enabling a combined concept *left of the red wall*.

Before these studies, two lines of evidence suggest that language indeed plays a role in the developmental change in reorientation performance. First, the age at which children begin to use landmarks to reorient highly correlates with their accurate production of the phrases *left of* X and *right of* X (Hermer-Vasquez et al., 2001). This correlation suggests a connection between linguistic ability and the conceptual underpinnings of successful navigation by landmarks. By contrast, no other aspects of cognitive development that were explored, such as spatial and verbal working memory, IQ, and vocabulary size, significantly correlated with performance on reorientation tasks.

The second line of evidence comes from adults. When adults do a verbal interference task at the same time as the reorientation task, they fail to use landmarks, suggesting that access to the language system is necessary to perform the task correctly. By contrast, when adults are asked to shadow a rhythm instead of words, they succeed in using the colored wall to reorient (Hermer-Vasquez et al., 1999). Adults' superior performance during the rhythm shadowing task is probably not attributable to the greater difficulty of the verbal shadowing task, since a set of parallel studies suggested that the rhythm shadowing condition was at least as difficult. Importantly, these studies revealed that verbally shadowing adults both used the shape of the room to reorient and used a nongeometric landmark as a direct cue to the hidden object's location. Verbal interference specifically impaired adults' ability to use the nongeometric information in the reorientation task.

While both of these findings suggest that language is involved in the developmental change in spatial representation described here, neither provides a direct, causal link between language acquisition and novel conceptual combination. Concerning the developmental correlation between "left" and "right" production and reorientation performance, correlation does not imply causation. The child's spatial representations may change first, enabling better reorientation performance, and fostering the acquisition of spatial language. Indeed, there is no intuitive reason why language should precede conceptual change; it is just as likely that a purely nonlinguistic maturation in spatial cognition would make the terms *left* and *right* meaningful in a way that they weren't before, enabling the child to learn these terms.

The verbal interference studies with adults also fail to show that language acquisition causes the change in spatial cognition. Mature cognitive systems are considerably different from those of two-year-old children: adults have years of practice sharing spatial concepts with each other through language, and a large body of data in various domains suggests that habitual patterns of language use have cognitive consequences for nonlinguistic tasks (e.g., Boroditsky & Schmidt, 2000). Adults' extended use of language, therefore, may promote more verbalized spatial representations than those of children. Adults might even construct a completely different representational system for reorientation from that of children. Consequently, verbal interference may impair adults' navigation, even if language played no role in the initial acquisition of the spatial representations that are uniquely human.

In an attempt to address these alternative explanations for the apparent involvement of language in reorientation tasks, we have embarked on two studies of the effect of language on children's navigation and spatial representation. The first study investigates whether the presentation of linguistic information alters children's attention to, memory for, and use of nongeometric information in a navigation task. The second study investigates whether training in spatial language can enhance children's landmark-based navigation and spatial representation.

2 Does Verbal Cueing Enhance Children's Use of Nongeometric Landmarks?

The point of departure for our first study is the finding that rats, fish, and monkeys can learn to use a nongeometric landmark as a direct cue to the location of a hidden object, allowing search for the object both in accord with the shape of the environment and in accord with the object's proximity to the landmark. In the studies with animals, subjects learned over a series of training trials to locate the hidden object at a particular landmark. It seemed possible, however, that linguistic communication could substitute for this kind of learning and facilitate an association between the reward object and the nongeometric landmark.

To test whether language might help children to explicitly represent, remember, and orient to the correctly colored wall, we conducted an experiment using a language cue (Shusterman et al., in prep.). The design of the study was very simple: During some trials, the experimenter said, while she was hiding the sticker, "Look! I'm hiding it by the red wall!" or "Look! I'm hiding it by the white wall!" If language can serve to direct attention and memory to task-relevant information in the ways that associative learning processes do, then the verbal cue should lead children to search for the object in the ways that trained rats and fish do, using room shape to reorient and using nongeometric landmarks as direct cues to the object's location.

We ran 16 experimental and 16 control subjects in this study, changing only the presence or absence of the verbal cue. All of the children participated in four trials of the reorientation task. The task was conducted in a four- by six-foot rectangular apparatus built according to the original specifications in Hermer and Spelke (1994), with three walls covered with white fabric and one of the short walls entirely covered with bright red fabric. The door was made of a loose flap of white fabric and could not be distinguished from the other walls when closed. Blue flaps hanging in each of the four corners served as hiding places for the stickers.

On each trial, children watched the experimenter hide a sticker in one of the four hiding corners. Then the child put on a blindfold and turned around slowly four to five times. Before removing the blindfold, the experimenter ensured that the child was truly disoriented (indicated by the child's inability to correctly point to the door). The experimenter turned the child to face a particular wall and removed the blindfold, and the child was allowed to search for the sticker. Each child saw the sticker being hidden in the same corner on all four trials. Equal numbers of children in each group were tested with each hiding corner. In the

98 Architecture

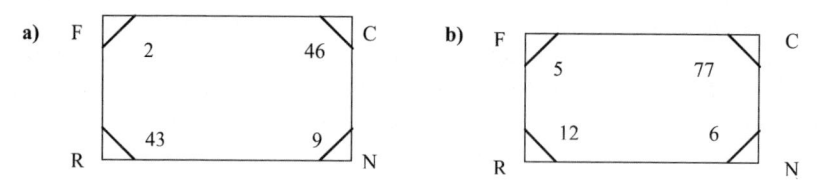

```
a)  F ╱‾‾‾‾‾‾‾‾‾╲ C        b)  F ╱‾‾‾‾‾‾‾‾‾╲ C
      |  2    46  |              |  5    77  |
      |           |              |           |
      | 43     9  |              | 12     6  |
    R ╲_____╱ N          R ╲_____╱ N
```

FIGURE 6.2 Mean search rates for a) control subjects ($n=16$) and b) cued subjects ($n=16$). Rates are expressed as percentage (%) of trials with first search at the corner. C: correct; R: rotated; N: near; F: far.

"cue" group, the experimenter told the child, as she was hiding the sticker, "Look! I'm hiding it by the red (or white) wall!"[1] In the "no cue" group, the experimenter talked with the child during the experiment but without explicitly referring to the color of the wall at the hiding place.

The verbal cue greatly enhanced children's performance on the reorientation task (fig. 6.2). In the no-cue condition, children showed the same geometric search patterns demonstrated in previous studies, choosing the correct corner and the opposite corner equally. In the verbal cue condition, by contrast, children relied both on the shape of the room and on the landmark.

This finding raises two questions. First, what navigation processes are engaged by talking about the nongeometric landmark? Studies of animals provide evidence that nongeometric landmarks are used as direct cues to a hidden object's location but not as cues for reorientation. Is the same true for the children in our study, or do children who hear that an object is being hidden at a nongeometric landmark actually reorient themselves by that landmark? Several incidental observations in this experiment suggest that children used the red or white wall as a direct cue to the object's location, not as a cue to reorientation. First, response latencies were longer in this study than in previous reorientation studies, suggesting that attending to the red wall elicited a further process not elicited by search in the rectangular room without landmarks. Second, children often appeared to hesitate, looking to both geometrically appropriate corners before choosing one. These observations are consistent with the thesis that two processes guided children's search: a reorientation process based solely on geometry and a landmark-guided process for selecting among the geometrically correct corners.

The second question is more speculative: if talking about the color of a wall allows children to use it as a direct cue to the hidden object's location, then why do children not provide themselves with this cue in the reorientation task? Peter Carruthers (personal communication, December 3, 2003) has offered an explanation why children may need to learn *left* and *right* in order to succeed independently in the reorientation task, even though the current studies show that *at*

---

1. While intuitively this might seem likely to have confused the children who heard a cue about the white wall, since there were actually *three* white walls (two long and one short), children immediately and correctly assumed that we were referring to the *short* white wall directly across from the short red wall.

would suffice. *Left of the red wall* specifies a unique corner in the room, while *at the red wall* does not, being ambiguous about which side of the red wall contains the toy. It does not make sense to remind oneself of a location with an ambiguous phrase, so children who don't know *left* and *right* don't encode the situation verbally at all. All this is a consequence (and a demonstration) of the deep encapsulation of the geometric information: because children, like adults, do not realize that they implicitly know which side of the red wall to search, they cannot use this fact in their explicit encoding and reasoning in the task.

We suspect that children also fail to encode and use the nongeometric cue spontaneously for the same reason that untrained animals do: because such cues are rarely as valid or useful as is the geometric information by which animals reorient. When animals are tested in symmetrical environments in which the shape of the surface layout provides ambiguous information, they learn over trials to supplement their normal navigation processes by attending to and using nongeometric information as direct landmark cues. Similarly, when children are told that an object is being hidden near a named, direct landmark, they incorporate this information into their search strategy. In the absence of either training or verbal cueing, however, animals and children fail to use this information.

If our speculations are correct, then neither rats who are trained to use a nongeometric landmark nor young children who hear talk about a nongeometric landmark truly combine geometric and nongeometric information into a unitary representation of an object's position. Adults, in contrast, do appear to form a single, unitary representation that combines these sources of information. When adults are disoriented in a rectangular room with a distinctively colored wall, they search immediately for objects in their correct locations, exhibiting none of the vacillations and hesitations shown by the children in our study. When asked why they searched where they did, adults typically report at once that they saw the object hidden, for example, "left of the red wall." Our next experiment was undertaken to provide more direct evidence for the hypothesis that language acquisition is causally related to this change in reorientation behavior. Specifically, we used a language training study to ask whether the acquisition of spatial language both precedes and gives rise to the developmental change in spatial representation and behavior.

3   Does Learning Spatial Language Change Reorientation Behavior?

In order to test the causal effect of language on reorientation, we taught children the words *left* and *right* and then tested their reorientation in a small rectangular room with a single nongeometric landmark, a red wall. Previous research has indicated that children under five typically fail to use landmarks in the reorientation task and that children begin reorienting successfully between the ages of five and six. Therefore, we chose to use children between four and four and a half years old for our study on the assumption that these children would fail to exhibit landmark-based reorientation behavior without any intervention, but that they would probably have the conceptual readiness to acquire the necessary knowledge for success in the reorientation task.

We created a language training protocol based on findings and intuitions in the literature on children's acquisition of spatial terms like *front* and *back* as well as *left* and *right* (Kuczaj & Maratsos, 1975; Piaget & Inhelder, 1948/1967; Rigal, 1994). It seemed likely to us that children learn these terms most easily on their own body parts. However, we were not sure that learning *left* and *right* on one's own body parts would be sufficient to affect reorientation behavior; after all, understanding the position of a moveable, hidden object relative to a landmark (in a thought like *the toy is to the left of the red wall*) seems qualitatively different and more difficult than identifying one's own left arm, which is much more stable than either a hidden object or a red wall landmark. Therefore, we used a combined training procedure that attempted to teach children to map the words *left* and *right* first onto their own bodies and then onto moveable objects placed at their sides.

The training procedure consisted of two comprehension games that followed an identical structure, the first focusing on body parts and the second focusing on objects. In the body parts game, children stood in the center of the room and followed instructions like "raise your right arm" or "shake your left leg," interspersed with filler commands like "touch your toes." In the objects game, children stood in the center of the room with four objects around them (in front, in back, and at their sides) and were asked to "show me the one on your left" or "give me the toy on your right," with filler trials asking for the object in front or back of the child or referring to the object by color. Both language games followed the same basic structure of pretest, feedback training, and posttest.

Children were observed over two sessions, typically a week apart. In the first session, children participated in our language training procedure, preceded and followed by tests of comprehension of the terms *left* and *right*. The second session began with language posttests to see whether children remembered what they had learned in the first session training. Then children walked to a separate room with a reorientation chamber and participated in up to eight trials of the reorientation task. Additional children were tested only in the reorientation experiment and never participated in language training.

Our first finding is that it is possible to teach some children the terms *left* and *right* under the present conditions. Of the 19 children who participated in training and returned for a second session, 8 passed both comprehension tests at the start of the second session. Thus, about 40 percent of the children demonstrated an improved comprehension of the terms *left* and *right*. (See table 6.1.)

How did language training affect children's behavior in the reorientation room? To address this question, we classified all of the subjects into one of two groups on the basis of their second session language assessments. The 8 *learners* passed both the body parts and objects games during the second session, and the 11 *nonlearners* did not. Consistent with the data from previous reorientation studies, both learners and nonlearners searched primarily in the two geometrically appropriate corners. Learners, however, searched in the *correct* geometric corner significantly more often than nonlearners. We also compared the reorientation behavior of learners and nonlearners to untrained controls who came into the lab for a single visit and participated only in the reorientation task. The behavior of control subjects was essentially identical to that of the nonlearners and significantly below the

Language and the Development of Spatial Reasoning   101

TABLE 6.1 Numbers of subjects succeeding following training on two left-right tasks immediately after training (Session 1) and approximately 1 week later (Session 2).

	Session 1			Session 2	
	Participating in training	Participating in post-test	Passing post-test	Participating in check-up	Passing check-up
Body parts	22	21	14	19	11
Objects	18	11	6	17	10
Both games	18	11	6	17	8

Children who passed the pre-test are counted here as participating in pre-test and post-test and passing post-test. Passing is defined as 75% or more correct.

performance of learners. Figure 6.3 shows mean search rates for learners, non-learners, and untrained controls.

The results confirm and extend the findings of Hermer-Vasquez and collaborators that knowledge of *left* and *right* correlates with higher accuracy in a reoriented search task. These findings provide the strongest evidence to date that the acquisition of spatial language closely mirrors the development of reorientation abilities within an individual child. At the same time, these results leave open a number of questions. One fundamental question is whether language training truly causes a change in reorientation performance. While our findings are consistent with this possibility, they do not rule out the possibility that the children designated as learners in our study might have succeeded on reorientation prior to our language intervention. Perhaps the children whom we classified as learners had advantages over the nonlearners in the reorientation task aside from the factor of language. For example, perhaps these children were simply better problem-solvers, and

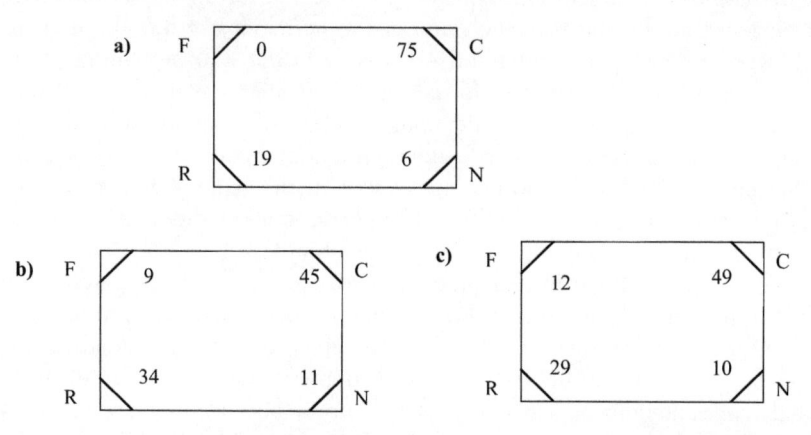

FIGURE 6.3 Mean search rates for a) learners $(n-7)$*, b) non-learners $(n=11)$, and c) untrained controls $(n+12)$. Rates are expressed as percentage (%) of trials with first search at that corner. C: correct; R: rotated; N: near; F: far. *One of the 8 children as Learners refused to cooperate during the orientation task, so the 7 remaining children contribute to this analysis.

therefore succeeded at the language games and the reorientation game independently. Language would then have no causal role as part of the learning mechanism in this case.

On the basis of Hermer-Vasquez and colleagues' (2001) report that IQ and other general problem-solving measures failed to predict reorientation behavior, we doubt that this explanation is correct. Nevertheless, it is an alternative that we take seriously, and further work in the lab is aimed at better probing the causal direction of the demonstrated correlation between language learning and increased success on the reorientation task.

4 Developing Systems for Representing Space

If spatial language does cause a change in reorientation performance, what is the nature of this effect? We now turn to a discussion of possible mechanisms by which language could exert influence over spatial representation and reorientation.

4.1 Linguistic Control of Attention and Memory

According to the initial hypothesis motivating this study, language learning allows the contents of separate modules to combine via natural language syntax, enabling a new thought like "the toy is to the left of the red wall." Alternatively, language learning may enable a novel ability to reorient in some other way than what is proposed in this hypothesis, without combining information from isolated modules. In particular, language may draw attention to nongeometric information or make that information more memorable.

Our first experiment showed that language can indeed direct a child's attention to task-relevant information. However, there are reasons to suggest that the language training in our second experiment played a different role. First, the children who learned *left* and *right* tended to search for the object directly, performing like adults and showing none of the hesitations of the children in the earlier experiment, whose attention was drawn to the wall by naming it. Their direct search suggests that they formed a unitary representation of the object's position, combining geometric and nongeometric information. Second, nothing about the language training specifically mentioned or called the child's attention to the kind of landmark information present in the reorientation task. On the contrary, children were taught *left* and *right* in quite a different context from the environment available during the reorientation task.

There remain three further potential explanations for the apparent training effect in the second experiment. First, domain-general cognitive control systems, such as attention and memory, may have benefited from the training, for reasons unrelated to the linguistic combination hypothesis. One might argue that the initial representations appear encapsulated simply because they are too weak to interact with each other or to drive behavior (for example, see Munakata, 2001). Language learning might make existing knowledge more explicit by strengthening weak representations. Training a child to label explicitly a location might make the location less taxing to remember, allowing the child to hold onto the concept *left of the long wall* at the same time as the concept *red wall*. By making both representations explicit at the same time, a child might be able to reorient more successfully than before, without any significant role of natural language or any requirement that the initial representations were combined in any special way.

Second, spatial language training may enhance children's performance by drawing their attention to the relevant spatial relationships. On this view, the spatial relationships need to be noticed by the child, but they do not need to be represented linguistically. In this case, children might benefit equally from training in a nonlinguistic task that emphasizes the same spatial relationships.

Third, language learning may enhance children's navigation performance by helping them to perform a two-step computation: they orient to the short red wall or the short white wall (wherever the object was hidden), and they choose between the left and right corners based on geometric information. This computation does not require a combined concept; furthermore, children already have all of the ingredients they need to perform each step (which can occur in any order). And, most pointedly, the results of the verbal cueing experiment described earlier show that children are capable of behaving in this way. Nevertheless, we think it is unlikely that our language training on phrases with the words *left* and *right* somehow prompted children to perform the two-step computation. A critical step in this computation is to orient to the correct colored wall, a step that children dramatically *fail* to make before they have a rich understanding of left and right, despite the fact that the difference between the two walls is salient to them. Apparently, this step is not as trivial as it seems. Moreover, it is utterly mysterious why learning *left* would help a child pay attention to wall color.

The current training study does not rule out these three possibilities, but we find them less plausible than the hypothesis that specific properties of spatial language led to the results presented here. We now address this hypothesis in more detail.

4.2 Linguistic Combination of Modular Representations

We hypothesize that learning a particular linguistic structure (left of X) enables children to construct a unitary representation of a concept like *left of the red wall*. There are several ways to imagine the benefit of such a representation. On the linguistic combination hypothesis, concepts that were previously unusable for a particular task, like wall color in a reorientation task, become usable by virtue of their connection to information that is automatically used in the task, in this case a sense of *left* from the geometric module. On a variant of this view, learning a phrase like "to the left of the red wall" might help the child remember the red wall, because the concept *red* is only remembered (for the purposes of a reorientation task) when its status is elevated from a visual feature of the environment to a noun phrase in a combinatorial spatial description. Regardless of whether the critical role of language is to combine modular representations or to redescribe and make explicit otherwise unusable information, both suggestions share an underlying mechanism: the unitary representation of piecemeal concepts.

One question for the linguistic combination hypothesis is whether the proposed mechanism uniquely solves the reorientation problem, or whether it is simply one of many possible mechanisms that might underlie this developmental transition. We suspect that the majority of children end up learning via some version of the linguistic combination process, but there may be different paths to the same end. We would not be surprised if the occasional child found an alternative way to solve the reorientation game, as did trained animals and children in our first experiment. In fact, we think we have witnessed a handful of these children over the various experiments we have conducted. Nevertheless, the critical point about the linguistic combination hypothesis is *cognitive flexibility*. Language learning, in one fell swoop, affords the ability to solve many tasks. If children were taught, or discovered on their own, some mnemonic device for reorientation, it would probably not help them succeed on many other tasks. Teaching children *left* and *right*, however, is likely to help them succeed on a wide range of novel tasks. Therefore, even if language does not provide a *unique* solution to the reorientation problem, it arguably provides the *best* (i.e., most flexible) solution to the reorientation problem.

Another challenge for the linguistic combination hypothesis is specifying exactly how language promotes flexible navigation. If language helps to combine the contents of encapsulated systems, how do we know which contents are combined by what bits of language? According to the hypothesis as originally described (Spelke, 2003), the word *left* maps onto a sense relation available from the output of the geometric module; the words *red wall* map onto the output of the object processing system; and these concepts become combined by natural language into a coherent, unified phrase. But what exactly does it mean to learn *left*? Does the meaning of the word in the child's mind actually reflect the geometric content of a navigation-specific mechanism?

The data here and from other training studies conducted in our lab suggest that children map the words *left* and *right* onto body parts earlier and more easily than onto sensed spatial relations between objects (Shusterman & Spelke, unpublished data; Shusterman & Abarbanell, 2004). At the same time, a large body of work suggests that animals, including humans, simultaneously hold multiple language-independent representations of space (Colby, 1999), including multiple representations of sense relations (i.e., left and right). Two simple examples of representations that hold sense information are proprioception (the sense of one's own body in space) and the sense of left and right conveyed by the geometric module. What is the relation between the spatial representations used for word learning and those used in language-independent tasks? Which systems contain the sense relations that link up with the word *left*? These questions remain wide open. The linguistic combination hypothesis requires direct tests of the claim that the word *left* in fact captures some of the content of the reorientation module.

4.3 Training Studies as an Approach to Exploring Learning Mechanisms

We hope that this case study on developmental change in spatial reorientation can make a methodological contribution on possible roles of training studies, as well as an empirical contribution to the literature on conceptual development. In order to understand mechanisms of learning and conceptual change, psychologists need to describe adequately the initial state of representations, the computations performed by the learning mechanism, and the content of the representations arrived at by the learning mechanism. Training methodologies can speak to each of these questions.

Training studies grant insight into the initial state of representations by allowing researchers to compare the ease of learning various concepts. In cases where there is a discrepancy in children's ability to grasp different meanings of words, the meaning that is *easier* to learn might be presumed to be more conceptually available than meanings that are more difficult to learn. Through careful investigation of which meanings children adopt easily and not so easily, the conceptual structure of the preexisting, putatively isolated representations in core knowledge become more transparent. This approach takes word learning as a window into prelinguistic conceptual structure, and the relative ease of word learning as a mirror of prior conceptual availability. In other research, we have begun using this approach to understand something about how children initially represent and learn words like *left* and *right* (Shusterman & Abarbanell, 2004). This approach is notably not unique to this study (for example, see Gentner & Boroditsky, 2001; Macario, 1991). Ideally, these sorts of studies will help to determine the grain of individual concepts that might get joined in a combinatorial system, as well as the boundaries of the domains that house these concepts.

In order to understand the computations performed by children in instances of conceptual development such as the one here, various types of training can be worked out to reflect different theorized learning mechanisms. The success of any particular training method could then serve as an indicator of the match between the hypothesized learning process and the computations that actually go on in the minds of children in more natural learning experiences. In this way, training studies might be used in parallel with computational models of learning algorithms to assess the plausibility of any hypothesized learning mechanism. This approach has been used fruitfully in studies of children's learning of adjectives (e.g., Gasser & Smith, 1998).

Finally, in order to understand the extent of children's knowledge at the end of a learning process, one can use training studies to test generalization to untrained contexts. Reorientation might be seen as one kind of a test of generalization; if the linguistic combination hypothesis stands a chance of being correct, then we should be able to find other test cases that require conceptual combination mediated by the words *left* and *right*.

5 Summary

In this chapter, we explore the developmental shift in human reorientation, a process that appears to be modular in animals and young children, but not in adults. We also address some challenges to claims about modularity in reorientation and the role of language in conceptual combinations. We present empirical evidence in support of the claim that language plays a causal role in this developmental shift, and we argue that the specific role of language is to allow the isolated contents of encapsulated representations to combine into unified representations. In particular, we hope that by elaborating the process and consequences of spatial language acquisition, we will be able to elucidate the role of language in this developmental shift and extend these hypotheses and methodologies to other tasks and domains where adult competence transcends the bounds of core knowledge.

RICHARD SAMUELS

The Complexity of Cognition
Tractability Arguments for Massive Modularity

A core commitment of contemporary nativism is that human beings possess innate, domain-specific mental structure, not merely for low-level perceptual processes but also for various "higher" cognitive tasks—paradigmatically, involving reasoning and decision-making—that would traditionally be viewed as parts of *central cognition*. One would be hard pressed to find any nativist who did not subscribe to this general thesis; and yet the precise nature of the specialized endowment on which central cognition depends remains a point of considerable controversy.

According to one venerable proposal that continues to exert a profound influence on psychological theorizing, the specialized structures on which central cognition depends primarily take the form of *representational* items, such as beliefs and bodies of mentally represented information somewhat akin to theories (Carey, 1985; Fodor, 2000; Gopnik & Meltzoff, 1998). This kind of nativism figures prominently in the rationalist tradition that traces from Plato, through Descartes, to Chomsky's work on language; and for this reason I refer to it as *psychological rationalism* (or just "rationalism" for short).

In recent years, however, an alternative and more radical nativist proposal has attained a certain prominence—not to mention notoriety. The view in question is sometimes called *massive modularity* (MM) and maintains that, in addition to whatever innate representational structure we may possess, central processes also rely on a multitude of innate, special-purpose information processing mechanisms or "modules" (Cosmides & Tooby, 1994; Fodor, 2000; Samuels, 1998; Sperber, 1994, 2001). So, for example, it has been suggested that we possess modules for folk

---

I would like to thank Peter Carruthers, Keith Hossack, Stephen Laurence, David Papineau, Gabe Segal, and Mark Textor for commenting on earlier drafts of this chapter. I would also like to thank Joanna Bryson for helpful discussion of the material in section 7.

biology, naive physics, theory of mind, and arithmetic. Thus construed, massive modularity differs from its more traditional, rationalist counterpart in being primarily a nativism about cognitive *mechanisms* as opposed to cognitive contents (Fodor, 2000; Samuels, 1998).

The commitments of MM and psychological rationalism overlap to a considerable degree. Both acknowledge that central cognition depends on substantial amounts of innate, domain-specific structure. Moreover, contemporary advocates of both positions almost invariably adopt some version of the *peripheral modularity hypothesis*, on which both perceptual (or input) processes and motor (or output) processes are subserved by an array of innate modules (Fodor, 1983). In view of this, it is seldom easy to discriminate between the two views on experimental grounds alone. Even so, advocates of MM maintain that their conception of cognition is independently plausible in the light of various general, theoretical considerations, of which perhaps the most prominent and widely invoked is what we might call the *tractability argument* for massive modularity. According to this argument, central cognition must be subserved by modular mechanisms because the alternatives—including psychological rationalism—are *computationally intractable*.

The central aim of this chapter is to assess the scope and limits of the tractability argument. In doing so, I argue for two claims. First, I argue that when explored with appropriate care and attention, it becomes clear that the argument provides no good reason to prefer massive modularity to the more traditional rationalist alternative. Second, while I deny that tractability considerations support massive modularity per se, I do not claim that they show nothing whatsoever. In particular, I argue that a careful analysis of tractability considerations suggest a range of characteristics that any plausible version of psychological rationalism is likely to possess.

Before arguing for these claims, however, there are a number of preliminary issues that need to be addressed. In section 1, I outline and clarify the general form of the tractability argument; and in section 2 I explain how massive modularity is supposed to resolve intractability worries. The remainder of the chapter—sections 3 to 7—is largely concerned with highlighting the deficiencies of the main extant arguments for claiming that nonmodular mechanisms are intractable. In section 8, I conclude by sketching some of the general characteristics that a plausible rationalist alternative to massive modularity—one capable of subserving tractable cognitive processes—is likely to possess.

1 Tractability Arguments for Massive Modularity

Although versions of the tractability argument vary considerably in detail, they all share the following pair of commitments. First, they assume that the *classical computational theory of mind* (CTM) is true:[1]

---

1. Though sometimes only tacitly and sometimes only for the sake of argument.

CTM: Human cognitive processes are classical computational ones—roughly, algorithmically specifiable processes defined over syntactically structured mental representations.

As has been commonly observed, however, the truth of CTM requires more than *mere* computability, since there are many algorithms that demand more time and resources—memory, information, and computational power—than actual human beings possess. Rather, what it requires is that mental processes are in some suitable sense *tractably* computable: roughly speaking, that they are specifiable in terms of algorithms that do not require more time or resources than humans can reasonably be expected to possess.[2] It is on this point that advocates of the tractability argument seek to undermine alternatives to MM. That is, they endorse the following *intractability thesis* (IT):

IT: Nonmodular cognitive mechanisms—in particular mechanisms for reasoning—are computationally intractable.

As will soon become apparent, the arguments for IT vary considerably. Nonetheless, the *source* of intractability is almost invariably assumed to be what many have called the "frame problem,"[3] though it is perhaps more accurately (and less contentiously) referred to as the *problem of relevance*. Nomenclature aside, the problem is this: How can a device determine in a computationally tractable manner which operations, options, or items of information are relevant to the cognitive task at hand? A satisfactory computational theory of mind must address this problem. Yet, according to IT, non-MM theories are unable to do so because relevance poses an insurmountable problem for nonmodular reasoning mechanisms. So, it would seem to follow that:

MM: The mind—including those parts responsible for reasoning—is composed of modular mechanisms.

And this is, of course, precisely what the massive modularity hypothesis requires.

---

2. According to one characterization of tractability familiar from computer science, an algorithm for solving some problem is *tractable* if, in the worst case, it is *polynomial* in the size of the input; that is, the resources required to compute a solution to every input can be expressed as a polynomial (or better) function of input size—e.g., n^2 or n^{300}. In contrast, an algorithm is intractable if, in the worst case, it is *superpolynomial*, in the sense that resource requirements increase *exponentially* (or worse) as a function of input size and can thus only be expressed as superpolynomial functions, such as 2^n or 100^n. But for current purposes this characterization of (in)tractability is doubly unsuitable. First, it is very widely assumed on inductive grounds by those who model cognitive processes that pretty much any interesting computational problem is superpolynomial in the *worst* case. Thus, the current criterion for intractability does little more than characterize those problems that are *not* of interest to a computational account of cognition. Second, it is entirely possible for a superpolynomial algorithm to very frequently— indeed *normally*—be significantly less expensive than the worst case. In which case, it's hard to see why intractability, in this sense, poses a problem for CTM. After all, it may just be that performance limitations prevent the algorithm being used in the worst case.
3. Dennett (1987); Fodor (1983, 2000); Sperber (1994); Tooby and Cosmides (1992).

In the following discussion I assume for the sake of argument that CTM is true and focus on the intractability thesis. What I aim to show is that a commitment to IT is built on shaky foundations, since the main arguments for it are deeply unsatisfactory. But first I need to explain how MM is supposed to secure tractability where the alternatives allegedly fail.

2 How Does Massive Modularity Help Resolve Tractability Problems?

The answer to the above question can be divided into two parts. First, according to MM—and in contrast to an earlier, well-known thesis defended by Fodor (1983) and others—modularity is not restricted to the periphery of the mind: to those *input systems* responsible for perception and *output systems* responsible for the production of action. According to MM, *central systems* for reasoning and decision-making can be divided into modules as well (Jackendoff, 1992). Thus MM maintains that our minds are modular in precisely those places where relevance is traditionally assumed to pose the greatest threat to tractable computation.

Second, according to the proposal, modules themselves possess certain core characteristics that engender feasible computation: in particular, *domain specificity* and *informational encapsulation*. The rough idea is that by virtue of possessing either or both of these, modular mechanisms can avoid the sorts of tractability problems that (allegedly) plague nonmodular devices. In the remainder of this section I explain this suggestion in more detail. But first a terminological point: The term "module" is notoriously ambiguous;[4] and it is often unclear how theorists intend it to be understood. But since we are concerned primarily with how modularity helps address tractability problems, we can safely restrict our attention to those characteristics of modules that are supposed to resolve such problems: namely, domain specificity and encapsulation. In what follows, then, I adopt a minimal definition of modules as computational mechanisms that possess one or both of these characteristics.

2.1 Domain Specificity and Feasible Computation

What is domain specificity and how is it supposed to engender feasible computation? To a first approximation, a mechanism is domain specific if it operates only in a highly restricted cognitive domain.[5] Standard candidates include mechanisms for face recognition, language, and arithmetic. There are, however, at least two broad views about cognitive domains that give rise to different conceptions of domain specificity. According to the first, the domain of a cognitive mechanism is the class of

---

4. See Segal (1996) and Samuels (2000) for discussions of the various uses of "module" in cognitive science.
5. It should go without saying—though I'll say it anyway—that the notion of domain specificity *admits of degree* and that researchers who use the notion are interested in whether we possess mechanisms that are domain specific to some *interesting* extent. The same points also apply to the notion of informational encapsulation.

representations that it can take as input: its *input domain*. On this conception of domains, a cognitive mechanism is domain specific to the extent that it can only take as input a highly restricted range of representations. According to the second conception of cognitive domains, the domain of a mechanism is the *task* (or function) that it performs: its *task domain*. On this conception of domains, a mechanism is domain specific if it is dedicated to performing a highly restricted task.

Why suppose that domain specificity in either of these senses engenders feasible computation? The claim cannot be that domain specificity is *sufficient* for tractability, since many of the paradigms of intractable computation—such as algorithms for solving the traveling salesman problem—are very domain specific indeed.[6] Nevertheless, if a mechanism is sufficiently domain specific, then it becomes possible to utilize a potent design strategy for reducing computational load, namely, to build into the mechanism substantial amounts of information about the domain in which it operates. This might be done in a variety of ways. It might be only implicit in the organization of the mechanism, or it might be explicitly represented; it might take the form of rules or procedures or bodies of propositional knowledge and so on. But however this information gets encoded, the key point is that a domain-specific mechanism can be *informationally rich* and, as a result, capable of rapidly and efficiently deploying those strategies and options most relevant to the domain in which it operates. Such mechanisms thereby avoid the need for computationally expensive search and assessment procedures that might plague a more general-purpose device. For this reason, domain specificity has seemed to many a plausible candidate for reducing the threat of combinatorial explosion without compromising the reliability of cognitive mechanisms (Sperber, 1994; Tooby & Cosmides, 1992).

2.2 Informational Encapsulation and Feasible Computation

I turn now to the notion of informational encapsulation. According to the standard definition, an encapsulated cognitive mechanism or faculty is one that "has access, in the course of its computations, to less than all of the information at the disposal of the organism whose cognitive faculty it is" (Fodor, 1987, p. 25). Paradigmatic examples—such as mechanisms for length perception or phonological processing—cannot draw upon the full range of the organism's beliefs, goals, and intentions. In contrast, a highly *unencapsulated* mechanism—paradigmatically for reasoning—would be one that has access to (virtually) all of our beliefs, goals, and intentions (Fodor, 1983; Stanovich, 1999).

A number of further comments are in order. First, although it is not uncommon to confound informational encapsulation and domain specificity (in particular with regard to the specificity of *input* domains), they are distinct properties. Both concern

---

6. In brief, the traveling salesman problem is to find the shortest path that a salesman can take between a network of cities. This is a highly specialized task and, moreover, the inputs to the process—the names of cities and representations of inter-city distances—are highly restricted as well. Yet it is notoriously hard to solve in a computationally tractable manner. This suggests that domain specificity is not plausibly viewed as sufficient for tractability.

the *access* that a mechanism has to representations. Yet the kind of access is quite different. Input-specificity concerns the class of representations that a mechanism can take as input: that "trigger" it or "turn it on." In contrast, the informational encapsulation of a mechanism concerns the class of representations that it can use as a resource once it has been so activated. Paradigmatically, encapsulation concerns the information encoded in memory that the mechanism is able to consult in the course of providing solutions to the particular inputs that it receives.

Second, encapsulation proper is not just any sort of restriction on access. Rather, it is supposed to be *architecturally* imposed. Minimally, this implies the following. First, encapsulation is a relatively enduring characteristic of the device. Second, it is not a mere product of *performance* factors, such as fatigue, lack of time or lapses in attention. Finally, and most important for my purposes, the encapsulation of a device is supposed to be *cognitively impenetrable* (Pylyshyn, 1984). To a first approximation: it is not a property of the mechanism that can be changed as a result of alterations in the beliefs, goals, and other representational states of the organism. Or roughly equivalently: it is not a property of the mechanism that can be changed by *psychological processes* alone.

Third, although there are various ways encapsulation might be architecturally imposed, the standard suggestion is that encapsulated mechanisms have access to only the information contained within a restricted, *proprietary database*. One important implication is that such mechanisms are unable to deploy information located elsewhere in the system even when that information is relevant to the task at hand. Suppose, for example, that mechanisms for face recognition only have access to a database of previously encountered faces. Such a device would be unable to utilize other sorts of information—for example, geographic or autobiographical information—even though it might sometimes be highly relevant to the task of recognizing faces

Finally, it is worth noting an ambiguity in the standard definition of encapsulation between a synchronic and a diachronic reading:

A mechanism M is *synchronically encapsulated* if, at any time, there is at least some (kind of) information possessed by the organism that is inaccessible to M.

A mechanism M is *diachronically encapsulated* if there is some (kind of) information that is inaccessible to M, not merely at some particular time but over a long period—paradigmatically the entire history of the mechanism.

I assume for two reasons that it is the *diachronic* notion that should concern us here. First, the paradigmatic examples of encapsulated modules are clearly diachronically encapsulated. So, for example, the perceptual mechanisms implicated in the production of persistent illusions—such as the Muller-Lyer or phi phenomenon—are not merely synchronically encapsulated with respect to our beliefs about the illusory phenomena.[7] (It is not as if, for example, two years hence

---

7. In the case of the Muller-Lyer illusion, the mechanisms responsible for visual length perception do not have access to the belief that, contrary to appearances, the lines are of identical length.

they might access the relevant beliefs and the illusions dissipate.) Rather, the claim is that such beliefs are never accessible to the mechanism. Second, the synchronic notion is *too liberal* and classifies as encapsulated mechanisms that would not normally be counted as such. So, for example, it will count as encapsulated (1) any deterministic computational device that does not engage in exhaustive memory search,[8] and (2) any reasoning mechanism whose access to information is mediated via a limited working memory.[9] But not all such systems would ordinarily be construed as encapsulated.

How, then, is encapsulation supposed to facilitate feasible computation? As with domain specificity, encapsulation is not *sufficient* for feasibility; and again the traveling salesman illustrates the point. Algorithms designed to solve this task typically have access to only the information contained in the input to the process; yet they are computationally very expensive indeed. Even so, there are two plausible explanations of how encapsulation might engender tractability: a superficial and a deeper one.

According to the superficial explanation, encapsulation reduces computational load in two ways. First, because the device only has access to a highly restricted database or memory, the costs incurred by memory search are considerably reduced. (There just isn't that much stuff over which the search can be performed.) Second, by reducing the range of accessible items of information, there is a concomitant reduction in the number of relations *between* items—paradigmatically, relations of confirmation and relevance—that can be computed.

Yet one might reasonably wonder what all the fuss is about. After all, computer scientists have generated a *huge* array of methods—literally hundreds of different search and approximation techniques—for reducing computational overheads (Russell & Norvig, 2003). What makes encapsulation of *particular* interest? Here's where the deeper explanation comes into play. Most of the methods that have been developed for reducing computational load require that the implementing mechanisms treat the assessment of relevance as a *computational* problem. Roughly: they need to implement computational procedures that select from the available information some subset that is estimated to be relevant. In contrast, encapsulation is supposed to obviate the need for such computational solutions. According to this view, an encapsulated device (at least paradigmatically) only has access to a very small amount of information. As a consequence, it can perform (near) exhaustive search on whatever information it can access, and thereby avoid the need to assess

---

8. Consider, for example, a domain-general reasoning device with sole access to a general encyclopedic memory system that contains all the information possessed by the organism of which it is a part. Such a reasoning mechanism would ordinarily be construed as a paradigm of nonmodularity. But if it were deterministic and also deployed procedures (e.g., heuristics) for delimiting which portion of the database to access, then it would, on the synchronic reading, count as encapsulated.

9. Consider a mechanism that can access any part of encyclopedic memory but does so via a working memory of the Miller "magic number seven" variety. Since at any specific time it would only have access to seven items of information (give or take a bit), it would, on the synchronic reading, be highly encapsulated.

relevance. There is a sense, then, in which highly encapsulated devices avoid the relevance problem altogether (Fodor, 2000).

Assume that the above is correct—that domain specificity and informational encapsulation help engender feasible computation—then it should be clear how MM is supposed to address the threat that intractability poses for CTM. What it does is ensure that reasoning mechanisms are architecturally constrained with respect to what options and items of information they can consider. Yet it is one thing to claim that modularity is an important way to engender tractability and quite another to claim that it is the *only* plausible way. The former is compatible with a broad range of architectural hypotheses—including a psychological rationalism that posits radically nonmodular reasoning mechanisms—while the latter demands that computationalists adopt an extreme form of MM. In the following sections, I consider arguments that purport to establish this stronger claim—the intractability thesis—and show that they are unsatisfactory.

3 Informational Impoverishment

Perhaps the most prominent argument for IT is one made popular by the evolutionary psychologists Leda Cosmides and John Tooby (Cosmides & Tooby, 1994). The argument proceeds from the assumption that a nonmodular, hence domain-general, mechanism "lacks any content, either in the form of domain-specific knowledge or domain-specific procedures that can guide it towards the solution of problems" (Cosmides & Tooby, 1994, p. 94). As a consequence, it "must evaluate all the alternatives it can define" (p. 94). But as Cosmides and Tooby observe, such a strategy is subject to serious intractability problems, since even routine cognitive tasks are such that the space of alternative options tends to increase *exponentially*. Nonmodular mechanisms would thus seem to be computationally intractable: at best intolerably slow and at worst incapable of solving the vast majority of problems they confront.

Though frequently presented as an objection to non-MM accounts of cognitive architecture, this argument is really only a criticism of theories that characterize cognitive mechanisms as suffering from a particularly extreme form of informational impoverishment. Any appearance to the contrary derives from the stipulation that domain-general mechanisms possess no specialized knowledge. But this conflates claims about the need for *informationally rich* cognitive mechanisms—a claim that I do not wish to deny—with claims about the need for modularity; and although modularity is one way to build specialized knowledge into a system, it is not the only way. Another is for nonmodular devices to have access to bodies of specialized knowledge. Indeed, it is commonly assumed by nonmodular—especially rationalist—accounts of central possessing that such devices have access to *huge* amounts of information. This is pretty obvious from even the most cursory survey of the relevant literatures. Fodor (1983), for example, maintains explicitly that nonmodular central systems have access to huge amounts of information; as do Gopnik, Newell, and many others who adopt a nonmodular conception of central systems (Gopnik & Meltzoff, 1997; Newell, 1990). The argument currently under discussion thus succeeds only in refuting a straw man.

4 Optimality

Another argument for IT turns on the claim that nonmodular reasoning mechanisms implement *optimization* processes. In this context, "optimization" refers to reasoning that broadly conforms to standards of *ideal rationality*, such as those characterized by Bayesian accounts of probabilistic inference or standard approaches to decision theory. There are a range of results that show such reasoning processes are computationally very expensive indeed (Osherson, 1995);[10] and for this reason they are commonly termed *unbounded* or even *demonic* conceptions of reasoning (Gigerenzer, 2001; Simon, 1972). So if advocates of nonmodular reasoning mechanisms are committed to optimization, then the view they endorse would be subject to serious intractability worries as well.

It is not at all clear to me that anyone *explicitly* endorses the above argument, though it is strongly suggested by some recent discussions of nonmodular reasoning architectures (Dietrich & Fields, 1996; Gigerenzer, 2001; Gigerenzer et al., 1999). The argument is not, however, a good one. Though optimal reasoning is (at least in the general case) intractable,[11] nonmodularists are in no way committed to such a view of human reasoning. What *is* true is that for a mechanism to optimize it needs to be *unencapsulated*, hence nonmodular; and this is because, as ordinarily construed, optimization demands the updating of all one's beliefs in the light of new information. But the converse is not true: an unencapsulated mechanism need not be an optimizer. On the contrary, since the inception of artificial intelligence (AI) it has been commonplace to combine a nonmodular conception of reasoning with the explicit denial of optimization. Consider, for example, Newell and Simon's seminal work on the general problem solver (GPS). As the name suggests, GPS was designed to apply across a very wide range of content domains without architectural constraint on what representations is could use. It is thus not plausibly viewed as modular. But, to use Simon's famous expression, it was designed to *satisfice*—to arrive at solutions that were *good enough*—not to optimize. The same could be said for many other nonmodular accounts of central processing, including Anderson's ACT-R theory and Laird and Newell's SOAR architecture (Anderson, 1993; Newell, 1990). These are among the paradigms of nonmodular approaches to cognition, yet they are in no way committed to optimization.

---

10. To use one well-known example, on standard Bayesian accounts, the equations for assessing the impact of new evidence on our current beliefs are such that if one's system of beliefs has n elements, then computing the new probability of a single belief, B, will require 2^n additions (Harman, 1986). Such methods thus involve an exponential growth in number of computations as a function of belief system size. To give some idea of just how expensive this is, on the hyperconservative assumption that we possess 100 beliefs, calculating the probability assignment of a belief B on the basis of new information will require the performance of more than 10^{30} additions, which is considerably more than the number of microseconds that have elapsed since the Big Bang!

11. Though there is lots of good research that aims to discover tractable methods for applying ideal standards of rationality to interesting—but restricted—domains. See, for example, the literature on Bayesian networks (Pearle, 1988).

5 Exhaustive Search

Still, even if optimization *as such* is not a problem for nonmodular accounts of reasoning, it might still be that there are properties of optimal reasoning to which the nonmodularist *is* committed and that these properties are sufficient to generate intractability problems. Exhaustive search is perhaps the most plausible candidate for this role. The rough idea is that nonmodular reasoning mechanisms must perform *exhaustive* searches over our beliefs. But, given even a conservative estimate of the size of any individual's belief system, such a search would be unfeasible in practice. In which case, it would seem that nonmodular reasoning mechanisms are computationally intractable.

Again, it's not at all clear to me that anyone really endorses this argument, though some have found it hard not to view advocates of nonmodular central systems as somehow committed to exhaustive search (Carruthers, 2004; Glymour, 1985). Yet this view is incorrect. What the nonmodularist does accept is that unencapsulated reasoning mechanisms have *access* to huge amounts of information—paradigmatically, all the agent's background beliefs. But the relevant notion of access is a *modal* one. It concerns what information—given architectural constraints—a mechanism *can* mobilize in solving a problem. In particular, it implies that any background belief can be used, not that the mechanism *in fact* mobilizes the entire set of background beliefs—that is, that it engage in exhaustive search. And this is just as well, since it would be absurd to hold a nonmodular view of reasoning if it implied exhaustive search (Fodor, 1985).

Of course, the fact that the nonmodularist does not *endorse* the claim that central systems engage in exhaustive search is perfectly consistent with there being an argument that shows such processes would need to occur if a nonmodular account of reasoning were true. In the next section, I consider a recent argument from Fodor (2000) that has been widely interpreted by advocates of MM as supporting this conclusion.

6 The Locality Argument

Fodor's argument is a complex one, but the core idea can be framed in terms of a tension between two claims. The first is that classical computational processes are *local* in roughly the following sense: what computations apply to a particular representation is determined solely by its *constituent structure*—that is, by how the representation is constructed from its parts (Fodor, 2000, p. 30). To take a very simple example, whether the addition function can be applied to a given representation is solely determined by whether or not it has the appropriate syntactic structure—for example, whether it contains a permissible set of symbols related by "+."

The second claim is that much of our reasoning is *global*, in that it is sensitive to *context-dependent* properties of the *entire* belief system. In arguing for this, Fodor focuses primarily on abductive reasoning (or inference to the best explanation).[12]

---

12. Though he thinks that the same considerations apply to decision-making or planning as well.

Such inferences routinely occur in science and, roughly speaking, consist in coming to endorse a particular belief or hypothesis on the grounds that it constitutes the best available explanation of the data. One familiar feature of such inferences is that the relative quality of hypotheses are not assessed merely in terms of their ability to fit the data but also in terms of their simplicity and conservativism.[13] According to Fodor, however, these properties are not intrinsic to a belief or hypothesis but are global characteristics that a belief or hypothesis possesses by virtue of its *relationship* to a constantly changing system of background beliefs. The problem, then, is this: If classical computational operations are local, how could global reasoning processes, such as abduction, be computationally tractable?

Notice that if the above is correct, then a classical abductive process could not operate merely by looking at the hypotheses to be evaluated. This is because, by assumption, what classical computations apply to a representation is determined solely by its constituent structure, whereas the simplicity and conservativism of a hypothesis, H, depend not only on its constituent structure but its relations to our system of background beliefs, K. In which case, a classical implementation of abduction would need to look at both H *and* whatever parts of K determine the simplicity and conservativism of H. The question is: How *much* of K needs to be consulted in order for a classical system to perform reliable abduction? According to Fodor, the answer is that lots—indeed, very often, the totality—of the background will need to be accessed, since this is the "only *guaranteed* way" of classically computing a global property. But this threatens to render reliable abduction computationally intractable. As Fodor puts its:

> Reliable abduction may require, in the limit, that the whole background of epistemic commitments be somehow brought to bear on planning and belief fixation. But feasible abduction requires in practice that not more than a small subset of even the relevant background beliefs are actually consulted. (2000, p. 37)

In short: if classicism is true, abduction cannot be reliable. But since abduction presumably is reliable, classicism is false.

If sound, the above argument would appear to show that classicism itself is untenable. So, why would anyone think it supports MM? The suggestion appears to be that MM provides the advocate of CTM with a way out: a way of avoiding the tractability problems associated with the globality of abduction without jettisoning CTM (Sperber, 2001; Carruthers, chapter 5 here). Fodor himself put the point as well as anyone:

> Modules are informationally encapsulated by definition. And, likewise by definition, the more encapsulated the informational resources to which a computational mechanism has access, the less the character of its operations is sensitive to global properties of belief systems. Thus to the extent that the information accessible to a device is architecturally constrained to a proprietary database, it won't have a frame

---

13. Very roughly: (1) one hypothesis is *simpler* (or more parsimonious) than another if it posits fewer entities/causes/parameters, and (2) one hypothesis is more *conservative* than another if it requires less revision to our belief system.

problem and it won't have a relevance problem (assuming that these are different); not, at least, if the database is small enough to permit approximations to exhaustive searches. (2000, p. 64)

The modularity of central systems is thus supposed to render reasoning processes sufficiently *local* to permit tractable computation.

There are a number of serious problems with the above line of argument. One that I will *not* address here concerns the extent to which MM provides a satisfactory way of shielding CTM from the tractability worries associated with globality.[14] What I will argue, however, is that although simplicity and conservativism are plausibly context dependent, Fodor provides us with no reason whatsoever to think that they are *global* in any sense that threatens nonmodular versions of CTM.

First, when assessing the claim that abduction is global, it is important to keep firmly in mind the general distinction between normative and descriptive-psychological claims about reasoning: claims about how we *ought* to reason and claims about how we *actually* reason. This distinction applies to the specific case of assessing the simplicity and conservativism of hypotheses. On the normative reading, assessments of simplicity and conservativism ought to be global: that is, normatively correct assessments ought to take into consideration one's total background epistemic commitments. But of course it is not enough for Fodor's purposes that such assessments *ought* to be global. Rather, it needs to be the case that the assessments humans make are, *in fact*, global; and to my knowledge, there is no reason whatsoever to suppose that this is true.

A comparison with the notion of consistency may help to make the point clearer. Consistency is frequently construed as a normative standard against which to assess one's beliefs (Dennett, 1987). Roughly: all else being equal, one's beliefs ought to be consistent with each other. When construed in this manner, however, it is natural to think that consistency should be a global property in the sense that any belief ought to be consistent with the entirety of one's background beliefs. But there is absolutely no reason to suppose—and indeed some reason to deny—that human beings conform to this norm (Cherniak, 1986). Moreover, this is so in spite of the fact that consistency really does play a role in our inferential practices. What I am suggesting is that much the same may be true of simplicity and conservativism. When construed in a normative manner, it is natural[15] to think of them as global properties, but when construed as properties of the beliefs that figure in actual human inference, there is no reason to suppose that they accord with this normative characterization.

Second, even if we suppose that the simplicity and conservativism are global properties of actual beliefs, the locality argument still does not go through, since it turns on the implausible assumption that we are guaranteed to make successful assessments of simplicity and conservativism. Specifically, in arguing for the conclusion that abduction is computationally unfeasible, Fodor relies on the claim that "the only guaranteed way of Classically computing a syntactic-but-global property" is to take

---

14. Though see Samuels (forthcoming) for an extended discussion of this issue.
15. Though by no means mandatory.

"whole theories as computational domains" (2000, p. 36). But guarantees are *beside the point*. Why suppose that we always successfully compute the global properties on which abduction depends? Presumably we do not. And one very plausible suggestion is that we fail to do so when the cognitive demands required are just too great. In particular, for all that is known, we may well fail under precisely those circumstances that the classical view would predict—namely, when too much of a belief system needs to be consulted in order to compute the simplicity or conservativism of a given belief.

7 The Robot Argument

The final argument for IT that I will discuss consists in an induction from recent trends in AI and robotics (Carruthers, 2004; Goodie et al., 1999). The starting point for this argument is that if one wants to assess the computational feasibility of classical, non-MM architectures, then the repeated efforts of computer scientists to produce feasible intelligent systems—paradigmatically, robots—constitute an important source of evidence. According to the robot argument, however, research in the past decade or so has increasingly converged on one form or other of massive modularity. To mention just two examples, *behavior-based* approaches have had an enormous influence on robotics (Brooks, 1999) while so-called multiagent systems has been among the most rapidly developing areas of AI in recent years (Ferber). Moreover, so the argument continues, this convergence is largely a consequence of the problems that researchers encounter in trying to develop practically feasible real-time systems. Roughly: nonmodular systems have in practice turned out to be unfeasible, whereas modular ones have been far less prone to such problems. It would seem, then, that the pattern of successes and failures in AI and robotics provide us with good—albeit nondemonstrative—grounds for accepting MM (Carruthers, 2004; Gigerenzer, 2001, p. 43).

The general form of the argument is a perfectly respectable one. Indeed, if CTM is true, then careful and accurate analysis of contemporary AI and robotics might have much to tell us about the architecture of human cognition. My concern, however, is that the analysis on which the robot argument depends is neither careful nor accurate. What *is* true is that research—especially in robotics—has converged on the need for a kind of module that Rodney Brooks calls *reactive behaviors*. Such modules are a commonplace feature of contemporary robots and are designed to generate rapid, real-time responses—such as avoidance behavior—to prespecified sets of environmental conditions (Brooks, 1999; Bryson, 2000). Moreover, the popularity of these kinds of modules is, in large measure, a response to the dramatic failure of a less modular approach to robotics—the *sense-model-plan-act* paradigm—which assumed that virtually all robot behavior should be mediated by the activity of a general-purpose planning system (Bonasso et al., 1998; Brooks, 1999).[16]

But this alone does not constitute an argument for *massive* modularity. What the Robot Argument needs to show is that there has been convergence on the idea that

---

16. The most famous product of the SMPA paradigm was Shakey, the Stanford Research Institute robot (Nilsson, 1984).

central systems are modular; and no such convergence of opinion exists within the AI community. Even in robotics where tractable, real-time performance is of a premium, the dominant kind of computational architectures—so-called three-layered or hybrid systems—incorporate a *deliberative* layer of nonmodular mechanisms for planning and world-modeling quite similar to those that figured in the discredited sense-model-plan-act paradigm (Bonasso et al., 1998; Gat, 1998).[17] In contrast to earlier proposals, however, the hybrid approach incorporates two additional design principles. First, the system has a *reactive layer* that contains a multitude of Brookian modules that enable it to respond rapidly to environmental contingencies. Second, in large measure because of this, the reasoning mechanisms within the deliberative layer of the system can be "decoupled" from real-time activities—such as obstacle avoidance—and instead deployed to generate solutions to complex, informationally intensive, decision-making tasks. The result of combining these various features is a kind of system that is both more flexible than those composed solely of reactive behaviors and more capable of real-time performance than those that assign a larger role to reasoning mechanisms (Russell & Norvig, 2003).

8 Conclusion

The main burden of this chapter has been to argue that we currently possess no good reason to accept IT, hence no reason to endorse MM on the grounds of tractability. Thus formulated, the project is a largely negative one. But my discussion of the arguments for IT also yield a series of positive suggestions about the general properties that the kind of computational architecture proposed by psychological rationalists is likely to possess. None of these suggestions are, I think, particularly surprising; and many of them are utterly commonplace in those regions of cognitive science most concerned with the computational implementation of cognitive processes. In view of the confusions that surround debate over MM, however, it is perhaps worth concluding this chapter by assembling these claims.

1. *Informational richness* (sec. 3). In view of the sorts of problems that Cosmides and Tooby pose for informationally impoverished cognitive mechanisms, it seems highly likely that nonmodular reasoning systems will almost invariably possess specialized bodies of knowledge about the domains in which they operate. Indeed, on a rationalist construal of such systems, they are likely to possess lots of innate, domain-specific information.
2. *Suboptimality* (sec. 4). There are overwhelming reasons to think that "optimal" reasoning processes of the kind associated with ideal theories of rationality are computationally intractable. In view of this, the reasoning processes subserved by nonmodular central systems will be suboptimal or bounded.

---

17. Another prominent example of a nonmodular reasoning system in AI is the procedural reasoning system (PRS; Georgeff & Lansky, 1987; d'Inverno et al., 1997).

3. *Limited search* (sec. 5). Nonmodular central systems will also not engage in exhaustive search of the information available to them, since, given a reasonable estimate of the size of a human belief system, it would pose serious tractability problems.
4. *Limited sensitivity to the global properties of cognition* (sec. 6). Fodor is right to claim that a computational, reasoning mechanism would be intractable if it were both highly reliable and sensitive to global properties of the belief system. But as I argued in section 6, this does not imply there are no nonmodular, computational mechanisms for reasoning. All that follows is that our reasoning is not all that sensitive to global properties after all; and this is, I maintain, an entirely sensible position for the advocate of nonmodular reasoning mechanisms to adopt.
5. *Autonomy from real-time control of action.*(sec 7). If we are to take seriously the last two decades of research in robotics, it would seem that incorporating nonmodular reasoning mechanisms into a cognitive system while avoiding practical tractability problems requires that the operations of such devices are *decoupled* from fine-grained, real-time behavioral operations. Instead, nonmodular reasoning mechanisms are likely to operate at a more coarse-grained temporal scale in order to make crucial decisions, construct relatively long-term plans, and provide rich representations of the world that can aid in the pursuit of the agents epistemic and practical goals.
6. *The need for reactive behaviors* (sec. 7). Since human beings do succeed in responding in real time to environmental conditions, claim 5 implies that nonmodular reasoning mechanisms need to be located within an architecture that contains other mechanisms that are responsible for the production of fine-grained, real-time responses. This claim is not at all contentious among nativists, since, as mentioned earlier, they almost invariably assume that humans possess a variety of input systems and output systems that play this role. Nonetheless, I would suggest that the past few decades of research in robotics makes it plausible to posit an additional kind of mechanism that aids in the production of real-time behavior: modular "reactive behaviors" that produce rapid behavioral responses to stereotypic environmental conditions.

Where do these comments leave us? What I think they provide is a rough sketch of some characteristics that a cognitive architecture of the kind advocated by psychological rationalists would be likely to possess. Is there any reason to suppose that this rationalist view is *preferable* to a thoroughgoing MM that denies the existence of nonmodular reasoning mechanisms? Clearly, I have provided no argument for such a conclusion in the foregoing discussion. For what its worth, however, I suspect that a non-MM account of cognition is likely to do far better at explaining the peculiar flexibility of human behavior and cognition. But an explanation of why this is so will have to wait for another day.

8

TOM SIMPSON

Toward a Reasonable Nativism

In recent years, nativism has come under repeated attack from advocates of a new developmental program: *neuroconstructivism*.[1] Armed primarily with results from theoretical and empirical work by Annette Karmiloff-Smith and her colleagues, neuroconstructivists aim both to refute nativist models of neonate cognition and human cognitive development and to provide alternative cognitive models in which "by contrast with the nativists, it is the process of development (that is ontogeny itself)" that is to the fore (Karmiloff-Smith, 2000, p. 145). The neuroconstructivists' challenge is wide in scope and detailed in implementation and involves many interesting, unexpected, and highly significant empirical and theoretical results. Neuroconstructivism does not, however, present nativism with an unanswerable challenge, as neuroconstructivists believe (Marcus, 1998, 2001, 2004, chapter 2 here; Samuels, 1998, 2002).

Nonetheless, what the neuroconstructivists' challenge does indicate is that some misunderstanding continues to exist among certain self-titled nonnativists over what it is that practicing nativists actually claim, together with a mistaken belief that current neurodevelopmental data is not or cannot be compatible with the nativist program. This chapter aims to address both of these issues, first by providing further explication of the claims of practicing nativists and then by showing how these claims provide the basis for a reasonable nativism that is fully cognizant of and consistent with empirical data from all the developmental sciences, neuroconstructivism included.

I thank Peter Carruthers, Stephen Laurence, Sarah Clegg, and Kate Arrowsmith for their help with this chapter.
1. See, for example, Elman et al. (1996), Karmiloff-Smith (1997, 1998a, 2000), Laing et al. (2002), Paterson et al. (1999), and Quartz and Sejnowski (1997).

1 Where to Begin?

In developing the basis for a reasonable nativism, it will be useful to begin with an unreasonable version of nativism. In particular, it will be useful to begin with the unreasonable version of nativism that Karmiloff-Smith uses in her neuroconstructivist challenge to nativism. Karmiloff-Smith's version of nativism has the appearance of reasonableness, in part because it does seem to capture and make explicit much that many theorists and laypeople believe nativists to claim. An understanding of why Karmiloff-Smith's version is in fact extremely unreasonable will therefore provide a profitable way in which to clarify what it is that practicing nativists do and *do not* actually claim, and will also make possible the systematic introduction of the central elements that will underwrite the reasonable nativism developed in the rest of this chapter.

Karmiloff-Smith attacks what she refers to as "staunch nativism," a position she introduces largely by contrasting it with "empiricism" on the one hand and "neuroconstructivism" on the other (1998a).[2] According to Karmiloff-Smith, central to staunch nativism are:

- **Highly detailed genetic prespecification:** "For the staunch nativist, a set of genes specifically targets domain-specific modules as the end product of their epigenesis" (1998a, p. 389). Correspondingly, cognitive development "is under tight genetic control... [and] more or less everything must be specified in advance, and there are upper bounds on complexity" (2000, p. 153).
- **Minimal environmental input:** "For both the strict [*sic*] nativist and the empiricist, the notion of the 'environment' is a static one" (1998a, p. 390), and: "Under this nondevelopmental view [i.e., staunch nativism], the environment simply acts as a trigger for identifying and setting... (prespecified) parameters" (p. 389).
- **Presence at birth:** For staunch nativists, "domain specificity is the starting point of ontogenesis, and development relegated to a relatively secondary role" (1998a, p. 390), and this, according to Karmiloff-Smith, is because staunch nativists believe that "the newborn brain... [is] crammed with independently functioning tools, each designed for a specific problem that faced our hunter-gatherer ancestors" (2000, p. 146).

In addition, Karmiloff-Smith claims, staunch nativists believe that cognitive development "involves the independent development of different parts of the system" (2000, p. 153); that many of these parts are "domain-specific mechanisms

---

2. Despite the contrasts in Karmiloff-Smith (1998a), it is not always entirely clear what Karmiloff-Smith intends "staunch nativism" to mean, as she sometimes uses the terms "strict nativism" and simply "nativism" without explicit differentiation. However, it seems from Karmiloff-Smith's overall position that any version of nativism that she contrasts with neuroconstructivism should be taken as "staunch nativism," so I have read her this way throughout.

within innately specified modules" (1998a, p. 390); and that these mechanisms are themselves "dedicated to the exclusive processing of one and only one kind of input" (p. 390).

Karmiloff-Smith's staunch nativism is thus a complex and detailed version of nativism, and may well successfully capture what many theorists and laypeople believe nativism to be. In addition, staunch nativism has the apparent virtues of making explicit the various components of nativists' claims, and of illuminating the ways these components fit together. Why then do I claim that Karmiloff-Smith's version of nativism is in fact extremely unreasonable?

Put simply: because staunch nativism is a version of nativism to which *no practicing nativist does or would subscribe*. Rather, as will become apparent hereafter, practicing nativists make far more moderate claims, and staunch nativism is an unreasonable and undefended extension of such claims (albeit, perhaps, a natural one). Practicing nativists should not, therefore, be taken as believing staunch nativism, especially as a much more reasonable version of nativism can readily be extracted from the claims practicing nativists make.

1.1 How Did We End Up Beginning Here?

I claim, then, that staunch nativism is not a version of nativism that practicing nativists would or do defend. One might wonder, therefore, why staunch nativism appears to capture many theorists' and laypeople's intuitions regarding nativists' claims. And one might also wonder why Karmiloff-Smith believes her interpretation, in particular, to be correct. Well, in large part this is because, as Karmiloff-Smith and other nonnativists often point out, staunch nativism *is*, strictly speaking, consistent with what prominent nativists sometimes actually say. It is therefore quite easy to get the impression that staunch nativism is what prominent nativists actually believe. However, when we examine what these nativists say in more detail, what we find is that the consistency upon which staunch nativism depends in fact relies upon both an unwarrantedly strict interpretation of nativists' claims, and on a reduction of the complexity of these claims. Once such unwarranted interpretations and reductions are made explicit, however, the unreasonableness of staunch nativism becomes readily apparent.

In *Why Babies' Brains Are Not Swiss Army Knives*, Karmiloff-Smith (2000, p. 145) provides a series of quotations from prominent—indeed canonical—nativists that she claims support her "staunch" interpretation:

> "We argue that human reasoning is guided by a collection of innate domain-specific systems of knowledge [Carey & Spelke, 1994]."

> "[S]yntactic knowledge is in large part innately specified [Crain, 1991]."

> "[The human mind is] equipped with a body of genetically determined information specific to Universal Grammar [Smith & Tsimpli, 1995]."

> "The mind is likely to contain blueprints for grammatical rules . . . and a special set of genes that help wire it in place [Pinker, 1994]."

"If language, the quintessential higher cognitive process, is an instinct, maybe the rest of cognition is a bunch of instincts too—complex circuits designed by natural selection, each dedicated to solving a particular family of problems [Pinker, 1994]."

These are clearly and straightforwardly nativist, and Karmiloff-Smith is right to claim such quotations should form the basis of any interpretation of nativism.

However, what is equally clear is that what, say, Steven Pinker claims here is *not* that the "special set of genes" that provide the mind with "blueprints for grammatical rules" do all—or even *most*—of the work in the development of these rules during language acquisition. Rather, Pinker claims only that such genes *"help"* wire these blueprints in place. Pinker does not, therefore, make any claim in this extract that is equivalent to staunch nativism's **highly detailed genetic prespecification**. Similarly, Pinker clearly does not claim that the newborn brain is "crammed with" the dedicated, complex circuits that may constitute the "bunch of instincts" that make up (most of) "the rest of cognition." Rather, Pinker's claims here are *entirely neutral* as to when in ontogeny such circuits may appear. So Pinker does not defend staunch nativism's **presence at birth** here either.

In other words, while Karmiloff-Smith's "staunch" interpretation is perhaps not *in*consistent with what Pinker actually says in the quotations provided, there is absolutely no requirement that we interpret the passages quoted as staunchly as Karmiloff-Smith chooses to do. Moreover, Pinker himself makes exactly these kinds of points elsewhere:

> The genetic assembly instructions for a mental organ do not specify every connection on the brain as if they were a wiring schematic for a Heathkit radio.... [Rather, t]he families of neurons that will form the different mental organs, all descendents of a homogeneous stretch of embryonic tissue, must be designed to be opportunistic as the brain assembles itself. (Pinker, 1997a, p. 35)

> The claim that there are several innate modules is a claim that there are several innate learning machines, each of which learns according to a particular logic. (p. 33)

Despite Karmiloff-Smith's textual evidence, then, we can clearly see that Pinker neither believes nor defends staunch nativism's **highly detailed genetic prespecification**, **presence at birth**, or **minimal environmental input** (the latter following from the prominent role Pinker gives to "learning machines"). Pinker, therefore, is clearly not a staunch nativist.

Similar points apply to the other nativists Karmiloff-Smith cites. Susan Carey and Elizabeth Spelke, for example, have clearly and intentionally used the words "is guided by" rather than "stauncher" terms such as, say, "is determined by" or "consists in" when making their nativist claims. Similarly, Stephen Crain's claim that "syntactic knowledge is in large part innately specified" leaves open the possibility that a good deal of this knowledge is *not* innately specified, or even that *no* such knowledge is *fully* specified. Once again, there is no reason to interpret "innate" and "innately specified" as synonymous with "crammed in the newborn brain" in either case. Furthermore, Crain and Carey and Spelke themselves explicitly say as much elsewhere:

[C]hildren's initial cognitive endowment consists of a set of innate core systems of knowledge.... Most importantly, the mechanisms by which these core systems arise *during early development* are distinct from those that underlie theory construction later in childhood. (Carey & Spelke, 1996, p. 516, emphasis added)

[I]t would be absurd to claim that *grammars* are innate.... However, nativists claim that many aspects of grammars—e.g., universal linguistic principles like the Binding Theory—are *not* acquired in this fashion [i.e., nativists claim that these aspects are not determined by the child's experience of her linguistic community]. (Crain & Pietroski, 2001, p. 146–7)

Thus these other canonical nativists also defend claims that are clearly distinct from staunch nativism's **highly detailed genetic prespecification** and **presence at birth**. Crain and Carey and Spelke therefore clearly do not advocate staunch nativism either.

In sum, then, while staunch nativism is perhaps not inconsistent with the canonical nativists' quotations that Karmiloff-Smith provides (and is, no doubt, equally consistent with claims made elsewhere by these and other nativists), staunch nativism is clearly neither intended nor entailed by these quotations. Moreover, staunch nativism is in fact *directly contradicted* by various other claims made elsewhere by these same nativists. Thus, despite the textual evidence that Karmiloff-Smith provides, we can see that canonical nativists simply do not believe or defend the version of nativism that Karmiloff-Smith attributes to them. Staunch nativism should not, therefore, be taken as representative of current nativist theorizing, and practicing nativists should not be understood as believing or defending it.

2 Where Does This Leave Us?

I have just shown that one way we can dissolve much of the neuroconstructivists' challenge to nativism is by rejecting staunch nativism as an accurate interpretation of nativists' claims. However, it may appear that this success has been achieved by making explicit the claims of *particular nativists* at the expense of retaining *nativism* as a unified position or program. One virtue of the concept of staunch nativism, and no doubt one source of its appeal, is that it offers an understanding of nativism that is both relatively easy to grasp and relatively explicit in its claims and components. Its vice, as already mentioned, for both methodological and practical purposes, is that few (if any) practicing nativists believe or defend it. However, determining "what nativists actually believe" is no easy matter, and even the most cursory glance at the literature generates a range of apparently distinct alternatives.

Clearly what is important for nativists is that some particular (kinds of) cognitive properties are "innate." However, as the quotations in the previous section show, canonical nativists appear to differ quite significantly over which these properties are, and over how claims about the "innateness" of these properties should best be understood. As it happens, the first of these need not be particularly worrying, for in the given extracts Pinker, Crain, Spelke, and others are each focusing on aspects of cognition that lie within their own distinct investigative domains. However, the apparent differences between these theorists' proposals concerning how best to understand their claims about "innateness" may initially seem to pose a much more significant problem. Proposed understandings include, for example, the existence of "genetically determined information" or "special sets of genes" somehow related to particular aspects of cognition; design of these aspects "by natural selection"; the "early development" of such aspects, which may itself involve "distinct mechanisms"; and these aspects not being determined by the organism's experience of particular environmental properties. These claims involve a wide variety of factors that may initially seem quite distinct, and the existence of much common ground between different nativists' claims is not immediately apparent. Given this kind of evidence, one might well start to wonder what exactly one should take "nativists" to believe, and also to worry just how unified a position "nativism" really is.

Fortunately, more detailed analysis of this evidence will do much to dispel these fears, and in the following sections I will show that such apparent conflict actually provides the basis for a robust understanding of the nativist program. I will begin by clearing away some basic confusions that seem still to surround discussion of practicing nativists' claims, and I will then move on to discuss a reasonable nativism in more detail.

3 How to Get Started Properly

3.1 Presence at Birth

There are several features of innate cognitive traits to which nativists often refer but which should be set aside right at the start of my explication of a reasonable nativism. The first such feature is the presence of such traits "in the newborn brain." This feature simply is not an essential part of practicing nativists' claims. Physiological traits can be innate without being present at birth, for example, teeth, eye color, and pubic hair; cognitive traits equally so. However, what is the case is that nativists sometimes employ "presence at birth" as *evidence in favor of* the claim that a particular trait is innate, and this is because many innate traits are indeed contingently so present. However, nativists rightly consider such evidence as *no more than defeasible evidence* of innateness, and thus "presence at birth" is not and should not be taken as essential to a reasonable nativism.

3.2 Evolution

Similarly, that an innate trait be some kind of "evolutionary adaptation" is also not a required part of a reasonable nativism, despite the fact that evolutionary arguments are also often used by nativists to support their nativist claims (see, e.g., Atran, chapter 9 here; Pinker, 1994, 1997a, 2002; Tooby & Cosmides, 1992a; Tooby, Cosmides, & Barrett, chapter 18 here). Physiologically, both the existence of the human chin and the redness of human blood are innate traits, but neither of these is itself an "evolutionary adaptation." This is not to say that an evolutionary explanation of the existence of such traits cannot be given—clearly one can. But such explanations do not involve—let alone require—considering the trait in question to be an "evolutionary adaptation" (see, e.g., Gould & Lewontin, 1979; Pinker, 1997a). Nor are such explanations essential to the claim that the traits in question are innate. Moreover, both Noam Chomsky and Jerry Fodor explicitly *reject* any necessary connection between claims about innateness and arguments from evolution (Chomsky, 1987; Fodor, 1998b, 2000). Thus if claims regarding evolutionary adaptation were to be taken as central to a reasonable nativism, we would find ourselves in the seemingly bizarre position whereby Chomsky and Fodor cease to be even *mainstream* nativists, let alone canonical ones. And this, surely, is not the right result.[3] That innate traits are or must be "evolutionary adaptations" should not, therefore, be taken as essential to the nativist program.

However, nativists do perhaps make use of evolutionary arguments more readily or more frequently than other cognitive scientists do. This is, I think, because nativists' uses of evolutionary arguments are often derived from (or otherwise driven by) the belief that innate traits are in some way "genetically specified"—and this understanding of innateness *is* much more central to many nativists' claims (see sec. 4.4). If this is the case, however, then nativists' claims concerning the evolutionary origins of innate components should in fact be best thought of as "secondary" claims—resulting largely from nativists' desire to integrate claims concerning "innateness as genetic specification" into a wider naturalistic framework—rather than as direct appeals to evolutionary origins. So while the claim that a particular trait is an "evolutionary adaptation" is indeed often employed by nativists as evidence in favor of the claim that a particular trait is innate, this is largely because a trait's being an adaptation of this kind is seen by some nativists as the best explanation for how such a trait could be "genetically specified." As with "presence at birth," however, such evidence is no more than defeasible evidence, and thus a trait's being an "evolutionary adaptation" is not and should not be taken as an essential aspect of what it is for a trait to be innate. That a trait be an "evolutionary adaptation" should not, therefore, be taken as a required part of a reasonable nativism.

3.3 Nativism and Innateness

Finally, it should be emphasized that the task of developing a reasonable nativism *is not the same task* as that of providing constitutive or other definitional conditions for "innateness." All developmental cognitive scientists agree that *some* cognitive and noncognitive properties are innate, and must therefore employ at least—and perhaps no more than—roughly the same understanding of this term for meaningful disagreement to occur. What distinguishes nativists, empiricists, neuroconstructivists, and so on is the volume, detail, and complexity of the properties that each claims to be innate. As Karmiloff-Smith herself puts it:

> At some level, of course, we all concur in the existence of some degree of innate specification. The difference in positions concerns how rich and how domain-specific the innately specified component is.... The neuroconstructivist approach to normal

---

3. See Samuels (2002) for a more detailed discussion of why a reasonable nativism should respect and preserve the standard categorization of central figures in debates over nativism.

and atypical development fully recognizes innate biological constraints but, unlike the staunch nativist, considers them to be initially less detailed and less domain-specific as far as higher level cognitive functions are concerned. (1998a, p. 389)

Likewise, Quine famously pointed out that even the behaviorist "is knowingly and cheerfully up to his neck in innate mechanisms" (1969, pp. 95–6).

In developing a reasonable nativism, one is not, therefore, required to provide a constitutive definition of "innateness" or to explain "what it means to be innate." Rather, what a reasonable nativism requires is that nativists' claims that certain properties are "innate" be reasonable, and this in turn depends upon the properties involved, and the kinds of explanation in which these properties are employed. Of course, nativists may turn out to be either correct or not about the properties they claim to be innate, and may provide either good or bad explanations in which such properties figure. However, such judgments must always be made by comparing nativists' claims to those made by neuroconstructivists, empiricists, or even other nativists, and by accepting or rejecting such claims accordingly. Provided the notion of innateness in all of these claims is roughly the same—or plays roughly the same role—such evaluation can legitimately be made, and can be made without having specified for certain "what it is to be innate."

This initial ground-clearing work done, I now turn to the features that should form part of a reasonable nativism.

4 Developing a Reasonable Nativism

It is clear from the discussion so far, and from debates about nativism more generally, that what most nativists consider central to nativism is the claim that certain cognitive properties are "not determined by" or "develop robustly in the face of" or are in some other way "impervious to" the specific properties of the environment in which an organism develops. And, most usually, this independence from environmental factors is explained by claiming that either the developmental trajectory of these properties or their mature end-state is in some sense "genetically specified." Of course, the particular reasons *why* individual nativists make these claims differ enormously, as do the details of the properties with which such claims are concerned (as the other chapters in this volume attest). Nonetheless, some notion of "independence from environmental particulars, ultimately explained by genetic structure" lies at the heart of most nativists' claims. Consequently, the majority of the work on developing a profitable or robust construal of nativism has occurred in this area, as has the majority of criticism (e.g., Ariew, 1996, 1999; Bateson, 1991; Cowie, 1999; Godfrey-Smith, 2002; Griffiths, 2002; Maclaurin, 2002; Oyama, 1985; Samuels, 2002; Stich, 1975a; Wimsatt, 1986, 1999).

I will not present a detailed examination of these arguments here—there is simply insufficient space to do justice to the complexity and variety of the claims made by those involved. Rather, I will examine the methodology that underwrites many of these claims, and show how a proper understanding of this aspect of nativists' practice provides a sound basis for a reasonable nativism.

4.1 Specific Cognitive Properties and Particular Environments

Nativists' claims have the following abstract form: for organisms with genome G, under environmental conditions E, cognitive property P is innate. More explicitly, any properly formed nativist claim about the innateness of any particular cognitive property P is always made *in the context of and with reference to* an explanatory framework the parameters of which are provided by the particular values for G and E appropriate to the organism and environment concerned. Crain and Pietroski (2001), for example, claim that for organisms with a "normal human" genome, under the environmental conditions that consist of "the linguistic input children receive," the specific linguistic property "binding theory" is innate. Correspondingly, properly formed nativist claims about the innateness of any other similarly specific Ps with respect to organisms that have differing values for G (e.g., normal humans, chimpanzees, or those with Williams syndrome) or with respect to environmental conditions providing differing values for E (e.g., normal linguistic input, brain lesions, or toxic atmospheres) are also made from within the explanatory framework provided by the particular values for G and E that are appropriate to the investigation concerned.

Understanding nativist claims in the manner just described allows us to see that individual theorists who make what may appear to be substantively different claims nonetheless remain steadfastly nativist when (1) the differences between such claims correlate with different values for P, G, and E, and (2) what unites these theorists *as nativists* is that they claim that (more of) P is innate, in some specified sense, in contrast to other less nativist or nonnativist theorists *working with the same set of values for G and E*. Understanding nativist practice in this way, therefore, does much to clarify why it is that the theorists quoted in section 1 should be taken as canonically nativist despite the seemingly disparate nature of their particular claims: each theorist is using different values for P and, possibly, E.

The extent to which these theorists' claims should be accepted as *correct* is then determined by how good the overall explanation is in which these claims figure (recall sec. 3.3). Returning to the example, Crain and Pietroski argue that "binding theory" is innate by showing that there is *no plausible* explanation of the development of this cognitive property in which such development is determined by the child's experience. This example, therefore, represents what is in effect the nativists' limiting case with regard to explanatory efficacy. However, when we consider other possible values for P, G and E, alternative plausible explanations may well be possible. The issue then is to compare the relative plausibility of these explanations in the light of current evidence, and to accept whichever explanation is most plausible. And, as everyone agrees, the accepted explanation will necessarily require *some* innate components. It is the *quantity, complexity, and kind* of these components that then determines how strongly (non)nativist the explanation is.

Importantly, therefore, individual nativists' claims necessarily have limited explanatory scope. That is, such claims apply in the first instance *only* to the specific cases about which such claims are initially made, and can be applied to other cases *only* when such cases are relevantly similar to the cases that led to the original claims. In the example, were we to change the values of any of the variables (i.e., P, G, or E) about which Crain and Pietroski make their claims, we would have no grounds to demand that Crain and Pietroski defend nativism in these new circumstances unless all of the new values can be shown to be sufficiently similar to the original values to mandate such a defense. Otherwise, it is perfectly legitimate for Crain and Pietroski to refuse to make any claims, nativist or otherwise, about the resultant situation. Moreover, the "value-specific" nature of Crain and Pietroski's nativism can be seen in their explicit *rejection* of nativism when the specific cognitive properties (the Ps) concerned are the parameters that "determine whether direct objects come before or after verbs in transitive constructions" (2001, p. 146), even though these properties are no less structural or linguistically important than binding theory.

One further consequence of the value-specific nature of nativists' claims is that disagreements between nativists and their opponents, and, indeed, between nativists themselves, may in fact be disagreements not over which properties are innate but over *which genomes such properties are innate for,* or *which environmental conditions these innate properties develop in.* Moreover, when disagreement does concern the innateness of specific cognitive properties, the correct conclusion to draw from such disagreement may not be that the innateness claims of one or other party are incorrect but rather that the organisms or the environmental conditions involved are not as similar as they were initially thought to be. Making the values of the relevant variables clear is, therefore, an essential part of any properly formed nativist claim, and acceptance and respect of these values must similarly be part of any criticism of such claims. Unfortunately, nativists have been as guilty as anyone else of failing to provide this clarity—particularly when engaging in more generalized speculation in the light of results from more specific research—so nativists, as much as their opponents, should become (or remain) as explicit as possible about the scope and limits of the claims they make. However, when such explicitness is present, as it is with Crain and Pietroski, we are able to see precisely how nativist claims should be understood.

Crain and Pietroski thus provide a clear example of the way nativist claims should be made and of the underlying nature of such claims. They also provide an example of the standard nativist belief that one good *evidential* reason to claim that certain specific cognitive properties are innate is that this explanation is superior to any *existing* alternative explanation in which such properties are determined by the particular experiences of the organism concerned. Crain and Pietroski, therefore, provide an excellent exemplar of one kind of nativist practice as it is typically found in cognitive science. With this in mind, I now turn to nativist practice of a subtly different but similarly typical kind.

4.2 Global Capacities and Mature End-States

Nativists also often claim that cognitive properties much less specific than binding theory are innate—for example, cognitive capacities such as "core knowledge," "theory of mind" or "language." When doing so, the evidence nativists use to support such claims falls into two types: (1) evidence concerning the innateness of many (or all) of the important or domain-specific components of these "general capacities" where this evidence is similar to the evidence that indicates that binding theory should be thought of as innate (see sec. 4.1), or (2) evidence that indicates that these general capacities reliably, robustly, or rigidly develop in organisms with a given genome despite wide variation in environmental conditions. These types of evidence are not mutually exclusive, of course. If the majority of the components of, say, our language ability are as independent of particular experience as binding theory is, then we would expect our language ability to develop across a wide variety of environments. Similarly, the development of the language ability across a wide variety of environments might reasonably lead us to expect that either the majority or the most important of the components of this ability develop relatively independently of individual experience. However, while many nativists do indeed combine both kinds of evidence in precisely this way, nativism about these general capacities *need in fact require no more than* that these capacities develop in a robust manner. George Botterill and Peter Carruthers, for example, argue that

> [w]hatever the pathways of development, they are compatible with our [nativism] if in the normal case they lead to a common outcome ... from varied input. For it is this common outcome which will be innately prespecified. (1999, p. 55)

This understanding of nativism is also what motivates accounts of nativism that focus on the "invariance" or "canalization" of phenotypic traits in organisms with a particular genome (e.g., Ariew, 1999; Sober, 1999).

Those who defend nativism about these general capacities therefore focus primarily on what is taken to be the *mature end-state* of these capacities rather than on these capacities' development or constituent parts. However, as with specific properties such as binding theory, nativism in the case of general capacities is defended by arguing that considering these capacities to be innate provides a superior explanation to any existing explanation offered by nonnativists for the robust appearance of these capacities in the face of substantial environmental variation. However, it is important to note that nativism about general capacities does *not* claim that such capacities develop without any significant environmental input. In principle, such nativism is *entirely neutral* about the developmental process, as the quotation from Botterill and Carruthers demonstrates. Moreover, in practice, nativism about general capacities claims that, for example, language has a robust end-state that requires a distinctive developmental trajectory involving *both* specialized, domain-specific innate components such as binding theory *and* significant environmental input such as that which provides the parameters for the direct-object/transitive-verb relation as appropriate for the local environment.[4] It is, therefore, simply mistaken to claim that nativism about language, core knowledge, or any other general capacity *must* consider the environment as little more than a trigger for environmentally independent developmental processes. In fact, nativism

---

4. Recall the quotation from Crain and Pietroski in section 1, in which they say that despite their nativism about binding theory, "it would be absurd to claim that *grammars* are innate" (2001, p. 146).

about such capacities is entirely consistent with significant environmental involvement. It claims only that current evidence indicates that there is *significantly less* environmental involvement than nonnativists maintain. Nativism about general capacities, therefore, employs the same "relative to alternative explanations" methodology that is employed for nativism about specific cognitive properties, even though the initial motivation for such nativism differs significantly.

4.3 Interim Summary

We now have a clearer sense of the claims that nativists make, and of how to understand the way nativists use such claims to motivate and defend nativism. I have shown that nativism about different kinds of cognitive properties—the specific and the general—often reflects a difference in initial investigative focus: developmental processes and mature end-states, respectively. I have also shown how nativism appropriate to each of these kinds of cognitive properties can and often does interrelate, *and* that it need not do so. In addition, I have shown that nativism in both cases is driven by an evidence-based methodology in which nativists claim that the *best explanation* for the existence of the cognitive properties under investigation is, for specific properties, that such properties develop independently of the appropriate environment for the organism concerned and, for general capacities, that such capacities develop robustly in the face of substantial environmental variation. Moreover, I have also shown that explanations of the latter kind *allow and often involve* significant environmental input into the resultant cognitive capacity.

The preceding sections, therefore, provide much of the required basis for a reasonable nativism. Moreover, I have shown that all properly formed nativist claims are made in the context of and with reference to a framework provided by appropriate values for G and E—a framework that also specifies the limits of the conclusions that can be drawn. And this last observation is an important one, for there is one final role that this framework plays in nativist claims, and understanding this role is crucial to the completion of my basis for a reasonable nativism.

4.4 Claims about Genes

Nativists argue that the best explanation for a cognitive property's environmental independence or developmental robustness is its being innate. This conclusion is then often elaborated by claiming that this property must therefore be in some significant way "genetically specified." Such elaboration, however, is *not* equivalent to the much stronger claims that the property in question is fully genetically determined, or that the property is represented exclusively in the genome.[5]

---

5. Recall the quotation from Pinker in section 1: "The genetic assembly instructions for a mental organ do not specify every connection on the brain as if they were a wiring schematic for a Heathkit radio" (1997a, p. 35).

Nativists are well aware of the difficulties associated with attempting to isolate causal or representational contributions to phenotypic traits (difficulties well documented by nonnativists such as Oyama 1985, 2000, Griffiths & Gray, 1994, and Sterelny & Griffiths, 1999). Consequently, the elaboration that nativists offer is in fact both largely methodological and explicitly promissory. That is, this elaboration is intended *only* to indicate that as the origin of the property in question cannot be explained by reference to properties of the organism's particular developmental environment, *then from within the explanatory framework being used*, this origin must, it seems, be explained by reference to that organism's genome. In other words, given the tripartite form of nativists' claims, once the cognitive property (P) in question is agreed and the appropriate environmental conditions (E) are ruled out, the genome (G) is the only source of explanation left available. Nativists' references to "genetic specification," therefore, result largely from the nature of the framework in which nativist claims are made rather than from any necessary commitment to specific, isolable causal or representational genetic origins.

One example of exactly this kind of elaboration can be found in Botterill and Carruthers's claim that certain general cognitive capacities are innately prespecified, "at least in so far as genetic inheritance predisposes toward the development of such a cognitive system" (1999, p. 55). A similar elaboration is present in Pinker's claim (in sec. 1) that the mind is "likely to contain...a special set of genes" that help wire the blueprint for grammatical rules in place. Pinker's claim here is basically that as the child's developmental environment has been shown to be insufficient to wire such grammatical rules in place, the only other available source to complete this "wiring"—and thus the most likely—is the genome. But in both these cases these authors claim only that innate cognitive properties should (somehow) be attributed to the genome because such attribution seems to provide a better explanation of the occurrence of that property than is provided by attributing it to particulars of the environment of the developing organism.

Thus, despite nativists' explanatory references to genetic properties, nativism is *not* primarily a thesis about isolable genetic origins of cognitive properties. Rather, nativists' claims about "genetic specification" are the result of the nature of the explanatory framework that governs properly formed nativist claims. References to "genetic specification" indicate only that in the context of and with reference to the particulars of the framework being employed, the appropriate "genome" is a more likely locus than the appropriate "environmental conditions" for an explanation of the property concerned. Furthermore, there are good reasons to believe that even *direct reference to the genome* is a much stronger claim than many nativists have any real desire to make.

4.5 Samuels's Primitivism

Richard Samuels (2002) has argued that when nativists claim that certain properties are innate, what they are really claiming is that such properties should be considered as "primitive" from the point of view of the framework within which such claims are made. For Samuels, a property is primitive just in case there can be no correct scientific explanation of the acquisition (under normal circumstances) of that property from within the particular scientific domain to which that property belongs. So, in the context of the kinds of cognitive properties with which nativists are concerned, Samuels claims that

> to say that a cognitive structure S is primitive is to claim that, *from the perspective of scientific psychology*, S needs to be treated as one whose acquisition has no *explanation*. For although primitive cognitive structures are presumably acquired in the (baseline) sense that they are not possessed by an organism at one time but are possessed at some later time, psychology fails to provide an explanation of *how* they come to be possessed. Of course, that is not to say that there is no theory *whatsoever* that explains the acquisition of S. It may be the case and, indeed, presumably is the case that some other branch of science—e.g., neurobiology or molecular chemistry—can provide an explanation. It's just that psychology cannot furnish us with such a theory. (2002, pp. 246–7)

For Samuels, then, to claim that a structure is psychologically primitive is to claim that any explanation of the acquisition or development of that structure (under normal developmental circumstances) must lie outside the domain of scientific psychology. Furthermore, Samuels maintains, when we apply his "primitivism" to the debates surrounding nativism, what becomes clear is that when nativists claim that in the light of the available evidence the existence of certain *specific* cognitive properties is best explained by their being innate, what nativists are really claiming is that the best explanation of the acquisition or development of such properties is a *nonpsychological* explanation of this acquisition or development. In other words, according to Samuels, what nativism claims is that any explanation of such acquisition or development lies outside the domain of psychology, and thus presumably lies in the domain of neurobiology, or molecular chemistry, or some other science. Under primitivism, then, it seems that nativists' references to "genetic specification" as the source of specific cognitive properties should be taken as reference not to explanations involving specific properties of an organism's genome per se but rather to explanations in which such properties are not determined by the (normal) *psychologically relevant environment* of the organism in question.[6] And this, it seems, is precisely what is—and should be—claimed, given the value-specific nature of the framework within which properly formed nativist claims are made.

An accurate understanding of this framework, therefore, really does play a crucial role in providing the basis for a reasonable understanding of nativists' claims, and Samuels's primitivism provides one analysis of exactly why this is so. However, even if one were not inclined to accept Samuels's analysis, it should nonetheless be clear that nativism simply *does not require* specific cognitive

---

6. Consider, for example, Crain, Gualmini, and Pietroski's claim (chapter 11 here) that "children know specific contingent facts that apply to a wide range of constructions across different linguistic communities. Insofar as this aspect of linguistic competence is not plausibly a product of children's experience, it is presumably a product of their biological endowment." Crain et al. refer here neither to "genetic specification" nor to "the genome." Rather, the reference is to *biology*, and their thought is that it is *from biology* that the explanation of children's innate linguistic properties will come.

properties to have a directly or exclusively causal or representational genetic origin. Rather, nativism claims only that *from within the explanatory framework with respect to which any given properly formed nativist claim is being made*, these cognitive properties are not acquired from environmental particulars, and thus their occurrence is best explained by supposing them to be innate. And, at the risk of tedious repetition, such claims are always made relative to the claims of other theorists operating with respect to the same framework.

My explication of the basis for a reasonable nativism is thus complete. Finally, therefore, I will now turn to the relations between this reasonable nativism and current neurodevelopmental data.

5 Neurodevelopmental Data and the Neuroconstructivists' Challenge

From the explication of nativism just given, it should now be clear that much neurodevelopmental work occurs as part of an explanatory project that is in an important sense *distinct from* the project engaged in by most practicing nativists. That is, to the extent that neurodevelopmental work aims to provide a comprehensive causal "route-map" of the processes and elements involved in development from conception to mature cognitive end-state, much of this map will speak to nativists' concerns only as part of the much larger overall project of understanding developing organisms in general. Nativism, I showed, is primarily concerned only with the *psychological* properties that contribute to or constitute mature cognitive end-states. Investigation and explanation of the *non*psychological development of these properties—and in particular of the properties that are innate or "primitive"—thus falls outside nativists' primary scientific domain. Such explanations will, therefore, frequently speak neither for nor against nativists' concerns, even though nativists readily accept the importance of such explanations in the context of the overall project in which nativism plays a part. Neurodevelopmental data and nativism can in principle therefore be entirely *complementary*, with the former providing explanation of how the innate properties suggested by the latter develop. Moreover, neuro*constructivism* and nativism can also be entirely complementary, as much of the data championed by neuroconstructivists either does not speak directly to nativists' claims or can be accommodated within the nativist program (see, e.g., Marcus, 1998, 2004, chapter 2 here; Samuels, 1998). Understanding the scope and limits of the framework in which nativists' claims are made thus plays a crucial role in understanding how neurodevelopmental data may (and may not) impact upon a reasonable nativism.

Furthermore, neurodevelopmental data can be detached from nativism not only in virtue of the difference in appropriate scientific domains but also in virtue of the relation between *neural* properties on the one hand and *cognitive* properties on the other. Nativism primarily concerns the latter, neurodevelopment the former, and neuroconstructivism *both*. Thus while all those involved in developmental research accept that cognitive properties are *somehow* implemented in or by neural properties, care must be taken by those within each program to differentiate these properties appropriately when making explanatory claims. It is simply not the case that what is true of neural properties *must* also be true of cognitive properties, even if the latter are fully implemented by the former. Nonnativist developmental explanations of *neural* structures are thus entirely compatible with nativist explanations of *cognitive* structures, all else being equal. Failure to respect this relation will, therefore, result in misplaced criticism of both nativism and neuroconstructivism alike, and is also likely to make both positions seem more at odds than they actually are.[7] On the other hand, proper consideration will do much to support both positions, and to move forward our understanding of both cognitive *and* neural development (e.g., Gerrans, 2003).

Of course, the claims made by those working in these different disciplines *can* conflict. Changes in cognitive properties must somehow be correlated with changes in neural properties, and investigations at the neurodevelopmental (or other nonpsychological) level may turn out to support either nativist or nonnativist models of cognitive development. But for the moment it is by no means clear that data from either neurodevelopmental studies or, more specifically, from neuroconstructivist research, does or must support nonnativist models over nativist ones (see, e.g., Tager-Flusberg, 2003, chapter 16 here; Tager-Flusberg & Sullivan, 2000; Tager-Flusberg et al., 2003). A reasonable nativism of the sort developed here therefore has little to fear from current neurodevelopmental research.

6 Conclusion

In the first section of this chapter I showed that the "staunch" understanding of nativism that many neuroconstructivists employ is not one to which practicing nativists subscribe. In the following sections, I showed that careful consideration of the actual claims of practicing nativists provides an understanding of nativism that is innocent of the extremes of which nativists are often accused, and that practicing nativists' claims can in fact provide a sound basis for a reasonable nativism. Essential parts of this basis are that a reasonable nativism does not require innate cognitive properties either to be present at birth or to be "evolutionary adaptations," nor does it hinge on providing a constitutive definition of the term "innate." Rather, nativism requires adopting the best *available* explanation for the occurrence of certain cognitive properties in the light of both current data and the appropriate explanatory framework, and nativist explanations are those in which *more is innate*—in some mutually agreed sense—than is innate in the explanations

---

[7]. Karmiloff-Smith, for example, writes that "[o]ne could claim that the face-processing module was only 'turned on' at twelve months, i.e., that it is under maturational control. But surely a more parsimonious and more likely explanation is that by twelve months the infant has had sufficient experience of faces to cause the microcircuits in the neocortex to become progressively specialised and localised" (2000, p. 152). Karmiloff-Smith presents these two sentences as though they contain incompatible explanations. But in fact the (nativist) "turning on" of a cognitive property as a result of the (nonnativist) progressive specialization of neural properties is entirely unproblematic, given the different scientific domains and (largely unknown) implementation relations involved.

offered by other less nativist or nonnativist theorists. In consequence, a reasonable nativism about general cognitive capacities (e.g., language) involves and requires significant environmental input, and a reasonable nativism about more specific cognitive properties (e.g., binding theory) centers around the implausibility of explanations of such properties in terms of environmental particulars. Moreover, a reasonable nativism in the latter case is not *primarily* a thesis about the ultimate genetic origin of the cognitive properties concerned. Indeed, nativism in the latter case can quite plausibly be understood as not making claims about ultimate causal origins at all, but rather as making claims about what is and is not part of the explananda of scientific psychology. Furthermore, a reasonable nativism of this kind makes it clear why apparently disparate or competing nativist claims are in fact both compatible and nativist, and also how such claims can profitably be employed by nativist theorists.[8] I have also shown that the reasonable nativism developed here can be fully cognizant of and consistent with current neurodevelopmental data—neuroconstructivism included.

Finally, crucial to all of these results was understanding the "value-specific" methodological framework in which properly formed nativists' claims are made, and the scope and limits that this framework places on such claims. I showed that both nativists and their opponents must be as explicit as possible about the details of the framework appropriate for their claims, for only then can such claims can be properly understood and significant progress be made. Provided that such criteria are met, however, a reasonable nativism of the kind developed in this chapter can and will continue to be a profitable research program for the understanding of human cognition and its development.

---

8. Indeed, recent work by Peter Godfrey-Smith (2002) has given some indication of how such a combination can do useful work in understanding the evolution of our representational and interpretive abilities.

PART II

LANGUAGE AND CONCEPTS

9

SCOTT ATRAN

Strong versus Weak Adaptationism in Cognition and Language

In a sense, everyone who isn't a creationist and who thinks that Darwin's theory of natural selection isn't moonshine is an adaptationist when it comes to explaining the origins of human cognition. Nevertheless, there are serious differences in research strategy between "strong adaptationism" and "weak adaptationism." Strong adaptationists hold that researchers should first attempt to explain any distinctive (non-cultural) complex organic design in terms of task-specific adaptations to ancestral environments (Barkow et al., 1992; Daly & Wilson, 1995; Plotkin, 1997; Sober & Wilson, 1998). Weak adaptationists hold that strong adaptationist arguments from design often involve Panglossian "just-so" stories that are consistent with natural selection but lack evidentiary standards that could rule out indefinitely many alternative and even contrary explanations (Gould & Lewontin, 1979; Fodor, 2001b). Weak adaptationism is driven by traditional scientific assumptions of parsimony, attempting to deduce and cover the widest range of facts from the minimal set of axioms and hypotheses (Chomsky, 2001; Hauser et al., 2002). Each camp routinely claims that the other camp doesn't really understand Darwin or evolution; both routinely pay homage to George Williams's (1966) modest use of adaptationism.

For many evolutionary psychologists who take a strong adaptationist position, *any functional cognitive design that is too complex to result from pure chance must be either an adaptation or a by-product of an adaptation* (Andrews et al., 2003; Buss et al., 1998). Thus,

> given any sensible analysis of the probabilities involved, a system with so many complexly interdependent subcomponents that together interact to produce complex functional output cannot be explained as anything other than an adaptation, constructed by the process of natural selection. (Tooby & Cosmides, 1990, p. 761)

Moreover,

> each Darwinian adaptation contains in its functional design the data of the cause—the selective force—that created it. These data are both necessary and

sufficient to demonstrate scientifically the historical environmental problem that was causal in creating the adaptation. (Thornhill, 1997, p. 5)

This is supposed to be clear for human syntax, particularly in regard to the apparently universal and unique structure of linearized sounds that are used to convey and combine meanings (Pinker, 1997a).

Weak adaptationists consider that *most higher order human cognitions are by-products of earlier evolutionary by-products that were not adapted to fulfill a specific function relative to some particular ancestral environment.* These by-products originated as functionless spandrels that have been subsequently modified under cultural selection rather than natural selection. Biologically functionless, or nearly functionless, spandrels supposedly include: religion, writing, art, science, commerce, war, and play. These evolutionary by-products are cultural "mountains" to the biologically "adaptive molehill" (Gould, 1991, pp. 58–9). On this account, evolutionary psychology would have little to reveal about the emergence and structure of such culturally elaborated spandrels. Because "the number and complexity of these spandrels should increase with the intricacy of the organism under consideration," the complexity, variety and importance of useable and significant spandrels will have little, if anything, to do with evolved functional design (Gould, 1997c, pp. 10754–5; see Fodor, 1998b). As a matter of methodological principle, weak adaptationism is equally open to the possibility of explanations that do not directly rely on natural selection. Resort to task- and environment-specific adaptationist accounts of the origins of human cognitive systems, including language, should be used only when comparative (fossil or ethological) evidence strongly warrants it—which is rarely the case (Chomsky, 2000; Finlay et al., 2001; Fodor, 2001b; Gould & Vrba, 1982; Hauser et al., 2002).

It is difficult to decide whether and when strong versus weak adaptationists differ in theory and ontological assumption, or differ "only" in methodological principle and practice. Although strong adaptationists sometimes argue as if adaptedness to a *particular environment* or "niche" is key to understanding complex design, their primary concern is how complex design evolved to fulfill a *specific function*. The distinction is important. Consider the bullet shapes of fish. One plausible evolutionary account is this. Given initial random variations in fish shape, laws of fluid flow would cause those who were initially more bullet-like to swim faster and more efficiently. As a result, those individuals would likely have more descendents, and in time bullet shapes would become fixed in the population. If so, we may conclude that bullet shapes fulfill the function of enabling efficient motion in water. Notice that such explanation does not appeal to anything like a "niche" (unless water counts as a niche). Nevertheless, strong adaptationists seldom consider explanations of complexity in terms of general adaptive pressures (e.g., hydrodynamical structures in the earth's gravitational field), which have more to do with all-purpose laws of physics and broad-ranging physical conditions on the planet than with specific adaptive problems that arise from trying to keep up with changing biotic environments. In contrast, weak adaptationists often look first to these more general sorts of physical pressures and conditions in order to understand organic (including cognitive) structures (Chomsky, 2001; Leiber, 2002; Turing, 1952).

It is also often unclear whether strong adaptationism is rooted in an ontological assumption that functional specialization underlies complexity—and that complexity is sufficient for inferring function—or whether evidence of complexity is primarily a "motivation" for research into function. Weak adaptationists can point to many examples of complexity—from the fractal structure of a sea-coast to crystals, snowflakes, and pentamerous forms among a host of biologically unrelated organisms—for which no function is readily (or even remotely) inferable. Weak adaptationists do not see evidence of complexity and constancy as a demonstration—or even as a sufficient reason to suspect and look for—some historical configuration of means being functionally appropriate to an end.

In what follows, I concentrate on the issue of methodological usefulness of a strong versus weak adaptationist position in attempting to gain significant insight and to make scientifically important advances and discoveries in human cognition. I argue that in cases of certain domain-specific cognitive competencies (e.g., folk biology) strong adaptationism has proven useful but not necessary to recent progress in the field. In other cases (e.g., language), a weak adaptationist strategy has been arguably most productive in advancing scientific understanding, without precluding that the structures uncovered by other means are actually adaptations.

1 Strong Adaptationism: The Case for Folk Biology

To get along in the world, people need to be able to understand and predict the general properties and behaviors of physical objects and substances (physics), the more specific properties of plants and animals (biology), and the particular properties of their fellow human beings (psychology). Recent developmental, cognitive and crosscultural experiments strongly indicate that all (non-brain-damaged) humans have distinct core faculties of mind with privileged access to these distinct but overlapping domains of nature: folk mechanics (object boundaries and movements), folk biology (biological species configurations and relationships), folk psychology (interactive agents and goal-directed behavior) (for reviews see Geary & Huffman, 2002; Hirschfeld & Gelman, 1994; Sperber et al., 1995a; Pinker, 1997a). These plausibly innate (but maturing), domain-specific faculties are candidates for naturally selected adaptations to relevant and recurrent aspects of ancestral environments. Under analytic idealization they are "universal" and "autonomous" from other cognitive faculties the way the visual system is universal and autonomous from other cognitive and biological systems (with significant individual genetic variation, and viability only in functional interaction with other faculties; Medin & Atran, 2004).

Take the case of folk biology. Humans and their ancestors undoubtedly depended for their survival on intimate interaction with plants and animals, which probably required anticipatory knowledge of at least some plant and animal species (it doesn't really matter which individual apple you can eat, or whether it's Leo or Larry the tiger who can eat you). This makes it likely (but not necessary) that adaptations for special dealings with plants and animals evolved. In addition, there is growing and converging evidence for innateness and domain specificity in human folk biological understanding. Although domain specificity is a weaker claim than adaptation (and innateness is a weaker claim than domain specificity), evidence for domain specificity helps to focus claims and research on adaptations.

Evidence for domain specificity in folk biology comes from a variety of converging sources (Atran, 2001a). These include: ethology (comparative studies of species recognition), crosscultural studies (universality of special taxonomic design), developmental psychology (precocity and regularity in acquisition of essentialized species concepts and ranked taxonomic groupings), cognitive psychology (independence from perceptual experience of biological essentialism and taxonomic organization), pathology (selective cerebral impairment of folk biological taxonomies and distinct taxonomic levels), social and educational studies (hyperactive use of biological essentialism and taxonomization, and their resistance to inhibition through formal or informal instruction or changing social conditions), and cognitive anthropology (rapid cultural transmission, easy mnemonic retention, and enduring historical survival of any given folk biological taxonomy under varied and changing conditions of experience). No single condition may be necessary for domain specificity; however, joint satisfaction of these conditions constitutes strong evidence for it (although they provide no causal explanation of it).

Phylogenetic comparisons of humans with other primates show some evidence for homology, and thus provide a good base from which to speculate about adaptation. For example, some nonhuman species can clearly distinguish several different animal or plant species (Cerella, 1979; Herrnstein, 1984; Lorenz, 1966b). Vervet monkeys even have distinct alarm calls for different predator species or groups of species: snake, leopard and cheetah, hawk eagle, and so forth (Hauser, 2000). Chimpanzees may even have rudimentary hierarchical groupings of biological groups within groups (Brown & Boysen, 2000).

Only humans, however, appear to have a concept of (folk) species as such, as well as taxonomic rankings of relations between species. The human taxonomic system for organizing species appears to be found in all cultures (Atran, 1990; Berlin, 1992; Berlin et al., 1973). It entails the conceptual realization that, say, apple trees and turkeys belong to the same fundamental level of (folk) biological reality, and that this level of reality differs from the subordinate level that includes Winesap apple trees and wild turkeys as well as from the superordinate level that includes trees and birds. This taxonomic framework also supports indefinitely many systematic and graded inferences with respect to the distribution of known or unknown properties among species (Atran, 1998).

In every human society, people seem to think about plants and animals in the same special ways. These special ways of thinking, which can be described as "folk biology," are basically different from the ways humans ordinarily think about other things in the world, such as stones, tools, or even people:

> From the most remote period in the history of the world organic beings have been found to resemble each other in descending degrees, so that they can be classed into groups under groups. This classification is not arbitrary like the grouping of stars in constellations. (Darwin, 1859, p. 431)

The structure of these hierarchically organized groups, such as *white oak/oak/tree* or *mountain robin/robin/bird*, is referred to as "folk biological taxonomy."

These nonoverlapping taxonomic structures can often be interpreted in terms of speciation (related species descended from a common ancestor by splitting off from a lineage).[1]

At each level the biological groups, or taxa, are mutually exclusive and partition the locally perceived biota in a virtually exhaustive manner. Lay taxonomy is composed of a small number of absolutely distinct hierarchical levels, or *ranks* (Berlin, 1992): the levels of *folk kingdom* (e.g., animal, plant), *life form* (e.g., bug, fish, bird, mammal, tree, herb/grass, bush), *generic species* (gnat, shark, robin, dog, oak, clover, holly), *folk specific* (poodle, white oak), and *folk varietal* (toy poodle; spotted white oak). Ranking is a cognitive mapping that projects living kind categories onto a structure of absolute levels, that is, fundamentally *different levels of reality*. Taxa of the same rank tend to display similar linguistic, biological, and psychological characteristics.

Ranks, not taxa, are universal. Biological ranks are second-order classes of groups (e.g., species, family, kingdom) whose elements are first-order groups (e.g., lion, feline, animal). Ranks are intended to represent fundamentally different levels of phenomenal (readily perceived) reality, not convenience (Berlin, 1992). In principle, this ranking system allows incorporation of indefinitely many folk species into an inductive compendium that "automatically" connects properties of the new species to the properties of all other species. This taxonomic framework supports indefinitely many systematic and graded inferences about the distribution of known or unknown properties among species (Atran, 1998).

Folk biological taxonomies are structurally anchored to the level of the "generic species" (Atran, 1990; Berlin et al., 1973), the common man's (folk) species (Wallace, 1889, p. 1). Generic species often correspond to scientific species (e.g., dog, apple tree); however, for a majority of perceptually salient organisms, such as vertebrates and flowering plants, a scientific genus frequently has only one locally occurring species (e.g., bear, oak). There is growing experimental and crosscultural evidence of a commonsense assumption that each generic species is presumed to have underlying causal nature, or essence, that is uniquely responsible for the typical appearance, behavior, and ecological preferences of the kind (Atran et al., 2001; Gelman & Wellman, 1991; Hickling & Gelman, 1995; Sousa et al., 2002).

People in all cultures, it appears, consider this essence responsible for the organism's identity as a complex entity governed by dynamic internal processes that are lawful even when hidden. This essence maintains the organism's integrity even as it causes the organism to grow, change form, and reproduce. For example, a tadpole and frog are conceptualized as the same animal although they look and behave very differently and live in different places. Western philosophers, such as Aristotle and Locke, attempted to translate this commonsense notion of essence into some sort of metaphysical reality, but

---

1. Within a single culture, there may be different sorts of "special-purpose" folk-biological classifications organized by particular interests for particular uses (e.g., beneficial/noxious, domestic/wild, edible/inedible, etc.). Ever since the pioneering work of Berlin and colleagues (Berlin et al., 1973), ethnobiological evidence has accumulated showing that societies everywhere also employ "general-purpose" taxonomy that supports the widest possible range of inductions about living kinds that are relevant to everyday life (Atran, 1998).

evolutionary thinkers reject the notion of essence as such (Hull, 1965; Mayr, 1982). Nevertheless, biologists have traditionally interpreted this conservation of identity under change as due to the fact that organisms have genotypes separate from phenotypes.

Although biological science does not abide metaphysical essentialism, there is a wide variety of evidence supporting the notion of psychological essentialism (Ahn et al., 2001); that is, even when people do not have specific ideas about essences, they may nonetheless have a commitment to the idea that there is an underlying nature (i.e., they may have an "essence placeholder," Medin & Ortony, 1989). This hidden, causal essence is presumably responsible for the manifest properties of the kind. The special causal presumptions inherent in essentialism cannot apparently be derived from more domain-general notions of causality (e.g., a three-legged tiger is still presumed to be a quadruped by nature, but a three-legged or bean-bag chair is not, although most chairs are quadrupedal; Atran, 1987). The fact that biological science can overturn psychological essentialism in theory construction doesn't imply that psychological essentialism is dismissible from everyday thought, any more than rejection of constant intervals of space and time in physics implies abandoning ordinary use of space and time (Atran, 1990).

Briefly, then, there is a folk biological system (FBS) of the human mind. It discriminates and categorizes parts of the flux of human experience as "biological," and develops complex abilities to infer and interpret this highly structured domain. In a general sense, there is nothing intrinsically different about FBS—in terms of innateness, evolution or universality—than the visual system (VS) or any other evolved cognitive system. The FBS is no more (or less) "autonomous" from the surrounding social environment, or from other mental systems, than VS is detachable from surrounding light and object patterning or from other physical systems (including linguistic and other cognitive systems; Marr, 1982).

The FBS and VS do not exist, and cannot develop, in isolation but only as subsystems of even more intricate structures. Moreover, to function properly, such systems require adequate access and exposure to the appropriate environmental input that triggers or enables them; otherwise they tend to degenerate (Hubel, 1988). Thus, claims about the biological "autonomy" or "modularity" of FBS or VS refer only to a specifiable level of systemic functioning, within a system hierarchy, under appropriate environmental conditions. Claims for "innateness" refer only to special biological preparedness that canalizes maturing and developing manifestations of FBS under environmental constraints. This does not imply genetic uniformity among individuals. A difficult empirical issue concerns the extent to which other cognitive systems, such as folk psychology and folk mechanics, are themselves geared to interface with folk biology.

The FBS constrains and guides the way biological inferences are generalized from particular instances (experiences, observations, exemplars). The particular persons observed, actual exemplars targeted, and specific inferences made can vary a lot from person to person. Nevertheless, much as rain falling anywhere in a mountain valley converges into the same natural mountain-valley river basin (Waddington, 1959), so each person's knowledge will converge (in the appropriate cultural idiom) toward the same basin of thought and action (Sperber, 1996).

Thus, many different people, observing many different exemplars of dog under varying conditions of exposure to those exemplars, all still generate more or less the same general concept of *dog*. The concept *dog*—or any other basic sort of living-kind concept—represents more than just "correlational features in the world." It is hard to imagine how a categorization system exclusively attuned to perceptually based "correlational structure" (see Berlin, 1992; Rosch et al., 1976) could possibly predict the classification of Pekinese with Saint Bernards and not Persian cats, and huskies with Chihuahuas and not wolves—much less the convergence across cultures of people's understanding that tadpoles belong with frogs, caterpillars with butterflies, and so forth. Rather, correlated surface features, together with deep inferential principles that go beyond given appearances (e.g., essentialism), spontaneously create natural living-kind categories that capture and predict organic relationships at roughly the level of human ecological proclivity (including larger vertebrates and flowering plants; Atran, 1990).

Within the emerging paradigm of cognitive domain specificity, there is much speculation and controversy, as might be expected in any young and dynamic science. For example, there are competing accounts of how human beings acquire basic knowledge of the everyday biological world, including the categorical limits of the biological domain and the causal nature of its fundamental constituents. Susan Carey and her collaborators have articulated one influential view of conceptual development in folk biology (Carey, 1985; Carey & Spelke, 1994; Solomon et al., 1996). On this view, young children's understanding of living things is embedded in a folk psychological, rather than folk biological, explanatory framework. Only by age 7 do children begin to elaborate a specifically biological framework of the living world, and only by age 10 does an autonomous theory of biological causality emerge that is not based on children's understanding of how humans think and behave. A competing view is that folk biology and folk psychology emerge early in childhood as largely independent domains of cognition that are clearly evident by ages four or five, and that may be innately differentiated (Atran, 1987; Gelman & Wellman, 1991; Hatano & Inagaki, 1999; Keil, 1994).

To address this issue, a series of cross-cultural experiments were carried out (Atran et al., 2001; Ross et al., 2003; Sousa et al., 2002). One set of experiments shows that by the age of four to five years (the earliest age tested in this regard) urban American, rural Yukatek Maya, and urban and rural Brazilian children employ a concept of innate species potential, or underlying essence, as an inferential framework for understanding the affiliation of an organism to a biological species, and for projecting known and unknown biological properties to organisms in the face of uncertainty (Atran et al., 2001; Sousa et al., 2002). For example, young children overwhelmingly believe, like adults, that the identity of animals and plants follows that of their progenitors, regardless of the environment in which the progeny matures (e.g., progeny of cows raised with pigs, acorns planted with apple seeds; see Gelman & Wellman, 1991).

Another set of experiments shows that whereas young urban American children exhibit strong anthropocentric construals of nonhuman biological kinds, the youngest Maya children, as well as Native American (Menominee) and rural majority-culture American children, do not (Atran et al., 2001; Ross et al., 2003). These children do not initially need to reason about nonhuman living kinds by analogy to human kinds. The fact that urban American children show anthropocentric bias appears to owe more to a difference in cultural exposure to nonhuman biological kinds than to a basic causal understanding of folk biology per se (see Inagaki, 1990). Together, the first two sets of experiments suggest that folk psychology can't be the initial source of folk biology. They also indicate that to master biological science, people must learn to inhibit activation of universal dispositions to view species essentialistically and to see humans as inherently different from other animals.

A third set of experiments reveals significant crosscultural agreement in folk taxonomic structures, and in correspondence of folk taxonomies with evolutionary taxonomy (Atran, 1999; Bailenson et al., 2002; Lopez et al., 1997). A final set of results shows the same taxonomic rank being cognitively preferred for biological induction in two diverse populations: people raised in the midwestern United States and Itza' Maya of the Lowland Mesoamerican rainforest (Atran et al., 1997; Coley et al., 1997). This is the generic species—the level of *oak* and *robin*. These findings cannot be explained by domain-general models of similarity, because such models cannot account for why both cultures prefer species-like groups in making inferences about the biological world, although Americans have relatively little actual knowledge or experience at this level. In fact, general relations of perceptual similarity and expectations derived from experience produce a "basic level" of recognition and recall for many Americans that corresponds to the superordinate life-form level of folk biological taxonomy—the level of *tree* and *bird* (Rosch et al., 1976). Still, Americans prefer generic species for making inductions about the distribution of biological properties among organisms, and for predicting the nature of the biological world in the face of uncertainty. Together, these findings suggest the generic-species level to be a partitioning of the universal (folk) ontological domains of *plant* and *animal* into mutually exclusive essences that are assumed (but not initially known) to have unique underlying causal natures.[2] The findings intimate that folk biology represents evolutionary design; that is, universal taxonomic structures, centered on essence-based generic species, are routine "habits of mind," which may be in part naturally selected to grasp relevant and recurrent "habits of the world." Pigeonholing generic species into a hierarchy of mutually exclusive taxa allows incorporation of new species and biological properties into an inductively coherent system that can be extended to any habitat, arguably facilitating adaptation to many habitats (a hallmark of *Homo sapiens*).

In the case of folk biology, adaptationism may justifiably serve as a heuristic that guides research; however, it has no descriptive or explanatory role. Domain specificity is as far as the scientific account goes (for now). A strong adaptationist stance also helps to counter claims that folk biology develops ontogenetically as an "exapted learning mechanism" (Andrews et al., 2003).[3] For example, in the controversy over whether folk biology develops out of folk psychology or constitutes a functionally autonomous and preexisting mode of construing the world, initial arguments focused on the fact

---

2. By "(folk)-ontological" is meant the apparent structure of the world that panhuman cognitive structures—especially domain-specific ones—intuitively (and to some extent, innately) present us with.
3. *Exaptation* (Gould & Vrba, 1982) is a modern rendition of Darwin's concept of *preadaptation*. It is a preexisting trait that has already evolved (e.g., feathers for insulation) but acquires a new functional effect (feathers for flight) without being naturally selected for this effect.

that the structural representation of species (essentialized taxonomy) in the adult state is more or less uniform across individuals and cultures. If so, it is unlikely that widely varying learning conditions are responsible for such a relatively stable and uniform state; however, evidence for developmental specificity was lacking.

The recent studies cited suggest that the apparent effects of folk psychology on developing folk biology (e.g., anthropocentric interpretations of animals and plants) weaken or disappear for "nonstandard" populations, that is, for any human group other than children or students linked to major research universities. One interpretation is that nonstandard societies more closely approximate ancestral conditions of intimate interaction with nature. By contrast, standard populations (the nearly exclusive focus of most developmental and cognitive psychology) need compensatory learning strategies for lack of sufficient exposure to triggering conditions that enable folk biological knowledge, including strategies derived from folk psychology and even folk mechanics (Au & Romo, 1999).

From this vantage, the study of "standard" populations reveals more about the effects of devolutionary cultural processes on innate knowledge than about the character of innate knowledge as such — much as the study of language acquisition in feral children tells us more about how the language faculty degenerates than about how it evolved to develop (Medin & Atran, 2004). Notice, though, that the evidence cited against exaptation stems from crosscultural research. This research may be compatible with heuristic use of prior or post hoc adaptationist interpretation but by no means requires it for description or explanation. Other aspects of folk biology might benefit from a weak adaptationist strategy that looks at general physical and processing constraints (e.g., economy of information through taxonomic organization), as may important aspects of folk mechanics and even folk psychology (e.g., embedding of mental states; see hereafter).

2 Weak Adaptationism: The Case of Language

Strong adaptationists and weak adaptationists alike accept the premise that natural selection is the only known (noncultural) explanation for functionally complex design — a functionally complex design being one that is "workable" (Gould, 1997c) or "goal-directed" (Pinker, 1997a). But this doesn't really say much. Natural complexity in itself doesn't warrant considerations of natural selection (e.g., snowflakes, crystals, the structure of organic molecules, the fractal structure of a sea-coast, etc.). A workable complex design means little more than a complex design that exists (if it weren't workable, it wouldn't survive). A "goal-directed" complex design is more of a vaguely metaphorical anthropomorphic idea than a formalizable or testable concept of biology. Pinker (1997a) uses "goal-directed" as a fuzzy sort of "as if" notion — as if evolution were purposely designed by an "intelligent designer" (Wallace, 1889, p. 138), blind watchmaker (Dawkins, 1986), "stupid" designer (Williams, 1992, p. 73), tinkerer (Jacob, 1977), or whoever. All one can really say is that nonrandom biological design is produced by cumulative natural selection of more or less random mutations.

One possibility consistent with this is that much complex design has no presently known explanation (most human cognitive architecture; Fodor, 2001b), and there may be some functional complexity that results largely from more general physical, chemical; or biological processes governing complex systems. Such textbook adaptations as the strikingly analogous aerodynamic designs of bird and bat wings, insect wings, and windborne seeds of certain trees (e.g., mahogany) may result chiefly from general physical laws and mechanical processes. Similarly, hydrodynamic laws place general constraints on the structural design of aquatic organisms, so that they tend to be bullet-shaped. Such traits as wings or bullet-shaped bodies are adapted principally to general conditions on earth (gravity, wind, water) distinctive of no particular environment. Talk of adaptation to "ancestral conditions" has little, if any, meaning in such cases.

To be sure, these general constraints on the "design space" of airborne and aquatic structure and movement are components of selective forces operating in particular environments. At each stage in the evolution of these traits, natural selection probably produced encoding in the genes. Nevertheless, further research into the gradual and cumulative action of natural selection on the production of wings and bullet-shaped bodies in particular historical environments and phyletic lineages seems warranted only within the framework of a general design space that is already clearly in view.

Take the case of language. Strong adaptationist scenarios for the emergence of language include stories about bee dances, bird songs, fish courtship, dog barking, simian aggression displays, ape signing, hominid tool-making, object recognition, gesturing, sensorimotor intelligence, self-awareness, food sharing, hunting, spatial mapping, cheater detection, gossiping, social planning, and so forth. Most can be dismissed from serious consideration because they ignore panhuman structural ("design") features of language, such as syntactic structures. Pinker and Bloom (1990) provide the most compelling story for language learning as a strong adaptation for communicating propositional structures over a serial channel.

Pinker and Bloom's proposal has two parts: demonstrating biological preparedness (using "poverty of stimulus" reasoning) and inferring adaptation. The first part is widely accepted by strong and weak adaptationists. Indeed, it is a virtual tautology. As Hume stressed, the ability to "automatically" extend a few (or finitely many) instances of experience to an indefinitely large (virtually infinite) set of complexly related cases logically requires the prior existence of projecting structures that do the work of generalization. For those who accept human minds to be biological systems that evolved under natural selection (as both strong and weak adaptationists do), the issue is decided and decidedly uninformative.

But biological preparedness doesn't imply "hence, adaptation for language learning" (as Andrews et al., 2003, suggest). The claims for syntax as an adaptation at best involve retrodictions of syntactic structures discovered through weak adaptationist reasoning and research (mostly through generative grammar). No novel predictions ensue. Reasonable people can argue over whether strong adaptationism provides novel predictions or discoveries for *any* higher order cognitive process.[4] Many adaptationist arguments for higher order cognition are mere consistency arguments. They lack even

---

4. For example, on the so-called cheater detection module as an adaptation (Cosmides, 1989; Fiddick et al., 2000; Gigerenzer & Hug, 1992), see Sperber et al. (1995a), Atran (2001c).

the power of retrodiction because they so easily accommodate conflicting and contrary adaptationist accounts.[5]

Finally, this one seriously strong adaptationist argument for language may be nearly circular, at least in its strongest claim that language was selected to communicate subject-predicate relations. There is no example I'm aware of indicating subject-predicate structures in any creature save language-competent humans. Even that stellar bonobo, Kanzi, consistently fails to apprehend such structures; his novel "sentences" are maximally just two concatenated arguments with no subjects, such as "chase bite," which humans shun (Atran & Lois, 2001). So this strongest of adaptationists proposal may reduce to: language was naturally selected to communicate what only language can formulate (propositions).

The proposal that language emerged as a vehicle for "thoughts struggling to get out" isn't logically circular, as it's logically possible for a mind to internally represent subject-predicate relations (or any other format for structured thought) without having means to encode and externalize them (e.g., a program running on a computer with no keyboard, speaker, or screen).[6] If the claim were merely for communicating predicate-argument relations, without any argument being distinguished as the subject, there would be some independent support by analogy (although no direct empirical test or confirmation). First, theories of a variety of forms of information representation (relational databases, formal logic, computer programming languages) and information processing (human vision, conceptual memory, real-time reasoning) hypothesize manipulation of predicate-argument relations.[7] Second, whatever the format, communication of information (which has evolved repeatedly in the animal and plant kingdoms) has fitness benefits when uncertainty is reduced: for example, if transaction costs for information exchange are lower than costs of individually rediscovering the information (Pinker, 1997a, p. 573).

Nevertheless, for the stronger claim that syntax is selected to communicate subject-predicate relations, there may be little prospect for independent support by analogy, let alone empirical support that directly tests the argument. A syntactic subject combines a logical function (a particular thematic role, typically agent) with the pragmatic function of topic in a topic-comment structure (allowing sentences to be pragmatically linked together in discourse). According to Pinker and Bloom (1990), the grammatical subject has this character because the medium of human communication is serial and attention is finite. Because attention is finite in all animals and other forms of serial communication exist in other animals, the subject in mind must have evolved to accommodate the medium of communication, and not the other way around. But the only known case of an agent-focused thought (the

---

5. For example, according to Sedikides and Skowronski (1997, p. 80) the symbolic self is a "flexible and multifaceted cognitive representation of an organism's own attributes" that "serves adaptive functions"; supporting arguments are speculative, uninformative as to any specific computational structures, and too vague to assess their truth or falsity.
6. Peter Carruthers, personal communication, November 5, 2002, on why Pinker's strong adaptationist view of language isn't circular (as Atran, 2003, suggests).
7. Steven Pinker, personal communication, November 8, 2002, on why his proposal is noncircular.

logical-pragmatic subject) being structurally fit to a serial communication medium is human language. How and where the fitting process got "kick-started" is left to the dark recesses of pure speculation. "Bootstrapping" only fudges the issue.

One alternative, weak adaptationist approach assumes no direct natural selection (no task-specific adaptation to distinctive features of ancestral environments) for language's "creative core," that is, the computational faculty of syntactic recursion that allows potentially infinite production of words and well-formed word-combinations with relatively few and finite means (Chomsky, 2000). Putting aside the argument from design as too open-ended or nearly circular, this "minimalist program" operates on the (huge but bold) assumption that language's creative core is a recently evolved accommodation to more general physical or biological processes—in ways analogous to the apparent optimization of information flow in a material medium through minimization of "wire length," as in microchip design, nematodes, and human brains (Cherniak, 1995). The idea is that recursion in language may be a *physically optimal* sort of interface (internal accommodation) between two physically suboptimal (but perhaps genetically optimal and adapted) systems of more ancient evolutionary origins: the sensorimotor system (including phonation) and the conceptual-intentional system (including categorization, reference, and reasoning).[8]

The idea of physical optimality has a distinguished tradition in natural philosophy (Galileo, Newton) and natural history (Blumenbach, A. L. Jussieu) as well as in modern cosmology (Einstein, Hawking) and in studies of biological form and development (D'Arcy Thompson, 1961/1917, Maynard Smith et al., 1985). For evolutionary biology in particular, the primary objective is to discover and predict,

---

8. The minimalist program uses Occam's razor to reduce the computational component for human language, which interacts with the two "external" systems, to only those elements warranted by conceptual necessity (Epstein, Thráinsson, & Zwart, 1996). Beyond Occam, though, is the metaphysical supposition that nature itself operates on principles of bare necessity, whenever it can get away with it. Chomsky's working assumption is that we can go a long way—perhaps even all of the way—in understanding the computational component of language that maps meaning onto form by attempting to reduce much of the descriptive richness and crosslinguistic variation in human syntax to the following: (1) a few invariant principles for all humanly possible syntactic systems (e.g., every sentence must have a subject), (2) a very limited number of parameter settings from which irreducible crosslinguistic variation derives (e.g., subjects are either morphophonologically overt, as in English *I desire* or optionally covert, as in Spanish (*yo*) *deseo*), (3) legibility conditions imposed by the sensorimotor system (e.g., linearization of sounds required for pronunciation imposes linear ordering on the interface representations that encode grammatical information, which yields phrase-structural properties), and (4) legibility conditions imposed by the conceptual-intentional system (e.g., positioning of semantic items in the contour of events requires the assignment of lexical items to thematic roles, such as agent, patient, instrument, and so forth). An open empirical issue is which aspects of syntactic theory should be retained (if any) as principles or parameters, which should be transferred from syntax proper to the interface with the two external systems, and which should be eliminated after reduction to principles, parameters, or interface conditions. Note, however, that the minimalist program itself is not a theory (contrary to what Pinker and Jackendoff, in press, contend) and makes no empirical claims; it is an inspired guess as to how general properties of organic systems might guide research and constrain empirical theses about the nature of human grammar for example, that perhaps there are no levels of representation (e.g., d- or s-structure) beyond the two interface levels.

through strictly physical and chemical means, the set of organic forms (molecular, morphological, neuronal) that are likely to emerge from a given starting point. Only then is it worthwhile to inquire into which of those forms might be selected and how. For example, extensive sharing of genomic structure among all vertebrates, and even vertebrates and invertebrates, suggests that many of the same "master genes" program body plan and the control mechanisms of development (Gehring, 1998). Even eyes, which were thought to have evolved analogously and independently in different phyla, may be in each case a homologous derivation from the same DNA (*Pax-6*). Physical law and mechanical processes appear to be responsible for much of what follows: development of each component of the eye is narrowly constrained by the laws of optics and mechanical contingencies involved in sharply projecting images of three-dimensional objects onto a planar surface of receptors.

In line with Turing's (1952) vision of biological explanation, much the same organic architecture and behavior may evolve in very different historical environments, just as basically similar cognitive architectures and behaviors may be developed in very different physical media (see Hodges, 1983; Leiber, 2002). If so, it is plausible to try to explain significant aspects of the structure and emergence of these architectures and behaviors without considering how they have been accommodated to (selected for) particular historical environments and physical media. Indeed, further understanding of particular historical and physical accommodations (e.g., the "Cambrian explosion" of multicellular organisms, the "real-time" processing of information) may depend crucially on such non-teleological insights. The worthiness of this approach depends on success in providing significant and surprising predictions and discoveries. In the minimalist program, these arguably (if controversially) far exceed what its originators previously thought possible (for a formalization, see Chomsky, 2001). At most, strong adaptationist arguments retrodict old discoveries. This isn't to deny that adaptationist arguments may ultimately prove insightful into language structure. For example, recent studies identifying multiple genetic loci for language disorders and delays seem to belie any single mutation account for language. Moreover, at least one of these genes seems to have been a target for selection, although the gene at issue (*FOXP2*) concerns speech and processing of morphology rather than syntactic recursion (Enard et al., 2002). In any event, even without an eventual recourse to adaptationism, novel biological and evolutionary understanding of language (and other cognitive structures) can occur beforehand.

Weak adaptationist (not necessarily minimalist) investigation of language crucially uses aspects of the strong adaptationist program, especially the comparative approach (Hauser et al., 2003). Thus, arguments for natural selection of phonation have involved claims about the uniqueness of categorical auditory discrimination and descent of the larynx in humans. Comparative studies prove otherwise: chinchillas and other mammalian species categorically discriminate human phones; deer and several bird species drop the larynx (possibly to exaggerate size, Fitch & Reby, 2001). Perhaps human phonation is itself a by-product of a jury-rigged combination of other by-products and adaptations: the (originally prevertebrate) alimentary system and the respiratory system of terrestrial vertebrates interface at the larynx (which drops in humans), hence by chance enabling production of phones later "exapted" to language. Other comparative studies show contrary evidence for prehominid antiquity in parts of the conceptual-intentional system. Intriguing experiments purporting to show that subordinate chimps can take the perspective of dominant chimps (Hare et al., 2001) have yet to be replicated in different laboratories (Povinelli, 2001a). In any event, chimps don't seem able to repeatedly embed states of mind: [Danny thinks that [Marc believes that [Brian knows that... etc. Short-term memory typically limits iterated embedding of mental states to five levels (L. Barrett et al., 2002); however, as with embedding of linguistic clauses (also usually limited to just a few levels), computational machinery allows for indefinitely many embeddings.[9]

For any apparent limit, simply embed the maximal thought or phrase into the further belief or clause: "(Do) you really think that..." or something of the sort. By giving a person more time and external memory, more embedding is interpretable in a unique and uniform way (not predicted by associationist models, connectionist or other). Other parts of the conceptual-intentional system may be more ancient in primates, including perceptually based reference (Gallistel, 1990), categorization (Brown & Boysen, 2000), and reasoning (Povinelli, 2000).

3 Conclusion

The intention in this essay has been to explore and evaluate the methodological usefulness of strong versus weak adaptationist positions as ways to gain insight and to make scientifically significant advances in the study of in human cognition. Although it remains unclear whether or not there are real differences in the theoretical and ontological assumptions of strong versus weak adaptationists, there is often a clear and deep methodological divide. So what works best? My answer is mixed.

In folk biology, as with perhaps other universal and "modular" cognitive domains (e.g., folk psychology), a strong adaptationist approach does seem to provide some genuine insight with testable consequences. Such insight has proven useful but perhaps not necessary to progress in the field. To the extent that phylogenetic homologies are apparent, a strong adaptationist approach may be warranted.

Neither the inferential structure of human folk biological taxonomy nor the recursive representational structure of human folk psychology have obvious homologies; however, more rudimentary and phylogenetically prior aspects of these two systems do. Accordingly, one may profitably consider which functional advantages the more recently evolved aspects of the folk biological and folk psychological systems might have provided relative to older aspects of these systems, given what is known about corresponding changes in hominid ecological and

---

9. Noam Chomsky, personal communication, October 27, 2002, referring to embedding experiments he performed with George Miller in the early 1960s. For developmental research linking syntactic structures to the representational format for false beliefs, see de Villiers and Pyers (2002).

social environments (e.g., wider roaming range, larger group size). In the case of folk biology, such considerations underscored the claim that folk biology and folk psychology are evolutionarily distinct domains of (primate) cognition; and this speculative claim, in turn, motivated experiments showing that folk biology and folk psychology are developmentally distinct domains of (child) cognition.

For language, strong adaptationism does not appear to have produced any new understanding, despite more intense effort by strong adaptationists in this domain than perhaps in any other. Here, a weak adaptationist strategy has arguably proved most productive in advancing scientific understanding, without precluding that the structures uncovered by other means are actually adaptations. In a sense, weak adaptationism is more scientifically demanding than strong adaptationism. For weak adaptationism's methodological stance follows from the belief that evidentiary standards for deciding between competing lines of research must go beyond mere consistency (which does not disallow contrary explanations), or even retrodiction, to include surprising deductions and significant empirical confirmations.

Now, I have argued as if insight and awareness on the one hand and prediction and discovery on the other are the same things when judging the relative scientific merit of one methodological stance versus another. But someone could think that the language faculty is an adaptation (claiming that this hypothesis is better warranted than any alternative on the market) and thereby gain some insight and awareness into how things fit together, without believing that an evolutionary explanation of language is likely to lead to new predictions and discoveries in linguistics.

In the end, a good way to obtain knowledge about a domain of human cognition may involve approaching a problem from both ends, initially keeping apart strong and weak strategies, then combining their respective appreciations to generate new knowledge. Viewing progress in understanding the emergence of human cognition exclusively through a lens of strong adaptationism (search first and always for the adaptation that a complex trait might represent) or weak adaptationism (if in doubt about some adaptation as a trait's explanation—which is usually the case—give nonadaptationist accounts the benefit) could lead science into blind alleys. To conclude that attempting a modest use and mix of strong and weak adaptationist approaches could prove most effective in producing knowledge about human cognition may appear obvious, even lame. But why, then, do so few attempt it?

10

MARK C. BAKER

The Innate Endowment for Language

Underspecified or Overspecified?

Some linguists argue that people have explicit innate knowledge not only of the universal aspects of language but even of the options that define different languages. Other researchers find this view unparsimonious and perplexing from an evolutionary perspective. They claim that linguistic diversity shows that our innate knowledge of language is incomplete, and is filled in by nonlinguistic learning—a view that they claim should be preferred on a priori grounds. This chapter questions whether the underspecification view is really feasible and whether it is more parsimonious than the overspecification view, drawing on examples from certain African languages. It also shows that the perplexity evoked by overspecification theories disappears if language has a concealing purpose as well as a communicating purpose, similar to a code.

1 A Fundamental Puzzle of Language

Since the beginning of the cognitive science research paradigm, language has provided some of the strongest evidence that the human mind has substantial innate structure. Noam Chomsky has forcefully presented the basic arguments for more than 40 years, and they have been confirmed, extended, and supplemented by many others. Adult speakers of a language have robust and reliable judgments about which sentences are or are not possible, and what their range of interpretations can be. These judgments exist for configurations that speakers have no prior experience with and for which there is no simple account by analogy to simpler sentences. Typological work has revealed important linguistic universals that are not a priori true of any moderately well designed communication system but that are contingently true of all human languages. Developmental research has shown that children acquiring a language never make certain types of errors that seem like reasonable inductive conjectures. Children do make mistakes, but only mistakes that fall within the constrained range of possibilities that are attested in actual natural languages (see Crain, Gualmini, & Pietroski, chapter 11 here, and references cited there). Studies of creolization and deaf populations have shown that people spontaneously create a complete and orderly language out of the unsystematic semimeaningful chaos that surrounds them. These lines of evidence converge into a powerful argument that humans are born with the foundational principles of human language. This idea is so important to much linguistic research that we linguists have our own name for the innate endowment as it applies to the human capacity for language: universal grammar (UG).

Yet language is not completely and uniquely specified in human minds from birth. Humans obviously speak different languages. And the differences reach to the deepest levels of sentence structure and interpretation. Compare, for example, the Japanese sentence in (1) with its English translation.

(1) John-ga Mary-ni hon-o ageta.
John Mary-to book gave
'John gave the book to Mary.'

In addition to the individual words in Japanese being different, they are arranged quite differently. In Japanese the verb comes at the end of the sentence, after the direct and indirect objects, whereas in English the verb comes before such elements. Moreover, in Japanese the preposition meaning 'to' comes after the noun 'Mary', whereas in English it comes before. Overall, the Japanese rules for ordering words into phrases, clauses, and sentences are systematically different from the English rules. For some domains of cognitive science—visual perception, or motor coordination, perhaps—it might be reasonable to suppose that all the interesting cognitive structure is uniquely innately specified, but this is not plausible for language. Indeed, the differences among languages are usually more striking than the similarities. It takes education and sophistication to see the similarities among languages, whereas the differences are manifest, and torment us in foreign language classes and train stations.

The study of language is thus particularly interesting for cognitive science, in part because one cannot ignore either its universal features or its culturally variable ones. It is an ideal domain for investigating the interplay of similarity and difference.

Granted that the innate endowment for language does not specify one grammatical structure for all human languages, there are only two logical possibilities. The first is that UG could *under*determine the grammar of particular languages. This would mean that some grammatical points are left open to be filled in from the environment using general learning devices of some kind. The alternative is to say that UG *over*determines the grammar of particular languages. On this second view, UG specifies multiple choices at certain points, with the result that young children in some sense "know" many grammars. Grammatical development can then be thought of as identifying which choices characterize the ambient language and discarding the rest. These choices are known as *parameters* (see Baker, 2001, for details). On the first view, the innate endowment contains less information than is needed to construct a coherent natural language; on the second view it contains more than is needed. A foundational question is which of these views is correct. Is UG like an unfinished novel with the ending left to the reader's imagination or like a book with several endings from which the reader may pick? Is it like a recipe that says nothing about how the dish should be spiced or like a recipe that specifies different spicing formulas depending on whether one wants it hot, or sweet, or bland?

Both views have their proponents. Among psychologists, the underdeterminist view predominates. Pinker and Bloom (1994), for example, endorse it in the following passage:

> Parameters of variation, and the learning process that fixes their values for a particular language, as we conceive them, are not individual explicit gadgets in the human mind.... Instead, they should fall out of the interaction between the specific mechanisms that define the basic underlying organization of language ('Universal Grammar') and the learning mechanisms, some of them predating language, that can be sensitive to surface variation in the entities defined by these language specific mechanisms. (1994, p. 183)

The linguist Frederick Newmeyer also takes this view:

> It... strengthens the case for individual parameter settings being learnable without demanding that the child literally choose from an innately specified set.
>
> However, it does seem clear that one does have to reject the idea that all principles, and their range of possible parametric variation, are innate. (1998, pp. 363–4)

Most so-called functionalist linguists would concur, since they generally downplay the Chomskian notion of universal grammar anyway.

In contrast, Chomsky since about 1980 and many linguists who follow him are overdeterminationists. Some representative passages from Chomsky's writings include:

> Each of the systems of [universal grammar] has associated with it certain parameters, which are set in terms of data presented to the person acquiring a particular language. The grammar of a language can be regarded as a particular set of values for these parameters, while the overall system of rules, principles, *and parameters* is UG, which we may take to be one element of human biological endowment, namely, the "language faculty." (1982, p. 7)
>
> Languages may select from among the devices of UG, setting the parameters in one or another way, to provide for such general processes as those that were considered to be rules in earlier work. (1981, p. 7)
>
> Within the P&P approach the problems of typology and language variation arise in a somewhat different form than before. Language differences and typology should be reducible to choice of values of parameters. (1995, p. 6)[1]

Here the child's task is seen not as filling in what is left open but as choosing among several specified options. Encouragement for this view comes from properties

---

1. It is debatable whether the "minimalist program" outlined in the later chapters of Chomsky (1995) represents an important shift in this conception or not. I do not explore this issue here.

of phonological development. Very young infants are able to distinguish pairs of sounds from any language when they hear them, but they lose this ability for all but the sounds in their native language after about six months (Pinker, 1994, pp. 253–64, and references cited there). In a sense, the youngest infants "know" more sounds than older ones do. Overdeterminists believe that this extends to other domains of language as well.

Ultimately, the choice between overdeterminism and underdeterminism is an empirical one. But relevant facts are not easy to come by in this area. Babies are complex and squirmy, and there are limits to what one can do to them. This chapter thus explores some of the more conceptual dimensions of the issue, so that we can judge more precisely what to look for and how hard to look for it. I argue against "easy underdeterminism," the attitude that underdeterminism is self-evidently true, or at least so plausible that it should be abandoned only in the face of overwhelming evidence to the contrary. After reviewing the embryonic arguments that are offered for underdeterminism, I show that, when one looks at some realistic cases of crosslinguistic variation, it is not so obvious that underdeterminism is feasible, or that it is simpler than overdeterminism. I also claim that there could be a useful function for overdeterminism, in that natural languages can be used as ciphers—tools that reveal information to your friends while concealing it from your rivals. I conclude that cognitive scientists should be open to the idea that the innate endowment is so rich that it specifies more than is necessary for any one organism to function—at least in the domain of language, and perhaps in other cognitive domains as well.

2 The Appeal of Underdeterminism

Why do most cognitive scientists not under Chomsky's direct influence find themselves drawn toward the underdeterminist view? I think their reasons can be boiled down to three key themes: underdeterminism seems *possible* and *parsimonious*, whereas the existence of an overdetermined UG would be *perplexing* from an evolutionary perspective. Therefore, underdeterminism is to be preferred.

The argument from possibility goes roughly as follows. Some features of language seem easy to characterize with relatively little language-specific knowledge. Word order in Japanese as opposed to English is a good example. We certainly have a nonlinguistic ability to detect differences in the temporal order of two stimuli: we can distinguish a "beep" followed by a "thunk" from a "thunk" followed by a "beep," for example. Now every transitive sentence in Japanese has the object before the verb, and (almost) every transitive sentence in English has the object after the verb (see [1]). There is nothing subtle or obscure about this grammatical difference, nothing that obviously puts it beyond the capacity of relatively unsophisticated nonlinguistic cognition. If children can hear objects as "beep" and verbs as "thunk," they should be able to learn the word-order difference reliably without the help of UG. Parameters such as these can therefore be left unspecified by the innate endowment without jeopardizing the reliability of language learning. So underdetermination seems possible.

Given that underdetermination is possible, it seems clear that it is more parsimonious. Underdeterminism by definition attributes less innate knowledge/ structure to the human mind than overdeterminism does, and less is better.

General considerations of scientific simplicity and elegance thus favor underdeterminism without compelling evidence to the contrary. Evolutionary theory might give additional bite to this parsimony argument. An underdetermined UG that represents less information should be easier to represent in the genome, should require fewer mutations to arise in the course of evolution, and thus should be easier to explain in evolutionary terms.

Evolutionary considerations also feed into the argument from perplexity. There seems to be no good reason why UG should bother encoding multiple parametric possibilities when one possibility would fully serve the need to communicate. On the overdeterminist view, children "forget" (lose access to) those grammatical options that they do not detect in the language spoken to them. This information thus plays no role in the cognitive life of a child after a certain age—an age after which children do most of their surviving and reproducing. So there seems to be no evolutionary benefit to having an overdetermined universal grammar. If UG exists to make it possible for us to acquire quickly and reliably a language rich enough to encode propositional information, then parameters seem like a design flaw; they make language learning harder with no increase in function.

Nowack, Komarova, and Niyogi (2001) purport to study mathematically the conditions under which a parametrized UG could evolve, but they make one very unrealistic assumption. They assume that different languages are better suited to talking about some kinds of evolutionarily significant contingencies than others. It is easy to see how their result follows if we grant this assumption. If (say) one can describe how to survive a sandstorm better with English-style subject-verb-object order and how to hunt walruses better with Japanese-style subject-object-verb order, then it will be advantageous to children to be able to acquire either type of language, depending on where they happen to grow up. But the assumption is wildly implausible. Either "First, the headman the walrus spears" or "First the headman spears the walrus" will do perfectly well in the Arctic. And (not surprisingly) there is no ecological or cultural regularity to how the major linguistic types are distributed around the world (see Baker, 2001). But if there is no difference in the evolutionary fitness of different languages in different environments, then there is no advantage to being able to learn different languages. Under these conditions, Nowack and colleagues' mathematics shows that a parameterized UG is disfavored, because it makes language learning less reliable. There seems to be no evolutionary advantage to having an overdetermined UG, making its existence perplexing if true.

Here are two sample quotations from underdeterminists. In each quotation, I have highlighted and tagged phrases that communicate considerations of possibility, parsimony, or perplexity.

> Often *there are plausible explanations* for a typological pattern that do not involve appeal to an innate UG principle [possibility]. In such cases, harm is done by assuming innateness. What we would then have are two contrasting explanans: one that says the pattern results from such-and-such motivated principle or force, the other that says that it is *merely a genetic quirk* [perplexity]. *All other things being equal*, we should choose the former [parsimony]. (Newmeyer, 1998, p. 362)

Why is there more than one language at all?... Some aspects of grammar *might be easily learnable from environmental inputs* by cognitive processes that may have been in existence prior to the evolution of grammar, for example, the relative order of a pair of sequenced elements within a bounded unit [possibility]. For these aspects *there was no need to evolve a fixed value*, and they are free to vary across communities of speakers [perplexity].... *It may be difficult* to evolve a huge innate code.... The size of such a code would *tax the time available to evolve* and maintain it in the genome in the face of random perturbations from sexual recombination and other stochastic genetic processes [parsimony]. (Pinker and Bloom, 1990, p. 716)

These, then, I take to be the three main strands of underdeterminist thought about linguistic variability. Underdeterminists seem to have a powerful argument—if not that underdetermination is true, at least that it deserves to be the null hypothesis.

Or do they? In the next three sections, I consider each strand individually, to show that it does not seem so compelling when one knows more about the details of linguistic variation and when one considers alternative hypotheses about what the purpose of language might be.

3   Is Underdetermination Possible?

In explaining their underdeterminist intuitions, Pinker, Bloom, and Newmeyer illustrate with what I call the head directionality parameter (HDP), which distinguishes Japanese-type word order from English-type word order. I begin by giving some more information about this parameter, and how it compares with other putative parameters. Although it seems reasonable that this particular parameter, taken alone, could be handled underdeterminist-style, it is not at all obvious that that is true for other parameters.

The HDP characterizes the difference between the Japanese sentence in (1) and its English equivalent. This parameter's net effect on sentence structure is huge. Examples (2) and (3) highlight this by comparing a more complex English sentence with its rough equivalent in Japanese:

(2)   Taro might think that Hiro showed a picture of himself to Hanako.

(3)   Taroo-ga   Hiro-ga   Hanako-ni zibun-no syasin-o   miseta to   omotte   iru.
      Taro-SUBJ Hiro-SUBJ Hanako to self-POSS pictureOBJ show   that thinking be
      'Taro thinks (literally, is thinking) that Hiro showed a picture of himself to Hanako.'

Yet the rule that underlies these observed differences is remarkably simple: English forms new phrases by adding words at the beginning of already constructed phrases, whereas Japanese forms new phrases by adding words at the end. Both languages make prepositional phrases out of noun phrases; English does it by putting *of* before the noun phrase (*of himself*), and Japanese does it by putting *no* after the noun phrase (*zibun-no* 'himself of'). English puts a noun before a prepositional phrase to make a noun phrase (*pictures of himself*); Japanese puts a noun after a prepositional phrase to make a noun phrase (*zibun-no syasin* 'himself-of picture'). English puts a verb before a noun phrase to make a verb phrase (*show pictures of himself*); Japanese puts a verb after a noun phrase to make a verb phrase (*zibun-no syasin-o miseta* 'himself of picture show'). This difference applies to the full range of phrases found in either language (see Baker, 2001, ch. 3). Although it is a simple rule, it has a huge impact on the character of a language, because it applies many times in a sentence of moderate complexity. This parameter is one of the most elegant, robust, and high-impact parameters known. About 45 percent of the languages in the world are clearly of the Japanese-type, and another 45 percent are of the English type. This was also one of the first parameters to be discovered, having its roots in Greenberg's (1963) pioneering study of universals in language. As such, it is a favorite of linguists, and a natural case for underdeterminists to consider.

How can this property of natural languages be captured? In the overdeterminist version, UG would somehow express the following disjunctive statement:

(4) The head directionality parameter (HDP) (overdetermination version):

When a word is combined with a phrase to make a larger phrase, the added word comes first *or* it comes last.

English chooses the "first" option; Japanese chooses the "last" option. Underdeterminists want to get the same effect without having (4) as part of the innate endowment for languages. They want to get by with only a statement like (5).

(5) Form a new phrase by adding a word to a phrase. (Undeterminist version.)

The underdeterminist idea is that when language users put (5) to use, they come up against the fact that speech is a serial medium, with each word strictly ordered with respect to all other words in an utterance. When one combines a word and a phrase into a grammatical unit, there are only two possibilities: the added word can come before the phrase, or it can come after it. There is no a priori reason to prefer one order to the other, and users have no innate knowledge that guides them on this. Therefore, they look to their environment to learn which order is in fact used in the language around them. As already mentioned, it is well within the power of our nonlinguistic cognitive system to detect the difference between the sequence A-B and the sequence B-A. In this way, children in a Japanese-speaking environment learn one version of the parameter and children in an English-speaking environment learn the other. This is not unreasonable, so far as it goes.

There is, however, much more to grammar than the HDP. Linguists know of at least 15 fairly well established large-scale parameters that concern syntax (see Baker, 2001, ch. 6, for a list), plus many others that govern other aspects of language. Furthermore, linguists frequently propose new parameters to handle fine-grain distinctions among familiar languages or the large-grain distinctions that characterize less familiar languages. It is reasonable to ask if the underdeterminist account is as plausible for other known parameters as it is for the HDP.

In order to assess this, I consider briefly a new parameter, which comes up in my current research in collaboration with Christopher Collins. This parameter, which we may call the "target of agreement parameter" (TAP), concerns a systematic difference between Indo-European (IE) languages and Bantu languages. In languages of both families, tensed verbs have an affix that agrees with the features of their subject. Example (6) shows this for English and Kinande (spoken in the Congo).

(6) Abakali *ba*-gula amatunda v. Omukali *a*-gula amatunda.
Women AGR2-buy fruits woman AGR1-buy fruits
'The women buy fruits.' v. 'The woman buys fruits.'

In other sentence types, the behavior of agreement on the verb diverges in the two language families. For example, in certain passive sentences either a noun phrase or a prepositional phrase can come before the passive verb, as shown in (7) in English.

(7) a. John put some peanuts/a peanut on the table. (active sentence)

b. Some peanuts *were* put on the table. (passive sentence, Noun Phrase moved)
A peanut *was* put on the table.

c. On the table *were* put some peanuts. (passive sentence, Prepositional Phrase moved)
On the table *was* put a peanut.

In English, the form of the verb *be* is determined by whether the remaining noun phrase is singular or plural. It does not matter where that noun phrase appears in the sentence. Bantu languages allow a similar range of word orders, but the agreement patterns are different, as shown in (8) from Kinande.

(8) a. Kambale a-hira ehilanga oko-mesa. (active sentence)
Kambale AGR1-put peanuts on-table

b. Ehilanga hya-hirawa oko-mesa. (passive, NP moved)
peanuts AGR2-were.put on-table

c. Oko-mesa kwa-hirawa ehilanga. (passive, PP moved)
on-table AGR3-was.put peanuts

The agreement prefix in (8c) is different from (8b), even though the number of the noun phrase 'peanuts' does not change. When the prepositional phrase is the preverbal element in a Kinande passive, the verb agrees with it, rather than with the noun phrase.

A related difference is found when direct objects are brought to the beginning of a transitive sentence. Many languages allow this in one form or another (e.g., *That woman, I met in town*). In some, when the object is moved to the front the verb also moves, so that it comes between the fronted object and the subject. This is known as the "verb second" phenomenon. It is found in most Germanic languages and survives to some extent in an archaic/poetic register of English:

(9) a. I have never seen a more beautiful woman.

b. ?A more beautiful woman have I never seen.

Notice that the verb agrees with *I* in (9b), not with the fronted object *a more beautiful woman*, even though the linear order is different: it is *have*, and could not be *has*. This fact holds true also in Dutch and German, in which (9b)-like word orders are commonplace.

Some Bantu languages also allow objects to be fronted in special discourse situations, with the verb coming second, between the fronted object and the subject. But in Bantu object-fronting does affect the agreement on the verb. Without object-fronting, the verb agrees with the subject; with object-fronting, it agrees with the object.

(10) a. A*ba*kali si-*ba*-lisenya olukwi l'omo-mbasa.
Women not-AGR1-chop wood with-axe
'Women do not chop wood with an axe.'

b. O*lu*kwi si-*lu*-lisenya bakali omo-mbasa.
Wood not-AGR2-chop women with-axe
'Wood, women do not chop with an axe.'

This is a second systematic difference between IE languages and Bantu languages.

These two differences in the behavior of agreement (and several others not reviewed here) can be unified under the following parameter:

(11) The target of agreement parameter (TAP):

The "subject" agreement affix associated with a verb must match either:

(a) the noun phrase on which it licenses nominative case,

or:

(b) the phrase that immediately precedes it.

Requirement (11a) is the IE value of the parameter. It capitalizes on the fact that there is a correlation between nominative forms of pronouns and other noun phrases and the presence of tense on the verb. For example, the nominative form *I* is found in (12a), where the following verb is tensed, but when the verb is an infinitive (as in [12b]) the accusative form *me* is required.

(12) a. They believe *I am* a fool.

b. They believe *me to be* a fool.

So tensed verbs make possible nominative case subjects. Tensed verbs also bear agreement affixes, and in IE languages the phrase they agree with is the same as the phrase that they induce nominative case on. As a result, agreement is not affected by minor variations in word order in IE languages, as shown in (7) and (9). The Bantu languages, in contrast, use (11b). In simple cases like (6), the two rules give the same result. But since the Bantu version is keyed specifically to linear order, agreement in Bantu languages is very sensitive to minor permutations of the sentence, as shown in (8) and (10). The TAP thus accounts for a cluster of differences in how agreement works in IE languages, as opposed to Bantu languages. It provides a fair example of how new parameters emerge routinely in the ongoing task of doing large-scale comparative linguistics.

Now the question is what would be involved in translating this parameter out of the overdeterminist format in (11), with its explicit disjunction, and into the underdetermined format recommended by Pinker, Bloom, and Newmeyer. It is hard to see how it would work out in this case. The starting point would presumably be something like (13).

(13) The tensed verb must agree in person (gender) and number with some phrase in its environment.

So far so good. But language learners now must infer from the underspecified statement in (13) that there are exactly two ways of identifying possible targets of agreement: linear precedence and nominative case. But why should that be? Why shouldn't they also consider the phrase that immediately follows the verb, or the phrase to which the verb assigns accusative case, or any of a variety of plausible grammatical relations, together with their Boolean combinations? The space of hypotheses for the HDP is plausibly constrained by the external condition that spoken language takes place in a serial medium. But there are not such obvious external constraints on (13).

The next step in the underdeterminist account would be to use language-independent learning gadgets to decide how (13) should be filled out by the learner. This too is tricky. It is fairly easy to see how one can learn the order of two adjacent elements with language-independent cognition. But how could one learn whether a verb agrees with a nominative noun phrase or a noun phrase that immediately precedes it using cognitive processes that are evolutionarily prior to language? What is a language-independent analog of a verb agreeing with a noun phrase? The closest thing that comes to mind is our ability to detect when one thing has a feature in common with something else, perhaps because there has been contact between the two. One might say that a mud patch "agrees" with the deer that left a footprint in it, for example. But that seems like a rather remote analogy to the case at hand. More problematic still, what is a language-independent version of "noun phrase whose nominative case is licensed by the verb"? This parametric choice seems intrinsically tied to concepts that are only meaningful within the language faculty itself, raising doubt that it can be learned by cognitive principles that are not part of that faculty. I am sure that it is *possible* for one to learn the value of (11) without using the language faculty; presumably that is what I did, using my science-forming ability. But that isn't what children in the Congo are doing. And the TAP is probably more typical of parameters in general than the HDP in these respects. The intrinsic plausibility of the underdeterminist view of the HDP thus does not carry over to other plausible parameters. We cannot take it for granted that the underdeterminist option is a viable approach, sufficient to answer the questions about typology and acquisition that parameters were created to solve.[2]

4 Is Underdeterminism More Parsimonious?

Next let us consider whether the underdeterministic approach is more parsimonious than the overdeterministic one, hence to be preferred on general grounds of scientific simplicity and because it minimizes the mystery of how UG evolved.

Considerations of simplicity, of course, apply only to theories that can be shown to do the basic explanatory work. One does not ultimately prefer a simple and inadequate theory to a more complex but more adequate one. The putative parsimony of underdeterminism is only relevant if its possibility has been established. And that still remains to be done, as already discussed.

But there is another point to make as well, which is that simplicity must usually be evaluated relative to the particular representation system in which the theory is couched. To see how this general point could apply to questions about UG, consider once again the HDP. Pinker, Bloom, and Newmeyer take it for granted that a UG that is silent about word order like (5) has a smaller and simpler mental representation than a UG that includes explicit disjunctive statements about word order like (4). Maybe this is so, but it is not *necessarily* so.

Imagine two ways in which linguists could express how sentences like (2) or (3) are structured into phrases. One possibility is that they could type the sentences on their word processors, and include labeled brackets to indicate which groups of words constitute phrases. A second possibility is that they could build Calder-style mobiles in which a symbol for every word is attached by pieces of wire to nodes that stand for the phrases that the word is contained in, the whole mobile then being hung from the ceiling. Both representations could be perfectly adequate expressions of phrasal grouping; indeed they could be logically equivalent (although the reader can probably guess which method is in common use). But the two differ markedly in how they would treat word order. In the mobile style of representation, no intrinsic order is implied. Two words X and Y could be part of the same phrase by virtue of being hung from the same piece of the mobile, but sometimes X might be to the right of Y, and other times X might be to the left of Y,

---

2. Further questions about the possibility of underdeterminism arise when one considers carefully the very first stages of language acquisition. Learning whether a language has verb-object or object-verb word order seems easy, since the information is there in any transitive sentence. But this presupposes that the learner already knows many other things—such as which word is the verb, which is the object (as opposed to the subject), and which sentences have basic word order (as opposed to an order affected by considerations of topic and focus). But these things cannot be taken as known when the very first parameters are learned. This makes the learning issues much harder. See Gibson and Wexler (1994) and Fodor (1998c) for discussion of this issue.

depending on the air currents in the room at the time. In this style of representation, it really does take something extra to specify a linear order for X and Y; one would have to solder in an extra piece of metal to prevent them from swinging in the breeze, for example. If mental representations are like Calder mobiles, then it is parsimonious to leave word order unspecified.

Things come out differently in the style of representation produced by word processors. This format automatically imposes an order onto any representation, whether one is desired or not. Even if one tries to type two characters at exactly the same time, the computer will detect tiny differences in timing and produce a strictly ordered representation, with X unambiguously to the right of Y or vice versa. In this representational medium, fixed order comes for free, and additional work is required to overcome it. For example, linguists who want to talk about verb phrases in a way that is neutral between Japanese-like languages and English-like languages have to add an additional tag, like "[$_{VP}$ *eat spinach*], *order irrelevant*," or create some notational convention to this effect. It is intrinsically difficult to leave order unspecified in this medium, so one resorts to explicit disjunctions or the equivalent. If mental representations are like word processors in these respects, then a UG that leaves word order open could be less parsimonious, rather than more.

So the parsimony issue hinges on whether the mental representations of languages are more like Calder mobiles or word processors. Which is the case? I think we must admit that we do not know. We know nothing about the details of how the innate endowment for language is realized that would allow us to make a firm judgment. It is true that the brain is a three-dimensional structure rather than a two-dimensional structure. Maybe this is a relevant similarity to the Calder mobile. But the brain is also known to be full of topographic mappings in (for example) the visual system, where adjacent points on the retina are represented by adjacent sets of neurons of the brain (see Marcus, chapter 2 here). Thus there is reason to think that one- or two-dimensional order is often significant in the neural medium. This could be a relevant similarity to the printed page. In this state of ignorance, we should not be too swayed toward underdeterminism by claims of parsimony.

There is also a detail about word order in languages of the world that suggests that linguistic representations are intrinsically ordered in a way that makes more sense within the overdeterminist picture. Examples (14) and (15) repeat the two versions of the HDP.

(14) Overdeterminist version:

  Combine a word with a phrase to make a larger phrase by putting the new word first *or* by putting the new word last.

(15) Underdeterminist version:

  Combine a word with a phrase to make a larger phrase.

The overdeterminist version includes an explicit disjunction, whereas the underdeterminist version leaves order open, to be fixed by some kind of learning. But notice that there is nothing in (15) that implies that a language learner must settle on a fixed order. The nature of the speech stream implies that each token of a verb phrase that gets uttered must have the verb come before the object or after it. But why couldn't the order vary from verb phrase to verb phrase within a single language? One can imagine a language in which it was possible to say either *Mary ate spinach* or *Mary spinach ate*, depending on one's whim or stylistic considerations. One can also imagine a language in which some verbs are used with verb-object order and others are used with object-verb order, so that one consistently says *Mary ate spinach* but *Mary spinach cooked*. In fact there are no such languages. Order within the verb phrase varies from language to language, but not internally to the same language.[3] This elementary fact is made mysterious by (15). It is not as mysterious in the overdetermined version in (14): one can imagine that the disjunction is really an exclusive *or*, accompanied by some kind of tag saying "learn which." But it makes little sense to append "learn which" to (15), since the options are not explicitly enumerated. This suggests that the human language capacity cares deeply about word order, and order is built into it from the beginning—like a word processor, not a mobile.

An underdeterminist might try to deflect this point by saying that people are such creatures of linguistic habit that they don't tolerate freedom. Even if a grammatical option exists in principle, we always settle into one routine or another in practice. But this is not true in other comparable domains. To see this, consider another feature of the Bantu languages. In all Bantu languages, direct objects ordinarily come after the verb, as in English, not before it, as in Japanese. Example (16) shows this for Chichewa (spoken in Malawi) and Kinande.

(16) a. Njuchi   zi-na-luma   alenje.   (Chichewa)
        Bees   AGR-past-bit   hunters.
        'The bees stung the hunters.' (Not: *Njuchi alenje zi-na-luma*.)

    b. Omukali   a-gula   eritunda.   (Kinande)
       woman   AGR-bought   fruit
       'The woman bought a fruit.' (Not: *Omukali eritunda a-gula*.)

Bantu languages also allow "object dislocation structures," in which the object-noun phrase appears at the edge of the sentence, and a pronoun is attached to the verb. (Colloquial English allows something similar, as in *That dress, I really like it*.) But there is a difference. Chichewa allows the dislocated object to appear either at the beginning of the sentence, or at the end:

(17) a. *Alenje*   njuchi   zi-na-wa-luma   (Chichewa)
        hunters   bees   AGR-past-them-bit.
        'The hunters, the bees stung them.'

---

3. There are languages with free word order, but these languages do not build phrases of the kind assumed by both (14) and (15) at all (Baker, 1996). Languages that allow both *Mary ate spinach* and *Mary spinach ate* also allow *Spinach Mary ate* and *Ate Mary spinach*, in which the object and the verb do not constitute a phrase. A very different parameter is at work in such languages, which I do not consider here.

b. Njuchi   zi-na-wa-lum-a   *alenje*
   Bees   AGR-past-them-bit   hunters.
   'The bees stung them, the hunters.'

In contrast, Kinande only allows the dislocated object to appear at the beginning:

(18) a. Eritunda,   omukali   a-ri-gula.   (Kinande)
        fruit   woman   AGR-it-buy
        The fruit, the woman bought it.

   b. Impossible: *Omukali   a-ri-gul-a   eritunda.
                    woman   AGR-it-buy   fruit
                    The woman bought it, the fruit.

The Chichewa examples in (17) show that humans are not intrinsically adverse to a degree of freedom being left open in language. The underdeterminist thus has no quick and easy answer as to why comparable freedom is not tolerated in the ordinary verb phrase structures formed by (15).

This point can be underscored in another way. The differences between Chichewa and Kinande imply that there is another parameter at work. This parameter can be expressed in overdeterminist fashion as in (19).

(19) The dislocation parameter:

   (a) Dislocated noun phrases appear at the beginning of the clause, *or*

   (b) they appear at either edge of the clause.

Kinande adopts (19a) and Chichewa (19b). Now (19) translates into the underdeterminist idiom roughly as (20).

(20) Dislocated noun phrases appear at the edge of the clause.

But (20) is no different in its basic structure from (15). How could children know that (20) does not need to be restricted down to a particular word order (see Chichewa), whereas (15) must be? Underdeterminists are on the horns of a dilemma. They must choose whether young humans have a general urge to fill out their general innate knowledge into more rigid and specific rules or not. If they do, then the dislocation pattern in Chichewa is mysterious. If they do not, then the fact that no language tolerates free word order inside verb phrases is mysterious. This dilemma does not arise within the overdeterminist view. That view is committed to explicitly spelling out the possible values for each parameter. Therefore, it is not at all surprising that two similar-looking parameters might specify a different range of admissible choices—"beginning" or "end" in one case, and "beginning" or "either" in the other.

5 Is Overdetermination of Language Perplexing?

Finally, consider the third pillar of underdeterminist intuitions: that the existence of a superrich innate endowment for language would be perplexing. To many people influenced by the "blank slate" model of human nature, the idea that the structure of a human language is built into our minds is hard to swallow. Given this predisposition, it is even harder to swallow the idea that the structure of *all* human languages is built in from the beginning. The overdeterminist seems to be saying that the infant knows not only the basic principles of English but also (in a sense) the basic principles of Japanese, Yoruba, Mohawk, Ancient Akkadian, and whatever will be spoken on the lunar colony a thousand years from now. That seems absurd. The mature human actually speaks only one or two languages, not tens of thousands. It seems that there is no purpose to all this extra knowledge in the ultimate scheme of things. Thus it is perplexing to think we have it.

The crucial point to make here is that our perplexity depends on our notions of purpose. The degree to which something is perplexing is in proportion to the degree to which it has complexity that serves no purpose. Therefore, whether we find an overdetermined language faculty perplexing or not depends on what we think the purpose of human language is.

Most people who think in these terms at all take it to be self-evident what the purpose of human language is. It is some variation on the following (see, e.g., Pinker, 1994, pp. 367–9):

(21) The purpose of language is to permit the communication of complex propositional information.

This is accepted almost without argument by a wide range of language specialists. If this is the purpose of language, then I agree that it would be perplexing to find that we have an overdetermined UG. We can, it seems, communicate whatever propositions we want using only one or two languages (contra Nowack et al., 2001), so why make explicit provision for more than that in our minds? There could be no evolutionary advantage to this capacity, given that we make little use of it in our ongoing lives. At best it could be an evolutionary accident of some kind.

But (21) is not set in stone. It could be correct but incomplete, in ways that affect our judgments of perplexity. Suppose, for example, we say that the purpose of human language is (22) instead.

(22) The purpose of language is to permit the communication of complex propositional information *to your collaborators, while concealing the information from possible competitors.*

This is a rather minor variation on (21), falling within the same conceptual scheme.[4] But it renders the existence of many potential linguistic systems unperplexing. Basically, it says that human language has the same purpose as those products of human engineering known as codes and ciphers. To be effective, such systems make explicit provision for variation, indeed for the setting of parameters. For example, the famous German Enigma machines of World War II could produce many different codes, depending on how certain "parameters" were set: which alphabet wheels were chosen, what their initial positions were, and how the crosswiring was done. Perhaps the human capacity to learn languages that superficially look quite different can be understood in the same way.

This idea is made plausible by the fact that natural languages do make very effective ciphers in practice. The most famous example is the use that the United States Marine Corps made of the Navajo code talkers in World War II. Navajo Indians speaking their native language to each other over the radio proved to be more efficient, more effective, and harder to decipher than the most sophisticated products of human engineering at the time.

From this perspective, it might not matter if underdeterminist intuitions turn out to be correct, and it is more costly to represent a language faculty with explicit parameters built in. The extra complexity might be justified by the advantages of having a better code, one that conceals strategic information better. This could be an instance of adaptive complexity, built into the account of the origins of the innate endowment of language from the beginning. Linguistic diversity would then not be an evolutionary accident or a residual imperfection but part of the point of language in the first place.

According to Pinker and Bloom (1990), claims about adaptive complexity gain support if one can point to instances of biology replicating the strategies used by engineering to accomplish some goal. This seems possible in the case at hand. Just as vertebrate eyes are much like cameras, so the human language faculty is structured rather like artificial encryption systems (see, for example, Singh, 1999). This comparison can be pursued at two levels.

At the gross level, every code is factored into two parts: the general encryption algorithm and the specific key. The general algorithm is public information available to all; the key is some crucial piece of secret information that needs to be plugged into the algorithm before the message can be decoded. For example, the algorithm for the Caesar shift cipher (used by Julius Caesar in his campaigns) is to replace every letter in the message with the nth subsequent letter in the alphabet. The secret key is the value for n—how far the alphabet is shifted. Choosing different values makes possible 25 different ciphers, giving the user flexibility for staying ahead of the enemy. Similarly, the RSA cipher, which is the basis

---

4. A more radical version of this critique, brought up from time to time by Chomsky, is to deny that language has a purpose. Not everything in the natural world does have a purpose that explains its structure, after all. Rocks, for example, do not have an intrinsic purpose, even though we use them for a variety of purposes. Language could be like a rock in this respect.

for modern internet security, is based on the algorithm of translating one's message into a huge number using its ASCII code, and then calculating the new number (message)^k (mod n), where n is the product of two large prime numbers. Anyone can know this, but your messages are safe unless someone knows the prime factorization of n, which is the mathematical key for decoding. Since there are an infinite number of primes, there are an infinite number of ciphers in this family. I suggest that the distinction between the invariant principles of UG and the parameter values needed to define a particular language is analogous. The invariant principles are like the general encryption algorithm, which is available to all humans. The parameter settings are like the key; they are kept "secret" within a particular speech community, and can only be revealed to children and others who come into the community by a rather lengthy process of language acquisition.

The comparison between UG and cryptography is also interesting at a more detailed level. If one looks at the kinds of tricks that UG uses to create a diversity of languages, they match up rather well with the ciphers of the sixteenth century. Sixteenth-century espionage used steganography—the art of hiding messages, for example, concealing a letter in the bottom of a barrel. Natural language does something similar by using different distinctive features in different languages. Each language contains certain distinctions between sounds that carry differences in meaning but are virtually undetectable to speakers of other languages; examples include Hindi's difference between aspirated 't' and unaspirated 't', which is inaudible to the English ear, or English's 'r' versus 'l', which is mysterious to a Japanese speaker. Sixteenth-century spies used ciphers that replace the elements of a message letter by letter; similarly, natural languages use different inventories of sounds. Sixteenth-century spies also used codes, which replaced whole words with other words or symbols; natural language uses Saussurean arbitrariness, according to which domestic canines can be indicated with *dog, chien, perro, erhar,* or *ekita*. Sixteenth-century spies used homophones (different symbols that represent the same meaningful unit) and nulls (symbols that represent nothing) to throw off code-breaking by frequency analysis. Similarly, natural languages contain allophonic variation in sounds, synonymous words, idioms, and apparently meaningless words. Sixteenth-century spies removed the spaces between words in coded messages, so it would not be clear where one word stopped and another began; natural languages have rules of sound assimilation that have the same effect. Finally, sixteenth-century spies made use of transposition, scrambling the elements of the message according to some regular procedure that a knowledgeable receiver could undo. Word-order parameters such as the head directionality parameter and the dislocation parameter can be seen as the analog in natural language. Overall, there are enough parallels to make one think that it is not an accident that the innate endowment for language is structured like a code—in which case, the existence of parameters is not perplexing after all.

This comparison between UG and espionage may not in the end be the most accurate one available. I am not wedded to the idea that (22) is the perfect statement of the purpose of language. Other views that attribute a concealing function to language as well as a revealing function would work just as well. For example, it could be that linguistic diversity has the desirable function of making it hard for a valuable member of your group to defect to a rival group, taking his resources and skills with him. He will not be as valuable to another group, because they cannot talk to him.[5] Reversing the scenario, it could be that linguistic diversity has the desirable function of making it hard for a greedy or dangerous outsider to join your group and get access to your resources and skills. You are less vulnerable to manipulation or deception by a would-be exploiter who cannot communicate with you easily. It is not my purpose to choose which of these scenarios is the most promising; I simply want to take away the certainty that (21) is correct, thereby dispelling some of perplexity associated with an overdetermined innate endowment for language.

6 Conclusion

Linguistic practice often makes use of an overdetermined innate endowment, one that explicitly specifies grammatical options from which language learners are invited to choose on the basis of their environment. That the innate endowment should be "superrich" in this way has been considered perplexing and unparsimonious by some researchers. They claim that the innate endowment should underdetermine language instead. In response, I have argued that this kind of underdetermined universal grammar may not be possible—that not all parameter values can be learned reliably by prelinguistic cognitive capacities. Second, I have argued that an underdetermined universal grammar is not necessarily more parsimonious than an overdetermined one; this depends on unknown details of the representation scheme. Third, I have argued that there are plausible purposes for an overdetermined universal grammar: it could make possible a form of communication that conceals information from some even as it reveals it to others. Overall, then, there is no compelling reason, prior to detailed inquiry, to think that the innate endowment must underdetermine the structures of particular human languages. This does not establish the superrich, overdetermined view of the innate endowment for language. But it does mean that if the most successful theories of

---

5. I thank the participants in the AHRB "Innateness and the Structure of the Mind" workshop, 12–14 October 2001, for bringing up this possibility.

Evolutionary psychology is committed to a somewhat stronger position: something can be attributed to the innate endowment only if it would have been beneficial in the context of small bands of hunter-gatherers in the ancestral environment. It is not clear that (22) meets this additional condition. Not being an evolutionary psychologist, I do not consider this crucial to my interests. Even so, it is not obvious to me that linguistic diversity would not have had code talker–like advantages in traditional societies, albeit on a smaller scale. Warfare is an important feature of all such societies; where possible it is directed against other linguistic groups, and its practice depends heavily on cooperation and treachery (see, e.g., Divale, 1973). These are precisely the boundary conditions under which it is plausible that a code-like function for language might have evolved.

People have pointed out to me that multilingualism is extremely widespread in traditional societies, suggesting that natural languages are not very effective codes in practice. This might only mean that the natural code-breakers have gained the advantage on the natural code-makers in a kind of evolutionary arms race at this particular point in human development. (This was also true of cryptography in the sixteenth century; Singh, 1999.)

language typology and syntactic acquisition (continue to) make important use of overdetermination, we should feel free to pursue them, not judging them out of bounds on evolutionary or methodological grounds.

This inquiry into one corner of the innate mind also means that we should be alert to parallel issues in other corners. For other mental modules, too, it might make sense to consider the rarely raised possibility that the innate structure might be more than is necessary to produce a certain result, rather than less. It could be that hypernativism is sometimes the right amount of nativism.

STEPHEN CRAIN, ANDREA GUALMINI, & PAUL PIETROSKI

Brass Tacks in Linguistic Theory
Innate Grammatical Principles

In the normal course of events, children manifest linguistic competence equivalent to that of adults in just a few years. Children can produce and understand novel sentences, they can judge that certain strings of words are true or false, and so on. Yet experience appears to dramatically underdetermine the competence children so rapidly achieve, even given optimistic assumptions about children's nonlinguistic capacities to extract information and form generalizations on the basis of statistical regularities in the input. These considerations underlie various (more specific) poverty of stimulus arguments for the innate specification of linguistic principles. But in our view, certain features of nativist arguments have not yet been fully appreciated. We focus here on three (related) kinds of poverty of stimulus argument, each of which has been supported by the findings of psycholinguistic investigations of child language.

The first argument hinges on the observation that children project beyond their experience in ways that their experience does not suggest. It is untendentious that children project beyond their experience, in the sense of acquiring a state of linguistic competence that they apply to novel constructions. The issue is *how* children project beyond their experience. That is, do children induce (or abduce) in the fashion of good scientists, on the basis of experience characterized in (more or less) observational terms; or do they project in more idiosyncratic and language-specific ways? To what degree is human language acquisition "data driven," and to what degree is it determined by the human genome? Clearly, experience matters. Typical children growing up in Tokyo achieve a state of linguistic competence that differs in some respects from the state achieved by typical children growing up in Topeka. According to the theory of universal grammar (UG), however, the differences between natural human languages—like English and Japanese, which any normal child can learn in the right context—are relatively small as compared with the differences between natural human languages and other logically coherent systems (equally compatible with the experience of human children) for associating signals with meanings. If so, this supports the nativists' contention that children use their experience simply to determine which of the highly constrained natural human languages adults around them speak. Evidence in favor of the nativist perspective comes from experimental studies of child language showing that children's projections do not violate any core principles of universal grammar, even in cases where children might be tempted to violate such principles if they adopted general-purpose learning algorithms.

A second poverty of stimulus argument is based on the kinds of nonadult constructions children produce. Children appear to follow the natural seams (or parameters) of natural language, even when child language diverges from the local adult language. On an experience-dependent approach to language learning, the pattern of children's nonadult linguistic behavior would presumably look quite different from this. From a data-driven perspective, children's nonadult productions would be expected to be simply less "filled out" than those of adults in the same linguistic community. Children's productions would be adult-like, except that they would be missing certain words or word-endings, for example. The UG-based approach, by contrast, is consistent with the continuity assumption, which supposes that child and adult languages can differ only in limited ways—specifically in ways that adult languages can differ from each other. If so, children are expected to project beyond their experience in ways that are attested in natural languages. The nonadult linguistic behavior of children is not expected to match the input (as experience-based approaches to learning suggest); rather, the input is seen to guide children through an innately specified space of hypotheses made available by universal grammar. So children are free to adopt hypotheses that differ from those of local adults, as long as they can later be retracted using positive evidence, until they hit upon a grammar that is sufficiently like that of other speakers of the local language; at that point, language change is no longer initiated by the input (see Crain, 2002; Crain & Pietroski, 2001, 2002; Thornton, 1990).

A third argument is based on the gap—Chomsky (1986) speaks of a chasm—between a typical child's experience and the linguistic principles that govern children's competence. The key observation here is that linguistic principles unify and explain (superficially) disparate phenomena. We focus on this last kind of argument in the most detail, in order to show that children know specific contingent facts that apply to a wide range of constructions across different linguistic communities. Insofar as this aspect of linguistic competence is not plausibly a product of children's experience, it is presumably a product of their biological endowment. This raises further questions about how human biology gives rise to such knowledge. But in our view, these are precisely the questions that need to be asked.

Critics cannot insist that our shared biology cannot give rise to knowledge of specific contingent linguistic facts if the available evidence suggests that our shared biology does just this. The "contingencies" of human language may not be accidental, however. They may reflect deep facts about human biology (or underlying physical constraints on that biology), as it has emerged under various pressures, including, perhaps, evolutionary pressures imposed by the kinds of signals and meanings that primates can employ. One can view certain aspects of Chomsky's "minimalist program" as an invitation for nativists to ask just what aspects of language must be attributed to biology—and to start asking how our shared biology might give rise to universal grammar without supposing that specific linguistic principles are biologically encoded as such; see Chomsky (1995, 2000). Perhaps a perspicuous characterization of what is innate will lead to a hypothesis about how (and why) human biology implements such constraints. But as Marr (1982) argued, one usually needs to know what is implemented before one can fruitfully speculate about implementation.

1 The Form of Linguistic Generalizations

One version of the poverty of stimulus argument proceeds from the following sort of observations. In simple sentences like (1), the reflexive pronoun *himself* is referentially dependent on another term, *Bill*, which appears nearby in the sentence. But in (2a–c), *himself* is anaphorically related to *John*, which is some distance away. This leaves open the possibility that (3a) is ambiguous. But adults know that (3a), like (3b), is unambiguous.

(1)   Bill washed himself.

(2)   a. John said to Bill that he wants to wash himself.

    b. John wants to shave Bill and wash himself.

    c. John said that he thinks he should wash himself.

(3)   a. John said that he thinks Bill should wash himself.

    b. John said that Bill washed himself.

By age two or three, normal children know how reflexive pronouns work. For example, they know that *himself* can*not* be anaphorically dependent on *John* in (3). But how could they infer this "negative" fact, about what (3a) can*not* mean, based on "positive" input? There is no general prohibition against ambiguity in natural language. So why don't children acquire a grammar that is more permissive than the adult grammar, according to which (3a) is ambiguous—in the way that (1) and (2) might suggest to an observer?

One can speculate that, first, children notice that adults (almost?) never use constructions like (3b) while intending *himself* as a device for referring to the person picked out by the distant name, and second, this leads children to infer that (3a) and (3b) are both unambiguous. But learning the rule for reflexive pronouns in this way requires rather substantial cognitive resources, for recognizing adults' intended referents and keeping track of the word strings children encounter and the interpretations that are assigned to those strings. Such an account is possible, but it does not seem very plausible. For one thing, children's specific knowledge about linguistic expressions does not end with reflexive pronouns. They also know how ordinary pronouns work. In *Bill washed him*, the accusative pronoun cannot be referentially dependent on the name; but in *John wants to feed Bill and wash him*, the pronoun can be linked back to *Bill* (but not *John*). So how do children (and adults) know that *John said that he thinks Bill should wash him* cannot be interpreted with the pronoun dependent on *Bill*? To complicate matters, children encounter sentences like *That man over there is him* (say, in response to a question about who John is). Therefore, a child can hardly assume that adults never intend to use *him* as a device for referring to someone picked out by a nearby expression. Linguistic principles, known as the binding theory, determine how pronouns can and cannot be interpreted. This component of UG governs the anaphoric relations among different kinds of noun phrases (e.g., Chomsky, 1981).

In attempting to characterize the knowledge that underlies the judgments in (1)–(3), linguists initially set aside issues about acquisition and its relation to experience, in order to look for a principle that explains a range of linguistic phenomena. In this quest, linguists (unlike children) elicited and considered judgments about what expressions can and cannot mean for adults; they conducted crosslinguistic research; and they looked for a principle that holds across human languages (and thus applies to many particular phenomena). Armed with a hypothesis about the operative linguistic principle, they then asked whether children could plausibly learn the principle that evidently characterizes adult competence. If not, the tentative conclusion is that the principle is not learned but is rather part of universal grammar. Or, more cautiously, the principle is due at least largely to human nature, as opposed to human experience. Such conclusions were bolstered when it was found that children adhered to the principle from an early age, because this compresses the learning problem, making it less plausible that all normal children encounter the data that would be needed on experience-based accounts.

This quick sketch of one poverty of stimulus argument illustrates several key points about such arguments. In particular, the much-discussed "logical problem of language acquisition" is not simply that the competence children achieve is underdetermined by their experience. This would be the case even if children induced linguistic principles from examples. Again, what impresses nativists is not the mere fact that children project beyond their experience but rather the fact that children project beyond their experience in ways that the input does not even suggest. Correlatively, the nativist is not just saying that children are born with a disposition to acquire a language. The nativist is saying that children are born with a disposition to acquire a natural human language; where the distinctive character of these human systems for associating signals with meanings are revealed by investigating what adults know and how that knowledge goes beyond the experience of typical children. Investigations of adult languages have revealed that there are universal grammatical principles, and experimental investigations of child language have found that these principles hold children's hypotheses in check. While universal grammar establishes boundaries on the space of hypotheses children can explore, children are free to explore this space as long as they do not exceed the boundaries. This observation forms the basis of the continuity assumption, to which we now turn.

2   The Continuity Assumption

The innate principles of universal grammar define a space of possible human languages for children to explore, under pressure from experience, until they stabilize on a grammar that is equivalent to that of adults in the same linguistic community. This means that young children are free to "try out" constructions that are unattested in the local language, but only if those constructions are from a possible human language. (If the actual adult languages exhaust the relevant space of possibilities, then young children will only try out constructions attested in some adult language spoken somewhere.) At any given time, children will be speaking a possible human language, just not the language spoken around them. This is the continuity assumption: child languages can differ from the local adult language only in ways that adult languages can differ from each other. According to this assumption, the possible mismatches between child and adult language follow the natural seams (the so-called parameters) of human languages; children are not expected to violate any core principles of universal grammar, since language acquisition is constrained by those principles. If the continuity assumption is correct, one would expect children to exhibit constructions with features of adult languages found elsewhere on the globe, but not in the local language. If this expectation is confirmed, it provides dramatic support for nativists. Given an experience-dependent learning algorithm, one will be hard pressed to explain why children learning English produce constructions exhibited in (say) German, Japanese, or Italian but not in English. Obviously, everyone thinks there are examples of mismatches between child and adult language. But it is worth pausing to be clear about the form of the argument.

Given a data-driven perspective, one would expect children's nonadult linguistic constructions to simply be less articulated than those of adults. A child in the process of learning a (first) human language on the basis of experience would not yet display full linguistic competence in any human language; at best, such a child would have an imperfect grasp of the local language. If this is the position children find themselves in, one would expect them to gradually modify their deviant constructions, in response to environmental input. But where experience provides abundant evidence of statistical regularities, a data-driven learner should be faithful to the patterns in question (and in that sense "match" the input). So it is worth attending to the respects in which children diverge from adults, since attention to the details might reveal something about just how children project beyond their experience.

Several examples of children's nonadult productions support the continuity assumption, as opposed to a data-driven account of language acquisition. A parade case is the medial-Wh phenomenon first reported by Thornton (1990). The finding is that some English-speaking children produce Wh-questions that are attested in many languages but not in English. These children consistently introduce a copy of a bare Wh-phrase in their tensed long-distance Wh-questions, as in (4).

(4) What do you think what that is?

In adult languages that allow such constructions (like Bavarian dialects of German), there is a prohibition against medial Wh-phrases with lexical content, as in (5).

(5) *Which boy do you think which boy that is?

There is also a crosslinguistic prohibition against medial constructions in which the original extraction site (of the Wh-phrase) is inside an infinitival complement clause, as in (6). Accordingly, American children who freely produce questions like (4) refrain from producing questions like (5). And they refrain from producing ones like (6); they use adult-like questions such as (7) instead.

(6) *Who do you want who to play with?

(7) Who do you want to play with?

The fact that American children produce questions like (4), in the absence of evidence for medial constructions in English, is interesting. But the really important fact, from the nativists' perspective, is what such children don't say, as illustrated in (5) and (6). For children appear to be obeying the very constraints that adult speakers of other languages obey. Given a data-driven perspective, it is hard enough to explain why Bavarian children who hear examples like (4) learn that examples like (5) and (6) are impermissible in the local language.[1] But why do some American children achieve a state of (perhaps partial) linguistic competence with this character, which matches (in this respect) the linguistic competence of faraway adults? Such facts are unsurprising, however, given a nativist perspective that includes the continuity assumption. (See Crain & Pietroski, 2002, and Thornton, 2004, for detailed discussions of another example concerning American children whose nonadult use of *why*-questions seems to match the adult Italian use of '*perche*'-questions; see Crain, 2002, for further examples.)

3 Deep Linguistic Principles

One goal of linguistic theory is to find principles that unify disparate linguistic phenomena. And as we have been stressing, the search for unifying principles is based only in part on what people say and the conversational contexts in which they say things. Just as important are facts about linguistic expressions that people don't use, and the meanings they do not assign to expressions they use. Moreover, human languages exhibit patterns at various levels of abstraction from what children hear. In addition to the various "construction patterns" that various languages exhibit—permissible ways of forming questions from declaratives, ways of extending sentences by means of relative clauses, and so on—there are generalizations (often characterized as constraints that hold crosslinguistically) across the patterns that careful observers of a particular language might note. As generalizations gradually emerge in linguistic analysis, therefore, their explanatory power is tested across languages, and against increasingly expanded sets of positive and negative data. Progress is difficult because the space of logically possible

---

1. Moreover, the wh-phrases that children consistently avoid in questions like (5) and (7) are well-formed fragments of the local language; they appear in embedded questions: e.g., "He asked me *which boy that is*." "I know *who to play with*." Therefore, these questions could be formed by the kinds of "cut-and-paste" operations that experience-based approaches invoke to explain how complex constructions are formed by combining simple constructions (e.g., Goldberg, 2003; Tomasello, 2000).

grammatical principles is so immense. For it appears that many linguistic phenomena reflect contingent aspects of human psychology, which in turn may reflect demands imposed by the kinds of signals and meanings that human beings are able to process; and as yet little is known about these demands. Nevertheless, linguists have uncovered grammatical principles with broad empirical coverage and explanatory power.

Child language acquisition proceeds without the benefit of the vast array of (crosslinguistic and negative) data available to linguists, yet every normal three-year-old knows many, perhaps most, of the grammatical principles known by adults. And these principles include nontrivial generalizations that tie together clusters of apparently unrelated linguistic phenomena that are common to languages around the globe—and that turn out, upon close scrutiny, to be interestingly related. In the absence of an alternative account of the relevant generalizations and lacking a learning-theoretic account of how young children come to know them, we find it reasonable to conclude that humans are innately endowed with substantive universal principles of grammar, and that children can only acquire languages that conform to these principles.

There is another view of the relation between linguistic theory and the primary linguistic data available to children. For example, in a recent challenge to nativism, Pullum and Scholz (2002) argue that it is an open question "whether children learn what transformational/generative syntacticians think they learn." On their view, the evidence does not suffice to conclude that children are innately endowed with "specific contingent facts about natural languages." They contend that positive evidence alone could suffice for language learning, which could consist of shallow linguistic representations that are hypothesized and tested using the same kind of domain-general cognitive mechanisms that children use to learn about other (nonlinguistic) things.

We take up this recent challenge to nativism by (re)considering the extent to which linguistic theory needs to postulate abstract grammatical principles that explain "specific contingent facts about natural languages," including abstract principles that lie beyond the grasp of even intricate methods of statistical sampling. We concentrate on three likely candidates for innate linguistic knowledge: (1) the meanings of determiners, (2) the basic interpretation of disjunction, and (3) the structural configurations in which pronouns, negative polarity items, and the disjunction operator must appear, with respect to the linguistic expressions that license them.

3.1 What Determiners Can Mean

One specific contingent fact about natural languages is that determiner meanings are conservative (Barwise & Cooper, 1981). Determiners (Det) are quantificational words (or phrases)—like *every, no, some, most, both, three, seventeen, more than 9 but fewer than 20*—that can combine with a noun (or noun phrase [NP]) to form a grammatical unit, like *every boy*, which can in turn combine with a verb (or verb-phrase [VP]) to form a sentence, like *Every boy swam*.[2] In this respect, a determiner is like a transitive

---

2. This is not to say that every expression that combines with a noun to form a grammatical unit is a determiner. Determiners have other properties, like not combining with verbs to form grammatical units.

verb, which combines with an "internal" argument to form a grammatical unit, which in turn combines with an "external" argument to form a sentence; though in the linear order of words, the external argument of a transitive verb comes first, while the external argument of a determiner comes last. There are various ways of characterizing the relevant semantic property of determiners. But let's say (for simplicity) that noun phrases and verb-phrases are semantically associated with sets of individuals, that a determiner expresses a binary relation between sets, and that such a relation is conservative iff: the internal set s bears relation R to the external set s' iff s bears R to s ∩ s'. Then the (perhaps improper) subset relation is conservative, since: s ⊆ s' iff s ⊆ (s ∩ s').

Consider again the example *Every boy swam*. Since the determiner *every* is conservative, the boys form a subset of the swimmers iff the boys form a subset of the boys who swam. But the converse relation of inclusion is not conservative, since it is false that: s ⊇ s' iff s ⊇ (s ∩ s'). It isn't a true biconditional that the boys include the swimmers iff the boys include the boys who swam. Trivially, the boys include the boys who swam; but it doesn't follow from this trivial truth that the boys include the swimmers. Intuitively, every F is G is true iff the Fs form a subset of the Gs. So, unsurprisingly, the following biconditional is sure to be true: every boy swam iff every boy is a boy who swam. Likewise, most boys swam iff most boys are boys who swam, and no boy swam iff no boys are boys who swam. Indeed, every natural language biconditional of this form is sure to be true: [(Det NP)(VP)] iff [(Det NP)(NP who VP)].

This is, upon reflection, a striking fact. No natural language determiner expresses the converse relation of inclusion.[3] Likewise, no natural language determiner expresses the relation of equinumerosity. But one can imagine a language in which *Equi boys swam* means that the boys are equinumerous with the swimmers. And in this language, the following biconditional would be false: Equi boys swam iff equi boys are boys who swam. (If every boy swam, then equi boys are boys who swam; but it doesn't follow that the boys are equinumerous with the swimmers.) This demonstrates that it is a contingent generalization that [(Det NP)(VP)] iff [(Det NP)(NP who VP)]. Of course, given what *every* means, it is a logical truth that every boy swam iff every boy is a boy who swam; and similarly for each natural language determiner. But it hardly follows that "logic alone" determines that determiners (individuated syntactically, as expressions with a certain *form*) have the precise semantic character that they do have, as a matter of fact. There are many (simple) nonconservative relations of the same logical type as actual determiner meanings, and there is no *logical* reason why determiners cannot indicate such relations (see e.g., Chierchia & McConnell-Ginet, 2000).

To underscore the point, it has been proposed that *Every boy is riding an elephant* is true — on a reading available to children (but not adults) — only if (1) every boy is riding an elephant *and* (2) every elephant is ridden by a boy (e.g., Drozd &

---

3. There is a sense in which *Only boys swam* captures the converse of *Every boy swam*. But *only*, which can combine with just about anything, is not a determiner. Compare *He only seems nice* with *He every/no/three seems nice* (see Herburger, 2000, for further discussion and defense). Notice also that *only* does not comply with the biconditional associated with conservativity. *Only boys are boys who dance* does not entail that only boys dance, since *Only boys are boys who dance* is a tautology, whereas *Only boys dance* is not.

van Loosbroek, 1998; Philip, 1995). If so, then children assign a nonconservative interpretation to the determiner *every*; in effect, the hypothesis is that children interpret *every* as though it meant what *equi* means in the imagined language (that no human adults speak). But if nonconservative determiner meanings are possible for children, and thus *not* ruled out by universal grammar, then one needs some other explanation for the absence of nonconservative determiner meanings in adult languages. If human children can operate with a determiner that expresses equinumerosity, why don't adult languages contain such a determiner? If the human language system is compatible with some nonconservative determiners, shouldn't we expect to find the semantic converse of *every* in some adult languages? In short, there is a nonlogical "conservativity generalization" for adult languages. And if this generalization is not a reflection of universal grammar, it is hard to see what it is a reflection of. It would seem apparent then that there is a significant theoretical cost to hypothesizing that children assign nonconservative interpretations to determiners. (See sec. 4.1).

3.2 Disjunction Is Inclusive-or

We claim that a second contingent fact, known by speakers of natural language, is that natural language disjunction is inclusive-*or* (as in classical logic); see Horn (1989) for references to researchers who argue that natural language disjunction is exclusive-*or*. Let the ampersand and wedge have their usual meanings, so that *P* & *Q* is true iff both *P* and *Q* are true, while *P* v *Q* is false iff both *P* and *Q* are false; and let's say that *P* X-or *Q* is true iff (*P* v *Q*) & not(*P* & *Q*), with X-*or* thus corresponding to exclusive disjunction. Then we endorse the view that the English word *or* corresponds semantically to v, as opposed to X-*or*; pragmatics is responsible for appearances to the contrary in examples like *You can have cake or (you can have) ice cream* (see Chierchia & McConnell-Ginet, 2000; Grice, 1975). One can certainly imagine a language with a sentential connective that sounds like *or* but corresponds semantically to X-*or*. Indeed, from a data-driven perspective, one might well expect children to conclude (at least for a while) that English is such a language. For the vast majority of children's experience suggests that *or* is used to indicate exclusive disjunction. Nonetheless, children as young as two appear to know that *or*-statements have a basically inclusive meaning. If this is correct, it ends up providing a double argument for nativism. For not only does it suggest that children essentially ignore the abundant evidence suggesting that *or* expresses exclusive disjunction, it raises the question of how children determine the relevant pragmatic implicatures in the right situations. And, as we shall show, the details suggest that children are (without learning) sensitive to quite subtle grammatical properties of sentences.

It is an obvious—but upon reflection, theoretically interesting—fact that English *or*-statements conform to DeMorgan's law for (classical inclusive) disjunction. It is a logical truth that not(*P* v *Q*) iff (not-*P* & not-*Q*); whereas it isn't a logical truth that not(*P* X-or *Q*) iff (not-*P* & not-*Q*). More specifically, not(*P* v *Q*) entails (not-*P* & not-*Q*), while not(*P* X-or *Q*) does not entail (not-*P* & not-*Q*). And in English, *You shouldn't kick the dog or pull his tail* pretty clearly entails that you shouldn't kick the

184 *Language and Concepts*

dog *and* you shouldn't pull his tail. Likewise, *Luisa doesn't want beans or rice* entails that Luisa doesn't want beans *and* doesn't want rice.[4] One can imagine languages in which the disjunction operator has the different semantic character of *X-or*: In such languages, the sentence that sounds just like *You shouldn't kick the dog or pull his tail* would be understood as an instruction to refrain from doing just one or the other (but it's okay to kick the dog and pull his tail).[5] No natural human language works like this. And it is a striking fact that children evidently "know" this at a remarkably early age. That is, without instruction and in apparent disregard for any evidence suggesting that English *or* is exclusive, children interpret negated *or*-statements as having conjunctive entailments.

Notice that even if young children have a tacit grasp of DeMorgan's law, in the sense of knowing (innately?) that not($P \vee Q$) entails (not-P & not-Q), this does not yet explain what they know about English *or*-statements. For any such "logical" knowledge would have to be combined with a conjecture about how children learn *which* logical operator the natural language expression *or* is associated with, that is, inclusive or exclusive disjunction. Of course, if inclusive disjunction is the only available candidate for the meaning of *or*, then children's immediate grasp of DeMorgan's law might suffice to explain how they interpret negated disjunctions. But if there is just one available candidate for the meaning of *or*, there is no learning to be done, which is hardly an embarrassment for nativists (though interesting facts about pragmatic implicatures remain). But it turns out that children know much more about how *or* contributes to the meanings of complex expressions: the DeMorgan facts are just the tip of an iceberg, and the relevant generalization concerning what children know about the extended class of statements with disjunction appears to track other logically contingent features of natural language, such as the linguistic environments that permit negative polarity items, and constraints on the anaphoric relations of different kinds of noun phrases. Taken together, these features form the basis for abstract generalizations that children apparently know as early as they can be tested. We now describe these other features of the abstract generalizations.

3.3 *Downward Entailment*

We said that the DeMorgan facts are just the tip of an iceberg. To expose more of it, notice that in English, disjunctive claims have conjunctive entailments in many contexts that (at least from the observable surface) do not appear to involve negation. Consider (8)–(10).

---

4. A related point is that the following biconditional is sure to be true: P or Q iff [(P or Q) or Q]. But this wouldn't be so if *or* expressed exclusive disjunction. And note, reminiscent of conservativity, that the following biconditionals are also sure to be true: P and Q iff [(P and Q) and Q]; P if Q iff [(P if Q) if Q].

5. The discussion presupposes that disjunction appears in the scope of negation, as suggested by the brackets in the logical notation. We discuss later how the logical notion of scope is related to structural properties of natural language sentences.

(8) Chris goes to the gym before linguists or philosophers arrive.

(9) Every linguist or philosopher admires Chomsky.

(10) If a linguist or philosopher arrives, Chris leaves.

If (8) is true, Chris goes to the gym before the linguists arrive *and* Chris goes to the gym before the philosophers arrive; similarly for (9) and (10). By contrast, (11)–(13) do not have conjunctive entailments.

(11) Chris goes to the gym after linguists or philosophers arrive.

(12) Every linguist admires Chomsky or Fodor.

(13) If Chris arrives, a linguist or philosopher leaves.

A comparison of (8) and (11) shows that linguistic expressions with clearly related meanings (*before* v. *after*) have divergent semantic properties. The contrast between (9) and (12) is even more striking. A disjunctive internal (NP) argument of the determiner *every* creates a conjunctive entailment, as in (9); while a disjunctive external (VP) argument, as in (12), does not create a conjunctive entailment. On the contrary, an utterance of (12) is naturally heard as conveying the pragmatic (and thus defeasible) implicature—that it's false that every linguist admires Chomsky *and* Fodor. Similarly, disjunction in the antecedent clause of a conditional statement creates a conjunctive entailment, as in (10), but disjunction in the consequent clause does not; (13) is naturally understood as implicating that at least sometimes when Chris arrives, it's false that both a linguist and a philosopher leave. We return to this point presently. For now, it suffices to note that disjunctive claims have conjunctive entailments in some but not all grammatical contexts, and that mere knowledge of DeMorgan's law does not provide knowledge of which contexts do and which do not have conjunctive entailments.

There is, however, a generalization here. Negated contexts are a special case of downward-entailing contexts, which can be characterized as contexts that license inferences from claims about things to claims about subsets of those things. For example, if Noam didn't buy a car, it follows that he didn't buy an Italian car.[6] Using this diagnostic of downward-entailing contexts, we see that the contexts in (8)–(10), where *or* had conjunctive entailments, were also downward-entailing (DE) contexts. This is illustrated in (14)–(16).

(14) a. Chris sang before the linguists danced.

b. Chris sang before the tall linguists danced.

---

6. Without negation, the entailment goes the other way: if Noam bought an Italian car, he bought a car.

(15) a. Every linguist admires Chomsky.

b. Every tall linguist admires Chomsky.

(16) a. If a linguist arrives, Chris leaves.

b. If a tall linguist arrives, Chris leaves.

In each case, the first claim entails the second. By contrast, *or* is not in a DE context in (11)–(13). For example, if every linguist is a singer, it doesn't follow that every linguist is a tall singer.

If young children apparently know these facts, then this would bolster the hypothesis that children know that English *or* is inclusive. For suppose that every linguist exclusive-*or* (X-*or*) philosopher admires Chomsky; that is, every individual *z* such that *z* is a linguist X-*or z* is a philosopher is an individual who admires Chomsky. It doesn't yet follow that every linguist admires Chomsky. Perhaps someone who is both a linguist and a philosopher doesn't admire Chomsky. (It's unlikely, but possible.) That is, exclusive disjunction doesn't create a conjunctive entailment in the first (NP) of the universal quantifier. Likewise, suppose Chris arrived before every individual *z* such that *z* is tall X-*or z* is a singer. It doesn't follow that Chris arrived before every *z* such that *z* is tall. The exclusive disjunctive claim leaves open the possibility that tall singers arrived before Chris. One can imagine a language in which this is how the entailments work for sentences with a connective that sounds like *or*. But English isn't such a language, and young children evidently know this—again, despite evidence suggesting otherwise.

Of course, given that English *or* is inclusive and that the first argument of *every* is a DE context, it follows that sentence (3) has the relevant conjunctive entailment. But it isn't a matter of logic that English *or* is inclusive. Neither is it a matter of logic that the first argument of the determiner pronounced *every* is a DE context, any more than it is a matter of logic that this determiner has a conservative meaning. Once the child knows that the word pronounced *every* is a determiner—a kind of second-order predicate (satisfying certain semantic restrictions) that takes an internal and an external argument—associated with the subset relation, the child is in a position to know that *Every boy swam* is true iff the boys form a subset of the swimmers (and that *Every tall boy swam* is true iff the tall boys form a subset of the swimmers). It doesn't take much more to know that the internal argument of *every* is a DE context. For if s $\subseteq$ s', and s'' $\subseteq$ s, then s'' $\subseteq$ s'. But the question is how the child comes to have all this knowledge about *every* (and what it means), and similarly for all the other expressions that create DE contexts.[7]

If the only linguistic generalizations concerning DE contexts concerned patterns of entailment, the point would be of interest but not yet a clear argument for linguistic nativism (as opposed to a version of empiricism that allows for innate logical concepts

---

7. A further complication is the overlap in meaning between *every* and other expressions, e.g., *lots of*. Whenever every boy swam, presumably lots of boys swam. But *lots of* is not DE: *Lots of boys swam* does not entail that lots of tall boys swam.

and some corresponding innate knowledge of logic). But, as we have already noted and now want to stress, adults and children know that *or*-statements have exclusive pragmatic implications in non-DE contexts. In such contexts, the use of *or* implies "not both" but does not entail it. To take an example, the truth-conditional content of a sentence with *or*, such as (17a), is taken to be that in (17b). That is, (17a) is true in a variety of different situations, including ones in which Geraldo is drinking and driving. However, disjunction triggers an implicature in ordinary contexts, such that sentence (17a) implicates (17c). Intuitively, the implicature stems from the fact that if a speaker uses *or* to describe a situation, then she does not plausibly intend *and*. If this were the intended interpretation, then a more cooperative description of the situation is a sentence like (17d), where *or* is replaced by *and*.

(17) a. Geraldo is drinking or driving.

b. drinking(g) ∨ driving(g)

c. ¬ [drinking(g) ∧ driving(g)]

d. Geraldo is drinking and driving.

This is, in effect, to treat *or*-statements in ordinary contexts as having a "secondary meaning" corresponding to X-*or*, but one that can also be characterized in terms of inclusive-*or*, negation, and conjunction: (P ∨ Q) & not(P & Q). But the reverse is also imaginable. That is, one can imagine a language in which the sentential connective pronounced *or* expresses exclusive disjunction as its "basic meaning" and *or*-statements in DE contexts have a secondary meaning characterized as follows: not(not-P & not-Q). The negation of this secondary meaning would be: not-P & not-Q. So a speaker of such a language would know that *Don't kick the dog or pull his tail* does not semantically entail that (just) kicking the dog is disallowed but that an utterance of this sentence pragmatically implicates that both actions are disallowed. This isn't how English works.[8] But how do children come to know this at an early age?

3.4 Negative Polarity Items

Another much-discussed phenomenon is that so-called negative polarity items (NPIs)—expressions like *ever*, as in *I wouldn't ever lie to* you—are licensed in DE contexts. For example, *ever* can appear in the first (NP) but not the second (VP) argument of *every* as indicated in (18)–(19).

---

8. Pragmatic implications are cancelable. One can say *He sang or danced, and he may have done both*. And there are pragmatic contexts that suspend implicatures. If you bet that Chris will sing or dance, you win if Chris does both; and if you promise to sing or dance, and do both, you keep your word. But it is a contradiction to say *He didn't kick the dog or pull his tail, but he may have done both*. Likewise, if the sign says *No parking or loitering*, you can't beat the ticket by saying that you parked and loitered: laws depend on primary meanings and not pragmatic implicatures.

(18) Every linguist who ever met Chomsky admires him.

(19) *Every linguist ever met Chomsky.

By contrast, *ever* can appear in both arguments of *no* and in neither argument of *some*, as indicated in (20)–(23).

(20) No linguist who ever met Chomsky admires him.

(21) No linguist ever met Chomsky.

(22) *Some linguist who ever met Chomsky admires him.

(23) *Some linguist ever met Chomsky.

And both arguments of *no* are DE contexts, while neither argument of *some* is a DE context. (If no linguist sang, then it follows that no tall linguist sang well. But if some linguist sang, it doesn't follow that some tall linguist sang; nor does it follow that some linguist sang well.)

Again, it may be that, given what negative polarity items mean, there is something semantically amiss with using them in non-DE contexts; though while there is something amiss with overt contradictions like *He is both tall and not tall*, they don't "sound bad" in the same way that (19), (22), and (23) do.[9] But even if knowing what negative polarity items and determiners mean would somehow determine which argument positions license such items (and similarly for other DE contexts), this just highlights the striking fact that children know what words like *any* and *ever* mean. And it's not enough to just say, for each expression in the "logical" vocabulary, that a child will know the relevant inferences once the child knows what the expression means. On the assumption that lexical meanings (together with some composition rules) determine entailment relations, knowledge of meaning (and perhaps a little logic) will presumably suffice for knowledge of entailment relations. But for just this reason, one wants to know how knowledge of meaning is achieved. And if there are (logically contingent) generalizations across the meanings of natural language expressions, that calls for explanation.

From a data-driven perspective, this poses the perhaps unanswerable question of how children learn all the (perhaps lexical) semantic facts in question on the basis of experience. Our view is rather that children effectively assume that natural languages contain determiners (all of which are conservative), that some argument positions of determiners create DE contexts, and that such contexts are grammatically significant. From this perspective, the child's task is "simply" to figure out which

---

9. And see Ludlow (2002) for an argument that negative polarity licensing should be explained in structural/grammatical terms.

adult words are determiners, and which sounds go with which of the determiner meanings countenanced by universal grammar. As we noted earlier, such nativist conclusions raise (hard) questions about how human biology could give rise to a universal grammar with this particular character. But in our view, these are the questions linguists are stuck with. At this point, it's no good insisting that some (yet to be specified) learning account will reveal that what we regard as "assumptions" are really "conclusions" based on experience. For our point is not that blaming unknown biological mechanisms is somehow better than blaming unknown learning mechanisms. It is rather that the available evidence strongly suggests that child experience is just too thin to be the basis for the logically contingent features of natural languages. Like it or not, detailed study reveals that human linguistic competence has a distinctive character that is not due to the environment in which it develops. (In this respect, human linguistic competence is like every other biologically based capacity that has been studied.)

Still, it is a persistent idea that knowledge—and in particular, knowledge of language—is the product of experience and a little logic. So we want to mention a third range of facts known by children that runs across the other phenomena we have been discussing—and cuts across them in a logically contingent way.

3.5 The Structural Property of C-Command

The facts under consideration are governed by the structural notion of c-command, which plays a central role in linguistic theory. If we think of phrase markers as trees (in the mathematical sense) with nodes (partially) ordered so that one can speak of the "ancestors" of any given node (except the root), we can provide a simple characterization of c-command: one node c-commands another if the immediate ancestor of the first is an ancestor of the second.[10] In the following tree, node 2 c-commands each of 3–7; node 3 c-commands 2; node 4 c-commands 5–7; and so on.

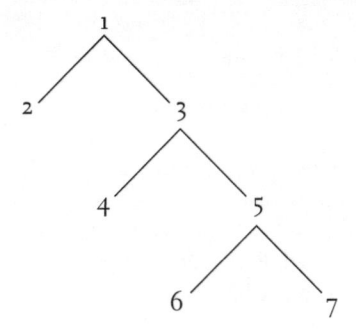

---

10. There may be empirical reasons for introducing slightly different definitions. But this one will do for present purposes.

This structural notion figures in the description and explanation of many phenomena. For example, the negative adverb *never* creates a DE context, which licenses the negative polarity item *any*, as in (24).[11]

(24) The man who laughed never expected to find any dogs at the party.

But what is the extent of the DE context created? As (25) illustrates, it is nothing so simple as the string of words that follow the adverb.

(25) *The man who never laughed expected to find any dogs at the party.

Rather, the negative polarity item must be c-commanded by *never*. In (24), *never* c-commands *to find any dogs at the party*; in (25), *never* c-commands only the verb *laughed* (see Fromkin et al., 2000, ch. 4).[12] It is customary to describe this fact, known by children, by saying that the "scope" of a licenser is the expression it c-commands. In our view, this importation of logical terminology is appropriate. The expression c-commanded by *never*, in each sentence, is relevantly like the expression surrounded by brackets in a formal language with expressions of the form *never* [...]. But this analogy—or if you like, the fact that the logical notion of scope is implemented in natural language by the structural notion of c-command (see Hornstein, 1984)—hardly shows that the natural language generalization (NPIs must be c-commanded by a suitable licenser) is not logically contingent.

One could try to formulate a more shallow generalization, not based on c-command, but in terms of linear order. One possibility, similar in kind to representations that Pullum and Scholz (2002) seem to endorse, would be something along the lines of (26), where (26a) illustrates a construction type in which *some*, but not *any*, are permitted; by contrast, (26b) is a construction type in which both *some* and *any* are permitted.

(26) a. ...never+V+V+NP+P+some

b. ...V+never+NP+P+some/any

Of course, one is left to wonder how children know to keep records of this sort, as opposed to others. It seems implausible, to say the least, that children are recording everything they hear and searching for every possible pattern. But even setting such issues aside, the proposal that c-command is the relevant structural relationship for the licensing of NPIs has much to recommend it, as opposed to the

---

11. We restrict attention, in this discussion, to *any* on its "true universal" as opposed to "free choice" uses of *any* (see, e.g., Horn, 2000; Kadmon & Landman, 1993; Ladusaw, 1996).
12. While some linguists seem to use the licensing of NPIs as a diagnostic of c-command, its precise definition and the level of representation at which it applies (d-structure, s-structure, LF, semantic representation) is the subject of considerable debate (see, e.g., the essays in Horn & Kato, 2000).

construction-type approach advocated by Pullum and Scholz. For the c-command account has independent support from other linguistic constructions. We will mention two.

A structural constraint, based on c-command, is operative in the interpretation of disjunction. To illustrate, because the negative adverb *never* does not c-command disjunction in (27a), an exclusive-*or* reading is available, on which the girl under consideration may have received just one thing—a coin or a jewel. By contrast, the conjunctive interpretation of disjunction is enforced in (27b) because the negative adverb *never* c-commands disjunction—the girl did not receive a coin, and she did not receive a jewel.

(27) a. The girl who never went to sleep received a coin or a jewel.

b. The girl who stayed awake never received a coin or a jewel.

Continuing in the same vein, the same structural notion that determines the extent of DE contexts is also germane to the interpretation of pronouns. To take a familiar kind of example, in (28), the pronoun cannot be referentially dependent on the referring expression *The Ninja Turtle*; whereas this relationship is possible in (29). And in (30), the reflexive pronoun *himself* must be referentially dependent on *the father of the Ninja Turtle* (but not *Grover* or *the Ninja Turtle*)

(28) He said the Ninja Turtle has the best smile.

(29) As he was leaving, the Ninja Turtle smiled.

(30) Grover said the father of the Ninja Turtle fed himself.

One standard explanation for the prohibition against referential dependence in (28) is that a pronoun cannot be referentially dependent on a referring expression that it c-commands. In (29), the pronoun does not c-command *the Ninja Turtle*, so anaphoric relations are permitted. In addition, reflexive pronouns must be referentially dependent on a "local" antecedent that c-commands it, as (30) illustrates.

3.6 Summary

Evidence from experimental investigations of child language suggests that young children grasp the distributional facts about NPI licensing, the interpretive facts about disjunction, and the interpretive facts about pronouns, as soon as they can be tested, that is, by age two or three. And this calls for explanation, presumably in terms of some biologically imposed constraint on the space of alternatives children consider in the course of acquiring a natural language. Even if children were meticulous record-keepers, there is no reason we can think of to suppose that, on a learning-theoretic account, children would notice that the very same linguistic environments require the conjunctive interpretation of disjunction. On the other hand, if these phenomena follow from syntactic and semantic principles that children have under their belts from the earliest stages of language development, then there should be no stage at which children know that some linguistic expression permits *any* but does not also require the conjunctive interpretation of disjunction. Similarly, they should know that c-command constrains these phenomena, as well as the anaphoric relations among different kinds of noun phrases. In the absence of an account of how children attain the specific linguistic knowledge underlying these different phenomena, we are left to infer that innate syntactic and semantic principles guide children as they navigate through their linguistic experience to discover where NPIs are permitted, and where to interpret disjunction as inclusive-*or*, and where to tolerate an exclusive-*or* reading, and where to tolerate coreference.

As we noted earlier, logic alone does not dictate that scope is implemented by c-command in natural language. But there may be opponents of linguistic nativism who would not object to the hypothesis that human minds do indeed implement structural hierarchies in terms of trees (nodes and ancestors), with the result that c-command is a "natural" implementation of the logician's notion of scope. One might even speculate that this is due to the fact that the language system interfaces (somehow) with a general system of inferencing, for which the notion of scope is important. But even if this is correct, one wants to know why children treat the relation of negative polarity items to their licensers as relevantly like the relation of a variable to the quantifier that binds it. Why should children view the relation of a negative polarity item to its licenser as an instance of scope, understood as a logical notion, if the relevant notion of scope comes from (innate) knowledge of how variables are related to quantifiers? One can speculate that the NPI/licenser relation is relevantly like the variable-quantifier relation. But if this speculation is correct, it just raises another poverty of stimulus challenge: how do children come to understand negative polarity constructions as instances of variable-binding, given their limited experience?[13]

Extending the argument, one also wants to know why children treat the relation of a pronoun to its antecedent as relevantly similar to variable-quantifier and NPI/licenser relations. This question remains, even if we assume that (because of simplicity, or some such constraint) children would not introduce a second notion of scope without severe experiential pressure. To repeat an earlier example, children know that in (30) *the Ninja Turtle* cannot be the antecedent of *himself*.

(30)   Grover said that the father of the Ninja Turtle fed himself.

One can describe this fact by saying that the pronoun is not in the scope of *the Ninja Turtle*, with scope implemented as c-command. But how does the child know that scope is what matters here? Many theorists have held that the pronoun/

---

13. And one should not discount the possibility, which we won't explore here, that the logician's notion of scope is a theoretical extension of c-command, a notion we implicitly grasp prior to any knowledge of logic. If this is correct, then viewing c-command as a natural-language implementation of scope gets things backward.

antecedent is indeed relevantly like the variable/quantifier relation; and while the jury is still out on the details, we have no doubt that some version of this suggestion will prove correct. But we see no reason for thinking that children abstract the relevant generalization from their experience. Rather, it seems that independently of experience, children are disposed to treat variable/quantifier, pronoun/ antecedent, and NPI/licenser relations as instances of linguistic relations governed by c-command. One wants to know the source of this disposition. What is it about the human language system that leads children to group together phenomena whose surface manifestations do not suggest an underlying unity? In our view, this is the question to ask. (And one does not answer it by stipulating that the various relations are all instances of "scope.") The unity does not seem to be a by-product of generalizing, in some language-independent way, from a typical child's experience. It is rather a by-product of the mental system, whose contours remain largely shrouded, that makes it possible for humans to associate signals with meanings in the distinctive way that comes naturally to human children.

4 Children's Emerging Linguistic Competence

This section summarizes some of the recent research relevant to this discussion of how children attain mastery of linguistic knowledge in the absence of decisive evidence in the input. Except where noted, the findings we report were gathered over the past few years in interviews with three- to six-year-old children at the Center for Young Children at the University of Maryland. (This research was conducted in collaboration with Luisa Meroni, Amanda Gardner, and Beth Rabbin.)

4.1 Constraints on Pronominal Reference

Children's knowledge of constraints of pronominal reference have been studied extensively for the past 20 years. For discussion of individual principles, see Crain and McKee (1985), and Crain and Thornton (1998) (for principle C); Thornton and Wexler (1999) (for principle B), and Chien and Wexler (1990) (for principle A).

4.2 The Universal Quantifier: Past Mistakes

Different investigations of sentences with the universal quantifier *every* have led to qualitatively different conclusions about children's linguistic knowledge. One line of research has uncovered systematic nonadult responses by even school-age children (e.g., Drozd & van Loosbroek, 1998; Philip, 1995). In certain experimental conditions, for example, young children sometimes reject (31) as an accurate description of a picture in which every boy is riding a donkey if there is an "extra" donkey, that is, one that is not ridden by a boy. For adults, the sentence is true despite the "extra" donkey. When these children are asked to explain why they reject (31), they often point to the "extra" donkey as the reason. It is as if these children think the question is asking about the symmetry between boys and donkeys. This response is therefore referred to as the symmetrical response.

(31) Every boy is riding a donkey.

Research that evoked the symmetrical response from (some) children typically used pictures, and perhaps brief verbal comments about what was depicted in them. Using a different experimental technique, the truth-value judgment task, Crain et al. (1996) found that children consistently produced adult-like affirmative responses to sentences like (31). In a truth-value judgment task, one experimenter acts out a short story in front of the child and a puppet, using props and toys. The story constitutes the context against which the child judges the target sentences. Following a story, the target sentence is uttered by the puppet, which is manipulated by a second experimenter (Crain & Thornton, 1998).

The Crain et al. study also adopted a specific feature of research design, which they call the condition of plausible dissent. This condition involved the introduction of another animal in the context for (31), for example, an elephant—in addition to the "extra" donkey (see Crain et al., 1996; Freeman et al., 1982). It was made clear to children that the boys could have ridden the elephant, though in the end they all decided to ride donkeys. There is considerable independent evidence that providing a different possible outcome in the experimental context significantly reduces children's uncertainty about the question being asked of them; this feature of the design satisfies the felicity conditions associated with tasks that require a decision about whether a sentence matches the context or not (see Guasti & Chierchia, 2000). The intuition is that it is felicitous to ask if every boy is riding a donkey in situations in which the outcome is in doubt at some point in the story. Since the symmetrical response failed to emerge in the truth-value judgment task, Crain et al. suggest that children's nonadult behavior in previous research may have been due to the failure of researchers to satisfy the felicity conditions associated with the target sentences, in particular the condition of plausible dissent. This rescues the claim that the meaning of the determiner *every* is conservative.

4.3 Downward Entailment in Child Language

Previous research has shown that children as young as four have mastered one of the linguistic phenomena associated with downward-entailing linguistic expressions, namely, the licensing of the negative polarity item *any* (O'Leary & Crain, 1994). In a recent study, we tried to find out, further, if children know another property of downward-entailing linguistic expressions—that they license the conjunctive entailments. The construction we used was negation, and the experimental technique of choice was the truth-value judgment task. On one trial, a story was acted out about some pirates who were looking for treasure in an Indian camp, where a jewel and a golden necklace were hidden. At the end of the story, none of the pirates had found the jewel, but one pirate had found the golden necklace. Children were then asked to judge the truth or falsity of Kermit the Frog's assertion in (32).

(32) None of the pirates found the necklace or the jewel.

(33) a. None of the pirates found the necklace *and* none of the pirates found the jewel.
   b. None of the pirates found the necklace *or* none of the pirates found the jewel.

Children who know that negation gives rise to conjunctive entailments for statements with disjunction should interpret (32) as (33a). Therefore, they should reject (32) in the context under consideration. By contrast, children who lack such knowledge could interpret (32) as equivalent to (33b), and could accept it (since it is true that none of the pirates found the jewel). The finding was that children consistently rejected the test sentences.

4.4 An Asymmetrical Universal Quantifier

As we indicated in section 4.1, previous researchers have reached the conclusion that children and adults assign different semantic representations to sentences with the universal quantifier *every* (Drozd & van Loosbroek, 1998; Philip, 1995). A common assumption in these accounts is that children fail to distinguish between the internal argument (NP) and the external argument (VP) of the determiner *every*. We conducted a study to determine if children know one semantic property that distinguishes between these arguments, the interpretation of disjunction. As we discussed, the truth conditions associated with exclusive-*or* are available in the external argument of *every*, but disjunction has conjunctive entailments in the internal argument. We used the truth-value judgment task to investigate children's interpretation of disjunction in the internal and in the external arguments of the determiner *every*. In one study, two groups of three- to six-year-old children were interviewed in the different conditions illustrated in (34)–(35). To satisfy the felicity conditions for (34), there was a Smurf who did not choose an apple or a jewel in the situation, but every Smurf who did choose an apple or a banana received a jewel, making the sentence true on the conjunctive interpretation of disjunction. There was also an "extra" jewel in the context. In the situation for (35), there was a character in addition to the Smurfs, and there was a highly salient "extra" apple and an "extra" banana. In the story corresponding to (35), every Smurf chose both an apple and a banana; this makes (35) true, but infelicitous, due to the implicature of exclusivity that is associated with disjunction in non-downward-entailing linguistic contexts, such as the external argument of the determiner *every*.

(34) Every Smurf who chose an apple or a banana got a jewel.

(35) Every Smurf chose an apple or a banana.

The group of child subjects who heard sentences like (34) accepted them over 90 percent of the time. The second group of children, who heard sentences like (35), accepted them only half of the time; and, in rejecting them, these children pointed out the improper use of disjunction (i.e., they indicated that "and" should have been used). No children pointed to the extra apple or banana.

Two previous studies assessed the truth conditions children associate with the internal and external arguments of the universal quantifier. One assessed children's knowledge that the truth conditions associated with exclusive-*or* are available in the external argument of *every*, as in (36), and a second study assessed children's knowledge that disjunction has conjunctive entailments in the internal argument of *every*, as in (37).

(36) Every lady bought an egg *or* a banana.

(37) Every lady who bought an egg *or* a banana got a basket.

The first of these studies was by Boster and Crain (1994), who showed that children correctly accept the exclusive-or interpretation of disjunction in the external argument of the determiner *every*, as in (36). The second study, by Gualmini, Meroni, and Crain (2003) found that disjunction is assigned the conjunctive entailments by children in sentences like (37). Children were presented with sentences like (37) in a context in which only the girls who had bought an egg received a basket. The child subjects rejected the test sentences over 90 percent of the time, showing mastery of the semantic property of downward entailment.

These results are unexpected under the account on which children lack knowledge of the semantic properties of the universal quantifier *every*, including the fact that it is downward entailing in its internal argument but upward entailing in its external argument. The findings add further support for the proposal by Crain and colleagues—that children's nonadult linguistic behavior in earlier work was an experimental artifact: children produce adult-like behavior when attention is paid to the felicity of the target sentences in experimental tasks.

4.5 The Structural Property of C-Command in Child Language

As we observed, for a downward-entailing operator to have scope over a linguistic expression, it must c-command that expression. To determine if child language is subject to the c-command constraint, we conducted an experiment using the Truth-value Judgment task (Crain & Thornton, 1998). The children who participated in the experiment were divided in two groups. Group 1 children encountered sentences in which negation c-commanded the disjunction operator, whereas group 2 children encountered sentences in which c-command did not hold. The experiment draws upon the observation that the disjunction operator *or* receives "conjunctive" interpretation when it occurs in the scope of a downward-entailing operator, but not if it is simply preceded by a downward-entailing operator. To illustrate, on one trial, children were told a story about two girls who had both lost a tooth and were waiting for the Tooth Fairy to come. One girl went to sleep, but the second girl decided to stay awake to see what the Tooth Fairy looked like. At this point, the puppet (Merlin the magician) made a prediction. Group 1 children heard (38) and group 2 children heard (39).

(38) The girl that stayed up late will not get a dime or a jewel.

(39) The girl that didn't go to sleep will get a dime or a jewel.

Then the story resumed, and the Tooth Fairy rewarded the girl who was sleeping with both a dime and a jewel but only gave a jewel to the girl who had not gone to sleep. For adults, (38) is equivalent to (40) and therefore false in the context under consideration. By contrast, (39) is equivalent to (41) and is therefore true in the context.

(40) The girl that stayed up late will not get a dime *and*
the girl that stayed up late will not get a jewel.

(41) The girl that didn't go to sleep will get a dime *or*
the girl that didn't go to sleep will get a jewel.

The main finding was that children in group 1 rejected sentences like (38) more than three-quarters of the time, whereas children in group 2 accepted sentences like (39) 90 percent of the time. The results lead us to conclude that children know that c-command is a necessary condition in creating downward-entailing contexts.

SUSAN A. GELMAN

Two Insights about Naming in the Preschool Child

Psychological models often assume that young children learn words and concepts by means of associative learning mechanisms, without the need to posit any innate predispositions. For example, Smith, Jones, and Landau (1996) propose that children learn concepts by hearing specific linguistic frames while viewing specific object properties. The environment provides all the information that children need; the conjunction of sights and sounds is proposed to be sufficient to enable children to construct word meanings. On their view, children make use of "associative connections and direct stimulus pulls," which Smith and colleagues dub "dumb attentional mechanisms."

In this chapter I suggest that this empiricist learning model is insufficient to account for two early-emerging insights that children possess about the nature of naming. These insights are: (1) *essentialism*: certain words map onto nonobvious, underlying causal features (e.g., dogs are alike in internal and subtle respects, even if they look quite different on the surface), and (2) *genericity*: certain expressions map onto generic kinds (e.g., *dogs* as an abstract category) as opposed to particular instances (e.g., one or more specific dogs). I will discuss empirical studies with preschool children to support the contention that essentialism and genericity emerge early in development and that neither insight is directly taught. I will also explore the question of whether these insights can be derived wholly from a direct reading of cues that are "out there" in the world, and I conclude that they cannot. I then explore the implications of these findings for innateness. Specifically, both essentialism and genericity provide cues regarding plausible candidates for innate conceptual knowledge in children.

This research was supported by National Institute of Child Health and Human Development grant number HD36043.

1 Empiricist Models of Concepts

In an influential essay, Smith, Jones, and Landau (1996) suggest that "associative connections and direct stimulus pulls...underlie children's novel word interpretations" (pp. 145–6). They go on to explain that language-learning children "repeatedly experience *specific* linguistic contexts (e.g., "This is a _____" or "This is some _____") with...*specific* object properties...(e.g., shape or color plus texture)." For example, a child can learn the distinction between count and mass nouns by noting that count nouns are uttered in the presence of consistent shapes (e.g., "This is *a book*" in the presence of rectangular solids; "This is *a banana*" in the presence of crescents), whereas mass nouns are uttered in the present of consistent colors and textures (e.g., "This is *some rice*" in the presence of white, sticky stuff; "This is *some sand*" in the presence of tan, granular stuff). By tracking the empirical regularities of linguistic form and perceptual cues, children learn familiar words and build up expectations about novel words.

In support of these arguments, the input that children hear seems to provide a rich source of data regarding such linkages between object shape and count nouns. For example, the first count nouns that children learn tend to refer to categories for which shape is a salient dimension, suggesting that the input children hear focuses heavily on shape-based count nouns. Furthermore, attention to shape appears to undergo a characteristic developmental time-course in which it grows more powerful as children acquire more experience with their own language—therefore suggesting that it may be the outcome rather than the source of word learning. Exposure to different language inputs results in somewhat different word-learning biases, also implicating experience as an important influence on children's early assumptions about word meaning. Relatedly, experimental manipulation of the input by teaching shape-based nouns results in stronger noun learning in early childhood (Smith, 2000).

From a theoretical perspective, this empiricist position has several intuitive appeals. It promises to provide a mechanistic model for *how* development takes place, it would make use of well-known psychological mechanisms, and it has generality that could account for a broad range of data. Furthermore, findings focused on other phenomena demonstrate the power of statistical learning procedures for rapid learning even in infancy (e.g., Saffran et al., 1996). Statistical learning procedures are important—but are they the full story for how children learn word meanings?

One reason to suspect that statistical learning procedures cannot provide a complete answer to the problem of word learning is that nonassociational information powerfully influences children's word learning at an early age. Numerous studies demonstrate the importance of the child's construal of the social context in determining the nature of early word meanings (Baldwin, 1993; Diesendruck & Markson, 2001; Tomasello & Akhtar, 2000; Woodward, 2000). For example, temporal contiguity between word and object is less important than direction of the speaker's gaze. Even young two-year-olds make use of subtle pragmatic information (such as whether the speaker's actions are intentional or accidental) to guide their interpretation of novel words.

Booth and Waxman (2002) have also demonstrated that conceptual information (in the form of verbal descriptions) powerfully influences children's word extensions. In two experiments, three-year-old children received a word-extension task with simple abstract objects, in which the objects were described as having either animal-relevant properties (e.g., "This dax has a mommy and daddy who love it very much... when this dax goes to sleep at night, they give it lots of hugs and kisses") or artifact-relevant properties (e.g., "This dax was made by an astronaut to do a very special job on her spaceship..."). Children sorted the objects differently, depending on the conceptual information provided in the story. The data strongly argue against the idea that children automatically activate purely perceptually based associations between the presence of eyes and the dimension of shape.

Smith and colleagues have also argued that young children have difficulty mapping words onto higher level conceptual information, such as function, but more recent studies demonstrate that preschool children—in some studies as young as two years old—can take function into account in early naming (Kemler Nelson et al., 2000).

Keil, Smith, Simons, and Levin (1998) provide a cogent critique of the empiricist view. They point out that associative learning models require constraints on the properties to be associated (Goodman, 1972; Murphy & Medin, 1985) and that no one has yet articulated a plausible account of how the perceptual system would provide such constraints. They also point out that in some cases children possess abstract expectations *before* a concrete knowledge base (Simons & Keil, 1995).

This argument extends these critiques by providing two specific examples of early capacities or expectations young children have about naming. Although naming is a domain that has been taken as an example par excellence for the power of empiricist models, it falls short in some crucial ways. The problems with empiricist accounts of acquisition in these examples raise the question of what is innate, which I take up in the final section.

2 Two Insights about Naming

When thinking about word learning, what typically comes to mind is the simple case of learning to label a single object with a count noun. It is this sort of context for which the associative learning models have most success. When one examines children's early word learning, however, one immediately sees that the problem is more complex. Children are learning not just nouns but also verbs (Tomasello & Merriman, 1995). Children are learning not just to label shapes but also to take into account speakers' intentions (Tomasello & Akhtar, 2000; Bloom, 2000). And the concepts to which nouns refer include more than available percepts.

There are at least two ways that words convey concepts that are not directly observable—even for young word-learners. First, words can map onto nonobvious, underlying features. And second, words can map onto abstract *kinds* (not just specific, individual instances). I will characterize each of these insights below, referring to the first as *essentialism* and referring to the second as *genericity*. Neither insight is directly or explicitly provided in the input, and it would appear that neither insight is derived from "dumb attentional mechanisms." This will then raise the question of how children acquire these insights. I will suggest that there are domain-general innate distinctions or biases that give rise to these understandings.

3   Essentialism: An Overview

Essentialism is a term that has been used broadly in different disciplines, with widely varying meanings. Medin (1989) draws an important distinction between metaphysical essentialism (a claim about the structure of the world) and psychological essentialism (a claim about human beliefs); my focus is psychological essentialism. I use the term "essentialism" to refer to a three-part belief: (1) that certain categories are "natural kinds": real (v. artificial), discovered (v. invented), and stable or unchanging, (2) that some unobservable part, substance, or quality (the essence) causes observable similarities,[1] and (3) that many everyday words map onto this real-world structure. When we learn words such as *dog, oak tree, gold*, or *schizophrenic*, we believe that we are learning something about real kinds in the world.

Fodor (1998a) suggested that essentialism is the outgrowth of modern science. As people gain more knowledge about the world, they understand it at a deeper, less obvious level. They learn about modern technology and concepts that provide access to the rich internal structure of animals: microscopes, x-rays, DNA, and modern scientific taxonomies (e.g., whales are mammals, not fish). Perhaps all of this information accounts for why people assume there are hidden properties shared by members of a category.

Children provide a critical test case for studying the origins of essentialism, precisely because they lack detailed scientific knowledge. If essentialism requires knowledge of modern science and technology, then it should emerge late in development, only after the acquisition of detailed biological knowledge. However, if preschool children essentialize, then we would have to look elsewhere to explain this early appreciation. Furthermore, if children can look beyond the obvious in their classifications, it would also pose a challenge to standard claims about children's thinking as concrete, perceptual, focused on the obvious, and so forth (Piaget, 1970; Siegler, 1998) and would challenge long-held assumptions about the nature of early concepts.

What would be evidence for essentialism, in children or adults? Medin and Ortony (1989) suggest that essentialism is a "placeholder" notion—one can believe *that* categories possess an essence without knowing *what* the essence is. For example, a child might believe that there exist deep, nonobvious differences between males and females but have no idea just what those differences are. If essentialism is a placeholder notion, then the evidence for essentialism will be indirect. Figure 12.1 illustrates this notion. The essence placeholder would imply that categories are immutable, have sharp boundaries, permit rich inductive inferences, capture nonobvious properties, have some underlying causal force, and have innate potential.

Elsewhere I have detailed at length the evidence that preschool children expect certain categories to have all of these properties (Gelman, 2003). I will not have space to review all the evidence in this chapter. However, I summarize below

---

1. There is some debate as to how strongly people adhere to a single essence, whether this essence needs to be an internal aspect of the entity as opposed to relational, and how articulated this aspect is. (See Strevens, 2000; Wilson, 1999.) I think these are constructive debates, though irrelevant for current purposes.

202 Language and Concepts

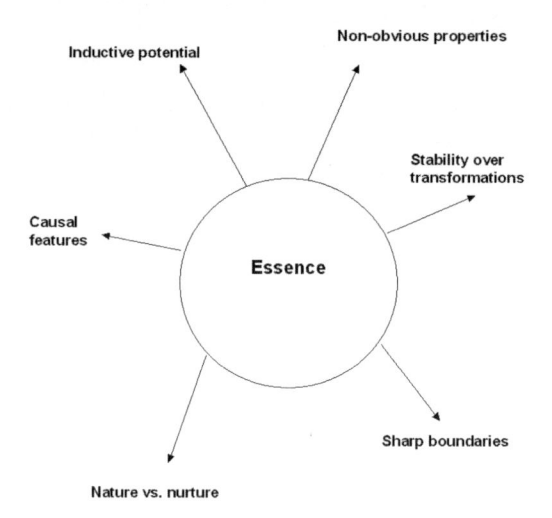

FIGURE 12.1 Implications of essentialism.

some of the major points from two of these essentialist implications: inductive potential and innate potential. Additional claims regarding essentialism that will not be covered here include: (1) children treat certain categories as immutable; (2) children treat certain categories as having relatively sharp boundaries; (3) nonobvious properties are central to certain of children's categories; (4) causal properties are central to certain of children's categories.

3.1 Inductive Potential

One of the major essentialist assumptions is that category members share more than surface similarities; they also have important nonobvious properties in common. We see this with children's inductive inferences. One experimental paradigm provides children with item sets in which category membership conflicts with outward appearances. Figure 12.2 provides an example. The blackbird and the bat are overall more similar: both are black, with outstretched wings. However, if told the category membership of each item ("bird," "bat," "bird") and asked to draw novel inferences about the blackbird, children rely on category membership as conveyed by the label. Once children learn a new fact about one member of a category, they generalize the fact to other members of that category, even if the two category members look substantially different. This effect holds up for animals (bird, fish, rabbit), for natural substances (gold, cotton), for gender (boy, girl), for traits (smart, shy). (See Gelman, 2003.)

These results are not due to a simple reliance on matching labels, as children rely on information about kind membership (not names per se). When the labels are distinct but refer to the same kind (e.g., "puppy," "baby dog"), children still use kind membership as the basis of nonobvious inferences. Conversely, when the labels are identical but fail to refer to kinds (e.g., "sleepy," "wide awake"), then

FIGURE 12.2 Sample item (from Gelman & Markman, 1986).

children ignore the labels in their inferences. Recent studies show that even one- and two-year-old children draw category-based inferences (Graham et al., 2001; Jaswal & Markman, 2001). Thus, the appreciation that words can signal nonobvious properties seems to be in place at the very start of word learning.

3.2 Innate Potential

One of the most important kinds of evidence for essentialism is the belief that properties are fixed at birth, and even passed down from parent to child. We can refer to this as "innate potential." There is now a sizeable database of studies examining children's beliefs about innate potential. Details vary, but the basic paradigm is the same. Children learn about a person or animal that has a set of biological parents, and then is switched at birth to a new environment and a new set of parents. The question is, which do children think is more important: birth parents or upbringing? For example, in one item set, Henry Wellman and I told children about an infant kangaroo that went to live with goats: would it be good at hopping or good at climbing? Would it have a pouch or no pouch (Gelman & Wellman, 1991)?

Overall, when one poses this sort of question to children, they show a powerful nativist bias. This is so when children reason about animal kinds, plant kinds, racial identity, and gender-linked properties. Intriguingly, children tend to be *more* nativist than adults (Taylor, 1996). For example, five-year-olds predict that a child who is switched at birth will speak the language of the birth parents rather than that of the adoptive parents (Hirschfeld & Gelman, 1997).

3.3 Summary

A range of studies using varied methods suggests that preschool children expect members of a category to be alike in nonobvious ways. They treat certain categories as "natural kinds": with inductive potential, an innate basis, immutable kind membership, and sharp boundaries between contrasting categories.

4 Where Does Essentialism Come From? Some Negative Conclusions

Where does essentialism come from? I first give four negative answers to this question, by considering and then rejecting four accounts that fail to match the available evidence. Specifically, essentialism is *not* simply derived from the structure of the world, it does *not* reflect a particular cultural stance, it is *not* explicitly taught by parents, and it *cannot* simply be deduced by language use. All of these negative conclusions would seem to suggest that some form of essentialism is spontaneously emerging in children. In the following section, I will consider the nature of this early predisposition.

4.1 Structure of the World?

Essentializing extends to social categories that are constructed and have no true underlying essence (Gil-White, 2001; Hirschfeld, 1996). Essentializing of race, caste, and occupation are not grounded in an accurate biological description of the world (Mahalingam, 1998). Even when considering biological species, essentialism seems to misstate the evidence. Biological species evolve; they are not immutable (Mayr, 1982); they are population based rather than reflecting properties inherent in each individual (Sober, 1994; Wilson, 1999), and rather than their being a single, real classification of species, there may be numerous valid classifications, each of which captures some cluster of relevant properties (Dupré, 1993). The essentialist view, therefore, seems to be a human construction rather than a perceived reality (see also Kornblith, 1993).

4.2 Particular Cultural Input?

It is also not the case that essentialism results from the particular cultural milieu of the typical experimental subject (middle-class, educated, U.S.). Recent work suggests essentializing in a broad range of samples, including Favela-dwelling children in Brazil (Diesendruck, 2001), Torguud adults in western Mongolia (Gil-White, 2001), Vezo children in Madagascar (Astuti et al., 2003), and Itzaj Maya adults and children in Guatemala (Atran et al., 2001). More work is needed to examine different cultures; certainly one cannot conclude universality on the basis of sampling a handful of cultures. Another caveat is that there is cultural variation in which categories are essentialized, especially evident in variation in construal of human kinds (Bloch et al., 2001; Chandler, 2001). Nonetheless, the variety of contexts in which essentialism emerges suggests that essentialism is relatively "easy to think."

4.3 Explicit Instruction by Parents?

How do children learn about essentialism? Children's fiction contains a rich source of essentialist stories (e.g., "The Ugly Duckling"), but it also contains a rich source of antiessentialist stories (e.g., *Horton Hatches an Egg*). Moreover, it is unclear whether children incorporate fictional input into their construal of the real world. Presumably, certain sorts of input from fiction are buffered from beliefs about reality (e.g., that animals can talk, as seen in many storybooks and cartoons). Therefore, it is crucial to see how parents talk to children outside of storybooks or other mass media.

My collaborators and I set out to examine the nature of the input in a context that should strongly encourage talk about essences (Gelman et al., 1998). Parent-child dyads received a picture-book reading task, where each page depicted several animals or objects in a realistic setting. Notably, each page displayed appearance-reality contrasts: two horses and a zebra; two bats and a bird; and so on. We videotaped the sessions, and transcribed and coded the videotapes.

It was clear that the pages did set up the desired contrast between appearance and reality, as children often mislabeled the pictures. The key question was how parents explained these contrasts to children. Most important for our purposes, parents provided very little in the way of explicit input concerning the nonobvious basis to category membership. Table 12.1 lists the mean percentage of properties of a given type that parents provided: using "all" as a universal quantifier to signal that a property was true of an entire kind; reference to insides; reference to kinship; and reference to appearance-reality conflicts. As can be seen, all of these explicit essentialist statements were exceedingly rare, and most were no more common for animals than for artifacts. The only property that parents expressed with any frequency concerned appearance-reality distinctions. Even here, however, the appearance-reality discussions did not provide explicit lessons in essentialism but rather indirectly alluded to the notion that appearances might be deceiving. For example:

CHILD: That's kangaroo. [pointing to aardvark]

MOTHER: Well, that looks like a kangaroo but it's called an aardvark.

CHILD: Aardvark.

What is striking about this otherwise commonplace exchange is that the child readily accepts the mother's relabeling, without any elaboration or explanation. Altogether, parental input seems rather minimal and indirect, even in a highly educated sample with much category knowledge.

TABLE 12.1 Parental input concerning essentialism: Mean percentage of properties (from Gelman, Coley, Rosengren, Hartman, & Pappas, 1998).

Properties	Animals	Artifacts
"All" as referring to entire category	0.18	0.00
Insides	0.00	0.58
Kinship	0.07	0.00
Appearance-reality conflict	1.36[a]	0.65[a]

[a]Indicates significant domain difference.

4.4 Provided by Language Use?

Some have proposed that essentialism can be deduced by language use: hearing the word "bird" for a wide variety of dissimilar birds (hummingbirds, eagles, ostriches) signals to the child that something other than surface similarity must bind these instances together (Hallett, 1991; Mayr, 1991). On this view, language has a powerful causal force in implying essentialism to children. Certainly children respond differently to tasks in which language is or is not used (Gelman & Markman, 1986; Markman & Hutchinson, 1984; Waxman & Markow, 1995; Xu, 1999). Moreover, hearing a label for a concept does provoke a more essentialist construal (e.g., "carrot-eater" implies a more stable, immutable category than "someone who eats carrots whenever she can" (Gelman & Heyman, 1999)).

However, one problem with assigning too central a role to language is that names need not—and do not—automatically cue essentialism, in children or adults. Children learn homonyms (*Lily* as a name v. *lily* as a flower) and nonkind terms, both adjectives (sleepy) and nouns (*passenger; pet*). When learning novel words, children do not automatically assume that the words are kind referring, if perceptual cues compete (Davidson & Gelman, 1990). One striking example of children's willingness to interpret a word for two dissimilar things as homonyms rather than essentialist similarities came from my daughter, who at about age three and a half remarked: "Isn't it funny—'chicken' sounds just like 'chicken'"—not realizing that the bird and the food were indeed manifestations of the same kind!

These examples suggest that language may be an important cue regarding *when* to essentialize, but it is not the mechanism by which essentializing emerges to begin with. If sameness of naming is to convey underlying sameness, children must first have the capacity to understand that appearances can be deceiving. Armed with such an understanding, naming practices could provide important information to children about the structure of concepts. However, that initial understanding must already be in place in order for children to benefit from naming.

4.5 Summary

Essentialism appears to be an early predisposition, not supplied by the structure of the world, the logic of language, or parental instruction. Certainly aspects of the world, of language, and of cultural teachings get incorporated into essentialist understandings, but the conclusion I reach is that essentialism is fundamentally a construction of the human mind (see also Kornblith, 1993).

5 Genericity: An Overview

I turn now to a second insight that preschool children have regarding naming. This is an appreciation that nouns can be used to refer not only to particular or indefinite *instances* but also to *generic kinds*. To appreciate the distinction, consider "My bat lives in this cave" versus "Bats live in caves." The first (nongeneric) refers to a particular bat; the second (generic) refers to bats as an abstract kind. Generic noun phrases are also known as *kind-referring expressions* (Carlson & Pelletier, 1995).

Generics relate to essentialism in two respects. First, both generics and essentialism reflect how people construe categories, and particularly categories referred to by count nouns. Second, generic language may foster essentialist thought, by expressing inherent properties that members of a category have in common. When a child hears "Birds fly south for the winter," she is learning a property that is not simply accidentally true of a subset of birds but rather something that is inherently true of birds as a class. Furthermore, generics may imply that members of a category cohere, regardless of property content. Even when the property expressed is highly familiar (e.g., "Birds fly"), the generic form of the noun phrase may emphasize the coherence of the category in question.

Recent studies from my lab suggest that generics are frequent in the speech that children hear (Gelman & Tardif, 1998; Gelman et al., 1998; Pappas & Gelman, 1998) and that children both produce and understand generics at an early age. One set of analyses rests on longitudinal studies of eight children followed over the ages of two to four years, during in-home, real-life interactions (thanks to the CHILDES database; MacWhinney & Snow, 1990). In this project, nearly 45,000 child noun phrases were analyzed, and we are in the process of analyzing as many adult utterances. The eight children we studied produced over 3,000 generic noun phrases during the sessions recorded. At every age (two, three, and four years), every child we studied produced generics. By age four, generics constituted nearly 4 percent of children's total utterances—a high rate, comparable to that of children's talk about mental states and processes (Bartsch & Wellman, 1995). Detailed analyses of parent-child conversations reveals that children initiate generic talk a good portion of the time, even at preschool age (Goetz & Gelman, 2005). That is, for each generic that was produced, we traced backward to determine who first introduced the topic, and who first introduced the topic generically. Children frequently took the lead in initiating a generic level of talk.

Importantly, children are not simply adept at *producing* generics; they *comprehend* them appropriately as well. Four-year-olds appreciate that generics are generally true of a category but allow for exceptions (Hollander et al., 2002). Thus, children do not confuse generics with either indefinite noun phrases (e.g., "some") or universal quantifiers (e.g., "all"). Like "all," generics are appropriate for category-wide generalizations (e.g., "[All] fires are hot"). Yet, like "some," generics are appropriate for properties true of a subset (e.g., "[Some] girls have curly hair"). Generics differ from nongenerics in content as well as scope: they more typically express actions and less typically express physical appearances, compared to nongenerics (Hollander et al., 2002). Children's generics are also distributed differently from nongenerics in the focus of conversation concerning important social categories.

Crossculturally and crosslinguistically, we found very similar patterns in Chinese to those in American children, and even in the "home sign" gestures of deaf children without a conventional language (Gelman & Tardif, 1998; Goldin-Meadow et al., 2003). We selected Mandarin because it does not include several of the cues that are so central to generic identification in English, including articles, plurality, and tense. Therefore, whereas in English we distinguish between "The duck is waddling" (nongeneric) and "Ducks waddle" (generic), in Mandarin both ideas could be expressed with the same sentence. Despite radically different linguistic models for the expression of generics across these three groups (including no conventional model for the children producing home signs), the patterns of use are remarkably similar. In all the groups, generics disproportionately refer to animals and people, even controlling for the amount of overall talk about each domain, thus suggesting that generics more readily map onto essentialized categories.

Another important point is that children extend a generically learned property more broadly to other items of the same category than to a nongeneric property (Gelman, Star, & Flukes, 2002). In a series of studies, we taught children novel facts about a series of animals, in one of three forms: generic (e.g., "Bears like to eat ants"), indefinite (e.g., "Some bears like to eat ants"), and universal quantifier (e.g., "All bears like to eat ants"). Hearing the facts in generic form led to inferences that were broad (unlike indefinites) but allowing for exceptions (unlike universal quantifiers). Thus, children's patterns of inductive inference are influenced by hearing generic language. This finding has potentially far-reaching implications, given the frequency of generics in parental speech.

Children are highly sensitive to the formal linguistic and contextual markers of generics, acquiring them by three years of age (Gelman & Raman, 2003). For example, if shown a picture of two penguins, preschool children interpret "Do birds fly?" differently from "Do the birds fly?" Simple presence or absence of the article "the" has powerful implications for the interpretation children assign. Generics draw children's attention away from the particulars in the context and bring to mind the larger category. Moreover, children use not just formal linguistic cues but also contextual cues. For example, the very same sentence, "Do they have short necks or long necks?" is interpreted differently, depending on whether it is prefaced by a picture of *two* short-necked giraffes and the sentence "Here are two giraffes" (thereby leading to the answer "short necks") or whether it is prefaced by a picture of *one* short-necked giraffe and the sentence "Here is a giraffe" (thereby leading to the answer "long necks"). In the former case, children interpret the sentence as referring to the giraffes in the picture (nongenerically), but in the latter case, children interpret the sentence as referring to giraffes as a generic kind. Altogether, this work suggests that preschool children exploit multiple sources of information (including formal morphosyntactic cues, contextual cues, and theory-based knowledge) to solve the problem of generic language.

Despite preschool children's early appreciation for generics, there are also important developmental changes in the preschool years. Generics are almost nonexistent in productive speech before about age two and a half. Between the ages of two to four, there is a dramatic increase in the frequency of generics, even controlling for amount of nongeneric talk, even when we focus only on those children who already have command of the formal linguistic markers (e.g., articles, plurality, tense; Gelman, 2003). The cues that children use to recognize generics change with age: two-year-olds use formal linguistic cues only (e.g., differentiating "dogs" from "the dogs"), whereas three-year-olds additionally use context (e.g., whether the linguistic form matches or mismatches the nonlinguistic context; Gelman & Raman, 2003). Finally, the scope of generics changes as well: three-year-olds fail to differentiate generic questions from questions involving "all" or "some," whereas four-year-olds make a three-way distinction between generics, "all," and "some." Interestingly, however, the patterns of response to generic questions does not change from age three to adulthood; rather, three-year-olds' problem involves treating both "all" and "some" as if they too were generics (Hollander, Gelman, & Star, 2002).

6 How Are Generics Acquired?

From an acquisitional standpoint, generics pose in bold relief the induction problem discussed by Pierce, Goodman, Quine, and others. First, the generic concept is never perceptually available to the learner. Thus, when one hears "dogs," the generic category of dogs can never be displayed or pointed to. At most a subset of the category may be visible, but never the entire kind. Note that this is a more basic problem than even Quine proposed. With Quine's gavagai example, perceptual displays are always ambiguous and open to alternative construals (thus a point to a rabbit need not imply the entire rabbit, but at least the entire rabbit is visible and could be linked to the act of naming ["Gavagai!"]). With generics, perceptual displays can *never* display the referent (even ambiguously). Second, the semantics of generics are potentially confusing, because they refer to a category as a whole but also allow for exceptions (e.g., "Boys play with trucks" is not invalidated by counterexamples). Third, the formal cues to genericity are varied, and provide no one-to-one mapping between form and meaning. To elaborate: generics can be expressed with multiple forms in English:

Bare plural: Dogs are mammals.

Indefinite singular: A dog is a mammal.

Definite singular: The dog is a mammal.

Definite article plus adjective: The elderly need better health care.

Interestingly, for three of these four examples, the same noun phrase can also be used nongenerically:

Bare plural: Dogs were playing frisbee in the park yesterday.

Indefinite singular: A dog is barking outside my window.

Definite singular: The dog next door dug up an old bone.

Thus, children cannot simply learn that a fixed linguistic form has generic meaning. They must use context effects to figure out the intended scope of a noun phrase in context (see Gelman, 2004, for details).

One further illustration underscores the complexity of the mapping problem:

- Do you like the mango? (nongeneric, specific)
- Do you like mango? (generic)
- Would you like mango? (nongeneric, indefinite ['some'])
- Would you like mango, if you were a monkey? (generic)

Whether or not the noun phrase includes the determiner is not decisive, nor is the verb decisive. It is the combination of the determiner and the verb that is important. However, even here the formal cues are not entirely decisive, as can be seen when we consider

"Would you like mango, if you were a monkey?" (in which "mango" could have a generic reading, even though the first portion is identical to the nongeneric indefinite sentence). Thus, even when one considers all formal cues simultaneously, they are insufficient to determine with any certainty whether a noun phrase is generic or not.

If generics were to be acquired by means of "dumb attentional mechanisms," then one would need to identify a small set of formal linguistic properties that are consistently linked to a set of perceptual properties that would cue a generic interpretation. Yet, as I've tried to sketch out, there is no small set of formal linguistic cues, and there are no perceptual instantiations of generic concepts.

I propose that generics are a default interpretation for children (Gelman, 2004). Generics are not marked by means of clear or unambiguous cues. Instead, in many languages, generics are the unmarked (or relatively less marked) form: an interpretation reached when the sentence *lacks* determiners, tense, aspect markings, number, or any other cue that an utterance is linked to a specific time or place. This is certainly true for both English and Mandarin. There are many devices in language for indicating that something is particular, and it would be extraordinarily difficult (perhaps impossible) to enumerate them all. These include (but are not limited to): form of the determiner; precise number; deictics (including pointing); tense. All of these devices serve to locate an utterance within an identifiable context (*this* place, *that* time, *those* entities). Generics contrast with specific utterances in that they cannot be pinned down to a context—they hold generally over time and situations. Thus, there is not a limited set of features or contexts that correspond to the set of generic utterances. Rather, I hypothesize that language users assume that an utterance is generic unless that interpretation is blocked.

The implications of this view for acquisition are as follows. In learning generics (at least in English), the child's task is *not* to acquire a particular form, nor to map one formal set of cues onto a set of properties in the world (à la Smith, Jones, & Landau, 1996). Rather, the child's task is to filter out the specific. This can be done most successfully by considering multiple cues, given the breadth and variety of means of indicating specificity. Thus, my position is that acquisition of the generic system in English requires a theory-driven assessment of when an utterance picks out specific referents, and when an utterance does not. (See also Downing, 1996, for further arguments that generics are a default.)

6.1 Summary

Children learning English readily produce and understand the distinction between generic noun phrases and nongeneric noun phrases, despite the lack of clear formal linguistic cues marking the distinction, and despite the impossibility of instantiating entire kinds in the real world.

7 Failure of Empiricist Models to Account for Early Essentialism and Early Generics

To review, evidence from both essentialist reasoning and genericity provide challenges to the empiricist view that concept learning consists entirely of relating perceptual features in the input to elements of speech. For essentialism, the problem with the "dumb attentional" model is twofold: that essentialism entails thinking about nonobvious or nonperceptual features, and that children do not receive explicit instruction in any case. For genericity, the problem is also twofold: that generic kinds (the referents to generic noun phrases) cannot be displayed or presented in perceptual form, and that the linguistic input is ambiguous.

This is not to say that environmental cues or statistical learning mechanisms are irrelevant or unimportant. Such cues and mechanisms may be central—when taken in conjunction with other conceptual underpinnings. For example, naming practices seem to provide important information regarding *when* to essentialize. Providing a noun label encourages the belief that a novel category is stable and resistant to change (Gelman & Heyman, 1999), and providing a generic encourages drawing inferences from a category (Gelman et al., 2002). For generics, children's interpretation in English may be guided by parents' frequent practice of using plural nouns in the presence of a single exemplar to figure out that what is meant is something *other* than the individual in context (Pappas & Gelman, 1998). However, the question is whether such learning mechanisms are sufficient to build essentialism or genericity within the first two or three years of life. At present, such cues seem insufficient to generate the patterns of conceptual understanding we see by preschool age.

8 What Is Innate?

Preschool children appreciate two insights about naming: that certain words capture nonobvious properties and map onto essentialized kinds, and that words can refer to generic kinds as well as individuals. Empiricist models do not fully account for either capacity. What then can we conclude about the nature of innate knowledge?

One approach would be to assume that essentialism is the result of innate domain-specific knowledge: if the form of knowledge is domain specific, than the mechanism itself is domain specific. For example, essentialism is applied to animals more than artifacts, and generics are applied more to animals than artifacts, so essentialism and genericity could be domain-specific expressions of a folk biology module. An example of this position can be found in the writings of Atran, Estin, Coley, and Medin (1997), Gil-White (2001), and Pinker (1997a), each of whom propose that people have an innate folk biology module that results in essentializing of animal kinds and related categories.

One appeal of such a position is that essentialism seems to fit better with categories of animal kinds than categories of artifacts (Gelman, 2003). Another appeal is that this provides a potential reason *why* people essentialize, in evolutionary adaptationist terms. However, this interpretation also faces some empirical problems. Children and adults treat a variety of *non*biological entities as having underlying, nonobvious commonalities: including both nonbiological human kinds (including race; Hirschfeld, 1996) and nonbiological natural substances (e.g., gold, water; Gelman & Markman, 1986; but see Malt, 1994). Although one might argue that human kinds could be part of folk biology, or included on the basis of analogy to animals (e.g., Gil-White, 2001; but see Hirschfeld, 1996), it seems implausible to suggest that inanimate natural substances could be part of a folk biology.

A further potential problem is that we see essence-like (though not essentialist) constructs outside the realm of biology, including: contagion and contamination (e.g., Hitler's sweater; Rozin & Nemeroff, 1990), fetishes (e.g., Jacqueline Onassis's fake pearls were sold at auction for many times more than their material worth), and judgments of authenticity (e.g., an original Picasso is worth so much more than a reproduction). In such cases, people seem to believe that something nonobvious underlies surface appearances, and that origins are especially important. I stop short of calling these examples of essentialism (though see Bloom, 2000). But as a working hypothesis, one might speculate that some general capacities underlie both essentializing and these other intuitions. Whatever prompts these intuitions is probably not a strictly biological capacity, for then it would not readily apply to such entities as sweaters, jewelry, or paintings (see Gelman, 2003, for further elaboration of this point).

In contrast, I suggest an alternative position: that domain-specific effects, in both essentialism and generics, may emerge from domain-general causes (see also Keil, 1994; Smith, 2000). This possibility is sketched out below.

8.1 Essentialism Results from a Conspiracy of Domain-General Predispositions

Rather than being a single predisposition, essentialism may emerge from a cluster of other early-emerging skills that are fundamental to early cognition. Studies of early development suggest that young children have a variety of domain-general skills by two years of age (or earlier) that are relevant to forming information-rich categories. Each of these capacities individually has functional significance in development, and each has implications for some aspect of the essentialist phenomena I have sketched out earlier.

Appearance-reality distinction. A prerequisite to essentialist understanding is a distinction between appearance and reality. Specifically, an appearance-reality distinction seems necessary for thinking about nonobvious properties, for accepting category anomalies (e.g., that a bat is not a bird), and for distinguishing what something "is" from what it "is like." Although it is not until about four years of age that children can reflect on the appearance-reality distinction in a metacognitive way (Flavell, Flavell, & Green, 1983), a basic appreciation seems well in place much earlier. The two-year-old's capacity to accept her mother's word that a pterodactyl is a dinosaur, not a bird, is evidence of this core understanding. Basic appreciation of an appearance-reality distinction would be important and useful to a broad range of concerns, not just essentialism but also reasoning about a range of human interactions and physical events.[2]

---

2. An unresolved question is why appearance-reality distinctions are available to young children in certain contexts before they pass appearance-reality tasks of the sort tested by Flavell and colleagues. One possibility is that the Flavell et al. tasks are especially challenging because they require both appearance and reality to be kept in mind simultaneously. Alternatively, perhaps children achieve a mentalistic understanding of the appearance-reality distinction first in the context of language interpretation (see Happé & Loth, 2002; Sperber & Wilson, 2002, for related claims; thanks to Peter Carruthers for suggesting this possibility).

Induction from property clusters. People may assume (implicitly) that property clusters attract other properties. The more commonalities you have learned about a category in the past, the stronger your inferences about that category are in the future. Conversely, a category that lacks such property clusters will not be expected to attract new properties. This core assumption could grow into categorical realism, the belief that the world consists of natural kinds. It would favor essentialism for categories that have demonstrated inductive potential (e.g., basic-level object kinds) but not for, say, superordinate categories (tools) or single properties with little inductive potential (striped things). This assumption might also contribute to domain differences, given the richer property clusters for natural kinds versus simple artifacts (Boyd, 1999; Gelman, 1988; Keil, 1989; Kornblith, 1993). However, the assumption need not be domain specific in its basic architecture.

To be clear: the suggestion here is not simply that categories permit induction (although they do). Instead, people generate the second-order inference that categories permit even more inductions into the future, including *as-yet-unknown* properties. This appreciation seems to be in place even before children learn language (Baldwin et al., 1993).

Causal determinism. This is the assumption that properties and events are caused. In the case of natural events, causal determinism means that events without external cause demand some sort of mediating, inherent cause. The power of causal determinism for essentialism is in generating a search for hidden, nonobvious, as-yet-unknown properties. A number of scholars have suggested that children early on adhere to something like causal determinism (Brown, 1990; Bullock et al., 1982; Gelman & Kalish, 1993; Shultz, 1982). Recent evidence provides some compelling demonstrations of how this might work in detail (Gopnik & Sobel, 2000). Of interest for this context, causal determinism would seem to apply broadly across domains (e.g., in understanding mechanical devices as well as natural kinds). Where it could engender domain-specific reasoning would be with the different causal relations entailed in natural kinds versus artifacts. Whereas many artifact features can be attributed to an external agent (e.g., the person who made a chair gave it four legs), many natural-kind features cannot be so attributed, and so would lead to positing nonobvious causal forces (e.g., there is no person who gave a dog four legs).

Tracking identity over time. Recognizing offspring, tracking relative position in a social hierarchy, even thinking about ownership all require that one recognize the same object over time. The capacity to track identity over time is therefore broad and early emerging. It is crucial to reasoning about object permanence and object identity, even for preverbal infants (Baillargeon, 1993; Spelke et al., 1995b; Xu & Carey, 1996). By preschool age, children can track the identity of individuals when applying proper names (Gutheil & Rosengren, 1996; Hall, 1996; Sorrentino, 2001). What is crucial to determining individual identity is historical path, not the physical properties that were present at the original naming.

The centrality of this concept for essentialism is potentially profound. Tracking an individual over time requires the insight that a thing can retain identity despite outward changes in appearance (the appearance-reality distinction again). For example, as an animal grows, it changes dramatically. This capacity also seems implicated in reasoning about kind essentialism. Indeed, kind essentialism seems in some ways an extension of the insights about individual identity (Kripke, 1972; Schwartz, 1979). Just as an individual remains the same over outward variations, so too are members of a kind the same as one another despite outward variations. Just as the identity of an individual is decided by consulting the historical record, so too is the identity of a living kind decided by consulting its origins (namely, parentage).

Deference to experts. I also suggest that children honor a *tacit* division of linguistic labor, in which they defers to others as the ultimate arbiter of correct naming. Children can consult experts (such as parents) to find out what something *truly* should be called (see Putnam, 1973). This principle dovetails with the appearance-reality distinction, as it entails a willingness to suspend the evidence of our own eyes: "That looks like a bird to me, but you say it's a dinosaur—so it must be a dinosaur."

Adults defer to experts in matters of naming natural kinds (Malt, 1990; but see Kalish, 1995), and children do so even more strongly (Kalish, 1998). As we have seen, children readily accept experimenter-provided labels, even when such labels are surprising and counterintuitive (e.g., Gelman & Markman, 1986). Children also distinguish names made up on the spot from conventional names (Sabbagh & Baldwin, 2001). It would be interesting to know the depths and origins of children's deference to experts. Does it extend across the board in all knowledge domains, perhaps as a result of children's genuine ignorance about most things, or is it particularly strong in the case of naming? Are young children *most* open to expert knowledge, because they are themselves least knowledgeable? Or does deference to expert knowledge grow as children become more aware of their own limitations?

Each of the core capacities just described is plausibly an early-emerging (perhaps innate) propensity in human infants. Each of the core capacities also appears to be domain general in scope. Yet each of these capacities has special implications when applied to the domain of natural kinds.

8.2 Generics Are Domain-General but Interact with How Readily One Construes Things as Kinds versus Individuals in Different Domains

A similar argument can be made regarding generics. Generics are grammatical and appropriate for any domain, including both animals and artifacts (e.g., "*Dogs* bark"; "*Refrigerators* are heavy"). Yet a striking feature of both parental and child generics is that they are domain specific, appearing significantly more frequently for animals than artifacts (Gelman, 2003). Domain specificity in children emerges as soon as children start to produce generics, between two and three years of age (Gelman, 2003). Domain differences in maternal usage obtain even when one controls for familiarity of the category, similarity among category members, thematic relatedness among category members, and amount of maternal talk (Gelman et al., 1998). The domain differences are also unlikely to be attributable to lack of sufficient knowledge about the artifacts (see Gelman et al., 1998, for argument), although this issue requires more systematic study.

Why, then, do animals elicit so many more generics than artifacts? My colleagues and I interpret this result as reflecting conceptual differences between animal and artifact categories. If mothers construe animal kinds as more richly structured than artifact kinds (with deeper commonalities and greater coherence), they may more easily conceptualize animals as category members. In other words, the larger category to which an animal belongs may be relatively more salient. Although people can think about any object both as a category member and as an individual, the relative emphasis may vary by domain. Once again, what emerges early is a domain-general understanding (that entities can be construed either as individuals or as kinds), which gets instantiated to differing degrees in different domains.

9 Conclusions

In this chapter I have sketched out two insights children achieve at an early age regarding naming: that words can refer to essentialized kinds, and that generic kinds can be distinguished from individuals. In contrast to developmental theories that portray children as focused on concrete, observable properties that are present in the "here and now" of the child's immediate context, these early acquisitions highlight young children's capacity to think about nonobvious, underlying, abstract entities. These early understandings also pose challenges to the idea that children acquire language wholly by means of "dumb" attentional mechanisms linking observable features of the world to regularities in the language stream. Associative learning processes undoubtedly contribute to learning in many realms of thought but appear to be insufficient for essentialism and genericity.

Both understandings also appear to be domain specific: children essentialize animal kinds more readily than artifact categories, and generics are used more frequently for animal than artifact categories. However, I argue against the conclusion that children therefore possess an innate, domain-specific folk biology module. Instead, the data are consistent with the idea that children have an early, *domain-general* set of understandings that interact with domain differences to result in the concepts children display.

STEPHEN LAURENCE & ERIC MARGOLIS

Number and Natural Language

One of the most important abilities we have as humans is the ability to think about number. Without it, modern economic life would be impossible, science would never have developed, and the complex technology that surrounds us would not exist. Though the full range of human numerical abilities is vast, the positive integers are arguably foundational to the rest of numerical cognition, and they will be our focus here. Many theorists have noted that although animals can represent quantity in some respects, they are unable to represent precise integer values. There has been much speculation about why this is so, but a common answer is that it is because animals lack another characteristic feature of human minds—natural language.

In this chapter, we examine the question of whether there is an essential connection between language and number, while looking more broadly at some of the potential innate precursors to the acquisition of the positive integers. A full treatment of this topic would require an extensive review of the empirical literature, something we do not have space for. Instead, we intend to concentrate on the theoretical question of how language may figure in an account of the ontogeny of the positive integers. Despite the trend in developmental psychology to suppose that it does, there are actually few detailed accounts on offer. We'll examine two exceptions, two theories that give natural language a prominent role to play and that represent the state of the art in the study of mathematical cognition. The first is owing to C. R. Gallistel, Rochel Gelman, and their colleagues; the second to Elizabeth Spelke and her colleagues. Both accounts are rich and innovative, and their proponents have made fundamental contributions to the psychological study of number. Nonetheless, we will argue that both accounts face a range of serious objections and that, in particular, their appeal to

---

This essay was fully collaborative; the order of the authors' names is arbitrary. We would like to thank Rosanna Keefe, Stephen Stich, and audience members and participants at the AHRB "Structure of the Innate Mind" conference, Sheffield, England, July 2002, and the UQÀM Summer Institute in Cognitive Sciences, Montreal, July 2003. We'd also like to thank Rice University for its support of this research.

language isn't helpful. Of course, this isn't enough to show that the acquisition of number doesn't depend on natural language. But it does raise the very real possibility that, although language and number are both distinctively human achievements, there is no intrinsic link between the two.

1 Gallistel and Gelman

We will begin with Gallistel and Gelman's treatment of the positive integers. As they see it, the power of language stems from the way it interacts with an innate and evolutionarily ancient system known as the *Accumulator*. Before explaining their theory, it will help to have a basic understanding of what this system is and how it is motivated.

1.1 The Accumulator

Much of the motivation for the Accumulator derives from the study of nonhuman animals (for a review, see Gallistel, 1990). It turns out that many animal species are able to selectively respond to numerosity (that is, numerical quantity) as such, though not, it seems, to precise numerosity. For example, in one experimental design, a rat is required to press a lever a certain number of times before entering a feeding area to receive food. The rat can press more than the correct number of times, but if it enters the feeding area early it receives a penalty. On experiments of this sort, rats were shown to respond appropriately to numbers as high as 24 (Platt & Johnson, 1971; see also Mechner, 1958). While they don't reliably execute the precise number of required presses, they do get the approximate number correct, and their behavior exhibits a predictable pattern. First, they tend to overshoot the target, pressing a few more times than necessary rather than incurring the penalty. Second, and more important, their range of variation widens as the target number of presses increases (see fig. 13.1).

What makes this data interesting is that it looks as though the rats really are responding to numerosity rather than some closely related variable, such as duration. In a related experiment, Mechner and Gueverkian (1962) were able to control for duration by varying the hunger levels of their subjects. They found that hungrier rats would press the lever faster but with no effect on the number of presses. So the rats weren't simply pressing for a particular amount of time. Moreover, rats are equally good with different modalities (e.g., responding to numbers of lights or tones) and can even combine stimuli in two different modalities (Meck & Church, 1983). In short, the evidence strongly points in the direction that rats are able to respond to number; they just don't have precise numerical abilities.

Related studies with pigeons suggest that animals can respond to even larger numbers and that their discriminative capacity, though not as precise as the positive integers, is surprisingly fine grained. In these experiments, pigeons face a panel with three buttons and have the task of pecking the center button while it is illuminated. The experimenter controls things so that the illumination ceases after either 50 pecks or some other specified number, n. If the pigeon ends up pecking 50 times, it is supposed to peck the right button next, but if it pecks n times, then it is supposed to peck the left button next. Under these conditions, whether the

218 *Language and Concepts*

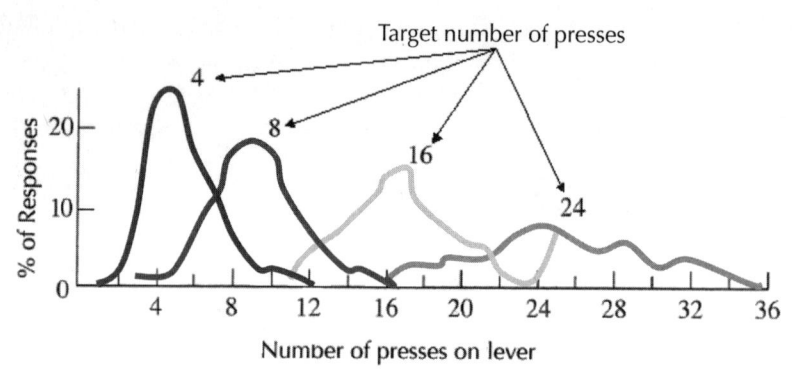

FIGURE 13.1 Data from Platt & Johnson's Experiments. In Platt & Johnson's experiments, rats were required to press a lever a certain number of times before moving to a feeding area. As the target number of presses increases, the range of variation in the number of presses widens (adapted from Platt & Johnson, 1971).

pigeons are able to reliably peck on the left or the right in appropriate circumstances indicates whether they are able to discriminate n from 50. Rilling and McDiarmid (1965) found that pigeons are able to correctly discriminate 40 from 50 90 percent of the time and 47 from 50 60 percent of the time.

The data from these sorts of experiments conform to two principles—the *magnitude effect* and the *distance effect* (see Dehaene, 1997).

The Magnitude Effect

Performance for discriminating numerosities separated by an equal amount declines as the quantities increase. For instance, it's harder to tell 10 from 12 than to tell 2 from 4, even though the difference between the two pairs is the same.

The Distance Effect

Performance for discriminating two numerosities declines as the distance between the two decreases. For instance, it's harder to tell 3 from 4 than to tell 3 from 8.

Together these principles illuminatingly describe the approximate character of animals' numerical abilities.

Gallistel and Gelman, following others, posit the existence of the Accumulator to explain the animals' pattern of results (Gallistel, 1990; Gallistel & Gelman, 2000). As we'll see, the interpretation of this system is a matter of some disagreement, and Gallistel and Gelman have their own peculiar way of understanding it. What is widely agreed upon, however, is that the Accumulator represents numerosity via a system of mental magnitudes. In other words, instead of using discrete symbols, the Accumulator employs representations couched in terms of a continuous variable.

Gallistel and Gelman employ an analogy to convey how the Accumulator works (Gallistel & Gelmans, 2000; Gallistel et al., forthcoming). Imagine water being poured into a beaker one cupful at a time and one cupful per item to be enumerated.[1] The resulting water level (a continuous variable) would provide a representation of the numerosity of the set: the higher the water level, the more numerous the set. Moreover, with an additional beaker, the system would have a natural mechanism for comparing the numerosities of different sets. The set whose beaker has the higher water level is the larger set. Similarly, the Accumulator could be augmented to support simple arithmetic operations. Addition could be implemented by having two beakers transfer their contents to a common store. The level in the common store would then represent their sum.

The Accumulator's variability has several possible sources. One is an inaccuracy in the measuring cup. Perhaps slightly more or less than a cupful gets into the beaker on any given pouring. Another possibility is that the beakers are unstable. Perhaps water sloshes around once inside them. In any event, the suggestion is that the variability is cumulative, so that the higher the water level, the greater the variability. This would explain why a system along these lines is only approximate and why pairs of numbers separated by equal distances are harder to distinguish as the numbers get larger.

Gallistel and Gelman make a good case for the importance of the Accumulator in accounting for the numerical abilities of nonhuman animals. But, as they note, rats and pigeons aren't the only ones who employ approximate representations of numerosity (Gallistel & Gelman, 2000). Humans do as well, and this suggests that humans have the Accumulator as part of their cognitive equipment too. In an important recent study, Fei Xu and Elizabeth Spelke set out to test the view held by many psychologists that preverbal infants aren't capable of discriminating numerosities beyond the range of one to three (Xu & Spelke, 2000). They presented six-month-old infants with displays of dots. One group of infants saw various displays of 8 dots while the other group saw displays of 16. After reaching habituation (i.e., a substantial decrease in looking time), both groups of infants were shown novel displays of both 8 and 16 dots and their looking times were measured (see fig. 13.2). In both the habituation phase and the test phase, Xu and Spelke were extremely careful to control for features of the stimuli that correlate with numerosity—display size, element size, stimulus density, contour length, and average brightness. What Xu and Spelke found was that the infants who were habituated to one numerosity recovered significantly more to the novel numerosity, indicating that they *are* able to distinguish 8 from 16 after all. However, infants under the same experimental conditions showed no sign of being able to discriminate 8 from 12. Xu and Spelke's conclusion was that infants at this age can discriminate between large sets of differing numerosity "provided the ratio of difference between the sets is large" (p. 87). Within the framework of the

---

1. Put without the analogy, the model maintains that a fixed amount of energy is stored for each item enumerated and that the process is iterative in that only one unit is stored at a time. However, a major point of disagreement among defenders of the Accumulator is whether the process is in fact iterative. For a noniterative model, see Church and Broadbent (1990). Another point of disagreement worth mentioning is whether one and the same mechanism—the Accumulator—underlies both numerical and temporal discriminations. Gallistel and Gelman maintain that the Accumulator, functioning in different modes, underlies both types of discriminative ability.

Habituation

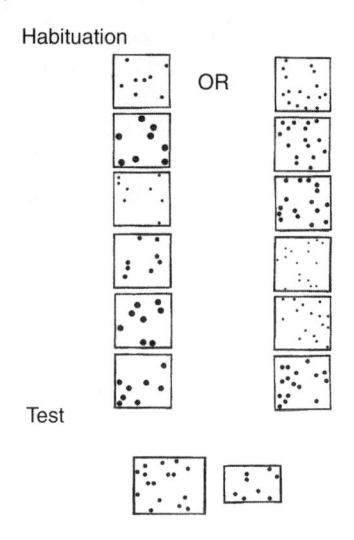

Test

FIGURE 13.2 Sample stimuli from Xu & Spelke's experiments. In Xu & Spelke's experiments 6-month-old infants were habituated to displays of either 8 dots or 16 dots. In the testing phase they were shown new displays with both 8 and 16 dots. The infants dishabituated more to displays with the novel numerosity, indicating that they were able to discriminate 8 from 16 (Xu & Spelke, 2000). Reprinted from *Cognition*, vol. 74, no. 1, F. Xu et al., "Large Number Discrimination in 6-Month-Old Infants," p. B5, copyright 2000, with permission from Elsevier.

Accumulator model, this all makes sense. Like the rats and pigeons, infants are able to discriminate some numerosities from others. It's just that their Accumulator isn't fully developed and so isn't as sensitive as the one found in (mature) rats and pigeons.

Evidence for the accumulator can also be found in adult humans. For example, Whalen, Gallistel, and Gelman (1999) gave adults tasks comparable to the ones previously given to rats. In one of their experiments, adults had to respond to a displayed numeral by tapping a key the corresponding number of times as rapidly as possible. The speed of the tapping ensured that the subjects couldn't use subvocal counting, and Whalen and colleagues were able to rule out a reliance on duration as well. The results were that Whalen et al.'s subjects performed in much the same way as Platt and Johnson's rats. Their responses were approximately correct, with the range of key presses increasing as the target numbers increased. The conclusion Whalen et al. drew was that adults employ "a representation that is qualitatively and quantitatively similar to that found in animals" (p. 134).[2]

So there is substantial evidence for the existence of an innate number-specific system of representation that provides humans and animals with an ability to respond to approximate numerosity by means of a system of mental magnitudes. This system explains the distance and magnitude effects and a wealth of experimental results (of which we have only been able to present a small sample here). Though the Accumulator's

---

[2]. For further evidence concerning the Accumulator's role in adult human cognition, see Dehaene (1997) and Barth, Kanwisher, and Spelke (2003).

representational resources may seem rather crude compared to the concepts for the positive integers, Gallistel and Gelman's position is that they form the basis for how we acquire the positive integers. We are now in a position to turn to their theory.

1.2 The Theory: Getting the Integers from the Reals

Psychologists typically assume that the positive integers form our most basic system of precise numerical representation. Systems incorporating zero, negative integers, fractions, real numbers, and so on are thought to be cultural inventions. Indeed, the cultural origin of many of these systems is taken to be part of the historical record.

Gallistel and Gelman's theory boldly challenges this conventional wisdom. As they see it, the Accumulator plays a foundational role in the acquisition of the positive integers. But they offer a distinctive interpretation of the Accumulator and what its states represent that provides the point of departure for a truly radical account of the relationship between the integers and the reals. For Gallistel and Gelman, it's the *reals*, not the integers, that are the more basic:[3]

> We suggest that it is the system of real numbers that is the psychologically primitive system, both in the phylogenetic and the ontogenetic sense. (Gallistel et al., forthcoming, p. 1)

> Our thesis is that this cultural creation of the real numbers was a Platonic rediscovery of the underlying nonverbal system of arithmetic reasoning. The cultural history of the number concept is the history of learning to talk coherently about a system of reasoning with real numbers that predates our ability to talk, both phylogenetically and ontogenetically. (Gallistel et al., forthcoming, p. 3)

For Gallistel and Gelman, the integers are a psychological achievement but one that occurs only against the background of representational resources that most others take to be a *far greater* psychological achievement.

On the standard interpretation of the Accumulator, its representations are of approximate numerosity (see, e.g., Carey, 2001; Dehaene, 1997). They represent, in Elizabeth Spelke and Sanna Tsivkin's useful phrase, "a blur on the number line" (2001, p. 85). Instead of picking out 17 (and just 17), an Accumulator-based representation indeterminately represents a range of numbers in the general vicinity of 17. A good deal of the evidence in favor of this interpretation—and likewise, a good deal of evidence in favor of the Accumulator—comes from the variability in animal and human performance under a variety of task conditions. But Gallistel and Gelman have a different take on this variability. Their interpretation is that it traces back to problems with memory. "[T]he reading of a mental magnitude is a noisy process, and the noise is proportional to magnitude being read" (forthcoming, p. 5). That is, the accumulator represents precise numerosities that are systematically distorted when stored and retrieved. Mental magnitudes, as they see it, aren't approximate. It's the processes that are defined over them that make them seem as

---

3. See also Gallistel and Gelman (2000) and Gelman and Cordes (2001).

if they are. How precise are the representations that feed into memory? Gallistel and Gelman's answer is that they are extremely precise, that mental magnitudes by their very nature are so fine grained as to represent the real numbers.[4]

Given this understanding of the Accumulator, arriving at representations of the positive integers is not a matter of trying to make precise the approximate representations used by the Accumulator. The representations in the Accumulator are already perfectly precise; in fact, precise representations of all the positive integers are already present in the Accumulator, since the positive integers are a subset of the reals. What's needed is some way to pick out the positive integers from among the reals. This is where Gallistel and Gelman appeal to natural language.

One of Gallistel and Gelman's major contributions to the study of numerical cognition is the characterization of a set of principles whose mastery is constitutive of learning to count. There are four principles in all (see Gelman & Gallistel, 1978):

Gelman and Gallistel's Counting Principles

1. *The one-one principle*: one and only one tag is to be used for each item in a count.
2. *The stable-order principle*: the tags used in counting must be applied in a fixed order.
3. *The cardinal principle*: the final tag in a count gives the cardinality of the set of items being counted.
4. *The abstraction principle*: principles 1–3 apply to any collection of entities; in other words, there is no restriction on the sorts of things one can count.

For Gallistel and Gelman, counting plays a critical role in the acquisition of concepts of positive integers. They argue that the preverbal system—the Accumulator—effectively embodies the counting principles[5] and that children may come to perceive the correspondence between nonverbal and verbal counting processes. This leads children to conclude that counting terms represent the same thing as the preverbal mental

---

4. Gallistel and Gelman's claim that mental magnitudes represent the reals isn't a metaphor. It's to be taken quite literally. Oddly, though, they are not entirely explicit about why they think this is so. We suspect that their reasoning may be something like the following. Since a single system, the Accumulator, functions to represent both number and duration (see note 1), the representations involved must have the same basic features when representing number and time. And since time can be measured in terms of arbitrarily finer and finer units, the representations must be capable of being divided in ever finer ways, ultimately to the point of representing any real numbered unit of time. Anything less would be to impose a discrete structure on what is by all accounts a continuous, nondiscrete vehicle of representation. The upshot is that it is supposed to be intrinsic to the format of representation that it picks out quantities in terms of real numbers. So when the Accumulator is working with numerosities, that can hardly change. It's built into the nature of the representations themselves.
5. Returning to the beaker analogy, each water level resulting from adding a cupful of water corresponds uniquely to the next item enumerated (one-one principle). Likewise, the beaker states occur in a fixed order (stable-order principle), with the final beaker state giving the cardinal value of the set (cardinal principle). Finally, the Accumulator is not tied to any particular modality; it can be used to evaluate the numerosity of visual stimuli, auditory stimuli, tactile stimuli, and so on (abstraction principle).

magnitudes, namely, numerosities. What's more, language, according to Gallistel and Gelman, acts as a kind of filter.[6] Its discrete character invariably selects the integers from the rest of the reals:

> [T]he integers are picked out by language because they are the magnitudes that represent countable quantity. Countable quantity is the only kind of quantity that can readily be represented by a system founded on discrete symbols, as language is. (Gallistel et al., forthcoming, p. 19)

For Gallistel and Gelman, the nonverbal system gives children a head start in learning the verbal system, in that it directs them to the verbal system and shapes their understanding of its significance. But in learning the verbal system, children are able to go beyond the limitations of the preverbal system and beyond the capacities of animals and infants. Language brings the positive integers into focus and eliminates the variability that is so characteristic of the preverbal system.

1.3 Objections

Unfortunately, Gallistel and Gelman's theory faces a number of serious objections, and ultimately, we believe, it cannot be made to work.

Let's start with their understanding of the Accumulator and its representational states. Granting that the representations in the Accumulator are given by mental magnitudes, should we take the system to be capable of representing the full range of real numbers? The answer quite simply is *no*. For example, there is no reason to suppose that Platt and Johnson's rats are capable of representing 3.5, much less 7.4121326769 or $\sqrt{2}$. Certainly the rats' *behavior* doesn't show sensitivity to these numerosities. To be sure, they can't reliably determine whether they should press 7, 8, 9, or 10 times, when the required value is precisely 8. But this would only seem to indicate a failure to discriminate among various *whole number* values.

Of course, it may be that experiments that are sensitive enough to detect the presences of more fine-grained representational capacities have not yet been conducted. Perhaps future experiments will show that the rats' representations of numerosity do encompass the full range of the real numbers and that they can distinguish between, say, 7.4121326768 and 7.4121326769. Similarly, we suppose one could try to insist that the rats have the far more powerful representational system embodying the reals but are unable to manifest it in their behavior. At present, however, we have no reason to take either of these possibilities seriously.[7]

---

6. Alternatively, Gelman and Cordes describe the process as making explicit what was previously implicit through a process of "rerepresentation" (2001, p. 294).
7. Though we don't have space to discuss it here, there is reason to doubt whether the mental magnitudes employed in measuring duration are as fine grained as the reals either. It's hardly obvious that we ever represent to ourselves durations of π or $\sqrt{2}$ seconds. Certainly, there is no behavioral evidence for this. Nor is there evidence that for any two durations there is always a representable duration between then. Much the same is true of other mental magnitudes. There is no reason to believe that the visual system can always represent a length between any two lengths no matter how fine-grained, or that the auditory system can always represent a volume between any two volumes.

Moreover, the situation isn't just that there is a lack of evidence to support Gallistel and Gelman's position. There is also an inherent tension in their account. Assuming that the Accumulator's states do represent the reals, it's hard to see how the Accumulator could embody the counting principles. The idea that there is a "next tag" makes no sense with respect to the reals. The problem is that the reals are *dense* in that between any two real numbers there is always another real number. So "2" is no more "the next tag" after "1" than "1.5" is (or, for that matter, than any other number greater than 1 is). Putting this problem aside, even if there was some sense in which "the next tag" could be defined for a system representing the reals, the Accumulator would still have to operate with impossibly perfect precision to ensure that the same accumulator levels are applied in the same order for each count. In all likelihood the level corresponding to "1" would rarely be followed by the level corresponding to "2"; rather, it would sometimes be followed by "2.0000000000103," sometimes by "2.000010021," and so on. But that's just to say that the stable-order principle wouldn't hold. And if two items were being counted and the final tag were anything other than precisely "2," the cardinality principle wouldn't hold either, since the cardinal value of a two-membered set is *precisely* 2, not, 2.0000000000103 or 2.000010021.[8]

What has gone wrong? Our diagnosis is that Gallistel and Gelman have taken features of the representational format to necessitate features of the content of the representation. In particular, they have assumed that if the vehicle of representation is a continuous magnitude, then what it represents must also be a continuous magnitude. However, this assumption is mistaken. There is nothing at all incoherent about mental magnitudes representing discrete values.

What about the second half of Gallistel and Gelman's model, namely, the role that they assign to language? Recall that on their view natural language acts as a sort of filter, selecting the positive integers from among the reals. Natural language is able to do this because it is discrete, and discrete representations are supposed to readily represent only countable quantities. Unfortunately, this feature of their theory is indefensible, quite apart from the troubles with their interpretation of the Accumulator.

The main problem is their assumption about what language can and cannot readily represent. The fact that language is discrete does not in any way limit it to representing discrete contents. Language has no difficulty representing imprecise, nondiscrete properties such as *being bald, being red*, or *being tall*. Far from it; vagueness is a pervasive feature of language (Keefe, 2000). Likewise, language isn't limited to terms like "pencil," which pick out countable entities. It can happily

---

8. These problems also undermine Gallistel and Gelman's claim that the correspondence between verbal and nonverbal counting will help in picking out the integers from the reals. Since there won't be any Accumulator states consistently correlated with verbal counting symbols, there won't be any correspondence to notice. Moreover, this problem remains on the alternative interpretation of Accumulator states, where such states represent a "blur on the number line." In that case, the "correspondence" would be between "*n*" and a blur somewhere in the general vicinity of *n*. But this isn't really a correspondence at all. Indeed, the problem remains even if we suppose that the Accumulator states represent *precise integer values*—albeit ones that can only be accessed via the noisy and distorting process of memory. Since the precise values cannot be accessed as such to be compared with the verbal counts, again it seems there would be no correspondence that the child could notice.

accommodate mass terms, such as "salt," which pick out substances or stuffs. Mass terms can also be incorporated into expressions of quantity ("more salt," "less salt," "a little salt," "a lot of salt," "loads of salt"). And it should also go without saying that language has numerous devices for expressing inexact quantities of differing sizes ("some," "plenty," "a few," "a handful," "a bunch of," "an army of").

Language can also readily represent specific real number quantities via names and descriptions ("pi" and "the square root of two"). And by incorporating a system of decimal notation, language can of course represent arbitrarily fine-grained real values, allowing us to discuss such things as whether the current interest rate of 5.867 percent is likely to rise.

We take it that these considerations undercut any hope that the discrete character of language accounts for how the integers emerge from the reals. Once again, the difficulties for Gallistel and Gelman's theory appear to stem from a conflation of representational formats, or vehicles, and representational contents. In this case, the problematic assumption is that discrete vehicles—linguistic symbols—can only readily express discrete contents. But it should now be abundantly clear that this assumption is false. Discrete systems like language are not limited to representing countable quantities. The relation between vehicles and contents just isn't as tight as Gallistel and Gelman would have us assume.

We have argued that Gallistel and Gelman's account of the ontogeny of the integers faces a number of serious objections. Their interpretation of the Accumulator as representing the reals is unwarranted, their commitment to this interpretation is in direct conflict with their claim that the Accumulator operates in accordance with the counting principles, and their view about language's role as a filter is based on mistaken assumptions about what language can and cannot readily represent. These objections go to the heart of Gallistel and Gelman's account. Without their interpretation of the Accumulator and without their view of language acting as a filter, their account simply cannot be made to work. All the same, Gallistel and Gelman are right to emphasize the importance of the Accumulator. It is a number-specific system that is plausibly innate and likely to play a role in the ontogeny of the integers. In the next section we will examine another theory that also makes use of the Accumulator, but in very different way.

2 Spelke

We turn now to Elizabeth Spelke's theory of the positive integers. Like Gallistel and Gelman, Spelke makes use of the Accumulator, but she also emphasizes a second cognitive system. And, importantly, she identifies a new and interesting role for natural language to play.

2.1 Language as the Basis for Conceptual Change

Spelke's treatment of the positive integers is based on a general account of conceptual change that aims to explain, among other things, why the human conceptual system is far more expressive and flexible than that of other animals. At the center of Spelke's account is natural language. According to Spelke, human beings are endowed with a variety of innate domain-specific, task-specific modules. These modules function independently of one another, and their internal workings are inaccessible to other parts of the mind. As Spelke sees it, the richness of adult human thought isn't a matter of the contents of any particular module; most of these modules are supposed to be present in other species. Rather, the key difference is owing to the human ability to bring together the contents of two or more modules. Crucially, the way this is done is through natural language. "Natural languages provide humans with a unique system for combining flexibly the representations they share with other animals. The resulting combinations are unique to humans and account for unique aspects of human intelligence" (Spelke, 2003, p. 291). Language's power stems from two of its central features—its domain generality and its compositionality:

> First, a natural language allows the expression of thoughts in any area of knowledge. Natural languages therefore provide a domain-general medium in which separate, domain-specific representations can be brought together. Second, a natural language is a combinatorial system, allowing distinct concepts to be juxtaposed and conjoined. Once children have mapped representations in different domains to expressions of their language, therefore, they can combine those representations. Through these combinations, language allows the expression of new concepts: concepts whose elements were present in the prelinguistic child's knowledge systems but whose conjunction was not expressible, because of the isolation of these systems. (Spelke & Tsivkin, 2001, p. 71)

Spelke's primary and most developed illustration of this account focuses on spatial reorientation (Shusterman & Spelke, chapter 6 here; Spelke, 2003; Spelke & Tsivkin, 2001). In reorienting, one could rely on geometrical information about the layout of the environment, landmark cues, or both. Surprisingly, many nonhuman animals seem unable to combine these two types of information; for example, they don't take advantage of concepts like LEFT OF THE BLUE WALL.[9] Moreover, while adult humans *do* employ combinations of this sort, children who have yet to master the spatial vocabulary don't, and neither do adults who are engaged in tasks that interfere specifically with language processing. These results seem to provide strong support for Spelke's general account of conceptual change. Natural language, as she puts it, has the "magical property" of compositionality. "Thanks to their compositional semantics, natural languages can expand the child's conceptual repertoire to include not just the preexisting core knowledge concepts but also any new well-formed combination of those concepts" (Spelke, 2003, p. 306).

2.2 The Theory of Positive Integers: Old Concepts, New Combinations

Spelke's account of how the positive integers are acquired is supposed to follow the same pattern as the spatial reorientation case, once again drawing upon the domain generality and combinatorial structure of language.

---

9. Here and below we employ the standard small capitals notation for concepts and mental representations.

> The foregoing analysis of spatial orientation prompts a different [i.e., novel] account of number development. Children may attain the mature system of knowledge of the natural numbers by conjoining together representations delivered by their two preverbal systems. Language may serve as a medium of this conjunction, moreover, because it is a domain-general, combinatorial system to which the representations delivered by the child's two nonverbal systems can be mapped. (Spelke & Tsivkin, 2001, p. 84)

What, then, are the two preverbal systems on the basis of which the positive integers are formed? Unfortunately, Spelke doesn't have a lot to say about them. The first she and Sanna Tsivkin characterize as a *small-number system*, saying that it "serves to represent small numerosities exactly" (p. 83). The second, in contrast, is supposed to be a *large-number system*, one that "serves to represent large sets" but whose "accuracy decreases with increasing set size in accord with Weber's Law" (p. 83). We take it that the large-number system is the Accumulator. Though Spelke doesn't come right out and say this, the evidence that she and Tsivkin cite on behalf of the large-number system is exactly the sort that is generally associated with the Accumulator. Things are a little trickier with their so-called small number system. But the sort of evidence they cite in connection with this system suggests that what they have in mind is what is elsewhere known as the *object indexing system* (or the *object file system*).

The object indexing system is a psychological mechanism that supports the visual tracking of a small number of objects. Several similar models have been proposed, but the basic idea in each case is to have reassignable indexes that function as abstract representations of individual objects (see, e.g., Leslie et al., 1998). In adult humans, the number of indexes is about four—a number that derives from work on object-based attention studies in vision (Trick & Pylyshyn, 1993). The indexes are abstract in that they don't inherently represent the color, shape, texture, or any of the features of an object. They are sometimes likened to fingers, which can point to a thing without thereby conveying any of its features. Object indexes are able to do this because they track objects, in the first instance, by responding to their spatial-temporal properties.[10] As a result, once an index is assigned to an object, it "sticks" to it simply on the basis of such things as the object's maintaining a continuous path (with allowances for brief occlusions).

The object indexing system has a great deal of explanatory power. Here we have space for only one example—its ability to account for an influential finding of Karen Wynn's. Wynn (1992) showed five-month-old infants scenes that instantiated simple additions and subtractions, followed by outcomes that were either arithmetically correct or incorrect. In one experiment, after a doll was placed on an empty stage, a screen came up to hide the doll from view. While the screen was still up, a second doll was visibly added. The screen was then withdrawn, revealing either two objects

---

10. This isn't to say, however, that an object's features aren't represented by the object indexing system. Leslie et al. (1998) emphasize that features may be recorded and may even be used in the assignment of object indexes. It's just that the use of spatial-temporal properties is more basic and can govern the assignment of indexes independently of information about features.

(the correct outcome) or one object (an incorrect outcome). The infants' looking time (relative to their base preference levels) was significantly greater for the incorrect outcome, suggesting to Wynn that five-month-olds know that $1+1=2$ (see fig. 13.3). Wynn's conclusion is controversial, but for present purposes the interesting fact is that her results hold only for small numbers. This is part of the reason Spelke and Tsivkin claim that there is a system that represents only small numerosities.

The object indexing system explains this cap in terms of its limited stock of indexes; it can track no more than four objects simultaneously. The looking-time patterns in Wynn's experiments can also be explained under the assumption that attention is allocated when an active index loses its object or when a new object necessities the activation of a new index. In the $1+1$ scenario, infants look longer at the incorrect outcome ($1+1=1$) because they end up with an active index that has lost its object.

Having introduced Spelke's two preverbal number modules, we turn now to her account of how they come together to yield the integers. Representations from the small-number system (the object indexing system) are supposed to be conjoined with representations from the large-number system (the Accumulator), through the power of natural language. According to Spelke and Tsivkin, exposure to number words leads children to notice that representations from the two systems apply to the same sets of entities for small numbered sets:

> [B]ecause the words for small numbers map to representations in both the small-number system and the large-number system, learning these words may indicate to the child that these two sets of representations pick out a common set of entities, whose properties are the union of those picked out by each system alone. This union of properties may be sufficient to define the set of natural numbers. (2001, p. 85)

A variety of cues then suggest that all number words should be treated alike, even though the small-number system is limited to very small sets:

> Because all the number words appear in the same syntactic contexts (see Bloom & Wynn, 1997) and occur together in the counting routine, experience with the ambient language may lead children to seek a common representational system for these terms. (p. 85)

And finally it all comes together, the result being representations of the positive integers:

> [B]ecause the terms *one*, *two* and *three* form a sequence in the counting routine, children may discover that each of these number words picks out a set with one more individual than the previous word in the sequence, and they may generalize this learning to all the words in the counting sequence. (pp. 85–6)

In support of this account, Spelke cites two further sources of evidence linking language to number. One source of evidence involves cases of brain-damaged patients who have impaired language and are also unable to perform exact calculations (yet retain the ability to approximate). The other source of evidence involves experimental work on bilinguals who were trained to do certain sorts of exact calculations and approximations in one of their languages and then tested on these tasks in both of their languages. Interestingly, the bilinguals were able

Correct Outcome   **Incorrect Outcome**

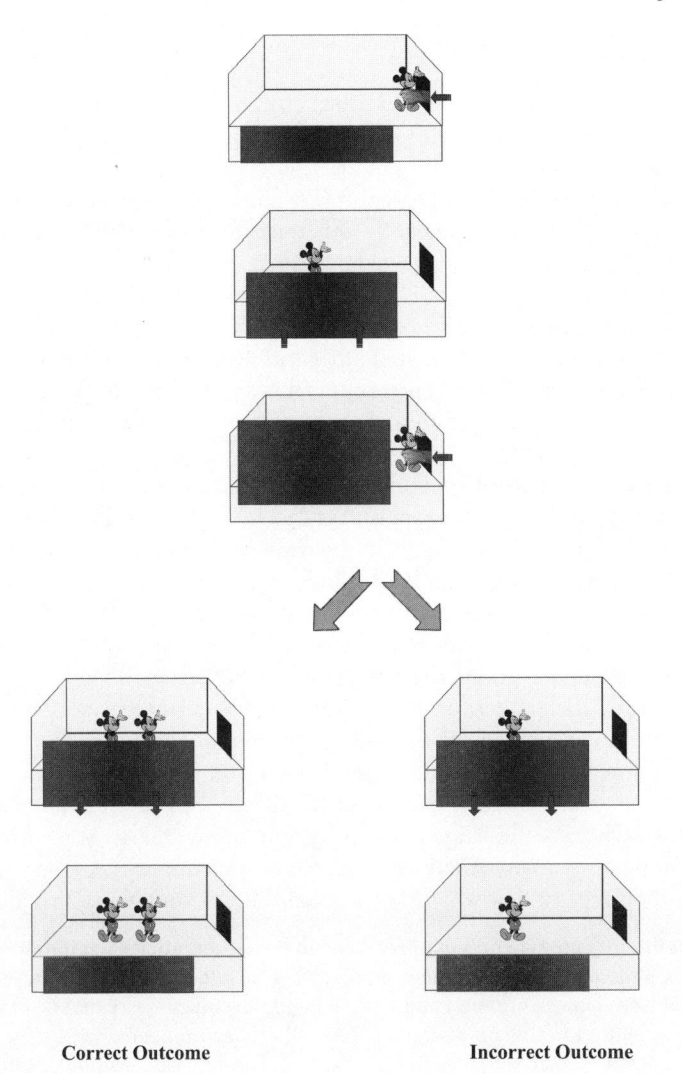

FIGURE 13.3 Schematic Depiction of one of Wynn's Addition/Subtraction Experiments. After a doll was placed on an empty stage, a screen came up to hide the doll from view. While the screen was still up, a second doll was visibly added. The screen was then withdrawn revealing either two objects (the correct outcome) or one object (the incorrect outcome) (adapted from Wynn, 1922).

to transfer the new approximation skills across languages but were unable to transfer their new skills with exact calculations. Spelke and her collaborators take this to suggest that language is essentially involved in the representation of large exact numerosities—a view that is a natural corollary of her theory of development.

2.3 Objections

Spelke's account faces a number of serious objections, and, ultimately, we believe it is no more promising than Gallistel and Gelman's. Much of the trouble with Spelke's account comes right at the beginning. In particular, it isn't clear which representations are to be drawn from the two modules. Spelke gives several answers that are significantly different from one another if not simply inconsistent.

As we showed in section 2.2, Spelke and Tsivkin (2001) claim that the small-number system "serves to represent small numerosities exactly." This remark is embedded in a larger discussion where they introduce the small number system by noting that "the capacity for representing the exact numerosity of small sets is common to humans and other animals and emerges early in human development" (pp. 82–3). Likewise, writing with Marc Hauser, Spelke refers to "a system for representing the exact number of object arrays or events with very small numbers of entities" (Hauser & Spelke, 2004, p. 9). Yet in a related discussion, Spelke says that the system "does not permit infants to discriminate between different sets of individuals with respect to their cardinal values" (2003, p. 299). These claims, if not simply inconsistent, are in strong tension with one another. How could a system represent the exact numerosity of different small sets without at least permitting infants to discriminate among them with respect to their cardinality?

Other times the concern isn't inconsistency but rather that what are supposed to be the same components of the theory are presented in ways that aren't at all equivalent. For example, at one point Spelke and Tsivkin say that the small-number system represents a two-member set as "an object x and an object y, such that $y \neq x$," whereas the large-number system represents it as "a blur on the number indicating a very small set" (Spelke & Tsivkin, 2001, p. 85). Elsewhere, however, they suggest that what the two contribute is something very different:

> From the small number system may come the realization that each number word corresponds to an exact number of objects, that adding or subtracting exactly one object changes number, and that changing the shape or spatial distribution of objects does not change number. From the large-number system may come the realization that sets of exact numerosity can increase without limit, and that a given symbol represents the set as a unit, not just as an array of distinct objects." (p. 86)

Given all of these different pronouncements, it's hard to say which should be taken as Spelke's considered view of the representations that the two modules are supposed to deliver.

If that weren't bad enough, it's doubtful that any of her answers are especially promising. For instance, take the representations (i) and (ii):

(i) AN OBJECT X AND AN OBJECT Y, SUCH THAT $Y \neq X$

(ii) ──── ["────" indicates a specific blur on the number line corresponding to approximately 2]

Spelke and Tsivkin talk repeatedly about "conjoining" representations from the small and large number systems. But conjoining these two representations results in the bizarre representation (iii):

(iii)   AN OBJECT X AND AN OBJECT Y, SUCH THAT Y ≠ X AND ⎯⎯⎯⎯

The problem is that it is anything but clear what this representation means.

Since the target is a concept like SEVEN (exactly seven, not approximately seven), perhaps a more promising suggestion is to combine the generic concept of EXACT NUMEROSITY with a given approximate numerical range. The generic concept may be what Spelke has in mind when she emphasizes that the small number system "represents small numerosities exactly." Suppose, then, that the combination is a representation of exact numerosity with a blur corresponding to approximately 7—SEVENISH, for lack of a better expression. The question is what the result would be. We see no reason to think that there is a determinate answer to this question or one that Spelke would find particularly favorable. To see why, consider a close analogy. RED indeterminately applies to a range of colors with no precise boundary separating red and its neighboring colors, such as orange. What happens when the concept RED is combined with the concept EXACT COLOR? What would the content of this concept be? The answer isn't at all clear. Notice that adding COLOR to RED doesn't add anything at all, so in combining EXACT COLOR and RED, EXACT does all the work. But what does EXACT add to RED? Something can be such-and-such percentage red, or such-and-such shade of red, but not exactly red. Perhaps the best that can be said here is that EXACT + RED just means red. In that case, EXACT NUMEROSITY + SEVENISH would just mean sevenish. This hardly brings us closer to SEVEN.

What's more, the situation doesn't improve even if one insists that EXACT NUMEROSITY + SEVENISH must refer to some more specific numerosity, since there are many specific contents that would be candidates. These include (but aren't limited to) the range 7–8, the range 6–7, the range 6–8, the number 7.5, the number 8, and so on. All of these are different ways of making SEVENISH more precise. Modifying SEVENISH by EXACT NUMEROSITY does nothing to single out seven.

Things get even worse in that Spelke can't assume that a concept of numerosity is in the small-number system in the first place. If this system is the object indexing system, as we suggested earlier, then its representational powers are far more modest. What it does is attend to a small number of objects by employing a small number of indexes, one per object. Its representations are the indexes, each of which only represents the object it temporarily tracks. Of course, whenever the system responds to two objects, it will activate exactly two indexes. But that doesn't mean that the system is employing the concept EXACTLY TWO or representing the two-ness of the set. Rather, it's just a reflection of the parallel activation of two indexes, each of which continues to represent no more than its object. The same considerations extend to other numerical or quasi-numerical concepts that Spelke may wish to appeal to—EXACT NUMEROSITY, EXACT, NUMEROSITY, ONE, TWO, EXACTLY ONE, EXACTLY TWO, and so on. None of

232 *Language and Concepts*

these are present in the object indexing system, and none can be taken for granted.[11]

Up until now we have been taking at face value Spelke's claim that her treatment of the positive integers follows the same model as her treatment of spatial reorientation. It may be, however, the two aren't so closely related and that what Spelke ought to say is that the common ground between them is just the importance given to language. In that case, it may be that the compositional structure of language is what's important for spatial reorientation but that language functions rather differently when it comes to number. If this is right, then Spelke's view of number isn't grounded in her general theory of conceptual change (or else that theory is described very misleadingly). On the other hand, the departure from her general theory of conceptual change would make sense of the fact that Spelke suggests a variety of different contributions from the preverbal number modules. It would also make sense of Spelke and Tsivkin's remarks about different "realizations" coming from the two number systems.

Suppose, then, that the theory isn't that the representations of the small and large number systems are combined compositionally. The remarks about realizations suggest a more intellectual process where information made available by the two modules is subjected to reflection and a certain amount of theorizing takes place, leading somehow to a new stock of concepts. One problem that this raises for Spelke is *where* the reflection takes place. Spelke's inventory of innate mechanisms includes the modules we share with animals plus language. Clearly reflection of the required sort isn't something that could occur in a domain-specific, task-specific module; and language, while it may provide a domain-general medium, isn't a mechanism that can be counted on to embody any inference you like. So it may turn out that the seat of conceptual change has yet to be identified.

More generally, though, we need to ask what exactly the initial information to be combined looks like, how exactly the process works, and how any new concepts emerge from it. Since the alternative model of conceptual change that we are considering is not explicitly discussed in Spelke's work, it cannot be evaluated in any detail. But to get a feel for the difficulties it is likely to face, consider just the question of what initial information is to be combined. In several places, Spelke indicates that the small-number system may contribute something like the concept of an individual, while the large-number system contributes something like the concept of a set. For instance:

> One system represents small numbers of persisting, numerically distinct individuals exactly and takes account of the operation of adding or removing one indi-

---

11. One might try to argue that, though these are not explicitly represented in the object indexing system, one or more are *implicitly* represented. We should note that we don't think that this is a promising suggestion. Part of the problem is that Spelke would then need a mechanism that could make them explicit. Moreover, such a mechanism would threaten to make her language-based theory of conceptual change superfluous. Any cognitive mechanisms that could render a concept explicit in the envisioned sense would be capable of formulating an entirely novel concept. Language would no longer be the driving force for conceptual change.

vidual from the scene. It fails to represent the individuals as a set, however, and therefore does not permit infants to discriminate between different sets with respect to their cardinal values. A second system represents large numbers of objects or events as sets with cardinal values, and it allows for numerical comparison across sets. This system, however, fails to represent sets exactly, it fails to represent the members of these sets as persisting, numerically distinct individuals, and therefore it fails to capture the numerical operations of adding or subtracting one. (2003, p. 299)

Learning the meaning of small number words is supposed to bring these two representations together, thereby laying the groundwork for concepts of the positive integers:

> To learn the full meaning of two, however, children must combine their representations of individuals and sets: they must learn that two applies just in case the array contains a set composed of an individual, of another, numerically distinct individual, and of no further individuals. (p. 301)

One point to note here is that it is puzzling how the combination of such varied information is supposed to be achieved. The suggestion is that the likes of (1) and (2) are brought together to yield (3):

(1) The information that there is a set consisting of a small indeterminate number of individuals that aren't represented as persisting or as being numerically distinct form one another

(2) The information that there is a persisting individual and a different persisting individual

(3) The belief that there is a set consisting of a persisting individual and a different persisting individual and no other individuals

A major problem with this proposal, to the extent that we understand it, is the very different assumptions about "individuals" in the two systems. In one case the individuals are persisting and numerically distinct. In the other, they are neither of these. There would seem to be little point of contact between the two, making it difficult to see how they could come to support a common belief, short of equivocation. Similarly, the notion of set that is supposed to be derived from the large-number system is a peculiar one. Our ordinary notion of a set is one that is defined in terms of its members (where these are numerically distinct, persisting individuals). But Spelke can't avail herself of this notion. Another concern is that, while Spelke may be right that the small-number system doesn't represent the set of objects as such—that it only represents the individuals in the set—whatever justification there is for this claim could be applied to the Accumulator as well. The only thing the Accumulator patently represents is a property of sets, namely, their approximate numerosity. This no more requires that the sets themselves be represented than representing the redness of an individual requires representing the individual as such. As a result, Spelke isn't in a position to assume that the Accumulator has any explicit representation of a set to begin with.

Together these considerations cast doubt on Spelke's theory insofar as it breaks away from the spatial reorientation example. Because Spelke says so little about how the imagined combination proceeds, it's hard to say more. Still, we do want to mention one final potential difficulty. The current model requires that both the small-number system and the large-number system are responsive to smaller numbers, each in its own way. For example, both are supposed to be able to respond to sets of two items, particularly in the course of learning the word "two." The result is supposed to be that learning the first few number-words precipitates, and in some sense causes, a conceptual shift, giving rise to the positive integers. It goes without saying that for any of this to work, the large-number system—the Accumulator—has to function for small numbers. Our last concern is that there is a very real possibility that it doesn't. In the Xu and Spelke study cited in section 1.1, it was found that infants who could distinguish 8 from 16 couldn't distinguish between 8 and 12 (Xu & Spelke, 2000). And in a subsequent work, Xu has found that infants who can distinguish between 4 and 8 nonetheless can't distinguish between 2 and 4 (Xu, 2003). Xu concludes that infants at this age have an Accumulator that requires a 1:2 ratio but, in addition, doesn't respond to small numbers (thus the failure with 2 v. 4). Why not? There are several possibilities. One is that, as Xu puts it, the Accumulator's "computations are unstable or undefined for small values" (p. B23). This would be a likely outcome, particularly if its operations aren't iterative—as is assumed by Gallistel and Gelman—but instead compute approximate number in some other way.[12] Another possibility is that "the output of the object tracking system inhibits the output of the number estimation system [the Accumulator]" (p. B24). Either way, Spelke's treatment of the positive integers would be problematic, since she couldn't assume that children have representations from both preverbal systems at the level at which they are supposed to be compared. The result is that they would have no basis for formulating concepts for the integers 1, 2, and 3, and the account wouldn't even get off the ground.

Finally, before closing this section, we should say a word or two about the evidence linking language to number. This includes evidence from brain-damaged patients and from bilinguals, both pointing to a link between language and the representation of exact number, including exact calculation. The question is whether the link is so strong that it argues that language is intrinsic to the representation of the positive integers, making language a condition for their emergence. We would suggest that the evidence is, at best, inconclusive. This is for the simple reason that, among language users, language may come to play an important role in the representation of the integers without being the original source of these concepts. Though extremely interesting, the data aren't developmental data; consequently, they don't tell one way or the other about the fact of ontogeny.

Of course, even if these data did establish that language is essential to number, this wouldn't argue for Spelke's theory in particular. The data are equally compatible with Gallistel and Gelman's theory or any of a large number of different possible theories that take language to play a crucial role in the ontogeny of number. Moreover, there are also data suggesting that number isn't essentially dependent on language. Though we lack the space to go into much detail here, it's worth mentioning in this context that there are cases of patients with severe

---

12. Spelke herself has argued for a noniterative model in Barth, Kanwisher, and Spelke (2003).

linguistic deficits who can perform exact calculation. For instance, Hermelin and O'Connor (1990) describe a speechless autistic man who can identify five-figure prime numbers and who can factorize numbers of the same magnitude, all based on exposure to a few examples. The examples involve the use of symbols — standard Arabic notation. However, the important point is that Arabic notion isn't anything like a natural language and can hardly vindicate Spelke's model of development. At the very least, it lacks the domain generality that is supposed to allow language to bring together representations from distinct modules.

In this section we have argued that Spelke's account faces a number of serious objections. Many of these concern the representations that are supposed to be contributed by the preverbal number modules. In particular:

- It isn't clear what these representations are.
- Spelke's suggestions aren't always consistent.
- The reasonable candidates involve concepts that aren't explicitly represented (EXACTLY ONE, NUMEROSITY, SET, etc.).
- The reasonable candidates aren't able to get us closer to the positive integers when combined via the compositional semantics of natural language.

Further, if compositionality isn't the mechanism of conceptual change, then it just isn't clear what the alternative is supposed to be. And finally, all of the suggestions and hints that Spelke makes assume that both preverbal systems contribute representations in connection with the first few integers. But there is evidence to suggest that the Accumulator doesn't function for these numbers, in which case Spelke's account can't even get off the ground.

In light of these problems, Spelke's account of the positive integers is not promising. At the same time, Spelke does identify an innate cognitive mechanism (the object indexing system) that, like the Accumulator, may well play an important role in the ontogeny of the integers. But the question remains of how exactly the two could be combined to yield the integers and what other ingredients might be needed.[13]

3 Conclusion

Are language and number essentially linked? In this essay we have examined two of the most important current accounts of the origins of number concepts. Though they have their own distinctive commitments, both identify language as one of the core innate capacities that subserve the development of number. We have argued that neither account is defensible. Still, work by Gallistel, Gelman, Spelke, and others has done much to advance our understanding of the origins of number. So the answer to our question is, so far as anyone knows, *no*. Though it is still too early to say whether the ontogeny of number depends on language, the situation at present is that we have little reason to suppose that it does.

---

13. For our views on these questions, and a more detailed discussion of the ontogeny of number, see Laurence and Margolis (in prep.).

PART III

THEORY OF MIND

14

DANIEL J. POVINELLI, CHRISTOPHER G. PRINCE, & TODD M. PREUSS

Parent-Offspring Conflict and the Development of Social Understanding

Human infants exhibit a number of behaviors that have been interpreted as evidence of an early ability to represent and reason about mental states (theory of mind). We reconsider these behaviors in light of evolutionary theory concerning parent-offspring conflict. We speculate that some of these that intuitively appear to provide evidence of an ability to reason about the mental states of others might in fact reflect a history of selection for behaviors that only appear to be generated by such an ability. We hypothesize that certain infant behaviors might have evolved in order to extract higher levels of parental and caretaker investment. All other things being equal, parents will invest more when the perceived quality of the infant is higher. In this case, we suggest that parents would have invested more in infants who exhibited behaviors similar to their own, especially when the behaviors caused adults to attribute a higher degree of infant social understanding.

In what follows, we briefly review the theory of parent-offspring conflict and consider the role of this conflict in the cognitive development of human infants. Next, we discuss the evolution of theory of mind—which we take to have its origins in human evolution—and consider how this human cognitive specialization might have interacted with existing parent-offspring dynamics. We show how the epigenetic systems of infants might have responded by elaborating upon existing cognitive and behavioral systems, or by canalizing later developing ones earlier into development, in order to recruit higher degrees of parental investment. We assess the merits of our framework in the context of the development of behaviors considered by some researchers to be indicative of a certain degree of social understanding, namely, gaze-following, pointing, social smiling, and neonatal imitation. We

This research was supported by National Science Foundation Young Investigator Award number SBR-8458111 and a Centennial Fellowship from the James S. McDonnell Foundation to Daniel J. Povinelli and James S. McDonnell Foundation grant number 2002029 to Todd M. Preuss.

conclude by showing how this proposal makes several longstanding theoretical and methodological difficulties for the field of cognitive development even more vexing.

1 Parental Investment and Parent-Offspring Conflict

The theoretical underpinnings of parental investment strategies were first worked out by Trivers (1974), who realized that the different genetic interests of parents and their offspring can account for behavioral conflicts between the two. From Hamilton's (1964) landmark work on inclusive fitness, Trivers was able to derive the following asymmetry of interest.

> At any moment in the period of [parental investment] the female is selected to invest that amount [in her infant] which maximizes the difference between the associated cost and benefit.... The infant is selected to induce that investment which maximizes the difference between the benefit and cost devalued by the relevant [degree of relatedness]. (1974, p. 252)

Because social mammals typically reproduce more than once, and because they typically invest a substantial amount of resources in caring for their young after birth, parents must seek some way of limiting investment in any given infant. Simply put, too much energy investment in a current infant might be at the expense of the production and care of future or related infants (or kin). Trivers showed that the optimal amount of investment in a current infant can be understood as a mathematical function that maximizes the chance that the infant will survive to the point at which it can reproduce but minimizes costs to potential future infants (or closely related kin). In contrast to parental efforts in minimizing investment, the infant should favor increases in parental investment. Examples of the conflicts that emerge from the partial asymmetry of interests between infant and parents are widespread (for a classic study with nonhuman primates, see Altmann, 1980). Presumably, weaning conflict has evolved precisely because of the differential interests of the mother and the infants. Maestripieri (2002) has recently reviewed the literature in this area and argues that parent-offspring conflict remains an important and valuable explanatory framework in primate biology.

In humans, evidence of parent-offspring conflict can be seen even before birth. First, up to half of all pregnancies end in spontaneous abortions, abortions that might be due to the mother's physiological evaluation of the fetus (Gaulin & McBurney, 2001). Second, the normal physiological relationships between the fetus and mother might reflect such conflict. Haig (1993), for example, considered mother-fetus conflicts in which the fetus attempts to manipulate maternal physiology for its own benefit, and the maternal physiology responds to counteract these manipulations. Examples of fetal manipulations include actions that reduce the probability of miscarriage, actions that increase nutrient supply in maternal blood, and actions that increase the duration of pregnancy. Each of these manipulations, while providing direct benefits to the fetus, can be problematic for the mother. When the fetus is of low fitness value, reducing the probability of a miscarriage is advantageous only to the fetus. Increased nutrient supply in maternal blood also benefits the fetus, but extreme variations of blood sugar (for example) might produce gestational diabetes in the mother. In addition, increases in the duration of pregnancy, while providing more resources to the fetus, can be dangerous to the mother due to increased size of the infant at term. Thus, even before birth, infants might engage in a parental conflict over investment (in this case, with their mother).

2   Infant Cognitive Development in Light of Parent-Offspring Conflict

Trivers (1974) anticipated the application of parent-offspring conflict for understanding the evolution and ontogeny of infant cognitive skills. In describing the infant as a "psychological manipulator" (p. 257), Trivers noted that the asymmetry in physical size between the parents and infants has selected infants to deploy psychological tactics in order to induce parents to provide higher levels of investment than they have been selected to give. He noted that once a system of "honest" communication has evolved between the infant and its mother about the infant's immediate needs,

> the infant can begin to employ it out of context. The offspring can cry not only when it is famished but also when it merely wants more food than the parent is selected to give. Likewise, it can begin to withhold its smile until it has gotten its way. Selection will then of course favor parental ability to discriminate the two uses of the signals, but still subtler mimicry and deception are always possible. (p. 257)

It is important for our purposes here to note that Trivers used this logic to explain parent-offspring conflict that is widespread among species that provide investment in their offspring after birth.

Two additional points should be made in relation to Trivers's observations. First, the domains of parent-offspring conflict within a species would presumably become fairly well defined over time. That is, there would be some circumscribed arenas in which the evolutionary dance of the appearance of new infant behavioral strategies, followed by the emergence of adult counterstrategies, would continue. Within these arenas, there would be a continual tweaking of such strategies, but the basic arenas in which this evolutionary cycle would go on should be relatively fixed until some further changes were introduced into the behavioral repertoire of the species (for other reasons) — modifications that enabled infant, parent, or both to exploit this new behavioral arena. To anticipate, we suggest hereafter that the emergence of a new kind of social understanding in the course of human evolution was one such modification.

Another point in relation to Trivers's (1974) argument should be made. At least two different means of parental exploitation are available. Trivers emphasized that infants would exploit parental resources by behaving in a manner less mature, and thus in need of more resources, than their chronological age would suggest. For example, a child might use a strategy of crying to obtain more food or attention. As a young infant is "more helpless and vulnerable... its parents will have been more strongly selected to respond positively to signals of need emitted by the offspring, the younger that offspring is" (p. 257) or appears to be. Of course, it is also highly likely that age-related changes in crying might have been selected for in order to maximize investment. However, there are clearly limits on the use of such a strategy, even at ages when some crying might be beneficial. Experimental research has shown that exposure to the sight and sound of crying increases various indicators of stress-induced arousal in adult observers, and can increase frustration and aggression (Donovan & Leavitt, 1985; Donovan et al., 1978; Frodi & Lamb, 1980; Murray, 1985). Thus, although some degree of crying is likely to extract a higher degree of parental investment, extreme crying might also place infants at risk. For example, crying is the most widely cited cause of "shaken baby syndrome" (Becker et al., 1998; Dykes, 1986) and might be the "primary reason for aggression" directed at children less than two years of age (see Norman, 1983).

Another means by which infants can exploit additional resources is through social behaviors that generate positive regard and affect from caregivers. For example, parents might delight in the imitations of their new infant (Meltzoff & Moore, 1977), in the social smiling of their two-month-old (Wolff, 1963), or in the speech-like vocalizations of their three-month-old (Beaumont & Bloom, 1993). Such behaviors might lead to parental attribution of a high level of social understanding to the infant and, in combination with other factors (e.g., breast-feeding; see review in DiGirolamo et al., 2001), increase the degree of attachment between caregiver and infant (Klaus et al., 1995). By producing behaviors that lead to positive regard and affect, and increasing the attachment between caregiver and infant, the infant's behaviors can reduce the very real possibilities of suffering neglect, abuse, or abandonment (Klaus & Kennell, 2001; Sameroff & Chandler, 1975), and thus these strategies for recruiting resources have quite different limits than those faced by immaturity-based strategies. Indeed, the emotional regard and attachment generated by these behaviors might constitute a core basis for caregivers providing additional resources.

3 Evolution of Theory of Mind in Humans: New Strategic Fodder for Infants

In what follows, we outline our hypothesis that the evolution of the human capacity for reasoning about mental states (theory of mind) opened up a new arena in the ongoing parent-offspring conflict. The evolutionary emergence of theory of mind might have provided infants with a new avenue for recruiting additional parental investment. Once parents began to respond to the psychological states of their infants, in addition to their overt behavioral states, infants could begin to evolve behaviors that would, in effect, manipulate this ability for their own benefit.

We assume (on the basis of our assessment of the current evidence) that the capacity to reason about mental states evolved sometime *after* the separation of humans from other hominoids (see Povinelli & Bering, 2002), but it is important to note that our hypothesis does not depend upon this inference. Even if the time-frame we advocate turns out to be incorrect (that is, if theory-of-mind abilities are more widespread than we believe), this would only mean that humans are simply an example of a more widespread phenomenon. Nonetheless, it is important to make some assumption about the timing of the evolution of theory of mind in order to explain how it was integrated into earlier psychological systems. We recognize that this claim is controversial, and so we direct the reader's attention to other authors who believe the evidence supports a wider distribution of this ability in living primates or other taxa (e.g., Boesch & Boesch-Achermann, 2000; Call & Tomasello, 2003; Hare et al., 2000; Suddendorf & Whiten, 2001).

Our current conclusion that theory of mind is restricted to our species does not imply that only humans exhibit complex social behaviors; indeed, many social species produce behaviors that, on the surface, resemble behaviors often associated in our species with the functioning of theory of mind. Certain complex social behaviors seem especially elaborated in primates, especially in chimpanzees (e.g., deception, gaze-following, reconciliation and "holding grudges" after fights: de Waal, 1982, 1986, 1989; Goodall, 1986; Povinelli & Eddy, 1996a; Tomasello et al., 1998; Whiten & Byrne, 1988).

Some scholars will wonder how chimpanzees and other nonhuman animals could lack an understanding of mental states when they share with us so many of the behaviors that, when exhibited by humans are interpreted as prima facie evidence of the ability to represent mental states. We have offered one possible solution to this apparent problem: namely, that the connection between our representation of each other's mental states and our overt behavior is far more complex than introspection suggests (e.g., Povinelli & Giambrone, 1999, 2000; Povinelli & Prince, 1998). In short, many behaviors that our folk psychology tells us are being generated by inferences about what others are thinking or feeling might in fact have multiple causes; furthermore, many of these behaviors might have originally been supported by psychological systems unrelated to theory of mind. Gaze-following is an excellent case in point. Although we are certainly capable of attending to and following the gaze of others as a consequence of wondering what it is that they see, it is not at all clear that this is always or even usually the proximate cause of gaze-following in adult humans. Recent research hints at the operation of precisely such a dual system of responding to gaze in human adults (e.g., Driver et al., 1999; Kingstone et al., 2000; Langton & Bruce, 1999). The general point is that systems that enable reasoning about the behavior of others and its relationship to other observable events might often suffice.

Based on the foregoing line of thinking, we have argued that the ability to reason about mental states evolved as a unique specialization of the human species, and its *initial* function was to understand ancient, already-existing behaviors in a novel way (a mentalistic way), and therefore more flexibly deploy them—not to endow us with a multitude of fundamentally new behaviors (for detailed descriptions of this hypothesis, see Povinelli & Giambrone, 1999, 2000; Povinelli & Prince, 1998). In short, the initial selective advantage of theory of mind was for greater flexibility in combining and recombining old behavioral patterns. The psychological system for representing the mental states of others might therefore reside alongside (and interact in complicated ways with) more ancient systems for keeping track of and reasoning about the behavior of others. The significance of this framework is that it leads one to expect, a priori, that chimpanzees and humans would share numerous, nearly identical behavioral patterns, and yet understand them differently (with chimpanzees reasoning strictly about the behavioral propensities of others and humans reasoning about *both* behavioral propensities and mental states). In our view, this is what the experimental data suggest. Because this interpretation holds that humans evolved a cognitive specialization that allowed our species to interpret existing behaviors in new ways, we have referred to it as the "reinterpretation" hypothesis (Povinelli & Giambrone, 1999, 2000).

The reinterpretation hypothesis has two important implications for the model that we are proposing. First, it suggests a particular evolutionary time-point for the emergence of a new arena for parent-offspring conflict in ancestral hominoids: the evolutionary appearance of theory of mind in humans. If theory of mind is a novel (or even largely novel) specialization of the human lineage, then this addition to the parent-offspring conflict occurred sometime after the split of humans and chimpanzees. Second, just as chimpanzees might engage in behaviors like deception without appreciating how they connect to the underlying mental states of others, so too might human infants. For example, when a two-month-old infant smiles in response to her mother gazing at her, this smile might not be driven by sophisticated social recognition or knowledge of the mother's emotional or mental states. Rather, as we shall show, it might be the result of a finely honed evolutionary strategy in which smiling yields more investment.

4 Parent-Offspring Conflict and the Evolution of Behavioral "Impostors"

We use the term "impostor" to indicate a subclass of behaviors exhibited by human infants that evolved to exploit the human adult's theory-of-mind system. When a parent attributes a high degree of social understanding to his or her infant, there are several possible psychological bases for the infant's behaviors. On the one hand, the infant's behaviors might indicate the presence of precisely the kind of social understanding attributed to him or her by the parent. At some point in development, most children will develop the ability to explicitly reason about mental states, because the child will develop the same social understanding that is modally present in human adults. Conversely, the parent's attribution could be incorrect. A given behavior exhibited by the infant, while appearing to result from an ability to reason about mental states, could instead be caused by other psychological systems. Because of their purported evolutionary history, we label these latter class of behaviors "impostors." These proposed "impostors" would be, of course, *ontogenetic adaptations* (Oppenheim, 1981), or transient processes enabling an infant to adapt to particular stages of development. Only when viewed through the lens of progression to more adult-like or mature states are these "impostors" really impostors. Hereafter, we propose three processes by which such "impostors" could have originated through selection on infants to act as though they possess a theory of mind, without necessarily having the ability to represent mental states. In each process, the evolution of the infants' behavior is being driven by the ability to extract additional levels of parental investment.

1. Neurological substrates for the behavior were present in the infants of the common ancestor of humans and the African apes; however, human infants evolved subtle alterations in these behaviors once a developmental pathway in humans was established for representing mental states and hence allowing adults to (incorrectly) construe these behaviors in terms of the infant's ability to reason about mental states (for example, by shifting the behaviors earlier and earlier into development).
2. Specific neurological substrates for the behavior were not present in the infants of the common ancestor of humans and the African apes but rather the evolution of a theory of mind in adult humans led to the evolution of some entirely novel behaviors in infancy.
3. Finally, the neurological substrates were present in the infants of the common ancestor of humans and African apes but they subserved a different function. Once human adults began to evolve a theory of mind, some behaviors (e.g., smiling) could be interpreted very differently by human parents, and were therefore evolutionarily modified by infants to gain additional resources based on this new parental interpretation.

Hereafter, we examine some infant behaviors that might be outcomes of the three processes just isolated.

4.1 Gaze-Following

Certain aspects of gaze-following in early infancy might have been shaped by the first process. Human infants, starting at six months or younger, develop an ability to follow the gaze of others (e.g., Butterworth & Jarrett, 1991; Corkum & Moore, 1998; D'Entremont et al., 1997; Scaife & Bruner, 1975). Infants of this age will follow an adult's gaze within their own visual field, and orient to the first object along their scan path from the adult's face. After the age of 12 months, infants' gaze-following is said to progress to a "geometric" mechanism that enables localization of the specific target of an adult's gaze—provided the object is within the infant's visual field (e.g., Butterworth & Jarrett, 1991). Similar gaze-following abilities are present in chimpanzees and other Old and New World anthropoid primates, but possibly not prosimians (Anderson & Mitchell, 1999; Emery et al., 1997; Itakura, 1996; Povinelli & Eddy, 1996a, b, 1997; Tomasello et al., 1998; Tomasello et al., 2001).

Given its phyletic distribution among living primates, we can be very confident that at least major components of a gaze-following system were present in the common ancestor of humans and apes. However, we hypothesize that once a theory-of-mind system evolved and was firmly established in the development of modern humans, human infants began to take advantage of the new, mentalistic construal of gaze direction now present in older children and adults. Infants might have shifted aspects of the gaze-following system earlier and earlier in development. Further, and consistent with both the first and third processes identified earlier, infants might have also evolved subtle alterations in their behaviors related to gaze-following. For example, they might have begun to yoke affective expressions with gaze alternations from the parent to other objects of interest, leading to parental attributions of higher levels of social awareness. In this case, infants would have preserved the general function of their behavior but tweaked it to maximize resource investment. Because gaze-following is present in many social primate species and therefore must have a shared ontogenetic trajectory, its form in human infancy is an impostor only to the extent that selection might have shaped its specific expression precisely so that it would more readily trigger the adult theory-of-mind system. Of course, at some point in *human* development (and the exact age is still a matter of empirical controversy), infants do begin to construe gaze in a mentalistic fashion.

4.2 Indexical Pointing

Pointing in infancy might be an example of a behavior that arose through the second process. Younger than three months, infant humans spontaneously display early forms of "pointing" by extending their index fingers from their otherwise closed fist (Hannan & Fogel, 1987). However, throughout much of their first year, infants' index finger extensions are not coordinated with their gaze direction toward adults or objects in the world. By 12 months, pointing involves extension of the arm, use of the index finger, and gaze coordination with another person (e.g., Franco & Butterworth, 1996), with infants looking in the general direction of another's pointing gesture (e.g., Morissette et al., 1995). By about 15 months, infants are able to precisely localize the intended targets of the pointing gestures of others (Lempers, 1979; Morissette et al., 1995). Pointing by young infants might be well characterized as "protoimperative" (Bates et al., 1975), involving an infant instrumentally using a parent (see also Mosier & Rogoff, 1994). Although chimpanzees raised with humans do develop whole arm, hand, and even index finger extensions toward objects that they want when interacting with humans (review by Leavens & Hopkins, 1999), they do not use such gestures with each other, and there is substantial reason to suppose that they do not understand that the gesture connects to the mental states of others (review by Povinelli et al., 2003). Indeed, the conspicuous absence of pointing in free-ranging chimpanzees (e.g., Plooij, 1978) is perhaps best highlighted by the ambiguity of the single published instance of a possible example of pointing by chimpanzees in the 40 years this species has been intensively studied in its natural habitats (Vea & Sabater-Pi, 1998). (Interestingly, specialization of the action of the tendons of the index finger that might be relevant to the topographical form of the gesture has been noted in humans, but not chimpanzees; see Povinelli & Davis, 1994.)

We interpret the lack of pointing behavior in chimpanzees and other great apes to indicate that the behavior of pointing was not present in the common ancestor of humans and the great apes. Rather, it appears to have evolved exclusively in the human lineage. We propose that pointing in young human infants evolved after adult humans had evolved the capacity to reason about mental states and had begun to incorporate the pointing gesture into their behavior. Aspects of the topographic form of the gesture might have become canalized into infancy without any supporting relationship from an understanding of mental states. We suggest that it is not until late infancy (around 18–24 months) that pointing begins to develop into a gesture directly related to human infants' understanding of reference and communication (see Moore & D'Entremont, 2001)—both related to an understanding of mental states.

4.3 Social Smiling

Finally, early social smiling might be an example of a behavior that arose through the third process we described earlier. Social smiling emerges in young human infants at around two months of age. It is produced when the infant views the face and eyes of an observer, and also appears to be related to the contingency of the observer's behavior with the child's behavior. Young infants inspect a face presented to them, then focus on the eyes of the observer, and break out suddenly "into a broad smile or grin," and "this sequence of events [can] be repeated many times" (Wolff, 1963, pp. 122–3). Prior to four to six weeks, infants will smile to some external stimuli (e.g., light touches) and also to some internal stimuli (e.g., during REM sleep; Emde & Koenig, 1969). From four to six weeks through approximately six months, the most effective stimuli for evoking smiling in the infant is a moving "en face" approximate configuration of the face (Spitz & Wolf, 1946). Infants of this age vary their smiling on the basis of stimulus features, including eye-gaze (Hains & Muir, 1996a; Symons et al., 1998) and contingency (Hains & Muir, 1996b; Tronick et al., 1978; Watson, 1972). Chimpanzees and other nonhuman primates display facial gestures that resemble bare teeth smiles, but the social function of these gestures differs radically from the function of smiling in humans. Often, these facial displays indicate fear or submission (van Hooff, 1972).

We suggest that a specific behavioral substrate for smiling was present in the common ancestor of humans and other great apes, but once social smiling in adults began to have meanings such as appeasement, expression of empathy, acknowledgment, and attraction, infants began to utilize smiling as a facial gesture to ingratiate themselves in their parents' eyes.

4.4 Other Candidate Behaviors

Thus far, we have considered only a handful of behaviors that human infants might display in the absence of the mature, folk psychology that typically accompanies their production in older humans. Table 14.1 lists a number of additional behaviors that might be productively analyzed using the general framework outlined here.

Thus, although some researchers have interpreted the behaviors listed in Table 14.1 as evidence that infants represent aspects of the mental states of others, it is possible that some of these behaviors might be supported by other kinds of representations—ones not specifically involved in reasoning about mental states per se. After all, if our general model is correct, the initial selective advantages that led to the sculpting of new social behaviors in infants (or the modification of existing ones) resulted from the fact that these behaviors elicited increased levels

TABLE 14.1 Behaviors susceptible to a 'behavioral imposter' analysis.

Behavior	Example reference
Crying	Leger et al. (1996)
Neonatal imitation	Meltzoff & Moore (1977)
Deferred imitation	Meltzoff & Moore (1994)
Sensitivity to contingency of others	Hains & Muir (1996b)
Sensitivity to maternal still face	Field (1977)
Sensitivity to being imitated	Meltzoff (1990)
Sensitivity to varying affect intensities	Thompson (1987)
Gaze alternation	Carpenter et al. (1998b)
Gaze re-direction	Bates et al. (1975)
Mutual gaze	Trevarthen (1979)
Social referencing	Feinman (1982)
Sensitivity to adult eye gaze	Symons et al. (1998)
Conventionalized gestures	Butterworth & Grover (1990)
Early word production	Bloom (1973)
Proto-declarative pointing	Camaioni (1991)

of parental investment, regardless of whether those behaviors reflect sophisticated social understanding or not.

5 Behavioral Impostors versus Early Theory of Mind: A Comparison of Explanatory Frameworks

It is important to note that even if the proposal advanced here has merit, the new arenas of parent-offspring conflict that might have been opened up by the evolutionary emergence of theory of mind could have led to selection pressures for earlier (if more fragile) manifestations of genuine social understanding related to theory of mind (as opposed to selection for impostors alone). For example, it might be the case that what was canalized was a general representational code linking self and other—as proposed, for example, by Meltzoff and Gopnik (1993; see also Gopnik & Meltzoff, 1997). According to these authors, the existence of neonatal imitation demonstrated by Meltzoff and colleagues (e.g., Meltzoff & Moore, 1977, 1994) suggests that human infants begin life with a system of abstract crossmodal representation that provides them with an experiential similarity in their representations of self and other. With this system, they are "launched on their career of interpersonal relations with the primary perceptual judgement 'Here is something like me'" (Meltzoff & Gopnik, 1993, p. 336). This innate representational system is seen as laying the foundation for the child's conception of the social world in terms of theory-like structures. Thus, although the initial developmental pathway for theory of mind might have been present in older individuals, through time, there might have been selection for these abilities to appear earlier and earlier in development. Alternatively, as we have proposed here, instead of dragging these later emerging representational systems toward earlier ontogenetic time points, selection might have acted to favor infants who expressed behaviors that structurally resembled behaviors interpretable by adults as expressing those abilities.

Meltzoff and Gopnik's (1993) proposal suggests that there is substantial continuity or overlap between the mechanisms responsible for neonatal imitation and those that support adult imitation. This possibility can be evaluated from a neurobiological standpoint. Functional imaging studies have implicated several divisions of cortex in adult imitation; results vary somewhat across studies, but activation of inferior parietal area 40 and frontal opercular area 44 (also known as area F5 of ventral premotor cortex) are commonly noted (see, for example, Chaminade et al., 2002; Decety et al., 2002; Goldenberg, 2001; Iacoboni et al., 1999; Nishitani & Hari, 2000). The involvement of the inferior parietal and frontal opercular areas in gestural imitation is consistent with reports that both areas represent orofacial and upper limb movements, and both areas are known to be responsive when subjects view or execute movements (Buccino et al., 2001). Nonhuman primates appear to possess parietal and frontal areas homologous to those that support imitation in humans (Johnson, 2002; Preuss, 1995; Rizzolatti & Arbib, 1998), and these areas contain matched motor and visual representations of movement. These areas are also strongly interconnected (review by Wise et al., 1997). It is worth remembering, however, that the ability to intentionally copy observed movements is quite limited in species other than humans, and therefore the parietal and frontal territories that support adult-like imitation were likely modified recently in human evolution.

If adult imitation depends critically on the cortical structures just discussed, then it is unlikely that neonatal and adult imitation share the same substrates, if only because human cortex is very immature at birth. This immaturity is manifest in many aspects of anatomy and physiological organization, including synaptic density, dendritic elaboration, myelination, electrical activity, and metabolic activity (Albert et al., 1999). It is conceivable that the specific cortical structures and circuits involved in adult imitation follow an accelerated developmental schedule relative to neighboring areas, but there is no evidence of this. It seems more likely, on neurobiological grounds, that neonatal imitation is supported by different mechanisms from those of adult imitation, and specifically by subcortical systems, which are more mature at birth than cortical systems (Johnson, 1990). One structure that should be considered in this role is the superior colliculus (see Johnson, 1990). Although often treated by primate neuroscientists merely as an eye-movement center, it is substantially more than that: the colliculus contains spatially matched visual, auditory, and somatosensory maps, providing a basis for multimodal sensory integration (reviewed by Preuss, 2005). Moreover, in addition to eye movements, it organizes movements of the mouth, face, and forelimbs (Dean et al., 1989; Werner, 1993). The superior colliculus receives projections from parietal and frontal cortex in nonhuman primates (Fries, 1984); assuming that similar connections are present in humans, these could provide the basis for the transition of the control of imitation to cortical systems as the latter mature. Of course, given that there is no solid evidence that nonhuman primates exhibit neonatal imitation, our suggestion that the colliculus is involved in human neonatal imitation implies that aspects of this structure were functionally modified during hominid evolution. Likewise, we must assume that the cortical structures involved in adult imitation were modified, as nonhuman primates are not specialized for the intentional copying of observed movements.

Whatever the exact mechanisms supporting neonatal imitation, our model posits a history of selection for neonates and infants that expressed behaviors superficially resembling later developing behaviors (i.e., true imitation). In the context of facial imitation, such behaviors might have been especially important, given the relatively greater amount of face-to-face interactions in human development (as opposed to developmental patterns found in other primates)—a difference that might itself be a by-product of the evolution of theory of mind during the course of human evolution.

Thus, infants who reacted to adult facial expressions with gestures that were structurally matched and temporally coordinated would be likely to receive higher levels of attribution of social awareness, hence more and earlier investment. We emphasize that our behavioral impostors are not necessarily fixed-action-patterns (cogently argued against by Meltzoff and colleagues). Indeed, our model does not deny that neonatal imitation is a process of "active intermodal mapping" and thus does not deny the diversity of evidence gathered in this area (e.g., Meltzoff & Moore, 1997). Instead, it posits that this mapping principally involves subcortical systems, rather than the cerebral structures that seem to be involved in the kinds of imitation seen in older infants, children, and adults. In contrast, whereas Meltzoff and Gopnik (1993) seem to posit a continuity of cortical functions from birth forward, our account posits a major role for multimodal, but subcortical, representations at birth, which become integrated with cortical systems later in development. Thus, whereas both accounts acknowledge the common coding of visual and motor information at birth in humans, our model questions whether the mere expression of this common coding in overt behavior (through imitation) warrants the attribution of any kind of intentional understanding on the part of the infant (for a related account of neonatal imitation, also see Bjorklund, 1987). Interestingly, however, if our model is correct, the neonatal system for imitation might have been exquisitely designed to yield precisely such attributions by our naive folk psychology.

At this point, one might argue that the sheer diversity of evidence for early social understanding in infants already constrains the possibilities for what the outcome of parent-offspring conflict must have been: early social understanding of intentional states (e.g., Johnson, 2000). Scholars sympathetic to such a view differ widely in their opinions about the nature of such early understanding. Some see the evidence as supporting the view that infants possess a genuine, but more circumscribed or different, understanding of intentional states, while others see the knowledge as starkly domain specific; still others characterize the infants' understanding of intentional states as neither genuinely mentalistic nor strictly behavioral. Despite such diversity of opinion, these scholars could, in principle, accept the general proposal we have made but still conclude that the best evidence now suggests that the long-term outcome of this evolutionary arms race was to select for the increasingly earlier development of sophisticated social understanding. In other words, parent-offspring conflict might have favored infants who developed theory-of-mind-like abilities earlier in development. Some evidence that could be used to bolster this view is presented in table 14.2. It should be noted that this evidence has been gathered in the context of efforts to explicitly test predictions concerning alternative ideas about the kinds of social understanding present in infancy.

However, it could be the case that despite such targeted analyses, researchers are actually uncovering the very areas in which infants were selected to detect and respond to the statistical regularities that exist in the actions of their caregivers. The detection and use of these regularities does not necessarily imply a system for understanding mental states, but it might provide the means by which infants could maximally exploit their caregivers. That there are statistical regularities in the behavior of others is not particularly controversial; indeed, it can be shown that not only must such regularities exist, they must be detectable in many social species who use such information in their interactions with each other (see Povinelli, 2001b), and in the case of human development, some researchers are now demonstrating precisely such abilities (Baird & Baldwin, 2001). That these regularities are detectable by infants might not be, from the perspective we have outlined here, altogether surprising. For one thing, such a system for statistically based parsing of action might be phylogenetically quite old (and thus unrelated to theory of mind). Furthermore, to the extent that there was additional selection pressure on infants during human evolution to act as if they possessed a mentalistic type of social understanding, then infants might have further elaborated upon this ability. They might have latched onto a specific class of regularities in the behavior of their caregivers that could be exploited—ones precisely coinciding with the intentional parsing of action made by our adult folk psychology (Baird & Baldwin, 2001).

Of course, one might counter that such heretofore unnoticed competences on the part of infants—competences that were only discovered by the application of procedures designed to probe for intentional understanding in infancy (see table 14.2)—by themselves show that infants' understanding goes beyond what would be needed to exploit parents into providing more investment. After all, the abilities revealed by the research summarized in table 14.2 might not be detectable by parents as they interact with their infants. Conversely, however, one could argue that selection for behaviors that could be noticed by parents (the ones described

TABLE 14.2 Selected experimental evidence supporting the idea of early social understanding of intentional states in human infants.

Phenomenon	Reference
Encoding the goal of an actor's reach	Woodward (1998)
Parsing of the behavior stream at intentional joints	Baldwin et al. (in press)
Selective gaze-following of objects that establish contingency with infant	Johnson et al. (1998)
Connecting gaze and emotional expression to intentional actions	Phillips et al. (2002)
Connecting gaze and object of gaze	Woodward (in review)
Understanding referential of others' emotional outbursts in cases of discrepant focus	Moses et al. (2001)

earlier, and perhaps many of those listed in table 14.1), might have carried with them precisely some of the ancillary skills that developmental psychologists are now uncovering (e.g., see table 14.2). It is also possible that more sophisticated research with parents might reveal that they do detect these subtle aspects of behavior without being aware that they do so.

Compounding the problem is the likelihood that at least two systems—or perhaps more precisely, two kinds of systems—might be operating in parallel in adult humans: one for detecting the statistical regularities in the behavior of others, and another that maps intentional ascriptions onto that behavior (see Povinelli & Giambrone, 2000; Povinelli & Prince, 1998; from a human developmental point of view, see Baird & Baldwin, 2001). The difficulty arises in that independent of any selection for human infants to either actually understand (or act as if they understand) the intentional states of others, socially competent primates will have already evolved systems for detecting and analyzing many of the statistical regularities that exist in the behavior of others—precisely those regularities, in fact, upon which humans now map their intentional understandings (see Baird & Baldwin, 2001; Povinelli, 2001b). If it is the case that such systems for detecting and using the fine-grained regularities in the behavior of the self and others existed long before theory-of-mind systems evolved, then it might be aspects of these systems, not the ones for reasoning about mental states, that were canalized earlier and earlier in human development in the manner predicted by parent-offspring conflict theory.

6 Future Directions and Conclusions

Parent-offspring conflict theory suggests that as a new system for social understanding (the ability to explicitly represent mental states) emerged in human evolution, a new arena for parent-offspring would have been opened, and human developmental systems would have responded in predictable ways. For example, competences for genuine social understanding might have been dragged earlier into ontogeny. Alternatively, other systems that would lead infants to be perceived as if they possessed such competences might have been modified or pulled earlier into development as well. Finally, some complex combination of the two processes might have occurred.

The framework we have outlined here adds to the already-existing list of possible explanations of behavioral patterns in infancy that resemble in important ways adult behavioral patterns. Our account does not necessarily make the methodological task of choosing among these alternative explanations any easier. When an infant exhibits a behavior that looks similar to a behavior in later development (e.g., smiling, pointing, gaze-following, imitation), the early-arising behavior might or might not have relevance to the pathway for a psychological system causally involved in the similar, later arising behavior. Thus, our exploration of parent-offspring conflict theory offers developmental psychologists another principled, theoretical reason for delving deeper than the surface resemblance of behaviors in trying to understand the development of social understanding. One theoretical position that is particularly challenged by our model is the notion that very early in development, infants possess an understanding or representation of the intentional dimension of behavior in themselves or others. Furthermore, our model challenges traditional theoretical accounts of human development as seamless, causal transitions from earlier behaviors to later ones, in which behaviors that are present at each successive age are the basic building blocks for later ones. Earlier behaviors, though structurally similar to later ones, might not, in fact, be the right causal precursors. One outcome of accepting the view presented here is that far more data need to be rallied, and especially data that have some hope of testing the hypothesized causal relationships between antecedent behaviors in infants and later developments in social understanding and theory of mind.

Our proposal might be extended by considering the possibility that theory of mind, although a specialization of the human species, appeared only gradually during the course of human evolution, or in step-wise increments. We speculate that the emergence of even the earliest components of theory of mind in adults would have established the kind of selection pressures on human infants that we have discussed. Furthermore, because parent-offspring conflict is a continual, dynamic process (e.g., Trivers, 1974), once infants began evolving behavioral "impostors" to exploit the adult's theory of mind, adults, in turn, might have needed to advance their theory-of-mind skills in order to offset the resource losses brought on by their own infants' behaviors. So, while behavioral "impostors" might not play the kind of proximate causal role in the ontogeny of individual social understanding that is claimed by some researchers, these "impostors" might nonetheless have played an evolutionary role. The ontogenetic appearance of behavioral "impostors" such as early gaze-following, pointing, social smiling, and neonatal imitation might have caused the evolutionary honing of initial social understanding systems after these systems had started to appear in primate evolutionary history.

SUSAN C. JOHNSON

Reasoning about Intentionality in Preverbal Infants

Researchers disagree over whether to grant preverbal infants any true understanding of other minds. There seem to be at least two sources of hesitation among researchers. Some doubt that infants have any concepts as sophisticated as that implied by the term "intentionality." Other researchers simply doubt that infants understand *anything* in a conceptual way. The goal of this chapter is to provide arguments in favor of infants' abilities in both respects. My strategy is twofold. Following other researchers, I will adopt a general class of empirical strategies that may help us to decide between intentional and nonintentional interpretations of infants' earliest putative theory-of-mind behavior. Tomasello (1995) has suggested that arguments for intentional attributions in infancy would be strengthened if it were shown that attributions across multiple behavioral contexts emerge within the same developmental window. Heyes (1998), discussing a similar debate within the animal literature, suggested that target attributions be demonstrated across multiple behavioral contexts within the same individual. I aim to strengthen the evidence for intentional attributions by describing studies in which infants use similar object features to categorize novel objects as intentional across multiple behavioral contexts. For instance, if object characteristics that induce infants to follow a novel object's "attentional" orientation also induce "goal"-imitation, that would be important. It would suggest that those characteristics invoke an intermediary representation (intermediary in the processing stream between perception and action) of intentional agent that is available to support multiple behaviors across divergent methodological paradigms. Objections based on local interpretative issues of individual methods will no longer obtain. Finally, I will describe data from one study, in which the method itself was designed to assess conceptual representations abstracted away from perception-action systems.

I am supported by a grant from the National Institutes of Health, number RO1 HD38361.

1 What Is Meant by Intentionality?

Intentional states are unobservable constructs that must be inferred by observers rather than perceived directly. They are distinguished from other sorts of unobservables or internal states by the specific kind of relationship they hold with the world. That is, intentional states are *directed at* the world; they are *about* things (Lycan, 1999). The ability to construe ourselves and others as agents with intentional states such as perceptions, attention, desires, and beliefs is critical. With this "mentalizing" ability, we can communicate referentially, predict and explain others' behaviors, and manipulate both our own and others' mental/intentional states for the purposes of complex problem-solving and learning, not to mention deception.

1.1 What Is the Possible Evidence for an Understanding of Intentionality?

There are many ways of organizing the available evidence on infants' understanding of intentionality. Two obvious ways are in terms of the knowledge being assessed or the methods used for assessment. Because the argument in this chapter will hinge heavily on the convergence of evidence across differing behaviors and methodologies, that organization will be used with the one caveat that knowledge of people will be reviewed separately from knowledge of nonhuman agents. The reason for this will hopefully become clear.

2 Infants' Interpretation of People

2.1 Methods for Assessing Infants' Interpretation of People

2.1.1 Joint Attention Behaviors: Gaze-Following, Pointing, and Other Communicative Gestures
The onset of gaze-following and communicative gestures between the ages of 9 and 12 months is typically seen as the first plausible sign of intentional attributions. At this age, infants begin to reliably produce and respond to gestures such as pointing, showing, and requesting (Bretherton, McNew, & Beeghly-Smity, 1981; Butterworth & Grover, 1988; Carpenter et al., 1998b). Under the mentalistic view, these behaviors result from the infant's active attempt to direct the attention of others toward some aspect of the world. Around this age infants are also seen to follow the attention of adults by alternating their own gaze between adults and events or objects in the environment (Butterworth & Jarrett, 1991; Carpenter et al., 1998b; Corkum & Moore, 1998; Scaife & Bruner, 1975). Under very simplified conditions, infants as young as three months have also been shown to follow gaze (D'Entremont et al., 1997; Hood et al., 1998).

2.1.2 Imitation
Evidence for the comprehension of goal-directedness has also been reported. For instance, Carpenter, Akhtar, and Tomasello (1998a) found that 14- to 18-month-olds would readily imitate an adult's action if it were linguistically

marked as purposeful ("There!") but not if marked as accidental ("Whoops!"). Also using an imitation technique, Meltzoff (1995) showed that 18-month-olds manually reproduced the object-directed goals of adult modelers at rates far above those of spontaneous object manipulations, even in cases where the adult's goals were never actually achieved and therefore had to be inferred by the infants. In a control condition in which a set of mechanical pincers acted as the "agent," infants failed to reproduce the incompleted action, thereby eliminating explanations in terms of characteristics of the objects or action-paths alone.

2.1.3 *Language and Emotional Referencing* Evidence comes from other domains as well, including early comprehension of the referential aspects of language and emotion. Baldwin (1995) has shown that 18-month-olds consistently restrict their interpretations of new words to the referents of a speaker's gaze at the moment of utterance rather than the referent of their own gaze. Though 14- to 16-month-olds are not yet able to reliably make the correct mappings between a novel word and a referent when the object of the speaker's gaze conflicts with their own, they can nonetheless use the speaker's gaze to prevent themselves from wrongly mapping the word onto the object they themselves were attending to. Baldwin and Moses (1996) have shown even earlier understanding of the referents of emotions in 12-month-olds using similar methods. Infants seem able to use their understanding of emotional reference as an index of an individual's desire by 18 months at the latest. Tomasello, Strosberg, and Akhtar (1996) found that 18-month-olds could use a speaker's emotional expression to disambiguate the referent of a novel word from a series of sequentially presented objects, and Repacholi and Gopnik (1997) showed that infants of the same age were able to fulfill an adult's request for food on the basis of that adult's previous emotional responses to the food choices.

2.1.4 *Looking-Time Studies* Other possible evidence that infants attribute intentional states to people is based on infants' tendency to increase their visual attention to test events that fail to correspond to their interpretations of previous familiarization events. Using this method, Woodward, Phillips, and Spelke found evidence that suggested an attribution of perception to people (reported in Spelke et al., 1995c). They showed that seven-month-olds looked longer when a moving person collided with another person than when inanimate objects were involved in the same collisions. Furthermore, Phillips, Wellman, and Spelke (2002) reported evidence that 12-month-olds understand that desires (as indexed by facial expressions and direction of gaze) predict actions. They showed that 12-month-olds looked longer at a person who smiled at (expressed desire toward) one object but then picked up a different object than at a person who smiled at and picked up the same object.

Using the same looking-time measures, Woodward (1998) has shown that even five-month-olds appear to interpret human hands as goal-directed relative to comparable inanimate objects. Woodward familiarized five-month-olds to either a hand or a similarly configured rod repeatedly approaching one of two possible objects. The infants seemed to interpret the two displays differently, encoding the hand's movement in relation to the object it approached (i.e., its *goal*) but the rod's movement in isolation. This conclusion was inferred from the fact that, in test trials, they looked longer if the target object of the hand changed but not if the hand's approach path to the original target object changed. In contrast, their reactions to the same changes in the rod condition did not show this effect. Woodward has found similar results for infants' understanding of the point gesture, though at slightly later ages (Woodward & Guajardo, 2002).

2.2 The Interpretative Problem with People

While the above evidence is suggestive, there are problems with granting anyone a notion of intentional agent on the basis of such evidence. Individual behaviors based on mental states that are correlated with reality (e.g., perception-guided behavior or goal-directed behaviors in the absence of false beliefs) can always be interpreted in either intentional or nonintentional frameworks (Dennett, 1978).

For instance, one leading alternative explanation for infants' apparent precocity in the studies described above invokes the presence of conditioned responses in the infant (Corkum & Moore, 1998). Throughout the first year, the infant has ample opportunity to observe the covariation of people and actions in the world. In principle, the infant could learn the appropriate associations without needing to impute intentional states to people. Similar arguments apply to *any* common behavior an infant might engage in with other people, such as gaze-following, pointing, or other potentially communicative gestures. For instance, extensive experience interacting with their caretakers may condition infants to anticipate interesting events occurring in the direction of the caretakers' head turns. In support of this position, Corkum and Moore (1998) demonstrated that gaze-following can be partially shaped by conditioning in eight- to nine-month-old infants who otherwise fail to follow gaze spontaneously. Similarly, some authors argue that 12-month-olds produce points and requests because of their instrumental effectiveness long before they are *understood* for their communicative nature (Butterworth & Grover, 1988).

Of course, the alternative to such learning accounts is not necessarily a mentalistic account. For instance, some researchers have argued for evolutionarily specified mechanisms, such as signal releasers, to account for gaze-following (e.g., directional movement of the head or eyes; Butterworth & Jarrett, 1991; Povinelli & Eddy, 1996a; Povinelli, Prince, & Preuss, chapter 14 here). Such mechanisms, while unlearned, would not require the attribution of any conceptual understanding of other minds to the infant. They would, however, allow infants to share important information about the environment with caretakers without attributing a mind-world relationship to the gazer. And, as Povinelli argues, such mechanisms could also induce stronger attachment to infants by their caretaking adults (Povinelli, Prince, & Preuss, chapter 14 here). Povinelli's argument is based in part on work with chimpanzees. In work by Povinelli and Eddy (1996a), chimpanzees who could *follow* the gaze of humans did not use humans' gaze-direction to constrain their own requests. That is, they were just as likely to direct request gestures at humans whose vision was occluded as those who could see them (but see more recent work by Hare, Call, and Tomasello, 2001, for a theory-of-mind explanation of these results). Corkum and Moore also suggest the existence of an inherent signal value in head turns based on evidence that eight-month-olds can be conditioned to follow gaze in the same direction as observed head turns, but not in the opposite direction (1998). On such accounts, it is not until the end of the second year, when infants begin to use language productively, that these theorists grant infants the ability to construe people as having intentional states.

Given the possibility of accounts such as these, as long as the agents used to test infants' competency are highly familiar to the infant, as people are, nonintentional explanations remain difficult to rule out. Nonetheless, most of the work in this area has presupposed the role of people in infants' attributions of mental states. A small but growing body of work suggests that this presupposition may be unwarranted, however, for theoretical reasons as well as methodological ones. A number of researchers have pointed out that knowledge domains that entail domain-specific reasoning (as the intentional domain seems to) may also entail domain-specific object-identification processes (Carey & Spelke, 1994). The object-identification processes leading to the recognition of an intentional agent could be isomorphic with those for the recognition of people, but they *need* not be.

3 Infants' Interpretation of Nonhuman Agents

Several theoretical proposals have been offered about the information that lay thinkers, infants and adults alike, might use to identify the presence of intentional agents (Baron-Cohen, 1995; Carey & Spelke, 1994; Leslie, 1994, 1995; Premack, 1990). The features proposed fall into several overlapping classes: morphological features such as faces and eyes; asymmetry along one axis; nonrigid transformation; self-propulsion; the ability to engage in contingent and reciprocal interactions with other agents. In general, the ability of infants to *detect* these features goes uncontested. However, the degree to which any of these features might serve specific functions in infants' reasoning in the intentional domain, as opposed to other domains (e.g., the social or biological domains), is still largely unexamined.

It bears noting that two previously mentioned studies included nonhuman "agents" as experimental controls—Meltzoff's (1995) imitation study and Woodward's (1998) hand-rod study. In both cases, it was crucial to the interpretation of goal-attributions that infants treated the human agents and nonhuman control "agents" differently. In neither case, however, did the control "agent" clearly exhibit any of the putatively intentional cues mentioned above. Therefore, a domain-specific perception view, such as that described above, would predict the same results.

3.1 Methods for Assessing Infants' Interpretation of Nonhuman Agents

3.1.1 *"Gaze"-Following: Nonhuman Agents* On the basis of these domain-specific object-recognition speculations, Virginia Slaughter, Susan Carey, and I reasoned that if 12-month-olds have a concept of agent, and infants' ability to follow another's gaze or attentional focus reflects that concept, then any object that exhibits one or more of these features should elicit gaze-following in 12-month-olds (Johnson et al., 1998.) To test this, we built a small novel object that we could

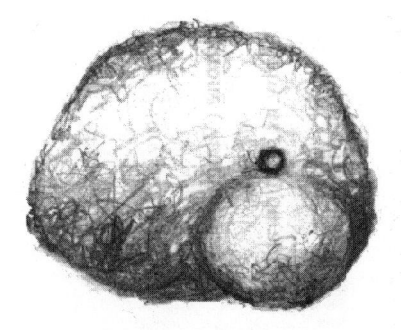

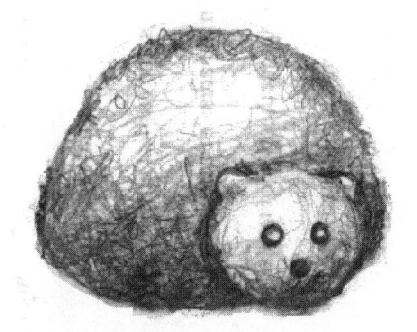

FIGURE 15.1 The object from Johnson, Slaughter, & Carey (1998) in its faceless and faced versions. Reprinted from Johnson et al., "Whose Gaze Will Infants Follow? Features That Elicit Gaze-Following in 12-Month-Olds," *Developmental Science*, Vol. 1, with permission from Blackwell.

introduce to 12-month-olds in a standard gaze-following paradigm in which the object would stand in for the person (fig. 15.1).

The object was the size of a small beach ball, made of natural-looking fuzzy brown fur. It had a naturalistic shape that was symmetrical along only one axis, and it had a small cone-shaped bulge at one end. It was originally designed so that we could vary two features: the presence or absence of facial features (as seen here) and the quality of its behavior—specifically whether or not its behavior was contingently interactive with the infant or not. Its "behavior" was generated via a small remote-controlled beeper and light hidden inside it. For instance, it was possible to control the object from a hidden vantage point such that when the baby babbled, the object babbled back.

Babies were brought into the experimental room and seated with their caretakers, in front of the novel object. A brief, 60-second familiarization period followed in which either the infant experienced the object reacting contingently to the infant's own behavior—if the baby vocalized, the object beeped; if the baby moved, the object flashed its light. Or the infant saw equivalent amounts of apparently self-generated beeping and flashing, but in a sequence that was random with respect to the baby's own behavior.

After this familiarization, the object turned and oriented itself toward one of two targets placed on either edge of the setup. The object made a series of four turns, each of which began with an attention-grabbing beep and then persisted with a silent seven- to eight-second fixation on the target.

The degree to which an infant's eye movements reflected active "gaze"-following by the infant was inferred by subtracting the looks in the unpredicted direction (opposite to the object's turn) from those in the predicted direction (same direction as the object's turn) for each trial. The resulting average difference scores per trial were then compared to a chance level of zero for each condition.

Infants were found to follow the "gaze" of the object by shifting their own attention in the same direction under three of the four familiarization conditions; if the object had a face or if, when the infant babbled or moved, the object beeped back and flashed lights, or both (see fig. 15.2).

260   Theory of Mind

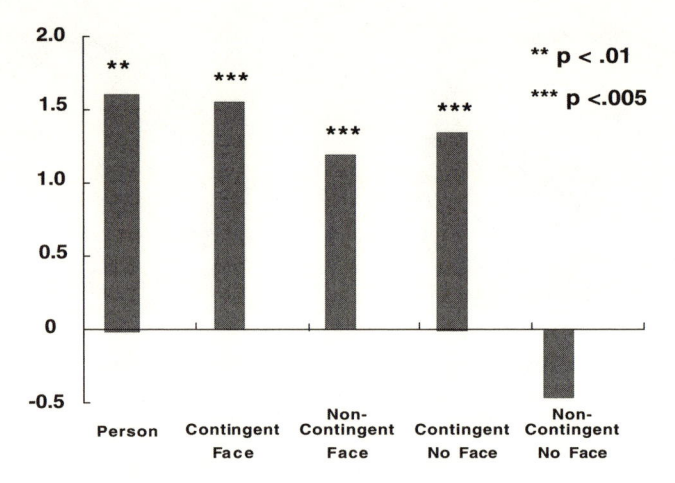

[Bar chart showing values approximately: Person ~1.6 (**), Contingent Face ~1.55 (***), Non-Contingent Face ~1.2 (***), Contingent No Face ~1.35 (***), Non-Contingent No Face ~-0.35. Legend: ** p < .01, *** p <.005. Y-axis from -0.5 to 2.0.]

FIGURE 15.2 Data from Johnson, Slaughter & Cary (1998). The score in the Y-axis equals the total number of looks in the predicted direction minus the total number of looks in the unpredicted direction.

Importantly, the object in the noncontingent, faceless condition embodied the same shape and movement cues as it did in the other conditions, but infants showed no reliable sign of following its "gaze." A further comparison condition with unfamiliar adults revealed no difference between the likelihood that infants would follow a contingently interacting person (with a face) and a contingently interacting fuzzy brown object with a face. Taken together, these results seem to show that infants do use quite specific information to decide when an object does or does not have the ability to perceive or attend to its surroundings, in this case the presence of a face, or the propensity to interact contingently. To the extent that the infants in this study had no prior experience with this particular novel object, and the object in the unsuccessful conditions superficially resembled humans or familiar animals just as much as the object in the successful conditions, it is difficult to argue that these results could be due to infants' generalization from previously learned behaviors. The results seem more consistent with the operation of a dedicated input system, as previously speculated.

The study just described suggests that infants can use either morphological or behavioral information to categorize a novel object as an agent. The evidence for either as entirely sufficient in its own right was not shown. For instance, in the attentional following studies of Johnson et al. (1998), neither the presence of a face nor the ability to interact contingently was necessary to elicit following from infants — either bit of information could elicit the behavior without the other. However, in all cases the object was also animated and had familiar animal-like, if not human, morphology. A face stenciled onto an inert plastic blob might not be a convincing agent; nor might a faceless, plastic blob, even if it were animated in appropriately mentalistic ways.

In the following studies we have concentrated on the ability of just one of these cues — behavior — to elicit mentalistic attributions on its own. Are infants willing to

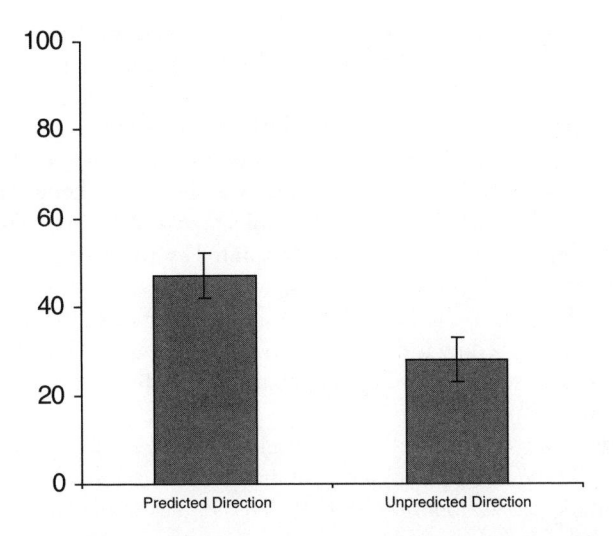

FIGURE 15.3 Percentage of infants' first looks in the predicted and unpredicted directions after the green blob turned (in Johnson, Bloz, Carter, Mandsager, Teichner and Zettler, under review).

categorize a novel object as an agent even if it bears no perceptual similarity to any familiar agent? To address this issue, we created a new novel object that was intended to be as perceptually unlike any familiar agent as we could make it. The object was the approximate size and shape of an adult's shoe, draped in bright green fiberfill. It could make beeping noises and move on its own around a large black table. It was symmetrical both front to back and side to side and had no distinguishing marks anywhere on its surface. Unlike the original furry brown agent, adults never spontaneously labeled this "agent" as anything other than an inanimate object. Anecdotally, when shown the object sitting inactive on the table, adults typically described it as a slipper, lint, cotton candy, and so on.

In our first study with this object (Johnson et al., under review), 14-month-old infants were seated in front of the experimental display and shown the location of two toy target objects at each front corner. Infants then observed an adult confederate engaging the object in small talk, as before. After the confederate left the room, the infant watched as the object turned to one side or the other. Again, infants' responses were coded as being in either the predicted or unpredicted direction. If infants' responses to the original agent were due to its similarity to familiar animals, looks in this condition, with a very unanimal like object, should be evenly split in the two directions. Figure 15.3 shows the relative percentages of infants' first looks in each direction. As in the case with the original furry brown agent, infants looked significantly more often in the direction in which the object turned, even though the agent in this case was more perceptually reminiscent of a shoe than an animal.

3.1.2 *Assigning Perceptual/Attentional Orientation to Nonhuman Agents*   Although the results just described were predicted on the view of the importance of behavior in the categorization of agents, they did pose a puzzle of sorts. By stripping the object of any recognizable facial or body features, we also stripped it of a distinctive front and back. It's one thing to realize that an unfamiliar object is an agent with the ability to perceive the world, it's possibly a separate thing altogether to determine that agent's perceptual orientation. That is, in the absence of eyes and the absence of any relevant asymmetry in the object's shape, how did the infants know which end was the front? Put another way, because of the object's symmetry and rigidity, a single clockwise rotation of the object could be interpreted by an observer as either the end proximal (or nearest to the observer) turning to the observer's left or as the distal end turning to the observer's right. Regardless of the interpretation, the objective spatio-temporal event witnessed by the observer would be the same. Nonetheless, infants were able to make a systematic judgment about this, without which they would not have produced systematic behaviors.

Given the absence of any detectable facial or head-like features, we hypothesized that infants would use the apparent ability of the object to *perceive* the confederate and targets to disambiguate its front from its back. That is, they would assume that the side facing the confederate and targets was the front, independent of their own orientation. Of course, this prediction holds only on the assumption that infants do categorize the object as agent—that is, as an object whose behavior is directed at the world. Importantly, this prediction is agnostic with respect to which, if any, specific modality infants assume the perception is embedded in (i.e., vision, audition, electromagnetic sensors, etc.).

If this hypothesis is correct, we should be able to control which end infants designate as the object's "front," and thus which direction they look, by manipulating the location of the confederate and the targets during the interaction. Again, such a result would imply that infants interpreted the behavior of the object in terms of its *inferred relationship with the world*—a notion at the heart of agency—rather than simply responding to nonrelational characteristics of its appearance or movement.

In a second study, 14-month-old infants participated in one of two conditions (Johnson et al., under review). In both, the infants were first shown the targets. They then observed a human confederate engaging the agent in the same scripted "conversation" used before. The two conditions varied only with respect to where the confederate stood during her conversation with the agent and where the targets were placed on the platform. In one condition, the confederate stood next to the seated infant, facing the proximal end of the agent. In the other, the confederate stood across the table from the infant, facing the distal end of the agent (see fig. 15.4). The targets were placed on the same side as the confederate. After interacting for approximately 60 seconds, the confederate left the room and the agent executed four test trials in which it first beeped loudly and then rotated approximately 45 degrees in one direction or the other.

In the proximal condition, significantly more of infants' first looks away from the object were in the same direction that the proximal end of the object turned than was predicted by chance. This replicated the results shown in the previous study. The interesting question is what they did in the distal condition. The observed test event was exactly the same. However, if infants were categorizing the object as an agent with a distinct front through which it perceived the world, the inferred event should have been reversed. That is, infants should now preferentially look in the same direction as the end of the object most distal to themselves.

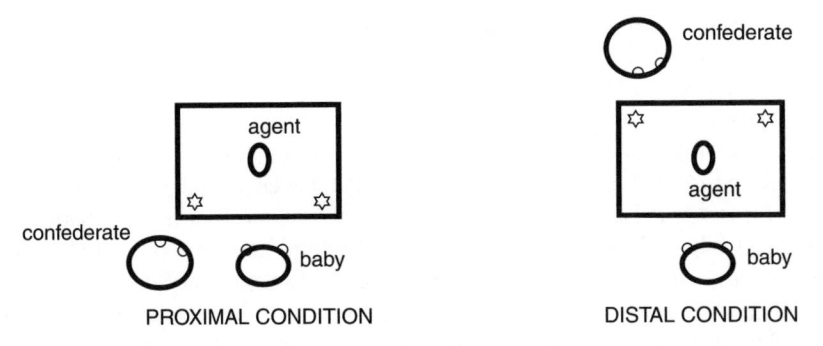

FIGURE 15.4 Schematics of the relative positions of the green blob, confederate, and infant in the orientation assignment study of Johnson, Bloz, Carter, Mandsager, Teichner and Zettler (under review).

That is what they did. Infants in the distal condition reversed their looking behavior relative to infants in the proximal condition. Significantly more of the first looks away from the object were in the direction of the distal end rather than the canonical proximal end. In effect, infants behaved as though they were watching an agent from behind. These results are remarkable not only because infants in this context did not need facial features to cue their looking but also because they were able to override any potential prepotent egocentric tendencies to treat the side facing them as the front. How exactly infants accomplished this and how they represented the hidden "face" to themselves remains to be seen.

On the basis of these results, we can tentatively conclude that around the end of the first year, infants are able to categorize a completely novel object as an intentional agent on the basis of its behavior alone. In the studies described so far, they seem to be reasoning about not only the ability of the object to perceive or attend to the world but also the actual geometric orientation of the object that would make that most plausible.

3.1.3 *Imitation: Nonhuman Agents*   In the hopes of providing evidence from a methodology distinct from gaze-following, Amy Booth, Kirsten O'Hearn, and I adapted Meltzoff's (1995) goal-reenactment paradigm for use with novel agents (Johnson et al., 2001). Although there are alternative accounts of this paradigm, such as object affordances and social enhancement, they are sufficiently different from the alternatives in the gaze-following case that similar results with novel agents in the two paradigms would have to be marked up to either the result of a single underlying concept influencing both or a striking coincidence.

With respect to Meltzoff's own person-centered account of the development of theory of mind, we questioned the extent to which infants, in fact, restrict their attribution of goals to human actors. We reasoned that unlike the novel object used in the gaze-following study just described, Meltzoff's mechanical pincers failed to embody any of the characteristics thought to imply a mind, and certainly had neither a face nor the ability to engage in contingent interactions. Therefore, in the first version of this study, we replicated Meltzoff's design and procedure, replacing the human actor with an animated stuffed monkey that had both a face and the ability to interact contingently with the infant.

Fifteen-month-olds participated in three conditions; baseline, completed target actions, and incompleted target actions. The infant was seated on the caretaker's lap at a table. The novel agent, created out of an infant-sized, stuffed orangutan toy, was seated on top of the table directly across from the infant. Its arms and hands were modified so that a hidden experimenter could extend her or his own arms into the arms of the orangutan like a puppeteer. Thus the agent possessed a full array of possible cues for characterizing intentional agents, including hands and a face, self-generated and contingent interaction with the infant, and visually guided, goal-directed actions.

As in Meltzoff's paradigm, infants observed the agent acting on a series of objects in turn. In the complete and incomplete conditions, an infant first saw the agent either successfully complete a goal with the objects (that is, drop a string of beads into a cup) or unsuccessfully complete the same goal (for instance, accidentally drop the string of beads just outside the cup), after which the infant was given the objects to play with for 20 seconds. In the baseline condition, the infant received each object first, and afterward watched the agent handle each toy in a non-goal-directed way.

Infants produced the target outcomes only 10 percent of the time in the baseline condition, thus confirming that these outcomes were rarely produced spontaneously by infants of this age. On the other hand, infants produced the target outcomes 52 percent and 37 percent of the time in the complete and incomplete conditions, respectively—rates that differed significantly from the baseline rate but not from each other. Overall, these results reveal the same patterns seen in Meltzoff's original reenactment paradigm. Not only were infants able to reproduce the same literal outcomes of a series of actions produced by an agent on objects but they were also able to produce the same target outcomes even when the agent tried but failed to produce them itself. As argued by Meltzoff, this suggests that the infants interpreted the agent's actions in terms of the agent's goals rather than the spatiotemporal characteristics of the movements themselves. The major difference between these results and Meltzoff's, of course, is that the goals in this study were attributed to a nonhuman agent.

3.1.4 *Communicative Gestures: Nonhuman Agents* In Johnson, Booth, and O'Hearn (2001), we reasoned that if imitation of goals reflects an interpretation of the orangutan as an agent, that interpretation might be manifested in other ways as well. Communicative gestures such as showing, requesting, and waving are all behaviors reflecting putative mentalistic attributions of agents. Informal coding of the infants in the goal reenactment study revealed that the majority of infants in all three conditions directed some sort of social/communicative behavior at the agent at least once, including waving, showing or giving objects, requesting objects, or alternating attention between the agent's face and a toy.

We ran a further study to rule out the possibility that the infants were simply taking their cues from the experimenter, either by imitating the experimenter's gestures directly or by more generally imitating the experimenter's stance toward the agent. To do this, we built another novel object out of a common table lamp that was roughly matched to the orangutan for visual interest without actually having any intrinsically agentive features of its own. It had comparable shape, color patterns, and moving parts. The experimenter then deliberately tried to induce in the infant a mentalistic stance toward the lamp on the basis of the experimenter's behavior alone. The experimenter talked to the lamp, called it by name ("Bob"), and invited infants to communicate with the lamp by giving and requesting objects. Despite these direct attempts to induce the mentalistic stance, infants were quite reluctant to treat it as an agent themselves. Though they waved to the orangutan, showed it objects, offered it objects, requested objects from it, and actually withdrew physically from the orangutan, these behaviors were rarely used with the lamp.

3.1.5 *Looking-Time Studies: Nonhuman Agents* Returning again to our original empirical strategy of collecting converging results from multiple methods, Shimizu and Johnson (2004) hoped to show that the same novel green blob that had previously elicited attentional following in infants (see above) was also capable of eliciting goal attributions. Whereas Johnson, Booth, and O'Hearn (2001) showed that infants would attribute goals to an agent that looked in many ways like a human, the current study was designed to test whether infants would also attribute goals to an agent that was entirely unlike any agent they were likely to have seen.

We chose Woodward's (1998; see above) looking-time method as one that would be both sensitive to goal attributions and also appropriate for use with infants of this age given this simplified agent. Like Meltzoff (1995), Woodward (1998) argued that infants' reasoning about goals and mental states is restricted to their reasoning about humans. However, like Meltzoff, Woodward only showed that infants exclude some objects from their agent category, not that they include only humans. Like Meltzoff's nonagentive pincers, Woodward's rod, though grossly similar to a human arm and hand, showed none of the specific putative behavior or morphology of agents.

Shimizu and Johnson (2004) thus showed 12-month-olds the novel green blob in a procedure based on Woodward's (1998) dishabituation paradigm that compared changes in spatiotemporal path to changes in target object. To make the behavioral test as strong as possible, two groups of infants were tested with the same green blob. The only difference between the two groups was the behavior of the novel object in the introduction and habituation phases of the study. In an agent condition, infants were introduced to the object with our now-standard confederate conversation. The confederate talked to the object, and the object beeped back. In the nonagent condition, the confederate remained silent while the object beeped its way through the same script (thus appearing random). In addition, at the beginning of each habituation trial, the agentive blob began its action facing the "nongoal" object, thus requiring a deliberate "choice" to turn toward the "goal" before beginning its approach. In comparison, the nonagentive blob simply began each habituation trial facing in the same direction that it ultimately moved—toward the target object.

Infants in both conditions saw exactly the same test events—one in which the green blob's trajectory was changed but its target object was not, and one in which the blob's target object was changed but the trajectory itself remained unchanged.

Unlike in the habituation trials, in the test trials the green blob always began its action oriented in the direction it moved, regardless of condition.

Nonetheless, these two conditions, the interactive choice-making agent versus the noninteractive mechanical-like nonagent, yielded quite different interpretations from the infants. Infants in the nonagent condition treated the two test outcomes (changes in trajectory versus changes in target) equivalently. Nothing in their behavior suggested that they selectively attended to the relationship between the blob and the objects in its immediate world. Infants in the agent condition acted quite differently, however. They looked significantly longer at the test events in which the target of the blob's action changed compared to those events in which the trajectory of the blob's action changed. As in Woodward's studies, this suggests that infants coded the relationship between the blob's actions and a specific object in the world to the exclusion of other more superficial or perceptual aspects of the events that they could have attended to. Thus, we can conclude that infants considered the interactive, choice-making blob to be an agent, just like a human. The fact that infants in the other condition did not reach that conclusion when they observed the very same object behave in nonagentive ways strengthens the case that it was the behavior, not the appearance, of the object that infants used in making their interpretations.

3.1.6 Other Looking-Time Studies with Computer-Animated Shapes In other work testing infants' interpretations of the behavior of nonhuman agents, Gergely and his colleagues (1995) showed that 12-month-olds develop visual expectations about the movements of computer-animated dots based on apparent interpretations of the dots' goal-directedness. The dots in Gergely and his colleagues' study presented several putatively mentalistic characteristics, including nonrigid transformations, contingent interactions, and self-propelled motion.

Interestingly, the existence of specialized object identification processes based on *object* cues, as opposed to *event* structures, has been questioned in a recent followup to that study. Csibra and colleagues (1999) stripped the animated dots themselves of all obvious intentional cues and found that infants still interpreted their behaviors as goal directed. The exact difference between the agents (or events) in Meltzoff's and Woodward's studies on the one hand and Csibra and colleagues' on the other is not yet resolved.

4 Imitative Generalization: A Conceptual Measure

The results presented so far are consistent with the notion that infants' behaviors at the end of the first year of life, including productive behaviors like gaze-following and imitation, as well as more passive attentional measures, reflect an incipient sensitivity to the "aboutness" quality of human behaviors. Furthermore, infants are also capable of detecting this quality in the behavior of novel, morphologically ambiguous objects. These facts are consistent with an account grounded in a domain-specific recognition system. They are less consistent, however, with either straightforward conditioning or signal releaser accounts. Such accounts rest on the assumption that infants learn their behaviors in the context of other humans (or evolution created them in the context of other humans) and that infants deploy them with nonhumans only to the extent that nonhumans resemble humans. Thus such accounts would need to specify which dimensions of humans infants are likely to use for generalization to nonhumans. Given the specificity of the actual dimensions infants do use (e.g., contingent interactivity is used by infants, but the presumably equally salient quality of self-propulsion is not always used), such attempts run the risk of collapsing onto the domain-specific perception account.

Nonetheless, the presence of a dedicated input system for agents does not entail that infants actually have a conceptual interpretation of the output of that system, even if the output is available to action systems like gaze and direct imitation or is triggered by the statistical regularities embodied in the looking-time studies described. It would be useful to find a more explicit measure of conceptual understanding in prelinguistic infants. If infants can be shown to have not only a specialized system for detecting agents but also a conceptual understanding of those agents, the arguments for an incipient theory of mind will be considerably strengthened.

The imitative generalization technique pioneered by Mandler and her colleagues is just such a measure. They have argued that infants' first conceptual categories are broad global categories that correspond more closely to adults' superordinate categories, like *animal*, than adults' basic-level categories, like *dog* or *cat*. Mandler and McDonough (1996; McDonough & Mandler, 1998) found that infants will generalize animal-typical behaviors to members of the animal category but not to members of the vehicle category, and vice versa with vehicle-typical actions. That is, infants who observe an adult demonstrate a toy dog drinking from a toy cup will then reproduce that action on a toy cat but not a toy car. Conversely, if infants see someone demonstrate "motor-revving" on a toy truck and are then given a toy cat and a toy car, they will make the car go vroom but not the cat. Thus this method not only documents the possession of the inferential category *animal* (or *agent*) in very young, prelinguistic infants but also provides a technique for examining the types of inferences infants are willing to make over that category.

The last study described here capitalized on Mandler and McDonough's method to provide a more explicit test of the concept of agents. In this preliminary study, nonhuman agents were represented by familiar animals like those used by Mandler and McDonough. If infants' representation of mentalistic agents is available to conceptual processes, that category should support the generalization of intentional properties, in addition to the bodily properties of sleeping and drinking already documented by Mandler and McDonough. Fourteen-month-olds were therefore tested on their willingness to generalize the behaviors "looking" and "listening" from one animal to another, while simultaneously denying the behaviors to vehicles.

Exemplars from two animal categories (dogs and cats) and two vehicle categories (cars and trucks) were used, along with four object-related behaviors, including two from the bodily behavior category (sleeping on a bed and drinking from a bowl) and two from the mental behavior category (looking at a picture and listening into a phone). The bodily behaviors were demonstrated as described in Mandler and McDonough (1996; McDonough & Mandler, 1998) and the mental behaviors were modeled in the following way.

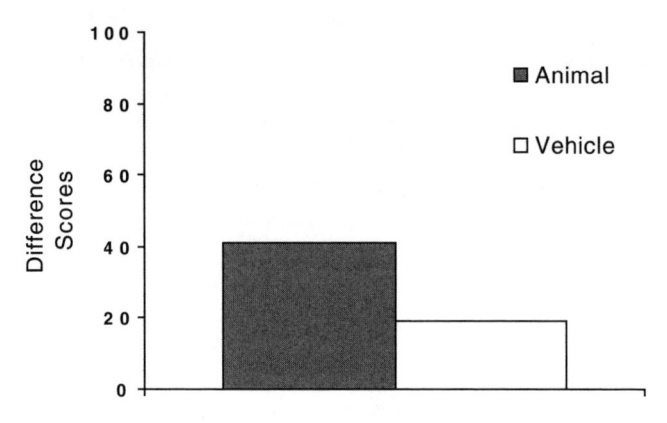

[Bar chart showing Difference Scores for Animal (~42) and Vehicle (~20)]

FIGURE 15.5 Percentage target actions produced in the modeled minus baseline conditions on either the animal or vehicle exemplar for all properties (drink, sleep, look, and listen) combined, $p < .03$.

For the looking behavior, a bright drawing of a star was attached to one side of an upright toy street sign. The demonstration animal was made to approach the side of the sign with the picture on it, while the experimenter exclaimed "Look at the picture! Isn't that pretty! Look at the picture!" For the listening behavior, the demonstration animal was made to approach a telephone handset while the experiment exclaimed "Ring ring! Hello! Who's there?" In both cases, the orientations of the target behaviors had to resemble that of the actual behavior—eyes forward in the looking behavior, and head turned with the ear and side of the face aligned with the handset for the talking behavior.

Trials began with a baseline for measuring spontaneous target actions followed by the demonstration. Each demonstration was followed by a test of the infants' interpretation of the target behavior relative to the animal and vehicle categories. Infants were presented first with the relevant target prop (e.g., the picture) and then simultaneously with a new exemplar from each of the animal and vehicle categories (if the behavior was demonstrated on a cat, it was tested on a dog, and vice versa). Infants were then given the opportunity to act on the objects in any way they chose until they had touched both exemplars at least once. Infants' behaviors were videotaped and later coded by a blind coder. A difference score for each animal and vehicle was calculated for each behavior by subtracting the rate of target production in the baseline from that in the test.

An overall analysis of the four items showed a clear replication of Mandler and McDonough's own findings. That is, infants were more likely to produce the four animal-typical behaviors on animals than they were on vehicles (see fig. 15.5).

Further analysis examined the two classes of behaviors independently, particularly to see whether the mental behaviors could produce the effect on their own. Analysis of the bodily behaviors virtually replicated the overall results and those of Mandler and McDonough. That is, infants were more likely to attempt to make a cat drink or sleep than a car (see fig. 15.6).

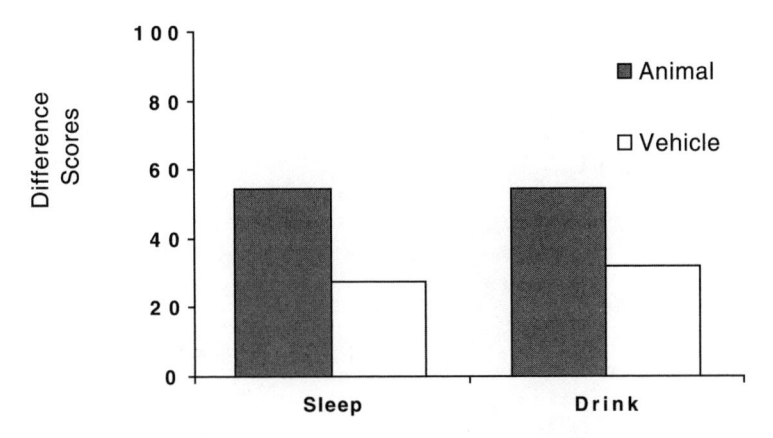

FIGURE 15.6 Percentage target actions produced in the modeled minus baseline conditions on either the animal or vehicle exemplar for bodily properties (drink and sleep) combined, $p < .06$.

Finally, analysis of the mental properties showed the same finding (see fig. 15.7). Infants consistently reproduced the intentional action "looking," in a way that appeared no different from the properties of drinking or sleeping. The rate of production for mental properties overall might have been even higher had difficulties with the telephone prop not become a problem in this preliminary study. Telephone props of the appropriate size for use with toy animals were very difficult to manipulate for both the experimenter and the infant and had a tendency to break when handled by a 14-month-old. Larger props, on the other hand, tended to prompt the infant to reproduce the "listening" behavior on themselves, thereby distracting them from the task at hand. Infants' willingness to reproduce the action on themselves suggests that it is well within their comprehension at this age. In addition, these results would be stronger if the contrasting case of vehicle-based properties were included (e.g., "vroom vroom"). As Mandler and McDonough (1996; McDonough & Mandler, 1998) argued, this condition is necessary in order to rule out the possibility that infants are simply less interested in the vehicle toy. Future research might also examine whether infants would perform the same sort of imitative generalizations with morphologically novel agents.

Nonetheless, these results provide evidence of the sort sought. At least by 14 months, the productive behaviors that infants have begun to produce in the presence of agents, such as gaze-following, imitation, and communicative gestures, are accompanied by an ability to perform relatively sophisticated actions on objects that have no obvious instrumental benefit to the infant but nonetheless reflect inductive inferences about intentional behaviors over the category of animal and/or agent.

5 Conclusions

Researchers disagree over whether to grant preverbal infants any true understanding of other minds. A general class of empirical strategies that may help to us

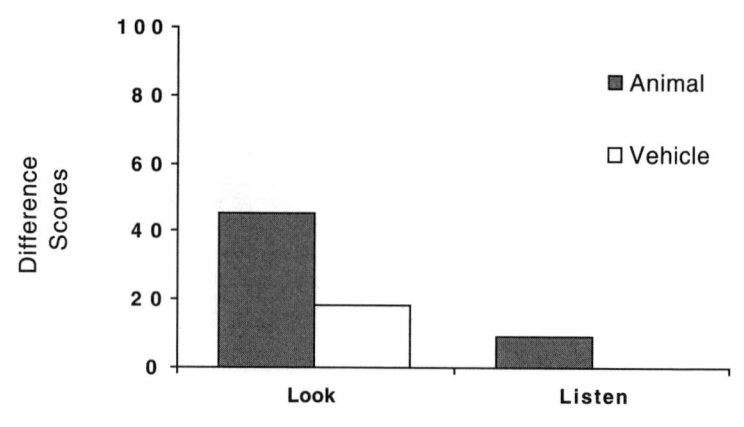

FIGURE 15.7 Percentage target actions produced in the modeled minus baseline conditions on either the animal or vehicle exemplar for intentional properties (look and listen) combined, $p < .06$.

decide between intentional and nonintentional interpretations of infants' earliest putative theory-of-mind behaviors has emerged. Tomasello (1995) suggested that arguments for intentional attributions in infancy would be strengthened if it were shown that attributions across multiple behavioral contexts emerge within the same developmental window. Heyes (1998), discussing a similar debate within the animal literature, suggested that target attributions be demonstrated across multiple behavioral contexts within the same individual.

Finally, in the work described here, I have aimed to strengthen the evidence for intentional attributions in two ways. First by attempting to elicit them across multiple behavioral contexts with the same restricted set of object-recognition cues. For instance, if the object characteristics that induce infants to follow a novel object's directional orientation do so because they invoke an intermediary representation (intermediary in the processing stream between perception and action) of intentional agent, that representation should also be available to support other behaviors thought to be based on intentional attributions, such as goal-imitation. If results consistent with intentional interpretations are obtained in divergent methodological paradigms, objections based on local interpretative issues of individual methods will no longer obtain. Second, I have attempted to elicit intentional attributions from infants using one behavior—imitative generalization—that seems unlikely to reduce to a perception-action system under any interpretation and is therefore less susceptible to nonconceptual construals.

The evidence gathered is promising. By the age of 12 to 15 months, infants will follow the directional orientation, reenact unseen goals, gesture communicatively, dishabituate to changes in the goals, and imitatively generalize intentional actions, like "looking," to nonhuman agents. Many, though not all, of these measures have been used with agents that bear no perceptual similarity to humans. The feature these objects do share with humans seems to be quality of "aboutness" in their behavior. This quality is most likely perceived in a variety of forms, including at least (1) temporal/contingent interactivity with other behaving beings—this ability implies the ability to perceive others and possibly to interpret communicative signals—and (2) nonrandom spatial directedness; again, this ability implies the ability to perceive the world. Exactly how infants calculate "aboutness" from the spatial and temporal characteristics of objects' actions will require a great deal more study.

16

HELEN TAGER-FLUSBERG

What Neurodevelopmental Disorders Can Reveal about Cognitive Architecture
The Example of Theory of Mind

Over the past two decades, cognitive scientists have become increasingly interested in how the study of children and adults with neurodevelopmental disorders might inform theories of neurocognitive architecture. This interest has not been without controversy, and the extent to which research on neurodevelopmental disorders provides new insights for cognitive science has been hotly debated both on theoretical and empirical grounds. In this chapter, I provide a brief overview of this controversy and weigh the arguments for and against what we might learn from studying individuals who have fundamental biological impairments. I then discuss the example of research on theory of mind in two different disorders, autism and Williams syndrome (WMS), which has highlighted a number of important aspects of how this core cognitive capacity develops in both normal and atypical populations.

1 Neurodevelopmental Disorders

1.1 Defining Neurodevelopmental Disorders

The majority of neurodevelopmental disorders are caused by genetic abnormalities that may be classified into several categories. These include disorders that result from mutations in a single gene (e.g., phenylketonuria or fragile-X syndrome) and chromosomal disorders in which an entire chromosome (e.g., Down syndrome or Turner syndrome) or segments of a chromosome (e.g., WMS or Prader-Willi syndrome) are either missing or duplicated. A third group of disorders is referred to as polygenic, or complex, because they are assumed to be caused by several interacting genes. These disorders (e.g., autism, specific language impairment, or dyslexia)

Preparation of this chapter was supported by National Institutes of Health grants numbers PO1/U19 DC 03610 and RO1 HD 33470.

typically involve inherited quantitative cognitive, behavioral, or personality traits (Tager-Flusberg, 1999a).

Across all neurodevelopmental disorders, genetic abnormalities disrupt the normal course of brain development, beginning early during the prenatal period. These developmental brain abnormalities lead to distinct cognitive and behavioral phenotypic outcomes, including mental retardation or learning disabilities, which are characteristic of the majority of individuals with specific disorders. In some disorders, we find quite unusual profiles of cognitive functioning, which may include striking differences between specific cognitive domains (Tager-Flusberg, 2003). For example, people with WMS have relatively strong language skills coupled with severely impaired visual-spatial skills, whereas people with Down syndrome have significantly impaired verbal short-term memory, in contrast to their spatial skills, which are commensurate to their mental age levels. These contrasting patterns of cognitive skills are sometimes interpreted as evidence for dissociations between different mental processes and brain systems.

1.2 Neurodevelopmental Disorders and Cognitive Science

Within cognitive science there has been a rich and lengthy tradition of using evidence from people with brain damage to inform cognitive theory, including how cognitive systems are structured and organized. The use of adults with *acquired* lesions in discrete brain regions, which result in disorders such as amnesia, aphasia, or agnosia, has enriched our understanding of the memory, language, and visual systems (see Gazzaniga, 2000). Adult patients with acquired disorders are assumed to have developed normally and reached a mature end-state before the lesion damaged their previously intact cognitive system. Much of what we have learned from studies of these adult patients has involved the comparison of patients, often at the individual subject level, who have contrasting lesion sites and demonstrate dissociated deficits (e.g., Dunn & Kirsner, 2003; Gabrieli et al., 1995; Sternberg, 2001).

The assumptions that underlie studies of adult patients with acquired lesions do not hold for people with neurodevelopmental disorders, for whom disruptions in early brain development influence not only the end-state but also the *development* of cognitive systems. Children with such disorders provide a window onto the developmental processes that underlie these atypical patterns, but there are no discrete neural lesions associated with particular disorders that are comparable to those found in acquired disorders. Instead, studies using *in vivo* brain imaging methods with children or adults suggest that there are subtle differences in the volume and morphology of particular structures in both cortical and subcortical regions associated with different disorders (Lyon & Rumsey, 1996; Thatcher et al., 1996). The differences between acquired and developmental disorders are as fundamental as the differences between static and dynamic neurological and neurocognitive systems (Oliver et al., 2000), leading some to question whether evidence from children or adults with neurodevelopmental disorders can be used to make claims about the architecture of human cognitive systems, especially claims regarding modularity.

Karmiloff-Smith (1997) has articulated most clearly the key differences between adult and developmental disorders. Her main arguments focus on the fact that brain development in neurodevelopmental disorders differs from normal brain development beginning early in neurogenesis (see Courchesne et al., 1995). Karmiloff-Smith points out that there is no one-to-one mapping between specific genes and specific cognitive abilities. Genetic influences operate on the trajectory of neural development in complex ways that we are only beginning to understand. These are important points that are often missed by cognitive scientists outside the field of neurodevelopmental disorders.

Karmiloff-Smith (1998b) further argues that the developing brain is significantly more plastic than we have appreciated from earlier research on adult acquired disorders. On her view, brain specialization or modularity is not the starting point that directs the course of cognitive development; rather it is the *product* of development (Karmiloff-Smith et al., 2003). In neurodevelopmental disorders, because development has gone awry, cognitive structure and function will also not be normal. There may be cases where behavioral patterns will resemble normal functioning, but Karmiloff-Smith argues that even superficially preserved abilities are the result of atypical underlying developmental processes and brain organization (Karmiloff-Smith et al., 2003; Paterson et al., 1999). These arguments suggest that individuals with neurodevelopmental disorders cannot provide evidence about how cognitive systems are organized, but these claims rest on assumptions about the degree and type of plasticity that is available for the development of neurocognitive systems in different populations.

One might question how far we can take the plasticity claim; put another way, are there more constraints on the organization and structure of the developing brain than Karmiloff-Smith and her colleagues suggest? At some level, this remains an empirical question. Elsewhere I have argued that there are far fewer differences from normal development in developmental disorders than others have assumed (Tager-Flusberg, 2000a). For example, as noted earlier, despite some variation in relative size (either smaller or larger) and other surface features, in fact, across a wide range of disorders it is actually quite remarkable how similar the brains of different populations are to one another and to normally developing children. Sensory and motor systems are located in similar cortical brain regions, and higher level cognitive functions are also organized in quite parallel neural structures. While there is some functional variation, this does not go much beyond the degree that is observed in normal people. This suggests that the brain is a dynamic system that develops along moderately flexible but fairly bounded and directed pathways that are essentially similar in both normal and disordered populations. On this view, neurodevelopmental disorders can provide cognitive science with converging evidence about cognitive organization. Because there are sometimes striking developmental asynchronies (but not aberrant pathways) and protracted developmental periods in children with different disorders, they may reveal aspects of neurocognitive architecture that are not clearly evident in normally developing children in whom there is close synchrony and rapid timing across many developmental domains.

Despite the fact that neurodevelopmental disorders do not create discrete brain lesions, it may still be the case that certain cognitive systems or subsystems will be differentially affected by particular genetic abnormalities. This remains an empirical question. It may hold for some disorders but not others, for some cognitive systems but not others. Nevertheless, we should keep Karmiloff-Smith's cautions in mind; especially since the identification of specific cognitive modules or domains that have been disrupted in any specific neurodevelopmental disorder has been more elusive that we had anticipated (e.g., Frith & Happé, 1998).

1.3 Methodological Issues

Studies of neurodevelopmental disorders have been used as evidence for strong theoretical claims, even when they have employed highly questionable methodology that would not be viewed as acceptable in other areas of cognitive science. Supporters of widely different theoretical perspectives have been guilty of taking this relatively uncritical view of the literature on neurodevelopmental disorders, including both nativists (e.g., Pinker, 1994) and nonnativists (e.g., Karmiloff-Smith et al., 2003).

One of the major issues that must be addressed in the study of all neurodevelopmental disorders is the significant *heterogeneity in phenotype expression* within each syndrome, which may be related to nongenetic as well as genetic variation. Significant individual differences in performance are related to variations in the experiences of people with neurodevelopmental disorders. One important experiential factor is the effect of remediation that is likely to influence a person's performance on cognitive as well as functional neuroimaging tasks. For example, the neural and behavioral outcomes in adults with a history of severe dyslexia differ considerably for those who have been able to compensate as a result of extensive intervention compared to those who remain severely impaired in their reading ability (Shaywitz et al., 2003). Although this is not a factor that can be effectively controlled in all studies, it needs to be considered as a potential contributor to performance variation within any study sample. A second factor is age: older people have had significantly more cognitive experience than younger people, which contributes to their task performance. All developmental research acknowledges this important influence, yet it is not unusual to find studies on neurodevelopmental disorders that include young children as well as adults as subjects in the same experiment (e.g., Deruelle et al., 1999).

The two variables that have the most significant impact on cognitive performance in studies of neurodevelopmental disorders are level of intellectual functioning and language. As noted earlier, most neurodevelopmental disorders include mental retardation as part of the phenotype. However, within every disorder, IQ shows the same bell-shaped distribution of scores as in the normal population, though the average will be significantly lower than 100 and the range will vary (Tager-Flusberg, 1999b). For example, in WMS, the average IQ score is about 60, with some people scoring within the normal range of 85–100, while others have scores of 40 or below. The range is even wider in autism spectrum disorders: about 70 percent of the autism population have mental retardation (Bailey et al., 1996), but the full range may be from below 20 to above 150. The IQ significantly impacts performance across all cognitive tasks. Its influence is on general rather than domain-specific cognitive processes (e.g., attention, memory, processing speed) and may be linked to cognitive or neural efficiency (Detterman, 1999). Language skills also significantly impact task performance. Many people with neurodevelopmental disorders are language impaired, performing below expectations for age on standard tests of linguistic ability. Impaired language may affect comprehension of task instructions, the content of verbal tasks, or the ability to use language directly or indirectly in responding to an experimental task.

The cumulative effects of IQ and language variation can potentially obscure syndrome-specific patterns of performance across cognitive tasks. In turn, this will have considerable impact on the inferences that can be drawn from studies of neurodevelopmental disorders regarding cognitive structure and organization. Specifically, these nonmodular influences on task performance may override what might be revealed about the modular architecture of cognitive systems that have been differentially affected by neurogenetic factors.

The methodological challenges posed by investigating neurodevelopmental disorders cannot be disregarded or completely controlled. We are limited by the availability of study participants diagnosed with syndromes that are often quite rare. Nevertheless, well-controlled studies will select experimental subjects representing a relatively narrow age range, document the IQ and language skills of their participants, and include control tasks or comparison groups that are appropriately matched on these key variables. (See Tager-Flusberg et al., 2003.)

2 Theory of Mind in Neurodevelopmental Disorders

2.1 Background on Theory of Mind

Successful social interactions depend on the ability to understand other people's behavior in terms of their mental states, such as beliefs, desires, knowledge, and intentions. Social situations and events cannot be interpreted on the basis of overt behavior without representing the mental states underlying people's actions. Understanding people as intentional, mental beings is at the core of social cognition, within which the ability to interpret people's behavior in a mentalistic explanatory framework using a coherent, causally related set of mental constructs is central to a theory of mind (Astington et al., 1988; Carruthers & Smith, 1996; Perner, 1991; Wellman, 1990; Whiten, 1991).

The past two decades witnessed an exponential increase in research on the development of theory of mind. Studies suggest that the earliest signs of social understanding appear in infancy, including the ability to detect biological motion, goals and intentions, preferential gaze toward people rather than objects, imitation, and joint attention (e.g., Baldwin & Moses, 1996; Csibra, 2003; Hood et al., 1998; Meltzoff, 1995; Meltzoff & Decety, 2003; Repacholi, 1998; Woodward, 1998; see also Johnson, chapter 15 here). By the time children reach the preschool years, they understand mental concepts and are able to predict and explain human actions by inferring the contents of people's mental states. Understanding that a person's behavior can be interpreted on the basis of the person's belief about a situation, which may differ from reality (i.e., a false belief), has been considered a hallmark of a representational theory of mind, which is based on the capacity for metarepresentation. Other types of evidence for a mentalistic construal of persons emerging in the preschool years consist of children's capacity to use mental states (e.g., desire and belief terms) to explain human action (Bartsch & Wellman, 1995), children's capacity to use information about a person's perceptual access or knowledge to judge whether an action was intended or accidental (Schult & Wellman, 1997; Pillow, 1988), and children's preference for psychological explanations over behavioral descriptions of action scenarios (Lillard & Flavell, 1990; Tager-Flusberg & Sullivan, 1994). These abilities are the main ingredients of a theory of mind, and have been shown to develop in normally developing children between two and five years of age.

Since entering the "canon" of cognitive systems, findings from studies of neurodevelopmental disorders have been taken as central in arguments regarding the structure, architecture, and neural basis of theory of mind (see Baron-Cohen et al., 2000). This began with the influential studies of theory of mind in autism (Baron-Cohen et al., 1985) and has continued more recently with investigations of theory of mind in WMS (Karmiloff-Smith et al., 1995; Tager-Flusberg & Sullivan, 2000), specific language impairment (Miller, 2001), and even deaf (de Villiers & de Villiers, 2000; Peterson & Siegel, 1995; 1998) and blind (Brown et al., 1997) children. The findings from these studies have been the subject of considerable controversy, in part because of the methodological problems discussed earlier. In the remainder of this chapter, I review evidence from studies of autism and WMS in favor of a new model for the organization of theory of mind, with special attention to how particular components of this cognitive system may be integrally linked to specific aspects of language.

2.1 Theory of Mind in Autism

Baron-Cohen and his colleagues were the first to demonstrate that the majority of children with autism failed false belief tasks, in contrast to normally developing preschoolers and children with Down syndrome (Baron-Cohen et al., 1985). Follow-up experimental studies provided further support for their hypothesis that autistic children are impaired in their acquisition of a theory of mind: they fail to understand stories that involve deception or false belief (Baron-Cohen et al., 1986), they do not understand the connection between perception and knowledge (Baron-Cohen, 1989), they lack imagination (Scott & Baron-Cohen, 1996), and they do not engage in spontaneous pretend play (Baron-Cohen, 1987; Lewis & Boucher, 1988). In naturalistic settings, children with autism do not use mental state terms such as *think* and *know* in everyday conversation (Tager-Flusberg, 1992), and they lack social skills that depend on mentalizing (Frith et al., 1994; for a review see Baron-Cohen, 2000).

The significance of the theory-of-mind hypothesis of autism, as it came to be known in the literature (Baron-Cohen et al., 1993), was that it not only explained the failure of children with autism on tasks tapping theory-of-mind abilities but also provided a unified cognitive explanation for the primary diagnostic impairments in pretence, social functioning, and communication (Baron-Cohen, 1988; Frith, 1989; Leslie, 1987). It revolutionized research on autism and had important influences on theoretical models of theory of mind. The selective deficits in theory of mind among people with autism were taken as evidence in support of the modularity of theory of mind (e.g., Baron-Cohen, 1995; Leslie & Roth, 1993). More recent neuroimaging studies also suggest that the neural circuits that subserve theory of mind may be fundamentally impaired in autism (e.g., Frith & Frith, 1999; 2000).

2.2 Theory of Mind in Williams Syndrome

Williams syndrome is a rare neurodevelopmental disorder caused by a hemizygous microdeletion on the long arm of chromosome 7 (7q11.32), which includes between 16 and 25 genes (Bellugi et al., 1999; Osborne & Pober, 2001). The syndrome is characterized by a unique phenotype that typically includes physiological abnormalities of the heart and other organs, a variety of connective or soft tissue disorders, cranio-facial dysmorphology, and an unusual combination of cognitive, personality, and behavioral features (Morris & Mervis, 1999).

Although the majority of individuals with WMS are mentally retarded, some aspects of their cognitive functioning appear to be relatively spared, including vocabulary knowledge (Bellugi et al., 1992; Mervis et al., 1999; Volterra et al., 1996), face processing (Bellugi et al., 1988a; Tager-Flusberg et al., 2003), and auditory rote memory (Mervis et al., 1999; Robinson et al., 2003; Udwin & Yule, 1991). The behavior and personality of people with WMS also suggest some unique characteristics. The most remarkable feature of both children and adults with WMS is their extreme interest in people. They have a warm, outgoing, cheerful, and friendly personality style (Klein-Tasman & Mervis, 2003; Udwin & Yule, 1991). They are described as being empathic toward other people (Gosch & Pankau, 1994); they are less reserved toward strangers, more approaching, curious and extroverted, and overly friendly and affectionate (Gosch & Pankau, 1997; Sarimski, 1997; Tomc et al., 1990; Van Lieshout et al., 1998).

The cognitive and personality profile associated with WMS led several researchers to propose that WMS may be characterized by sparing in the domain of theory of mind (Karmiloff-Smith, et al., 1995; Tager-Flusberg et al., 1998). The combination of relatively good language skills, excellent face processing abilities, strong social interest, and attention to faces and people (Mervis et al., 2003) helped to foster the view that theory of mind might be spared in this population. The initial evidence came from a study by Karmiloff-Smith and her colleagues (1995), who used a set of standard theory-of-mind tests, including first- and second-order false belief tasks and a higher order task that involved attributing intentions to linguistic utterances. Karmiloff-Smith and her colleagues found that the majority of the subjects with WMS passed the first-order tasks, and some even passed the second- and higher order tasks. They concluded from their findings that WMS involves an "islet of relatively preserved ability" (Karmiloff-Smith et al., 1995, p. 202) in theory of mind.

Of particular interest to theory-of-mind scholars is the striking contrast between autism and WMS. In autism there are fundamental impairments in language (Kjelgaard & Tager-Flusberg, 2001; Lord & Paul, 1997), face processing (e.g., Langdell, 1978; Joseph & Tanaka, 2003), and severe social deficits (Klin et al., 2000)—exactly those cognitive skills that are relatively preserved in WMS. Furthermore, visual-spatial skills (as measured for example by block design tasks) are spared in autism (e.g., Joseph et al., 2002; Shah & Frith, 1993), but are severely impaired in WMS (Bellugi et al., 1988b; Hoffman et al., 2003; Mervis et al., 2000). These contrasting profiles suggest a double dissociation: in autism, theory of mind is impaired while visual-spatial skills are spared; in WMS, theory of mind is spared while visual-spatial skills are impaired. These arguments provide support for the view that these domains are separable in terms of their underlying cognitive and neural mechanisms.

2.3 Criticisms of the Theory-of-Mind Hypothesis in Autism and WMS

Despite its wide-ranging appeal, the theory-of-mind hypothesis of autism has come under attack (see Tager-Flusberg, 2001). Researchers have questioned the selectivity or uniqueness of theory-of-mind impairments in autism, because studies show that nonautistic children and adolescents with mental retardation also fail standard theory-of-mind tasks at a higher rate than would be expected given their age and developmental level (Benson et al., 1993; Yirmiya et al., 1998; Zelazo et al., 1996). The same is true for other populations, such as oral deaf children (de Villiers & de Villiers, 2000; Peterson & Siegel, 1995, 1998) and people with schizophrenia (Corcoran, 2000). If these groups also have difficulty on theory-of-mind tasks, can theory of mind be interpreted as the unique deficit in autism?

Other concerns voiced by some researchers include the fact that autism symptoms emerge in infancy long before normally developing children would pass theory-of-mind tasks, such as false belief (Klin & Volkmar, 1993). Furthermore, there are features of autism that are not so clearly interpreted in terms of a core cognitive impairment in theory of mind. These include the primary symptoms of repetitive behavior and restricted or obsessive interests (Turner, 1999) and other secondary features such as savant abilities (such as outstanding memory for facts, perfect pitch, calendrical calculators, or artistic talent), deficits in the ability to generalize, exceptionally good visual perceptual skills, and atypical sensory sensitivities. Impairments in theory of mind do not explain these features of the disorder (Happé, 1999; Plaisted, 2000).

One final criticism of the theory-of-mind hypothesis comes from the fact that some children with autism pass theory-of-mind tasks, including false belief (Baron-Cohen et al., 1985). The numbers who pass varies from one study to the next, but even a small percentage (e.g., 20 percent in Baron-Cohen et al., 1995) must be accounted for in any theory. If autism involves a failure to develop a theory of mind, how could these participants with autism pass the tasks? One explanation is that theory of mind may be seriously delayed in autism, and most people never achieve the same endpoint as nonautistic people. Others argue that in autism, failure on tasks that tap theory-of-mind abilities may be more directly interpreted in terms of domain-general deficits in either executive functions (e.g., Russell, 1997) or language (e.g., Eisenmajer & Prior, 1991; Tager-Flusberg, 2000b). The latter argument challenges the view that difficulties on false belief and related tasks directly reflect domain-specific impairments to theory of mind.

At the same time, recent evidence suggests that theory of mind may not be as spared in WMS as originally believed. We systematically investigated performance on false belief and other theory-of-mind tasks in children with WMS. The children with WMS were matched to two comparison groups on age (4 to 10 years), IQ, and standardized language measures. The comparison groups included children with Prader-Willi syndrome (PWS), another genetically based neurodevelopmental disorder, and children with nonspecific mental retardation. In each experiment, between 15 and 25 children were included in each group. On three different first-order theory-of-mind tasks—false belief, explanation of action (Tager-Flusberg & Sullivan, 1994), and understanding of intended action (Joseph & Tager-Flusberg, 1999)—we found that the children with WMS performed no better than the matched comparison groups (Plesa-Skwerer & Tager-Flusberg, in press; Tager-Flusberg & Sullivan, 2000).

We also investigated higher order theory-of-mind tasks in adolescents with WMS, and matched groups of adolescents with PWS and mental retardation. Again, no differences were found among these groups in second-order belief reasoning (Sullivan & Tager-Flusberg, 1999), distinguishing lies and jokes (Sullivan et al., 2003), or using trait information to attribute intentionality (Plesa-Skwerer & Tager-Flusberg, in press). Thus, our more recent studies on theory of mind in WMS provide no evidence of relative sparing in this domain for either children or adolescents with WMS compared to age, IQ, and language-matched controls (see the earlier discussion on methodology issues in sec. 2.3).

3 Model of Theory of Mind

3.1 Two-Component Model

Research on theory of mind in autism and Williams syndrome has left us with contradictory hypotheses and findings. On the one hand, it has been proposed that these disorders represent dissociation in theory-of-mind abilities, reflecting their contrasting social profiles. On the other hand, current data suggest that there may be little to distinguish between these groups in their performance on theory-of-mind tasks (see also Pearlman-Avnion, 2003). To resolve this apparent paradox, I have recently proposed a componential model of theory of mind in which there are several interacting hierarchically organized component levels within the domain of theory of mind (Tager-Flusberg, 2001; Tager-Flusberg & Sullivan, 2000). The advantages of this model are that it accounts for a broader range of phenomena than original theoretical accounts (e.g., Leslie & Thaiss, 1992) that encompass traditional conceptions of theory of mind as well as more general mentalizing abilities: it incorporates known developmental aspects of theory of mind from infancy through middle childhood; it is consistent with neurobiological models of social neuroscience; and it can explain the pattern of findings from autism and WMS (as well as other disordered populations). The model presented here is quite preliminary; I limit discussion to two key components of theory of mind: the perceptual, and cognitive components. No doubt, as research in this area advances, these will be further divided into additional discrete components.

On this model, there are two levels or components where mental states are represented: a primary *social-perceptual* level and a higher order *social-cognitive* level. The perceptual component refers to the online immediate or intuitive representation of a person's mental state, based on information directly available in faces, voices, and body posture and movement. The cognitive component refers to our metarepresentational capacity to make more complex cognitive inferences about the content of mental states, and it requires integrating information across time and events. This distinction between perceptual and cognitive levels of representation corresponds roughly to the categories of "intuitive belief" and "reflective beliefs" proposed by Sperber (1997).[1]

3.2 Social-Perceptual Component

The social-perceptual component of theory of mind builds on the innate preferences of infants to attend to human social stimuli, especially faces and voices (e.g., Fernald, 1989, 1993; Johnson & Morton, 1991; Mehler & Dupoux, 1994). The route to interpreting mental state information from these stimuli lies in the interaction of innately specified mechanisms with social information in the world, which is obtained through continued interactions with people. The social preferences of infants that promote continued interactions with people might be driven by affective motives—the intrinsic reward of social stimuli. By the latter half of the first year of life, infants use perceptual information from faces, voices, and gestures to interpret the intentions and emotional states of other people; they may also use more subtle cues, such as eye-gaze, to judge what another person is attending to or planning to do (see Baldwin, 1993; Baron-Cohen, 1994; Repacholi, 1998). Thus, the perceptual component of theory of mind emerges first in development, and is available to infants for making a range of mental state judgments about other people based primarily on sensory inputs. Over the course of development, social-perceptual judgments may also entail other cognitive inputs (e.g., memory).

3.3 Social-Cognitive Component

The social-cognitive component of theory of mind builds on the earlier emerging perceptual component. This component is involved in making mental state inferences that depend on integrating information not only from perceptual cues but also from sequences of events over time. The social-cognitive component of theory of mind is more closely linked to other cognitive or information-processing systems,

---

1. There have been other researchers who have proposed more complex models of theory of mind: for example, Wellman (1990) and Baron-Cohen (1995). Their models share certain features with the model presented here, but they also differ in terms of either the nature of the core components (Wellman) or the more limited developmental framework (Baron-Cohen, 1995) that is endorsed here. The model presented here was explicitly developed to account for the detailed evidence of both spared and impaired aspects of mentalizing found in autism and Williams syndrome (Tager-Flusberg, 2001; Tager-Flusberg & Sullivan, 2000).

such as working memory (needed for integrating information) and language. The development of the cognitive component of theory of mind begins during the early preschool years when children begin to talk and reason about epistemic states (Bartsch & Wellman, 1995). It is firmly in place by four years of age, when young children have the metarepresentational capacity to pass false belief and other related tasks. Language plays an especially significant role in the development of this component of theory of mind (de Villiers, 2000; Hale & Tager-Flusberg, 2003).

3.4 Neurobiological Evidence

In this model, each of the two main components of a theory of mind has its own developmental time-course, and each is dependent on different underlying neurocognitive mechanisms. Converging evidence comes from studies of brain function, particularly from research on the neurobiological substrate of what Leslie Brothers (1990) refers to as the "social brain." The primary areas of the brain that are involved in social-perceptual information processing include the amygdala and associated regions of medial temporal cortex, including the superior temporal sulcus (Allison et al., 2000). The amygdala is central to the processing of emotion (e.g., Adolphs et al., 1994; Adolphs et al., 1998) and other complex social stimuli (Brothers et al., 1990; Perrett et al., 1990). Functional brain-imaging studies show that the amygdala and areas of the medial temporal cortex are activated in tasks tapping the recognition of facial expressions of emotions and other mental states (Baron-Cohen et al., 1999; Breiter et al., 1996) as well as the perception of biological or intentional motion (Bonda et al., 1996).

The brain areas that subserve the social-cognitive component of theory of mind include regions in the prefrontal cortex. The orbito-frontal cortex is involved in reasoning about the social appropriateness of action (Eslinger & Damasio, 1985) and in making lexical judgments about cognitive mental state terms (Baron-Cohen et al., 1994). Areas in the medial frontal cortex are closely associated with other theory-of-mind abilities, especially tasks tapping advanced social-cognitive capacities (Fletcher et al., 1995; Goel et al., 1995). In summary, there is preliminary evidence that different neural substrates underlie the components of theory of mind described here (see also Frith & Frith, 2003; Siegal & Varley, 2002). These brain regions form a complex neural circuit for processing a range of social information, from basic perception of biological motion to inferring the contents of other people's minds.

4 Application of the Componential Model to Neurodevelopmental Disorders

4.1 Theory-of-Mind Deficits in Autism

The componential model provides for two levels of representing mental states: the perceptual and cognitive. The perceptual component is the primary level, in that it directly computes mental states on the basis of available information, it emerges early in development, and it is based in both subcortical and cortical brain regions. The cognitive component, while it builds on the perceptual level and is closely interconnected, is a higher order level, interacting with other cognitive systems, including memory and language, to compute *the contents* of mental states in prefrontal cortical regions. On this view, theory of mind is conceived in broader terms than the original metarepresentational theories (see Leslie & Roth, 1993). Within this model, the fundamental domain-specific deficits in autism are in the social-perceptual component of theory of mind: children and adults with autism are fundamentally impaired in computing mental states on the basis of information available from social stimuli, especially faces and voices.

The roots of the social-perceptual impairments in autism may be seen in the social orienting deficits that are evident in infants (Dawson et al., 1998; Klin, 1991; Osterling & Dawson, 1994). These deficits are correlated with their failure to perceive behavior in others as intentional or to appreciate others' perspectives, as exemplified in the joint attention deficits that are among the hallmark symptoms of the disorder (Mundy & Sigman, 1989; Mundy et al., 1990, 1993). Thus, children with autism below the age of three demonstrate significant impairment in the range of behaviors that are among the early developments in the social-perceptual component of theory of mind (see Klin & Volkmar, 1993). Even older high-functioning people with autism or Asperger syndrome perform poorly on tasks that measure the perception of biological motion (Blake et al., 2003), the ability to read mental states from the eye region of the face (Baron-Cohen et al., 1997), or the attribution of intentional and social significance to ambiguous visual stimuli (Klin et al., 2000; Klin et al., 2003).

The majority of children with autism are also impaired on social-cognitive measures of theory of mind, as evidenced by their failure to pass false belief tasks (Baron-Cohen et al., 1985) or to explain human behavior using mental-state terms (Tager-Flusberg, 1992). These deficits in the cognitive aspects of theory of mind grow out of the earlier deficits in social perception, because these components are closely interconnected, with cognition building on social perception. Nevertheless, as noted earlier, some children with autism pass theory-of-mind tasks. Within the componential framework, I argue that these children depend on *language* (not theory of mind) to hack out solutions to such tasks, which they treat as logical problems (Tager-Flusberg, 2001). At the same time, these children remain fundamentally impaired at the social-perceptual level, and in their conceptual understanding of mental states. Later I provide evidence for this claim that children with autism can pass theory-of-mind tasks via language.

4.2 Theory-of-Mind Deficits in WMS

Children and adults with WMS are fundamentally different from people with autism, in that they show an extremely strong interest in and sensitivity to others (Jones et al., 2000). On the basis of evidence from two preliminary studies, Tager-Flusberg & Sullivan (2000) argued that these aspects of their behavior reflect relative *sparing* in the social-perceptual component of theory of mind. On this view, the dissociation between autism and WMS is at the social-perceptual level of representing mental states. At the same time, there is no dissociation between autism and WMS at the social-cognitive level; both groups generally perform poorly on classic theory-of-mind tasks relative to age-matched peers. Thus, there is no double dissociation between these populations within these two components of theory of mind.

We conducted two small-scale studies on the social-perceptual component of theory of mind in WMS. Tager-Flusberg et al. (1998) compared adults with WMS to a well-matched group of adults with Prader-Willi syndrome on the eyes task (Baron-Cohen et al., 1997), for which a subject is asked to select which of two terms best describes the mental state expressed in a photograph of the eye region of a face. At noted earlier, Baron-Cohen and colleagues (1997) found that high-functioning adults with autism performed significantly worse than controls on this task. In our study, the adults with WMS performed significantly better than the adults with Prader-Willi syndrome. In fact, half the WMS group performed at the same level as normal age-matched adults. These findings were taken as evidence that WMS involves sparing in theory of mind; some people with WMS may be spared in the absolute sense (i.e., those performing within the limits of the normal population) while other were spared in the relative sense (compared to matched adults with Prader-Willi syndrome). In another study, Tager-Flusberg and Sullivan (1999) found that young children with WMS showed significantly greater empathy than a matched group of children with Prader-Willi syndrome. Their task involved comparing the verbal and nonverbal responses of the subjects to the distress exhibited by an experimenter when she feigned hurting her knee. The children with WMS showed greater concern and more appropriate affect and made more relevant verbal empathic comments than the comparison group. Both of these studies involved measures of the social-perceptual component of theory of mind, in that they tapped the ability to read facial expressions of mental states rather than the ability to make inferences about the contents of another person's mind.

We are currently following up on these earlier studies using tasks that are better controlled and larger, more heterogeneous groups of adolescents and adults with WMS. On the basis of preliminary analyses of our data, we can say that it is no longer so clear that people with WMS are spared in their ability to compute mental-state information from facial or vocal expressions. Across several experiments, the WMS subjects performed worse than normal controls, although their *pattern* of performance was similar, suggesting the use of the same cognitive mechanisms (Plesa-Skwerer et al., 2003). Thus, it seems that even social-perceptual theory-of-mind tasks entail some domain-general processing skills, such as attention or response speed, that are most likely to be compromised in any person with mental retardation. It remains to be seen whether the unusual sociability that is a central feature of the WMS phenotype is related to theory of mind or is a reflection of unique arousal and emotional functioning.

5 Language and Theory of Mind

5.1 *Language and the Social-Cognitive Component*

One of the fundamental differences between the perceptual and cognitive components of theory of mind lies in the role of language. The social-cognitive component is integrally linked to language. Evidence for this close relationship between language and a representational understanding of mind comes from several sources, including developmental studies of preschoolers. Numerous studies have found a significant correlation between standardized language measures and performance on theory-of-mind tasks in preschoolers (e.g., Cutting & Dunn, 1999; Hughes & Dunn, 1997; Jenkins & Astington, 1996). Astington and Jenkins (1999) conducted a longitudinal study in order to identify the direction of this relationship. Their findings confirmed that language predicted later performance on theory-of-mind tasks but not the reverse. Furthermore, syntactic knowledge was the major factor predicting later theory of mind.

What is significant about syntax in relation to false belief? De Villiers and her colleagues (de Villiers, 2000; de Villiers & de Villiers, 2000; de Villiers & Pyers, 2002) argue that sentential (or tensed) complements are a prerequisite to the child's acquisition of a representational theory of mind. Sentential complements, which allow for the embedding of tensed propositions under a main verb, have unique syntactic and semantic properties. Two classes of verbs take sentential complements: verbs of communication (e.g., "John *said* that Fred went shopping") and verbs of mental state (e.g., "Mary *thought* that Fred went to the movies"). In sentential complements, the embedded clause is an obligatory linguistic argument that may have an independent truth-value. Therefore, the main clause may be true (e.g., John said X; Mary thought Y) while the embedded clause may be false (e.g., Fred went neither shopping nor to the movies). The syntax and semantics of sentential complements allow for the explicit or meta representation of a falsely embedded proposition.

A few studies have documented a significant correlation between knowledge of sentential complements and performance on theory-of-mind tasks in preschool-aged children (e.g., de Villiers & Pyers, 2002; Tager-Flusberg, 1997, 2000b). In a longitudinal study carried out over the course of a year, de Villiers and Pyers (2002) found that mastery of sentential complements predicted later theory-of-mind performance independent of general language change, but that the reverse did not hold. Two recent training studies have provided further evidence that explicit training on the syntax of sentential complements promotes the acquisition of false belief (Hale & Tager-Flusberg, 2003; Lohmann & Tomasello, 2003), even when mental-state verbs were not incorporated into the training phase of the study. These studies highlight the significance of language, specifically sentential complements, in acquiring the social-cognitive component of theory of mind. At the same time, contrary to de Villiers's (2000) predictions, the training studies demonstrated that for normally developing preschoolers, acquisition of sentential complements was not a *necessary* prerequisite to passing false belief tasks. Hale and Tager-Flusberg (2003) included a group of children who were trained only on the false belief task (not including complex complement constructions). After the training phase, these children performed as well as the group of children trained on complements on the theory-of-mind posttests; however, they had not mastered sentential complements. Similarly, Lohmann and Tomasello (2003) found significant advances in theory-of-mind abilities in a group of children whose training consisted of exposure to perspective-shifting discourse (again, no complex syntax) in the context of deceptive objects. Thus, while sentential complements may strongly facilitate the acquisition of theory of mind because the linguistic representations for complements are isomorphic to the representational format needed for propositional attitudes (see de Villiers, 2000), they do not constitute the sole developmental pathway to achieving this new level of metarepresentational capacity in normal preschoolers.

5.2 Language and Theory of Mind in Neurodevelopmental Disorders

In this section, I discuss how the componential model, specifically the role of language in the social-cognitive component, might help to reconcile the contradictory perspectives on theory of mind in children with autism and WMS. Recall that one major concern about the theory-of-mind hypothesis of autism is that it does not explain why some children with autism *pass* false belief tasks. At the same time, our data showed that contrary to initial speculation, children with WMS do not perform especially well on such tasks, compared to matched control groups. If, as I argued in the previous section, language plays a significant role in the social-cognitive component, exemplified by false belief tasks, then we should find that variation in theory-of-mind performance in both autism and WMS is predicted by linguistic ability.

In autism, deficits in pragmatic aspects of language communication are universal, and are among the core diagnostic symptoms that define the syndrome. At the same time, linguistic development is much more variable. About 25 percent of high-functioning children with autism acquire a rich vocabulary and fully master the grammar of their native language, while about 75 percent of verbal high-functioning children remain language impaired to different degrees of severity (Kjelgaard & Tager-Flusberg, 2001). If language plays an important determining role in performance on theory-of-mind tasks, then this variability in linguistic ability may explain why some children with autism are able to pass false belief tasks: they do so via language.

Across many studies on false belief in children with autism, performance is significantly correlated with standardized measures of language, including measures of verbal mental age and pragmatics (Eisenmajer & Prior, 1991), vocabulary (Dahlgren & Trillingsgaard, 1996; Happé, 1995; Sparrevohn & Howie, 1995; Tager-Flusberg & Sullivan, 1994), and syntax (Fisher, 2002; Tager-Flusberg & Sullivan, 1994). We followed up these studies on the influences of general language measures with both cross-sectional and longitudinal studies that investigated whether this relationship between language and theory of mind in autism was more specifically related to mastery of sentential complements. Tager-Flusberg (2000b) compared autistic with age-, IQ-, and language-matched mentally retarded adolescents on three experiments that tested knowledge of the syntactic and semantic properties of sentential complement constructions, including both communication and mental-state verbs. In all three experiments, performance by participants in both groups on the complementation tasks was significantly related to whether they passed or failed false belief tasks, and in regression analyses, complement knowledge was the single best predictor (over and above IQ and general language measures) of performance on the false belief task. However, for the autistic subjects, false belief was only significantly related to performance on communication verbs, and, in contrast to the mentally retarded group, subjects with autism showed little sensitivity to the conceptual or linguistic properties of the cognitive mental-state verbs used in these studies.

In a more recent longitudinal study of over 50 children with autism between the ages of 5 and 14, we replicated these findings (Tager-Flusberg & Joseph, in press). At two time-points, spaced about one year apart, we collected data on theory-of-mind performance and comprehension of sentential complements for communication and mental state verbs, as well as measures of general language ability. The cross-sectional data collected at the first time-point found that knowledge of complements, but only for communication verbs, accounted for 25 percent of the variance in theory-of-mind score, beyond the variance explained by age and general language level (which accounted for 43 percent of the variance). The longitudinal data were analyzed, looking at which variables at the first time point predicted theory of mind one year later. Not surprisingly, general language and the children's original theory-of-mind scores accounted for 74 percent of the variance in later theory of mind. Again, additional unique variance (about 8 percent) was accounted for by performance on the sentential complements task for communication verbs.

These findings show that children with autism who have more advanced language skills, specifically those who have acquired sentential complements for communication verbs, are able to use this linguistic knowledge to master tasks that tap the social-cognitive component of theory of mind. Some children with autism, the minority with normal or nearly normal linguistic ability, can use language to reason logically through false belief tasks. On the basis of this evidence, we have argued that in contrast to normally developing preschoolers, for people with autism, language provides the *sole route* to understanding propositional attitudes; for these people, there is no independent language-of-thought in the domain of theory of mind. There is some evidence, from functional imaging studies using theory-of-mind tasks, that higher functioning adults with autism activate brain regions that are not typically associated with theory of mind, suggesting that they are using different neurocognitive mechanisms (see Frith & Frith, 2000).

Turning now to children with WMS: why did they perform relatively poorly on false belief and other related tasks (Tager-Flusberg & Sullivan, 2000)? In our studies we carefully matched the children with WMS to two other groups of mentally retarded children, one with Prader-Willi syndrome and one with unspecified retardation. All three groups were matched on age, IQ, and language, including both vocabulary and syntactic measures. Because performance on theory-of-mind tasks is so closely linked to language, it is not surprising that the matched WMS children did not perform better than the other retarded children. Indeed, these findings provide further evidence for the significant role that language (and perhaps other domain-general cognitive processes) plays in solving classic theory-of-mind tasks. In these studies on theory of mind, we gave a small number of children with WMS a sentential complements task (the same one used in Tager-Flusberg, 2000b). Although our sample was not large, within this group of 10 children we found that mastery of sentential complements was highly correlated with performance on the false belief tasks, replicating our earlier cross-sectional work on autism. Taken together, the studies summarized here provide strong evidence from normally developing children, children with autism, and children with WMS to support the claim that language, especially sentential complements, plays an important role in the acquisition of a representational theory of mind.

6 Conclusions

Our studies on theory of mind in autism, WMS, and other comparison groups with neurodevelopmental disorders have led us to new insights about the cognitive structure and organization of this important domain of human cognition. Nevertheless, it is important to stress the fact that the componential model outlined here is based on *converging* evidence, not only from the study of autism and Williams syndrome but also from developmental and neurobiological research. Our claim for the distinction between the perceptual and cognitive levels for representing mental states is also consistent with other accounts of the hierarchical nature of representational systems (Sperber, 1997), including the significant role played by language at the metarepresentational level (Sperber, 2000).

The research program presented here supports the view that we can indeed learn from well-designed studies involving children with neurodevelopmental disorders, though we may easily be led astray if our research designs are not adequate. Despite the fact that children with autism or WMS have genetic abnormalities that no doubt influence brain development in significant ways, there are still important and consistent similarities found across all children. At the same time, unusual phenotypic profiles reveal a great deal about the mechanisms that underlie cognitive performance. Thus, our studies have led us to hypothesize that autism involves *selective* impairments to those brain areas that are critical for perceiving and representing socially relevant information such as biological motion and facial and vocal expression. In WMS there is no such impairment, though these brain areas may also not be specifically spared—the evidence thus far is equivocal. Future research with these and other populations will ultimately provide a more complete and detailed picture of the neurocognitive architecture of theory of mind; our componential model is simply a first step in this endeavor.

PART IV

MOTIVATION

JOSHUA D. DUNTLEY & DAVID M. BUSS

The Plausibility of Adaptations for Homicide

A partner of mine said he might come over to my pad with some broads, so I hurried over to the liquor store right around the corner to get a case of beer. As I was walking across the parking lot of the store, this guy almost ran me over. I flipped him off. The driver and his partners jumped out of the car and rat-packed me. They knocked me down, and the driver pushed my head into the dirt next to the cigarette butts. . . . In my mind I suddenly thought, "I've got to get back at these dirty motherfuckers," and I ran back to my pad for my rifle.

I got back to the liquor store as fast as I possibly could and waited for them about twenty yards from the front door of the store. Finally his two partners popped out the door. I said to myself, "Fuck it, I'll shoot all of them." I fired two quick, wild shots but missed them both, and they got away. I decided then that I better put the barrel to the chest of the motherfucker who I really wanted—the driver—and make sure that I didn't miss him. I had stone hatred for him, and I righteously couldn't wait to see the look on his face when I blew him away. As soon as he popped out of the liquor store door, I charged right up to him, rammed the barrel in his chest, and pulled the trigger.

—Quoted in Lonnie Athens, *Violent Criminal Acts and Actors Revisited* (1997)

People kill other people in every known culture around the world. The question is why. This chapter presents a new theory of homicide, homicide adaptation theory, which proposes that humans evolved adaptations to facilitate killing. The new theory is contrasted with two competing conceptions of why people kill: The by-product hypothesis and the evolved goal hypothesis. Prior to presenting these competing views of homicide, we discuss the concept of "innateness" in relation to our conception of evolved homicide adaptations.

1 The Concept of Innateness from the Perspective of Evolutionary Psychology

The term "innateness" is used to refer to many different phenomena (see, e.g., Elman et al., 1996). Our conceptualization of innateness falls in line with the standard definition used by evolutionary psychologists and biologists when referring to any adaptation. Selection has shaped the genes that pattern human ontogeny. These genes provide the blueprint for the development of adaptations. Like the blueprints for a house, they rely on resources and information present in the environment to construct the adaptations for which they code. These features of the environment were presumably recurrent in all or most generations of individuals in the evolutionary history of an adaptation in order for selection to have made them an integral part of reliable adaptation development.

Tooby and Cosmides (1992) refer to the statistical composite of selection pressures that shaped an adaptation as its environment of evolutionary adaptedness (EEA). Different sets of selection pressures contributed to the evolution of every individual adaptation, tailoring each to have a specific function in contributing to the solution of a specific problem of survival and reproduction. Thus, each adaptation has its own unique history of selection pressures and therefore its own unique EEA.

The function of a given adaptation can be affected by recurrent adaptive problems in three primary ways. First, by their presence or absence, characteristics of the environment can determine *whether or not an adaptation develops at all*. Take, for example, the visual system. If a person were forced to live in an environment without any visual light from the time he was born until adolescence, his visual system would not develop normally. If he were suddenly exposed to visual light during adulthood, he would have difficulty focusing his eyes, distinguishing between objects, and orienting himself with visual cues (Sacks, 1995). The human visual system evolved in ancestral environments where visual light was a recurrent feature. The visual system depends on the presence of this environmental feature in abundance for its reliable development.

Second, the presence, absence, or amount of a feature of the environment may contribute to the *developmental trajectory* of an adaptation. At certain points in a lifetime, particularly during childhood, a person comes to a developmental fork in the road. The contingency of environmental features that she faces or has faced thus far in her development determines in large part her future developmental trajectory. Belsky, Steinberg, and Draper (1991), for example, argue that pubertal onset and patterns of adult sexual behavior are influenced by father presence or absence in the home. Their research findings suggest that, among female offspring, father absence is associated with earlier onset of menarche, earlier first intercourse, and a greater number of sexual partners. This pattern is proposed to be the result of adaptations fashioned to recognize that there is a low probability of reliable male investment in reproduction. Such psychological adaptations are argued to function outside of conscious awareness.

Third, adaptations can be designed by selection to be prepared with *different adaptive contingencies* in different environments. As situations change, one adaptive contingency may be reversed or abandoned in favor of a different contingency. For example, the skin, like any organ, is vulnerable to injury. Depending on the kinds of tasks in which an individual routinely engages, some areas of the skin may be more likely to be injured than others. As a protective measure, callous production has evolved as a defense mechanism against repeated friction, preventing injury to the skin (Buss, 2004). Callous production is an adaptive contingency that is active only in response to specific environmental inputs (repeated friction to the skin). When the friction disappears, callous production may stop as well.

Each of these examples describes an innate adaptation. They are evolved, functional solutions to adaptive problems that reliably develop in normal environments. They evolved in response to recurrent features of ancestral environments and require the presence of the same features during ontogeny to develop and function normally. The conceptualization of innateness explained in this section forms the foundation of our hypotheses about adaptations for homicide.

2 Adaptations for Homicide

We propose that humans possess adaptations that evolved to produce homicide (Buss & Duntley, 1998, 2003, 2004). Psychological adaptations for homicide were selected when they contributed to better fitness outcomes, on average, than competing designs present in the population at the time. Certain information-processing adaptations in our brains were shaped by selection specifically to scrutinize and sometimes produce *homicidal* behavior when an individual faces an adaptive problem similar to one recurrently solvable by homicide in the evolutionary past. In this chapter, we will (1) discuss our theory that humans evolved adaptations for homicide, (2) discuss two alternative evolutionary theories of homicide, and (3) review relevant homicide evidence that will help to evaluate the plausibility of our theory and the other theories of homicide.

2.1 The Nature of Selection Pressures for Homicide Adaptations

A description of adaptations for homicide begins with the recurrent adaptive problems they evolved to solve. We hypothesize that a combination of simultaneously relevant contextual factors, not any one single factor, acted as selection pressures that shaped psychological adaptations for homicide. Therefore, it is not possible to point to just one feature of a context that will activate a psychology of homicide in every instance, in every person. There are always other, mitigating environmental factors present in any real-world situation that were also part of the overall selection pressures that shaped homicide adaptations. In other words, any set of contextual cues to an adaptive problem that was ancestrally solvable by homicide is made up of multiple inputs. The presence or absence, as well as the magnitude, of inputs demonstrated to contribute to the activation of homicide adaptations can help us to predict when homicide will be more or less likely to occur. Homicidal behavior is not under the control of a simple "on/off" switch that can be manipulated with a push from a single factor. The activation of evolved psychological mechanisms for homicide requires the presence of co-occurring sets of circumstances, made up of factors such as: (1) the degree of genetic relatedness between killer and victim, (2) the relative status of the killer and victim, (3) the sex of killer and victim, (4) the size and strength of the killer's and victim's families and social allies, and (5) the relative reproductive values of the killer and victim.

2.2 Recurrent Adaptive Problems Solvable by Homicide

Homicide could not have evolved as a strategy unless it was ancestrally associated with greater reproductive success than competing strategies. In most sets of circumstances, the extremely high costs of committing homicide would have outweighed the benefits of adopting it as a strategy. We propose, however, that rare sets of circumstances reliably recurred in our evolutionary history in which the benefits of homicide would have outweighed the costs, selecting for a psychology that would lead to homicide when a person confronted such circumstances.

This characterization of the ancestral costs and benefits of homicide, leading to the evolution of psychological adaptations for homicide, is different from arguing that humans decide whether or not to kill by actively weighing the costs and benefits of killing in the present moment. The first argument is about the cumulative effects of the costs and benefits of a strategy over multiple generations of our evolutionary history. The second argument is about decision-making conducted by existing psychological mechanisms in the present. When we make arguments about the costs and benefits of homicide, they are arguments about ancestral fitness costs and benefits that we hypothesize shaped adaptations for homicide. It may intuitively seem as though a person is consciously weighing the costs and benefits of a homicidal strategy in the present. We caution, however, that this interpretation may be misleading (see Carruthers, 2003b; Wegner, 2002).

In outlining some of the adaptive problems for which homicide would have been a possible solution, we are making the case that homicide could have been beneficial enough to our ancestors' reproductive success to lead to the evolution of adaptations for murder. We are *not* arguing that homicide would have evolved to be the *preferred strategy* for each or any of these adaptive problems. Different strategies are appropriate in different contexts. In *certain sets* of recurrent circumstances, we propose that homicide was the best of available strategies. Specifically, we hypothesize homicide was functional in contributing to the solution of adaptive problems such as:

1. Preventing the exploitation, injury, rape, or killing of self, kin, mates, and coalitional allies by conspecifics in the present and future
2. Reputation management against being perceived as easily exploited, injured, raped, or killed by conspecifics
3. Protecting resources, territory, shelter, and food from competitors
4. Eliminating resource-absorbing or costly individuals who are not genetically related (e.g., stepchildren)
5. Eliminating genetic relatives who interfere with investment in other vehicles better able to translate the investment into genetic fitness (e.g., deformed infants, the chronically ill or infirm)

This list represents a sample of some of the more obvious adaptive problems that could have been addressed with homicide. The purpose in outlining them is to demonstrate that adaptive problems solvable by homicide are numerous. The strategic deployment of homicide to solve them could have substantially increased the reproductive success of ancestral killers. If conspecific killing were a good strategy in specific contexts that included these adaptive problems, there would have been significant and unique selection pressures for the evolution of adaptations for homicide. There is no a priori reason, therefore, to dismiss the possibility that homicide adaptations could have evolved.

3 The Fitness Costs of Being Killed

Homicide is the elimination of another individual. Once eliminated, his or her ability to impact the future disappears. A murder victim's death, however, has a much larger impact on his inclusive fitness than just the loss of the genes housed in his body. Death by homicide often has cascading deleterious effects on a victim's inclusive fitness, including the following.

3.1 Loss of Future Reproduction

A victim of murder loses all chances of future reproduction with all the mates he may have had during the rest of his life. Thus, the average reproductive costs are greater for those killed at younger ages.

3.2 Damage to Existing Children

The child of a murdered parent receives fewer resources, is more susceptible to being exploited or injured by others, and may have greater difficulty negotiating his future status trajectory or mating relationships, which probably will lead to poorer fitness outcomes. Children of a murdered parent may see their surviving parent's investment in them diverted to a new mating relationship and to children who are the product of that relationship. A single parent, who can invest only half of the possible investment of two parents, would be more likely to abandon children in favor of better mating prospects in the future. And the children of a murdered parent risk becoming stepchildren, a condition that brings with it physical abuse and homicide risks that are 40–100 times greater than among children who reside with two genetic parents (Daly & Wilson, 1988).

3.3 Damage to Extended Kin Group

A homicide victim cannot protect or invest in his extended kin. A victim's entire kin network can gain the reputation of being vulnerable to exploitation as a result of his murder. A murder victim cannot affect his family members' status trajectories or mating relationships. The open position left by the murder victim in a kin network's status hierarchy could create a struggle for power among the surviving family members. In sum, the death of a key member of a kin group imposes important costs on his surviving relatives.

3.4 A Murder Victim's Fitness Losses Can Become a Rival's Gains

The residual reproductive and parenting value of the mate of a homicide victim may go to a rival, often at the expense of the victim's children with that mate. The murder of a man or woman creates an opening in a social group's hierarchy into which a rival can ascend. The children of rivals who had two surviving genetic parents would thrive relative to the victim's children, who would be deprived of the investment, protection, and influence of two parents.

Human intuition tells us that it is bad to be killed. But being the victim of murder is much worse than intuition or previous theories of homicide have fully appreciated. The costs of being killed cascade down through successive generations of a victim's kin group, damaging not only his immediate fitness and that of his children, but the fitness of his family members and descendants for generations. Many who would have survived if the person lived will die before they can reproduce. And many more will never be born.

4 Homicide Defenses

We propose that the great costs resulting from being murdered would have selected for adaptations to: (1) avoid being killed, (2) punish killers who damage one's inclusive fitness by murdering kin, mates, or coalitional allies, and (3) eliminate or otherwise control individuals who presented a persistent threat of homicide to the larger social group of which an individual, his kin, and coalition are a part (e.g., psychopaths, hostile members of other groups). We propose that inflicting costs on killers is part of an evolved strategy to avoid or staunch the inclusive fitness costs of being victimized by another individual or group.

In order to avoid being killed, the intended victim must be sensitive to cues indicative of situations in which someone else might want him dead. Individual insight into the likelihood that one will be the victim of homicide before the homicide occurs requires that murders be committed in predictable sets of circumstances. If homicide reliably occurred in response to predictable sets of circumstances over our evolutionary history, the selection pressure created by the recurrent killings would have shaped homicide defense mechanisms capable of recognizing those circumstances and trying to change or avoid them. The evolution of such homicide defense mechanisms, in turn, would have selected for homicide strategies that could circumvent the evolved homicide defense strategies. In this way, adaptations to avoid being murdered would have served as selection pressures for the refinement of psychological adaptations for homicide over evolutionary time. These new homicide adaptations would have selected for further refinements in homicide defense adaptations—homicide and homicide defense locked in a perpetual, coevolutionary arms race through the generations.

Demonstration of the existence of a psychology of homicide defense that appears to have been designed to defeat specific homicidal strategies would provide evidence that: (1) homicide was a recurrent feature of ancestral environments, (2) homicidal strategies occurred in predictable patterns over our evolutionary history, and therefore

```
        Selection Pressure
```

[Homicide] ⇄ [Anti-Homicide]

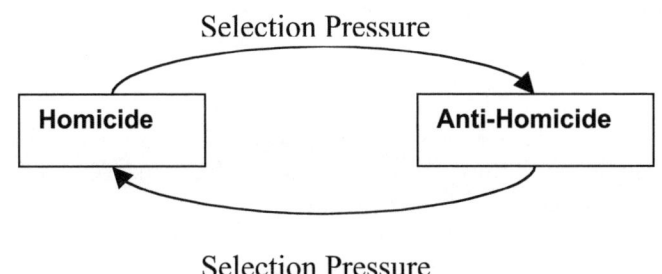

```
        Selection Pressure
```

FIGURE 17.1 The co-evolution of adaptations for homicide and anti-homicide.

(3) there may be adaptations specifically for homicide. The greater the *corresponding specificity of design* in the psychologies of homicide and homicide defense, the stronger the evidence that the two have had a coevolutionary relationship.

5 Alternative Evolutionary Explanations for Homicide

A number of alternative hypotheses and theories have been proposed to explain why people kill. For the purposes of this chapter, we will focus on two explicitly evolutionary hypotheses. (For a more complete discussion of alternative theories of homicide, please refer to Buss & Duntley, under review.)

At least three competing evolutionary theories have been proposed to explain why people kill. The first, which is the primary focus of this chapter, argues that humans possess adaptations specifically for homicide. Others have also suggested this possibility (Ghiglieri, 1999; Pinker, 1997b) though none have gone into depth in exploring the adaptive design of these adaptations (see a notable exception dealing with warfare: Tooby & Cosmides, 1988).

5.1 The By-Product Hypothesis

One evolutionary explanation of killing was proposed first by Daly and Wilson in their book *Homicide* (1988). They hypothesize that homicide may be considered an overreactive mistake, the by-product of psychological adaptations designed for nonlethal outcomes. For example, the behavior of a teenage mother who abandons her newborn in a dumpster to die may be explained by the failure of her psychological mechanisms for parenting to engage. Similarly, in the case of a husband who kills his wife for being sexually unfaithful, Daly and Wilson have argued that male mechanisms for sexual jealousy and the coercion and control of their mates may slip, leading the man to mistakenly kill his wife. Although these two contexts are drastically different, the same explanation is applied to both—homicide is an overreactive mistake, a by-product of mechanisms designed by selection to serve other functions.

Wilson, Daly, and Daniele (1995) argue that "using homicides as a sort of 'assay' of the evolved psychology of interpersonal conflict does not presuppose that killing *per se* is or ever was adaptive" (p. 12). If it is the case that homicide has never been adaptive, then selection could not have fashioned adaptations for homicide.

The only remaining possibilities are that homicide was neutral in terms of selection or that it had negative selective consequences. In contexts where homicide yielded recurrently negative fitness consequences, there would have been active selection pressure against homicide.

How could a behavior with negative selective consequences be maintained over our evolutionary history? To our knowledge, Daly and Wilson have not directly addressed this issue. But there are at least two possible explanations. First, it could be the case that the overall benefits of psychological adaptations that sometimes produce homicide as a by-product have outweighed the occasional costs associated with killing a conspecific over our evolutionary history. Another, related possibility is that selection *has* operated to eliminate by-product homicide in contexts where it was too costly, modifying or fashioning new psychological mechanisms for this purpose. This explanation, however, is no longer a strict by-product hypothesis of the origins of homicide. It suggests that selection has acted to inhibit homicide in some contexts, while allowing it to persist in others. Instead of an argument against adaptations for homicide, this seems a plausible explanation for the origins of homicide adaptations—through the gradual recognition of the rare subset of situations in which homicides lead to greater benefits than costs.

5.2 Evolved Goal Hypothesis

Another evolutionary explanation for homicide proposes that humans and other species have evolved specific goals that were ancestrally associated with greater reproductive success. These are not suggested to be general goals, like "maximize fitness." Instead, they are more specific, such as "ambitiously strive for status" or "acquire a mate." These goals are reached through the use of evolved problem-solvers that function to figure out ways to achieve them. By this argument, there need not be any evolved mechanisms to engage in any specific behavior, including killing. In order to produce adaptive behavior, selection needed only to fashion some knowledge of what goals to achieve and the psychological machinery required to figure out how to achieve them. According to the strong form of this argument, there are no evolved psychological mechanisms for homicide per se. Instead, there are general problem-solving mechanisms that become aware of homicide as a means to achieve goals through exposure to the environment or through rational means-ends calculations. According to the weak form of the argument, there may be some psychological adaptations specifically for homicide, such as a desire to kill certain individuals. The majority of the information processing that needs to take place in deciding whether or not to kill, however, is done by a general problem-solving mechanism or a small number of mechanisms, capable of figuring out solutions to problems as diverse as which travel agent to use, who to pursue as a mate, and when it's appropriate to commit murder. The ultimate or evolved goals may or may not be part of the conscious awareness of the person who has them, but the proximate goals are thought to be consciously articulated.

Little has been written about this perspective in the academic literature. The most specific account we have found comes from Sarah Hrdy's book *Mother Nature* (1999), where she wrote:

My own guess is that the behavior of infanticidal men is homologous to that of their primate cousins in only the most general sense. They are motivated to strive for status, to compete for access to females, to avoid investing in unrelated infants, to adopt patterns of behavior more likely to enhance than to decrease long-term inclusive fitness. The specific similarities, then, are merely analogous solutions to common problems these variously endowed animals confront. (p. 244)

Human raiders consciously evaluate costs and benefits, as well as future consequences of their actions. They calculate contingencies: How much more slowly, for example, are mothers burdened by infants likely to travel? What are the chances that a son spared will grow up to avenge his father? Might these children be useful alive? (p. 243)

In both examples, Hrdy argues that the *goals* of homicidal behavior evolved, but not homicide as a strategy itself. Instead, she proposes that a general calculus of costs and benefits would arrive at homicide as the best solution in certain situations.

6 Comparison of Explanations Based on Available Evidence

It is important to note that, of the three evolutionary theories of homicide discussed, our homicide adaptation theory provides the most detailed explanation of the functions of mechanisms involved in producing homicidal behavior. The by-product theory and perhaps, in some instances, the evolved goal theory require that homicide be a by-product of many different sorts of mechanisms or many different sorts of goals. The mechanisms of which homicide may be a by-product or goal need to be specified before either of the two theories can be appropriately evaluated. Because of the lack of explicitness and detail provided by authors of these alternative hypotheses, comparison of the three explanations is an extremely difficult task. Our theory has generated specific, a priori predictions about the evolutionary past of adaptations for homicide and the present functioning of homicide adaptations. We have had less success in generating specific, a priori predictions that follow directly from the by-product or evolved goal hypotheses.

6.1 Comparative Evidence

Humans are not the only species that kill their own kind. Numerous species kill conspecifics in predictable contexts. Among insects (including mantids, black widow spiders, jumping spiders, and scorpions), the female murder of her male mate is quite common when her subsequent consumption of the male leads to a greater number and increased viability of her offspring. Males of these species are not willing food sources for their mates. In the sexually cannibalistic black widow spider *Latrodectus mactans*, for example, males that survive copulation can often fertilize multiple partners (Breene & Sweet, 1985). Males across sexually cannibalistic species use a diverse array of strategies to decrease their chances of being eaten by their mates: Male scorpions sometimes sting their mates after depositing their spermatophore (Polis & Farley, 1979); male crab spiders (Bristowe, 1958) and black widows (Gould, 1984) often restrain females in silk before mating with them.

Among mammals there are many well-documented patterns of conspecific killing. Male lions, wolves, hyenas, cougars, and cheetahs have been observed to kill the offspring of rival males (Ghiglieri, 1999). Killers often benefit because the mothers of the infants that are killed often go into estrus sooner, allowing the infanticidal males to impregnate them with offspring of their own. Among primate species, conspecific infanticides have been documented in similar contexts among a number of species, including langur monkeys (Hrdy, 1977), red howler monkeys (Crockett & Sekulic, 1984), mountain gorillas (Fossey, 1984), chimpanzees (Bygott, 1972), and others (Hausfater & Hrdy, 1984). The killing of rival, adult males has also been well documented among mountain gorillas (Fossey, 1984) and the chimpanzees of Gombe (Wrangham & Peterson, 1996), two of our closest genetic relatives.

6.1.1 Evolutionary Explanations of the Comparative Evidence

Homicide adaptation theory. Most researchers do not doubt that conspecific killings in other animal species are the product of adaptations to kill (Crockett & Sekulic, 1984; Ghiglieri, 1999; Hrdy, 1977; Johnson et al., 2002). Because they occur in such predictable circumstances that benefit the reproductive success of the killer, most animal researchers hypothesize or assume implicitly that killings are the product of adaptations designed by selection to solve specific adaptive problems. The widespread occurrence of conspecific killings in predictable contexts across multiple, different animal species provides support for the hypothesis that adaptations for conspecific killing also could have evolved in humans, perhaps having early roots in the homicide adaptations of a common ancestor with extant primates or even further back in our evolutionary heritage. If it is possible for other animals to have coevolved strategies of homicide and homicide defense, there is no reason a priori to be skeptical about the hypothesis that selection could have fashioned psychological adaptations for homicide and antihomicide in humans as well.

By-product hypothesis. If conspecific killings in animals are by-products of mechanisms that evolved for other purposes, what are those mechanisms? How do they function to reliably produce homicide in response to such predictable and similar circumstances across different species? It seems unlikely that humans would have been immune to essentially the same selection pressures that shaped adaptations for killing conspecifics in other species.

Evolved goal hypothesis. If conspecific killings in animals are the products of evolved goals, what are those goals and how does an organism figure out how to achieve them? The burden of proof falls on the shoulders of the evolved goal hypotheses to specify this information. To date, this has not been done in a way that is empirically testable.

6.2 Homicide Rates

Roughly 1 in 15,000 people is murdered in the United States each year (Stolinsky & Stolinsky, 2000). At first glance, this seems like a fairly rare event. But computed over a 75-year lifespan, this equates to a 1 in 200 chance of being murdered at some point during an individual lifetime (Ghiglieri, 1999). Between the years of 1999 and 2002, homicide ranked fourteenth among the leading causes of death for men and women of all ages in the United States. But for men between the ages of 15 and 24, it was the second leading cause of death. For men between the ages of 25 and 34, it was the third leading cause of death. For black men between 15 and 34, homicide was the leading cause of death (Centers for Disease Control and Prevention National Center for Injury Prevention and Control, 2002).

Homicide rates in the United States are much higher than in many industrialized nations, exceeding those in the United Kingdom and Japan by a factor of 10; exceeding those in France, Austria, Sweden, and Germany by a factor of 9; and exceeding the rates in Canada, Italy, Portugal, Korea, and Belgium by a factor of 5. But the homicide rates in many other countries are equivalent to or exceed those in the United States (United Nations, 1998). The lifetime likelihood of being murdered in Venezuela and Moldova is 1 in 90, twice that of the United States. In Estonia and Puerto Rico, the likelihood is 1 in 60, three times that of the United States. And in Colombia and South Africa, the likelihood is better than 1 in 20 that a person will die at the hands of a murderer, more than 10 times the lifetime homicide risk in the United States.

These within-culture rates of homicide typically do not include casualties of warfare or genocide. The murder rates in these nations would undoubtedly be *much higher* were it not for emergency medical interventions that were not available to our ancestors for most of our evolutionary history. This is precisely the point made by Harris and colleagues (2002) in their ambulance-homicide theory. They found that faster ambulances and better emergency room care were significantly responsible for the decrease in homicide rates over the last three decades. In fact, they estimate that there would be 30,000 to 50,000 *additional* murders in the United States each year—doubling or tripling the current rate—without advanced emergency care technology.

The homicide rates in the industrialized nations discussed pale in comparison to the risk of being murdered in many primitive cultures. Homicides account for roughly 1 in 10 deaths of adult men among the Huli; 1 in 4 deaths among the Mae Enga; and 1 in 3 deaths among the Dugum Dani and Yanomamo (Chagnon, 1988). Even among the so-called gentle or peaceful !Kung San of Botswana, there were 22 murders over a 25-year period among a population of 1,500, more than four times the rate of homicide in a typical year in the United States (Lee, 1984).

6.2.1 Evolutionary Explanations of Homicide Rates

Homicide adaptation theory. If the rates of killing, particularly in tribal cultures, are similar to the rates of killing over our evolutionary history, it is quite plausible that selection was powerful enough to construct a psychology in humans, both to commit homicide and to avoid being killed. Selection over deep time is a powerful force for change. As Nilsson and Pelger (1994) have demonstrated, a complex adaptation can evolve in as few as 364,000 generations, even when (1) each improvement on its design confers only a 1 percent advantage in reproductive success, (2) any surviving mutation has only a 50 percent chance of making it to the next generation, and (3) only one part of the adaptation can change in each generation. We propose that, given the likely frequency of homicide in ancestral environments, the tremendous costs of being killed, and the substantial benefits that can accrue to killers, there was more than ample selection pressure for the evolution of adaptations for homicide.

By-product hypothesis. This hypothesis differs from the homicide adaptation hypothesis in arguing that homicide most likely is not the product of adaptations specifically for killing. Despite the fact that they have drawn parallels between the lives of people in isolated, tribal groups and the lives of our ancestors (1988), Daly & Wilson (1999) are clear in their arguments that homicide probably was too costly over our evolutionary history for homicide adaptations to evolve.

Evolved goal hypothesis. On the surface, the evolved goal hypothesis is consistent with evidence about homicide rates from around the world. The psychological mechanisms that determine how to best achieve a particular goal are assumed to be domain-general and sometimes choose homicide. It is likely, however, that there were recurrently high costs associated with choosing homicide inappropriately, and recurrently high benefits of killing in appropriate contexts over our evolutionary history. Many of these historic costs and benefits of homicide are probably hidden from individuals who are trying to figure out the best course of action in the present. An individual with evolved thinking biases that function to account for the likely ancestral costs and benefits of homicide in a particular situation would be at a significant advantage in choosing whether or not to kill.

6.3 Homicidal Ideation

Although homicides are statistically rare, making them difficult to study, people's homicidal thoughts or fantasies are not. Kenrick and Sheets (1993) conducted two studies of homicidal fantasies on a total of 760 undergraduate participants. They asked participants to provide demographic information and then describe their most recent fantasies about killing someone else. They also asked for descriptions of the circumstances that triggered the fantasies and their content, such as how the participant thought of committing the murder. Finally, they asked about the frequency of participants' homicidal fantasies and how the participants knew the person they thought of killing.

The studies yielded similar findings, so our discussion will focus only on the second. The survey of homicidal fantasies found that more men (79 percent) than women (53 percent) reported having at least one homicidal fantasy in their lifetime. Men (38 percent) also were more likely than women (18 percent) to report having more than one homicidal fantasy in their lifetime. And men's homicidal fantasies tended to last longer than those experienced by women.

The sexes also differed in the triggers of their homicidal fantasies. Men's homicidal fantasies more often than women's were triggered by personal threats, theft of their belongings, a desire to know what it is like to kill, conflict over money, and public humiliation.

6.3.1 Evolutionary Explanations of Patterns of Homicidal Ideation

Homicide adaptation theory. According to the homicide adaptation theory, homicidal ideation can provide a window into the functioning of psychological adaptations for homicide. The accuracy of the information about actual homicide that can be gleaned from homicidal fantasies is an open question. But some of the characteristics of homicidal thoughts can provide us with clues to help evaluate evolutionary hypotheses for homicide.

Given the existence of adaptations for homicide, we would expect that men would be more likely to have homicidal thoughts than women, to have more frequent thoughts, and to have thoughts for longer periods of time, just as they are more likely to actually commit homicide. We would also expect that their thoughts would be triggered by contexts that are likely to precipitate the commission of actual homicides and that the end product of homicidal thoughts, just as in homicidal reality, is the willful killing of another person. All of these characteristics of homicidal thoughts are consistent with homicidal reality.

By-product hypothesis. Homicidal ideation is much less consistent with the by-product hypothesis. If homicide is the by-product of mechanisms designed for other purposes, what might be the function of producing thoughts of killing someone else? If the function of an adaptation (that occasionally produced homicide as a by-product) was coercion and control, wouldn't fantasies of coercion and control better serve this function than fantasies of killing the person? It has been proposed that homicidal thoughts may make coercive threats more convincing, enabling those wishing to control the behavior of others to have greater leverage in exerting their control. A difficulty with this explanation is that the introduction of elaborate homicidal thoughts into the stream of information processing in a given context may have the effect of increasing the likelihood that homicide would actually be committed. Finally, the by-product hypothesis cannot account for premeditated murders, where careful thought and elaborate planning of a murder occur and absolutely no attempt is made to control the behavior of another individual beyond ending his or her life.

Evolved goal hypothesis. Patterns in homicidal ideation present a number of problems for the evolved goal hypothesis. The hypothesis does not explain why homicide would be chosen as the topic of scenario building at such high frequencies. Why would almost 80 percent of college-age men in the United States have had a homicidal fantasy, when only a tiny fraction of all men actually commit homicide? It also does not explain how homicidal content is brought into scenario building in the first place. The causal process that is responsible must be described for adequate empirical comparisons of the evolved goal hypothesis and homicide adaptation theory.

7 Conclusions

Humans kill other humans at nontrivial frequencies across cultures. Homicide, as well as the varieties of homicide, must be explained. Our theory of evolved homicide adaptations proposes the existence of certain circumstances over human evolutionary history in which the fitness benefits of killing outweighed the costs. These circumstances are highly varied—those promoting killing a deformed infant differ from those promoting going to war.

In this chapter, we have considered just three of many sources of evidence bearing on the competing theories of homicide—comparative evidence from other species, homicide rate data, and studies of homicidal ideation (see Buss & Duntley, under review, for a more extensive discussion of sources of evidence). We have also evaluated three evolutionary theories of homicide for their conceptual power and adequacy in explaining these sources of evidence. Given the recency of homicide adaptation theory, definitive conclusions about its power, scope, and explanatory adequacy would be premature. Nonetheless, the theory of evolved homicide adaptations appears to account for existing empirical data better than competing theories and generates specific and novel predictions not generated by the competing theories. Although future empirical work is needed to properly evaluate the theory that humans have evolved specialized adaptations for killing, no compelling evidence or arguments currently rule out the possibility of evolved adaptations for murder.

18

JOHN TOOBY, LEDA COSMIDES, & H. CLARK BARRETT

Resolving the Debate on Innate Ideas

Learnability Constraints and the Evolved Interpenetration of Motivational and Conceptual Functions

1 On the Sociological Need to Find Arguments That Are Effective as Well as True

> Plato says... that our "necessary ideas" arise from the preexistence of the soul, are not derivable from experience—read monkeys for preexistence.
>
> Charles Darwin, M Notebooks (entry 128)

In order for the study of the human mind and brain to become a successful natural science, a sufficiently large number of researchers must organize their research on the basis of theoretical commitments and methodologies that reflect, in broad outline, the realities of their object of study. Yet there has been, for over a century, enormous resistance to incorporating into the human sciences the most fundamental truth about the species they study: our functional, species-typical design is the organized product of ancestral natural selection (for discussion, see Pinker, 2002; Tooby & Cosmides, 1992a; for opposing views, see Fodor, 2000; Gould, 1997a, b). The brain came into existence and acquired a functional organization to the extent that its arrangements acted as a computational system whose operations regulated the organism's behavior to promote propagation. Studying psychology and neuroscience without the analytical tools offered by evolutionary theory is like attempting to do physics without using mathematics. It may be possible, but the rationale for inflicting needless damage on our ability to understand the world is obscure.

We warmly thank Pascal Boyer, Peter Carruthers, Martin Daly, Tim German, Steve Pinker, Dan Sperber, Steve Stich, Don Symons, and Margo Wilson, the participants in the Innateness Workshops, and the members of the Center for Evolutionary Psychology for many illuminating conversations on these issues.

Why treat natural selection as central to psychology, neuroscience, and the human sciences? Why does it have a privileged organizational and explanatory role? Why is the neglect, peripheralization, or dismissal of natural selection in these sciences necessarily misguided? The reason inheres in what makes organisms (self-replicating physical systems) different from all other natural phenomena: organisms differ from other natural phenomena in that they manifest a profusion of thermodynamically improbable arrays of extraordinarily attuned interrelationships—states that are simultaneously highly ordered and highly functional (Dawkins, 1986; Schrödinger, 1944; Tooby & Cosmides, 1992a; Tooby et al., 2003). This physically unspontaneous order would collapse in a fraction of a second were it not for the ceaseless operation of complexly engineered chemical and computational arrangements designed to combat the ubiquitous encroachments of entropy, in service of bringing about those narrowly targeted outcomes that facilitate propagation. To put it more simply, the second law of thermodynamics is the first law of psychology: functional order in organisms requires explanation (Tooby et al., 2003). This high level of functional organization is not a brute fact of the world, produced randomly or inexplicably. Instead, this functional organization has a known explanation, an explanation that is unique, well established, and beautifully principled. Physics and biology, considered together, inform us that natural selection is the only known natural process that pushes populations of organisms thermodynamically uphill into higher degrees of functional order, or counterbalances the otherwise inevitable increases in disorder that plague ordered systems. In other words, all complex (i.e., significantly better than random) functional organization in the designs of organisms traces back to the prior operation of natural selection, and must necessarily be explained in terms of it. Natural selection builds developmental adaptations into the designs of organisms, and the operation of these adaptations assembles each organism's functional machinery, and calibrates it to its circumstances. To use a nineteenth-century scientific idiom, it might be said that the second law of psychology is that ancestral natural selection is the cause of the functional order in brains and allied regulatory systems.

Psychology and neuroscience, if they are to be successful as sciences, must recognize, describe, and explain the functional order[1] to be found in minds and brains. Since this functional order derives uniquely from the evolutionary process, any accurate, theoretically principled psychology that humans might eventually build must inevitably become an evolutionarily centered science. The essential elements of this argument were clear in 1859 to Darwin, and are not hard to follow. Yet the 145 years since the publication of *The Origin of Species* have not seen the steady, linear growth of a reasoned appreciation of the Darwinian framework,

---

1. Of course, there are other characteristics of the evolved architectures of organisms in addition to their largely species-typical functional organization. These include transient and idiosyncratic features, as well as by-products of adaptations, which emerge as concomitants of the aspects of the architecture that have been selected (Tooby & Cosmides, 1992a). There are indefinitely many by-products, because there are indefinitely many ways of describing organisms without making reference to their evolved adaptations.

especially in the psychological and behavioral sciences. In contrast, the value of far more conceptually taxing advances in quantum mechanics and relativity (not to mention the Newtonian revolution, or electrodynamics) were rapidly recognized, accepted, and disseminated throughout the relevant disciplines. Although there have been a few efforts to integrate Darwinism, these were generally followed by periods when evolutionary research went into near eclipse. Even at the high-water marks of these Darwinian infiltrations, evolutionarily informed psychology always remained a minority enterprise. To this day, evolutionary biology is not taught routinely, along with statistics and mathematics, as an indispensable element of professional training. Many researchers in the neural, psychological, and social sciences have only the vaguest idea about what is known in the evolutionary sciences and are often prey to lay mythology about Darwinism. Generally speaking, the biologists to whom nonbiological audiences are exposed are seen as both representative of biological thought and authoritative in proportion to their tendency to reassure their audiences of the fundamental irrelevance of Darwinism to the human sciences (Gould 1997a, b; Lewontin, 1998; Rose & Rose, 2000).

As a result of this strangely endemic resistance to Darwinism, the presuppositions of most of the research enterprises in the psychological and social sciences clash with the core nature of the phenomena they investigate. In consequence, over the last century efforts have been misdirected, results confused, and progress (where there is any)[2] made painfully slow (Tooby & Cosmides, 1992a; Pinker, 2002). Otherwise gifted people advance and laboriously defend arguments whose obvious weakness they themselves would readily detect in other contexts (e.g., Chomsky, 1987; Fodor, 2000).[3] The rationalizations for peripheralizing Darwinism have impeded the emergence of a critical mass of researchers who appreciate its analytic centrality and inferential power. The institutional entrenchment of these rationalizations interferes with ordinary research and training, requiring responses that

---

2. Sociocultural anthropology, for example, has been moving backward for decades, and large segments of it are dead as a science.
3. Two striking examples are Fodor's argument that Darwinian conceptions of function are superfluous to building a functionalist cognitive science (Fodor, 2000) and Chomsky's argument that the understanding of language will be better elucidated "in molecular biology, in the study of what kinds of physical systems can develop under the conditions of life on earth and why, ultimately, because of physical principles," than through the analysis of the organizing effects of natural selection on cognitive architectures (Chomsky, 1987, p. 167).

That such arguments are advanced and defended by such typically strong thinkers is evidence of how unpalatable natural selection is even to leaders of the cognitive science community—a fact of considerable sociological importance.

Fodor (echoing many others) justifies his claim that natural selection is superfluous in the analysis of cognitive function by pointing out that the identification of the function of the heart preceded Darwin. That is, one can employ functionalist reasoning without being forced to traffic in unholy knowledge of evolutionary biology. In what other science would one find large numbers of people defending the use of a folk concept (common-sense function) in order to avoid the use of a well-established, technically rigorous, formally derived scientific concept (evolved function)—a concept, indeed, that connects cognitive science logically and empirically to the rest of the natural sciences?

siphon off much of the effort that would otherwise go into the progressive mapping of our evolved architecture.

Of greatest concern, the intellectual history of the last century makes it clear that a consensus that lacks good scientific justification can maintain itself through sociological processes for long periods of time, and perhaps indefinitely (Pinker, 2002; Tooby & Cosmides, 1992a). This brings us to the heart of the issue to be addressed. The fact that resistance to Darwinism in the human sciences has been profound and enduring and yet not supported by an adequate scientific justification is significant. It makes it clear that we are not dealing with purely scientific objections that can be surmounted solely by addressing issues of logic and evidence. Instead we are confronted with a formidable practical problem in the sociology of science. If the intellectual ecology of the psychological, neural, and social sciences is to change for the better, it will be necessary to do more than come up with arguments of scientific merit. We need to find valid arguments that in addition have the potential to be sociologically successful. Revising one's set of scientific beliefs by getting rid of propositions that are inconsistent with facts from the evolutionary sciences is painful. We need to identify arguments that make the effort of adhering to poorly founded positions greater than the effort of correcting them. It is this problem that must be addressed and solved if our sciences are to move ahead. Where might such arguments be found?

We have folk notions of heat and temperature from boiling water, but through the use of concepts derived from thermodynamics, engineers can build (for example) power stations with tens of thousands of intricate, efficiency-promoting features that could not have been designed, manufactured, managed, or understood without the scientific concept of heat. Why have a kitchen science of psychology using folk function when we can have a vastly larger, far more rigorous genuine science? The architectures of animals are far more complexly engineered than any human-built system, so the correct idea of functionality (together with the long list of functions known to biologists) will be even more necessary for the understanding of humans. This is particularly true because the biological definitions of functionality that predict the principles of our construction often depart radically from folk notions, which often lead psychologists astray (see, e.g., the theory of intragenomic conflict, Cosmides & Tooby, 1981). Are incestuous desires evolutionarily functional or dysfunctional? What about jealousy, guilt, aggression, in-group favoritism, infanticide in langurs, within-family conflict, the perception of beauty, pregnancy sickness, mitochondrially induced pollen sterility, fever, avian siblicide, play, and gestational diabetes? Biological theories of function provide clear and often quantitative criteria in these and hundreds of other cases that folk functionality has not and cannot.

With respect to Chomsky's argument, brief reflection reminds us that the number of designs for physically possible systems is vast beyond all possible analysis but is known to include circuits for honeybee dancing, web spinning, spotting nests suitable for brood parasitism by cowbirds, killing male rivals' still-nursing offspring in langurs, echolocation, bat detection in moths, throat targeting by wolves, reverse peristalsis, reciprocal blood regurgitation in vampire bats, nuptial gift analysis in insects, alarm call discrimination in vervets, copulation continuation after decapitation in the praying mantis, upstream salmon homing, sex change upon receipt of dominance information in the coral reef living wrasse, as well as every known human and nonhuman neural syndrome, impairment, developmental anomaly, and embryological experiment. In the absence of natural selection, physical principles are not a very plausible or significant source of information about why the language system has one set of computational properties rather than another. Again, it seems the kind of argument that is advanced more to deny the relevance of Darwinism than because there is any compelling affirmative case for it.

2 The Debate over Innate Ideas Is a Possible Turning Point in the Integration of Darwinism with the Human Sciences

One arena in which such progress might be made is over the fiercely contested claim that our reliably developing, species-typical neurocomputational architecture includes what would once have been called innate ideas (see, e.g., the attack on representational nativism in Elman et al., 1996). This is an argument that matters: if it became recognized that human minds are infused with content many of whose specifics are the downstream consequence of natural selection, this would require revision throughout psychology, neuroscience, and the social sciences. Of course, for most of the last century, the default position of most learning theorists, cognitive scientists, and neuroscientists has been that the neurocomputational mechanisms and developmental programs that operate on experience to produce mental content are primarily content independent and general purpose. On this view, such mechanisms have no content-like organization built into their structure nor do they introduce evolved content of their own into the mind. That is, they lack any neurocomputational implementations of innate ideas, such as evolved, reliably developing conceptual primitives, content-specialized inferential procedures, representational formats that impose contentful features on different inputs, domain-specific skeletal principles, or anything else that was designed by evolution to process inputs, throughputs, or outputs differently by virtue of their content. We will call any perspective that makes content-specificity exceptional or peripheral to the mind's evolved architecture a *blank slate view* (for discussion, see Cosmides & Tooby, 1987; Pinker, 2002; Tooby & Cosmides, 1992a).[4]

For evolutionary psychologists, the blank slate view is both theoretically implausible (because a blank slate architecture would pointlessly and fatally handicap any animal so designed), and inconsistent with the comparative evidence (Cosmides & Tooby, 1987; Tooby & Cosmides, 1992a). Darwin and subsequent evolutionary

---

4. Fodor uses some terms differently from the way we do, leading to some considerable confusion in the literature. For example, he writes in his critique of us that "poverty of the stimulus arguments militate for *innateness*, not for *modularity*. The domain-specificity and encapsulation of a cognitive mechanism on the one hand, and its innateness on the other, are orthogonal properties"; and "[y]ou can have perfectly general learning mechanisms that are born knowing a lot, and you can have fully encapsulated mechanisms (e.g., reflexes) that are literally present at birth" (2000, pp. 68–9). We certainly agree that innateness is a different dimension from information encapsulation (e.g., driving may be encapsulated but is not innate). To us, however, information encapsulation is also distinct from domain specificity (in context, we are almost always talking about evolved domain specificity). We have also used the term *modularity* to mean the tendency of biological systems to evolve functional specializations and the term *module* to refer to an evolved specialization, regardless of the degree to which it exists in a heavily policed informational quarantine or operates on information available to other procedures in the architecture. In this usage, we did not mean to invoke Fodor's particular and narrow concept of modularity, which appears to make information encapsulation a defining feature rather than (in our view) an occasional concomitant. In particular, we are suspicious of the encapsulation spatial metaphor of cognitive mechanisms being *containers* that act on the informational *objects* they hold *inside* of them. This produces spurious problems of how information trapped inside one container could manage to touch and so interact with information walled off inside another container (see, e.g., Barrett, in press).

researchers have investigated numerous species in which organisms display knowledge and competences that they did not acquire ontogenetically from any general-purpose, content-independent neurocomputational procedure (Cosmides & Tooby, 1987; Tooby & Cosmides, 1992a; for specific examples, see e.g., Gallistel, 1990, 1995; Garcia & Koelling, 1966; Gaulin, 1995; Johnson & Morton, 1991; Mineka et al., 1984; see also Darwin, 1859, 1871). That is, many species develop knowledge that is either absent from the stimuli they have access to or is not uniquely entailed by those stimuli.

Natural selection provides an elegant, naturalistic explanation for the origin of such innate ideas, a point that Darwin himself realized shortly after developing the theory of natural selection (Darwin, 1974). In modern terms, mutations that cause neural machinery to reliably develop useful, world-reflecting mental contents (or organizing principles, categories, etc.) give their possessors a propagative advantage over blank slate designs that must consider an unconstrained set of possibilities, and are limited to applying the same procedures to all contents. Natural selection constitutes a second route, independent of the specific characteristics of individual experience, by which the mind might become endowed with knowledge, and endowed with the Kantian conceptual tools that shape and make use of experience in an evolutionarily functional way (for discussion, see e.g., Cosmides & Tooby, 1987; Tooby & Cosmides, 1992a).

Hence, from an evolutionary perspective, a primary roadblock to progress has been the persisting consensus that general-purpose, content-independent mechanisms are the null hypothesis: that hypotheses about the existence of content-specific mechanisms are (in the words of Farah et al., 1996) "a priori implausible."

Although we cannot specifically remember using the phrase *massive modularity* ourselves, we are happy to endorse it, provided it is taken to be a claim that the number of evolved functional specializations in the brain (regardless of whether they are encapsulated) is substantially greater than has been traditionally believed—and not that there are no content-independent operations whatsoever, or that all mechanisms are informationally encapsulated with respect to all others. Finally, *general* has been used by scholars in a diversity of ways, but in the nativism debate we have used it to refer to evolved mechanisms that lack attributes that were added by natural selection because they work for some specialized domains but fail for others. Such systems require design features that activate them for the contents or inputs they evolved to work on, and deactivate them outside of their specific functional domain. In particular, general learning mechanisms will include content-independent computational procedures. Antinativists doubt (while we conclude) that there exist different evolved, content-dependent procedures specialized (in some way) for computing about mothers (Lieberman et al., 2003), predators (Barrett, 2005; Barrett et al., under review), coalitions (Kurzban et al., 2001), social exchanges (Cosmides, 1989; Cosmides & Tooby, 1989, 2005), and so on. For this reason, we find Fodor's statement that "[y]ou can have perfectly general learning mechanisms that are born knowing a lot" baffling. If the learning system knows a lot (e.g., that there are two sexes, that it had a mother, to avoid open running sores on others), then it cannot be as prepared to face one environment (where things that it knows are not true) as another environment (where everything it knows is true). The system is not general with respect to the set of possible environments and inputs it might receive, nor with respect to the kinds of environments it might have to act in. In our experience, antinativists express their antinativism through their belief in the explanatory adequacy for humans of mechanisms that are innately equipped with general-purpose, content-indendent procedures, arriving into the world free of any preexisting innate knowledge.

For the majority who hold this view, the only scientific problem worth addressing is choosing among models of content-independent processes, perhaps occasionally noting some content-sensitive exceptions of no general significance. This extreme Bayesian a priori skepticism deployed against reported architectural content specificity is the scientifically respectable face for its obverse—an extreme credulity extended to the sociologically preferred, blank slate alternative. If for many, as experience suggests, this theoretical precommitment floats free of the evidence, then no amount of contrary evidence by itself may be able to displace it. The remedy for this sociologically rooted epistemological problem must therefore be to change the scientific culture so that both kinds of explanations are put on an equal footing, subject to the same burdens of evidence, consistency, testability, economy, and predictive power. How might this be accomplished?

3 The Role of Learnability Analyses in Testing the Computational Sufficiency of Content-Independent Cognitive Architectures to Account for the Development of Competences

Chomsky, influenced in part by this independent Darwinian tradition, was the most prominent cognitive scientist of the modern era to attempt to relegitimize nativism, at least within the domain of language (Chomsky, 1957, 1959, 1965). Indeed, the history of the Chomskian enterprise is illuminating with respect to the problem at hand. Citing biological principles, Chomsky (1959, 1965) famously made poverty of the stimulus arguments about the acquisition of language—arguments that were modern applications of Darwin's reasoning about the emergence in individual development of knowledge and competences that were not wholly extracted from individual experience. These arguments gained substantial formal weight from subsequent learnability analyses (see, e.g., Pinker, 1984). A competence is *learnable* by a given computational architecture in a given environment if the architecture's procedures, in interaction with the structure of the environment, cause the development within the architecture of the competence in question (whether knowledge, skill, or regulatory structure). If the proposed procedures are not computationally sufficient to construct the competence with the given set of inputs, then they cannot be a correct model of the computational design. This form of analysis requires one to fully and explicitly characterize the procedures that constitute the set of acquisition mechanisms, the relevant features of the developmental environment, and the competence (or behavioral output) that develops. Candidate models for human learning and other cognitive mechanisms can be evaluated as computationally sufficient or not based on the following criteria:

1. *They should produce the set of competences humans actually acquire.* Examples include the ability to speak one's local language grammatically (Chomsky, 1965); the observed distribution of aversion intensities at the prospect of sex with family members (Lieberman et al., 2003, in press, under review); the ability to make correct inferences about predator-prey interactions (Barrett, 2005; Barrett et al., under review);

the observed, complementary patterns of insensitivity to and use of local social categories such as "race" in person representation (Hirschfeld, 1996; Kurzban et al., 2001); the scaling of punitive sentiment directed at free riders according to the magnitude of the individual's anticipated contribution to a collective action (Price et al., 2002); the ability to detect possible violations of social contracts in contexts of social exchange (Cosmides, 1989; Cosmides & Tooby, 1989, 1992, 2005).

2. *They should refrain from producing those competences that humans fail to acquire.* For example, pattern associator architectures unguided by specializations predict the acquisition of large bodies of strange knowledge that real organisms, including humans, do not acquire (see, e.g., Marcus, 2002). More simply, content-free acquisition mechanisms should cause children in urban America to develop fears to local causes of injury and mortality, such as cars, stoves, and stairs. But these fears rarely develop, whereas fears concerning snakes, spiders, the dark, wild animals, and skeletons often do—even though they do not reflect local dangers (Maurer, 1965).

3. *Their success should not depend on the presence in the environment of properties that do not, in fact, exist* (e.g., specific forms of social instruction, reinforcement, or feedback; the direct observation of unobservable things such as mental states; signals of the objective value of a goal-state).

4. *They should produce the patterns of individual and cultural uniformity and variation that are actually observed, using the observed distributions of environmental conditions as inputs.* For example, despite enormous cultural differences in rates of exposure to predator-prey interactions, the predator-prey inference system develops precociously and in parallel in different cultures—a fact that any acquisition mechanism must account for (Barrett, 2005; Barrett et al., under review).

These are very stringent requirements. Indeed, well-specified domain-general models reliably fail learnability tests for language (e.g., Pinker, 1979, 1984; Pinker & Prince, 1988; Wexler & Culicover, 1980). The scope and informativeness of this kind of argument can be greatly expanded, however, by considering tests of learnability and computational sufficiency for an entire range of problem-types that we know ancestral (and modern) foragers had to be able to solve in order to exist, survive, reproduce, and take advantage of their fitness-promoting opportunities (Cosmides & Tooby, 1987, 1989; Tooby & Cosmides, 1992a). Learnability analyses for this broader set of competences can play a pivotal role in demonstrating that our species-typical cognitive architecture manifests an evolved, pervasive content sensitivity in its operation. There exist large sets of formally definable computational problems that humans routinely solve (and evolved to solve) that no content-independent architecture can solve, even in principle. To be worth considering as a viable candidate model for the human cognitive architecture, a domain-general model must generate the entire set of ancestrally necessary competences that human foragers (and humans in general) manifest, without also generating nonexistent competences (Cosmides & Tooby, 1987; Tooby & Cosmides, 1992a).

In the case of language, leaving aside the specific claims associated with particular models of language acquisition, we believe that Chomsky's arguments and Pinker's and others' learnability analyses logically demonstrated the need for positing some implementation of innate ideas that make possible the acquisition of language and, in particular, grammar. That is, the human neurocomputational architecture contains a language acquisition device in the form of a set of procedures at least some of which are language specific and whose embodied inferential strategies reflect structural or statistical regularities in the set of languages humans spoke ancestrally (as well as the contexts of meaning within which utterances were made). In our view, these Chomskian arguments should have established a scientific consensus that the blank slate viewpoint was mistaken, at least in the case of language.

However, despite the intellectual force of these arguments, and as influential as they have been in cognitive science, they have failed to bring about a consensus among psychologists, neuroscientists, and behavioral scientists of the kind one regularly sees in the other natural sciences. One possible reason for this failure is that the arguments over the acquisition of grammatical competence have become increasingly technical. The language system (whatever its nature) is very complex, making it difficult for researchers outside of language to arrive confidently at independent judgments of their value. This cannot, however, be the whole reason. After all, far more technical and counterintuitive theories were rapidly adopted in the quantum and relativistic revolutions. Another reason might be that Chomskian psycholinguistics, despite its various successes, has not clearly produced the step-by-step theoretical advances coupled to empirical demonstrations that aggregate into an ever-expanding circle of persuasively well-explained phenomena. Nevertheless, we think the key reason for the persistence of the debate lies in the fact that the grammatical patterns exhibited by human languages are widely believed to be objectively and publicly present in the world.

For the majority who are attracted to a blank slate view, the seemingly objective character of the learning task invites the perennial speculation that some presently unknown kind of cognitive architecture will be discovered that could detect such patterns without any assistance from computational machinery specialized for the task. Certainly substantial subcomponents of learning tasks appear to be tractable to content-independent operations such as pattern association, giving evidence of partial successes. Moreover, it takes a great deal of time and effort to explore the computational virtues and limitations of each new proposal, and for their explanatory deficiencies to become manifest (in the case of connectionism, see, e.g., Marcus et al., 1995; Marcus et al., 1992; Marcus, 2002; Pinker, 1999; Pinker & Prince, 1988). New variants on previously discredited approaches can be introduced at least as rapidly as they can be analyzed, especially if they contain large numbers of degrees of freedom that can be fitted to already gathered data (as is true of connectionist models). Most critically, it is impossible to show that unspecified models that might be developed in the indefinite future are computationally insufficient. The result in the scientific community has been a steady-state indeterminacy, where researchers continue to believe what they are disposed to believe, and fractionate into self-reinforcing communities of belief. As the decades pass, it is difficult to escape the conclusion that whatever the virtues of the Chomskian enterprise (we think it has many), sociologically it has been ineffective in generally legitimizing proposals of functional content specificity and its evolutionary basis.

Poverty-of-the-stimulus arguments similar to Chomsky's have been outlined in cognitive development, where there is a vigorous and increasingly evolutionary subcommunity of cognitive nativists studying a larger and more diverse set of evolved functional specializations (Atran, 1990; Baillargeon, 1986; Baron-Cohen, 1995; Boyer, 2001; Hirschfeld, 1996; Hirschfeld & Gelman, 1994; Leslie, 1987; Markman, 1989; Spelke, 1990).[5] However, learnability arguments in these areas suffer from the same vulnerabilities that have made the Chomskian argument inconclusive: the knowledge that develops is widely seen as reflecting objectively true sets of relationships manifested in the world. Consequently, it is hard to convince blank slate advocates that no possible architecture of truth-discovery or relationship extraction would be able to account for the development of these competences without recourse to evolved content-dependent functional specializations (Quartz & Sejnowski, 1997). To solve our problem, we need to look elsewhere.

4 Hume's *Ought From Is* Barrier Poses a Set of Learnability Problems for Content-Independent Architectures, Which Are Insurmountable Whatever Their Implementation

If the Chomskian debate has not produced a consensus because the knowledge to be learned is (believed to be) objectively present in the world,[6] this suggests a strategy of argument that might be effective if its preconditions could be satisfied. If it can be shown that organisms need to acquire—and do develop—competences based on patterns that are *not* sensorily available or objectively present in the external world, then no possible blank slate learning architecture could acquire

---

5. We deeply admire the achievements of the cognitive development community (and consider ourselves part of it). Moreover, we appreciate the widespread understanding within this community of the need for biological constraints on induction. At least since Quine, the interaction on this issue between philosophy and cognitive development has been extraordinarily fruitful. What baffles us, however, is that when it comes time to go looking for biology to inform the investigation of biological constraints on induction, so many researchers in cognitive development go looking only in philosophy. Cognitive scientists need to mature beyond the point of regarding evolutionary biology as a stigmatizing contaminant.

6. Of course, Chomskians argue that the local grammar is not objectively present in the external world, because there are an infinite number of possible grammars that are consistent with any finite set of observed utterances. We agree with this, but we have observed that, sociologically, this argument is ineffective, and it leaves blank-slate researchers unpersuaded. It cannot be argued that evidence about the local grammar is unavailable in observable utterances. In the defense of anti-Chomskians, one could argue that whatever the architecture of general-purpose learning engines turns out to be, it could provide, incidentally as a by-product of its implementation, the necessary constraints on the hypothesis space that are, for Chomskians, supplied by the design features of the language acquisition device.

those competences or extract the requisite knowledge. Acquisition would require the presence in the evolved architecture of content-specific systems (innate ideas). The impossibility of learning things that are not objectively present in the world to be observed would demonstrate conclusively the reality of innate ideas, resolving the issue sociologically (we are optimists) as well as analytically.

Hume's argument (Hume, 1740/1978) that one cannot derive an *ought* from an *is* suggests one major class of competences fitting this precondition: motivational competences. Hume's argument generalizes to any psychological phenomenon that requires valuation to operate. From the point of view of the valuer, value is not a physical property, or a set of patterned relationships among entities in the external world, or an observer-independent property. Because the value of a behavioral outcome is not objectively present in the external world, it is absent from inputs to the sensory systems. Accordingly, mental representations of the value of a behavioral outcome cannot, even in principle, be learned through the operation of any content-independent procedures, including logical operations, pattern association, or inductive processes as traditionally conceived. If organisms have motivational systems and concepts that play an embedded role in them, then both motivational systems and the concepts they employ must be, at least in part, developmentally architecture derived. That is, regardless of what environmental features they are designed to take as inputs during development, motivational machinery and the core concepts they require must be assembled by specialized developmental programs designed by natural selection for that function.

No stimulus intrinsically mandates any response, or any value hierarchy of responses. In the tangled bank of coevolved organisms that Darwin memorably contemplated at the end of the *Origin*, naturally selected differences in the brains of different species cause them to treat the same objects in a rich and conflicting diversity of ways: the infant who is the object of caring attention by one organism is the object of predatory ambition by another, an ectoparasitic home to a third, and a barrier requiring effortful trajectory change to a fourth. It is the brains of these organisms that introduce behavior-regulatory valuation into the causal stream, and it was natural selection that introduced into brains the neural subsystems that

---

Indeed, during the initial emergence of language, prior to the evolution of any rich set of specializations to support it, the primary constraints on language learning would have to have been supplied by nonlanguage components of the cognitive architecture (whether specialized or general purpose). In the final analysis, it boils down to claims about what the evolved functions of the implicated machinery are. The choices are: (1) all aspects of the system used for language acquisition evolved for general cognition, producing language for free; (2) at least some parts of the system evolved for specialized functions, but none specifically for language; or (3) some parts of the system evolved for specialized functions, and some of these evolved specifically for language. Whatever the truth turns out to be about grammar, mechanisms for the acquisition of meaning could not be blank slate, or no one could ever learn language. Our interpretation of likely messages must be informed by a rich set of content-specialized mechanisms that tells us what someone is likely to be saying under given circumstances. If meaning were unconstrained and indeterminate, this process could not take place (see e.g., Markman, 1989; Sperber, 1996; Sperber & Wilson, 1995; Tooby & Cosmides, 1992a).

accomplish valuation. The same stimulus set, by itself, cannot explain differences in the preferences and actions it provokes, or indeed, the preferences themselves. Value is not in the world, even for members of the same species. Members of the same species view the same objects differently: the very same object is one person's husband and another's father—an object of sexual preference in one case and sexual aversion in the other. Moreover, because each evolved organism is by design the center of its own unique web of valuations, evolved value by its nature cannot have an objective character (Cosmides & Tooby, 1981; Hamilton, 1964). Because of the structure of natural selection, social organisms are regularly in social conflict, so that the objective states of the world that are preferred by some are aversive or neutral to others (e.g., that this individual, and not that one, should get the contested food, mating opportunity, territory, parental effort, status, grooming, and so on). This gives value for organisms an intrinsically indexical quality. Indeed, fitness "interests"—the causal feedback conditions of gene frequency that value computation evolved to track—cannot be properly assigned to such a high-level entity as a person but are indexical to sets of genes inside the genome, defined in terms of their tendency to replicate under the same conditions (Cosmides & Tooby, 1981). Whatever else might be attainable by sense data and content-independent operations, value or its regulatory equivalents must be added by the architecture.

The architecture's evolved systems for assigning value and computing motivation were shaped by the relative fitness productivity of ancestral design variants, as matched against the set of evolutionarily recurrent choice problems. That is, content-specific value processing is done by mechanisms that ultimately were shaped according to whether their rankings and decisions were, on balance, reproduction-promoting under ancestral conditions. So value exists for animals solely because natural selection built neurocomputational circuitry into our minds to compute it as one of several kinds of representation necessary for regulating our behavior according to evolutionarily functional performance criteria.

The ramifications of integrating value into cognitive science will be far reaching because valuation is not a rare or peripheral neurocomputational activity. Valuation is cognitively *ubiquitous*. It goes on continuously, entering into the representation of almost all situations, and into the regulation of almost all behavior. Animals depend on motivational systems to assign tradeoffs, establish goal states, apportion effort, prepare plans, and trigger actions, assigning different kinds of valuation as a regular and necessary part of the generation of behavior. Valuation is intrinsically *content sensitive*. That is, valuation by its nature depends on discriminating situations from each other on the basis of their content. Predators but not prey must be avoided, substances with nutrients must be chosen over toxins or inorganic materials as food, offspring must be fed rather than eaten, fertile people as opposed to prereproductives or nonhumans courted, skills as opposed to eccentricities acquired, reliable as opposed to faithless cooperators preferred, free riding punished rather than rewarded, genetic relatives avoided rather than chosen as sex partners, injured legs favored rather than damaged further, role models attended to rather than ignored, friends cultivated, sexual rivals intimidated, coalitions formed, relatives assisted, and so on across an enormous range of ancestrally necessary and evolutionarily favored activities.

Valuation is intrinsically *content generative:* upon discriminating objects, situations, or prospects on the basis of their content, valuation intrinsically introduces its own proprietary forms of content into other representational structures. Persons, situations, objects, actions, and experiences are tagged as frightening, sexually attractive, appetizing, disgusting, dull, funny, glorious, grievous, embarrassing, beloved, horrifying, disturbing, shameful, fatiguing, irritating, fascinating, beautiful, fun, and so on (for an evolutionary-computational approach to the emotions and their relationship to motivation, see Cosmides & Tooby, 2000b; Tooby & Cosmides, 1990). Valuation processes and valuation ontologies are necessarily rich because of the large number of hetereogeneous mechanisms they need to orchestrate in preparation for action (e.g., flight, courtship, eating) and to recalibrate after action (e.g., guilt, shame, regret, satisfaction).

In short, many evolved motivational mechanisms, by virtue of the nature of the functions they serve, are necessarily functionally specialized rather than general purpose, are content dependent rather than content independent, introduce content not derived from the senses into the operation of the architecture, and do so ubiquitously.

The proprietary content introduced by the architecture constitutes a form of knowledge: the architecture must know (in some sense) that living children are better than dead children, social approval is better than disapproval, salt and sweet are better than acrid or putrefying, sex with your mother or father is to be avoided, helping siblings is (within certain tradeoffs) better than helping fungi, your mate copulating with your sexual rival is worse than his or her fidelity, spiders on your cheek are worse than in the garden, understanding is better than confusion, skill mastery is better than inept performance, and so on. Of course, the interaction of motivational systems with other cognitive activities occasioned by experience massively expands and enriches evaluative knowledge representations (e.g., from generalization along psychophysical dimensions; from the backward derivation of valuation of instrumentally useful intermediate steps to a primarily valued goal; for an analysis of various aesthetic activities as valuation processing, see Tooby & Cosmides, 2001). Nevertheless, there must be an irreducible core set of initial, evolved, architecture-derived content-specific valuation assignment procedures, or the system could not get started. The debate cannot sensibly be over the necessary existence of this core set. The real debate is over how large the core set must be, and what the proper computational description of these valuation procedures and their associated motivational circuitry is.

Valuation processes are often necessarily *domain specific* (Cosmides & Tooby, 1987): because the sets of outcomes that constitute biological success in some domains of adaptive problem are different from the sets of outcomes that are biologically successful in others, the same evolved definitions of success or valuation cannot be used to regulate action across them all. Indeed, this gives us a way of distinguishing evolved domains with respect to valuation and action regulation. The question is: can the criteria for valuation (or the criteria-deriving procedures) in two areas be developmentally derived from the same evolved core set? If the answer is "no," then two different evolved motivational domains are implicated. For example, humans do not and could not evaluate potential mates by using the same criteria they use to evaluate foods or dangers or interactions with their children or projects for advancing their status. Nor is there any possible evolved core set from which such diverse definitions of valued outcomes or successful action in these five domains (for example) could be derived (Cosmides & Tooby, 1987). Different adaptive problems require different computational properties for their solution when reliance on the same properties would lead to functional incompatibilities and poor performance. To see this, consider designing a computational program that chooses foods based on their kindness or one that chooses friends based on their flavor and the aggregate calories to be gained from consuming their flesh. This thought experiment suggests the kind of functional incompatibility issues that naturally sort motivational domains based on their incommensurability. Hence, by evolved design, different content domains activate different evolved criteria sets and evaluation procedures.

For those unused to thinking about the computational requirements for action, particularly as seen within an evolutionary framework, this argument will not seem as powerful as it is. After all, maybe humans do not solve motivational problems, or do so only very poorly. What sort of justification could there be in the endless parade of human folly for the claim that people are behaving functionally? Appreciating the argument from value computation depends on understanding that many species, including humans, are known to systematically perform substantially better than random in a growing number of well-studied domains, reaching narrow targets of evolutionarily defined behavioral success. This is what it means to say humans (and other species) are known to solve certain adaptive problems well. The very existence of individuals and populations depends on the ongoing successful computation of the answers to a range of value-dependent, action-regulatory problems to within very narrow tolerances. Although entropy is a formidable opponent, and our systems all break down sooner or later, animals on their passage through cycles of replication exhibit consistent, impressive, temporary triumphs over it. For example, the world is full of substances, but random selection of these, or random motor operations on these, will not prevent the organism from starving to death or poisoning itself. Courtship, mating, and parenting are far more complex. Explaining how this is regulated computationally is the task.

The study of motivational incommensurability gives us a method for setting an irreducible lower bound on the number of different evolved content-specific procedures or computational elements involved in valuation, as well as insight into their heterarchical organization into domains. (Of course, the actual number of evolved conceptual elements is likely to be larger because there are other kinds of computational advantages to content sensitivity than to serve as inputs to motivational operations). Cases of motivational incommensurability are numerous, and easily identified. Distinct and incommensurable evolved motivational principles exist for food, sexual attraction, parenting, kinship, incest avoidance, coalitions, disease avoidance, friendship, predators, provocations, snakes, spiders, habitats, safety, competitors, being observed, behavior when sick, certain categories of moral transgression, and scores of other entities, conditions, acts, and relationships. Consequently, evolved content specializations must also exist for these separate domains. (For the original versions of this argument, on why organisms cannot evolve a general-purpose inclusive fitness-maximizing device, and so necessarily depend on at least some content-specific machinery, see Cosmides & Tooby, 1987; Tooby & Cosmides, 1992a).

A motivational domain is a set of represented inputs, contents, objects, outcomes, or actions that a functionally specialized set of evaluative procedures was designed by evolution to act over (e.g., representations of foods, contaminants, animate dangers, people to emulate, potential retaliations to provocations). Not only is there an irreducible number of domains, but there is an irreducible set of domain-specific criteria or value-assigning procedures operating within each domain (e.g., for food: salt, sweet, bitter, sour, savory, fat affordances, putrefying smell avoidance, previous history with the aversion acquisition system, temporal tracking of health consequences by immune system, stage of pregnancy, boundaries on entities and properties considered by the system, perhaps maggot-ridden food avoidance, and scores of other factors). When the required assignments of value within a domain (such as food) cannot all be derived from a common neurocomputational procedure, then the number of motivational elements must necessarily be multiplied to account for the data.

The computational challenge with respect to motivation is to produce a set of programs that can duplicate human value-regulated behavior. As an important scientific goal, we need to begin the construction of an inventory of evolved value and choice criteria and procedures that are (in some way) built into our species-typical architectures, and of the evolved neurocomputational programs that derive, expand, and enrich them. To do this, we need to examine evolved valuation problems that humans can be shown to solve (or indeed any valuation-requiring behavior that humans are known to exhibit) and look at the set of valuation criteria that are needed to accomplish the task. We need to see how small the set of initial evolved value elements can be made that can still fully account for the data, being open to the parsimony considerations posed by the possible involvement of domain-general and domain-specific procedures for ontogenetically elaborating value criteria (e.g., the derivation of secondary reinforcers from primary reinforcers by pattern associator systems). If it can be shown at any point that the so-far-identified derivation procedures (operating realistically in a naturally structured environment) cannot derive the required valuation-regulated behavior from the so-far-identified list of evolved value elements, then either new value elements should be added to the list to account for the new sets of behaviors to be explained or a new procedure must be added (whichever the data supports). So, for example, at present we are not compelled to posit a separate motivation for locomotion, because locomotion is instrumental to achieving other valued outcomes (although we do need to posit a value-based effort computation system that transduces locomotion, among other things, to explain why the same individual will walk 10 feet for a given reward but not 10 miles). Nevertheless, we do need to posit separate evolved motivational elements to account for sexual behavior and feeding behavior, because well-engineered choice in both these areas cannot be achieved by the same value criteria. Altogether, there has not been very much progress over the last century toward constructing such an inventory, because we have been shrugging off the issue of motivational innateness through the shell game of implying that any given motivation is secondarily acquired, without obliging ourselves to computationally specify how and from what. The field needs to settle on a well-validated, irreducible set of motivational first movers. In our experience, a serious analysis of any domain often leads to the discovery that the irreducible minimum motivational feature set is surprisingly large (see, for an analysis of incest avoidance, Lieberman et al., 2003, in press, under review).

The outputs of these rich, indispensable systems of valuation computation are loosely referred to as *feeling*, saturating our experience with their voluminous, dense, intricate textures, and guiding our mental operations and bodies into fitness-enhancing realizations, choices, behaviors, and preparatory activities. They also deliver inputs to (but should not be confused with) a parallel, minimalist system of value distillation that produces a stripped down set of proprietary content that is used in certain aspects of decision-making. This subsidiary system provides the basis for intuitive and formal concepts such as utility, reward, payoff, and reinforcement. Why is this subsystem needed, in addition to the richer system it derives from? The realities of the physical world, the fact that we cannot be in two places at the same time, and the finite processing limitations on our neural circuits mean that many choices are necessarily mutually exclusive. In order to make choices in a way that usually promotes fitness, our architectures need to be able to discriminate alternative courses of action on the basis of computed indices of their probable fitness consequences. To serve this purpose, the minimum valuation-proprietary form of content is therefore a form of representational tagging with computed scalar utilities (or their equivalent) assigned to whatever representational parsing there is of goals, plans, situations, outcomes, or experiences. That is, the system must reliably develop so as to translate complex high-dimensional valuation representations involving rich content—such as *frightening* or *disgusting* or *irritating*—into unidimensional magnitudes. This is required so that situation-representations or sensory inputs can be ordered by payoff. Although the motivational system is far richer than just a utility computing system, we know this unidimensional neural currency must exist as one aspect of the motivational system, or the system could not be designed to make mutually exclusive choices nonreflexively in a way that tracked higher fitness payoffs. This form of payoff representation must be scalar so that magnitudes can be ordered, and should in addition have properties of a ratio scale so the computational system can arbitrate competing goals under different probability distributions. That is, this subsystem must be able to do more than ordinally rank outcomes, or it could not shift from one course of action to another upon discovering a shift in the probabilities of success among the alternatives (which common experience and conditioning studies show is routinely done).

Although only a small piece of the motivational system, this minimalist subsystem attracts disproportionate attention, and is often mistaken by certain research communities to constitute essentially the whole of motivation. This belief is seductive for researchers in fields like economics and learning theory because utility-style conceptualizations are easy to mathematically formalize and test. By focusing only on the question of what procedures would be needed to use pre-existing utilities to make choices, many researchers overlook the existence of the rest of the motivational architecture that encompasses it. There is all too little research, for example, into the irreducibly complex input and processing systems needed to transform the entire universe of human experience and situation representation into payoff magnitudes. When their attention is drawn to the contrast, most researchers will admit that the rich universe of feeling cannot be captured by a set of flat, unidimensional utilities, and so utilities by themselves cannot be an adequate model of or explanation for this universe of valuation. It is time to move cognitive science into an exploration of this larger realm.

5 Evolved Systems for Motivational Computation Use Conceptual Structure in Targeted Ways, so Motivational Computation and Knowledge Computation Cannot Be Isolated from Each Other into Separate Systems

Valuation processes typically involve many of the same elements of conceptual structure that are the traditional objects of cognitive science (representations of persons, foods, objects, animals, actions, events). This means that the evolution of innate motivational elements will mandate the evolution of an irreducible set of conceptual elements as well. Why? A valuation is not meaningful or causally efficacious in the regulation of behavior unless it includes some form of specification of what is valued. That is, the specification of what the value applies to generally involves conceptual structure.

For example, for natural selection to cause safe distances from snakes to be preferred to closeness to snakes, it must build the recognition of snake-like entities into our neurocomputational architecture. This system of recognition and tagging operations is computationally a snake concept, albeit a skeletally specified one. Evidence supports the view that humans and related species do indeed have a valuation system specialized to respond to snakes (e.g., Marks, 1987; Mineka & Cook, 1993; Mineka et al., 1984; Yerkes & Yerkes, 1936). This one consideration alone forces us to add to a fourth innate idea to Kant's space, time, and causality. Yerkes and Yerkes's finding counts as empirically based philosophical progress, and as straightforward progress in the cognitive science of knowledge as well—derived (*pace* Fodor) from evolutionarily motivated theories of function.

In other words, the evolved motivation argument not only establishes the necessity of evolved motivational elements: it also resurrects the argument for the necessity of innate knowledge-like conceptual structure. Moreover, it does this in a way that is not vulnerable to the counterargument that objective knowledge (putatively) can be discovered by some general learner alone. This is because evolved conceptual structure is not present in the architecture (only) as "objective" knowledge. For the purposes of this argument, the elements of conceptual structure under discussion evolved to be in the architecture in order to be the object of intrinsically unlearnable motivational valuations. It is the specificity of the coupling to the particular valuation procedure that individuates the concept with respect to this set of motivational functions (e.g., [your children: *beloved*], [snakes: *suspect*]). Of course, although we think the neurodevelopmental basis of a lot of conceptual structure was built in to the developmental programs by natural selection because it helped in computing accurate representations of evolutionarily important external relationships (see, e.g., Spelke, 1990), that is not the kind of selection pressure being discussed here. The requirements of motivation and action selected for certain aspects of conceptual structure, and these aspects of conceptual structure may or may not be the same features of conceptual structure that were favored because they promoted the efficient acquisition of accurate representations of the world. (It seems extremely likely that conceptual structure was shaped by both sets of selection pressures.) In any case, conceptual elements (sexual rival) that evolved to serve motivational functions must be innately individuated by the way the motivational system distinguishes them for its operations (like jealousy).

That is, the evolution of content-discriminating motivational systems necessarily involves the evolution of crosscoupled, motivation-discriminated conceptual structure. Our evolved architecture is riddled with valuation processes, including (but not limited to) systems for generating, specifying, distinguishing, and ranking goal-states. To compute actions that differentially increase the probability of reaching a given goal-state, that goal-state (and action-relevant aspects of the situation the goal-state is embedded in) must be computationally definable, recognizable, and distinguishable from non-goal-states and alternative goal-states. More generally, if the successful functioning of an evolved adaptation requires a valuation process underivable from anything else, and if that valuation process requires the participation of a specific concept or category whose relationship to the rest of the valuation process cannot be derived, then the conceptual element must be, in some sense, innately (that is, evolutionarily) specified. You cannot systematically hit narrow targets unless there is a specification of the target. And in the realm of motivation, findings from evolutionary biology, behavioral ecology, and evolutionary psychology provide domain after domain where animals, including humans, efficiently hit the evolved targets that natural selection predicts they should.

For example, normally developing humans were naturally selected to have sex with healthy, reproductively mature members of the opposite sex (Symons, 1979). For a computational system to cause this, there must be evolved, reliably developing conceptual machinery that distinguishes human from nonhuman, male from female, mature from immature or senescent, healthy from unhealthy, live from dead (and so on) in order to assign one attribute higher valuation than the other. As one surveys the conceptual requirements of each motivational system about which there is evidence, the list of reliably developing, evolutionarily discriminated concepts becomes inescapably long. In traditional cognitive and philosophical terms, evolved motivational computation requires massive nativism.[7] Of course, this is not the claim that every adult value discrimination is innate. For example, if the representation of *healthy* gives *living* for free by derivation, then the

---

7. We use the terms *innate*, *nativism*, and so on because, given the discourse practices of philosophers and cognitive scientists, they are the closest counterpart to a more biologically elaborate concept. That is, while genetic determinism is an incoherent position, so is environmental determinism.

live versus *dead* distinction need not be a separately selected component of the motivational system (although this distinction might be important, for different reasons, in systems motivating behavior around potentially dangerous animals; Barrett & Behne, in press).

These representations need not be rich representations—neural and genetic economizing will mean that they will often be encoded using what can be called *minimal sufficient specification*. The minimal sufficient specification is the most economical cognitive machinery necessary for recognizing a representation by some evolutionarily constant feature it manifests neurodevelopmentally. The specification must tag representations so that the specific motivational operation will be able to find its proper objects. For example, adult concepts of male and female are undoubtedly very rich. Yet all the developing sexual valence circuit might need (in principle) is a single innately privileged psychophysical cue that causes males to be reliably distinguished from females, binarily indicating which is which for motivational purposes, with another binary parameter for setting the sex targeted for attraction. The sorting of tokens into types by the conceptual projections of the motivational system then allows a richer psychophysical template to be formed than is initially used, and conceptual enrichment to occur. (Evidence suggests, for example, that the historically contingent concept of *race* is a projection of a coalitional categorization system that evolved for sorting individuals into alliance sets; Kurzban et al., 2001.) The specific psychophysical (or other) cues that motivational systems use as inputs to accomplish the initial sorting of represented entities are expected to be minimal, subtle, strange, and abstractly contentful,

---

Everything develops from a jointly codetermined interaction among the genes, the environment, and the state of the organism at a given time. More precisely, in addition to zygotic organization, the organism inherits two sets of determinants rather than just one—a genetic inheritance and a less well conceptualized environmental inheritance (Tooby & Cosmides, 1990, 1992a; Tooby et al., 2003). The environmental system of inheritance consists of the properties of the world that participate in the organism's development and life-processes and that persist from generation to generation. These two sets have been inherited together repeatedly across a number of generations. This repetition has allowed natural selection to coordinate the interaction of stably replicated genes with stably persisting environmental regularities, so that this web of interactions produces the reliable development of a highly organized, highly functional, and largely species-typical design. When we call something *innate*, we do not mean that it is "encoded entirely in the genes," that it is genetically determined, that it does not develop, that the environment played no role or a lesser role in its development, and so on—nothing real has those properties: not eyes, nor eye color, nor aortas, nor otoliths. What we mean is that it reliably develops across the species' normal range of environments. Reliable development (innateness) is caused by the interaction of the ancestrally coordinated set of environmental regularities and genetic regularities. We do not mean *present at birth* if by that one means *expressed at birth*. An innate feature could be the product of selection, a by-product of selection, or a property fixed by stochastic processes. In each of these cases, it is a regular part of the architecture of the organism. Regardless of whether something was itself selected, if it was a regular part of the architecture, it could have been a cause of selection. We are most interested in exploring innate *functional* organization, which is recognizable because it consists of reliably developing properties that are nonramdomly organized according to biologically functional engineering criteria: eyes see, and sexual jealousy interferes with one's mate's potential extrapair copulations, but the color of blood does not help it carry oxygen or nutrients.

compared to the richly elaborated adult representations we are familiar with. Of course, there is a balance between neural and genetic economy on the one side and worthwhile improvements in performance made through adding evolved criteria on the other. In the case of human sexual attraction, there is substantial evidence that the irreducible set of evolved criteria used and traded off against each other are complexly multidimensional (Buss, 1991) and not simply binary (or all members of each sex would be equivalently attractive).

Returning to our snake avoidance system, we can see it has a series of components. It has a psychophysical front end: one of its subcomponents assigns the evolved, internal tag *snake* through visual and biomechanical motion cues to a perceptual representation of some entity in the world. It has a second subcomponent that maps in a parameter *distance* between the *snake* and the valued entity (like *self* or *child*). Obviously, the distance-representing component is used by many systems. However, it also must have a component that assigns and updates different specific valuation intensities for different distances, so that further away is better than closer. The metric of valuation against distance (and its update rules) is proprietary to snakes, but the output value parameter it produces must be accessible to other systems (so that distance from snakes can be ranked against other goods, like getting closer in order to extract your child from the python's coils). Snake, distance, and the identity-distance valuation metric all necessarily operate together for this simple system to work. Snakes, the entity to be protected, and distance cannot be assigned to one computational process and valuation to another. Even in this simple example, conceptual and valuation functions indivisibly interpenetrate each other, with the representations necessarily coexisting within the same structure. As this form of analysis is applied to the other tasks humans perform, we think it will be impossible to escape the general conclusion that cognitive science intrinsically involves motivation, and the science of motivation intrinsically involves cognitive science. (Opposing views are not only implicit in the comparative neglect of motivation, except as a factor in learning, but are sometimes explicit. Fodor (2000), for example, considers the study of "cognitive"[8] processes and "conative" processes to be functionally separate, rather than co-evolved aspects of the same unified systems of representation and action.)

The snake system also must interface with other shared systems for planning, situation representation, emotion, and action (e.g., systems that produce inferences that some potential actions represent improvements; that some potential outcomes are negatively valued; that motivate the choice of better outcomes over worse ones). The emotion system is particularly interrelated (Cosmides & Tooby, 2000b; Tooby & Cosmides, 1990). The function of the rich representation *frightening*

---

8. It is important to clarify that when we use the word *cognitive*, we intend it to be understood solely as a synonym for *information-processing* or *computational*, and not as an adjective that distinguishes say, thinking or knowing from feeling or acting. We are looking for cognitive—that is, computational—models of motivation and knowledge. We also use the word *representation* more loosely than most (e.g., as any computational product), because limiting it to knowledge-like structures with counterparts in the environment invites the acceptance of folk concepts and intuitions that we resist.

(as opposed to mere negative utility) is that in its associated emotion mode, fear orchestrates perception, hormones, the cardiopulmonary system, memory, and so on, so that they perform better, given the kinds of imminent action the architecture is likely to decide on and the long-term recalibration it derives from the event. (Emotions are conceptualized as evolved modes of operation of the entire psychological architecture, rather than a separate kind of mental activity.) The snake avoidance system also has another component. Although the details are not clear, it presumably recalibrates on the basis of individual experience, possibly slowly habituating in the absence of negative experiences or observations, and increasing sharply if snake contact leads to injury. It also narrowly accepts inputs from the social world—a conspecific expressing fear toward a snake (but not toward rabbits or other stimuli) in order to recalibrate the individual's snake valuation (Mineka & Cook, 1993; Mineka et al., 1984). Presumably this evolved because the system operates more functionally by upregulating or downregulating fear as a function of the local distribution of fear intensities in others, which index to some degree the local rate at which venomous snakes are encountered.

The key point here is that even this apparently simple one-function motivational system involves a series of evolved content-specific conceptual elements, including snakes, distance, conspecifics, that fear-faces have specific referents in the world, that snakes are a privileged referent of a fear-face (for snake fear to be recalibrated), and the output of fear itself. Of course, not all of these elements are unique to the snake system (although several are), but their pattern of distribution among motivational systems is heterarchical and itself not something that could be derived by content-independent operations acting on experience.

It is important to recognize that many kinds of motivational architectures are possible, not just ones that specify a single privileged goal-state and initiate means-ends inference. That structure seems an unlikely candidate, for example, for snake avoidance or sexual attraction. A particular bad event (like an imagined snake bite) need not be specifically represented as a negative goal-state in the snake avoidance system, with distance acquiring its significance through backward induction and means-ends analysis. More probably, the distance-fear relationship fills the representation of space with a motivational manifold that itself motivates avoidance (closeness is increasingly unpleasant). In the case of sex, it seems likely that the motivational system has a great deal of structure, with an evolved multidimensional path of motivational elicitation that intrinsically motivates many steps that guide the organism (foresightfully or not) to what is functionally (but not necessarily representationally) the goal-state. Computationally speaking, action-inviting affordances are not the same thing as represented goal-states.

The relevant question that will need to be addressed as the cognitive science project proceeds is how complex and how specifically detailed the architecturally derived motivational and conceptual machinery has to be to account for known, well-defined cases of human behavioral success. Computational explicitness, if insisted on, can play an important role in pushing cognitive science to deal more productively with the issues raised by the fact that the human neurocomputational architecture solves a large family of complex, distinct, evolutionarily recurrent adaptive problems. It is illuminating to try to map out a subsystem that can handle even very simple, direct motivational phenomena. Such an attempt rapidly makes clear how much our intuitions hide the computational intricacy that underwrites the approximation humans achieve of evolutionarily adaptive valuation in their daily affairs. The requirement to build something program-like as opposed to labeling black boxes will awaken the field to the true magnitude of the scientific problems posed by motivation. It will correspondingly inhibit the tendency to imbue black boxes with magical powers.

The case of socially recalibrated intensities of snake avoidance show that natural selection can and does evolve procedures that accept social inputs when it is evolutionarily advantageous to do so. While the discussion of the machinery that underlies cultural phenomena lie beyond the scope of this chapter, we wish to warn against the casual acceptance of the widespread idea that social inputs processed by content-independent learning procedures are the primary explanation for the origin of human valuation. Here are a few reasons. Functionally well-calibrated valuation is indexical. What is good to value for some individuals is not good to value for others. Individuals are in daily social conflict over whose values prevail. (Because of inherent conflicts of interest in social species, a system that simply adopts others' values would be rapidly selected out. Others' values are processed [1] prudentially, in terms of the incentives they provide for the organism's own already-existing value system; and [2] as evaluated clues to what might lead to the best behavioral payoffs, given the individual's evolved meta-value criteria.) Although we cannot explore them here, there are insurmountable learnability barriers preventing the social acquisition of necessary values solely through content-independent procedures. For example, the courses of action the monitored individual did not choose and traded off against are invisible because they are counterfactual. Therefore, any observed course of action gives insufficient information from which to deduce the valuation systems of others. We only succeed at deducing some of the values of others because we share the same underlying sets of content-sensitive value systems, which allow us to know, a priori, what values others are likely to hold.

Even granting that some values could be acquired through content-independent processes operating on social inputs (which we dispute), the motivational unlearnability argument would continue to apply to the aspects of motivational systems whose parameters are not wholly accounted for by social information. It is easy to identify large numbers of these. For example, one major class involves valuations that develop independently of those held by others in the social group. The argument applies even more strongly for those values that develop in opposition to widely shared values, often eliciting strong negative sanctions from others. The idea that the child is a tape recorder passively absorbing values from others is easily contravened by ordinary experience: children resist foods urged by their parents; they resist treating objects valued by adults with the same care and reverence; they resist acquiring many skills valued by adults; most adolescents in religious and traditional schools notoriously do not adopt the urged or modeled values toward premarital sexual behavior. These and many similar observations lead us to the *social learnability test*: if it can be shown that the social world resists or fails to support certain motivations, then those motivations cannot have been acquired from the social world. Many value-related phenomena meet the conditions for this argument. Indeed, humans ubiquitously pursue goals for which they are punished—and the development of valuation for these goals develops in spite of, and not because of, the existence of the social world.

6   The Evolved Function of the Cognitive Architecture Is the Generation of Biologically Successful Action Rather Than the Fixation of True Belief

Value and action have been relatively neglected by cognitive scientists because a commonly held view is that "the proper function of cognition is" (as Fodor puts it) "the fixation of true beliefs" (2000, p. 68). A consideration of the evolutionary dynamics acting on cognitive architectures shows that this view is at best incomplete, and more usually misleading. Before going further, however, it is important to point out that such a starting point, as self-evident as it may seem to be, commits us to a set of philosophical concepts that have no clear definitions in engineering terms. Whenever we are dealing with the designs of organisms, we are dealing with engineering questions. Philosophically, of course, it has proven extremely difficult to specify exactly what it means to call something a belief, to call a belief true, or to explicate reference, at least in an uncontroversial way. Although we seem to have clear intuitions about the meaning of such concepts as truth, knowledge, belief, representation, and reference, this may not be because they are what they seem to be. Indeed, a synthesis of evolution and computationalism suggests that these intuitions have led us away from a correct scientific understanding of the organic engineering phenomena they are used to represent. The situation may not be so different from what happened to many other equally irresistible intuitive concepts under the onslaught of modern physics (e.g., intuitions about space, time, causality, solid objects, and empty space bear little resemblance to the scientific concepts). We need to be prepared to have these venerable epistemological concepts transformed by our understanding of the nature, origin, and function of the computational systems that they inhabit as control elements. A quite different possibility is that they seem self-evident because they are conceptual primitives built into our cognitive architecture—as naturally selected Kantian *a prioris*, so to speak. These primitives are needed, for example, in theory-of-mind computations (Leslie, 1987) and in other scope-setting operations (Cosmides & Tooby, 2000a).

An alternative approach to their elucidation is to start out with engineering concepts drawn from biology, physics, and computer science. From there, the task is to see if it is possible (in principle) to build systems that have the same competences that animals (including humans) do. Once that is done, then it is possible to reexamine the architecture and its operation and see (1) what causally clear, well-described properties might serve as the evolutionarily tailored computational counterparts to our intuitive concepts of truth, belief, representation, reference, and so on; (2) how our engineering counterparts to these concepts might differ in certain key respects from their use in other accounts; and (3) the evolutionary-functional reasons why natural selection engineered reduced and transformed versions of these concepts into our cognitive architectures as metarepresentational conceptual primitives (Cosmides & Tooby, 2000a).[9] Through this process, we might be able to get a fresh perspective on certain questions.

For animals, the accomplishment of sets of ancestral adaptive problems was enhanced by the evolution of *behavior regulatory systems*, which over evolutionary time coalesced into what, on histological grounds, is usually viewed as a single entity, the nervous system (as well as a few other architectural features, such as the endocrine system). The nervous system's functional identity is as a control system (or a set of control systems), analogous in many ways to control systems in manufacturing, robotics, engine design, architecture, and aviation. A control system is, by its very nature, a very different kind of thing from a scientist or a philosopher. Scientists and philosophers often stress the importance of arriving at true beliefs, while control systems exist solely to generate successful behavior. Correct action (action leading to successful propagation) is the functional product that the brain evolved to furnish, as disease resistance is the functional product of the immune system.[10]

For animals, knowledge only exists because ancestrally its production served as a means to correct action. Therefore, the designs of systems for the acquisition of knowledge in our architecture owe their functional organization to the evolved, systematic role they played ancestrally in regulating correct action. While this is sometimes acknowledged, less often explored are the downstream revisions this requires us to make in our thinking and scientific practice. The usual move is to argue that successful action self-evidently seems to depend on the attainment of true belief, so that the primary functional identity of the brain must be as a knower, a reasoner, and an acquirer of truths. Alternatively, some define cognition exclusively as knowledge-related mental operations, banishing by definition other operations from cognitive science. Either move justifies viewing the mission of cognitive science as primarily to explain the acquisition of knowledge (e.g., Fodor, 2000).

There have been a series of negative consequences for cognitive science that stem from its primary emphasis on knowledge acquisition. First, it assumes that at computational and neural levels, procedures for knowing are functionally separable from procedures for action regulation, and so can be successfully conceptualized and studied independently. We think that motivation, for the reasons discussed, shows that this is not the case. Second, it reduces the scope of cognitive science to a far smaller jurisdiction than what humans (and so human brains)

---

9. This project would require a book-length treatment, and in this chapter we can only offer a few remarks on the way to discussing motivational unlearnability. We do wish to warn the reader of our occasional departures from common accounts of truth, belief, reference, and representation; for further discussion, see, e.g., Cosmides and Tooby (1987, 2000a); Tooby and Cosmides (1992a).
10. Fodor (2000) dismisses this view because of its affinities with pragmatism. Pragmatism founders on the vagueness of its foundational standard: what *works*. In contrast, the engineering perspective of evolutionary functionalism is based on a very precise, formalizable concept: ancestrally, a systematic enhancement of successful design propagation.

actually do. From an evolutionary control theory perspective, there is not just a cognitive science of such things as language, intuitive physics, and number, but a cognitive science of parenting, eating, kinship, friendship, alliance, groups, mating, status, fighting, tools, minds, foraging, natural history, and scores of other ancient realms of human action. Third, it diverts cognitive scientists away from studying conceptual structure, motivation, and action as a single integrated system (which it seems likely to be), with motivation, in particular, in cognitive eclipse. Fourth, it ignores the many causal pathways whereby our evolved architecture should have been designed to manufacture, store, communicate, and act on the basis of representations that would not qualify as a rational architecture's efficient attempt at constructing true beliefs.[11] But the most intriguing reason to consider the implications of the brain as a control system is that it might give us better insight into what the phenomenon of knowledge is (i.e., insight into its ontology and engineering), as well as into the ontology of truth, belief, and representation.

7 Knowledge Is the Product of Evolutionarily Valid Inference and Came into Existence in Order to Serve as Potential Parameters for Biologically Successful Behavioral Regulation

From an evolutionary-functional perspective, knowledge is the total set of regulatory discriminations in the organism that allow its actions to be generated and adjusted so that they mesh successfully with the potentially variable features of its world. Of course, there are regulatory units in the genetic systems of bacteria that bind environmental factors (such as the lac operon) that qualify as embodying knowledge in this sense. However counterintuitive this engineering definition might initially seem to some, it becomes less so as regulatory problems get more complex and evolved regulatory systems get more sophisticated. As this happens, at least some sets of regulatory discriminations resemble more and more strongly our modern, intuitive conception of what knowledge ought to look like.

---

11. There are many evolutionary-functional reasons why "the fixation of true belief" is an inaccurate description of the goals or design criteria of the cognitive system, of which the following is a partial list. The first is discussed in the text: that values play an inextricable role in effectively setting truth criteria in systems engineered to take action that is designed to be successful (Neyman & Pearson, 1928, 1933). Leaving aside the necessary coparticipation of value in the definition of truth (discussed in the text), the existence of conflicts of interest in social life constitutes the source of many other deviations from truth-seeking as an engineered goal of all cognitive mechanisms. The system may be required to reason about value, and there is no truth of the matter for valuation. Individuals may adopt beliefs (e.g., God is three in one; Darwinism is irrelevant) because they socially coordinate them with others. The recomputation required to adopt the true belief may be too costly, at least for a period of time, so that temporary denial (as in grief) may be functional. The introduction of true information may be too disruptive to successful functioning, as when you choose not to look down when climbing a cliff face. To the extent a data store is computed for communication to others rather than to be acted on by oneself, then the optimal impact on others will be the criterion and not truth-value. The attribution of fault or blame to social rivals illustrates one of the many situations in which individuals may develop, disseminate, and "believe"—act as if—something is true that they have grounds for knowing is false.

In particular, many circuits for making discriminations in the service of action control will be indices that change in coordination with states of the external world. For example, one could imagine a binary neural register that is set to zero at night and one during the day, a register that evolved to regulate a single activity, such as sleep. Taken together, the parameter value of the index, and its location in the circuit structure, can for engineering purposes be called a representation, and its value constitutes a belief. From an engineering perspective, it is a true belief when it is successfully tracking the discriminated conditions that it evolved to parameterize. Representations are settings in a computational architecture designed to regulate behavior; they derive their existence and meaning from the causal properties of the architectures they inhabit. On this view, belief, truth, representation, and reference have a mechanism-relative, mechanism-anchored, and evolutionary function-specific character that delivers us from many of the puzzles that emerge when we attempt to make their character transcend mechanism (Cosmides & Tooby, 2000a; Tooby & Cosmides, 1992b; for kindred views see German & Leslie, 2000).[12] An indefinitely rich aspect of the external world such as night and day can be indexed to operation-defined parameters whose design is shaped to regulate a particular set of activities such as sleep or fear of leaving the concealment of one's home base. Operations on a belief do not have to be truth-preserving with respect to a superset of logical operations that might conjoin it with the total set of other beliefs in the system (assuming they were represented in such a way as to even make that possible). They only need to be success promoting within the scope of operations that regulate biologically significant behavior. What sets the definition this register uses for day and night are the engineering criteria built into its input and decision-making circuitry—that is, the circuitry that flips the register from one state to the other. These criteria will be set over evolutionary time by the relative fitness consequences of the various design variants made available by mutation. (I.e., it will hill-climb toward the variant that is "best" in the sense of producing the highest long-term fitness.) The register that results can be thought of as a "concept" of day versus night. The "meaning" of this concept can be explicated functionally and computationally in terms of the states of the world it evolved to track and, especially, the computational systems it evolved to interact with and regulate. Using this approach, one can isolate different

---

12. For some (but not for us), some kind of indexing of what a given representation is "about" (i.e., refers to or tracks) in the external world is diagnostic of representation. For a discussion of some of the functions of tags or representations about representations (metarepresentation), see Cosmides and Tooby (2000a) and Leslie (1987). The evolution of a capacity to tag some representations with respect to a system of common reference serves at least one obvious function: it allows different kinds of information about cognitively defined environmental entities to be brought together as likely to be inferentially relevant to each other. In our view, the idea of reference is coherent not because it involves a relationship between a representation and the world but because it involves the coordination between at least two systems of representation (such as a perceptual parsing and predicted consequences of action made on the basis of that parsing), embedded in a system (or communicating community of systems) that can take action on the basis of these representations in a way that can be evaluated using some criterion of success (such as biological success).

components of meaning in an engineering sense. Loosely speaking, reference constitutes the states of the world that the register evolved to track. Another component of meaning is the set of input criteria that sets the value of the register. A third component of meaning is the set of action-regulating procedures that take as input the representation in the register. And a fourth component of meaning—what might be called *sense*—has to do with the set of inferences that can be made using the content of the register as an input.

Among more sophisticated organisms, it will usually be the case that action must be regulated by a space of discriminations that cannot be parameterized by mapping sensory inputs directly. Better kinds of actions could be orchestrated if unobservable states of the world could be determined through computation. What is this predator intending (Barrett, 2005; Barrett et al., under review)? What is the degree of genetic relatedness between this person and me (Lieberman et al., 2003, in press, under review)? Which coalition is this person likely to ally with (Kurzban et al., 2001)? Because the world repeatedly faced by members of a species over evolutionary time has a rich, stable, recurrent causal and statistical structure (the environment of evolutionary adaptedness), this problem can be evolutionarily solved by an additional process: *evolutionarily valid inference*. By inference, we mean the application of any neurocomputational procedure that uses some registers to set the value of other registers. We in no way mean to limit the structure of these procedures to the set normatively recognized in logic, statistical inference, and decision theory. Indeed, we think traditional inferential methods, to the extent they may be neurally realized within some representational systems, constitute only a small subset of the procedures embodied in the mind. Most inferential procedures will be what we have called *ecologically rational*—that is, they improve the performance of the animal because the structure of the inferential procedure reflects some enduring relationships in the structure of the world (Cosmides & Tooby, 1996; Gigerenzer et al., 1999; Shepard, 1984, 1987; Tooby & Cosmides, 1992b). Logically or mathematically valid inferences are (within some representational systems) a small subset of evolutionarily valid inferences. An evolutionarily valid inference rule is any rule whose application produces (1) on average for a given species over its recent evolution, (2) within its proper cognitive domain, (3) a change in its set of computational parameters, so (4) the range of potential actions of the organism is adjusted, so that (5) they mesh with the potentially variable features of its world, with (6) greater biological success.

For example, among our mammalian ancestors, the female who nursed an infant was almost always its mother. This evolutionarily reliable statistical relationship meant that infant caretaking predicted genetic relatedness between mother and offspring, as well as relatedness among offspring cared for by the same mother. Another relatedness-predicting relationship ancestrally existed between the length of subadult coassociation and relatedness. Evidence supports the prediction that these enduring relationships in the world selected for a set of ecologically rational procedures specialized for inferring genetic relatedness. These evolved procedures take observations about the duration of coresidence and the existence of common caretaking as input, and transform them to set the values of a system of regulatory variables that evolved to track genetic relatedness between individuals (Lieberman et al., 2003, in press, under review). This neurocomputational system of regulatory variables was selected for because these variables are used to (1) upregulate or downregulate tradeoffs between one's own welfare and that of kin, and (2) generate appropriate intensities of aversion to sex with genetic relatives (incest avoidance). We believe that these representations also influence (to some extent) the formation of explicit, linguistically accessible representations of kinship, but are not isomorphic with them. They are simultaneously and inseparably motivational and cognitive. They drive inferentially constructed plans. At least with respect to these two action systems (and perhaps to others), these regulatory variables represent "true" genetic relatedness. However, because the scope and fitness consequences for helping and for incest avoidance are different, the brain may represent two different (but related) values for genetic relatedness between a given pair of individuals. Each is "true" (functionally well calibrated), with respect to the action-regulatory system it inhabits, but they may be different. Females may, for example, represent individuals as more highly related for purposes of incest avoidance than as objects of altruism, because the asymmetric consequences of a miss versus a false alarm are different for incest avoidance and kin assistance.

Evolutionarily valid inferential procedures can exploit the fact that some relationships among elements of the ancestral world remained statistically true during the species' evolution. This means that the determination of the state of some variables allowed the probabilistic inference of the state of other variables, using procedures whose principles of transformation reflect these enduring relationships (i.e., if i nursed j, then set the register tracking the genetic degree of relatedness between individuals i and j to .499). These relationships need not be sensorily detectable or logically warranted, because architectures that build in the best Kantian a priori assumptions about unobservable relationships (embodied in procedures, data formats, etc.) outcompete others that lack such assumptions (Tooby & Cosmides, 1992a, 1992b). Moreover, we expect that there are many internal systems of representation (involving what Fodor would call central processes) that are not set simply or primarily by the immediate mapping of perceptual systems. They consist of libraries of operations and networks of representations linked by tags. These tags identify the inferential procedures that can operate on them. There are also tags to identify which evaluation procedures, decision-making procedures, differential memory operations, and so on can operate on them. These include a very rich set of evolved systems of conceptual structure, including many specialized systems for the construction of representations of persons, predators (Barrett et al., under review), minds (Baron-Cohen, 1995; Leslie, 1987), coalitions (Kurzban et al., 2001; Price et al., 2002), social interactions (Cosmides & Tooby, 1989, 1992, 2005), kinship (Lieberman et al., 2003, in press, under review), artifacts (Boyer, 2001; German & Barrett, in press; German & Johnson, 2002), and many other classes of entities. If an evolved action-regulation system regularly requires distinctions of a certain kind (cheater, predator, coalition member, gender, manipulable object, own child, mother), then specialized systems of representation tagging may evolve to provide these distinctions or create an evolved cognitive ontology (Boyer, 2001; Cosmides & Tooby, 1989, 1992; Kurzban et al., 2001). Indeed, valuation processes may play a significant role in defining certain ontological domains (such as food, dangers, and exchanges) and the ontological affordances that invite domain-specific processes.

Selection should favor the evolution of ecologically rational procedures, concepts, and concept-generating systems on the basis of (1) how inferentially productive they are; (2) the degree to which they support informative distinctions in evolutionarily important valuation processes; (3) how easy it is to obtain relevant perceptual inputs (if these are required or useful); (4) how relevant they are to regulating important, evolutionarily recurrent activities for the organism; and (5) how naturally they can be derived from other reliably developing computational elements of the architecture. The aggregate effect of these functional criteria on shaping our cognitive architectures will make them look very different from what one would expect if knowledge acquisition alone were the criterion of functional performance. The developing picture is one of an evolutionary micro-Kantianism that shapes experience in far more detailed ways than giving form to space, time, and causality. These ecologically rational procedures pour experience into evolved, and often motivationally significant, categories such as *mother, predator, male, my child, coalition, domestic sharing unit, meat*, and so on. All together, these evolved procedures (and evolved metasystems for deriving procedures) constitute a very productive system for massively unpacking the fragmentary samples of perceptual and other inputs into a strongly structured set of representations of the world, and of the values of the actions that can be taken in it.[13]

8 The Computation of Truth Is Inextricably Bound to the Evolved and Computed Standards of Valuation Expressed in Our Evolved Architecture

The population of modern humans embodies neurocomputational architectures that acquired their engineering compromises from an immense series of encounters

---

13. There are many sources of input—initial parameter setting—in addition to sense data. For one thing, any somatic developmental interaction with the world could be used by natural selection to build a parameter setting system, and not just the senses as traditionally conceived. The organism may, in its developmental rules, be designed to assemble different computational settings on the basis of different nutrient flows, chemical exposures, endocrine levels, uterine environments, and so on—factors that provide another kind of grounding for inference aside from sense data. For example, a large number of regulatory parameter settings are unpacked from being on one of the two developmental pathways orchestrated by sex determination (i.e., organisms are often designed to think and choose differently depending on whether they are males or females). Moreover, the genetic material can itself receive signals when in the parent that are transmitted to the offspring and unpacked in the form of different developmental trajectories. This can happen, for example, through the setting and transmission of methylation patterns, piggy-backed on the outside of unchanged, inherited DNA sequences (Haig, 2002; Tooby et al., 2003). Third, there is nothing that would rule out knowledge from being inferentially developed from built-in premises and rules for their elaboration, whether or not at some processing stage it is admixed with inputs from the senses. Fourth, our species-typical endowment of evolutionarily valid inference procedures (which include the motivational assignment systems discussed earlier) can itself be viewed as an important kind of "input"—the introduction of content into our minds from the reliable development of the inherited design rather than from the senses.

that differentially preserved some design features and discarded others. This differential preservation was based on the degree to which they successfully solved recurrent ancestral adaptive problems in real, consequential environments. Our ancestors not only held beliefs (to use the folk concept) but acted on them, and the relative propagative success of those actions built some procedures for belief acquisition at the expense of others. Since the pioneering work of Neyman and Pearson (1928, 1933), it has been clear that for systems designed to realize values through making decisions that lead to actions, the optimal criteria for truth determination sensitively depend on the values the system is designed to realize (Tooby & Cosmides, 1990, 1992a).

Signal detection theory with its hits, misses, false alarms, and correct rejections, for example, is a well-known and straightforward application of Neyman-Pearsonian decision theory, in which the values of the four outcomes must be computed to set the threshold criterion for when to decide the signal has been detected. Since representational systems evolved as input parameters into action systems, the need to integrate value weighting into "truth" criteria would necessarily have ramified through every aspect of our cognitive architecture. Consider a simple dichotomous case (Tooby & Cosmides, 1990a): the shortest path to walk to a destination would take a hominid under the overhanging branches of a tree. There is either a leopard in the tree or there is no leopard in the tree. There are different payoffs to the four possible outcomes defined by act and state of the world: the hominid avoids walking under the tree, and there was a leopard in the tree (hit); the hominid avoids walking under the tree, and there was no leopard in the tree (a false alarm); the hominid walks under the tree, and there is no leopard in the tree (a correct rejection); and the hominid walks under the tree, and there is a leopard in the tree (a fatal miss). The cost of a leopard attack is large (death); the benefit of walking in a straight line is a few calories saved. The best strategy for the choice system (its truth setting for the purpose of action regulation) is to act as if the leopard is in the tree, even if in 999 times out of 1,000 it is not. On the other hand, if a group of hominids were hunting a leopard, they might not even bother to look in an unpromising tree that, under identical information conditions but with different purposes, each individually would have avoided for possibly harboring a leopard. Similar shifts in truth criteria can be expected in making judgments about whether a predator is dead or merely asleep, for example (Barrett & Behne, in press).

The coevolutionary dependence of truth standards on value applies to every component of our evolved neurocomputational architecture. The design of every system should have been impacted by this relationship. Because knowledge acquisition systems evolved to form the basis of action, the kinds of actions the system has evolved to engage in will build in different procedures for establishing truth criteria for different kinds of functions. This kind of Neyman-Pearsonian value shift is why genetic relatedness representation may effectively fractionate in its downstream passage to the incest avoidance system and to the kin-assistance system. Wherever there has been an evolutionarily recurrent relationship between a kind of knowledge to be acquired and the kinds of uses to which it is put, there is the possibility that natural selection has introduced procedures for calibrating differentiated sets of truth criteria. What the criteria for truth ought to be for an engineered cognitive system cannot be determined in the absence of value criteria. Even logical operations, which are supposed to be perfectly truth-preserving, cannot be trusted to give true conclusions in engineered systems, because the correspondence between the representations in the architecture and the conditions in the world they supposedly index cannot be made operationally perfect. There is always some possibility that a valid transformation will produce a conclusion outside of the scope within which the representational system evolved to work. Our architectures may be designed to disregard such logically valid conclusions, when they can be detected.

In the area of knowledge acquisition, value may play a more significant role than simply triggering occasions and activities within which knowledge is acquired. The motivational architecture may be constitutive of the organization and acquisition of children's knowledge, shaping or creating principles of knowledge acquisition. To take one out of many possible examples, valuation procedures may play an important role in setting the boundaries of concepts, shifting to some extent our understanding of prototypicality effects. To begin with the familiar, the perceived world "is not an unstructured total set of equiprobable co-occurring attributes" (Rosch, 1978, p. 29); it has a correlational structure. Attributes come in clusters: objects that share many properties—prototypical items—are information rich clusters of attributes. For prototypic items, knowing one property allows one to predict the presence of many other properties. Rosch argued that our cognitive architecture is designed to detect the correlational structure in the perceived world and produce categories that mirror it: categories with a family resemblance structure. Prototypes are "just those members of a category that most reflect the redundancy structure of the category as a whole" (p. 37). This is one clear area where domain-general learning procedures can produce a large and valuable set of data structures (although domain-specific skeletal organizing principles play at least as big a role in conceptual structure [Gelman, 1990]). Roschian prototype effects have been one experimentally validated theory for explaining perplexities that arise from considering instances where classical definitions of concepts conflict with people's intuitions: for example, is the pope a bachelor? Was Jesus? Is a eunuch? An infant boy? A homosexual male? However, whereas correlated attributes may explain some aspects of the rapidly fading concept of bachelor, it is possible that conceptual projections of valuation procedures are another. That is, concepts may be generated, and their properties partially determined, by a calculus of the value their constituent criteria play in predicting the value of the instance for regulating behavior. If a major, socially shared function of the concept of *bachelor* is to make inferences about potential marriage partners, then other criteria contributing to this function may be imported into the concept in addition to the most probabilistically informative threshold tests organizing the concept (being male and unmarried). These may also lead to patterns of exclusion or peripheralization of instances with low value for the contemplated activity (the pope, a child, etc.). This is a different explanation for prototypicality judgments from those that emphasize instances that "most reflect the redundancy structure of the category as a whole." At least in Austen's world of *Pride and Prejudice*, more attractive men and more prosperous men would be judged more prototypic, even though their attributes are rarer. Their use in choice and goal-state setting would explain the tendency of prototypic representations of instances to incorporate aspects of the ideal (based on valuation) rather than simply correlated attributes (based on frequencies). In addition, value criteria should play a role in defining the boundaries of the category over which correlations of attributes are computed. For example, there is no logical reason why early fruiting bodies should not count as fruit, but they are so distant from being edible that they are not considered instances that help to define the category. An experimental program to test this approach would see whether the internal structure of concepts reflected not only correlated attributes but also value criteria rendering them more or less valuable for the actions the category supports. Both ought to be present in stabilizing the meaning and boundaries of categories. Frequency-defined attributes are inferentially powerful; value-diagnostic attributes are motivationally informative. A typical prediction would be that (for example, in the case of fruit) prototype effects would only be partially accounted for by statistical frequencies of attributes, with prototypes shifted in the direction of increasing value. Rotten, unripe, or otherwise inedible fruit would not be considered central to the category even when their ecological frequency is greater (as it usually is). Indeed, the concept of *fruit* may be something like: any fruiting body whose appearance warrants further investigation as potentially edible enough in the near future to be worth harvesting.

9 Conclusion

We are not making any claims about information encapsulation. We are not claiming that all elements of each computational adaptation evolved from "the beginning" for the functions they presently serve. We are not claiming that, for example, all of the functional elements used for the operation of the snake avoidance motivational adaptation are unique to the snake avoidance system. We are not claiming that there are no general mechanisms for motivation. We are not claiming that the environment plays no role in the development of these systems, or that evolved systems operate the same way regardless of developmental environment. We do think that each adaptation is a collection of elements many of which are shared in different configurations among adaptations, some of them quite broadly. The specialization of an adaptation for a function does not lie in the specialization of all parts to its function. The specialization lies in the way the particular interrelationship of the parts is coordinated to solve the specialized adaptive problem with particular efficiency. This may require the evolved introduction of only a single new element into the evolved developmental programs—a minimal sufficient specification, for example, that can individuate an additional proper object of a certain class of motivations or inferences.

We are claiming that (1) an initial, irreducible set of category-recognizing, value-assigning, and value-responsive procedures must be built into our species-typical set of developmental programs; that (2) every evolved motivational system must have evolved conceptual machinery to express its necessary set of evaluative distinctions (e.g., in the case of sexual attraction, tags that distinguish the representational identities of adult from child, male from female, human from nonhuman, healthy from unhealthy); that (3) such evolved conceptual elements are numerous; because (4) the rules required for regulating action and assigning value will necessarily be different for each adaptive problem domain in which the criteria of biological success are functionally incompatible (e.g., you necessarily pick the best available mate by different criteria from those for picking the best food, the safest refuge, or the neediest child); that (5) many of these evolved elements will be by their nature functionally specialized, content sensitive, domain specific, and content generative; and that (6) the architecture operates jointly on values and representations of states of affairs within a given computational system, so that knowledge-representing cognitive processes often cannot be intelligibly separated from motivational processes. More generally, the claim is that successful performance on value-related adaptive problems poses an insurmountable *ought from is* learnability barrier that cannot be crossed, even in principle, by content-independent learning architectures, whatever their implementation. Given data about which valuation problems humans solve, this is a method not only for demonstrating the general case for innate ideas but also for identifying specific sets of such computational elements.

19

JOSHUA GREENE

Cognitive Neuroscience and the Structure of the Moral Mind

If you visit www.dictionary.com online and type in the word "innate," this is what you'll get:

adj
1. Possessed at birth; inborn.
2. Possessed as an essential characteristic; inherent.
3. Of or produced by the mind rather than learned through experience: *an innate knowledge of right and wrong.*

Of all the things in the world one might use to illustrate the concept of innateness, this dictionary offers *moral knowledge*. I find this amusing—the idea that someone who is not exactly sure what "innate" means would benefit from knowing that one of the most complex and least understood of human capacities could plausibly be described as "innate." And yet this choice, I suspect, is no accident. Our capacity for moral judgment, perhaps more than anything else, strikes people as both *within us* and *external to us*, as essentially human and at the same time possessing a mysterious external authority, like the voice of God or Nature calling us at once from within and beyond. But however obvious the reality of an innate capacity for moral judgment may be to theologians, lexicographers, and the like, it is not at all obvious from a scientific point of view, or even clear what such a capacity would amount to.

Any investigation into the possibility of an innate capacity for moral judgment must begin with what is known about moral psychology. Much of what we know comes from the developmental tradition, beginning with the work of Piaget (Piaget, 1965) and Kohlberg (Kohlberg, 1969). Some of the most compelling work on moral psychology has come from studies of the social behavior of our nearest living relatives, especially the great apes (de Waal, 1996; Flack & de Waal, 2000). Such studies

Thanks to Andrea Heberlein for many helpful suggestions.

reveal what Flack and de Waal call the "building blocks" of human morality. Likewise, anthropologists (Shweder et al., 1997), evolutionary psychologists (Cosmides, 1989; Wright, 1994), and evolutionary game theorists (Axelrod, 1984; Sober & Wilson, 1998) have made other important contributions. Perhaps the most striking work of all has come from "candid camera"–style studies from within the social psychological tradition that dramatically illustrate the fragility and capriciousness of human morality (Milgram, 1974; Ross & Nisbett, 1991). All of these disciplines, however, treat the mind as a "black box," the operations of which are to be inferred from observable behavior. In contrast, the emerging discipline of cognitive neuroscience aims to go a level deeper, to open the mind's black box and thus understand its operations in physical terms. The aim of this chapter is to discuss neurocognitive work relevant to moral psychology and the proposition that innate factors make important contributions to moral judgment.

1   Lesion Data

Imagine the following scenario. A woman is brought to the emergency room after sustaining a severe blow to the head. At first, and much to her doctors' surprise, her neurological function appears to be completely normal. And for the most part it is, but it soon becomes clear that she has acquired a bizarre disability. As a result of her accident, this woman can no longer play basketball. Her tennis game is still top-notch, as is her golf swing, and so on. Only her basketball game has been compromised. Could such an accident really happen? Almost certainly not. The way the brain is organized, it is virtually impossible that something like a blow to the head could selectively destroy one's ability to play basketball and nothing else. This is because the neural machinery required to play basketball isn't sitting in one place, like a car's battery (Casebeer & Churchland, 2003). Instead, this machinery is distributed throughout the brain, and its various components are used in the performance of any number of other tasks.

While no one claims to have seen a case of acquired "abasketballia," there have been cases in which brain damage has appeared to rob individuals of their moral sensibilities in a strikingly selective way. By far the most celebrated of such cases is that of Phineas Gage (Damasio, 1994), a nineteenth-century railroad foreman who worked in Vermont. One fateful day, an accidental explosion sent a tamping iron through Gage's cheek and out the top of his head, destroying much of his medial prefrontal cortex. Gage not only survived the accident; at the time he appeared to have emerged with all of his mental capacities intact. After a two-month recuperation period Gage, was pronounced cured, but it was soon apparent that he was damaged. Before the accident, he was admired by his colleagues for his industriousness and good character. After the accident, he became lawless. He wandered around, making trouble wherever he went, unable to hold down a steady job due to his antisocial behavior. For a long time no one understood why Gage's lesion had the profound but remarkably selective effect that it had.

More recent cases of patients with similar lesions have shed light on Gage's injury. Damasio and colleagues (Damasio, 1994) report on a patient named "Elliot" who suffered a brain tumor in roughly the same region that was destroyed in Gage.

Like Gage, Elliot has maintained his ability to speak and reason about topics such as politics and economics. He scores above average on standard intelligence tests, including some designed to detect frontal lobe damage, and responds normally to standard tests of personality. However, his behavior, like Gage's, is not unaffected by his condition. While Elliot did not develop antisocial tendencies to the extent that Gage did, he, too, exhibits certain peculiar deficits, particularly in the social domain. A simple laboratory probe has helped reveal the subtle but dramatic nature of Elliot's deficits. When shown pictures of gory accidents or people about to drown in floods, Elliot reports having no emotional response but comments that he knows that he used to have strong emotional responses to such things. Intrigued by these reports, Damasio and colleagues employed a series of tests designed to assess the effects of Elliot's damage on his decision-making skills. They asked him, for example, whether or not he would steal if he needed money and to explain why or why not. His answers were like those of other people, citing the usual reasons for why one shouldn't commit such crimes. Saver and Damasio followed up this test with a series of five tests of moral/social judgment (Saver & Damasio, 1991). As before, Elliot performed normally or above average in each case. It became clear that Elliot's explicit knowledge of social and moral conventions was as good or better than most people's, and yet his personal and professional life, like Gage's, deteriorated rapidly as a result of his condition. His inability to focus and make decisions cost him his job, and he eventually lost his savings in a series of misguided business ventures. His marriage ended in divorce. Elliot subsequently married a woman of whom his friends and family disapproved, and that marriage quickly ended in divorce as well. Amazingly, Elliot remained unruffled by these events. Damasio attributes Elliot's real-life failures not to his inability to reason but to his inability to integrate emotional responses into his practical judgments. "To know, but not to feel," says Damasio, is the essence of his predicament (Damasio, 1994).

In a study of Elliot and four other patients with similar damage and deficits, Damasio and his colleagues observed a consistent failure to exhibit normal electrodermal responses (a standard indication of emotional arousal) when these patients were presented with socially significant stimuli, though they responded normally to nonsocial, emotionally arousing stimuli (Damasio et al., 1990). A more recent study of patients like Elliot used the "Iowa gambling task" to study their decision-making skills (Bechara et al., 1996). In performing this task, patients like Elliot tend to make unwise, risky choices and fail to have normal electrodermal responses in anticipation to making those poor choices, suggesting, as predicted, that their failure to perform well in the gambling task is related to their emotional deficits. They can't *feel* their way through the problem.

While the subjects in the foregoing studies exhibit "sociopathic behavior" as a result of their injuries, they are not "psychopaths." Most often they themselves, rather than others, are the victims of their poor decision-making. However, a more recent study (Anderson et al., 1999) of two subjects whose ventral, medial, and polar prefrontal cortices were damaged at an early age (3 months and 15 months) reveals a pattern of behavior that is characteristically psychopathic: lying, stealing, violence, and lack of remorse after committing such violations. These developmental patients, unlike Elliot and the like, exhibit more flagrantly antisocial behavior, presumably because they did not have the advantage of a lifetime of normal social experience involving normal emotional responses. Both patients perform fairly well on IQ tests and other standard cognitive measures and perform poorly on the Iowa gambling task, but, unlike adult-onset patients, their knowledge of social/moral norms is deficient. Their moral reasoning appears to be, in the terminology of Kohlberg, "preconventional," conducted from an egocentric perspective in which the purpose is to avoid punishment. Other tests show that they have a limited understanding of the social and emotional implications of decisions and fail to identify primary issues and generate appropriate responses to hypothetical social situations. Grattan and Eslinger (1992) report similar results concerning a different developmental-frontal patient. Thus, it appears that the brain regions that are compromised in these patients include structures that are crucial not only for online decision-making but also for the acquisition of social knowledge and dispositions toward normal social behavior.

What can we learn from these damaged individuals? In Gage—the legend, if not the actual patient—we see a striking dissociation between "cognitive"[1] abilities and moral sensibilities. Gage, once an esteemed man of character, is transformed by his accident into a scoundrel, with little to no observable damage to his "intellectual" faculties. A similar story emerges from Elliot's normal performance on questionnaire-type assays of his social/moral decision-making. Intellectually, or "cognitively," Elliot knows the right answers, but his real-life social/moral decision-making is lacking. From this pattern of results, one might conclude that Gage, Elliot, and the like have suffered selective blows to their "morality centers." Other results, however, complicate this neat picture. Elliot and similar patients appear to have emotional deficits that are somewhat more general and that adversely affect their decision-making in nonsocial contexts as well as social ones (e.g., on the gambling task). And to further complicate matters, the developmental patients studied by Anderson and colleagues appear to have some "cognitive" deficits, although these deficits are closely related to social decision-making. Thus, what we observe in these patients is something less than selective damage to these individuals' moral judgment abilities but something more than a general deficit in "reasoning" or "intelligence" or "judgment." In other words, these data suggest that there are dissociable cognitive systems that contribute asymmetrically to moral judgment but give us little reason to believe that there is a discrete faculty for moral judgment or a "morality module."[2] Moreover, these data suggest that there is an important dissociation between affective and "cognitive" contributions to

---

1. The term "cognitive" has two uses. In some contexts, "cognitive" refers to information processing in a general. In other contexts, "cognitive" refers to a more narrow range of processes that contrast with affective or emotional processes (Greene et al., 2004). Here I use the term "cognitive" with quotation marks to indicate the second meaning.
2. There is a sizable literature reporting on patients with morally aberrant behavior resulting from frontal damage, and the cases discussed earlier are not necessarily representative (Grafman et al., 1996). I have chosen to focus on these cases because they involve what I take to be the most interesting examples of dissociations between moral and other capacities.

social/moral decision-making and that the importance of the affective contributions has been underestimated by those who think of moral judgment primarily as a reasoning process (Haidt, 2001).

2 Antisocial Behavior

The foregoing studies concern patients whose social behavior has been compromised by observable and relatively discrete brain lesions. There are, however, many cases of individuals who lack macroscopic brain damage and who exhibit pathological social behavior. These people fall into two categories: people with antisocial personality disorder (APD) and the subset of these individuals known as psychopaths. Antisocial personality disorder is a catchall label for whatever it is that causes some people to habitually violate our more serious social norms, typically those that are codified in our legal system (DSM IV, 1994). Psychopaths not only engage in antisocial behavior but exhibit a pathological degree of callousness, lack of empathy or emotional depth, and lack of genuine remorse for their antisocial actions (Hare, 1991). In more intuitive terms, the difference between APD and psychopathy is something like the difference between a hotheaded barroom brawler and a cold-blooded killer.

Psychopaths appear to be special in a number of ways (Blair, 2001). First, while the behavioral traits that are used to diagnose APD correlate with IQ and socioeconomic status, the traits that are distinctive of psychopaths do not (Hare et al., 1991). Moreover, the behaviors associated with APD tend to decline with age, while the psychopath's distinctive social-emotional dysfunction holds steady (Harpur & Hare, 1994). The roots of psychopathic violence in psychopaths appear to be different from those of similarly violent nonpsychopaths. In two ways, at least, psychopaths' violence appears to be less contingent on environmental input. First, positive parenting strategies appear to influence the behavior of nonpsychopaths, whereas psychopaths appear to be impervious in this regard (Wootton et al., 1997). Second, and probably not incidentally, the violence of psychopaths is more often instrumental rather than impulsive (Blair, 2001).

Experimental studies of psychopaths reveal further, subtler differences between psychopaths and other individuals with APD. Psychopaths exhibit a lower level of tonic electrodermal activity and show weaker electrodermal responses to emotionally significant stimuli than normal individuals (Hare & Quinn, 1971). A more recent study (Blair et al., 1997) compares the electrodermal responses of psychopaths to a control group of criminals who, like the psychopathic individuals, were serving life sentences for murder or manslaughter. While the psychopaths resembled the other criminals in their responses to threatening stimuli (e.g., an image of a shark's open mouth) and neutral stimuli (e.g., an image of a book), they showed significantly reduced electrodermal responses to distress cues (e.g., an image of a crying child's face) relative to the control criminals, a fact consistent with the observation that psychopathic individuals appear to have a diminished capacity for emotional empathy. An earlier study (Blair, 1995) revealed that psychopaths, unlike ordinary criminals, have an impoverished appreciation of what is known as the "moral"/ "conventional" distinction (Turiel, 1983). Most people believe that some social rules may be modified by authority figures while others may not. For example, if the teacher says that it's okay to speak without raising one's hand ("conventional" violation), then it's okay to do so, but if the teacher says that it's okay to hit people ("moral" violation), then it's still not okay to hit people. Psychopaths seem to lack an intuitive understanding of this moral/conventional distinction, and it has been suggested that they perceive all social rules as mere rules (Blair, 1995). Finally, a recent study suggests that psychopathic murderers, unlike other murders and non-murdering psychopaths, fail to have normal negative associations with violence (Gray et al., 2003).

According to Blair (Blair et al., 1997), "The clinical and empirical picture of a psychopathic individual is of someone who has some form of emotional deficit." This conclusion is bolstered by the results of a recent neuroimaging study (Kiehl et al., 2001) in which psychopaths and control criminals processed emotionally salient words. The posterior cingulate gyrus, a region that exhibits increased activity during a variety of emotion-related tasks (Maddock, 1999), was less active in the psychopathic group than in the control subjects. At the same time, other regions were more active in psychopaths during this task, leading Khiel and colleagues to conclude that the psychopaths were using an alternative cognitive strategy to perform this task.

Thus, so far, a host of signs point to the importance of emotions in moral judgment (Haidt, 2001). In light of this, one might come to the conclusion that a psychopath, with his dearth of morally relevant emotion, is exactly what we're looking for — a human being "with everything — hold the morality." Indeed, Schmitt and colleagues (Schmitt et al., 1999) found that psychopaths performed normally on the Iowa gambling task, suggesting that their emotion-based decision-making deficits are not general but rather related specifically to the social domain. As before, however, the empirical picture is not quite so simple, as psychopaths appear to have other things "held" as well. To begin, two studies, one of adult psychopaths (Mitchell et al., 2002) and one of children with psychopathic tendencies (Blair et al., 2001), found that psychopathic individuals do perform poorly on the Iowa gambling task. (These authors attribute the conflicting results to Schmitt and colleagues' failure to use the original task directions, which emphasize the strategic nature of the task.) Moreover, there are several indications that psychopaths have deficits that extend well beyond their apparently stunted social-emotional responses. They respond abnormally to a number of "dry" cognitive tasks, both in terms of their behavior (Bernstein et al., 2000; Lapierre et al., 1995; Newman et al., 1997) and their electrorencephalographic ("brainwave") responses (Kiehl et al., 1999a; Kiehl et al., 1999b; Kiehl et al., 2000). A common theme among these studies seems to be psychopaths' one-track-mindedness, their inability to inhibit prepotent responses and respond to peripheral cues.

The psychopathy literature sends mixed signals regarding the "impulsivity" of psychopaths. Psychopathic violence has been described as "instrumental" rather than "reactive" (Blair, 2001). At the same time, however, some of the aforementioned evidence suggests that psychopaths have a hard time inhibiting disadvantageous behavior, even during the performance of "dry" cognitive tasks. Compared to some antisocial individuals, psychopaths are "cool and collected," but a closer examination reveals that psychopaths have a kind of impulsivity, or one-track-mindedness, that subtly distinguishes them from normal individuals. The results of a neuroimaging study of "predatory" versus "affective" murderers (Raine et al., 1998) gestures toward a synthesis. Raine and colleagues argue that excessive subcortical activity in the right hemisphere leads to violent impulses but that "predatory" murderers, who, unlike "affective" murderers, exhibit normal levels of prefrontal activity, are better able to control these impulses. (In a more recent study, it was found that a sample of individuals diagnosed with APD—some of whom, however, may have been psychopaths—tended on average to have decreased prefrontal gray matter.) However, it's not clear how to reconcile the claim that "predatory" and "affective" murderers act on the same underlying impulses with the claim that psychopathic violence is "instrumental" rather than "impulsive."

In sum, psychopaths are not nature's controlled experiment with amorality. Psychopathy is a complicated syndrome that has subtle and not-so-subtle effects on a wide range of behaviors, including many behaviors that, superficially at least, have nothing to do with morality. At the same time, however, psychopathy appears to be a fairly specific syndrome. Psychopaths are not just people who are unusually antisocial. Using the proper methods, psychopaths are clearly distinguishable from others whose behavior is comparably antisocial, suggesting that the immoral behavior associated with psychopathy stems from the malformation of specific cognitive structures that make important contributions to moral judgment. Moreover, these structures seem to be rather "deep," in the sense that they are not well defined by the concepts of ordinary experience and, more to the point, ordinary learning. Psychopaths do not appear to be people who have, through some unusual set of experiences, acquired unusual moral beliefs or values. Rather, they appear to have an abnormal but stereotyped cognitive structure that affects a wide range of behaviors, from their willingness to kill to their inability to recall where on a screen a given word has appeared (Bernstein et al., 2000).

3 Neuroimaging Studies of Moral Judgment and Decision-Making

Consider the following moral dilemma (the *trolley* dilemma; Foot, 1978; Thomson, 1986). A runaway trolley is headed for five people who will be killed if it proceeds on its present course. The only way to save these people is to hit a switch that will turn the trolley onto an alternate set of tracks where it will run over and kill one person instead of five. Is it okay to turn the trolley in order to save five people at the expense of one? Most people I've tested say that it is, and they tend to do so in a matter of seconds (Greene et al., 2001).

Now consider a slightly different dilemma (the *footbridge* dilemma; Thomson, 1986). A runaway trolley threatens to kill five people as before, but this time you are standing next to a large stranger on a footbridge spanning the tracks, in between the oncoming trolley and the five people. The only way to save the five people is to push this stranger off the bridge and onto the tracks below. He will die as a result, but his body will stop the trolley from reaching the others. Is it okay to save the five people by pushing this stranger to his death? Most people I've tested say that it's not, and, once again, they do so rather quickly.

These dilemmas were devised as part of a puzzle for moral philosophers (Foot, 1978; Thomson, 1986) the aim of which is to explain why it's okay to sacrifice one life to save five in the first case but not in the second case. Solving this puzzle has proven very difficult. While many attempts to provide a consistent, principled justification for these two intuitions have been made, the justifications offered are not at all obvious and are generally problematic. The fact that these intuitions are not easily justified gives rise to second puzzle, this time for moral psychologists: How do people know (or "know") to say yes to the trolley dilemma and no to the footbridge dilemma if there is no obvious, principled justification for doing so? If these conclusions aren't reached on the basis of some readily accessible moral principle, they must be made on the basis of some kind of intuition. But where do these intuitions come from?

To try to answer this question, my colleagues and I conducted an experiment in which subjects responded to these and other moral dilemmas while having their brains scanned (Greene et al., 2001). We hypothesized that the thought of pushing someone to his death with one's bare hands is more emotionally salient than the thought of bringing about similar consequences by hitting a switch. More generally, we supposed that moral violations of an "up close and personal" nature, as in the footbridge case, are more emotionally salient than moral violations that are more impersonal, as in the trolley case, and that this difference in emotional response explains why people respond so differently to these two cases.

The rationale for this hypothesis is evolutionary. It is very likely that we humans have inherited many of our social instincts from our primate ancestors, among them instincts that rein in the tendencies of individuals to harm one another (de Waal, 1996; Flack & de Waal, 2000). These instincts are emotional, triggered by behaviors and other elicitors that were present in our ancestral environment. This environment did not include opportunities to harm other individuals using complicated, remote-acting machinery, but it did include opportunities to harm other individuals by pushing them into harm's way (e.g., off a cliff or into a river). Thus, one might suppose that the sorts of basic, interpersonal violence that threatened our ancestors back then will "push our buttons" today in a way that peculiarly modern harms do not.

With all of this in mind, we operationalized the "personal"/"impersonal" distinction as follows. A moral violation is personal if it is (1) likely to cause serious bodily harm (2) to a particular person (3) in such a way that the harm does not result from the deflection of an existing threat onto a different party. (See the "no new threat principle"; Thomson, 1986). A moral violation is impersonal if it fails to meet these criteria. One can think of these criteria for personal harm in terms of *me hurt you* and as delineating roughly those violations that a chimpanzee can appreciate. Condition (a) (*hurt*) picks out roughly those harms that a chimp can understand (e.g., assault v. tax evasion). Condition (b) (*you*) requires that the victim be vivid as an individual. Finally, condition (c) (*me*) captures the notion of "agency," the idea that the action must spring in a vivid way from the agent's will, must be "authored" rather than merely "edited" by the agent. Pushing someone in front of a trolley meets all three criteria and is therefore "personal," while diverting a trolley involves merely deflecting an existing threat, removing a crucial sense of "agency" and therefore making this violation "impersonal." Other moral dilemmas (about 40 in all) were categorized using these criteria as well.

Before turning to the data, the evolutionary rationale for the "personal"/"impersonal" distinction requires a bit more elaboration. Emotional responses may explain why people say no to the footbridge dilemma, but why do they say yes to the trolley dilemma? Here we must consider what has happened since we and our closest living relatives parted ways. We, unlike other species, have a well-developed capacity for general-purpose abstract reasoning, a capacity that can be used to think about anything one can name, including moral matters. Thus, one might suppose that when the heavy-duty, social-emotional instincts of our primate ancestors lie dormant, abstract reasoning has an opportunity to dominate. More specifically, one might suppose that in response to the trolley case, with its peculiarly modern method of violence, the powerful emotions that might otherwise say "No!" remain quiet, and a faint little "cognitive" voice can be heard: "Isn't it better to save five lives instead of one?"

That's a hypothesis. Is it true? And how can we tell? This hypothesis makes some strong predictions regarding what we should see in people's brains while they are responding to personal and impersonal moral dilemmas. The contemplation of personal moral dilemmas like the footbridge case should produce increased neural activity in brain regions associated with emotional response and social cognition, while the contemplation of impersonal moral dilemmas should produce relatively greater activity in regions associated with "higher cognition." This is exactly what was observed (Greene et al., 2001). Contemplation of personal moral dilemmas produced relatively greater activity in two emotion-related areas, the posterior cingulate cortex (the region Kiehl and colleagues (2001) found to exhibit decreased emotion-related activity in psychopaths) and the medial prefrontal cortex (one of the areas damaged in both Gage (Damasio et al., 1994) and Elliot (Bechara et al., 1996)), as well as in the superior temporal sulcus, a region associated with various kinds of social cognition in humans and other primates (Allison et al., 2000). A more recent replication of these results using a larger pool of subjects has revealed the same effect in the amygdala, one of the primary emotion-related structures in the brain (Greene et al., 2004). At the same time, contemplation of impersonal moral dilemmas produced relatively greater neural activity in two classically "cognitive" brain areas associated with working memory function in the inferior parietal lobe and the dorsolateral prefrontal cortex.

This hypothesis also makes a prediction regarding people's reaction times. According to the view I've sketched, people tend to have emotional responses to personal moral violations that incline them to judge against performing those actions. That means that someone who judges a personal moral violation to be appropriate (e.g., someone who says it's okay to push the man off the bridge in the footbridge case) will most likely have to override an emotional response in order to do it. That overriding process will take time, and thus we would expect that yes answers will take longer than no answers in response to personal moral dilemmas like the footbridge case. At the same time, we have no reason to predict a difference in reaction times between yes and no answers in response to impersonal moral dilemmas like the trolley case because there is, according to this model, no emotional response (or much less of one) to override in such cases. Here, too, the prediction holds. Trials in which the subject judged in favor of personal moral violations took significantly longer than trials in which the subject judged against them, but there was no comparable reaction time effect observed in response to impersonal moral violations (Greene et al., 2001).

Further results support this model as well. Earlier we contrasted the neural effects of contemplating "personal" versus "impersonal" moral dilemmas. But what should we expect to see if we subdivide the personal moral dilemmas into two categories, on the basis of difficulty (that is, on the basis of reaction time)? Consider the following moral dilemma (the *crying baby* dilemma). It's wartime, and you and some of your fellow villagers are hiding from enemy soldiers in a basement. Your baby starts to cry, and you cover your baby's mouth to block the sound. If you remove your hand, your baby will cry, the soldiers will hear, and they will find you and the others and kill everyone they find, including you and your baby. If you do not remove your hand, your baby will smother to death. Is it okay to smother your baby to death in order to save yourself and the other villagers? This is a very difficult question. Different people give different answers, and nearly everyone takes a relatively long time to answer.

Here's a similar dilemma (the *infanticide* dilemma). You are a teenage girl who has become pregnant. By wearing baggy clothes and putting on weight you have managed to hide your pregnancy. One day during school, you start to go into labor. You rush to the locker room and give birth to the baby alone. You do not feel that you are ready to care for this child. Part of you wants to throw the baby in the garbage and pretend it never existed so that you can move on with your life. Is it okay to throw away your baby in order to move on with your life? Among the people we tested, at least, this is a very easy question. All of them say that it would be wrong to throw the baby away, and most do so very quickly.

What's going on in these two cases? My colleagues and I hypothesized as follows. In both cases there is a prepotent, negative emotional response to the personal violation in question, killing one's own baby. In the crying baby case, however, there are powerful, countervailing, "cognitively" encoded considerations that push one toward smothering the baby. After all, the baby is going to die no matter what, and so you have nothing to lose (in terms of lives lost/saved) and much to gain by smothering it, awful as it is. In some people the emotional response ("Aaaahhhh!!! Don't do it!!!") dominates, and those people say no. In other people, a "cognitive," cost-benefit analysis ("But you have nothing to gain, and so much to lose...") wins out, and those people say yes.

What does this model predict that we'll see in the brain data when we compare cases like *crying baby* to cases like *infanticide*? First, this model supposes that cases like *crying baby* involve an increased level of "response conflict," that is, conflict between competing representations for behavioral response. Thus, we should expect that difficult moral dilemmas like *crying baby* will produce increased activity in a brain region that is associated (albeit controversially) with response conflict, the anterior cingulate cortex (Botvinick et al., 2001). Second, according to our model, the crucial difference between cases like *crying baby* and cases like *infanticide* is that dilemmas like *crying baby* involve "cognitive" considerations that compete with the prepotent, negative emotional response. Thus, we should expect to see increased activity in classically "cognitive" brain areas when we compare cases like *crying baby* to cases like *infanticide*, even though dilemmas like *crying baby* are personal moral dilemmas. As for emotion-related activity, the prediction is unclear. On the one hand, this model requires that emotional responses play an important role in both types of cases, leading to the prediction that there will be little observable difference in emotion-related areas of the brain. On the other hand, the type or level of emotional response that is involved in a protracted cognitive conflict as hypothesized to occur in *crying baby* may be different from the sort of quick emotional response that is hypothesized to be decisive in cases like *infanticide*. Thus, one might also expect to see some sort of additional emotion-related brain activity for the former cases.

The two clear predictions of this model have held (Greene et al., 2004). Comparing high-reaction-time personal moral dilemmas like *crying baby* to low-reaction-time personal moral dilemmas like *infanticide* revealed increased activity in the anterior cingulate (conflict) as well as the anterior dorsolateral prefrontal cortex and the inferior parietal lobes, both classically "cognitive" brain regions (Greene et al., 2004).

So far I have talked about neural activity correlated with the type of dilemma under consideration, but what about activity correlated with subjects' behavioral response? Does a brain saying "yes" to a question like this look different from a brain saying "no"? To answer this question we subdivided our dilemma set further by comparing the trials in which the subject says "yes" to difficult personal moral dilemmas like *crying baby* to trials in which the subject says no in response to such cases. Once again, we turn to the model for a prediction. If the cases in which people say yes are cases in which "cognition" wins, then we would expect to see more activity in the dorsolateral prefrontal cortex and parietal lobes in those cases. Likewise, if cases in which people say no are cases in which emotion wins, then we would expect to see more activity in emotion-related areas such as the posterior cingulate, medial prefrontal cortex, or the amygdala.

The first of these predictions held. "Cognitive" brain regions in both the anterior dorsolateral prefrontal cortex and in the inferior parietal lobes exhibited greater activity for trials in which personal moral violations were judged appropriate ("yes") as compared to trials in which such violations were judged inappropriate ("no"). No brain regions, however, showed the opposite effect (Greene et al., 2004).

The foregoing results, taken together, provide support for the model sketched earlier according to which moral decisions are produced through an interaction between emotional and "cognitive" processes subserved by anatomically dissociable brain systems. Another recent brain-imaging experiment further supports this model of moral judgment. Alan Sanfey, Jim Rilling, and colleagues (Sanfey et al., 2003) conducted a brain-imaging study of the ultimatum game in order to study the neural bases of people's sense of fairness. The ultimatum game works as follows. There is a sum of money, say $10, and the first player (the proposer) makes a proposal as to how to divide it up between herself and the other player. The second player, the responder, can either accept the offer, in which case the money is divided as proposed, or reject the offer, in which case no one gets anything.

When both players are perfectly rational, purely motivated by financial self-interest, and these facts are known to the proposer, the outcome of the game is guaranteed. Because something is better than nothing, a rationally and financially self-interested responder will accept any nonzero offer. A rationally and financially self-interested proposer who knows this will therefore offer the responder as small a share of the total as possible, and thus the proposer will get nearly all and the responder will get nearly none. This, however, is not what usually happens when people play the game, even when both players know that the game will only be played once. Proposers usually make offers that are fair (i.e., fifty-fifty split) or close to fair, and responders tend to reject offers that are more than a little unfair. Why does this happen?

The answer, once again, implicates emotion. This study reveals that unfair offers, as compared to fair offers, produce increased activity in the anterior insula, a brain region associated with anger, disgust, and autonomic arousal. Moreover, individuals' average levels of insula activity correlated positively with the percentage of offers they rejected and was weaker for trials in which the subject believed that the unfair offer was made by a computer program. But the insula is only part of the story. The anterior cingulate (the region mentioned earlier that is associated with response conflict) and the dorsolateral prefrontal cortex (one of the regions mentioned earlier that is associated with "higher cognition") were also more active in response to unfair offers. Moreover, for trials in which unfair offers were rejected, the level of activity in the insula tended to be higher than the level of activity in the dorsolateral prefrontal cortex, while the reverse was true of trials in which unfair offers were rejected. This result parallels very nicely the finding described earlier that increased (anterior) dorsolateral prefrontal cortex activity was observed when people judged personal moral violations to be appropriate (in spite of their emotions, according to our model).

Other neuroimaging results have shed light on the neural bases of moral judgment. Jorge Moll and colleagues have conducted two experiments using simple, morally significant sentences (e.g., "They hung an innocent.") (Moll et al., 2001; Moll et al., 2002a) and an experiment using morally significant pictures (e.g., pictures of poor abandoned children; Moll et al., 2002b). These studies, along with the ones described earlier, implicate a wide range of brain areas in the processing of morally significant stimuli, with a fair amount of agreement (given the variety of tasks employed in these studies) concerning which brain areas are the most important. In addition, many of the brain regions implicated by this handful of neuroimaging studies of moral cognition overlap with those implicated in neuroimaging studies of "theory of mind," the ability to represent others' mental states (Frith, 2001). (For a more detailed account of the neuroanatomy of moral judgment and its relation to related processes see Greene & Haidt, 2002.) While many big questions remain unanswered, it is clear from these studies that there is no "moral center" in the brain, no "morality module." Moreover, moral judgment does not appear to be a function of "higher cognition," with a few emotional perturbations thrown in (Kohlberg, 1969). Nor do moral judgments appear to be driven entirely by emotional responses (Haidt, 2001). Rather, moral judgments appear to be produced by a complex network of brain areas subserving both emotional and "cognitive" processes (Greene & Haidt, 2002; Greene et al., 2001; Sanfey et al., 2003).

4 What in Moral Psychology Is Innate?

In extracting from the foregoing discussion provisional answers to this question, it will be useful to distinguish between the form and content of moral thought. The *form* of moral thought concerns the nature of the cognitive processes that subserve moral thinking, which will surely be a function of the cognitive structures that are in place to carry out those processes. The *content* of moral thought concerns the nature of people's moral beliefs and attitudes, what they think of as right or wrong, good or bad, and so on. Thus, it could turn out that all humans have an innate tendency to think about right and wrong in a certain way without any tendency to agree on which things are right or wrong. With this distinction in mind, let us review the data presented earlier.

A number of themes emerge from studies of (1) patients with social behavioral problems stemming from brain injury, (2) psychopaths, and (3) the neural bases of moral judgment in normal individuals. Popular conceptions of moral psychology, bolstered by the legend of Phineas Gage and popular portrayals of psychopaths, encourage the belief that there must be a "moral center" in the brain. This does not appear to be the case. The lesion patients discussed earlier, both developmental and adult-onset, all have deficits that extend beyond the moral domain, as do the psychopaths who have been studied. Moreover, the results of brain-imaging studies of moral judgment reveal that moral decision-making involves a diverse network of neural structures that are implicated in a wide range of other phenomena. Nevertheless, the dissociations observed in pathological cases and in the moral thinking of normal individuals are telling. Most important, multiple sources of evidence tentatively point toward the existence of at least two relatively independent systems that contribute to moral judgment: (1) an affective system that (a) has its roots in primate social emotion and behavior; (b) is selectively damaged in psychopaths and certain patients with frontal brain lesions; and (c) is selectively triggered by personal moral violations, perceived unfairness, and, more generally, socially significant behaviors that existed in our ancestral environment, and (2) a "cognitive" system that (a) is far more developed in humans than in other animals; (b) is selectively preserved in the aforementioned lesion patients and psychopaths; and (c) is not triggered in a stereotyped way by social stimuli. I have called these two different "systems," but they themselves are almost certainly composed of more specific subsystems. In the case of the affective system, its subsystems are probably rather domain specific, while the system that is responsible for "higher cognition," though composed of subsystems with specific cognitive functions, is more flexible and more domain general than the affective system and its subcomponents. Mixed in with what I've called the affective system are likely to be cognitive structures specifically dedicated to representing the mental states of others ("theory of mind"; Greene & Haidt, 2002).

What does this mean for the innateness of moral thought? It seems that the *form* of moral thought is highly dependent on the large-scale structure of the human mind. Cognitive neuroscience has made it increasingly clear that the mind/brain is composed of a set of interconnected modules. Modularity is generally associated with nativism, but some maintain that learning can give rise to modular structure, and in some cases this is certainly true (Elman et al., 1996; Shiffrin & Schneider, 1977). My opinion, however, is that large-scale modular structure is unlikely to be produced without a great deal of specific biological adaptation to that end. Insofar as that is correct, the form of human moral thought is to a very great extent shaped by how the human mind happens to have evolved. In other words, our moral thinking is not the product of moral rules written onto a mental blank slate by experience. As the stark contrast between the trolley and footbridge dilemmas suggests, our moral judgment is greatly affected by the quirks in our cognitive design.

As for the *content* of human morality, there are good reasons to think that genes play an important role here as well. Many of our most basic prosocial tendencies are exhibited in other species such as the chimpanzee, suggesting that such tendencies stem from shared genes (Flack & de Waal, 2000). Moreover, insofar as one can take modularity as evidence for innate structure, the fact that psychopaths exhibit relatively normal cognitive function alongside dramatic deficits in emotional empathy suggests that normal empathic responses may depend on something like an innate "empathy module." (See also Tooby and Cosmides on innate motivation: Tooby, Cosmides, & Barrett, chapter 18 here). Finally, the fact that psychopathic tendencies, unlike ordinary violent tendencies, appear to be unaffected by differences in parenting strategy (Wootton et al., 1997) and socioeconomic status (Hare et al., 1991) suggests that psychopathy may result from compromised genes.

So far I've argued that the form of human moral thought is importantly shaped by the innate structure of the human mind and that some basic, prosocial tendencies probably provide human morality with innate content. What about more ambitious versions of moral nativism? Might there be detailed moral principles written into the brain? People seem to "know" intuitvely that it's okay to hit the switch in the trolley case and that it's not okay to push the man in the footbridge case. Moreover, they seem to know these things without knowing how they know them, that is, without any access to organizing principles. Such mysterious nuggets of apparent moral wisdom encourage the thought that somewhere, deep in our cognitive architecture, we're going to find the mother lode: an innate "moral grammar" (Harman, 2000; Mikhail, 2000; Rawls, 1971; Stich, 1993). (Or, more accurately, an innate "moral language," since such rules would have *content* as well as form.) Whether this more ambitious form of moral nativism will pan out remains to be seen. But already there is evidence suggesting that much of human moral judgment depends on dissociable "cognitive" and affective mechanisms that can compete with one another and that are not specifically dedicated to moral judgment (Greene & Haidt, 2002). It seems unlikely, then, that human moral judgment as a whole derives from a core moral competence that implements a set of normative-looking rules. Nevertheless, this motley picture of the moral mind is compatible with certain aspects of moral judgment's depending on cognitive structures that can be described as implementing something like a "grammar."

As noted earlier, I believe that the question of nativism in moral psychology commands attention because our moral thought is at once highly familiar and thoroughly alien. Our moral convictions are central to our humanity, and yet their origins are obscure, leading people to attribute them to supernatural forces, or their more naturalistic equivalents. For some, it seems, the idea of innate morality holds the promise of *validation*. Our moral convictions, far from being the internalization of rules that we invented and taught one another, would be a gift from a universe wiser than ourselves. There is, no doubt, much wisdom in our moral instincts, but they, like all of nature's fabrications, will have their quirks and flaws.

SHAUN NICHOLS

Innateness and Moral Psychology

Although linguistic nativism has received the bulk of attention in contemporary innateness debates, moral nativism has perhaps an even deeper ancestry. If linguistic nativism is Cartesian, moral nativism is Platonic. Moral nativism has taken a backseat to linguistic nativism in contemporary discussions largely because Chomsky made a case for linguistic nativism characterized by unprecedented rigor. Hence it is not surprising that recent attempts to revive the thesis that we have innate moral knowledge have drawn on Chomsky's framework. I will argue, however, that the recent attempts to use Chomsky-style arguments in support of innate moral knowledge are uniformly unconvincing.

The central argument in the Chomskian arsenal, of course, is the "poverty of the stimulus" (POS) argument. In section 1, I will set out the basic form of the POS argument and the conclusions about domain specificity and innate propositional knowledge that are supposed to follow. In section 2, I'll distinguish three hypotheses about innateness and morality: rule nativism, moral principle nativism, and moral judgment nativism. In sections 3–5 I'll consider each of these hypotheses in turn. I'll argue that while there is some reason to favor rule nativism, the arguments that moral principles and moral judgment derive from innate moral knowledge don't work. The capacity for moral judgment is better explained by appeal to innate affective systems rather than innate moral knowledge. In the final section, I'll suggest that the role of such affective mechanisms in structuring the mind complicates the standard picture about poverty of the stimulus arguments and nativism. For the affective mechanisms that influence cognitive structures can make contributions that are neither domain general nor domain specific.

I thank Peter Carruthers and Philip Robbins for very helpful comments on an earlier draft of this essay.

1 Poverty, Innateness, and Domain Specificity

Like most toweringly influential arguments in philosophy, Chomsky's POS argument is at its core quite simple. We can suppose that empiricist learning proceeds by applying domain-general learning mechanisms (e.g., hypothesis testing) to environmental input. The idea behind the POS argument is that the environment doesn't contain enough information to enable an empiricist learner to acquire the linguistic competence that children exhibit (Laurence & Margolis, 2001; see also Botterill & Carruthers, 1999; Cowie, 1999). This shows that children are not merely empiricist learners when it comes to language. This argument is only strengthened if it turns out that children acquire the capacity early in development (Samuels, 2002, p. 238).

It's important to distinguish two inferences drawn from the POS argument, a negative and a positive conclusion (see, e.g., Laurence & Margolis, 2001, p. 248). If the POS argument works at all, it delivers the *negative conclusion* that the acquisition of language can't be explained by the empiricist proposal. This antiempiricist conclusion is, of course, of signal importance. But the antiempiricist conclusion would not be very sticky without a positive proposal as well. One standard interpretation of Chomsky's POS arguments is that they are supposed to lead to a positive conclusion. Fodor puts it thus: "the bottom line of Poverty of Stimulus Arguments, as Chomsky uses them, is that innate domain-specific information is normally recruited in first language acquisition" (Fodor, 2001a, p. 107). Hence the positive conclusion is that first-language acquisition involves "innate, domain-specific information." The connection between these elements is fairly clear. The body of information is restricted to the domain of language, so the domain is specified by the information itself. And the body of information is innate.[1]

In the recent literature in developmental psychology and evolutionary psychology, there are a number of somewhat different notions of domain specificity (see, e.g., Carruthers, 2004; Karmiloff-Smith, 1992; Samuels et al., 1999). However, since the focus here will be on POS-style arguments, my interests will be in the notion of domain specificity that plays the central role in POS arguments. As Cowie puts it in her discussion of POS arguments, nativists invoke domain-specific mechanisms to explain the "gap between the information provided by experience about some domain...and the ideas or beliefs we acquire concerning that domain" (Cowie, 1999, p. 37; see also Laurence & Margolis, 2001). Hence, for my purposes, domain-specific mechanisms will be mechanisms that are not part of the stock of empiricist mechanisms but that are devoted to special functions or special tasks. The standard examples are mechanisms that are devoted to the domains of language, mind reading, and folk physics. Domain-specific databases constitute one kind of domain-specific mechanism. In addition, some cognitive mechanisms

---

1. There is much discussion about how to define innateness (see, e.g., Cowie, 1999; Samuels, 2002), but I am happy enough to rely on exemplars of innate traits (e.g., ears) and noninnate traits (e.g. scars) as a rough guide to whether a cognitive trait is innate (see Laurence & Margolis, 2001, pp. 219–20).

are thought to be domain-specific *processors*. Perhaps the best known species of this genus is the Fodorean module, a mechanism that processes only certain kinds of information, namely, information restricted to a particular domain. A nativist might invoke either domain-specific databases or processors (or both) to explain the acquisition of a capacity that outstrips the resources of the empiricist learner.

2 Three Kinds of Nativism about Norms

Now that the general background on nativism is in place, I can turn to focus on the status of nativism in the moral domain. There are a number of psychological joints at which the normative domain can be cut. I will distinguish three kinds of nativist claims about moral capacities: rule nativism, moral principle nativism, and moral judgment nativism.

2.1 Rule Nativism

People obviously have a capacity to recognize and reason about rules, and the basic capacity for rule comprehension is a natural candidate for a nativist proposal. To frame the nativist proposal, it will be useful to draw on Kant's distinction between hypothetical and nonhypothetical imperatives. Hypothetical imperatives are rules that serve one's interests like "Put oil in your car." This imperative applies to us because we desire to prevent our engine from seizing up. If for some reason we *want* our engine to seize up (say, because we're conducting an engine test) then the imperative no longer applies. Some imperatives, however, apply to us even if they don't serve our interests. Kant's examples here were moral imperatives, like "Don't lie"; this moral imperative applies to us even when lying is obviously in our best interests. However, in a widely influential essay, Philippa Foot argues that moral imperatives aren't the only cases of nonhypothetical imperatives. Foot begins by noting that on Kant's characterization, hypothetical imperatives are "those telling a man what he ought to do because . . . he wants something and those telling him what he ought to do on grounds of self-interest" (1972, p. 306). She then proceeds to give two examples of nonmoral norms that are not hypothetical in this self-interested sense. First, Foot offers an example from etiquette—the norm that invitations addressed in the third person should be answered in the third person—and she claims that "the rule does not *fail to apply* to someone who has his own good reasons for ignoring this piece of nonsense, or who simply does not care about what, from the point of view of etiquette, he should do" (p. 308). Even though I may have no interest in following the rule of etiquette, it still applies to me. Foot's second example invokes a club rule: "the club secretary who has told a member that he should not bring ladies into the smoking-room does not say, 'Sorry, I was mistaken' when informed that this member is resigning tomorrow and cares nothing about his reputation in the club" (pp. 308–9). Here again, even though the member has no interest in obeying the rule, if he takes a woman into the smoking room, it is still the case that he is breaking the rule—he is doing something that he is not supposed to do.

There are a number of further distinctions to draw between different kinds of imperatives.[2] But for my purposes, the class of nonhypothetical imperatives is central.[3] The capacity to recognize and reason about these nonhypothetical imperatives is plausibly a fundamental capacity implicated in moral judgment, and one might well maintain that we have innate mechanisms dedicated to this basic capacity. The precise label for this view would be "nonhypothetical-imperative comprehension nativism"; I'll abbreviate this to "rule nativism."

2.2 Moral Principle Nativism

In addition to a capacity for rule comprehension, people exhibit knowledge of distinctively moral principles. One might claim that certain of these moral principles are innately specified. Obvious candidates here are principles that seem to be universal. For instance, some claim that in every culture there are prohibitions against rape, violence, and murder (Pinker, 1994, p. 414; see Brown, 1991, pp. 138–9). These might be regarded as public expressions of innate moral principles. The analogy with grammatical principles leads some theorists to propose a counterpart to Chomsky's universal grammar, a "universal moral grammar" (Harman, 2000, p. 225; Mikhail, 2002, p. 1088). We can call this kind of view "moral principle nativism."

2.3 Moral Judgment Nativism

In the psychological literature, the capacity for moral judgment has perhaps been most directly and extensively approached empirically by exploring the basic capacity to distinguish moral violations from conventional violations (for reviews see Smetana, 1993; Tisak, 1995). Rather than attempt to define the moral and conventional domains, the easiest way to see the import of the data on moral judgment is to consider how subjects distinguish canonical examples of moral violations (e.g., hitting, pulling hair) from canonical examples of conventional violations (e.g., talking during storytime). From a young age, children distinguish canonical moral violations from canonical conventional violations on a number of dimensions. For instance, children tend to think that moral transgressions are generally less permissible and more serious than conventional transgressions. Children are also more likely to maintain that the moral violations are "generalizably" wrong, for example, that pulling hair is wrong in other countries too. And the explanations for why moral transgressions are wrong are given in terms of fairness and harm to victims. For example, children will say that pulling hair is wrong because it hurts the person. By contrast, the explanation for why conventional transgressions are wrong is given in terms of social acceptability—talking out of turn is wrong because it's rude or

---

2. For instance, there is the additional Kantian notion of the categorical imperative, which allegedly presents an action as "objectively necessary." Etiquette norms and school rules are clearly not categorical even if they are nonhypothetical.
3. The focus on nonhypothetical imperatives was suggested to me by recent work by Chandra Sripada and Stephen Stich.

impolite, or because "you're not supposed to." Further, conventional rules, unlike moral rules, are viewed as dependent on authority. For instance, if at another school the teacher has no rule against talking during storytime, children will judge that it's not wrong to talk during storytime at that school; but even if the teacher at another school has no rule against hitting, children claim that it's still wrong to hit.

These findings on the moral/conventional distinction are neither fragile nor superficial. On the contrary, the findings are quite robust. They have been replicated numerous times, using a wide variety of stimuli. Furthermore, the research apparently plumbs a fairly deep feature of moral judgment. For, as recounted earlier, moral violations are treated as distinctive along several quite different dimensions. Finally, this turns out to be a persistent feature of moral judgment. It's found in young and old alike. Thus, we might think of this as reflecting a kind of *core moral judgment*. Accordingly, one might maintain that some innate moral knowledge guides the child in developing such an early appreciation of the distinctive status of morality. Call this view "moral judgment nativism."[4]

3 The Case for Innateness of Rule Comprehension

A number of recent theorists have proposed something like rule nativism (e.g., Cummins, 1996; Sripada & Stich, forthcoming). Recall that the focal capacity is the ability to recognize and reason over nonhypothetical rules. Is it plausible that this ability derives from empiricist learning mechanisms? I'll sketch a kind of POS argument that might support rule nativism; this argument is enhanced by evidence on young children's facility with rules.

As empiricism was described earlier, the empiricist learner has a set of domain-general capacities (e.g., hypothesis testing) for processing input from the environment. In addition, in this context it will be important to allow the empiricist learner general purpose means-ends reasoning. The enthusiast for rule nativism might argue as follows. It's easy to see how the empiricist learner might come to hold *hypothetical imperatives*. For the empiricist learner just determines that certain actions get better results for him than other actions. Following certain rules helps him to get what he wants. However, there is no obvious story about how the empiricist learner might come to acknowledge *nonhypothetical imperatives*. When confronted with the environmental information concerning etiquette, for example, the empiricist learner might think that it's in his best interests to reply in the third person to invitations addressed in the third person. However, it's not at all clear how empiricist learning mechanisms would lead him to acknowledge that *even if it is not in his best interests*, he should reply in the third person. People clearly have this capacity to acknowledge nonhypothetical imperatives that apply even when they run against one's desires and interests. As a result, people's capacity for this kind of

---

4. These three nativist proposals might be teased apart in various ways. Rule nativism does not entail moral-principle nativism—the capacity for rule comprehension need not carry with it any particular principles. Neither does rule nativism entail moral-judgment nativism. For the recognition of nonhypothetical imperatives like etiquette rules does not deliver the moral/conventional distinction.

rule comprehension must depend on some innate contribution beyond what empiricists allow. The mind is apparently prewired to have a cognitive slot for nonhypothetical rules.[5]

As noted in section 1, a POS argument is only strengthened if we find that the capacity in question emerges early in development. And there is indeed evidence for the early emergence of rule comprehension. By the age of four, children are adept at detecting transgressions of both familiar precautionary rules and arbitrary novel rules (Cummins, 1996; Harris & Núñez, 1996). This evidence shows a strikingly early capacity for rule comprehension. In particular, it shows that young children are quite capable of assimilating information about which sorts of actions are prohibited and then using this information appropriately to judge whether a given action is a transgression.

The foregoing scarcely provides a knockdown argument for rule nativism. One salient fact is that the child is exposed to *lots* of admonitions and instruction in the normative domain. Parents and teachers are constantly telling kids what shouldn't be done, and perhaps the empiricist can concoct some story about how the cognitive slot for nonhypothetical imperatives emerges through general reasoning. Nonetheless, the arguments for rule nativism seem sufficiently promising to make rule nativism a contender. The case for rule nativism is also appreciably better than the other nativist arguments to be considered hereafter.

4 The Case for the Innateness of Moral Principles

Theorists arguing for distinctively moral nativism, as opposed to the broader kind of *rule* nativism considered earlier, have found the analogy with linguistics irresistible. In recent work, Gilbert Harman and John Mikhail suggest that just as we have an innate set of grammatical principles guiding our language acquisition, we also have an innate set of moral principles, a "universal moral grammar" (Harman, 2000; Mikhail, 2002; see also Stich, 1993). Harman and Mikhail advert to two key points to support the case for the existence of a universal moral grammar. People seem to be committed to a set of subtle, untaught moral principles, and this might be explained by positing a universal moral grammar; positing such a grammar would also explain the existence of crossculturally universal moral principles. I'll consider the merits of these arguments in turn.

4.1 Unlearned Moral Principles

According to the Chomskian POS argument, the child has knowledge of grammatical principles that could not possibly have been learned from the available evidence (using empiricist learning mechanisms); hence these principles must be

---

5. An obvious empiricist response is to maintain that the "nonhypothetical imperatives" are really just heuristics that the empiricist learner recognizes as being in his interests in the long run. But this seems to distort the facts about normative judgment. When children learn norms like the rules of etiquette, they often have no idea whether following the rule will benefit them or not.

part of the innate universal grammar. Harman maintains that a parallel argument might be made for moral principles. Just as there are unlearned syntactic principles, Harman suggests that there are "unlearned moral principles" that are part of a universal moral grammar (2000, pp. 224–5).

Harman draws on the large literature devoted to the "trolley problem" to make the case for unlearned moral principles. Philosophical research in this area resembles linguistic research, insofar as the project is to consider a wide range of test cases against our intuitions and to determine a set of principles that will capture our intuitions about the cases (Harman, 2000, p. 224). Here's Harman's gloss of the standard trolley case:

> You are driving a trolley and the brakes fail. Ahead five people are working on the track with their backs turned. Fortunately you can switch to a side track, if you act at once. Unfortunately there is also someone on that track with his back turned. If you switch your trolley to the side track, you will kill one person. If you do not switch your trolley, you will kill five people. (1977, p. 57)

Most people think that it is permissible to switch to the side track, killing one person but saving five. After all, the choice is between one person dying and five persons dying. However, this is hardly the end to it. For consider the variant in which you have to throw a person onto the tracks to stop the train from hitting the five people. In this case, most people regard the action as impermissible.[6]

Since the origin of the trolley literature (Foot, 1967), the doctrine of double effect (DDE) has been a prevailing candidate for capturing intuitions about a range of trolley cases. According to the DDE, it can be permissible to perform an act that has an unintended but foreseen side effect that one is forbidden from intending. Hence, in the initial trolley case, it is permissible to switch the trolley even though it has an effect (the killing of an innocent) that it would be impermissible to intend. It will serve us better to have a fuller characterization of the principle:

> The principle holds that under strict conditions it is permissible foreseeably to bring about an effect of a type that it is never permissible to intend. These conditions are: that the act itself... be morally good or indifferent; that the bad effect... be an unavoidable, unintended effect of the act which also achieves the good effect... and that the good effect be sufficiently weighty to warrant causing the bad effect. (Uniacke, 1998, p. 120)

Obviously, the DDE is subtle and sophisticated. And few people are explicitly taught this doctrine. As a result, Harman argues, if the DDE is "adequate to an ordinary person's I-morality [the moral idiolect of an individual]" this would provide reason to think that the principle is part of universal moral grammar:

> An ordinary person was never taught the principle of Double-Effect... and it is unclear how such a principle might have been acquired from the examples available to the ordinary person. This suggests that the relevant principle is built

---

6. These sorts of cases are discussed at length in Thomson (1986). For empirical confirmation of the pattern of intuitions described earlier, see Greene et al. (2001) and Mikhail (forthcoming).

into I-morality ahead of time, in which case we should expect it to occur in all I-moralities (or be a default case, or something of the sort). In other words, the principles should be part of universal moral grammar. (2000, p. 225)[7]

It is, as Harman notes, thoroughly implausible that people are taught the DDE. So if this principle is adequate to people's moral views, then, Harman suggests, the principle must be a built-in element of a "universal moral grammar."

The suggestion that we have a universal moral grammar is enticing, but the foregoing argument for unlearned moral principles fails to support any such innate moral knowledge. To begin, the claim that the DDE might turn out to be "adequate to an ordinary person's I-morality" (Harman, 2000, p. 225) is ambiguous on a crucial dimension that loomed important in philosophical discussions of linguistics. Grammatical intuitions, it was agreed by all sides, play a vital role in linguistics. However, it is important to distinguish between an *external* and an *internal* approach to linguistics (see Stich & Ravenscroft, 1994). On the external approach, the linguists' job is precisely to come up with a grammar that is *externally adequate* to the linguistic intuitions. That is, the goal is to assemble a set of principles that captures most of these intuitions. It's possible that there are a number of quite different grammars that will satisfy this goal, and this approach can be entirely neutral on the psychological details about how (or whether) this grammar is internally represented (see Stich, 1972). By contrast, on the internal approach to linguistics, the goal is not just to come up with a set of principles that *fit* the observed intuitions but to divine the set of principles that are causally responsible for, *inter alia*, the production of the grammatical intuitions (e.g., Fodor, 1981).

Now, as with linguistic theory, we need to distinguish between two approaches to the trolley cases. On an external approach, the goal is to produce a unified set of principles that would capture most of the trolley intuitions. On an internal approach, the goal is to determine the psychological elements that actually subserve the trolley intuitions. Many of the philosophers engaged in the trolley debates are clearly pursuing the externalist project of producing a set of principles that fits with the intuitions, and if it turns out that their favored set of principles is not psychologically realized in the average person, this is not a particular problem.

There is, of course, considerable disagreement in the trolley literature, and a number of philosophers deny that the DDE is externally adequate to our intuitions (e.g., Foot, 1967; Thomson, 1986). Nonetheless, the DDE, or something very like it, has an impressive cadre of admirers (e.g., Harman, 1977; Nagel, 1986; Quinn, 1989), and I'll simply grant the moral principle nativist the assumption that the DDE is externally adequate to trolley intuitions. However, this does not entail that the DDE is part of an innate universal moral grammar. While the explicit goal of the external project is to develop a single theory that accommodates the trolley intuitions, it is a bold assumption that internally there is a single unified set of principles that subserves trolley intuitions.

---

7. Harman credits unpublished work by John Mikhail here. Mikhail (forthcoming) makes an extensive empirical case that people's intuitions about trolley cases conform to the DDE.

So even if we assume that the DDE is externally adequate to a core set of trolley intuitions, we still need to determine the best internal account of those trolley intuitions. It is by no means clear that the appeal to an innate DDE principle is the best explanation of the pattern of intuitions. Here I want to sketch just one alternative internal account. The intuitions might implicate multiple cognitive mechanisms rather than a single unified set of complex principles.

It is independently plausible to think that people have both a set of nonhypothetical moral rules (like the prohibition against murder) and a separate, general capacity to reason about how to minimize bad outcomes.[8] It's natural to think of these two systems as deontological and utilitarian systems, respectively. These systems are at least partly independent. For the utilitarian system is deployed in thoroughly nonmoral domains, including the merely prudential; furthermore, the nonhypothetical rules of the deontological system are expressly *not* utilitarian—the rules apply independently of our wants and interests.

Acknowledging both a deontological and a utilitarian system also helps us to explain some apparently irresolvable tensions in commonsense moral thought. We have deeply conflicting intuitions about cases in which catastrophic utilitarian consequences—say, the destruction of a civilization—will follow unless we perform an action that is obviously forbidden, such as murdering a child. It seems wrong to murder the child, and it also seems wrong to allow the catastrophe (Nagel, 1972). The two-system approach would explain why we have this tension in our moral intuitions. The deontological system rebels at defying the moral rule; the utilitarian system balks at the catastrophic cost of sparing the child.

We can now exploit the two-system proposal to generate an internal account of the trolley intuitions: an action (or possible action) is assessed by the deontological system for whether it violates deontological prohibitions against, for example, intending to harm innocents.[9] If the action violates such a deontological principle, then the action is judged as impermissible.[10] Even if the action violates no deontological principle, it still gets assessed by the utilitarian system. If the action has not violated a deontological principle and does not run afoul of utilitarian considerations, then it is

---

8. Evolutionary psychologists have similarly proposed independent mechanisms for cheater detection and hazard management (e.g., Fiddick et al., 2000).
9. Of course, to fit the DDE, the formulation here is important. The prohibition is against actions intended to produce bad effects rather than against actions that cause unintended but foreseeable bad effects. But this is probably a feature even of many nonmoral prohibitions. Consider the following nonmoral variant of the trolley cases. Susie and Billy's mom says, "You are forbidden from breaking any of the cups." Billy subsequently sets up his toy train so that it is about to plow through five cups; then he calls for Susie as he leaves the scene. In one case, Susie can divert the train so that it will break only one cup; in another case, Susie must smash a cup in front of the train to prevent the train from breaking the five cups. It's plausible that only in the latter case would Susie be breaking the rule (even though her mother will presumably forgive the transgression).
10. I am supposing here that the deontological system is typically privileged in an important way over the utilitarian system, but the account I'm proposing doesn't explain why one system is privileged or how the systems might interact. An adequate account would obviously need to address these issues. One interesting possibility is that emotions play a role in the deontological system that they do not play for the utilitarian system (see Greene et al., 2001, for some suggestive evidence).

judged permissible. This two-system model might explain why trolley intuitions would fit with the DDE. According to the DDE, an action that has a foreseen effect that would be wrong to intend is permissible only if:

1. The intended action is permissible
2. The foreseen bad effect is not intended
3. There is no way to achieve the good effect without also causing the bad effect
4. The bad effect is not disproportionate to the good effect (e.g., Uniacke, 1998, p. 120)

The deontological system will ensure that whenever conditions 1 and 2 are not met, the action will be judged as impermissible. The utilitarian system, on the other hand, will deem the action impermissible when 3 or 4 is flouted.

So the two-system model would provide an internal explanation for why the DDE is externally adequate to our intuitions. However, the two-system model does not require that the principle itself be internally represented at all. Rather, the two-system model is aimed at elucidating how we could have intuitions that can be externally captured by the DDE, even while the DDE itself does not correspond to any internal item in our moral psychology.

Of course, the two-system model I've suggested is a bare sketch. It hardly counts as a serious psychological account. The goal here has not been to deliver a definitive internal account of trolley intuitions but rather to provide a model that explains people's intuitions without invoking the universal moral grammar. The two-system model does, I suggest, provide a viable alternative to the idea that the DDE is a part of a universal moral grammar. Indeed, to the extent that it is independently plausible that the mind includes separate deontological and utilitarian evaluative systems, the two-systems account of the trolley intuitions provides a significantly better explanation than the appeal to a universal moral grammar.

4.2 Universality

Even if the argument from "unlearned moral principles" fails, the nativist can still exploit the linguistic analogy to explain the universality of moral principles. My earlier discussion just takes for granted the rather striking fact that virtually everyone thinks that it's wrong to intentionally harm or kill innocent people. The moral nativist might complain that I've simply helped myself to a large part of what makes the nativist account attractive. For, as in the case of language, nativism provides an obvious explanation for why the range of moral systems seems to be significantly constrained. Indeed, as Mikhail notes, "even the most superficial comparison of morality and language suggests the development of moral competence is *more* constrained than the development of linguistic competence" (2002, p. 1110). For instance, it would seem that in every culture there are prohibitions against rape and murder (Brown, 1991, pp. 138–9; Mikhail, 2002, pp. 1107–10). The hypothesis of a universal moral grammar explains the universality that I have simply assumed.

Moral nativism does offer one explanation for the universality of moral principles. However, in many instances of universally held beliefs, nativism is not the *best* explanation for universality. A standard empiricist alternative is that some beliefs are universal because the relevant information is readily available in everyone's environment. So, for instance, the universal belief that many birds fly comes from the *fact* that many birds fly and that this fact is readily accessible through our experience. This empiricist explanation might be offered to explain why we have universal moral principles. The normative information is readily available in the environment: parents systematically instruct their children that it is wrong to hurt others. However, this parry only defers the question—why is it that the norms themselves are so widely present? Why do parents in every culture have these norms? The appeal to a universal moral grammar provides an answer.

If we concede that the standard empiricist explanation of universal moral beliefs is incomplete, does the universal moral grammar proposal count as the best explanation for the universality of norms prohibiting intentional harm?[11] It's far from obvious, and I want to sketch an alternative explanation for why prohibitions against intentional harm are virtually ubiquitous.

Why does every culture have norms prohibiting hurting others? Nativism does seem a natural answer, and it is at home both with the Chomskian approach and with various evolutionary accounts of morality (e.g., Ruse, 1993). Another alternative, however, is that harm norms are ubiquitous because they have an edge in cultural evolution. There are a number of cultural explanations for why harm norms arose. And it's quite possible that such norms arose for different reasons in different communities. But what seems clear is that once the harm norms did arise, they would find a powerful ally in the emotions. Accordingly, we might explain the universality of harm norms as follows.

(i) Harm norms prohibit actions to which we are predisposed to be emotionally averse.

(ii) Norms that prohibit actions to which we are predisposed to be emotionally averse enjoyed enhanced cultural fitness over other norms.

If these two claims are right, we should expect harm norms to become widely prevalent, and we thus would have an explanation for the ubiquity of harm norms.

Each of the two claims enjoys considerable support. Normal humans have strongly aversive emotional responses to suffering in others. These responses show quick onset, and they emerge quite early in development. Indeed, even newborn infants respond aversively to some cues of suffering (e.g., Simner, 1971). As with

---

11. Due to space considerations, I'm focusing on harm norms. But there are other candidates for moral universals, including the widely prevalent notion of fairness. A discussion of the hypothesis that there is an innate principle of fairness exceeds the ambitions of this chapter. But it's worth noting that there are important cultural evolutionary and game-theoretic explanations for the ubiquity of fairness principles that need not appeal to an innate notion of fairness (e.g., Skyrms, 1996).

"basic emotions" like sadness, anger, disgust, and fear, there is good reason to suppose that the emotional response to suffering in others is universal and innately specified. As a result, we should expect that in all cultures, harming people will tend to produce seriously aversive affect. Thus harmful actions themselves will be likely to arouse negative affect, all else being equal.

As for claim (ii), it is independently plausible that emotional responses would contribute greatly to the cultural viability of norms. For instance, emotionally salient cultural items will be attention grabbing and memorable, which are obvious boons to cultural fitness. In addition to these general theoretical virtues, (ii) also makes a clear prediction about the pattern of normative cultural evolution. *Ceteris paribus*, norms that prohibit actions that are independently likely to excite negative emotion should be more likely to survive than norms that are not connected to emotions. In some recent work on the cultural evolution of etiquette, this prediction was borne out. In Western European culture, sixteenth-century etiquette norms that prohibited disgusting actions were much more likely to survive than other sixteenth-century etiquette norms (Nichols, 2002b).

The predicted pattern of normative evolution is also found in moral norms themselves. It has become a commonplace in discussions of moral evolution that, in the long run, moral norms exhibit a characteristic pattern of development. First, harm norms tend to evolve from being restricted to a small group of individuals to encompassing an increasingly larger group. That is, the moral community expands. Second, harm norms come to apply to a wider range of harms among those who are already part of the moral community—that is, there is less tolerance of pain and suffering of others. The trends are bumpy and irregular, but this kind of characteristic normative evolution is affirmed by a fairly wide range of contemporary moral philosophers (e.g., Brink, 1989; Nagel, 1986; Railton, 1986; Smith, 1994). Since we are disposed to respond aversively to even low-level signs of distress, the trend in moral evolution further confirms the prediction that norms will have enhanced cultural fitness when they prohibit actions that we're predisposed to find emotionally aversive (see Nichols, 2004).

Thus, one doesn't need to appeal to innate moral principles to explain the ubiquity of harm norms. A cultural evolution account that appeals to the role of emotions can provide an explanation that is at least as promising as the moral nativist explanation. Indeed, given that the affect-based cultural evolution story is independently motivated, there is reason to think it is a *better* explanation than the nativist explanation. Of course, on this account, we still explain the ubiquity of harm norms as a function of innate biases, but the biases are innate affective systems rather than innate moral principles.

5 The Case for the Innateness of Moral Judgment

Finally, let's turn to the child's capacity for core moral judgment. As noted in section 2, from a young age, children treat moral transgressions as distinctive on a number of dimensions—seriousness, authority contingence, generalizability, and justification-type. The early emergence and the multidimensionality of this capacity make it an extremely attractive candidate for a nativist explanation. And, indeed, recently

Susan Dwyer has taken up this charge. Dwyer characterizes the child's competence with the moral/conventional distinction much as I did earlier, and she goes on to develop a kind of POS argument for moral nativism (Dwyer, 1999, pp. 171–7). According to Dwyer, "the fundamental mistake" of empiricist accounts like social learning theory is "the assumption that all the information the child needs to achieve moral maturity is available in her environment" (p. 172). More fully, she writes:

> Absent a detailed account of how children extrapolate distinctly moral rules from the barrage of parental imperatives and evaluations, the appeal to explicit moral instruction will not provide anything like a satisfactory explanation of the emergence of mature moral competence. What we have here is a set of complex, articulated abilities that (i) emerge over time in an environment that is impoverished with respect to the content and scope of their mature manifestations, and (ii) appear to develop naturally across the species. (p. 173)

Thus Dwyer draws the negative, antiempiricist conclusion from her POS argument. According to Dwyer, just as empiricist accounts can't explain the child's linguistic competence, empiricist accounts can't explain the child's *moral* competence (as revealed by the child's grasp of the moral/conventional distinction). Dwyer also goes on to propose an answer similar to the positive conclusion set out earlier (sec. 1) for language. She suggests that "we all come into the world equipped with a store of innate moral knowledge which, together with our experience, determines our mature moral competence" (pp. 176–7). Given the universality of the moral/conventional distinction, she speculates that children are "in possession of some knowledge that primes them for recognizing two normative social domains" (p. 177). So Dwyer draws both a negative and a positive conclusion from her POS argument. The negative conclusion is that the child's moral competence exceeds what an empiricist learner would be able to achieve, given the information available in the environment. The positive conclusion is that moral competence depends on innate domain-specific information, namely, knowledge of the moral domain.

Let's allow Dwyer the negative conclusion that there isn't enough information in the environment to explain the child's capacity for moral judgment. To assess Dwyer's positive conclusion we need to consider whether there is an alternative to innate moral knowledge that provides a better explanation of the capacity for moral judgment. Recent work suggests that a better explanation of this capacity adverts to affective response. In a series of important studies, James Blair found that psychopaths and children with psychopathic tendencies perform abnormally on the moral/conventional task. For instance, psychopaths tend to give social-conventional explanations for why moral transgressions are wrong (Blair, 1995). And children with psychopathic tendencies are more likely than other children with behavioral problems to judge moral transgressions as authority contingent; for example, they are more likely to say that hitting others would be okay if the teacher said it was okay (Blair, 1997). Blair also found that psychopaths tend to have diminished response to distress cues in others. Over a series of studies, Blair and colleagues found that normal children, autistic children, and nonpsychopathic criminals all show considerably heightened physiological response both to threatening stimuli and to cues that another is in distress; psychopaths, on the other hand, show considerably heightened physiological response to threatening stimuli but show abnormally low responsiveness to distress cues (Blair, 1999; Blair et al., 1997). The fact that the population that shows a deficit in moral judgment also shows a distinctive affective deficit suggests that the moral deficit might derive from the affective deficit.

Blair's explanation of the psychopath's deficit in moral judgment appeals to what he calls a "violence inhibition mechanism" (VIM; Blair, 1995). The idea derives from Lorenz's (1966a) proposal that social animals have evolved mechanisms to inhibit intraspecies aggression. When a conspecific displays submission cues, the attacker stops. Blair suggests that there's something analogous in our cognitive systems, the VIM, and that this mechanism underlies both our response to distress cues and our capacity to distinguish moral from conventional violations. This mechanism is damaged in psychopathy, according to Blair, and this explains the psychopath's failure on the moral/conventional task. In normals, the VIM produces negative affect, which generates moral judgment.

I think that there are a number of problems with Blair's VIM account of moral judgment (Nichols, 2002a). On the model that I prefer, the capacity for drawing the moral/conventional distinction depends on two quite different mechanisms. First, there is a body of information, a normative "theory" that specifies a set of harm-based normative violations. The child's knowledge of these rules presumably depends on the general capacity for rule comprehension (see sec. 3). Second, Blair's data suggest that affect also plays a role in mediating performance on the moral/conventional task. In the normal population, the affective response to suffering in others bestows the harm norms with a distinctive, nonconventional status. Since psychopaths have a deficiency in their affective response to harm in others, this plausibly explains why they show a diminished tendency to treat harm norms as distinctive.

The proposal that emotions play a crucial role in generating nonconventional judgment gains further support from recent work on judgments about disgusting transgressions (e.g., spitting into a glass of water before drinking from it). In recent experiments, disgusting transgressions were treated as nonconventional along the same dimensions as moral transgressions. Disgusting transgressions are regarded by children as generalizably wrong (Nichols & Folds-Bennett, 2003). Adults regard disgusting transgressions as less authority contingent and more serious than conventional transgressions. Furthermore, low-disgust-sensitivity subjects are more likely than high-disgust-sensitivity subjects to judge a disgusting action as authority contingent (Nichols, 2002a).

Although there are differences between Blair's proposal and the one just sketched, if either of these accounts is right, then the capacity for core moral judgment can be explained without appeal to innate moral knowledge. Of course, there is still a crucial innate contribution to distinctively moral judgment, but the contribution comes from innate affective systems rather than innate propositional knowledge.

After setting out her case for moral judgment nativism, Dwyer actually considers the possibility that emotions play a crucial role in the acquisition of moral judgment:

> [T]he moral environment might be richer that I supposed earlier. Indeed, it is quite plausible that affective cues help children distinguish between moral transgressions and conventional transgressions. But it is hard to see how the deployment of

emotional capacities could facilitate children's grasp of the distinction between rule-governed behavior and accidentally-regular behavior. (1999, p. 182)

Of course, I think that Dwyer is right to acknowledge that emotions might play a critical role in the development of moral judgment. However, Dwyer's initial concession here that "the moral environment might be richer" than she had supposed looks to abandon her POS argument altogether. For it threatens to give up entirely even on the negative conclusion of the POS argument against empiricist accounts of core moral judgment. I think that this concession is too early. Even if the moral/conventional distinction doesn't derive from innate moral knowledge, there might still be an important sense in which the tendency to treat the moral domain as distinctive is "unlearned." In the affect-based accounts, the contribution of affect is in the mind of the judger rather than in the cues in the environment, and on both accounts affect influences the emergence of moral competence in a way that doesn't conform to empiricist learning processes.

Thus, one can perfectly well accept the negative conclusion of Dwyer's POS argument while rejecting her positive proposal that we have innate moral knowledge. The foregoing emotion-based proposals do just that. However, Dwyer maintains that while emotion-based accounts might explain the child's capacity to distinguish moral from conventional violations, emotion-based accounts will not explain the child's appreciation of rule-governed behavior. This claim seems plausible, and it might bolster the kind of rule nativism discussed in section 3. However, it is worth emphasizing that this is a serious retreat for the moral nativist. If rule nativism remains the only stronghold, then there is no longer a case for innate moral knowledge or even for innate capacities that are distinctively moral. For, as I argued earlier, rule nativism does not entail moral judgment nativism; the capacity for rule comprehension is by no means a distinctively moral capacity.

6 Affective Constraints on Cognition

In the last several sections I've maintained that none of the arguments for innate moral knowledge succeeds. It is plausible, however, that innate affective mechanisms shape our moral capacities. In this final section, I will consider how this proposal reflects on broader issues about nativism. Clearly the influences of affective responses to suffering constitute innate biases that fall on the nature side of the nature/nurture divide. However, I'll suggest that the role of affective mechanisms in structuring the mind complicates the standard picture about poverty of the stimulus arguments and nativism.

I've assumed that some of the emotions that influence moral judgment are innately specified. As noted earlier, affective responses to suffering emerge very early and would seem to be culturally universal. It is also plausible that these emotion systems were designed by evolution. Presumably, having these emotional reactions generated motivation that enhanced biological fitness in some way. It is currently unclear exactly why these responses were fitness enhancing. Nonetheless, given that these innate emotion systems are tied so closely to behavioral response, it is prima facie plausible to take them to be adaptations to some problem in the ancestral environment.

Now let's return to the capacity for moral judgment. The evidence on the moral/conventional distinction suggests that the moral realm is organized into a domain that is quite distinct from the conventional domain. Transgressions apparently get sorted into cognitive domains of moral and conventional. Hence, moral judgment has the marks of domain specificity. However, the claim in the preceding section was that these domains are generated by emotion systems—in particular, affective systems that respond to suffering in others. If that's right, emotions can have a cascading influence on information bases, imposing important cognitive structure onto domains of knowledge. Of course an emotion-based explanation for the acquisition of a cognitive capacity can displace the appeal to innate propositional knowledge. Indeed, that was the thrust of the argument in section 5. But the role of affective mechanisms in structuring the mind has more interesting implications about domain specificity.

As noted earlier, it is plausible that the emotion systems that react to suffering in others evolved to address some problem in our ancestral environment. However, these emotion systems constrain cognitive structures in ways that are not domain specific. Let's suppose, in line with the proposal in section 5, that the affective response to suffering in others does marshal a division between conventional and moral transgressions. There's no reason to think that this emotion system affects *only* this set of cognitive states. That is, the emotions that influence the character of moral judgment are probably not specific to the domain of moral judgment; these emotions might influence the acquisition of other areas of knowledge. For instance, our responses to suffering in others might also play an important role in the way we think about natural disasters that cause immense human suffering.

Although the effects of these emotions on cognition are probably not domain specific, neither are they perfectly domain general. There are lots of knowledge structures that will be utterly unaffected by the emotional response to suffering in others. The class of conventional transgressions provides one obvious candidate. But these emotions don't affect our cognitions about mathematics, about music, or about growing vegetables either.

The case of moral judgment thus suggests that innate affective elements of the mind can shape cognitive structures in ways that do not fit the traditional distinction between domain general and domain specific. For the influence of emotion systems might be neither domain specific nor domain general but rather domain *diverse*. The emotional responses to suffering affect the development and character of certain cognitive structures, like the rules against intentional harm, but have no intercourse with other cognitive structures, like folk astronomy.

The existence of innate domain-diverse factors alters the landscape of nativist arguments. For a POS argument might succeed in showing that a given capacity can't have been reached by general purpose learning mechanisms, but it won't follow immediately that the capacity depends on a mechanism that is devoted to the domain of that capacity. The acquisition might depend rather on a *domain-diverse* mechanism like an emotion system.

There is one further implication of the account of moral judgment that I'd like to spin out. On the proposal set out in section 5, both the capacity for rule comprehension and the emotional response to suffering are implicated in core moral judgment. I've assumed that affective mechanisms that respond to suffering in others have an innate basis and that they are the product of natural selection. I have also been allowing throughout that we have an innate capacity for rule comprehension. It is quite possible that this capacity for rule comprehension is also an adaptation. Indeed, there is a range of intriguing adaptationist proposals about the capacity for rule comprehension (see e.g., Cummins, 1996; Sripada & Stich, forthcoming). Thus, both of the mechanisms that I've suggested contribute to moral judgment might well be adaptations. However, it is distinctly less plausible that the capacity for core moral judgment itself is an adaptation. It is more likely that core moral judgment emerges as a kind of by-product of (*inter alia*) the innate affective and innate rule comprehension mechanisms.[12] That is, if the emotion system and the rule system are innate adaptations, core moral judgment is plausibly a kind of cognitive spandrel. It isn't an adaptation, but it is a natural by-product of psychological mechanisms that are adaptations.

7 Conclusion

The linguistic analogy provides an attractive basis for advancing the idea that we come with innate moral knowledge. However, none of the recent arguments for innate moral knowledge is at all convincing. There is reason to think that moral psychology is profoundly shaped by innate biases. But the innate biases plausibly come in the form of affective mechanisms rather than propositional information. The human mind comes loaded with a set of affective systems that seem to shape cognitive structures in ways that are neither domain general nor specific to a particular domain. So if we are to understand the innate factors that influence the acquisition of knowledge structures and other cognitive capacities, we must attend to the distinctive role of our innate affective endowment.

---

12. This view is bolstered by the findings on disgusting transgressions (Nichols, 2002a). For, again, distinctively nonconventional judgments apparently emerge as a by-product of rules and emotions.

References

Adelson, E. (2000). Lightness perception and lightness illusions. In M. Gazzaniga (ed.), *The New Cognitive Neurosciences*, 2nd ed. MIT Press.

Adolphs, R., Tranel, D., and Damasio, A. (1998). The human amygdala in social judgment. *Nature*, 393.

Adolphs, R., Tranel, D., Damasio, H., and Damasio, A. (1994). Impaired recognition of emotion in facial expressions following bilateral damage to the human amygdala. *Nature*, 372.

Ahn, W., Kalish, C., Gelman, S., Medin, D., Luhmann, C., Atran, S., Coley, J., and Shafto, P. (2001). Why essences are essential in the psychology of concepts. *Cognition*, 82.

Albert, M., Diamond, A., Fitch, R., Neville, H., Rapp, P., and Tallal, P. (1999). Cognitive development. In F. Bloom, S. Landis, J. Robert, L. Squire, and M. Zigmond (eds.), *Fundamental Neuroscience*. Academic Press.

Alberts, B., Bray, D., Lewis, J., Raff, M., Roberts, K., and Watson, J. (1994). *Molecular Biology of the Cell.* 3rd ed. Garland.

Alexander, R. (1974). The evolution of social behaviour. *Annual Review of Ecology and Systematics*, 5.

Allison, T., Puce, A., and McCarthy, G. (2000). Social perception from visual cues: Role of the STS region. *Trends in Cognitive Sciences*, 4, 7.

Altmann, J. (1980). *Baboon Mothers and Infants*. Harvard University Press.

American Psychiatric Association (1994). *Diagnostic and Statistical Manual of Mental Disorders*. 4th ed. American Psychiatric Association.

Anderson, J. (1993). *Rules of the Mind*. Erlbaum.

Anderson, J., and Mitchell, R. (1999). Macaques but not lemurs co-orient visually with humans. *Folia Primatologia*, 70.

Anderson, S., Bechara, A., Damasio, H., Tranel, D., and Damasio, A. (1999). Impairment of social and moral behavior related to early damage in human prefrontal cortex. *National Neuroscience*, 211.

Andrews, P., Gangestad, D., and Mathews, D. (2003). Adaptationism—How to carry out an exaptationist program. *Behavioral and Brain Sciences*, 25.

Ariew, A. (1996). Innateness and canalisation. *Philosophy of Science*, 63.

Ariew, A. (1999). Innateness is canalisation: In defence of a developmental account of innateness. In V. Hardcastle (ed.), *Where Biology Meets Psychology*: Philosophical Essays. MIT Press.
Astington, J., and Jenkins, J. (1999). A longitudinal study of the relation between language and theory of mind development. *Developmental Psychology*, 35.
Astington, J., Harris, P., and Olson, D. (eds.). (1988). *Developing Theories of Mind*. Cambridge University Press.
Astuti, R., Solomon, G., and Carey, S. (2003). *Folkbiology and the Construal of Group Identity: A Study of Knowledge Acquisition in Madagascar*. Unpublished manuscript.
Athens, L. (1997). *Violent Criminal Acts and Actors Revisited*. University of Illinois Press.
Atran, S. (1987). Ordinary constraints on the semantics of living kinds: A commonsense alternative to recent treatments of natural-object terms. *Mind and Language*, 2.
Atran, S. (1990). *Cognitive Foundations of Natural History: Towards an Anthropology of Science*. Cambridge University Press.
Atran, S. (1998). Folkbiology and the anthropology of science: Cognitive universals and cultural particulars. *Behavioral and Brain Sciences*, 21.
Atran, S. (1999). Itzaj Maya folkbiological taxonomy. In D. Medin and S. Atran (eds.), *Folkbiology*. MIT Press.
Atran, S. (2001a). The case for modularity: Sin or salvation? *Evolution and Cognition*, 7.
Atran, S. (2001b). The trouble with memes: Inference versus imitation in cultural creation. *Human Nature*, 12.
Atran, S. (2001c). A cheater detection module? Dubious interpretations of the Wason Selection Task and logic. *Evolution and Cognition*, 7.
Atran, S. (2002). Modular and cultural factors in biological understanding: an experimental approach to the cognitive basis of science. In P. Carruthers, S. Stich, and M. Siegal (eds.), *The Cognitive Basis of Science*. Cambridge University Press.
Atran, S. (2003). Modest adaptationism (reply to Andrews et al.). *Behavioral and Brain Sciences*, 25.
Atran, S., and Lois, X. (2001). Reply to Shanker. *Current Anthropology*, 42.
Atran, S., Estin, P., Coley, J., and Medin, D. (1997). Generic species and basic levels: Essence and appearance in folk biology. *Journal of Ethnobiology*, 17.
Atran, S., Medin, D., Lynch, E., Vapnarsky, V., Ucan Ek', E., and Sousa, P. (2001). Folkbiology doesn't come from folkpsychology: Evidence from Yukatek Maya in cross-cultural perspective. *Journal of Cognition and Culture*, 1.
Au, T., and Romo, L. (1999). Mechanical causality in children's folkbiology. In D. Medin and S. Atran (eds.), *Folkbiology*. MIT Press.
Axelrod, R. (1984). *The Evolution of Cooperation*. Basic Books.
Bailenson, J., Shum, M., Atran, S., Medin, D., and Coley, J. (2002). A bird's eye view: Biological categorization and reasoning within and across cultures. *Cognition*, 84.
Bailey, A., Phillips, W., and Rutter, M. (1996). Autism: Towards an integration of clinical, genetic, neuropsychological, and neurobiological perspectives. *Journal of Child Psychology and Psychiatry*, 37.
Baillargeon, R. (1986). Representing the existence and the location of hidden objects: Object permanence in 6- and 8-month-old infants. *Cognition*, 23.
Baillargeon, R. (1987). Object permanence in 3.5- and 4.5-month-old infants. *Developmental Psychology*, 23.
Baillargeon, R. (1993). The object concept revisited: New direction in the investigation of infants' physical knowledge. In C. Granrud (ed.), *Visual perception and cognition in infancy*. Erlbaum.

Baillargeon, R. (1994). Physical reasoning in infancy. In M. Gazzaniga (ed.), *The Cognitive Neurosciences*. MIT Press.

Baillargeon, R. (1999). Young infants' expectations about hidden objects: A reply to three challenges. *Developmental Science*, 2.

Baillargeon, R. (2002). The acquisition of physical knowledge in infancy: A summary in eight lessons. In U. Goswami (ed.), *Blackwell Handbook of Child Cognitive Development*. Blackwell.

Baillargeon, R., Spelke, E., and Wasserman, S. (1985). Object permanence in 5-month-old infants. *Cognition*, 20.

Baird, J., and Baldwin, D. (2001). Making sense of human behavior: Action parsing and intentional inference. In B. Malle, L. Moses, and D. Baldwin (eds.), *Intentions and Intentionality: Foundations of Social Cognition*. MIT Press.

Baker, M. (1996). *The Polysynthesis Parameter*. Oxford University Press.

Baker, M. (2001). *The Atoms of Language: The Mind's Hidden Rules of Grammar*. Basic Books.

Baldwin, D. (1993). Infants' ability to consult the speaker for clues to word reference. *Journal of Child Language*, 20.

Baldwin, D. (1995). Understanding the link between joint attention and language. Development of joint visual attention in infants. In C. Moore and P. Dunham (eds.), *Joint Attention: Its Origin and Role in Development*. Erlbaum.

Baldwin, D., and Moses, L. (1996). The ontogeny of social information gathering. *Child Development*, 67.

Baldwin, D., Baird, J., Saylor, M., and Clark, M. (in press). Infants detect structure in human action: A first step toward understanding others' intentions? *Child Development*.

Baldwin, D., Markman, E., and Melartin, R. (1993). Infants' ability to draw inferences about nonobvious object properties: Evidence from exploratory play. *Cognitive Development*, 64.

Barkow, J., Cosmides, L., and Tooby, J. (eds.). (1992). *The Adapted Mind: Evolutionary Psychology and the Generation of Culture*. Oxford University Press.

Barlow, H. (1981). Critical limiting factors in the design of the eye and visual cortex. *Proceedings of the Royal Society of London*, series B, Biological Sciences, 212, 1186.

Baron-Cohen, S. (1987). Autism and symbolic play. *British Journal of Developmental Psychology*, 5.

Baron-Cohen, S. (1988). Social and pragmatic deficits in autism: Cognitive or affective? *Journal of Autism and Developmental Disorders*, 18.

Baron-Cohen, S. (1989). Perceptual role-taking and protodeclarative pointing in autism. *British Journal of Developmental Psychology*, 7.

Baron-Cohen, S. (1994). How to build a baby that can read minds: Cognitive mechanisms in mindreading. *Cahiers de Psychologie Cognitive/Current Psychology of Cognition*, 13.

Baron-Cohen, S. (1995). *Mindblindness: An Essay on Autism and Theory of Mind*. MIT Press.

Baron-Cohen, S. (2000). Theory of mind and autism: A fifteen-year review. In S. Baron-Cohen, H. Tager-Flusberg, and D. Cohen (eds.), *Understanding Other Minds: Perspectives from Developmental Cognitive Neuroscience*. Oxford University Press.

Baron-Cohen, S., Jolliffe, T., Mortimore, C., and Robertson, M. (1997). Another advanced test of theory of mind: Evidence from very high functioning adults with autism or Asperger Syndrome. *Journal of Child Psychology and Psychiatry*, 38.

Baron-Cohen, S., Leslie, A., and Frith, U. (1985). Does the autistic child have a "theory of mind?" *Cognition*, 21.

Baron-Cohen, S., Leslie, A., and Frith, U. (1986). Mechanical, behavioral, and intentional understanding of picture stories in autistic children. *British Journal of Developmental Psychology*, 4.

Baron-Cohen, S., Ring, H., Moriarty, J., Shmitz, P., Costa, D., and Ell, P. (1994). Recognition of mental state terms: A clinical study of autism, and a functional neuroimaging study of normal adults. *British Journal of Psychiatry, 165*.

Baron-Cohen, S., Ring, H., Wheelwright, S., Bullmore, E., Brammer, M., Simons, A., and Williams, S. (1999). Social intelligence in the normal and autistic brain: An fMRI study. *European Journal of Neuroscience*.

Baron-Cohen, S., Tager-Flusberg, H., and Cohen, D. (eds.). (1993). *Understanding Other Minds: Perspectives from Autism*. Oxford University Press.

Baron-Cohen, S., Tager-Flusberg, H., and Cohen, D. (eds.). (2000). *Understanding other Minds: Perspectives from Developmental Cognitive Neuroscience*. 2nd ed. Oxford University Press.

Barrett, H. C. (2005). Adaptations to predators and prey. In D. Buss (ed.), *The Handbook of Evolutionary Psychology*. Wiley.

Barrett, C. (in press). Enzymatic computation and cognitive modularity. *Mind and Language*.

Barrett, H. C., and Behne, T. (in press). Children's understanding of death as the cessation of agency: A test using sleep versus death. *Cognition*.

Barrett, H., Tooby, J., and Cosmides, L. (under review). Children's understanding of predator-prey interactions: Cultural dissociations as tests of the impact of experience on evolved inference systems.

Barrett, L., Dunbar, R., and Lycett, J. (2002). *Human Evolutionary Psychology*. Palgrave.

Barth, H., Kanwisher, N., and Spelke, E. (2003). The construction of large number representations in adults. *Cognition, 86*.

Bartsch, K., and Wellman, H. (1995). *Children talk about the mind*. Oxford University Press.

Barwise, J., and Cooper, R. (1981). Generalized quantifiers and natural language. *Linguistics and Philosophy, 4*.

Bates, E., Camaioni, L., and Volterra, V. (1975). The acquisition of performatives prior to speech. *Merrill-Palmer Quarterly, 21*.

Bateson, P. (1991). Are there principles of behavioural development? In P. Bateson (ed.), *The Development and Integration of Behaviour*. Cambridge University Press.

Beaumont, S., and Bloom, K. (1993). Adult's attributions of intentionality to vocalizing infants. *First Language, 13*.

Bechara, A., Tranel, D., Damasio, H., and Damasio, A. (1996). Failure to respond autonomically to anticipated future outcomes following damage to prefrontal cortex. *Cerebral Cortex, 62*.

Becker, J., Liersch, R., Tautz, C., Schlueter, B., and Andler, W. (1998). Shaken baby syndrome: Report on four pairs of twins. *Child Abuse and Neglect, 22*.

Bednar, J. (2003). The role of internally generated neural activity in newborn and infant face preferences. In O. Pascalis and A. Slater (eds.), *Face Perception in Infancy and Early Childhood*. NOVA Science.

Bednar, J., and Miikkulainen, R. (2003). Learning innate face preferences. *Neural Computation, 15*.

Bellugi, U., Bihrle, A., Neville, H., and Doherty, S. (1992). Language, cognition, and brain organization in a neurodevelopmental disorder. In M. Gunnar and C. Nelson (eds.), *Developmental behavioral neuroscience: The Minnesota symposium*. Erlbaum.

Bellugi, U., Lichtenberger, L., Mills, D., Galaburda, A., and Korenberg, J. (1999). Bridging cognition, brain and molecular genetics: Evidence from Williams syndrome. *Trends in Neurosciences, 5*.

Bellugi, U., Marks, S., Bihrle, A., and Sabo, H. (1988a). Dissociation between language and cognitive functions in Williams syndrome. In D. Bishop and K. Mogford (eds.), *Language development in exceptional circumstances*. Churchill Livingstone.

Bellugi, U., Sabo, H., and Vaid, J. (1988b). Spatial deficits in children with Williams syndrome. In J. Stiles-Davis, U. Kritchevshy, and U. Bellugi (eds.), *Spatial cognition: Brain bases and development*. Erlbaum.
Belsky, J., Steinberg, L., and Draper, P. (1991). Childhood experience, interpersonal development, and reproductive strategy: An evolutionary theory of socialization. *Child Development*, 62.
Benson, G., Abbeduto, L., Short, K., Bibler-Nuccio, J., and Maas, F. (1993). Development of theory of mind in individuals with MR. *American Journal on Mental Retardation*, 98.
Berbaum, K., Bever, T., and Chung, C. (1983). Light source position in the perception of object shape. *Perception*, 12.
Berlin, B. (1992). *Ethnobiological Classification*. Princeton University Press.
Berlin, B., Breedlove, D., and Raven, P. (1973). General principles of classification and nomenclature in folk biology. *American Anthropologist*, 74.
Bernstein, A., Newman, J., Wallace, J., and Luh, K. (2000). Left-hemisphere activation and deficient response modulation in psychopaths. *Psychological Science*, 115.
Bickerton, D. (1990). *Language and Species*. University of Chicago Press.
Bickerton, D. (1995). *Language and Human Behavior*. University of Washington Press.
Biederman, I. (1987). Recognition-by-components: A theory of human image understanding. *Psychological Review*, 94.
Biegler, R., and Morris, R. (1993). Landmark stability is a prerequisite for spatial but not discrimination learning. *Nature*, 361.
Bishop, K., Goudreau, G., and O'Leary, D. (2000). Regulation of area identity in the mammalian neocortex by Emx2 and Pax6. *Science*, 288, 5464.
Bjorklund, D. (1987). A note on neonatal imitation. *Developmental Review*, 7.
Blair, R. (1993). The development of morality. Ph.D. diss., University of London.
Blair, R. (1995). A cognitive developmental approach to morality: Investigating the psychopath. *Cognition*, 57.
Blair, R. (1997). Moral reasoning and the child with psychopathic tendencies. *Personality and Individual Differences*, 22, 5.
Blair, R. (1999). Psychophysiological responsiveness to the distress of others in children with autism. *Personality and Individual Differences*, 26, 3.
Blair, R. (2001). Neurocognitive models of aggression, the antisocial personality disorders, and psychopathy. *Journal of Neurology, Neurosurgery, and Psychiatry*, 71, 6.
Blair, R., Colledge, E., and Mitchell, D. (2001). Somatic markers and response reversal: Is there orbitofrontal cortex dysfunction in boys with psychopathic tendencies? *Journal of Abnormal Child Psychology*, 29, 6.
Blair, R., Jones, L., Clark, F., and Smith, M. (1997). The psychopathic individual: A lack of responsiveness to distress cues? *Psychophysiology*, 34, 2.
Blake, R., Tuner, L., Smoski, M., Pozdol, S., and Stone, W. (2003). Visual recognition of biological motion is impaired in children with autism. *Psychological Science*, 14.
Blakemore, C., and Cooper, G. (1970). Development of the brain depends on the visual environment. *Nature*, 228.
Bloch, M., Solomon, G., and Carey, S. (2001). Zafimaniry: An understanding of what is passed on from parents to children: A cross-cultural investigation. *Journal of Cognition and Culture*, 1.
Bloom, L. (1973). *One Word at a Time: The Use of Single Word Utterances before Syntax*. Mouton.
Bloom, P. (2000). *How Children Learn the Meanings of Words*. MIT Press.
Boesch, C., and Boesch-Achermann, H. (2000). *The Chimpanzees of the Taï Forest: Behavioural Ecology and Evolution*. Oxford University Press.

Bogartz, R., Shinskey, J., and Speaker, C. (1997). Interpreting infant looking: The event set [Not Defind] event set design. *Developmental Psychology*, 33.

Bonasso, R., Kortenkamp, D., and Murphy, R. (1998). Mobile robots: A proving ground for artificial intelligence. In D. Kortenkamp, R. Bonasso, and R. Murphy (eds.), *Mobile Robots and Artificial Intelligence*. AAAI Press.

Bonda, E., Petrides, M., Ostry, D., and Evans, A. (1996). Specific involvement of human parietal systems and the amygdala in the perception of biological motion. *Journal of Neuroscience*, 15.

Booth, A., and Waxman, S. (2002). Word learning is "smart": Evidence that conceptual information affects preschoolers' extension of novel words. *Cognition*, 84.

Boroditsky, L., and Schmidt, L. (2000). Sex, syntax, and semantics. *Proceedings of the Cognitive Science Society*, 22.

Boster, C., and Crain, S. (1993). On children's understanding of *every* and *or*. In C. Smith (ed.), *Conference Proceedings: Early Cognition and the Transition to Language*. University of Texas at Austin.

Botterill, G., and Carruthers, P. (1999). *The Philosophy of Psychology*. Cambridge University Press.

Botvinick, M., Braver, T., Barch, D., Carter, C., and Cohen, J. (2001). Conflict monitoring and cognitive control. *Psychological Review*, 1083.

Boyd, R. (1999). Homeostasis, species, and higher taxa. In R. Wilson (ed.), *Species: New Interdisciplinary Essays*. MIT Press.

Boyer, P. (1994). *The Naturalness of Religious Ideas: A Cognitive Theory of Religion*. University of California Press.

Boyer, P. (2000). Evolution of the modern mind and the origins of culture: Religious concepts as a limiting case. In P. Carruthers and A. Chamberlain (eds.), *Evolution and the Human Mind: Modularity, Language and Meta-Cognition*. Cambridge University Press.

Boyer, P. (2001). *Religion Explained*. Basic Books.

Brady, M., and Kersten, D. (2003). Bootstrapped learning of novel objects. *Journal of Vision*, 3, 6.

Brainerd, D., and Freeman, W. (1997). Bayesian color constancy. *Journal of the Optical Society of America*, 14.

Breene, R., and Sweet, M. (1985). Evidence of insemination of multiple females by the male black widow spider, *Latrodectus mactans* (Araneae, Theridiidae). *Journal of Arachnology*, 13.

Breiter, H., Etcoff, N., Whalem, P., Kennedy, W., Rauch, S., Buckner, R., Strauss, M., Hyman, S., and Rosen, B. (1996). Response and habituation of the human amygdala during visual processing of facial expression. *Neuron*, 17.

Bretherton, I., McNew, S., and Beeghly-Smith, M. (1981). Early person knowledge as expressed in gestural and verbal communications: When do infants acquire a "theory of mind"? In M. Lamb and L. Sherrod (eds.), *Infant Social Cognition*. Erlbaum.

Brink, D. (1989). *Moral Realism and the Foundation of Ethics*. Cambridge University Press.

Bristowe, W. (1958). *The World of Spiders*. Collins.

Brooks, R. (1999). *Cambrian Intelligence*. MIT Press.

Brothers, L. (1990). The social brain: A project for integrating primate behaviour and neurophysiology in a new domain. *Concepts in Neuroscience*, 1.

Brothers, L., Ring, B., and Kling, A. (1990). Responses of neurons in the macaque amygdala to complex social stimuli. *Behavioral Brain Research*, 41.

Brown, A. (1990). Domain-specific principles affect learning and transfer in children. *Cognitive Science*, 14.

Brown, A., Yates, P., Burrola, P., Ortuno, D., Vaidya, A., Jessell, T., Pfaff, S., O'Leary, D., and Lemke, G. (2000). Topographic mapping from the retina to the midbrain is controlled by relative but not absolute levels of EphA receptor signaling. *Cell*, 102, 1.

Brown, D. (1991). *Human Universals*. Temple University Press.

Brown, D., and Boysen, S. (2000). Spontaneous discrimination of natural stimuli by chimpanzees. *Journal of Comparative Psychology*, 114.

Brown, R., Hobson, P., Lee, A., and Stevenson, J. (1997). Are there "autistic-like" features in congenitally blind children? *Journal of Child Psychology and Psychiatry*, 38.

Brownlee, H., Gao, P., Frisen, J., Dreyfus, C., Zhou, R., and Black, I. (2000). Multiple ephrins regulate hippocampal neurite outgrowth. *Journal of Comparative Neurology*, 425, 2.

Bryson, J. (2000). Cross-paradigm analysis of autonomous agent architecture. *Journal of Experimental and Theoretical Artificial Intelligence*, 12 (2).

Buccino, G., Binkofski, F., Fink, G., Fadiga, L., Fogassi, L., Gallese, V., Seitz, R., Zilles, K., Rizzolatti, G., and Freund, H.-J. (2001). Action observation activates premotor and parietal areas in a somatotopic manner: An fMRI study. *European Journal of Neuroscience*, 13.

Bullock, M., Gelman, R., and Baillargeon, R. (1982). The development of causal reasoning. In W. Friedman (ed.), *The Developmental Psychology of Time*. Academic Press.

Buss, D. (1991). Mate preference mechanisms: Consequences for partner choice and intrasexual competition. In J. Barkow, L. Cosmides, and J. Tooby (eds.), *The Adapted Mind: Evolutionary Psychology and the Generation of Culture*. Oxford University Press.

Buss, D. (1999). *Evolutionary Psychology: The New Science of the Mind*. Allyn and Bacon.

Buss, D. (2004). *Evolutionary Psychology: The New Science of the Mind*. 2nd ed. Allyn and Bacon.

Buss, D., and Duntley, J. (1998). Evolved homicide modules. Paper presented to the annual meeting of the Human Behavior and Evolution Society, Davis, CA.

Buss, D., and Duntley, J. (2003). Homicide: An evolutionary perspective and implications for public policy. In N. Dess (ed.), *Violence and Public Policy*. Greenwood.

Buss, D., and Duntley, J. (2004). The evolution of gender differences in aggression. In S. Fein (ed.), *Gender and Aggression*. Guilford.

Buss, D., and Duntley, J. (under review). Homicide adaptation theory.

Buss, D., Shackelford, T., Bleske, A., and Wakefield, J. (1998). Adaptations, exaptation, and spandrels. *American Psychologist*, 53.

Butterworth, G., and Grover, L. (1988). The origins of referential communication in human infancy. In L. Weiskrantz (ed.), *Thought without Language*. Oxford University Press.

Butterworth, G., and Grover, L. (1990). Joint visual attention, manual pointing, and preverbal communication in human infancy. In M. Jeannerod (ed.), *Attention and Performance XIII*. Erlbaum.

Butterworth, G., and Jarrett, N. (1991). What minds have in common is space: Spatial mechanisms serving joint visual attention in infancy. *British Journal of Developmental Psychology*, 9.

Bygott, J. (1972). Cannibalism among wild chimpanzees. *Nature*, 238.

Byrne, R. (1995). *The Thinking Ape: Evolutionary Origins of Intelligence*. Oxford University Press.

Calder, A., Lawrence, A., and Young, A. (2001). Neuropsychology of fear and loathing. *Nature Review: Neuroscience*, 2.

Call, J., and Tomasello, M. (2003). Social cognition. In D. Maestripieri (ed.), *Primate Psychology: The Mind and Behavior of Human and Nonhuman Primates*. Harvard University Press.

Camaioni, L. (1991). Mind knowledge in infancy: The emergence of intentional communication. *Early Development and Parenting*, 1.

Campbell, D., and Holt, C. (2001). Chemotropic responses of retinal growth cones mediated by rapid local protein synthesis and degradation. *Neuron*, 32, 6.

Carey, S. (1985). *Conceptual Change in Childhood*. MIT Press.

Carey, S. (1995). On the origin of causal understanding. In D. Sperber, D. Premack, and A. Premack (eds.), *Causal Cognition*. Clarendon Press.

Carey, S. (2001). Cognitive foundations of arithmetic: Evolution and ontogenisis. *Mind & Language*, 16, 1.

Carey, S., and Spelke, E. (1994). Domain-specific knowledge and conceptual change. In L. Hirschfeld and S. Gelman (eds.), *Mapping the Mind: Domain Specificity in Cognition and Culture*. Cambridge University Press.

Carey, S., and Spelke, E. (1996). Science and core knowledge. *Philosophy and Science*, 63.

Carey, S., and Xu, F. (2001). Infant knowledge of objects: Beyond object files and object tracking. *Cognition*, 80, 1/2.

Carlson, G., and Pelletier, F. (eds.). (1995). *The Generic Book*. University of Chicago Press.

Carpenter, M., Akhtar, N., and Tomasello, M. (1998a). Fourteen- through eighteen-month-old infants differentially imitate intentional and accidental actions. *Infant Behavior and Development*, 21.

Carpenter, M., Nagell, K., and Tomasello, M. (1998b). Social cognition, joint attention, and communicative competence from 9 to 15 months of age. *Monographs of the Society for Research in Child Development*, vol. 63, no. 4, serial no. 255.

Carruthers, P. (2002a). The roots of scientific reasoning: Infancy, modularity, and the art of tracking. In P. Carruthers, S. Stich, and M. Siegal (eds.), *The Cognitive Basis of Science*. Cambridge University Press.

Carruthers, P. (2002b). Human creativity: Its evolution, its cognitive basis, and its connections with childhood pretence. *British Journal for the Philosophy of Science*, 53.

Carruthers, P. (2002c). The cognitive functions of language. *Behavioral and Brain Sciences*, 26.

Carruthers, P. (2003a). Moderately massive modularity. In A. O'Hear (ed.), *Mind and Persons*. Cambridge: Cambridge University Press.

Carruthers, P. (2003b). Is the mind a system of modules shaped by natural selection? In C. Hitchcock (ed.), *Great Debates in Philosophy: Philosophy of Science*. Blackwell.

Carruthers, P. (2003c). On Fodor's problem. *Mind and Language*, 18.

Carruthers, P. (2004). Practical reasoning in a modular mind. *Mind and Language*, 19, 3.

Carruthers, P., and Chamberlain, A. (eds.). (2000). *Evolution and the Human Mind: Modularity, Language and Meta-Cognition*. Cambridge University Press.

Carruthers, P., and Smith, P. (eds.). (1996). *Theories of Theories of Mind*. Cambridge University Press.

Casebeer, W., and Churchland, P. (2003). The neural mechanisms of moral cognition: A multiple aspect approach to moral judgment and decision-making. *Biology and Philosophy*, 18

Cassidy, K., and Ballaraman, G. (1997). Theory of mind ability in language delayed children. Biennial Meeting of the Society for Research in Child Development, Washington, DC.

Centers for Disease Control and Prevention National Center for Injury Prevention and Control. (2002). WISQARS Leading causes of death reports, 1999–2002, consulted January 6, 2005. Available online at: http://webapp.cdc.gov/sasweb/ncipc/leadcaus10.html.

Cerella, J. (1979). Visual classes and natural categories in the pigeon. *Journal of Experimental Psychology Human Perception and Performance*, 5.

Chagnon, N. (1988). Life histories, blood revenge, and warfare in a tribal population. *Science*, 239.

Chaminade, T., Meltzoff, A., and Decety, J. (2002). Does the end justify the means? A PET exploration of the mechanisms involved in human imitation. *Neuroimage*, 15.
Chandler, M. (2001). The time of our lives: Self-continuity in native and non-native youth. *Advances in Child Development and Behavior*, 28.
Cheng, K. (1986). A purely geometric module in the rat's spatial representation. *Cognition*, 23.
Cherniak, C. (1986). *Minimal Rationality*. MIT Press.
Cherniak, C. (1995). Neural component placement. *Trends in neuroscience*, 18.
Chien, Y.-C., and Wexler, K. (1990). Children's knowledge of locality conditions on landing as evidence for the modularity of syntax and pragmatics. *Language Acquisition*, 1.
Chierchia, G. (2000). Scalar implications and polarity phenomena. Paper presented at NELS 31. Georgetown University, Washington, D.C.
Chierchia, G., and McConnel-Ginet, S. (2000). *Meaning and Grammar: An Introduction to Semantics (2nd ed.)*. MIT Press
Chierchia, G., Crain, S., Guasti, M., and Thornton, R. (1998). "Some" and "Or": A study on the emergence of Logical Form. In *Proceedings of the Boston University Conference of Language Development*, 11. Cascadilla Press.
Chomsky, N. (1957). *Syntactic Structures*. Mouton.
Chomsky, N. (1959). Review of Skinner's "Verbal Behavior." *Language*, 35.
Chomsky, N. (1965). *Aspects of the Theory of Syntax*. MIT Press.
Chomsky, N. (1967). Recent contributions to the theory of innate ideas. *Synthese*, 17.
Chomsky, N. (1975). *Reflections on Language*. Pantheon Books.
Chomsky, N. (1980). *Rules and Representation*. Columbia University Press.
Chomsky, N. (1981). *Lectures on Government and Binding*. Foris.
Chomsky, N. (1982). *Some Concepts and Consequences of the Theory of Government and Binding*. MIT Press.
Chomsky, N. (1986). *Knowledge of Language: Its Nature, Origin and Use*. Praeger.
Chomsky, N. (1987). *Language and the Problems of Knowledge: The Managua Lectures*. MIT Press.
Chomsky, N. (1995). *The Minimalist Program*. MIT Press.
Chomsky, N. (2000). Minimalist inquiries. In R. Martin, D. Michaels, and J. Uriagereka (eds.), *Step by Step: Essays on Minimalist Syntax in Honor of Howard Lasnik*. MIT Press.
Chomsky, N. (2001). Beyond explanatory adequacy. *MIT Occasional Papers in Linguistics*, no. 20.
Chun, M. (2000). Contextual cueing of visual attention. *Trends in Cognitive Sciences*, 4.
Church, R., and Broadbent, H. (1990). Alternative representations of time, number, and rate. *Cognition*, 37.
Cohen, L., and Cashon, C. (2003). Infant perception and cognition. In R. Lerner, A. Easterbrooks, and J. Mistry (eds.), *Comprehensive Handbook of Psychology*. Vol. 6. *Developmental Psychology. II. Infancy*. Wiley.
Cohen, L., and Marks, K. (2002). How infants process addition and subtraction events. *Developmental Science*, 5.
Cohen, L., Amsel, G., Redford, M., and Casasola, M. (1998). The development of infant causal perception. In A. Slater (ed.), *Perceptual Development: Visual, Auditory, and Speech Perception in Infancy*. Psychology Press.
Colby, C., and Goldberg, M. (1999). Space and attention in parietal cortex. *Annual Review of Neuroscience*, 22.
Coley, J., Medin, D., and Atran, S. (1997). Does rank have its privilege? Inductive inferences within folkbiological taxonomies, *Cognition*, 64.

Corcoran, R. (2000). Theory of mind in other clinical samples: Is a selective theory of mind deficit exclusive to autism? In S. Baron-Cohen, H. Tager-Flusberg, and D. Cohen (eds.). *Understanding Other Minds: Perspectives from Developmental Cognitive Neuroscience*. 2nd ed.. Oxford University Press.

Corkum, V., and Moore, C. (1998). The origins of joint visual attention in infants. *Developmental Psychology*, 34.

Cosmides, L. (1989). The logic of social exchange: Has natural selection shaped how humans reason? Studies with the Wason selection task. *Cognition*, 31, 3.

Cosmides, L., and Tooby, J. (1981). Cytoplasmic inheritance and intragenomic conflict. *Journal of Theoretical Biology*, 89.

Cosmides, L., and Tooby, J. (1987). From evolution to behavior: Evolutionary psychology as the missing link. In J. Dupre (ed.), *The Latest on the Best: Essays on Evolution and Optimality*. MIT Press.

Cosmides, L., and Tooby, J. (1989). Evolutionary psychology and the generation of culture. Part 2. Case study: A computational theory of social exchange. *Ethology and Sociobiology*, 10.

Cosmides, L., and Tooby, J. (1992). Cognitive adaptations for social exchange. In J. Barkow, L. Cosmides, and J. Tooby (eds.), *The Adapted Mind: Evolutionary Psychology and the Generation of Culture*. Oxford University Press.

Cosmides, L., and Tooby, J. (1994). Origins of domain specificity: The evolution of functional organization. In L. Hirschfeld and S. Gelman (eds.), *Mapping the Mind: Domain Specificity in Cognition and Culture*. Cambridge University Press.

Cosmides, L., and Tooby, J. (1995). Beyond intuition and instinct blindness: Toward an evolutionarily rigorous cognitive science. *Cognition*, 50.

Cosmides, L., and Tooby, J. (1996). A logical design for the mind? *Contemporary Psychology*, 41, 5.

Cosmides, L., and Tooby, J. (2000a). Consider the source: The evolution of adaptations for decoupling and metarepresentation. In D. Sperber (ed.), *Metarepresentations: A Multidisciplinary Perspective*. Oxford University Press.

Cosmides, L., and Tooby, J. (2000b). Evolutionary psychology and the emotions. In M. Lewis and J. Haviland-Jones (eds.), *Handbook of Emotions*, 2nd ed. Guilford.

Cosmides, L., and Tooby, J. (2005). Neurocognitive adaptations designed for social exchange. In D. Buss (ed.), *Evolutionary Psychology Handbook*. Wiley.

Courchesne, E., Townsend, J., and Chase, C. (1995). Neurodevelopmental principles guide research on developmental psychopathologies. In D. Cicchetti and D. Cohen (eds.), *Developmental psychopathology. Vol. 1. Theory and Methods*. Wiley.

Cowie, F. (1999). *What's Within? Nativism Reconsidered*. Oxford University Press.

Crain, S. (1991). Language acquisition in the absence of experience. *Behavioral and Brain Sciences*, 4.

Crain, S. (2002). The continuity assumption. In I. Lasser (ed.), *The Process of Language Acquisition*. Lang.

Crain, S., and McKee, C. (1985). The acquisition of structural restrictions on anaphora. *Proceedings of NELS*, 15. GLSA.

Crain, S., and Pietroski, P. (2001). Nature, nurture and Universal Grammar. *Linguistics and Philosophy*, 24.

Crain, S., and Pietroski, P. (2002). Why language acquisition is a snap. *Linguistic Review*, 19.

Crain, S., and Thornton, R. (1998). *Investigations in Universal Grammar: A Guide to Experiments on the Acquisition of Syntax and Semantics*. MIT Press

Crain, S., Thornton, R., Boster, C., Conway, L., Lillo-Martin, D., and Woodams, E. (1996). Quantification without qualification. *Language Acquisition*, 3, 2.

Critchley, H., Elliott, R., Mathias, C., and Dolan, R. (2000). Neural activity relating to generation and representation of galvanic skin conductance responses: a functional magnetic resonance imaging study. *Journal of Neuroscience*, 20.

Crockett, C., and Sekulic, R. (1984). Infanticide in red howler monkeys. In G. Hausfater and S. Hrdy (eds.), *Infanticide: Comparative and Evolutionary Perspectives*. Aldine.

Crowley, J., and Katz, L. (1999). Development of ocular dominance columns in the absence of retinal input. *Nature Neuroscience*, 2, 12.

Cruz, Y. (1997). Mammals. In S. Gilbert and A. Raunio (eds.), *Embryology: Constructing the Organism*. Sinauer.

Csibra, G. (2003). Teleological and referential understanding of action in infancy. *Philosophical Transactions of the Royal Society, series B*, 358.

Csibra, G., Gergely, G., Bíró, S., Koós, O., and Brockbank, M. (1999). Goal attribution without agency cues: The perception of "pure reason" in infancy. *Cognition*, 72.

Cummins, D. (1996). Evidence of deontic reasoning in 3- and 4-year old children. *Memory and Cognition*, 24.

Cutting, A., and Dunn, J. (1999). Theory of mind, emotion understanding, language, and family background: Individual differences and interrelations. *Child Development*, 70.

D'Entremont, B., Hains, S., and Muir, D. (1997). A demonstration of gaze following in 3- to 6-month-olds. *Infant Behavior and Development*, 20.

d'Inverno, M., Kinny, D., Luck, M., and Wooldridge, M. (1997). A formal specification of dMARS. In M. Singh, A. Rao, and M. Wooldridge (eds.), *Intelligent Agents IV: Proceedings of the Fourth International Workshop on Agent Theories, Architectures and Languages*. Springer-Verlag.

Dahlgren, S., and Trillingsgaard, A. (1996). Theory of mind in non-retarded children with autism and Asperger's syndrome. A research note. *Journal of Child Psychology and Psychiatry*, 37.

Daly, M., and Wilson, M. (1988). *Homicide*. Aldine.

Daly, M., and Wilson, M. (1995). Evolutionary psychology: Adaptationist, selectionist and comparative. *Psychological Inquiry*, 6.

Daly, M., and Wilson, M. (1999). *The Truth about Cinderella*. Yale University Press.

Damasio, A. (1994). *Descartes' Error: Emotion, Reason, and the Human Brain*. Putnam.

Damasio, A., Grabowski, T., Bechara, A., Damasio, H., Ponto, L., Parvizi, J., and Hichwa, R. (2000). Subcortical and cortical brain activity during the feeling of self-generated emotions. *National Neuroscience*, 310.

Damasio, A., Tranel, D., and Damasio, H. (1990). Individuals with sociopathic behavior caused by frontal damage fail to respond autonomically to social stimuli. *Behavioral Brain Research*, 41, 2.

Damasio, H., Grabowski, T., Frank, R., Galaburda, A., and Damasio, A. (1994). The return of Phineas Gage: Clues about the brain from the skull of a famous patient. *Science*, 264, 5162.

Darwin, C. (1859). *On the Origins of Species by Means of Natural Selection*. John Murray.

Darwin, C. (1871). *The Descent of Man and Selection in Relation to Sex*. Murray.

Darwin, C. (1872). *The Expression of the Emotion in Man and Animals*. Murray.

Darwin, C. (1974). *Metaphysics, Materialism, and the Evolution of Mind: Early Writings of Charles Darwin*. Transcribed and annotated by Paul H. Barrett. University of Chicago Press.

Davidson, N., and Gelman, S. (1990). Inductions from novel categories: The role of language and conceptual structure. *Cognitive Development*, 5.

Dawkins, R. (1986). *The Blind Watchmaker*. Penguin.

Dawson, G., Meltzoff, A., Osterling, J., Rinaldi, J., and Brown, E. (1998). Children with autism fail to orient to naturally occurring social stimuli. *Journal of Autism and Developmental Disorders*, 28.

de Villiers, J. (2000). Language and theory of mind: What are the developmental relationships. In S. Baron-Cohen, H. Tager-Flusberg, and D. Cohen (eds.), *Understanding Other Minds: Perspectives from Developmental Cognitive Neuroscience*. 2nd ed. Oxford University Press.

de Villiers, J., and de Villiers, P. (2000). Linguistic determinism and the understanding of false beliefs. In P. Mitchell and K. Riggs. (eds.), *Children's Reasoning and the Mind*. Psychology Press.

de Villiers, J., and de Villiers, P. (2003). Language for thought: Coming to understand false beliefs. In D. Gentner and S. Goldin-Meadow (eds.), *Language in Mind: Advances in the Study of Language and Thought*. MIT Press.

de Villiers, J., and Pyers, J. (2002). Complements to cognition: A longitudinal study of the relationship between complex syntax and false-belief understanding. *Cognitive Development*, 17.

de Waal, F. (1982). *Chimpanzee Politics: Power and Sex among Apes*. Harper and Row.

de Waal, F. (1986). Deception in the natural communication of chimpanzees. In R. Mitchell and N. Thompson (eds.), *Deception: Perspectives on Human and Nonhuman Deceit*. SUNY Press.

de Waal, F. (1989). *Peacemaking among Primates*. Harvard University Press.

de Waal, F. (1996). *Good Natured: The Origins of Right and Wrong in Humans and Other Animals*. Harvard University Press.

Dean, P., Redgrave, P., and Westby, G. (1989). Event or emergency? Two response systems in the mammalian superior colliculus. *Trends in Neuroscience*, 12.

DeCasper, A., and Spence, M. (1986). Prenatal maternal speech influences newborns' perception of speech sounds. *Infant Behaviour and Development*, 9, 1.

Decety, J., Chaminade, T., Grezes, J., and Meltzoff, A. (2002). A PET exploration of the neural mechanisms involved in reciprocal imitation. *Neuroimage*, 15.

Dehaene, S. (1997). *The Number Sense: How the Mind Creates Mathematics*. Oxford University Press.

Dehaene, S. (forthcoming). Evolution of human cortical circuits for reading and arithmetic: The "neuronal recycling" hypothesis. In S. Dehaene, J. Duhamel, M. Hauser, and G. Rizzolatti (eds.), *From Monkey Brain to Human Brain*. MIT Press.

Dehaene, S., Dupoux, E., Mehler, J., Cohen, L., Paulesu, E., Perani, D., van de Moortele, P-F., Lehéricy, S., and LeBihan, D. (1997). Anatomical variability in the cortical representation of first and second languages. *NeuroReport*, 8.

Dennett, D. (1978). Response to Premack, D., and Woodruff, G. Does the chimpanzee have a theory of mind? *Behavioral and Brain Sciences*, 4.

Dennett, D. (1987). Making sense of ourselves. In *The Intentional Stance*. MIT Press.

D'Entremont, B., Hains, A., and Muir, E. (1997). A demonstration of gaze following in 3- to 6-month olds. *Infant Behavior and Development*, 20.

Deruelle, C., Mancini, J., Livet, M., Cassé-Perrot, C., and de Schonen, S. (1999). Configural and local processing of faces in children with Williams syndrome. *Brain and Cognition*, 41.

Detterman, D. (1999). The psychology of mental retardation. *International Review of Psychiatry*, 11.

Diamond, S. (1974). Four hundred years of instinct controversy. *Behavior Genetics*, 4.

Dibble, E., Condry, K., and Spelke, E. (2003). Toddlers' use of directional cues in a reorientation task. Poster presented at the Biennial Meeting of the Society for Research on Child Development, Tampa, FL.

Dickinson, A. (1994). Instrumental conditioning. In N. Mackintosh (ed.), *Animal Learning and Cognition*. Academic Press.

Dickinson, A., and Balleine, B. (2000). Causal cognition and goal-directed action. In C. Heyes and L. Huber (eds.), *The Evolution of Cognition*. MIT Press.
Dickinson, A., and Shanks, D. (1995). Instrumental action and causal representation. In D. Sperber, D. Premack, and A. Premack (eds.), *Causal Cognition*. Blackwell.
Diesendruck, G. (2001). Essentialism in Brazilian children's extensions of animal names. *Developmental Psychology, 37*.
Diesendruck, G., and Markson, L. (2001). Children's avoidance of lexical overlap: A pragmatic account. *Developmental Psychology, 37*.
Dietrich, E., and Fields, C. (1996). The role of the Frame Problem in Fodor's modularity thesis: A case study of Rationalist cognitive science. In K. Ford and Z. Pylyshyn (eds.), *The Robot's Dilemma Revisited*. Greenwood Press.
DiGirolamo, A., Grummer-Strawn, L., and Fein, S. (2001). Maternity care practices: Implications for breastfeeding. *Birth, 28*.
Divale, W. (1973). *Warfare in Primitive Societies*. Clio Press.
Donovan, W., and Leavitt, L. (1985). Physiology and behavior: parent's response to the infant cry. In B. Lester and C. Boukydis (eds.), *Infant Crying: Theoretical and Research Perspectives*. Plenum Press.
Donovan, W., Leavitt, L., and Balling, J. (1978). Maternal physiological response to infant signals. *Psychophysiology, 15*.
Downing, P. (1996). *Numeral Classifier Systems: The Case of Japanese*. Benjamins.
Driver, J. Davis, G. Ricciardelli, P., Kidd, P., Maxwell, E., and Baron-Cohen, S. (1999). Gaze perception triggers reflexive visuospatial orienting. *Visual Cognition, 6*.
Drozd, K., and van Loosbroek, E. (1998). Weak quantification, plausible dissent, and the development of children's pragmatic competence. *Proceedings of the Twenty-Third Boston University Conference on Language Development*. Cascadilla Press.
Dudchenko, P., Goodridge, J., Seiterle, D., and Taube, J. (1997). Effects of repeated disorientation on the acquisition of spatial tasks in rats: Dissociation between the appetitive radial arm maze and aversive water maze. *Journal of Experimental Psychology: Animal Behavior Processes, 23*.
Dunbar, R. (1999). Sociobiology. In R. Wilson and F. Keil (eds.), *The MIT Encyclopedia of the Cognitive Sciences*. MIT Press.
Dunn, J., and Kirsner, K. (2003). What can we infer from double dissociations? *Cortex, 39*.
Duntley, J., and Buss, D. (1998). Evolved antihomicide modules. Paper presented to the annual meeting of the Human Behavior and Evolution Society, Davis, CA.
Duntley, J., and Buss, D. (in prep.). The nature of selection pressure.
Dupré, J. (1993). *The Disorder of Things: Metaphysical Foundations of the Disunity of Science*. Harvard University Press.
Dwyer, S. (1999). Moral competence. In K. Murasugi and R. Stainton (eds.), *Philosophy and Linguistics*. Westview Press.
Dyer, F., and Dickinson, J. (1994). Development of sun compensation by honeybees: How partially experienced bees estimate the sun's course. *Proceedings of the National Academy of Science USA, 91*.
Dyer, F., and Dickinson, J. (1996). Suncompass learning in insects: Representation in a simple mind. *Current Directions in Psychological Science, 5*.
Dykes, L. (1986). The whiplash shaken baby syndrome: What has been learned? *Child Abuse and Neglect, 10*.
Edelman, G. (1988). *Topobiology: An Introduction to Molecular Embryology*. Basic Books.
Eisenmajer, R., and Prior, M. (1991). Cognitive linguistic correlates of "theory of mind" ability in autistic children. *British Journal of Developmental Psychology, 9*.

Elman, J., Bates, E., Johnson, M., Karmiloff-Smith, A., Parisi, D., and Plunkett, K. (1996). *Rethinking Innateness: A Connectionist Perspective on Development.* MIT Press.

Emde, R., and Koenig, K. (1969). Neonatal smiling and rapid eye movement states. *Journal of the American Academy of Child Psychiatry,* 8.

Emery, N., Lorincz, E., Perrett, D., Oram, M., and Baker, C. (1997). Gaze following and joint attention in rhesus monkeys (*Macaca mulatta*). *Journal of Comparative Psychology,* 111.

Enard, W., Przeworski, M., Fisher, S., Lai, C., Wiebe, V., Kitano, T., Monaco, A., and Pääbo, S. (2002). Molecular evolution of FOXP2, a gene involved in speech and language. *Nature,* 418.

Epstein, S., Thráinsson, H., and Jan-Wouter Zwart, C. (1996). Introduction. In, W. Abraham, S. Epstein, H. Thráinsson, and C. Jan-Wouter Zwart (eds.), *Minimal Ideas.* Benjamins.

Eslinger, P., and Damasio, A. (1985). Severe disturbance of higher cognition after bilateral frontal lobe ablation: Patient EVR. *Neurology,* 35, 17.

Farah, M., Meyer, M., and McMullen, P. (1996). The living/nonliving dissociation is not an artifact: Giving an a priori implausible hypothesis a strong test. *Cognitive Neuropsychology,* 13.

Feigenson, L., Carey, S., and Hauser, M. (2002). The representations underlying infants' choice of more: Object files versus analog magnitudes. *Psychological Science,* 13, 2.

Feinman, S. (1982). Social referencing in infancy. *Merrill-Palmer Quarterly,* 28.

Feldheim, D., Kim, Y., Bergemann, A., Frisen, J., Barbacid, M., and Flanagan, J. (2000). Genetic analysis of ephrin-A2 and ephrin-A5 shows their requirement in multiple aspects of retinocollicular mapping. *Neuron,* 25, 3.

Feldman, J. (1999). Does vision work? Towards a semantics of perception. In E. Lepore and Z. Pylyshyn (eds.), *What Is Cognitive Science?* Blackwell.

Feldman, J. (2000). Bias toward regular form in mental shape spaces. *Journal of Experimental Psychology: Human Perception and Performance,* 26.

Feldman, J. (2001). Bayesian contour integration. *Perception and Psychophysics,* 63.

Feng, G., Laskowski, M., Feldheim, D., Wang, H., Lewis, R., Frisen, J., Flanagan, J., and Sanes, J. (2000). Roles for ephrins in positionally selective synaptogenesis between motor neurons and muscle fibers. *Neuron,* 25, 2.

Ferber, J. (1999). *Multi-agent Systems: Introduction to Distributed Artificial Intelligence.* Addison Wesley.

Fernald, A. (1989). Intonation and communicative intent in mothers' speech to infants: Is the melody the message? *Child Development,* 60, 10.

Fernald, A. (1993). Approval and disapproval: Infant responsiveness to vocal affect in familiar and unfamiliar languages. *Child Development,* 64.

Fiddick, L., Cosmides L., and Tooby, J. (2000). No interpretation without representation: the role of domain-specific representations and inferences in the Wason selection task. *Cognition,* 77.

Field, T. (1977). Effects of early separation, interactive deficits, and experimental manipulations on infant-mother face-to-face interactions. *Child Development,* 48.

Finlay, B., Darlington, R., and Nicastro, N. (2001). Developmental structure in brain evolution. *Behavioral and Brain Sciences,* 24.

Fischer, K., and Biddell, T. (1991). Constraining nativist inferences about cognitive capacities. In S. Carey and R. Gelman (eds.), *The Epigenesis of Mind: Essays on Biology and Cognition.* Erlbaum.

Fischer, K., and Stewart, J. (1999). Into the middle of things: From dichotomies to grounded dynamic analysis of development. *Developmental Science,* 2, 2.

Fiser, J., and Aslin, R. (2001). Unsupervised statistical learning of higher-order spatial structures from visual scenes. *Psychological Science,* 12.

Fiser, J., and Aslin, R. (2002a). Statistical learning of higher-order temporal structure from visual shape-sequences. *Journal of Experimental Psychology: Learning, Memory and Cognition*, 28.

Fiser, J., and Aslin, R. (2002b). Statistical learning of new visual features by infants. *Proceedings of the National Academy of Sciences*, 99.

Fisher, N. (2002). How do they pass, and why do they fail? Language and false belief in children with autism and developmental delay. Presented at "Why Language Matters for Theory of Mind," international conference, University of Toronto, Toronto.

Fitch, W., and Reby, D. (2001). The descended larynx is not uniquely human. *Proceedings of the Royal Society, Biological Sciences*, 268, 15.

Flack, J., and de Waal, F. (2000). "Any animal whatever": Darwinian building blocks of morality in monkeys and apes. In L. Katz (ed.), *Evolutionary Origins of Morality*. Imprint Academic.

Flavell, J., Flavell, E., and Green, F. (1983). Development of the appearance-reality distinction. *Cognitive Psychology*, 15.

Fletcher, P., Happé, F., Frith, U., Baker, S., Dolan, R., Frackowiak, R., and Frith, C. (1995). Other minds in the brain: A functional imaging study of "theory of mind" in story comprehension. *Cognition*, 57.

Fodor, J. (1981). Introduction: Some notes on what linguistics is about. In N. Block (ed.), *Readings in the Philosophy of Psychology*, vol. 2. Harvard University Press.

Fodor, J. (1983). *Modularity of Mind: An Essay on Faculty Psychology*. MIT Press.

Fodor, J. (1985). Précis of modularity of mind. *Behavioral and Brain Sciences* 8 (1)

Fodor, J. (1987). "Frames, Fridgeons, Sleeping Dogs and The Music of The Spheres." In Z. Pylyshyn (ed.), *The Robot's Dilemma: The Frame Problem in Artificial Intelligence*. Ablex.

Fodor, J. (1998a). *Concepts: Where Cognitive Science Went Wrong*. Oxford University Press.

Fodor, J. (1998b). The trouble with psychological Darwinism. *The London Review of Books*, 20.

Fodor, J. (1998c). Unambiguous triggers. *Linguistic Inquiry*, 29.

Fodor, J. (2000). *The Mind Doesn't Work That Way: The Scope and Limits of Computational Psychology*. MIT Press.

Fodor, J. (2001a). Doing without What's Within. *Mind*, 110.

Fodor, J. (2001b). Review of P. Carruthers and A. Chamberlain (eds.), *Evolution and the Human Mind*. *British Journal for the Philosophy of Science*, 52.

Foot, P. (1967). The problem of abortion and the doctrine of the double effect. *Oxford Review*, 5. Reprinted in P. Foot (1978), *Virtues and Vices*. Oxford University Press. All page references to the reprinted version.

Foot, P. (1972). Morality as a system of hypothetical imperatives. *Philosophical Review*, 81.

Foot, P. (1978). The problem of abortion and the doctrine of double effect. In P. Foot, *Virtues and Vices*. Oxford University Press.

Ford, K., and Pylyshyn, Z. (1996). *The Robot's Dilemma Revisited*. Ablex.

Fossey, D. (1984). *Gorillas in the Mist*. Houghton Mifflin.

Franco, F., and Butterworth, G. (1996). Pointing and social awareness: Declaring and requesting in the second year. *Journal of Child Language*, 23.

Fraser, S., and Perkel, D. (1990). Competitive and positional cues in the patterning of nerve connections. *Journal of Neurobiology*, 21, 1.

Freeman, N., Sinha C., and Stedman, A. (1982). All the cars—which cars? From word to meaning to discourse analysis. In M. Beveridge (ed.), *Children Thinking through Language*. Edward Arnold.

Freeman, W. (1996). The generic viewpoint assumption in a framework for visual perception. *Nature*, 368.

Fries, W. (1984). Cortical projections to the superior colliculus in the macaque monkey: A retrograde study using horseradish peroxidase. *Journal of Comparative Neurology*, 230.

Frisen, J., Yates, P., McLaughlin, T., Friedman, G., O'Leary, D., and Barbacid, M. (1998). Ephrin-A5 (AL-1/RAGS) is essential for proper retinal axon guidance and topographic mapping in the mammalian visual system. *Neuron*, 20, 2.

Frith, C., and Frith, U. (1999). Interacting minds: A biological basis. *Science*, 286, 15.

Frith, C., and Frith, U. (2000). The physiological basis of theory of mind: Functional neuroimaging studies. In S. Baron-Cohen, H. Tager-Flusberg, and D. Cohen (eds.), *Understanding Other Minds: Perspectives from Developmental Cognitive Neuroscience*. Oxford University Press.

Frith, U. (1989). *Autism: Explaining the Enigma*. Blackwell.

Frith, U. (2001). Mind blindness and the brain in autism. *Neuron*, 326.

Frith, U., and Frith, C. (2003). Development and neurophysiology of mentalizing. *Philosophical Transactions of the Royal Society*, series B, 358.

Frith, U., and Happé, F. (1998). Why specific developmental disorders are not specific: Online and developmental effects in autism and dyslexia. *Developmental Science*, 1.

Frith, U., Happé, F., and Siddons, F. (1994). Autism and theory of mind in everyday life. *Social Development*, 3.

Frodi, A., and Lamb, M. (1980). Child abusers' responses to infant smiles and cries. *Child Development*, 61.

Fromkin, V. (ed.). (2000). *Linguistics: An Introduction to Linguistic Theory*. Blackwell.

Fukuchi-Shimogori, T., and Grove, E. (2001). Neocortex patterning by the secreted signaling molecule FGF8. *Science*, 294, 5544.

Gabrieli, J., Fleischman, D., Keane, M., Reminger, S., and Morell, F. (1995). Double dissociation between memory systems underlying explicit and implicit memory in the human brain. *Psychological Science*, 6.

Galef, B. (1996). Food selection: Problems in understanding how we choose foods to eat. *Neuroscience and Biobehavioral Reviews*, 20.

Gallistel, C. (1990). *The Organization of Learning*. MIT Press.

Gallistel, C. (1995). The replacement of general-purpose theories with adaptive specializations. In M. Gazzaniga (ed.), *The Cognitive Neurosciences*. MIT Press.

Gallistel, C. (1999). The replacement of general-purpose learning models with adaptively specialized learning modules. In M. S. Gazzaniga, (ed.). *The Cognitive Neurosciences*, 2nd ed. MIT Press.

Gallistel, C. (2000). The replacement of general-purpose learning models with adaptively specialized learning modules. In M. Gazzaniga (ed.), *The New Cognitive Neurosciences*, 2nd ed. MIT Press.

Gallistel, C., and Gelman, R. (2000). Non-verbal numerical cognition: From reals to integers. *Trends in Cognitive Sciences*, 4, 2.

Gallistel, C., Gelman, R., and Cordes, S. (forthcoming). The cultural and evolutionary history of the real numbers. In S. Levinson and P. Jaisson (eds.), *Culture and Evolution*. MIT Press.

Garcia, J., and Koelling, R. (1966). Relation of cue to consequence in avoidance learning. *Psychonomic Science*, 4.

Garfield, J. (1987). *Modularity in Knowledge Representation and Natural-Language Understanding*. MIT Press.

Gasser, M., and Smith, L. (1998). Learning nouns and adjectives: A connectionist account. *Language and Cognitive Processes*, 13.

Gat, E. (1998). Three-Layer Architectures. In D. Kortenkamp, R. Bonasso and R. Murphy (eds.), *Mobile Robots and Artificial Intelligence*. AAAI Press.

Gaulin, S. (1995). Does evolutionary theory predict sex differences in the brain. In M. Gazzaniga (ed.), *The Cognitive Neurosciences*. MIT Press.
Gaulin, S., and McBurney, D. (2001). *Psychology: An Evolutionary Approach*. Prentice Hall.
Gauthier, I., and Nelson, C. (2001). The development of face expertise. *Current Opinion in Neurobiology*, 11.
Gazzaniga, M. (ed.). (2000). *The New Cognitive Neurosciences*. MIT Press.
Geary, D., and Huffman, K. (2002). Brain and cognitive evolution: Forms of modularity and functions of mind. *Psychological Bulletin*, 128.
Gehring, W. (1998). *Master Control Genes in Development and Evolution: The Homeobox Story*. Yale University Press.
Geisler, W., and Diehl, R. (2002). Bayesian natural selection and the evolution of perceptual systems. *Philosophical Transactions of the Royal Society of London*, series B, 357.
Geisler, W., and Kersten, D. (2002). Illusion, perception, and Bayes. *Nature Neuroscience*, 5.
Gelman, R. (1990). First principles organize attention to and learning about relevant data: Number and the animate-inanimate distinction as examples. *Cognitive Science*, 14.
Gelman, R., and Cordes, S. (2001). Counting in animals and humans. In E. Dupoux (ed.), *Language, Brain, and Cognitive Development: Essays in Honor of Jacques Mehler*. MIT Press.
Gelman, R., and Gallistel, C. (1978). *The Child's Understanding of Number*. Harvard University Press.
Gelman, S. (1988). The development of induction within natural kind and artifact categories. *Cognitive Psychology*, 20.
Gelman, S. (2003). *The essential child: Origins of Essentialism in Everyday Thought*. Oxford University Press.
Gelman, S. (2004). Learning words for kinds: Generic noun phrases in acquisition. To appear in D. Hall and S. Waxman (eds.), *Weaving a Lexicon*. MIT Press.
Gelman, S., and Heyman, G. (1999). Carrot-eaters and creaturebelievers: The effects of lexicalization on children's inferences about social categories. *Psychological Science*, 10.
Gelman, S., and Hirschfeld, L. (1999). How biological is essentialism? In S. Atran and D. Medin (eds.), *Folkbiology*. MIT Press.
Gelman, S., and Kalish, C. (1993). Categories and causality. In R. Pasnak and M. Howe (eds.), *Emerging themes in cognitive development*, vol. 2, *Competencies*. Springer-Verlag.
Gelman, S., and Markman, E. (1986). Categories and induction in young children. *Cognition*, 23.
Gelman, S., and Raman, L. (2003). Preschool children use linguistic form class and pragmatic cues to interpret generics. *Child Development*, 74.
Gelman, S., and Tardif, T. (1998). Generic noun phrases in English and Mandarin: An examination of child-directed speech. *Cognition*, 66.
Gelman, S., and Wellman, H. (1991). Insides and essences: Early understandings of the nonobvious. *Cognition*, 38.
Gelman, S., Coley, J., Rosengren, K., Hartman, E., and Pappas, T. (1998). Beyond labeling: The role of parental input in the acquisition of righly-structured categories. *Monographs of the Society for Research in Child Development*, vol. 63, no. 1, serial no. 253.
Gelman, S., Star, J., and Flukes, J. (2002). Children's use of generics in inductive inferences. *Journal of Cognition and Development*, 3.
Gentner D., and Boroditsky, L. (2001). Individuation, relational relativity and early word learning. In M. Bowerman and S. Levinson (eds.), *Language Acquisition and Conceptual Development*. Cambridge University Press.
Georgeff, M., and Lansky, A. (1987). Reactive reasoning and planning. In *Proceedings of the Sixth National Conference on Artificial Intelligence (AAAI-87)*, Seattle.

Gergely, G., Nadasdy, Z., Csibra, G., and Biro, S. (1995). Taking the intentional stance at 12 months of age. *Cognition, 56* (2).
German, T., and Barrett, H. (in press). Functional fixedness in a technologically sparse culture. *Psychological Science*.
German, T., and Johnson, S. (2002). Function and the origins of the design stance. *Journal of Cognition and Development, 3*.
German, T., and Leslie, A. (2000). Attending to and learning about mental states. In P. Mitchell & K. Riggs (eds.), *Reasoning and the Mind*. Psychology Press.
Gerrans, P. (2003). Nativism and neuroconstructivism in the explanation of Williams Syndrome. *Biology and Philosophy, 18*.
Ghiglieri, M. (1999). *The Dark Side of Man: Tracing the Origins of Violence*. Perseus Books.
Gibson, E., and Walk, R. (1960). The "visual cliff." *Scientific American, 202*.
Gibson, E., and Wexler, K. (1994). Triggers. *Linguistic Inquiry, 25*.
Gierer, A. (1983). Model for the retino-tectal projection. *Proceedings of the Royal Society of London*, series B, *Biological Sciences, 218*, 1210.
Gigerenzer, G. (2001). *Bounded Rationality: The Adaptive Toolbox*. MIT Press.
Gigerenzer, G., and Hug, K. (1992). Reasoning about social contracts: Cheating and perspective change. *Cognition, 43*.
Gigerenzer, G., Todd, P., and ABC Research Group. (1999). *Simple Heuristics That Make Us Smart*. Oxford University Press.
Gilbert, S. (2000). *Developmental Biology*. 6th ed. Sinauer.
Gil-White, F. (2001). Are ethnic groups biological "species" to the human brain? *Current Anthropology, 42*.
Girotto, V., Kemmelmeir, M., Sperber, D., and van der Henst, J. (2001). Inept reasoners or pragmatic virtuosos? Relevance and the deontic selection task. *Cognition, 81*.
Glymour, C. (1985). Fodor's holism. *Behavioral and Brain Sciences 8* (1).
Godfrey-Smith, P. (2002). On the evolution of representational and interpretive capacities. *Monist, 85*.
Goel, V., Grafman, J., Sadato, N., and Hallett, M. (1995). Modeling other minds. *Neuroreport, 6*, 16.
Goetz, P., and Gelman, S. (2005). The patterning of generic use in parent and child natural language. Paper presented at the biennial meetings of the Society for Research in Child Development. Atlanta, GA.
Goldberg, A. (2003). Constructions: A new theoretical approach to language, *Trends in Cognitive Science, 7*, 5.
Goldenberg, G. (2001). Imitation and matching of hand and finger postures. *Neuroimage, 14*, 1 (2).
Goldin-Meadow, S., Gelman, S., and Mylander, C. (2003). Expressing generic concepts with and without a language model. Unpublished manuscript.
Gómez, J. (1998). Some thoughts about the evolution of LADS, with special reference to TOM and SAM. In P. Carruthers and J. Boucher (eds.), *Language and Thought*. Cambridge University Press.
Gomez, R., and Gerken, L.-A. (1999). Artificial grammar learning by 1 year-olds leads to specific and abstract knowledge. *Cognition, 70*, 1.
Goodall, J. (1986). *The Chimpanzees of Gombe: Patterns of Behavior*. Belknap.
Goodie, A., Ortmann, A., Davis, J., Bullock, S., and Werner, G. (1999). Demons versus heuristics in artificial intelligence, behavioral ecology and economics. In G. Gigerenzer, P. Todd, and the ABC Research Group, *Simple Heuristics That Make Us Smart*. Oxford University Press.
Goodman, N. (1972). Seven strictures on similarity. In N. Goodman (ed.), *Problems and Project*. Bobbs-Merrill.

Gopnik, A. (1996). Theories and modules: Creation myths, developmental realities, and Neurath's boat. In P. Carruthers and P. Smith (eds.), *Theories of Theories of Mind*. Cambridge University Press.

Gopnik, A. (2003). The theory theory as an alternative to the innateness hypothesis. In L. Antony and N. Hornstein (eds.), *Chomsky and His Critics*. Blackwell.

Gopnik, A., and Meltzoff, A. (1997). *Words, Thoughts and Theories*. MIT Press.

Gopnik, A., and Meltzoff, A. (1998). Theories vs. modules: To the max and beyond. A reply to Poulin-Dubois and to Stich and Nichols. *Mind and Language*, 13.

Gopnik, A., and Sobel, D. (2000). Detecting blickets: How young children use information about novel causal powers in categorization and induction. *Child Development*, 71, 12.

Gopnik, A., and Wellman, H. (1994). The theory theory. In L. Hirschfield and S. Gelman (eds.), *Mapping the Mind: Domain Specificity in Cognition and Culture*. Cambridge University Press.

Gosh A., and Pankau, R. (1994). Social-emotional and behavioral adjustment in children with Williams-Beuren syndrome. *American Journal of Medical Genetics*, 52.

Gosh A., and Pankau, R. (1997). Personality characteristics and behavior problems in individuals of different ages with Williams syndrome. *Developmental Medicine and Child Neurology*, 39.

Gould, J., and Gould, C. (1994). *The Animal Mind*. Freeman.

Gould, S. (1984). Only his wings remained. *Natural History*, 93.

Gould, S. (1991). Exaptation: A crucial tool for evolutionary psychology. *Journal of Social Issues*, 47.

Gould, S. (1997a). Darwinian fundamentalism. *New York Review of Books*. 44.

Gould, S. (1997b). Evolution: The pleasures of pluralism. *New York Review of Books*, 44.

Gould, S. (1997c). Evolutionary psychology: An exchange. *New York Review of Books*, 44.

Gould, S., and Lewontin, R. (1979). The spandrels of San Marco and the Panglossian paradigm: A critique of the adaptationist programme. *Proceedings of the Royal Society of London, B205*.

Gould, S., and Vrba, E. (1982). Exaptation: A missing term in the science of form. *Paleobiology*, 8.

Gouteux, S., and Spelke, E. (2001). Children's use of geometry and landmarks to reorient in an open space. *Cognition*, 81.

Gouteux, S., Thinus-Blanc, C., and Vauclair, J. (2001). Rhesus monkeys use geometric and nongeometric information during a reorientation task. *Journal of Experimental Psychology: General*, 130.

Grafman, J., Schwab, K., Warden, D., Pridgen, A., Brown, H., and Salazar, A. (1996). Frontal lobe injuries, violence, and aggression: A report of the Vietnam Head Injury Study. *Neurology*, 465.

Graham, S., Kilbreath, C., and Welder, A. (2001). Words and shape similarity guide 13-month-olds' inferences about nonobvious object properties. In J. Moore and K. Stenning (eds.), *Proceedings of the Twenty-Third Annual Conference of the Cognitive Science Society*. Erlbaum.

Grattan, L., and Eslinger, P. (1992). Long-term psychological consequences of childhood frontal lobe lesion in patient DT. *Brain Cognition*, 201.

Gray, N., MacCulloch, M., Smith, J., Morris, M., and Snowden, R. (2003). Forensic psychology: Violence viewed by psychopathic murderers. *Nature*, 423, 6939.

Greenberg, J. (1963). *Universals of Language*. MIT Press.

Greene, J., and Haidt, J. (2002). How (and where) does moral judgment work? *Trends in Cognitive Science*, 612.

Greene, J., Nystrom, L., Engell, A., Darley, J., and Cohen, J. (2004). The neural bases of cognitive conflict and control in moral judgment. *Neuron, 44.*

Greene, J., Sommerville, R., Nystrom, L., Darley, J., and Cohen, J. (2001). An fMRI investigation of emotional engagement in moral judgment, *Science, 293,* 21.

Grice, H. (1975). Logic and conversation. In P. Cole and J. Morgan (eds)., *Syntax and Semantics,* vol. 3, *Speech Acts.* Academic Press. Reprinted in *Studies on the Way of Words.* Harvard University Press.

Griffiths, P. (2002). What is innateness? *Monist, 85.*

Griffiths, P., and Gray, R. (1994). Developmental systems and evolutionary explanation. *Journal of Philosophy, 91.*

Gualmini, A., Meroni, L., and Crain, S. (2003). An asymmetric universal in child language. *Proceedings of Sinn und Bedeutung VI.* Arbeitspapiere des Fachbereichs Sprachwissenschaft.

Guasti, M., and Chierchia, G. (2000). Backward versus forward anaphora: Reconstruction in child grammar. *Language Acquisition, 8.*

Guasti, M., and Chierchia, G. (2002). Reconstruction in child language. *Language Acquisition, 8.*

Gutheil, G., and Rosengren, K. (1996). A rose by any other name: Preschooolers' understanding of individual identity across name and appearance changes. *British Journal of Developmental Psychology, 14.*

Haidt, J. (2001). The emotional dog and its rational tail: A social intuitionist approach to moral judgment. *Psychological Review, 108*

Haig, D. (1993). Genetic conflicts in human pregnancy. *Quarterly Review of Biology, 68.*

Haig, D. (2002). *Genomic Imprinting and Kinship.* Rutgers University Press.

Hains, S., and Muir, D. (1996a). Infant sensitivity to adult eye direction. *Child Development, 67.*

Hains, S., and Muir, D. (1996b). Effects of stimulus contingency in infant-adult interactions. *Infant Behavior and Development, 19.*

Haith, M. (1998). Who put the cog in infant cognition? Is rich interpretation too costly? *Infant Behavior and Development, 21.*

Haith, M., Hazan, C., and Goodman, G. (1988). Expectation and anticipation of dynamic visual events by 3.5-month-old babies. *Child Development, 59.*

Halder, G., Callaerts, P., Flister, S., Walldorf, U., Kloter, U., and Gehring, W. (1998). Eyeless initiates the expression of both sine oculis and eyes absent during Drosophila compound eye development. *Development, 125,* 12.

Halder, G., Callaerts, P., and Gehring, W. (1995). Induction of ectopic eyes by target expression of the *eyeless* gene in *Drosophila. Science, 267.*

Hale, C., and Tager-Flusberg, H. (2003). The influence of language on theory of mind: A training study. *Developmental Science, 6.*

Hall, D. (1996). Preschoolers' default assumptions about word meaning: Proper names designate unique individuals. *Developmental Psychology, 32.*

Hallett, G. (1991). *Essentialism: A Wittgensteinian Critique.* SUNY Press.

Halper, F. (1997). The illusion of "The Future." *Perception, 26.*

Hamilton, W. (1964). The genetic evolution of social behaviour, I and II. *Journal of Theoretical Biology, 7.*

Hannan, T., and Fogel, A. (1987). A case-study assessment of "pointing" during the first three months of life. *Perceptual and Motor Skills, 65.*

Happé, F. (1995). The role of age and verbal ability in the theory of mind task performance of subjects with autism. *Child Development, 66.*

Happé, F. (1999). Autism: Cognitive deficit or cognitive style? *Trends in Cognitive Sciences, 3.*

Happé, F., and Loth, E. (2002). "Theory of mind" and tracking speakers' intentions. *Mind and Language, 17.*

Hare, B., Call, J., Agnetta, B., and Tomasello, M. (2000). Chimpanzees know what conspecifics do and do not see. *Animal Behaviour,* 59.

Hare, B., Call, J., and Tomasello, M. (2001). Do chimpanzees know what conspecifics know? *Animal Behaviour,* 6.

Hare, R. (1991). *The Hare Psychopathy Checklis—Revised.* Multi-Health Systems.

Hare, R., and Quinn, M. (1971). Psychopathy and autonomic conditioning. *Journal of Abnormal Psychology,* 77

Hare, R., Hart, S., and Harpur, T. (1991). Psychopathy and the DSM-IV criteria for antisocial personality disorder. *Journal of Abnormal Psychology,* 1003.

Harel, D. (1992). *Algorithmics: The Spirit of Computing.* Addison-Wesley.

Harman, G. (1977). *The Nature of Morality.* Oxford University Press.

Harman, G. (1986). *Change in View—Principles in Reasoning.* MIT Press.

Harman, G. (2000). Moral philosophy and linguistics. In G. Harman (ed.), *Explaining Value.* Oxford University Press.

Harpur, T., and Hare, R. (1994). Assessment of psychopathy as a function of age. *Journal of Abnormal Psychology,* 1034.

Harris, A., Thomas, S., Gisher, G., and Hirsch, D. (2002). Murder and medicine. *Homicide Studies,* 6.

Harris, P. (2000). *The Work of the Imagination.* Blackwell.

Harris, P., and Núñez, M. (1996). Understanding of permission rules by preschool children. *Child Development,* 67.

Hatano, G., and Inagaki, K. (1999). A developmental perspective on informal biology. In D. Medin and S. Atran (eds.), *Folkbiology.* MIT Press.

Hauser, M. (2000). *Wild Minds: What Animals Really Think.* Penguin Press.

Hauser, M., and Carey, S. (1998). Building a cognitive creature from a set of primitives. In D. Cummins and C. Allen (eds.), *The Evolution of Mind.* Oxford University Press.

Hauser, M., and Spelke, E. (2004). Evolutionary and developmental foundations of human knowledge. In M. Gazzaniga (ed.), *The Cognitive Neurosciences,* III.3rd ed. MIT Press.

Hauser, M., Chomsky, N., and Fitch, W. (2002). The faculty of language. *Science,* 298, 19.

Hausfater, G., and Hrdy, S. (eds.). (1984). *Infanticide: Comparative and Evolutionary Perspectives.* Aldine.

Hebb, D. (1955). Drives and the C.N.S. (Conceptual Nervous System). *Psychological Review,* 62.

Helmholtz, H. (1867/1925). *Handbuch der physiologischen optik.* Leipzig: L. Voss. Published in English as *Treatise on physiological optics,* vol. 3, trans. J. Southal. Optical Society of America.

Herburger, E. (2000). *What Counts: Focus and Quantification.* MIT Press.

Hermelin, B., and O'Connor, N. (1990). Factors and primes: A specific numerical ability. *Psychological Medicine,* 20.

Hermer, L., and Spelke, E. (1994). A geometric process for spatial reorientation in young children. *Nature,* 37.

Hermer, L., and Spelke, E. (1996). Modularity and development: The case of spatial reorientation. *Cognition,* 61.

Hermer-Vasquez, L., Moffet, A., and Munkholm, P. (2001). Language, space, and the development of cognitive flexibility in humans: The case of two spatial memory tasks. *Cognition,* 79.

Hermer-Vazquez, L., Spelke, E., and Katsnelson, A. (1999). Sources of flexibility in human cognition: Dual-task studies of space and language. *Cognitive Psychology,* 39.

Herrnstein, R. (1984). Objects, categories, and discriminative stimuli. In H. Roitblat (ed.), *Animal Cognition.* Erlbaum.

Hershberger, W. (1970). Attached-shadow orientation perceived as depth by chickens reared in an environment illuminated from below. *Journal of Comparative and Physiological Psychology*, 73.

Heyes, C. (1998). Theory of mind in nonhuman primates. *Behavioral and Brain Sciences*, 21.

Heyes, C., and Huber, L. (eds.). (2000). *The Evolution of Cognition*. MIT Press.

Hickling, A., and Gelman, S. (1995). How does your garden grow? Evidence of an early conception of plants as biological kinds. *Child Development*, 66.

Higginbotham, J. (1991). Either/or. *Proceedings of NELS*, 21, GLSA.

Hirschfeld, L. (1996). *Race in the Making: Cognition, Culture, and the Child's Construction of Human Kinds*. MIT Press.

Hirschfeld, L., and Gelman, S. (1997). What young children think about the relation between language variation and social difference. *Cognitive Development*, 12.

Hirschfeld, L., and Gelman, S. (eds.). (1994). *Mapping the Mind: Domain Specificity in Cognition and Culture*. Cambridge University Press.

Hodges, A. (1983). *Alan Turing: The Enigma*. Simon and Schuster.

Hoffman, D. (1998). *Visual Intelligence: How We Create What We See*. Norton.

Hoffman, D., and Richards, W. (1984). Parts of recognition. *Cognition*, 18.

Hoffman, J., Landau, B., and Pagani, B. (2003). Spatial breakdown in spatial construction: Evidence from eye fixations in children with Williams syndrome. *Cognitive Psychology*, 46.

Hollander, M., Gelman, S., and Star, J. (2002). Children's interpretation of generic noun phrases. *Developmental Psychology*, 38.

Hood, B., Willen, J., and Driver, J. (1998). Adults' eyes trigger shifts of visual attention in human infants. *Psychological Science*, 9.

Hope, R., Hammond, B., and Gaze, R. (1976). The arrow model: Retinotectal specificity and map formation in the goldfish visual system. *Proceedings of the Royal Society of London*, series B, *Biological Sciences*, 194, 1117.

Horn, L. (1989). *A Natural History of Negation*. University of Chicago Press.

Horn, L. (2000). ANY and EVER: Free choice and free relatives. In A. Wyner (ed.), *IATL 15 (Proceedings of the 15th Annual Conference of the Israeli Association for Theoretical Linguistics)*. Association for Theoretical Linguistics.

Horn, L., and Kato, Y. (eds.). (2000). *Negation and Polarity: Syntactic and Semantic Perspectives*. Oxford University Press.

Hornberger, M., Dutting, D., Ciossek, T., Yamada, T., Handwerker, C., Lang, S., Weth, F., Huf, J., Wessel, R., Logan, C., Tanaka, H., and Drescher, U. (1999). Modulation of EphA receptor function by coexpressed ephrinA ligands on retinal ganglion cell axons. *Neuron*, 22, 4.

Hornstein, N. (1984). *Logical Form: From GB to Minimalism*. Blackwell.

Horton, J., and Hocking, D. (1996). An adult-like pattern of ocular dominance columns in striate cortex of newborn monekys prior to visual experience. *Journal of Neuroscience*, 16.

Howard, I. (1996). Alhazen's neglected discoveries of visual phenomena. *Perception*, 25.

Howard, I., Bergstrom, S., and Ohmi, M. (1990). Shape from shading in different frames of reference. *Perception*, 19.

Hrdy, S. (1977). Infanticide as a primitive reproductive strategy. *Americian Scientist*, 65.

Hrdy, S. (1999). *Mother Nature*. Random House.

Hubel, D. (1988). *Eye, Brain, and Vision*. Scientific American.

Hubel, D., and Wiesel, T. (1965). Binocular interaction in striate cortex of kittens reared with artificial squint. *Journal of Neurophysiology*, 28.

Hubel, D., and Wiesel, T. (1970). The period of susceptibility to the physiological effects of unilateral eye closure in kittens. *Journal of Physiology*, 206.

Hughes, C., and Dunn, J. (1997). "Pretend you didn't know": Young children's talk about mental states in pretend play. *Cognitive Development, 12.*
Hull, D. (1965). The effects of essentialism on taxonomy: Two thousand years of stasis. Part 1. *British Journal for the Philosophy of Science, 15.*
Hume, D. (1740/1978). *A Treatise of Human Nature.* Book 3. Oxford University Press.
Hummel, J., and Biederman, I. (1992). Dynamic binding in a neural network for shape recognition. *Psychological Review, 99.*
Hupbach, A., and Nadel, L. (2003). Geometric information does not predominate spatial reorientation in young children. Poster presented at the biennial meeting of the Society for Research on Child Development, Tampa, FL.
Iacoboni, M., Woods, R., Brass, M., Bekkering, H., Mazziotta, J., and Rizzolatti, G. (1999). Cortical mechanisms of human imitation. *Science, 286.*
Inagaki, K. (1990). The effects of raising animals on children's biological knowledge. *British Journal of Developmental Psychology, 8.*
Inhelder, B., and Piaget, J. (1964). *Early Growth of Logic in the Child: Classification and Seriation.* Routledge and Kegan Paul.
International Human Genome Sequencing Consortium. (2001). Initial sequencing and analysis of the human genome. *Nature, 409.*
Itakura, S. (1996). Manual action in infant chimpanzees: A preliminary study. *Perceptual and Motor Skills, 83.*
Jackendoff, R. (1992). *Languages of the Mind.* MIT Press.
Jacob, F., and Monod, J. (1961). On the regulation of gene activity. *Cold Spring Harbor Symposium on Quantitative Biology, 26.*
Jacob, F. (1977). Evolution and tinkering. *Science, 196,* 16.
Jaswal, V., and Markman, E. (2001). *Effects of language on thought in 24-month-old children.* Unpublished manuscript.
Jenkins, J., and Astington, J. (1996). Cognitive factors and family structure associated with theory of mind development in young children. *Developmental Psychology, 32.*
Johnson, C., Topoff, H., Vander Meer, R., and Lavine, B. (2002). Host queen killing by a slave maker ant queen: When is a host queen worth attacking? *Animal Behaviour, 64.*
Johnson, M. (1990). Cortical maturation and development of visual attention in early infancy. *Journal of Cognitive Neuroscience, 2.*
Johnson, M., and Morton, J. (1991). *Biology and Cognitive Development: The Case of Face Recognition.* Oxford University Press.
Johnson, M., Dziurawiec, S., Ellis, H., and Morton, J. (1991). Newborns' preferential tracking of face-like stimuli and its subsequent decline. *Cognition, 40,* 1–2.
Johnson, S. C. (2000). The recognition of mentalistic agents in infancy. *Trends in Cognitive Science, 4.*
Johnson, S. C., Bolz, M., Carter, E., Mandsager, J., Teichner, A., and Zettler, P. (under review). Inferring the attentional orientation of morphologically novel agents in agency.
Johnson, S. C., Booth, A., and O'Hearn, K. (2001). Inferring the goals of non-human agents. *Cognitive Development, 16.*
Johnson, S. C., Slaughter, V., and Carey, S. (1998). Whose gaze will infants follow? Features that elicit gaze-following in 12-month-olds. *Developmental Science, 1.*
Johnson, S. H. (2002). Cortical representations of human tool use. In S. Johnson (ed.), *Taking Action: Cognitive Neuroscience Perspectives on Intentional Movement.* MIT Press.
Johnson, S. P. (2003). The nature of cognitive development. *Trends in Cognitive Sciences, 7.*
Jones, W., Bellugi, U., Lai, Z., Chiles, M., Reilly, J., Lincoln, A., and Adolphs, R. (2000). Hypersociability in Williams syndrome. *Journal of Cognitive Neuroscience, 12* (supp.).

Joseph, R., and Tager-Flusberg, H. (1999). Preschool children's understanding of the desire and knowledge constraints on intended action. *British Journal of Developmental Psychology, 17*.

Joseph, R., and Tanaka, J. (2003). Holistic and part-based face recognition in children with autism. *Journal of Child Psychology and Psychiatry, 44*.

Joseph, R., Tager-Flusberg, H., and Lord, C. (2002). Cognitive profiles and social-communicative functioning in children with autism spectrum disorder. *Journal of Child Psychology and Psychiatry, 43*.

Kaas, J. (1997). Topographic maps are fundamental to sensory processing. *Brain Research Bulletin, 44*, 2.

Kaas, J., and Huerta, M. (1988). The subcortical visual system of primates. In H. Steklis and J. Erwin (eds.), *Comparative Primate Biology*, vol. 4, *Neurosciences*. Liss.

Kadmon, N., and Landmon, F. (1993). Any. *Linguistics and Philosophy, 16*.

Kahneman, D., and Tversky, A. (1972). Subjective probability: A judgment of representativeness. *Cognitive Psychology, 3*.

Kalish, C. (1995). Graded membership in animal and artifact categories. *Memory and Cognition, 23*.

Kalish, C. (1998). Natural and artificial kinds: Are children realists or relativists about categories? *Developmental Psychology, 34*.

Kanwisher, N., and Moscovitch, M. (2000). The cognitive neuroscience of face processing: An introduction. *Cognitive Neuropsychology, 17*.

Karmiloff-Smith, A. (1992). *Beyond Modularity: A Developmental Perspective on Cognitive Science*. MIT Press.

Karmiloff-Smith, A. (1997). Crucial differences between developmental cognitive neuroscience and adult neuropsychology. *Developmental Neuropsychology, 13*.

Karmiloff-Smith, A. (1998a). Development itself is the key to understanding developmental disorders. *Trends in Cognitive Sciences, 2*, 10.

Karmiloff-Smith, A. (1998b). Is atypical development necessarily a window on the normal mind/brain? The case of Williams syndrome. *Developmental Science, 1*.

Karmiloff-Smith, A. (2000). Why babies' brains are not Swiss army knives. In H. Rose and S. Rose (eds.), *Alas, Poor Darwin: Arguments against Evolutionary Psychology*. Cape.

Karmiloff-Smith, A., Brown, J., Grice, S., and Paterson, S. (2003). Dethroning the myth: Cognitive dissociations and innate modularity in Williams syndrome. *Developmental Neuropsychology, 23*.

Karmiloff-Smith, A., Klima, E., Bellugi, U., Grant, J., and Baron-Cohen, S. (1995). Is there a social module? Language, face processing and theory of mind in individuals with Williams syndrome. *Journal of Cognitive Neuroscience, 7*.

Katz, L., Weliky, M., and Crowley, J. (2000). Activity and the development of the visual cortex: New perspectives. In M. Gazzaniga (ed.), *The New Cognitive Neurosciences*, 2nd ed. MIT Press.

Keefe, R. (2000). *Theories of Vagueness*. Cambridge University Press.

Keil, F. (1989). *Concepts, Kinds, and Cognitive Development*. MIT Press.

Keil, F. (1991). The emergence of theoretical beliefs as constraints on concepts. In S. Carey and R. Gelman (eds.), *The Epigenesis of Mind*. Erlbaum.

Keil, F. (1994). The birth and nurturance of concepts by domains: The origins of concepts of living things. In L. Hirschfeld and S. Gelman (eds.), *Mapping the Mind: Domain Specificity in Cognition and Culture*. Cambridge University Press.

Keil, F., Smith, W., Simons, D., and Levin, D. (1998). Two dogmas of conceptual empiricism: Implications for hybrid models of the structure of knowledge. *Cognition, 65*.

Kemler Nelson, D., Frankenfield, A., Morris, C., and Blair, E. (2000). Young children's use of functional information to categorize artifacts: Three factors that matter. *Cognition*, 77.

Kenrick, D., and Sheets, V. (1993). Homicidal fantasies. *Ethology and Sociobiology*, 14.

Kersten, D., and Yuille, A. (2003). Bayesian models of object perception. *Current Opinion in Neurobiology*, 13.

Kersten, D., Mamassian, P., and Yuille, A (2004). Object perception as Bayesian inference. *Annual Review of Psychology*, 55.

Kiehl, K., Hare, R., Liddle, P., and McDonald, J. (1999a). Reduced P300 responses in criminal psychopaths during a visual oddball task. *Biological Psychiatry*, 45, 11.

Kiehl, K., Hare, R., McDonald, J., and Brink, J. (1999b). Semantic and affective processing in psychopaths: An event-related potential (ERP) study. *Psychophysiology*, 366.

Kiehl, K., Smith, A., Hare, R., and Liddle, P. (2000). An event-related potential investigation of response inhibition in schizophrenia and psychopathy. *Biological Psychiatry*, 48, 3.

Kiehl, K., Smith, A., Hare, R., Mendrek, A., Forster, B., Brink, J., and Liddle, P. (2001). Limbic abnormalities in affective processing by criminal psychopaths as revealed by functional magnetic resonance imaging. *Biological Psychiatry*, 50, 9.

Kim, K., Relkin N., Lee K., and Hirsch J. (1997). Distinct cortical areas associated with native and second languages. *Nature*, 388.

Kingstone, A., Friesen, C., and Gazzaniga, M. (2000). Reflexive joint attention depends on lateralized cortical connections. *Psychological Science*, 11.

Kjelgaard, M., and Tager-Flusberg, H. (2001). An investigation of language impairment in autism: Implications for genetic subgroups. *Language and Cognitive Processes*, 16.

Klaus, M., and Kennell, J. (2001). Commentary: Routines in maternity units: Are they still appropriate for 2002? *Birth*, 28.

Klaus, M., Kennell, J., and Klaus, P. (1995). *Bonding: Building the Foundations of a Secure Attachment and Independence*. Perseus.

Klein-Tasman, B., and Mervis, C. (2003). Distinctive personality characteristics of 8-, 9-, and 10-year-olds with Williams syndrome. *Developmental Neuropsychology*, 23.

Klin, A. (1991). Young autistic children's listening preferences in regard to speech: A possible characterization of the symptom of social withdrawal. *Journal of Autism and Developmental Disorders*, 21.

Klin, A., and Volkmar, F. (1993). The development of individuals with autism: Implications for the theory of mind hypothesis. In S. Baron-Cohen, H. Tager-Flusberg, and D. Cohen (eds)., *Understanding Other Minds: Perspectives from Autism*. Oxford University Press.

Klin, A., Jones, W., Schultz, R., and Volkmar, F. (2003). The enactive mind, or from actions to cognition: Lessons from autism. *Philosophical Transactions of the Royal Society*, series B, 358.

Klin, A., Schultz, R., and Cohen, D. (2000). Theory of mind in action: Developmental perspectives on social neuroscience. In S. Baron-Cohen, H. Tager-Flusberg, and D. Cohen (eds.), *Understanding Other Minds: Perspectives from Developmental Cognitive Neuroscience*, 2nd ed. Oxford University Press.

Knill, D., and Richards, W. (eds.). (1996). *Perception as Bayesian Inference*. Cambridge University Press.

Knill, D., Kersten, D., and Yuille, A. (1996). A Bayesian formulation of visual perception. In D. Knill and W. Richards (eds.), *Perception as Bayesian Inference*. Cambridge University Press.

Koehler, J. (1996). The base rate fallacy reconsidered: Descriptive, normative, and methodological challenges. *Behavior and Brain Sciences*, 19.

Kohlberg, L. (1969). Stage and sequence: The cognitive-developmental approach to socialization. In D. Goslin (ed.), *Handbook of Socialization Theory and Research*. Rand McNally.

Kornblith, H. (1993). *Inductive Inference and Its Natural Ground: An Essay in Naturalistic Epistemology*. MIT Press.

Kortenkamp, D., Bonasso, R., and Murphy, R. (eds.). (1998). *Artificial Intelligence and Mobile Robotics*. MIT Press.

Kosslyn, S. (1994). *Image and Brain*. MIT Press.

Krebs, J., and Davies, N. (eds.) (1984). *Behavioural Ecology: An Evolutionary Approach*. 2nd ed. Blackwell.

Krebs, J., and Davies, N. (eds.) (1991). *Behavioural Ecology: An Evolutionary Approach*. 4th ed. Blackwell.

Krebs, J., and Davies, N. (eds.) (1997). *Behavioural Ecology: An Evolutionary Approach*. 3rd ed. Blackwell.

Krifka, M. (1995). The semantics and pragmatics and polarity items. *Linguistic Analysis*, 25.

Kripke, S. (1972). Naming and necessity. In D. Davidson and G. Harman (eds.), *Semantics of Natural Language*. Reidel.

Kuczaj, S., and Maratsos, M. (1975). On the acquisition of front, back, and side. *Child Development*, 46.

Kurzban, R., Tooby, J., and Cosmides, L. (2001). Can race be erased? Coalitional computation and social categorization. *Proceedings of the National Academy of Sciences*, 98.

Ladusaw, W. (1996). Negation and polarity items. In S. Lappin (ed.), *Handbook of Contemporary Semantic Theory*. Blackwell.

Laing, E., Butterworth, G., Ansari, D., Gsödl, M., Longhi, E., Panagiotaki, G., Paterson, S., and Karmiloff-Smith, A. (2002). Atypical development of language and social communication in toddlers with Williams syndrome. *Developmental Sciences*, 5, 2.

Landau, B., and Gleitman, L. (1985). *Language and Experience: Evidence from the Blind Child*. MIT Press.

Langdell, T. (1978). Recognition of faces: An approach to the study of autism. *Journal of Child Psychology and Psychiatry*, 19.

Langton, S., and Bruce, V. (1999). Reflexive visual orienting in response to the social attention of others. *Visual Cognition*, 6.

Lapierre, D., Braun, C., and Hodgins, S. (1995). Ventral frontal deficits in psychopathy: Neuropsychological test findings. *Neuropsychologia*, 332.

Laurence, S., and Margolis, E. (2001). The poverty of the stimulus argument. *British Journal for the Philosophy of Science*, 52.

Laurence, S., and Margolis, E. (in prep.). Think of a Number.

Learmonth, A., Nadel, L., and Newcombe, N. (2002). Children's use of landmarks: Implications for modularity theory. *Psychological Science*, 13.

Leavens, D., and Hopkins, W. (1999). The whole-hand point: The structure and function of pointing from a comparative perspective. *Journal of Comparative Psychology*, 113.

Lee, R. (1984). *The Dobe !Kung*. Holt, Rinehart and Winston.

Leger, D., Thompson, R., Merritt, J., and Benz, J. (1996). Adult perception of emotion intensity in human infant cries: Effects of infant age and cry acoustics. *Child Development*, 67.

Leiber, J. (2002). Philosophy, engineering, biology, and history: A vindication of Turing's views about the distinction between the cognitive and physical sciences. *Journal of Experimental and Theoretical Artificial Intelligence*, 14.

Lempers, J. (1979). Young children's production and comprehension of nonverbal deitic behaviors. *Journal of Genetic Psychology*, 135.

Leslie, A. (1987). Pretense and representation: The origins of "theory of mind." *Psychological Review*, 94.
Leslie, A. (1994). ToMM, ToBY and Agency: Core architecture and domain specificity. In L. Hirschfeld and S. Gelman (eds.), *Mapping the Mind: Domain-Specificity in Culture and Cognition*. Cambridge University Press.
Leslie, A. (1995). A theory of agency. In D. Sperber, D. Premack, and A. Premack (eds.), *Causal Cognition: A Multidisciplinary Debate*. Clarendon Press.
Leslie, A., and Keeble, S. (1987). Do six-month-old infants perceive causality? *Cognition*, 25.
Leslie, A., and Roth, D. (1993). What autism teaches us about metarepresentation. In S. Baron-Cohen, H. Tager-Flusberg, and D. Cohen (eds.), *Understanding Other Minds: Perspectives from Autism*. Oxford University Press.
Leslie, A., and Thaiss, L. (1992). Domain specificity in conceptual development: Evidence from autism. *Cognition*, 43.
Leslie, A., Xu, F., Tremoulet, P., and Scholl, B. (1998). Indexing and the object concept: Developing what and where systems. *Trends in Cognitive Sciences*, 2.
Levelt, W. (1989). *Speaking: From Intention to Articulation*. MIT Press.
Lewis, V., and Boucher, J. (1888). Spontaneous, instructed and elicited play in relatively able autistic children. *British Journal of Developmental Psychology*, 6.
Lewontin, R. (1998). The evolution of cognition: Questions we will never answer. In D. Scarborough and S. Sternberg (eds.), *An Invitation to Cognitive Science*, vol. 4, *Methods, Models, and Conceptual Issues*. MIT Press.
Liebenberg, L. (1990). *The Art of Tracking: the Origin of Science*. Philip.
Lieberman, D., Tooby, J., and Cosmides, L. (2003). Does morality have a biological basis? An empirical test of the factors governing moral sentiments relating to incest. *Proceedings of the Royal Society London (Biological Sciences)*, 270.
Lieberman, D., Tooby, J., and Cosmides, L. (under review). The architecture of the human kin detection system.
Lieberman, D., Tooby, J., and Cosmides, L. (in press). The evolution of human incest avoidance mechanisms: An evolutionary psychological approach. In A. Wolf and J. Takala (eds.), *Evolution and the Moral Emotions: Appreciating Edward Westermarck*. Stanford University Press.
Lillard, A., and Flavell, J. (1990). Young children's preference for mental states versus behavioral descriptions of human action. *Child Development*, 61.
Liu, Z., Knill, D., and Kersten, D. (1995). Object classification for human and ideal observers. *Vision Research*, 35.
Locke, J. (1690). *An Essay Concerning Human Understanding*. Ed. P. Nidditch. (1975). Clarendon Press.
Loewenstein, W. (1999). *The Touchstone of Life: Molecular Information, Cell Communication, and the Foundations of Life*. Oxford University Press.
Lohmann, H., and Tomasello, M. (2003). The role of language in the development of false belief understanding: A training study. *Child Development*, 74, 14.
López, A., Atran, S., Coley, J., Medin, D., and Smith, E. (1997). The tree of life: Universals of folk-biological taxonomies and inductions. *Cognitive Psychology*, 32.
Lord, C., and Paul, R. (1997). Language and communication in autism. In D. Cohen and F. Volkmar (eds.), *Handbook of Autism and Pervasive Developmental Disorders*, 2nd ed. Wiley.
Lorenz, K. (1957). The nature of instincts. In C. Schiller (ed.), *Instinctive Behaviour*. International University Press.
Lorenz, K. (1966a). *On Aggression*. Harcourt, Brace, Jovanovich.
Lorenz, K. (1966b). The role of gestalt perception in animal and human behavior. In L. White (ed.), *Aspects of Form*. Indiana University Press.

Ludlow, P. (2002). LF and natural logic. In G. Preyer and G. Peter (eds.), *Logical Form and Language*. Oxford University Press.

Lycan, W. (1999). Intentionality. In R. Wilson and F. Keil (eds.), *MIT Encyclopedia of Cognitive Science*. MIT Press.

Lyckman, A., Jhaveri, S., Feldheim, D., Vanderhaeghen, P., Flanagan, J., and Sur, M. (2001). Enhanced plasticity of retinothalamic projections in an ephrin-A2/A5 double mutant. *Journal of Neuroscience*, 21, 19.

Lyon, R., and Rumsey, J. (eds.). (1996). *Neuroimaging: A Window to the Neurological Foundations of Learning and Behaviour in Children*. Brookes.

Macario, J. (1991). Young children's use of color in classification: Foods and canonically colored objects. *Cognitive Development*, 6.

Maclaurin, J. (2002). The resurrection of innateness. *Monist*, 85.

MacWhinney, B., and Snow, C. (1990). The child language data exchange system: An update. *Journal of Child Language*, 17.

Maddock, R. (1999). The retrosplenial cortex and emotion: New insights from functional neuroimaging of the human brain. *Trends in Neuroscience*, 227.

Maestripieri, D. (2002). Parent-offspring conflict in primates. *International Journal of Primatology*, 23.

Mahalingam, R. (1998). Essentialism, power, and representation of caste: A developmental study. Ph.D. diss., University of Pittsburgh.

Malt, B. (1990). Features and beliefs in the mental representation of categories. *Journal of Memory and Language*, 29.

Malt, B. (1994). Water is not H_2O. *Cognitive Psychology*, 27.

Mamassian, P., and Goutcher, R. (2001). Prior knowledge on the illumination position. *Cognition*, 81, B1–B9.

Mamassian, P., and Landy, M. (1998). Observer biases in the 3D interpretation of line drawings. *Vision Research*, 38.

Mamassian, P., Landy, M., and Maloney, L. (2002). Bayesian modeling of visual perception. In R. Rao, B. Olshausen, and M. Lewicki (eds.), *Probabilistic Models of the Brain: Perception and Neural Function*. MIT Press.

Mandler, J., and McDonough, L. (1996). Drinking and driving don't mix: Inductive generalization in infancy. *Cognition*, 59.

Marcus, G. (1993). Negative evidence in language acquisition. *Cognition*, 46.

Marcus, G. (1998). Can connectionism save constructivism? *Cognition*, 66.

Marcus, G. (2001). Plasticity and nativism: Towards a resolution of an apparent paradox. In S. Wermter, J. Austin, and D. Willshaw (eds.), *Emergent Neural Computational Architectures Based on Neuroscience*. Springer-Verlag.

Marcus, G. (2002). *The Algebraic Mind: Integrating Connectionism and Cognitive Science*. MIT Press.

Marcus, G. (2004). *The Birth of the Mind*. Basic Books.

Marcus, G., Brinkmann, U., Clahsen, H., Wiese, R., and Pinker, S. (1995). German inflection: The exception that proves the rule. *Cognitive Psychology*, 29.

Marcus, G., Pinker, S., Ullman, M., Hollander, M., Rosen, T., and Xu, F. (1992). Over-regularization in language acquisition. *Monographs of the Society for Research in Child Development*, vol. 57, no. 4, serial no. 228.

Marcus, G., Vijayan, S., Bandi Rao, S., and Vishton, P. (1999). Rule learning in 7-month-old infants. *Science*, 283.

Margules, J., and Gallistel, C. (1988). Heading in the rat: Determination by environmental shape. *Animal Learning and Behavior*, 16.

Markman, E. (1989). *Categorization and Naming in Children*. MIT Press.

Markman, E., and Hutchinson, J. (1984). Children's sensitivity to constraints on word meaning: Taxonomic versus thematic relations. *Cognitive Psychology*, 16.
Marks, I. (1987). *Fears, Phobias, and Rituals*. Oxford University Press.
Marler, P. (1991). The instinct to learn. In S. Carey and R. Gelman (eds.), *The Epigenesis of Mind: Essays on Biology and Cognition*. Erlbaum.
Marr, D. (1982). *Vision*. Freeman.
Maurer, A. (1965). What children fear. *Journal of Genetic Psychology*, 106.
Maynard Smith, J., Burian, R., Kaufman, S., Alberch, P., Campbell, J., Goodwin, B., Lande, R., Raup, D., and Wolpert, L. (1985). Developmental constraints in evolution. *Quarterly Review of Biology*, 60.
Mayr, E. (1982). *The Growth of Biological Thought*. Harvard University Press.
Mayr, E. (1991). *One Long Argument: Charles Darwin and the Genesis of Modern Evolutionary Thought*. Harvard University Press.
McBreartey, S., and Brooks, A. (2001). The revolution that wasn't. *Journal of Human Evolution*, 39.
McDonough, L., and Mandler, J. (1998). Inductive generalization in 9- and 11-month-olds. *Developmental Science*, 1.
McIntyre, A. (2001). Doing away with double effect. *Ethics*, 111.
Mechner, F. (1958). Probability relations within response sequences under ratio reinforcement. *Journal of the Experimental Analysis of Behavior*, 1.
Mechner, F., and Guevrekian, L. (1962). Effects of deprivation upon counting and timing in rats. *Journal of the Experimental Analysis of Behavior*, 5.
Meck, W., and Church, R. (1983). A mode control model of counting and timing processes. *Journal of Experimental Psychology: Animal Behavior Processes*, 9.
Medin, D. (1989). Concepts and conceptual structure. *American Psychologist*, 44, 14.
Medin, D., and Atran, S. (2004). The native mind: Biological categorization and reasoning in development and across cultures. *Psychological Review*, 111.
Medin, D., and Ortony, A. (1989). Psychological essentialism. In S. Vosniadou and A. Ortony (eds.), *Similarity and Analogical Reasoning*. Cambridge University Press.
Mehler, J., and Dupoux, E. (1994). *What Infants Know: The New Cognitive Science of Early Development*. Blackwell.
Meltzoff, A. (1990). Foundations for developing a concept of self: The role of imitation in relating self to other and the value of social mirroring, social modeling, and self-practice in infancy. In D. Cicchetti and M. Beeghly (eds.), *The Self in Transition*. University of Chicago Press.
Meltzoff, A. (1995). Understanding the intention of others: Reenactment of intended acts by 18-month-old children. *Developmental Psychology*, 31.
Meltzoff, A., and Decety, J. (2003). What imitation tells us about social cognition: A rapprochement between developmental psychology and cognitive neuroscience. *Philosophical Transactions of the Royal Society*, series B, 358.
Meltzoff, A., and Gopnik, A. (1993). The role of imitation in understanding persons and developing a theory of mind. In S. Baron-Cohen, H. Tager-Flusberg, and D. Cohen (eds.), *Understanding Other Minds*. Oxford University Press.
Meltzoff, A., and Moore, M. (1977). Imitation of facial and manual gestures by human neonates. *Science*, 198.
Meltzoff, A., and Moore, M. (1994). Imitation, memory, and the representation of persons. *Infant Behavior and Development*, 17.
Meltzoff, A., and Moore, M. (1995). Infants' understanding of people and things: From body imitation to folk psychology. In J. Bermúdez, A. Marcel, and N. Eilan (eds.), *The Body and the Self*. MIT Press.

Meltzoff, A., and Moore, M. (1997). Explaining facial imitation: A theoretical model. *Early Development and Parenting*, 6.

Mervis, C., Morris, C., Klein-Tasman, B., Bertrand, J., Kwitny, S., Appelbaum, L., and Rice, C. (2003). Attentional characteristics of infants and toddlers with Williams syndrome during triadic interactions. *Developmental Neuropsychology*, 23.

Mervis, C., Robinson, B., Bertrand, J., Morris, C., Klein-Tasman, B., and Armstrong, S. (2000). The Williams syndrome cognitive profile. *Brain and Cognition*, 44, 3.

Mikhail, J. (2000). Rawls' linguistic analogy: A study of the "generative grammar" model of moral theory described by John Rawls in *A Theory of Justice*. Ph.D. diss., Cornell University.

Mikhail, J. (2002). Law, science, and morality: A review of Richard Posner's *The Problematics of Moral and Legal Theory*. *Stanford Law Review*, 54.

Mikhail, J. (forthcoming). Aspects of the theory of moral cognition.

Milgram, S. (1974). *Obedience to Authority: An Experimental View*. Harper and Row.

Miller, C. (2001). False belief understanding in children with specific language impairment. *Journal of Communication Disorders*, 34.

Miller, K., Keller, J., and Stryker, M. (1989). Ocular dominance column development: analysis and simulation. *Science*, 245, 4918.

Mineka, S., and Cook, M. (1993). Mechanisms involved in the observational conditioning of fear. *Journal of Experimental Psychology: General*, 122.

Mineka, S., Davidson, M., Cook, M., and Keir, R. (1984). Observational conditioning of snake fear in rhesus monkeys. *Journal of Abnormal Psychology*, 93.

Mitchell, D., Colledge, E., Leonard, A., and Blair, R. (2002). Risky decisions and response reversal: Is there evidence of orbitofrontal cortex dysfunction in psychopathic individuals? *Neuropsychologia*, 40, 12.

Mithen, S. (1990). *Thoughtful Foragers: A Study of Prehistoric Decision-Making*. Cambridge University Press.

Mithen, S. (1996). *The Prehistory of the Mind*. Thames and Hudson.

Mithen, S. (2000). Palaeoanthropological perspectives on the theory of mind. In S. Baron-Cohen, H. Tager-Flusberg, and D. Cohen (eds.), *Understanding Other Minds*. Oxford University Press.

Mittelstaedt, M., and Mittelstaedt, H. (1980). Homing by path integration in a mammal. *Naturwissenschaften*, 67.

Moll, J., de Oliveira-Souza, R., Bramati, I., and Grafman, J. (2002a). Functional networks in emotional moral and nonmoral social judgments. *Neuroimage*, 163 pt. 1.

Moll, J., de Oliveira-Souza, R., Eslinger, P., Bramati, I., Mourao-Miranda, J., Andreiuolo, P., and Pessoa, L. (2002b). The neural correlates of moral sensitivity: A functional magnetic resonance imaging investigation of basic and moral emotions. *Journal of Neuroscience*, 227.

Moll, J., Eslinger, P., and Oliveira-Souza, R. (2001). Frontopolar and anterior temporal cortex activation in a moral judgment task: Preliminary functional MRI results in normal subjects. *Arquivos de Neuro-Psiquiatria*, 593-B.

Moore, C., and D'Entremont, B. (2001). Developmental changes in pointing as a function of parent's attentional focus. *Journal of Cognition and Development*, 2.

Morissette, P., Ricard, M., and Décarie, T. (1995). Joint visual attention and pointing in infancy: A longitudinal study of comprehension. *British Journal of Developmental Psychology*, 13.

Morris, C., and Mervis, C. (1999). Williams syndrome. In S. Goldstein and C. Reynolds (eds.), *Handbook of Neurodevelopmental and Genetic Disorders in Children*. Guilford Press.

Morton, J., and Johnson, M. (1991). Conspec and Conlearn: A two-process theory of infant face recognition. *Psychological Review*, 98.
Moses, L., Baldwin, D., Rosicky, J., and Tidball, G. (2001). Evidence for referential understanding in the emotions domain at twelve and eighteen months. *Child Development*, 72.
Mosier, C., and Rogoff, B. (1994). Infants' instrumental use of their mothers to achieve their goals. *Child Development*, 65.
Müller, M., and Wehner, R. (1988). Path integration in desert ants, Cataglyphis fortis. *Proceedings of the National Academy of Science USA*, 85.
Munakata, Y. (2001). Graded representations in behavioral dissociations.*Trends in Cognitive Sciences*, 5, 7.
Mundy, P., and Sigman, M. (1989). Specifying the nature of the social impairment in autism. In G. Dawson (ed.), *Autism: Nature, Diagnosis and Treatment*. Guilford Press.
Mundy, P., Sigman, M., and Kasari, C. (1990). A longitudinal study of joint attention and language development in autistic children. *Journal of Autism and Developmental Disorders*, 20.
Mundy, P., Sigman, M., and Kasari, C. (1993). The theory of mind and joint-attention deficits in autism. In S. Baron-Cohen, H. Tager-Flusberg, and D. Cohen (eds.), *Understanding Other Minds: Perspectives from Autism*. Oxford University Press.
Murphy, G., and Medin, D. (1985). The role of theories in conceptual coherence. *Psychological Review*, 92.
Murray, A. (1985). Aversiveness is the in the mind of the beholder: Perception of infant crying by adults. In B. Lester and C. Boukydis (eds.), *Infant Crying: Theoretical and Research Perspectives*. Plenum Press.
Nagel, T. (1972). War and massacre. *Philosophy and Public Affairs*, 1.
Nagel, T. (1986). *The View from Nowhere*. Oxford University Press.
Nakayama, D., and Shimojo, S. (1992). Experiencing and perceiving visual surfaces. *Science*, 257.
Nazzi, T., Bertoncini, J., and Mehler, J. (1998). Language discrimination by newborns: Towards an understanding of the role of rhythm. *Journal of Experimental Psychology: Human Perception and Performance*, 24.
Needham, A., and Baillargeon, R. (1993). Intuitions about support in 4.5-month old infants. *Cognition*, 47.
Newell, A. (1990). *Unified Theories of Cognition*. Harvard University Press.
Newell, A., and Simon, H. (1972). *Human Problem Solving*. Prentice-Hall.
Newman, J., Schmitt, W., and Voss, W. (1997). The impact of motivationally neutral cues on psychopathic individuals: Assessing the generality of the response modulation hypothesis. *Journal of Abnormal Psychology*, 106, 4.
Newmeyer, F. (1998). *Language Form and Language Function*. MIT Press.
Neyman, J., and Pearson, E. (1928). On the use and interpretation of certain test criteria for purposes of statistical inference. *Biometrika*, A20.
Neyman, J., and Pearson, E. (1933). On the problem of the most efficient tests of statistical hypotheses. *Philosophical transactions of the Royal Society*, A231.
Nichols, S. (2002a). Norms with feeling: Towards a psychological account of moral judgment. *Cognition*, 84.
Nichols, S. (2002b). On the genealogy of norms: A case for the role of emotion in cultural evolution. *Philosophy of Science*, 69.
Nichols, S. (2004). *Sentimental Rules: On the Natural Foundations of Moral Judgment*. Oxford University Press.
Nichols, S., and Folds-Bennett, T. (2003). Are children moral objectivists? Children's judgments about moral and response-dependent properties. *Cognition*, 90, 2.

Nichols, S., and Stich, S. (2003). *Mindreading*. Oxford University Press.
Nilsson, D., and Pelger, S. (1994). A pessimistic estimate of the time required for an eye to evolve. *Proceedings of the Royal Society of London*, series B, 2556.
Nilsson, N. (1984). *Shakey the Robot*. Technical Note 323. AI Center, SRI International.
Nishitani, N., and Hari, R. (2000). Temporal dynamics of cortical representation for action. *Proceedings of the National Academy of Sciences*, 97.
Noble, W., and Davidson, I. (1996). *Human Evolution, Language and Mind*. Cambridge University Press.
Nolfi, S., and Parisi, D. (1995). Genotypes for Neural Networks. In M. Arbib (ed.), *The Handbook of Brain Theory and Neural Networks*. MIT Press.
Norman, L. (1983). Child abuse. *Clinics in Laboratory Medicine*, 3.
Nowak, M., Komarova, N., and Niyogi, P. (2001). Evolution of Universal Grammar. *Science*, 291.
Núñez, M., and Harris, P. (1998). Psychological and deontic concepts: Separate domains or intimate connection? *Mind and Language*, 13.
O'Donovan, M. (1999). The origin of spontaneous activity in developing networks of the vertebrate nervous system. *Current Opinion in Neurobiology*, 9, 4.
O'Leary, C., and Crain, S. (1994). Negative polarity items (a positive result); positive polarity items (a negative result). Paper presented at the nineteenth annual Boston University Conference on Language Development, Boston.
O'Leary, D., and Stanfield, B. (1989). Selective elimination of axons extended by developing cortical neurons is dependent on regional locale: Experiments using fetal cortical transplants. *Journal of Neuroscience*, 9.
Oliver, A., Johnson, M., Karmiloff-Smith, A., and Pennington, B. (2000). Deviations in the emergence of representations: A neuroconstructivist framework for analyzing developmental disorders. *Developmental Science*, 3.
Oppenheim, R. (1981). Ontogenetic adaptations and retrogressive processes in the development of the nervous system and behaviour: A neuroembryological perspective. In K. Connolly and H. Prechtl (eds.), *Maturation and Development: Biological and Psychological Perspectives*. Lavenham Press.
Osborne, L., and Pober, B. (2001). Genetics of childhood disorders: XXVII. Genes and cognition in Williams syndrome. *Journal of the American Academy of Child and Adolescent Psychiatry*, 40.
Osherson, D. (1995). Probability Judgment. In E. Smith and D. Osherson (eds.), *Thinking*. MIT Press.
Osterling, J., and Dawson, G. (1994). Early recognition of children with autism: A study of first birthday home videotapes. *Journal of Autism and Developmental Disorders*, 24.
Oyama, S. (1985). *The Ontogeny of Information*. Cambridge University Press.
Oyama, S. (2000). *Evolution's Eye*. Duke University Press.
Palmer, S. (1999). *Vision Science: Photons to Phenomenology*. MIT Press.
Pappas, A., and Gelman, S. (1998). Generic noun phrases in mother-child conversations. *Journal of Child Language*, 25.
Pascalis, O., and Slater, A. (eds.). (2003). *Face Perception in Infancy and Early Childhood*. NOVA Science.
Paterson, S., Brown, J., Gsodl, M., Johnson, M., and Karmiloff-Smith, A. (1999). Cognitive modularity and genetic disorders. *Science*, 286, 28.
Pearl, J. (1988). *Probabilistic Reasoning in Intelligent Systems: Networks of Plausible Inference*. Kaufmann.
Pearlman-Avnion, S. (2003). ToM in Williams syndrome and autism: An inconsistent profile of proficiency on false belief attribution and irony understanding. *Cognitive Neuroscience Society*. New York.

Pearse, R., II, and Tabin, C. (1998). The molecular ZPA. *Journal of Experimental Zoology*, 282, 6.
Perner, J. (1991). *Understanding the Representational Mind*. MIT Press.
Perrett, D., Harries, M., Mistlin, A., Hietanen, J., Benson, P., Bevan, R., Thomas, S., Oram, M., Ortega, J., and Brierley, K. (1990). Social signals analyzed at the single cell level: Someone is looking at me, something touched me, something moved! *International Journal of Comparative Psychology*, 4.
Peterson, C., and Siegal, M. (1995). Deafness, conversation and theory of mind. *Journal of Child Psychology and Psychiatry*, 36.
Peterson, C., and Siegal, M. (1998). Changing focus on the representational mind: Deaf, autistic and normal children's concepts of false photos, false drawings and false beliefs. *British Journal of Developmental Psychology*, 16.
Philip, W. (1995). Event quantification in the acquisition of universal quantification. Ph.D. diss., University of Massachusetts, Amherst.
Phillips, A., Wellman, H., and Spelke, E. (2002). Infants' ability to connect gaze and emotional expression to intentional action. *Cognition*, 85.
Phillips, M., Young, A., Senior, C., Brammer, M., Andrew, C., Calder, A., Bullmore, E., Perrett, D., Rowland, D., Williams, S., Gray, J., and David, A. (1997). A specific neural substrate for perceiving facial expressions of disgust. *Nature*, 389, 6650.
Piaget, J. (1936). *The Origin of Intelligence in the Child*. Routledge.
Piaget, J. (1937). *The Construction of Reality in the Child*. Basic Books.
Piaget, J. (1959). *The Language and Thought of the Child*. 3rd ed. Routledge.
Piaget, J. (1970). Piaget's theory. In P. Mussen (ed.), *Carmichael's Manual of Child Psychology*, vol. 1. Wiley.
Piaget, J., and Inhelder, B. (1941). *The Child's Construction of Quantities: Conservation and Atomism*. Trans. A. Pomerans. Basic Books.
Piaget, J., and Inhelder, B. (1948). *The Child's Conception of Space*. Trans. F. Langdon and J. Lunzer. Routledge.
Piaget, J., and Inhelder, B. (1966). *The Psychology of the Child*. Routledge.
Pillow, B. (1988). The development of children's beliefs about the mental world. *Merrill-Palmer Quarterly*, 34.
Pinker, S. (1979). Formal models of language learning. *Cognition*, 7.
Pinker, S. (1984). *Language Learnability and Language Development*. Harvard University Press.
Pinker, S. (1994). *The Language Instinct*. Morrow.
Pinker, S. (1997a). *How the Mind Works*. Lane.
Pinker, S. (1997b). Why they kill their newborns. *New York Times*, November 2.
Pinker, S. (1999). *Words and Rules: The Ingredients of Language*. Basic Books.
Pinker, S. (2002). *The Blank Slate: The Modern Denial of Human Nature*. Viking Press.
Pinker, S., and Bloom, P. (1990). Natural language and natural selection. *Behavioral and Brain Sciences*, 13.
Pinker, S., and Bloom, P. (1994). Humans did not evolve from bats. *Behavioral and Brain Sciences*, 17.
Pinker, S., and Jackendoff, R. (in press). What's special about the language faculty? *Cognition*.
Pinker, S., and Prince, A. (1988). On language and connectionism: Analysis of a parallel distributed processing model of language acquisition. *Cognition*, 28.
Plaisted, K. (2000). Aspects of autism that theory of mind cannot easily explain. In S. Baron-Cohen, H. Tager-Flusberg, and D. Cohen (eds.), *Understanding Other Minds: Perspectives from Developmental Cognitive Neuroscience*. 2nd ed. Oxford University Press.

Plato. (1997). *The Dialogues of Plato*. Trans. and ed. B. Jowett. Thoemmes Press.
Platt, J., and Johnson, D. (1971). Localization of position within a homogenous behavior chain: Effects of error contingencies. *Learning and Motivation*, 2.
Plesa Skwerer, D., Faja, S., and Tager-Flusberg, H. (2003). Reading emotions and mental states in faces and voices: How do people with Williams syndrome do it? Paper presented at the annual meeting of the Society for Research in Child Development. Orlando, FL.
Plesa-Skwerer, D., and Tager-Flusberg, H. (in press). Social cognition in Williams syndrome. In C. Morris, H. Lenhoff, and P. Wang (eds.), *Williams-Beuren Syndrome: Research and Clinical Perspectives*. Johns Hopkins University Press.
Plooij, F. (1978). Some basic traits of language in wild chimpanzees? In A. Lock (ed.), *Action, Gesture and Symbol: The Emergence of Language*. Academic Press.
Plotkin, H. (1997). *Evolution in Mind*. Harvard University Press. Polis, G., and Farley, R. (1979). Behavior and ecology of mating in the cannibalistic scorpion *Paruroctonus mesaensis* Stahnke (Scorpionida: Vaejovidae). *Journal of Arachnology*, 7.
Povinelli, D. (2000). *Folk Physics for Apes*. Oxford University Press.
Povinelli, D. (2001a). Chimpanzee theory of mind and folk physics. Paper presented at AHRB "Innatencss and Structure of Mind" workshop, University of Sheffield, Sheffield, England.
Povinelli, D. (2001b). On the possibilities of detecting intentions prior to understanding them. In B. Malle, D. Baldwin, and L. Moses (eds.), *Intentionality: A Key to Human Understanding*. MIT Press.
Povinelli, D., and Bering, J. (2002). The mentality of apes revisited. *Current Directions in Psychological Science*, 11.
Povinelli, D., and Davis, D. (1994). Differences between chimpanzees (*Pan troglodytes*) and humans (*Homo sapiens*) in the resting state of the index finger: Implications for pointing. *Journal of Comparative Psychology*, 108.
Povinelli, D., and Eddy, T. (1996a). What young chimpanzees know about seeing. *Monographs of the Society for Research in Child Development*, vol. 61.
Povinelli, D., and Eddy, T. (1996b). Chimpanzees: Joint visual attention. *Psychological Science*, 7.
Povinelli, D., and Eddy, T. (1997). Specificity of gaze-following in young chimpanzees. *British Journal of Developmental Psychology*, 15.
Povinelli, D., and Giambrone, S. (1999). Inferring other minds: Failure of the argument by analogy. *Philosophical Topics*, 27.
Povinelli, D., and Giambrone, S. (2000). Escaping the argument by analogy. In D. Povinelli (ed.), *Folk Physics for Apes*. Oxford University Press.
Povinelli, D., and Giambrone, S. (2001). Reasoning about beliefs: A human specialization? *Child Development*, 72.
Povinelli, D., and Prince, C. (1998). When self met other. In M. Ferrari and R. Sternberg (eds.), *Self-Awareness: Its Nature and Development*. Guilford.
Povinelli, D., Bering, J., and Giambrone, S. (2003). Chimpanzee "pointing": Another error of the argument by analogy? In S. Kita (ed.), *Pointing: Where Language, Culture, and Cognition Meet*. Erlbaum.
Premack, D. (1990). The infant's theory of self-propelled objects. *Cognition*, 36.
Prestige, M., and Willshaw, D. (1975). On a role for competition in the formation of patterned neural connexions. *Proceedings of the Royal Society of London*, series B, *Biological Sciences*, 190, 1098.
Preuss, T. (1995). The argument from animals to humans in cognitive neuroscience. In M. Gazzaniga (ed.), *The Cognitive Neurosciences*. MIT Press.

Preuss, T. (2005). Evolutionary specializations of primate brain systems. In M. Ravoso, and M. Dagosto (eds.), *Primate Origins and Adaptations*. Kluwer Academic/Plenum Press.

Price, D., and Willshaw, D. (2000). *Mechanisms of Cortical Development*. Oxford University Press.

Price, M., Cosmides, L., and Tooby, J. (2002). Punitive sentiment as an anti-free-rider psychological device. *Evolution and Human Behavior*, 23.

Pullum, G., and Scholz, B. (2002). Empirical assessment of the stimulus poverty argument. *Linguistic Review*, 19.

Putnam, H. (1973). Meaning and reference. *Journal of Philosophy*, 70.

Pye, C. (1992). The acquisition of K'iché Maya. In D. Slobin (ed.), *The Crosslinguistic Study of Language Acquisition*, vol. 3. Erlbaum.

Pylyshyn, Z. (1984). *Computation and Cognition*. MIT Press.

Pylyshyn, Z. (1985). Plasticity and invariance in cognitive development. In J. Mehler and R. Fox (eds.), *Neonate Cognition: Beyond the Blooming Buzzing Confusion*. Erlbaum.

Quartz, S., and Sejnowski, T. (1994). Beyond modularity: Neural evidence for constructivist principles in development. *Behavioral and Brain Sciences*, 17.

Quartz, S., and Sejnowski, T. (1997). The neural basis of cognitive development: A constructivist manifesto. *Behavioral and Brain Sciences*, 20, 4.

Quine, V. (1969). Linguistics and philosophy. In S. Hook (ed.), *Language and Philosophy: A Symposium*. NYU Press.

Quinn, W. (1989). Actions, intentions, and consequences: The doctrine of double effect, *Philosophy and Public Affairs*, 18.

Railton, P. (1986). Moral realism. *Philosophical Review*, 95.

Raine, A., Lencz, T., Bihrle, S., LaCasse, L., and Colletti, P. (2000). Reduced prefrontal gray matter volume and reduced autonomic activity in antisocial personality disorder. *Archives of General Psychiatry*, 57, 2.

Raine, A., Meloy, J., Bihrle, S., Stoddard, J., LaCasse, L., and Buchsbaum, M. (1998). Reduced prefrontal and increased subcortical brain functioning assessed using positron emission tomography in predatory and affective murderers. *Behavioral Sciences and the Law*, 16, 3.

Ramachandran, V. (1988). Perception of shape from shading. *Nature*, 331.

Rao, R., Olshausen, B., and Lewicki, M. (eds.). (2002). *Probabilistic Models of the Brain: Perception and Neural Function*. MIT Press.

Rawls, J. (1971). *A Theory of Justice*. Harvard University Press.

Repacholi, B. (1998). Infants' use of attentional cues to identify the referent of another person's emotional expression. *Developmental Psychology*, 34, 15.

Repacholi, B., and Gopnik, A. (1997). Early reasoning of desires: Evidence from 14- to 18-month-olds. *Developmental Psychology*, 33.

Rigal, R. (1994). Right-left orientation: Development of correct use of right and left terms. *Perceptual and Motor Skills*, 79.

Rilling, M., and McDiarmid, C. (1965). Signal detection in fixed ratio schedules. *Science*, 148.

Rittenhouse, D. (1786). Explanation of an optical deception. *Transactions of the American Philosophical Society*, 2.

Rizzolatti, G., and Arbib, M. (1998). Language within our grasp. *Trends in Neuroscience*, 21.

Rizzolatti, G., Fadiga, L., Gallese, V., and Fogassi, L. (1996). Premotor cortex and the recognition of motor actions. *Cognitive Brain Research*, 3.

Roberts, S., and Pashler, H. (2000). How persuasive is a good fit? A comment on theory testing. *Psychological Review*, 107.

Robinson, B., Mervis, C., and Robinson, B. (2003). The roles of verbal short-term memory and working memory in the acquisition of grammar by children with Williams syndrome. *Developmental Neuropsychology*, 23.

Rock, I. (1983). *The Logic of Perception*. MIT Press.

Rosch, E. (1978). Principles of categorization. In E. Rosch and B. Lloyd (eds.), *Cognition and Categorization*. Erlbaum.

Rosch, E., Mervis, C., Grey, W., Johnson, D., and Boyes-Braem, P. (1976). Basic objects in natural categories. *Cognitive Psychology*, 8.

Rose, H., and Rose, S. (eds.). (2000). *Alas, Poor Darwin: Arguments against Evolutionary Psychology*. Cape.

Rosenbloom, L., and Newell, A. (1993). *Soar Papers*. MIT Press.

Ross, L., and Nisbett, R. (1991). *The Person and the Situation*. McGraw-Hill.

Ross, N., Medin, D., Coley, J., and Atran, S. (2003). Cultural and experiential differences in the development of folkbiological induction. *Cognitive Development*, 18.

Rozin, P., and Nemeroff, C. (1990). The laws of sympathetic magic: A psychological analysis of similarity and contagion. In J. Stigler, R. Shweder, and G. Herdt (eds.), *Cultural Psychology: Essays on Comparative Human Development*. Cambridge University Press.

Ruse, M. (1993). The significance of evolution. In P. Singer (ed.), *A Companion to Ethics*. Blackwell.

Russell, J. (1997). How executive disorders can bring about an inadequate "theory of mind." In J. Russell (ed.), *Autism as an Executive Disorder*. Oxford University Press.

Russell, S., and Norvig, P. (2003). *Artificial Intelligence: A Modern Approach*. 2nd ed. Prentice Hall.

Sabbagh, M., and Baldwin, D. (2001). Learning words from knowledgeable versus ignorant speakers: Links between preschoolers' theory of mind and semantic development. *Child Development*, 72, 10.

Sabra, A. (1978). Sensation and inference in Alhazen's theory of visual perception. In P. Machamer and R. Turnbull (eds.), *Studies in Perception: Interrelations in the History of Philosophy and Science*. Ohio State University Press.

Sacks, O. (1995). *An Anthropologist on Mars*. Vintage Books.

Saffran, J., Aslin, R., and Newport, E. (1996). Statistical learning by 8-month-old infants. *Science*, 274, 18.

Sameroff, A., and Chandler, M. (1975). Reproductive risk and the continuum of caretaking casualty. In F. Horowitz (ed.), *Review of Child Development Research*, vol. 4. University of Chicago Press.

Samet, J. (1999). Nativism, history of. In R. Wilson and F. Keil (eds.), *MIT Encyclopedia of Cognitive Science*. MIT Press.

Samuels, R. (1998). What brains won't tell us about the mind: A critique of the neurobiological argument against representational nativism. *Mind and Language*, 14.

Samuels, R. (2000). Massively modular minds: evolutionary psychology and cognitive architecture. In P. Carruthers and A. Chamberlain (eds.), *Evolution and the Human Mind: Modularity, Language and Meta-Cognition*. Cambridge University Press.

Samuels, R. (2002). Nativism in cognitive science. *Mind and Language*, 17.

Samuels, R. (forthcoming). *Descartes' Challenge*. Oxford University Press.

Samuels, R., Stich, S., and Tremoulet, P. (1999). Rethinking rationality. In E. LePore and Z. Pylyshyn (eds.), *What Is Cognitive Science?* Blackwell.

Sanfey, A., Rilling, J., Aronson, J., Nystrom, L., and Cohen, J. (2003). The neural basis of economic decision-making in the Ultimatum Game. *Science*, 300, 5626.

Sarimski, K. (1997). Behavioral phenotypes and family stress in three mental retardation syndromes. *European Child and Adolescent Psychiatry*, 63.
Saver, J., and Damasio, A. R. (1991). Preserved access and processing of social knowledge in a patient with acquired sociopathy due to ventromedial frontal damage. *Neuropsychologia*, 29, 12.
Scaife, M., and Bruner, J. (1975). The capacity for joint visual attention in the infant. *Nature*, 253.
Schlosser, G., and Wagner, G. P. (eds.) (2004). *Modularity in Development and Evolution*. University of Chicago Press.
Schmitt, W., Brinkley, C., and Newman, J. (1999). Testing Damasio's somatic marker hypothesis with psychopathic individuals: Risk takers or risk averse? *Journal of Abnormal Psychology*, 108, 3.
Scholl, B., and Leslie, A. (1999a). Explaining the infant's object concept: Beyond the perception/cognition dichotomy. In E. Lepore and Z. Pylyshyn (eds.), *What Is Cognitive Science?* Blackwell.
Scholl, B., and Leslie, A. (1999b). Modularity, development, and "theory of mind." *Mind and Language*, 14, 1.
Scholl, B., and Leslie, A. (2001). Minds, modules, and meta-analysis. *Child Development*, 72, 3.
Schrödinger, E. (1944). *What is Life? With Mind and Matter and Autobiographical Sketches*. Cambridge University Press (Reprint edition, 1992).
Schult, C., and Wellman, H. (1997). Explaining human movements and actions: Children's understanding of the limits of psychological explanation. *Cognition*, 62.
Schwartz, S. (1979). Natural kind terms. *Cognition*, 7.
Scott, F., and Baron-Cohen, S. (1996). Imagining real and unreal objects: An investigation of imagination in autism. *Journal of Cognitive Neuroscience*, 8.
Sedikides, C., and Skowronski, J. (1997). The symbolic self in evolutionary context. *Personal and Social Psychology Review*, 1.
Sedlmeier, P., and Gigerenzer, G. (2001). Teaching Bayesian reasoning in less than two hours. *Journal of Experimental Psychology: General*, 130.
Segal, G. (1996). The modularity of the theory of mind. In P. Carruthers and P. Smith (eds.), *Theories of Theories of Mind*. Cambridge University Press.
Sengpiel, F., Stawinski, P., and Bonhoeffer, T. (1999). Influence of experience on orientation maps in cat visual cortex. *Nature Neuroscience*, 2.
Shah, A., and Frith, U. (1993). Why do autistic individuals show superior performance on the block design task? *Journal of Child Psychology and Psychiatry*, 34, 14.
Shatz, C. (1996). Emergence of order in visual system development. *Proceedings of the National Academy of Sciences, USA*, 93.
Shaywitz, S., Shaywitz, B., Fulright, R., Skudlarski, P., Mencl, W., Constable, R., Pugh, K., Holahan, J., Marchione, K., Fletcher, J., Lyon, G., and Gore, J. (2003). Neural syndromes for compensation and persistence: Young adult outcome of childhood reading disability. *Biological Psychiatry*, 54.
Shepard, R. (1984). Ecological constraints on internal representation: Resonant kinematics of perceiving, imagining, thinking, and dreaming. *Psychological Review*, 91.
Shepard, R. (1987). Evolution of a mesh between principles of the mind and regularities of the world. In J. Dupre (ed.), *The Latest on the Best: Essays on Evolution and Optimality*. MIT Press.
Shiffrin, R., and Schneider, W. (1977). Controlled and automaitc information processing: part 2. perceptual learning, automatic attending, and a general theory. *Psychological Review*, 84.

Shimizu, Y., and Johnson, S. (2004). Infants' attribution of a goal to a morphologically unfamiliar agent. *Developmental Science*, 7, 4.

Shultz, T. (1982). Rules of causal attribution. *Monographs of the Society for Research in Child Development*, vol. 47, no. 1, serial no. 194.

Shusterman, A., Lee, S., and Spelke, E. (in prep.). Verbal cues in a reorientation task.

Shusterman, A., and Abarbanell, L. (2004). Fast mapping and generalization of spatial reference terms in four-year-olds. Presented at the 29th Boston University Conference on Language Development, Boston.

Shweder, R., Much, N., Mahapatra, M., and Park, L. (1997). The "big three" of morality (autonomy, community, and divinity), and the "big three" explanations of suffering. In A. Brandt and P. Rozin (eds.), *Morality and Health*. Routledge.

Siegal, M., and Varley, R. (2002). Neural systems involved in "theory of mind." *Nature Reviews Neuroscience*, 3.

Siegler, R. (1998). *Children's Thinking*. Prentice Hall.

Simner, M. (1971). Newborn's response to the cry of another infant, *Developmental Psychology*, 5.

Simon, H. (1972). Theories of bounded rationality. In C. Radner and R. Radner (eds.), *Decision and Organization*. North-Holland.

Simons D., and Chabris, C. (1999). Gorillas in our midst: Sustained inattentional blindness for dynamic events. *Perception*, 28.

Simons, D., and Keil, F. (1995). An abstract to concrete shift in the development of biological thought: The insides story. *Cognition*, 56.

Singh, S. (1999). *The Code Book: The Evolution of Secrecy from Mary, Queen of Scots, to Quantum Cryptography*. Doubleday.

Skyrms, B. (1996). *The Evolution of the Social Contract*. Cambridge University Press.

Smetana, J. (1993). Understanding of social rules. In M. Bennett (ed.), *The Development of Social Cognition: The Child as Psychologist*. Guilford Press.

Smith, E., and Winterhalder, B. (eds.). (1992). *Evolutionary Ecology and Human Behaviour*. Aldine.

Smith, L. (1999). Do infants possess innate knowledge structures? The con side. *Developmental Science*, 2.

Smith, L. (2000). Learning how to learn words: An associative crane. In R. Golinkoff and K. Hirsh-Pasek (eds.), *Becoming a Word Learner: A Debate on Lexical Acquisition*. Oxford University Press.

Smith, L., Jones, S., and Landau, B. (1996). Naming in young children: A dumb attentional mechanism? *Cognition*, 60.

Smith, M. (1994). *The Moral Problem*. Blackwell.

Smith, N., and Tsimpli, I-M. (1995). *The Mind of a Savant: Language-Learning and Modularity*. Blackwell.

Sober, E. (1994). *From a Biological Point of View*. Cambridge University Press.

Sober, E. (1999). Innate knowledge. *The Routledge Encyclopedia of Philosophy*. Routledge.

Sober, E., and Wilson, D. (1998). *Unto Others: the Evolution and Psychology of Unselfish Behavior*. Harvard University Press.

Solomon, G., Johnson, S., Zaitchik, D., and Carey, S. (1996). Like father, like son: Young children's understanding of how and why offspring resemble their parents. *Child Development*, 67.

Sorrentino, C. (2001). Children and adults represent proper names as referring to unique individuals. *Developmental Science*, 4.

Sousa, P., Atran, S., and Medin, D. (2002). Essentialism in folkbiology: Evidence from Brazil. *Journal of Cognition and Culture*, 2.

Sovrano, V., Bisazza, A., and Vallortigara, G. (2002). Modularity and spatial reorientation in a simple mind: Encoding of geometric and nongeometric properties of a spatial environment by fish. *Cognition*, 85.

Sovrano, V., Bisazza, A., and Vallortigara, G. (2003). Modularity as a fish (*Xenotoca eiseni*) views it: Conjoining geometric and nongeometric information for spatial reorientation. *Journal of Experimental Psychology: Animal Behavior Processes*, 29.

Sparks, D., and Nelson, J. (1987). Sensory and motor maps in the mammalian superior colliculus. *Trends in Neuroscience*, 10.

Sparrevohn, R., and Howie, P. (1995). Theory of mind children with autistic disorder: Evidence of developmental progression and the role of verbal ability. *Journal of Child Psychology and Psychiatry*, 36.

Spelke, E. (1988). The origins of physical knowledge. In L. Weiskrantz (ed.), *Thought without Language*. Oxford Science Publications.

Spelke, E. (1990). Principles of object perception. *Cognitive Science*, 14.

Spelke, E. (1994). Initial knowledge: Six suggestions. *Cognition*, 50.

Spelke, E. (1998). Nativism, empiricism, and the origins of knowledge. *Infant Behavior and Development*, 21.

Spelke, E. (2000). Core knowledge. *American Psychologist*, 55.

Spelke, E. (2003). What makes us smart? Core knowledge and natural language. In D. Gentner and S. Goldin-Meadow (eds.), *Language in Mind: Advances in the Study of Language and Thought*. MIT Press.

Spelke, E. (forthcoming). Developing knowledge of space: Core systems and new combinations.

Spelke, E., and Kestenbaum, R. (1986). Les origins du concept d'object. *Psychologie Francaise*, 31.

Spelke, E., and Tsivkin, S. (2001). Language and number: A bilingual training study. *Cognition*, 78.

Spelke, E., Breinlinger, K., Macomber, J., and Jacobson, K. (1992). Origins of knowledge. *Psychological Review*, 99.

Spelke, E., Gutheil, G., and Van de Walle, G. (1995a). The development of object perception. In S. Kosslyn and D. Osherson (eds.), *Visual Cognition*, vol. 2 of *An Invitation to Cognitive Science*, 2nd ed. MIT Press.

Spelke, E., Kestenbaum, R., Simons, D., and Wein, D. (1995b). Spatio-temporal continuity, smoothness of motion, and object identity in infancy. *British Journal of Developmental Psychology*, 13.

Spelke, E., Phillips, A., and Woodward, A. (1995c). Infants' knowledge of object motion and human action. In D. Sperber, D. Premack and A. Premack (eds.), *Causal Cognition: A Multidisciplinary Debate*. Clarendon Press.

Spelke, E., Vishton, P., and van Hofsten, C. (1994). Object perception, object-directed action, and physical knowledge in infancy. In M. Gazzaniga (ed.), *The Cognitive Neurosciences*. MIT Press.

Sperber, D. (1974). Contre certains a priori anthropologiques. In E. Morin and M. Piatelli-Palmarini (eds.), *L'unité de l'homme*. Paris, Le Seuil.

Sperber, D. (1994). The modularity of thought and the epidemiology of representations. In L. Hirschfeld and S. Gelman (eds.), *Mapping the Mind: Domain Specificity in Cognition and Culture*. Cambridge University Press.

Sperber, D. (1996). *Explaining Culture: A Naturalistic Approach*. Blackwell.

Sperber, D. (1997). Intuitive and reflective beliefs. *Mind and Language*, 12.

Sperber, D. (2000). Metarepresentations in an evolutionary perspective. In D. Sperber (ed.), *Metarepresentations: A Multidisciplinary Perspective*. Oxford University Press.

Sperber, D. (2001). In Defense of massive modularity. In E. Dupoux (ed.), *Language, Brain and Cognitive Development: Essays in Honor of Jacques Mehler*. MIT Press.
Sperber, D., and Wilson, D. (1986). *Relevance*. Blackwell.
Sperber, D., and Wilson, D. (1995). *Relevance: Communication and Cognition*. 2nd ed. Blackwell.
Sperber, D., and Wilson, D. (1996). Fodor's frame problem and relevance theory. *Behavioral and Brain Sciences*, 19.
Sperber, D., and Wilson, D. (2002). Pragmatics, modularity, and mind-reading. *Mind and Language*, 17.
Sperber, D., Cara, F., and Girotto, V. (1995a). Relevance theory explains the selection task. *Cognition*, 57.
Sperber, D., Premack, D., and Premack, A. (eds.). (1995b). *Causal Cognition*. Oxford University Press.
Sperry, R. (1963). Chemoaffinity in the orderly growth of nerve fiber patterns and connections. *Proceedings of the National Academy of Sciences*, 50.
Spitz, R., and Wolf, K. (1946). The smiling response: A contribution to the ontogenesis of social relations. *Genetic Psychology Monographs*, 34.
Sroufe, L., and Waters, E. (1976). The ontogenesis of smiling and laughter: A perspective on the organization of development in infancy. *Psychological Review*, 83.
Stanovich, K. (1999). *Who Is Rational?* Lawrence Erlbaum Associates.
Sterelny, K. (2003). *Thought in a Hostile world: The Evolution of Human Cognition*. Blackwell.
Sterelny, K., and Griffiths, P. (1999). *Sex and Death: An Introduction to the Philosophy of Biology*. University of Chicago Press.
Sternberg, S. (2001). Separate modifiability, mental modules, and the use of pure and composite measures to reveal them. *Acta Psychological*, 106.
Stich, S. (1972). Grammar, psychology, and indeterminacy, *Journal of Philosophy*, 69.
Stich, S. (1975a). *Innate Ideas*. University of California Press.
Stich, S. (1975b). Introduction: The idea of innateness. In S. Stich (ed.), *Innate Ideas*. University of California Press.
Stich, S. (1993). Moral philosophy and mental representation. In M. Hechter, L. Nadel, and R. E. Michod (eds.), *The Origin of Values*. De Gruyter.
Stich, S., and Nichols, S. (1998). Theory-theory to the max: A critical notice of Gopnik and Meltzoff's *Words, Thoughts, and Theories*. *Mind and Language*, 13.
Stich, S., and Ravenscroft, I. (1994). What *is* folk psychology? *Cognition*, 50.
Stolinsky, S., and Stolinsky, D. (2000). Suicide and homicide rates do not co-vary. *Journal of Trauma*, 48.
Stone, V., Cosmides, L., Tooby, J., Kroll, N., and Knight, R. (2002). Selective impairment of reasoning about social exchange in a patient with bilateral limbic system damage. *Proceedings of the National Academy of Sciences*, 99.
Strevens, M. (2000). The essentialist aspect of naive theories. *Cognition*, 74.
Stringer, C., and Gamble, C. (1993). *In Search of the Neanderthals*. Thames and Hudson.
Stromswold, K. (2000). The cognitive neuroscience of language acquisition. In M. Gazzaniga (ed.), *The Cognitive Neurosciences*. MIT Press.
Suddendorf, T., and Whiten, A. (2001). Mental evolution and development: Evidence for secondary representation in children, great apes and other animals. *Psychological Bulletin*, 127.
Sugiyama, L., Tooby, J., and Cosmides, L. (2002). Cross-cultural evidence of cognitive adaptations for social exchange among the Shiwiar of Ecuadorian Amazonia. *Proceedings of the National Academy of Sciences*, 99.

Sullivan, K., and Tager-Flusberg, H. (1999). Second-order belief attribution in Williams syndrome: Intact or impaired? *American Journal on Mental Retardation*, 104.

Sullivan, K., Winner, E., and Tager-Flusberg, H. (2003). Can adolescents with Williams syndrome tell the difference between lies and jokes? *Developmental Neuropsychology*, 23.

Sun, J., and Perona, P. (1998). Where is the sun? *Nature Neuroscience*, 1.

Sur, M., and Leamey, C. (2001). Development and plasticity of cortical areas and networks. *Nature Review: Neuroscience*, 2, 4.

Suzuki, S., Augerinos, G., and Black, A. (1980). Stimulus control of spatial behavior on the eight-arm maze in rats. *Learning and Motivation*, 11.

Swindale, N. (1996). The development of topography in the visual cortex: A review of models. *Network: Computation in Neural Systems*, 7.

Symons, D. (1979). *The Evolution of Human Sexuality*. Oxford University Press.

Symons, L., Hains, S., and Muir, D. (1998). Look at me: Five-month-old infants' sensitivity to very small deviations in eye-gaze during social interactions. *Infant Behavior and Development*, 21.

Tager-Flusberg, H. (1992). Autistic children talk about psychological states: Deficits in the early acquisition of a theory of mind. *Child Development*, 63.

Tager-Flusberg, H. (1997). Language acquisition and theory of mind: Contributions from the study of autism. In L. Adamson and M. Romski (eds.), *Communication and Language Acquisition: Discoveries from Atypical Development*. Brookes.

Tager-Flusberg, H. (1999b). Introduction to research on neurodevelopmental disorders from a cognitive neuroscience perspective. In H. Tager-Flusberg (ed.), *Neurodevelopmental Disorders*. MIT Press.

Tager-Flusberg, H. (2000a). Differences between neurodevelopmental disorders and acquired lesions. *Developmental Science*, 3.

Tager-Flusberg, H. (2000b). Language and understanding minds: Connections in autism. In S. Baron-Cohen, H. Tager-Flusberg, and D. Cohen (eds.), *Understanding Other Minds: Perspectives from Developmental Cognitive Neuroscience*, 2nd ed. Oxford University Press.

Tager-Flusberg, H. (2001). A reexamination of the theory of mind hypothesis of autism. In J. Burack, T. Charman, N. Yirmiya, and P. Zelazo (eds.), *The Development of Autism: Perspectives from Theory and Research*. Erlbaum.

Tager-Flusberg, H. (2003). Developmental disorders of genetic origin. In M. de Haan and M. Johnson (eds.), *The Cognitive Neuroscience of Development*. Psychology Press.

Tager-Flusberg, H. (ed.). (1999a). *Neurodevelopmental Disorders*. MIT Press.

Tager-Flusberg, H., and Joseph, R. (in press). How language facilitates the acquisition of false belief in children with autism. In J. Astington and J. Baird (eds.), *Why Language Matters for Theory of Mind*. Oxford University Press.

Tager-Flusberg, H., and Sullivan, K. (1994). Predicting and explaining behavior: A comparison of autistic, mentally retarded and normal children. *Journal of Child Psychology and Psychiatry*, 35, 15.

Tager-Flusberg, H., and Sullivan, K. (1999). Are children with Williams syndrome spared in theory of mind? *Society for Research in Child Development*. Albuquerque, NM.

Tager-Flusberg, H., and Sullivan, K. (2000). A componential view of theory of mind: Evidence from Williams syndrome. *Cognition*, 76.

Tager-Flusberg, H., Boshart, J., and Baron-Cohen, S. (1998). Reading the windows to the soul: Evidence of domain-specific sparing in Williams syndrome. *Journal of Cognitive Neuroscience*, 10.

Tager-Flusberg, H., Plesa-Skwerer, D., Faja, S., and Joseph, R. (2003). People with Williams syndrome process faces holistically. *Cognition*, 89.

Tardif, T. (1996). Nouns are not always learned before verbs: Evidence from Mandarin speakers' early vocabularies. *Developmental Psychology*, 32.

Taylor, M. (1996). The development of children's beliefs about social and biological aspects of gender differences. *Child Development*, 67, 15.

Tenenbaum, J. (1999). Bayesian modeling of human concept learning. *Advances in Neural Information Processing Systems*, 11.

Tenenbaum, J., and Griffiths, T. (2001). Structure learning in human causal induction. *Advances in Neural Information Processing Systems*, 13.

Tenenbaum, J., and Xu, F. (2000). Word learning as Bayesian inference. In L. Gleitman and A. Joshi (eds.), *Proceedings of the Twenty-Second Annual Conference of the Cognitive Science Society*. Erlbaum.

Thatcher, R., Lyon, G., Rumsey, J., and Krasnegor, N. (eds.). (1996). *Developmental Neuroimaging: Mapping the Development of Brain and Behavior*. Academic Press.

Thelen, E., and Smith, L. (1994). *A Dynamical Systems Approach to Development of Cognition and Action*. MIT Press.

Thompson, D. (1917/1961). *On Growth and Form*. Cambridge University Press.

Thompson, R. (1987). Empathy and emotional understanding: The early development of empathy. In N. Eisenberg and J. Strayer (eds.), *Empathy and Its Development*. Cambridge University Press.

Thomson, J. (1986). *Rights, Restitution, and Risk*. Harvard University Press.

Thornhill, R. (1997). The concept of evolved adaptation. In G. Bock and G. Cardew (eds.), *Characterizing Human Psychological Adaptations*. Wiley.

Thornton, R. (1990). Adventures in long-distance moving: Acquisition of complex wh-questions. Ph.D. diss., University of Connecticut.

Thornton, R. (1996). Elicited production. In D. McDaniel, C. McKee, and H. Cairns (eds.), *Methods for Assessing Children's Syntax*. MIT Press.

Thornton, R. (2004). Why continuity. *Proceedings of Boston University Conference on Language Development*, 26. Cascadilla Press.

Tisak, M. (1995). Domains of social reasoning and beyond. In R. Vasta (ed.), *Annals of Child Development*, vol. 11. Kingsley.

Tomasello, M. (1995). Joint attention as social cognition. In C. Moore and A. Dunham (eds.), *Joint Attention: Its Origins and Role in Development*. Erlbaum.

Tomasello, M. (2000). First steps in a usage based theory of first language acquisition. *Cognitive Linguistics*, 11.

Tomasello, M., and Akhtar, N. (2000). Five questions for any theory of word learning. In R. Golinkoff and K. Hirsh-Pasek (eds.), *Becoming a Word Learner: A Debate on Lexical Acquisition*. Oxford University Press.

Tomasello, M., and Call, J. (1997). *Primate Cognition*. Oxford University Press.

Tomasello, M., and Merriman, W. (eds.). (1995). *Beyond Names for Things: Young Children's Acquisition of Verbs*. Erlbaum.

Tomasello, M., Call, J., and Hare, B. (1998). Five primate species follow the visual gaze of conspecifics. *Animal Behaviour*, 55.

Tomasello, M., Hare, B., and Fogleman, T. (2001). The ontogeny of gaze following in chimpanzees, *Pan troglodytes*, and rhesus monkeys, *Macaca mulatta*. *Animal Behaviour*, 61.

Tomasello, M., Strosberg, R., and Akhtar, N. (1996). Eighteen-month-old children learn words in non-ostensive contexts. *Journal of Child Language*, 23.

Tomc, S., Williamson, N., and Pauli, R. (1990). Temperament in Williams syndrome. *American Journal of Medical Genetics*, 36.

Tooby, J., and Cosmides, L. (1988). The evolution of war and its cognitive foundations. *Institute for Evolutionary Studies, Technical Report*, 88-1.

Tooby, J., and Cosmides, L. (1990). The past explains the present: Emotional adaptations and the structure of ancestral environments. *Ethology and Sociobiology*, 11.
Tooby, J., and Cosmides, L. (1992a). The psychological foundations of culture. In J. Barkow, L. Cosmides, and J. Tooby (eds.), *The Adapted Mind*. Oxford University Press.
Tooby, J., and Cosmides, L. (1992b). Ecological rationality and the multimodular mind: Grounding normative theories in adaptive problems. *Center for Evolutionary Psychology Technical Report* 92-1. Reprinted in Tooby, J., and Cosmides, L. (in press) *Evolutionary psychology: Foundational Papers* (with a foreword by Steven Pinker). MIT Press.
Tooby, J., and Cosmides, L. (2001). Does beauty build adapted minds? Toward an evolutionary theory of aesthetics, fiction and the arts. *Substance, iss.* 94/95.
Tooby, J., Cosmides, L., and Barrett, H. (2003). The second law of thermodynamics is the first law of psychology: Evolutionary developmental psychology and the theory of tandem, coordinated inheritances. *Psychological Bulletin*, 129.
Trevarthen, C. (1979). Communication and cooperation in early infancy: A description of primary intersubjectivity. In M. Bullowa (ed.), *Before Speech: The Beginning of Interpersonal Communication*. Cambridge University Press.
Trick, L., and Pylyshyn, Z. (1993). What enumeration studies can show us about spatial attention: Evidence for limited-capacity preattentive processing. *Journal of Experimental Psychology: Human Perception and Performance*, 19.
Trivers, R. (1974). Parent-offspring conflict. *American Zoologist*, 14.
Tronick, E., Als, H., Adamson, L., Wise, S., and Brazelton, T. (1978). The infant's response to entrapment between contradictory messages in face-to-face interaction. *Journal of the American Academy of Child Psychiatry*, 17.
Turiel, E. (1983). *The Development of Social Knowledge: Morality and Convention*. Cambridge University Press.
Turing, A. (1952). The chemical basis of morphogenesis. *Philosophical Transactions of the Royal Society*, B237.
Turner, M. (1999). Repetitive behavior in autism: A review of psychological research. *Journal of Child Psychology and Psychiatry*, 40.
Udwin, O., and Yule, W. (1991). A cognitive and behavioral phenotype in Williams syndrome. *Journal of Clinical and Experimental Neuropsychology*, 13.
Ullman, S. (1979). The interpretation of structure from motion. *Proceedings of the Royal Society of London*, B203.
Uniacke, S. (1998). The principle of double effect. In E. Craig (ed.). *Routledge Encyclopedia of Philosophy*, vol. 3. Routledge.
United Nations. (1998). *United Nations 1996 Demographic Yearbook*. United Nations.
U.S. Department of Justice. (1993). *Crime in the United States, 1992*. U.S. Government Printing Office.
Vanderhaeghen, P., Lu, Q., Prakash, N., Frisen, J., Walsh, C., Frostig, R., and Flanagan, J. (2000). A mapping label required for normal scale of body representation in the cortex. *Nature: Neuroscience*, 3, 4.
Van der Henst, J., and Sperber, D. (2004). Testing the cognitive and communicative principles of relevance. In I. Noveck and D. Sperber (eds.), *Experimental Pragmatics*. Palgrave.
Van der Henst, J., Sperber, D., and Politzer, G. (2002). When is a conclusion worth deriving? A relevance-based analysis of indeterminate relational problems. *Thinking and Reasoning*, 8.
van Hooff, J. (1972). A comparative approach to the phylogeny of laughter and smiling. In R. Hinde (ed.), *Non-verbal Communication*. Cambridge University Press.

Van Lieshout, C., De Meyer, R., Curfs, L., and Fryns, J-P. (1998). Family contexts, parental behavior, and personality profiles of children and adolescents with Prader-Willi, Fragile-X, or Williams syndrome. *Journal of Child Psychology and Psychiatry, 39*.

Vea, J., and Sabater-Pi, J. (1998). Spontaneous pointing behavior in the wild pygmy chimpanzee (*Pan paniscus*). *Folia Primatologica, 69*.

Venter, J., Adams, M., Myers, E., Li, P., Mural, R., Sutton, G., et al. (2001). The sequence of the human genome. *Science, 291*, 5507.

Verhage, M., Maia, A., Plomp, J., Brussaard, A., Heeroma, J., Vermeer, H., Toonen, R., Hammer, R., van den Berg, T., Missler, M., Geuze, H., and Sudhof, T. (2000). Synaptic assembly of the brain in the absence of neurotransmitter secretion. *Science, 287*, 5454.

Vicari, S., Albertoni, A., Chilosi, A., Cipriani, P., Cioni, G., and Bates, E. (2000). Plasticity and reorganization during language development in children with early brain injury. *Cortex, 36*, 1.

Volterra, V., Capirci, O., Pezzini, G., Sabbadini, L., and Vicari, S. (1996). Linguistic abilities in Italian children with Williams syndrome. *Cortex, 32*.

von der Malsburg, C., and Willshaw, D. (1977). How to label nerve cells so that they can interconnect in an ordered fashion. *Proceedings of the National Academy of Sciences USA, 74*, 11.

Waddington, C. (1959). Canalisation of development and the inheritance of acquired characteristics. *Nature, 183*, 15.

Wagner Gunter, P., and Altenberg, L. (1996). Complex adaptations and the evolution of evolvability. *Evolution, 50*, 3.

Wallace, A. (1889). *Darwinism*. Macmillan.

Wang, R., Hermer, L., and Spelke, E. (1999). Mechanisms of reorientation and object localization by children: A comparison with rats. *Behavioral Neuroscience, 113*.

Watson, J. (1972). Smiling, cooing, and "the game." *Merrill-Palmer Quarterly, 18*.

Waxman, S., and Markow, D. (1995). Words as invitations to form categories: Evidence from 12- to 13-month-old infants. *Cognitive Psychology, 29*.

Wegner, D. (2002). *The Illusion of Conscious Will*. MIT Press.

Weiss, Y., Simoncelli, E., and Adelson, E. (2002). Motion illusions as optimal percepts. *Nature Neuroscience, 5*.

Weliky, M., and Katz, L. (1997). Disruption of orientation tuning in visual cortex by artificially correlated neuronal activity. *Nature, 386*.

Wellman, H. (1990). *The Child's Theory of Mind*. MIT Press.

Wellman, H., Cross, D., and Watson, J. (2001). Meta-analysis of Theory-of-Mind development: The truth about false belief. *Child Development, 72*.

Werner, W. (1993). Neurons in the primate superior colliculus are active before and during arm movements to visual targets. *European Journal of Neuroscience, 5*.

Wexler, K., and Culicover, P. (1980). *Formal Principles of Language Acquisition*. MIT Press.

Whalen, J., Gallistel, C., and Gelman, R. (1999). Non-verbal counting in humans: The psychophysics of number representation. *Psychological Science, 10*.

Whitelaw, V., and Cowan, J. (1981). Specificity and plasticity of retinotectal connections: a computational model. *Journal of Neuroscience, 1*, 12.

Whiten, A. (ed.). (1991). *Natural Theories of Mind: Evolution, Development and Simulation of Everyday Mindreading*. Blackwell.

Whiten, A., and Byrne, R. (1988). Tactical deception in primates. *Behavioral and Brain Sciences, 11*.

Wiesel, T., and Hubel, D. (1965a). Extent of recovery from the effects of visual deprivation in kittens. *Journal of Neurophysiology, 28*.

Wiesel, T., and Hubel, D. (1965b). Comparison of the effects of unilateral and bilateral eye closure on cortical unit responses in kittens. *Journal of Neurophysiology, 28*.

Williams, G. (1966). *Adaptation and Natural Selection*. Princeton University Press.
Williams, G. (1992). *Natural Selection*. Oxford University Press.
Willshaw, D., and von der Malsburg, C. (1976). How patterned neural connections can be set up by self-organization. *Proceedings of the Royal Society of London*, series B, *Biological Sciences*, 194, 1117.
Willshaw, D., and von der Malsburg, C. (1979). A marker induction mechanism for the establishment of ordered neural mappings: Its application to the retinotectal problem. *Philosophical Transactions of the Royal Society of London*, series B, *Biological Sciences*, 287, 1021.
Wilson, D., and Sperber, D. (2004). Relevance theory. In L. Horn and G. Ward (eds.), *Handbook of Pragmatics*. Blackwell.
Wilson, E. (1975). *Sociobiology: The New Synthesis*. Harvard University Press.
Wilson, E. (1978). *On Human Nature*. Harvard University Press.
Wilson, M., Daly, M., and Daniele, A. (1995). Familicide: The killing of spouse and children. *Aggressive Behavior*, 21.
Wilson, R. (1999). Realism, essence, and kind: Resuscitating species essentialism? In R. Wilson (ed.), *Species: New Interdisciplinary Essays*. MIT Press.
Wimsatt, W. (1986). Developmental constraints, generative entrenchment and the innate-acquired distinction. In W. Bechtel (ed.), *Integrating Scientific Disciplines*. Nijhoff.
Wimsatt, W. (1999). Generativity, entrenchment, evolution, and innateness: Philosophy, evolutionary biology, and conceptual foundations in science. In V. Hardcastle (ed.), *Where Biology Meets Psychology: Philosophical Essays*. MIT Press.
Wise, S., Boussaoud, D., Johnson, P., and Caminiti, R. (1997). Premotor and parietal cortex: corticocortical connectivity and combinatorial computations. *Annual Review of Neuroscience*, 20.
Wolff, P. (1963). Observations on the early development of smiling. In B. Foss (ed.), *Determinants of Infant Behavior II*. Methuen.
Wolpert, L. (1998). *Principles of Development*. Oxford University Press.
Woodward, A. (1998). Infants selectively encode the goal of an actor's reach. *Cognition*, 69.
Woodward, A. (2000). Constraining the problem space in early word learning. In R. Golinkoff and K. Hirsh-Pasek (eds.), *Becoming a Word Learner: A Debate on Lexical Acquisition*. Oxford University Press.
Woodward, A. (under review). Infants' developing understanding of the link between looker and object. Manuscript submitted for publication.
Woodward, A., and Guajardo, J. (2002). Infants' understanding of the point gesture as an object-directed action. *Cognitive Development*, 83.
Wootton, J., Frick, P., Shelton, K., and Silverthorn, P. (1997). Ineffective parenting and childhood conduct problems: The moderating role of callous-unemotional traits. *Journal of Consulting and Clinical Psychology*, 65, 2.
Wrangham, R., and Peterson, D. (1996). *Demonic Males*. Houghton Mifflin.
Wright, R. (1994). *The Moral Animal: Evolutionary Psychology and Everyday Life*. Pantheon.
Wynn, K. (1992). Addition and subtraction by human infants. *Nature*, 358.
Wynn, K. (1998). Psychological foundations of number: Numerical competence in human infants. *Trends in Cognitive Sciences*, 2.
Wynn, K. (2002). Do infants have numerical expectations or just perceptual preferences? *Developmental Science*, 5.
Wynn, T. (1991). Tools, grammar and the archaeology of cognition. *Cambridge Archaeological Journal*, 1.
Wynn, T. (2000). Symmetry and the evolution of the modular linguistic mind. In P. Carruthers and A. Chamberlain (eds.), *Evolution and the Human Mind*. Cambridge University Press.

Xu, F. (1999). Object individuation and object identity in infancy: The role of spatiotemporal information, object property information, and language. *Acta Psychologica, 102.*

Xu, F. (2003). Numerosity discrimination in infants: Evidence for two systems of representations. *Cognition, 89.*

Xu, F., and Carey, S. (1996). Infants' metaphysics: The case of numerical identity. *Cognitive Psychology, 30.*

Xu, F., and Spelke, E. (2000). Large number discrimination in 6-month-old infants. *Cognition, 74.*

Yerkes, R., and Yerkes, A. (1936). Nature and conditions of avoidance (fear) response in chimpanzee. *Journal of Comparative Psychology, 21.*

Yirmiya, N., Erel, O., Shaked, M., and Solomonica-Levi, D. (1998). Meta-analyses comparing theory of mind abilities of individuals with autism, individuals with mental retardation, and normally developing individuals. *Psychological Bulletin, 124.*

Zelazo, P., Burack, J., Benedetto, E., and Frye, D. (1996). Theory of mind and rule use in individuals with Down's syndrome: A test of the uniqueness and specificity claims. *Journal of Child Psychology and Psychiatry, 37.*

Index

abduction, 116–119. *See also* inference to the best explanation
accumulator, the, 217–225, 227, 228, 233, 234, 235
adaptation, evolutionary, 127–128, 137, 141–143, 292–293, 306, 322, 336, 369. *See also* adaptationism; homicide, adaptation theory of; natural selection
conditions for, 301
adaptation, ontogenetic, 244
adaptationism. *See also* natural selection
and folk biology, 148–149, 154–155
and homology, 154
and inferring function from complexity, 143, 149–150
and language, 142, 149–155
and rule comprehension, 369
strong versus weak, 17, 141–143, 148–149, 150–152, 153–155
affect. *See* emotion
African apes, 245
agency
concept of, 267, 345–346
representations of, 89
agents, nonhuman, infants' interpretation of, 258–266
Akhtar, N., 255–256
amygdala, 282, 346, 348
anaphoric relations, 177–178, 184, 191
Ancient Akkadian, 170
Anderson, S., 341

antisocial personality disorder (APD), 342, 344
appearance-reality distinction, 212, 214
Arabic number notation, 235
Aristotle, 145
Artificial Intelligence (AI), 115, 119–120, 121
ASCII code, 172
Asperger syndrome, 283
Astington, J., 285
Athens, L., 291
Atran, S., 10, 17, 211
auditory system, 223n7
Austin, J., 335–336
autism, 235, 272, 275–276, 365
and language, 283, 286–288
and theory of mind, 277–281, 282–283, 284, 286–288
autonomy, in robotics, 121

Baker, M., 17
Baldwin, D., 256
Bantu languages, 163, 164–165, 168
Baron-Cohen, S., 277, 281n1, 284
Barrett, C., 18
Bates, E., 24, 32
Bayes' theorem, 43–44. *See also* reasoning, Bayesian
behavioral ecology. *See* evolutionary psychology
Belsky, J., 292
Biederman, I., 27–28

bilingual subjects, 228–229
binding theory, 130, 131, 138, 178
Blair, J., 365–366
Blair, R., 343
blank slate view, 4, 23, 170, 309–311, 313–314, 351. *See also* empiricism
Bloom, P., 150–152, 158, 161, 165, 166, 171
Booth, A., 199–200, 263, 264–265
Boster, C., 196
Botterill, G., 132, 134
Boyer, P., 10
brain damaged patients
 and cognitive science, 273–274
 and moral psychology, 339–342
brain imaging studies, 273, 278, 282, 287
 of moral judgement, 344–350
Brooks, R., 119
Brothers, L., 282
Brown, A., 30–31
Buss, D., 18

Caeser shift cipher, 171
Calder mobiles, 166–167, 168
canalization, 132
Carey, S., 124–126, 147, 258–261
Carpenter, M., 255–256
Carruthers, P., 16, 98, 132, 134
categorical imperative, 356n2
categorical realism, 213
causal determinism, 213
C-command, 189–193, 196–197
Chabris, C., 60–61
cheater detection, 77, 150n4, 361n8
Cheng, K., 75, 91–92, 93, 94, 95
Chichewa, 168–169
chimpanzees, 130, 144, 154, 243–244, 245, 246, 247, 257, 300, 351
Chomsky, N., 3, 5, 6, 23, 54n1, 68, 107, 128, 156, 158, 159, 171n4, 176–177, 307n3, 311, 313, 314, 353, 354, 356
codes, ciphers., and cryptography, 170–173
cognition, function of, 327–329
cognitive efficiency, 62–66
 and relevance, 66–68
cognitive impenetrability, 112
cognitive neuroscience, 339, 351
Coley, J., 211
Collins, C., 163

communicative gestures, 255, 257, 264–265, 269, 270. *See also* gaze-following; pointing
compositionality, 226, 232, 235
computational theory of mind (CTM), 108–109
concepts, learning of. *See* learning, of words and concepts
conceptual change, role of language in, 86, 96, 105, 225–229, 232, 234–235
conceptual primitives, 309, 327–328
conditioning, 257, 266–267
contagion and contamination, 212
control systems, 328, 329
Cordes, S., 223n6
core knowledge, 37–38, 39n3, 40, 89, 90, 95, 105–106, 131
Corkum, V., 257–258
Cosmides, L., 18, 54n1, 77, 114, 120, 292
Cowie, F., 354
Crain, S., 17, 124–126, 130–131, 132n4, 135n6
creationism, 141
creativity, 83–84, 85
creolization, 157
Cruz, Y., 24
crying baby dilemma, 347–348
Csibra, G., 266
cultural evolution, 363–364

Daly, M., 297–298
Damasio, A., 339–340
Daniele, A., 297
Darwin, C., 11, 141, 144, 305, 306, 307n3, 309–310, 311, 315
deception, 241, 243, 244, 255, 277
Dehaene, S., 23, 59
De Morgan's law, 183–185
determiners, 181–183, 188–189
development, cognitive. *See also* development, neurobiological
 associationist models of, 17
 disorders in (*see* neurodevelopmental disorders)
 and domain specificity, 9–10, 38–39
 and folk biology, 147–149
 and language (*see* language acquisition)
 and nativism, 24, 33, 34, 37–40, 48–52, 123–126, 129, 131–138 (*see also* innateness and neurodevelopment)
 not a seamless transition, 252–253

and number concepts (*see* number cognition)
and parent-offspring conflict (*see* parental investment and parent-offspring conflict, and infant cognitive development)
plasticity of, 24
and spatial reasoning, 93–106
uniformity of, 8–10, 38–39
and word and concept learning (*see* learning, of words and concepts)
development, neurobiological, 16, 24, 136–137. *See also* neuralplasticitiy; neuroconstructivism; neurodevelopmental disorders
computer simulations of, 28–33
and innateness (*see* innateness and neurodevelopment)
developmental biology, 25–27
and innateness (*see* innateness and neurodevelopment)
"knockout" experiments in, 27, 30, 32
de Villiers, J., 285
Dickinson, A., 75
disjunction, 181, 183–184, 195
dislocation parameter, 169, 172
doctrine of double effect (DDE), 359–362
domain specificity, 5, 9, 55, 57, 71–72, 80, 89, 107, 110, 123, 143–144, 147, 250, 258, 266, 337. *See also* modularity, biological; modularity, cognitive; evolutionary psychology
and actual versus proper domains, 55
as distinct from encapsulation, 55–56, 111–114, 309n4
and domain diversity, 367–368
and domain generality, 53, 69, 72, 90, 211–215, 225–226, 317
and feasible computation, 110–111
and informational impoverishment, 111
and input and task domains, 111
and poverty of the stimulus arguments, 354–355, 367–368
Down syndrome, 272, 273, 277
downward entailment (DE), 184–187, 188, 190–191, 194–195, 196, 197
Draper, P., 292
Dugum Dani, 301
"dumb attentional mechanisms," 198, 200, 210, 211, 215

Duntley, J., 18
Dutch, 164
Dwyer, S., 365, 366–367
dyslexia, 272, 275

ecologically rational procedures, 331, 333
Elliot (patient), 339–341, 346
Elman, J., 24, 32
emotion, 19, 256, 317, 324–325
and emotional deficits, 340, 341–342, 343
and modularity, 351
and moral psychology (*see* moral psychology and the role of emotion)
role of the amygdala in, 282, 346
empiricism, 5, 35, 38, 69, 123, 128, 129, 186–187. *See also* blank slate view; nativism
and empiricist learning, 198, 199–200, 210–211, 354–355, 357–358, 363, 365, 367
and language acquisition (*see* language acquisition, inadequacy of data-driven accounts of)
as the null hypothesis for cognitive science, 8, 310–311
Emx-2 gene, 26
English, 157, 159, 161–162, 163, 164, 168, 170, 172, 175, 179–180, 183, 184, 186, 187, 207, 209, 210, 211. *See also* Japanese, and systematic differences from English
Enigma machine, 171
entropy, 306, 318
environment of evolutionary adaptedness (EEA), 292, 331
ephrin ligands and Eph receptors, 30–32
Eslinger, P., 341
essentialism
and biological species, 145–146, 204
and folk biology, 145–146, 147, 211
kind, 214
and language use, 206
metaphysical and psychological, 146, 201
origins of children's, 201, 204–206, 210–214, 215
as a "placeholder" notion, 146, 201
and word and concept learning (*see* learning, of words and concepts and essentialism)

Estin, P., 211
ethology, 144
even-skipped stripe 2 gene, 26
evolution, 11–12, 18–19, 26, 32, 54, 66, 75n2, 77, 79–80, 127–128, 141, 152–154, 160, 211, 240–242, 292–293, 296–297, 301, 305–308, 309–310, 314n5, 319, 327, 328, 329, 332, 333. See also adaptation, evolutionary; adaptationism; evolutionary psychology; natural selection
evolutionarily valid inference, 329–333
evolutionary biology, 11–12, 152–153, 322
  resistance to its incorporation into the human sciences, 305–308, 314n5
evolutionary psychology, 11–12, 71–72, 173n5, 322, 339, 354, 361n8
  concept of innateness in, 292–293
  criticism of, 12
  and domain specificity, 11, 71
  of homicide (see homicide)
  importance of debate on innate ideas for, 309–314
  and massive modularity, 71–72
  sociological status of, 305–308
  and strong adaptationism, 141–142
exaptation, 148, 148n3, 149, 154
exhaustive search, 116, 121

face recognition, 51, 58
false belief tasks, 39, 277, 278, 279, 280, 282, 283, 285
  role of language in passing, 285, 286–288
fish, 92, 97, 142
Fodor, J., 13, 14–15, 36, 54n1, 55, 56n2, 59, 60, 68, 68n6, 69–70, 72, 89, 110, 111, 114, 116–119, 121, 128, 201, 307n3, 309n4, 321, 324, 327, 328n10, 332, 354
folk biology, 10, 77
  as an adaptation, 143–149, 154–155
  development of, 147–149
  domain specificity of, 143–144, 147, 148
  and essentialism, 145–146, 147, 211–212
  evidence for homology of in humans and primates, 144
  and folk taxonomy, 144–145, 148
  innateness of, 143, 146, 149
  and modularity, 146, 154
  notions of rank and taxa in, 145

  relationship to theory of mind, 146–148, 149, 155
  and "standard"/"non-standard" populations, 149
  and word and concept learning (see learning, of words and concepts and folk biology)
folk mechanics. See folk physics
folk physics, 77, 143, 146, 149
folk psychology. See theory of mind
Foot, P., 355
footbridge dilemma, 344–346, 351. See also doctrine of double effect; personal/impersonal distinction
foraging, 76, 91
FOXP2 gene, 153
frame problem, 109, 117–118
fruit flies, 25–26
Fukuchi-Shimogori, T., 25
function, concepts of, 307n3
functionalism, 307n3, 328n10
functional linguists, 158

Gage, Phineas., 339–340, 341, 346, 350
Gallistel, R., 35m 36, 53, 91–92, 93, 95, 216, 217–225, 230, 234–235
Garcia effect, 58
gavagai, 209
gaze-following, 239, 243, 245–246, 252, 253, 255, 256, 257–258, 266, 269
  studies in infants, 258–263
Gelman, R., 216, 217–225, 230, 234–235
Gelman, S., 17
gene expression, 25–26
gene hierarchies. See regulatory networks
generics, 206
  acquisition of, 209–212, 214–215
  children produce and understand at an early age, 207
  and the differences between animal and artifact categories, 215
  and essentialism, 207
  semantics of, 209
  and word and concept learning (see learning, of words and concepts and generics)
genes, as "IF-THEN" rules, 31
Gergely, G., 266
German and Germanic languages, 164, 179–180

gestational diabetes, 240–241
Gibson, E., 57–58
Gil-White, F., 211
goal-reenactment paradigm, 263–264
Goodman, N., 209
Gopnik, A., 39n3, 114, 248, 249, 250, 256
Gould, S. J., 142
Gouteux, S., 94
Grattan, L., 341
great apes, 76, 246, 247, 338–339
　common ancestor of humans and, 245, 246, 247
Greenberg, J., 162
Greene, J., 19*
Grove, E., 25
Gualmini, A., 17, 135n6
Gueverkian, L., 217

habituation, 219
Haig, D., 240
Hale, C., 285
Hamilton, W., 240
Harman, G., 358–362
Harris, A., 301
Hauser, M., 230
head directionality parameter (HDP), 161–162, 165–166, 167, 172
Helmholtz, H., 42–43
Hermelin, B., 235
Hermer, L., 93, 94, 95, 97
Hermer-Vazquez, L., 73, 101, 102
Hershberger, W., 46–47
Heyes, C., 254, 270
Hindi, 172
"home sign" gestures of deaf children, 207
homicide
　adaptation theory of, 18, 291, 293–297, 299, 300, 301–304
　by-product theory of, 291, 297–298, 299, 300, 301–302, 303
　and comparative data, 299–300
　evolved goal theory of, 291, 298–299, 300, 302, 303
　and the fitness costs of being killed, 295–296
　and homicide defense strategies, 296–297
　rates, 300–301
　selection pressures due to, 293–295
　thoughts and fantasies about, 302–303
hominoids, 242, 244

homo
　cognition in early species of, 76–81
　ergaster, 77, 78, 79
　sapiens sapiens, 77n4, 78, 79, 80, 84, 148
Hrdy, S., 298–299
Hubel, D., 27, 50
Huli, 301
Hume, D., 150, 314–315
Hummel, J., 27–28
Hupbach, A., 94
hypothetical and nonhypothetical imperatives, 355–356, 357–358, 361

identity, tracking of over time, 213–214
imagination, evolution of, 78–79
imitation
　and infants' understanding of other minds, 254, 255–256, 258, 263–264, 266–267, 269, 270, 276
　neonatal and adult, 239, 248, 249–250, 252, 253
　neurobiology of, 249–250
imitative generalization
　good evidence for theory of mind, 266–269, 270
　technique, 267
immune system, 319, 328
I-morality. *See* universal moral grammar
inattentional blindness, 60–61
inclusive fitness, 240, 295, 296, 299
Indo-European (IE) languages, 163, 164–165
induction, problem of, 209
inductive inference, 202, 208, 213, 314n5, 325
infanticide dilemma, 347–348
inference to the best explanation, 86–87. *See also* abduction
informational encapsulation, 52, 55–56, 76, 89, 309n4, 336. *See also* modularity, cognitive, and informational encapsulation
　and computational tractability, 70, 72, 110, 111–114, 117–118
　synchronic and diachronic, 112–113
innate ideas. *See* innateness
innateness. *See also* core knowledge; nativism; poverty of the stimulus arguments concept of in evolutionary psychology, 292–293
　defining, 4–5, 128–129, 338

innateness (*continued*)
and evolutionary adaptation, no necessary connection with, 127–128, 137
of folk biology, 143, 146, 149
and incorporating evolution into the human sciences, 309–311
and learnability analyses, 311–314
and learning, 5, 7, 16, 35–37, 38, 40, 50, 51
and linguistic diversity, 156, 157–159, 160–161
and modularity, 39n3, 351
and moral psychology, 19, 338–339, 350–352, 353–369 (*see also* nativism, moral; moral psychology)
and natural language, 6–8, 17, 130, 131, 132, 135n6, 156–159, 160–161, 175–81, 183, 184, 186–187, 188–189, 191–193, 311–314, 353, 354 (*see also* language, faculty of; poverty of the stimulus arguments; universal grammar; universal grammar, overspecified versus underspecified views of)
and neurodevelopment, 23–33, 50–51, 136–137 (*see also* nativism and development)
and parameterization, 39, 52
presence at birth as only defeasible evidence of, 127, 322n7
representational, 24
and representations of number, 220, 225, 235
and research into in simpler cognitive processes, 34, 36, 52
and research into in simpler organisms, 35–36
and study of "standard" populations, 149
and systems for motivation and valuation, 19, 321–327, 336–337
and theory of mind, 38–39, 40, 327
and the visual system, 34, 36, 40, 46–52
and word and concept learning, 198, 204–206, 210–215
inner speech, 84, 88
insects, conspecific killing in, 299
intentionality, 89, 276
reasoning about in preverbal infants, 254–271

problems in attributing understanding of in infants and animals, 254, 257–258, 269–271
intentional states, 250, 251, 252, 255, 257
intractability thesis (IT), 109–110. *See also* massive modularity
exhaustive search argument for, 116
informational impoverishment argument for, 114
locality argument for, 116–119
optimality argument for, 115
robot argument for, 119–120
intrinsic signals, 25, 27, 32
Iowa gambling task, 340, 341, 343,
Italian, 179
Itza' Maya, 148, 204

Japanese, 159, 168, 172, 175, 179
its systematic differences from English, 157, 161–162
Jenkins, J., 285
Johnson, D., 218, 220, 223
Johnson, M., 24, 32
Johnson, S., 18
joint attention, 255, 276, 283
Jones, S., 198, 199

Kant, I., 321, 355
Kanzi, 151
Karmiloff-Smith, A., 24, 32, 122, 123–126, 128–129, 137n7, 274–275, 278
Katz, L., 25
Keil, F., 200
Kenrick, D., 302
Kiehl, K., 343
Kinande, 163, 168–169
kind-referring expressions. *See* generics
knowledge, and evolutionarily valid inference, 329–333
Kohlberg, L., 338, 341
Komarova, N., 160
!Kung San, 301

Laird, J., 115
Landau, B., 198, 199
language acquisition, 6–8, 17, 90, 95–97, 99–104, 135n6, 138, 149, 156–159, 175–177, 354, 358. *See also* language, faculty of; language, natural; poverty of the stimulus; universal grammar

Index   423

and children's characteristic errors,
    156–157, 178–180
and children's linguistic generalizations,
    177–178
and the contingencies of natural
    languages, 180–193
and the continuity assumption, 178–180
and creolization, 157
in deaf populations, 157
inadequacy of data-driven accounts of,
    175–177, 179–181, 183, 184, 186–187,
    188–189, 191–193
and innateness (see innateness and
    natural language)
and learnability analyses, 311–314
logical problem of, 178
role of positive and negative
    data in, 181
and the size of the innate endowment for
    language (see universal grammar,
    overspecified versus underspecified
    views of)
summary of recent experimental
    research on, 193–197
language, faculty of, 158, 307n3, 313. See
    also language, natural
and adaptationism, 149–155
and domain-specificity, 81
and language comprehension and
    language production, 81–84
as a modular integration mechanism (see
    modularity, massive, and the language
    faculty as an integration mechanism)
modularity of, 58, 70
overspecified versus underspecified
    views of (see universal grammar,
    overspecified versus underspecified
    views of)
as a "supermodule," 81
language impaired subjects, 228, 234–235,
    272, 277
language, natural, 6–8, 16, 17, 58, 90, 131,
    132, 256
combinatorial properties of, 73, 82–83,
    226–227, 232
the contingencies of, 176–177, 180–193
evolution of, 33, 75n2, 79–80, 83,
    149–154, 155, 176–177, 307n3, 314n6,
and false belief tasks (see belief tasks, role
    of language in passing)

and innateness (see innateness and
    natural language)
purpose of, 156, 159, 170–173
representations of discrete and
    nondiscrete properties in, 223–225
role in number cognition (see number
    cognition, role of language in)
role in spatial reasoning (see spatial
    reasoning, role of language in)
similarities to codes and cyphers, 170–173
and theory of mind (see theory of mind,
    and language)
use of in thought and reasoning, 83–88
and vagueness, 224
language of thought, 68, 80
larynx, 153–154
Laurence, S., 17
Learmouth, A., 94
learning, 4n2, 38, 50, 51, 58, 76, 89, 255, 257.
    See also poverty of the stimulus
    arguments
and adaptive specialization, 53
associative, 17, 90, 95–96, 198, 200, 215,
    312, 313, 315, 319
and domain specificity, 309n4, 313,
    314n6, 335, 337
language (see language acquisition)
and learnability, 311–315, 326–327,
    328n9, 337
statistical, 199, 211
theory, 309, 320
learning, of words and concepts, 104–105
aided by domain-general rather than
    domain-specific mechanisms, 211–215
empiricist models of, 17, 198, 199–200
and essentialism, 17, 198, 200, 201–206,
    207, 210–214, 215
and folk biology, 211–212, 215
and generics, 17, 198, 200, 206–212,
    214–215
inadequacy of empiricist models of,
    199–200, 210–211, 215
and innateness (see innateness and word
    and concept learning)
Leslie, A., 227n10
Levin, D., 200
linguistic diversity, 156–157, 158. See also
    universal grammar, overspecified
    versus underspecified views of
and evolutionary fitness, 160

424 Index

linguistic diversity (*continued*)
  function of, 170–173
  and the head directionality parameter, 161–162
  importance for cognitive science, 157
  and innate endowment for language (*see* innateness and linguistic diversity)
Locke, John, 4, 145
Lohmann, H., 285
looking-time studies, 256–257, 265–266, 267
Lorenz, K., 366

Mae Enga, 301
Maestripieri, D., 240
mammals, conspecific killing in, 300
Mandarin, 207
Mandler, J., 267–268, 269
Marcus, G., 16
Margolis, E., 17
Marr, D., 48, 64, 177
McDiarmid, C., 218
McDonough, L., 267–268, 269
Mechner, F., 217
Medin, D., 201
Meltzoff, A., 39n3, 248, 249, 250, 256, 258, 263–264, 265, 266
mentalese. *See* language of thought
mental magnitudes, 220, 221–224
mental models, 82, 88
Meroni, L., 196
metarepresentation, 277, 281, 282, 283, 285, 286, 288, 330n12. *See also* theory of mind
Mikhail, J., 358, 362
mindreading. *See* theory of mind
minimalist program, 152, 152n8, 153, 158n1, 176–177
mirror neurons, 249
modularity, biological, 54–57
  as condition of evolvability, 54
modularity, cognitive., 12–15, 53, 90. *See also* intractability thesis; modularity, massive
  and actual and proper domains, 55
  and adaptationism, 154
  of central processes, 14–15, 70–71, 72, 81–82, 107–108, 110
  computational, 13
  and computational tractability, 16, 59, 70, 72, 88, 108–111, 113–120
  danger of trivializing notion of, 56–57
  and development, compatibility with, 52, 57
  and domain specificity, 13, 55, 110–111, 114, 309n4
  of face recognition, 137n7
  Fodorian, 13, 14, 36, 52, 55, 59, 60, 69–70, 89, 309n4, 355
  of folk biology, 146
  and informational encapsulation, 52, 55–56, 70, 76, 89, 110, 111–114, 117–118, 309n4
  and innateness, 39n3, 351
  of input and output systems, 36, 59, 61, 69–70, 108
  as a kind of biological modularity, 54–57
  and language, 58, 79–85, 72–73
  and manditoriness, 59–61, 70, 71
  and moral psychology, 341, 349, 351
  and neurodevelopmental disorders, 273–275, 276
  of reading, 58–59
  representational, 13
  and spatial reasoning, 75, 81n6, 92, 94–95, 103, 104, 105–106
  "teeming," 59
  of theory of mind, 39, 277–278
  of the visual system, 36, 48, 52, 146
modularity, massive, 14, 16, 54, 59, 68, 69, 71–73, 88, 107–108, 310n4
  "abduction problem" for, 15, 86–87, 116–119
  and competition between modules, 61–68, 87
  and context sensitivity, 54, 59–68, 116–119
  and cycles of activity, 83, 85, 88
  and "distinctively human thinking," 69, 83–88
  and the language faculty as an integration mechanism, 16, 69, 72–73, 79–85, 87–88, 90, 95, 102–106, 225–226
  and theory of mind as an integration mechanism, 80n5
  tractability arguments for, 16, 72, 108–114 (*see also* intractability thesis)
modus ponens, 56n2
Mohawk, 170
Moll, J., 349

monkeys, 75, 92, 300
　rhesus, 91
　vervet, 144
Moore, C., 257–258
moral/conventional distinction, 342–343, 356–357, 368
morality, cultural evolutionary accounts of, 363–364
moral judgment and moral reasoning. See moral psychology
moral philosophy, 345
moral psychology, 338–339
　and brain lesion data, 339–342
　deontological and utilitarian systems underlying, 361–362
　and innateness (see innateness and moral psychology)
　linguistic analogy for, 356, 358–367, 369
　and modularity, 341, 349, 351
　and neuroimaging studies of moral judgment, 344–350
　and psychopathy, 342–344, 350, 351, 365–366 (see also psychopathy)
　and the role of emotion, 341–342, 343–344, 345–352, 365–369
Moses, L., 256
motivation and valuation
　learnability constraints in the domain of, 314–321
　necessity of domain specific procedures for, 317–318
　necessity of innate conceptual structure for, 19, 321–327, 336–337
mRNA., 32
Müller-Lyer illusion, 55, 112
Munc-18 gene, 25

Nadel, L., 94
naming. See learning, of words and concepts
nativism. See also empiricism; innateness; poverty of the stimulus
　and arguments from evolution, 11–12, 127–128, 137
　a brief history of, 4–5
　and canalization, 132
　and computer simulations of neurodevelopment, 28–33
　controversy about, 35, 36, 38
　and defining "innateness," 128–129, 137
　and development, 24, 33, 34, 37–40, 48–52, 131–138 (see also nativism, "staunch")
　diversity of, 5, 15, 38
　and environmental input, 123, 125–126, 129, 130–138, 322n7
　and the "gene shortage," 24
　and genetic specification, 123, 125–126, 129, 130–131, 133–134, 135–136, 138, 322n7
　and "global capacities and mature end-states," 131–133
　hypernativism sometimes the right amount of, 174
　linguistic (see innateness and natural language)
　Locke's arguments against, 4
　moral, 351–352, 353–367, 369
　and neuralplasticity, 24
　and neuroconstructivism, 122, 123, 126, 128–129, 136–138
　and presence of traits at birth, 123, 125–126, 127, 128, 137, 322n7
　and psychological primitivism, 134–136
　"rationalist" (see psychological rationalism)
　a reasonable understanding of, 129–136, 137–138
　resurgence of, 3, 35, 311
　"staunch," 123–126, 129, 137
　as a unified program in cognitive science, 126–127
　versus empiricism, 5, 8, 35, 309–311
natural kinds, 201, 203–204, 213–214
natural selection, 292, 310, 315, 316, 322, 323n7, 326, 333n13, 369. See also adaptationism; evolution
　and complex functional organization, 149–150, 306, 307n3
　and cultural selection, 142
　and innate ideas, 310
　and language, 150–154, 307n3
　neglect of in human sciences, 305–308
　and strong versus weak adaptationism, 141–143
Navajo code talkers, 171
navigation, 35–36, 90–92, 95, 96, 97–99, 103, 104
Neanderthals, 79

negative polarity items (NPI), 181, 187–189, 190, 191–193, 194
nervous system, 328
neural networks. *See also* neurogenetic simulator
  and genetics, 27, 28–29
  and innateness, 27, 28–33
neuralplasticity, 24, 274. *See also* neuroconstructivism
neuroconstructivism, 122, 123, 126, 128–129, 136–138
neurodevelopmental disorders
  differences from acquired disorders, 273
  defining, 272–273
  implications for cognitive science, 18, 272, 273–275, 288
  methodological issues concerning, 18, 275–276
  and modularity, 273–275
  and theory of mind, 18, 272, 276–284, 286–288
neurogenetic simulator, 29, 32, 33
neuroimaging studies. *See* brain imaging studies
Newcombe, N., 94
Newell, A., 114, 115
Newmeyer, F., 158, 160, 161, 165, 166
Neyman, J., 334
Neyman-Pearson decision theory, 334
Nichols, S., 19
Nilsson, D., 301
Niyogi, P., 160
norms, moral. *See* moral psychology
Nowack, M., 160
number cognition, 75, 77, 89, 90
  in animals, 216, 217–221, 223
  distance effect in, 218, 220
  Gallistel and Gelman's theory of and its problems, 217–225
  importance of, 216
  innate components of (*see* innateness and representations of number)
  and integers, 17, 216, 217, 221–225, 226–235
  magnitude effect in, 218, 220
  in preverbal infants, 219–221
  role of language in, 17, 216–217, 222–225, 226–235
  Spelke's theory of and its problems, 225–235

object cognition, 37–38, 39n3, 78–79
object dislocation structures, 168
object indexing system, 227–228, 231–232
Occam's razor, 152n8. *See also* parsimony; simplicity and conservatism
O'Connor, N., 235
ocular dominance columns, 25, 50–51
O'Hearn, K., 263, 264–265
optimality, physical., 152–153
Ortony, A., 201

parental investment and parent-offspring conflict
  and behavioral "impostors," 244–253
  and the development of social understanding, 239–253
  and infant cognitive development, 239, 241–242, 244–245, 248–253
  theory of, 240–241
Parisi, D., 24, 32
Palaeolithic period, 79
parsimony, 117n13, 137n7, 141, 156, 159–161, 166–167, 173, 319. *See also* inference to the best explanation; Occam's razor; simplicity and conservatism
Pax-6 gene, 26, 153
Pearson, E., 334
Peirce, C., 209
Pelger, S., 301
personal/impersonal distinction, 345–347
phenotype, 273, 275, 278, 284, 288
Phillips, A., 256
phi-phenomenon, 112
physics, 142, 146, 305, 306, 307, 313, 327
Piaget, J., 8–9, 338
pidgin and proto languages, 79, 80
Pietroski, P., 17, 130–131, 132n4, 135n6
pigeons, 217–219, 220
Pinker, S., 23, 124–125, 126, 133n5, 134, 150–152, 158, 161, 165, 166, 170, 171, 211
Plato, 4, 305
Platt, J., 218, 220, 223
Plunket, K., 24, 32
pointing, 239, 246–247, 252, 253, 255, 257
poverty of the stimulus arguments, 6–8, 17, 18–19, 150, 311, 314
  and acquisition of generic/non-generic distinction, 209–211
  and children's essentialism, 204–206, 210–211

and children's knowledge of the
  contingencies of natural languages,
  180–193
and the form of children's linguistic
  generalizations, 177–178
and innateness and domain specificity,
  354–355, 367–369
and modularity, 309n4,
for moral psychology, 353, 357–367
not necessary for innateness, 7–8
and the range of children's linguistic
  constructions, 178–180
and recent experimental work on
  children's linguistic knowledge,
  193–197
three kinds for language, 175–177
Povinelli, D., 18, 257
Prader-Willi syndrome, 272, 280, 284, 287
pragmatic implicatures, 183–184, 187,
  187n8,
pragmatism, 328n10
pretend play, 85, 277
Preuss, T., 18
primates, nonhuman., 59, 89, 144, 154,
  176, 240, 345, 346, 350. See also
  chimpanzees; great apes; *homo*;
  monkeys
  infanticide in, 299, 300
  social behavior and theory of mind
    in, 242–244, 245, 246, 247, 249, 250,
    252, 253
Prince, C., 18
procedural reasoning system, 120n17
property clusters, 213
propositional attitudes, 286, 287
prosimians, 245
psychological rationalism, 107–108, 114,
  120–121
psychopathy, 340, 342–344
  and moral psychology (*see* moral
    psychology and psychopathy)
Pullum, G., 181, 190–191
Pyers, J., 285

Quartz, S., 24
Quine, W. V., 129, 209

Raine, A., 344
rats, 73, 75, 91, 92, 93, 95, 97, 217–218, 219,
  220, 223

reactive behaviors, 119, 121
reading, 58–59
real numbers, 221, 223, 224, 225
  as more psychologically basic than
    integers, 221
reasoning,
  Bayesian, 43–44, 115, 115n10, 115n11
  causal, 75
  in mammals, 73–76
  in a massively modular mind, 120–121
  optimal, 115–116
  practical, 73, 74, 75–76, 80, 87–88
  spatial (*see* spatial reasoning)
  theoretical, 84, 85, 86–87
recursion, 152
regulatory networks, 25
relevance
  and computation, 113–114, 117–118
  first cognitive principle of, 67, 67n5
    (*see also* cognitive efficiency)
  problem of, 109, 117–118
  and relevance theory, 16, 62–63,
    67–68, 86
Repacholi, B., 256
representation, nature of, 330
retinal ganglion cells, 30–31
Rilling, J., 348
Rilling, M., 218
robotics. *See* Artificial Intelligence
Rosch, E., 335
RSA cipher, 171–172

Samuels, R., 13, 16, 107–121, 134–136
Sanfey, A., 348
Saussurean arbitrariness, 172
schizophrenia, 279
Schmitt, W., 343
Scholl, B., 16
Scholz, B., 181
Sejnowski, T., 24
sense-model-plan-act-paradigm, 119–120
sentential compliments, 285–288
sexual attraction, 322, 323, 324, 325, 336–337
shaken baby syndrome, 242
Shanks, D., 75
Sheets, V., 302
Shimizu, Y., 265
Shusterman, A., 16, 73
signal detection theory, 334
signal releaser mechanisms, 257, 266–267

Simon, H., 115
Simons, D., 60–61, 200
simplicity and conservatism, 86, 117–119, 160, 166. *See also* inference to the best explanation; parsimony; Occam's razor
Simpson, T., 16
Slaughter, V., 258–261
Smith, L., 198, 199
Smith, W., 200
snake avoidance, 312, 321–322, 324–325, 326, 336
SOAR architecture, 115
social smiling, 239, 242, 247, 253
sociobiology. *See* evolutionary psychology
Sonic Hedgehog protein, 26
spandrel, 142, 369
spatial reasoning, 89
  and encapsulation, 91–95, 98–99, 102–103, 105–106
  and modularity, 75, 81n6, 92, 94–95, 103, 104, 105–106
  role of language in, 90, 95–97, 99–104, 226–227
  and spatial reorientation, 90–106, 232
speciation, 145
specific language impairment. *See* language impaired subjects
Spelke, E., 9, 16, 23, 73, 124–126, 216, 219–220, 221, 225–235, 256
Sperber, D., 16
Sperry, R., 30
steganography, 172
Steinberg, L., 292
Strosberg, R., 256
Sullivan, K., 283, 284
supposing and pretending, 85

Tager-Flusberg, H., 18
target of agreement parameter (TAP), 163–166
theory of mind, 18, 38–39, 40, 77, 79–80, 90, 131, 143, 154, 349, 350
  and autism, 277–278, 279–281, 282–283, 284, 286–288
  and behavioral "impostors," 244–253
  componential model of, 280–284, 286–288
  and the development of folk biology, 146–148, 149, 155

evolution of, 239, 242–244, 245–246, 248, 250, 252, 253
imitative generalization as indicator of, 266–269, 270
and innateness (*see* innateness and theory of mind)
and language, 282, 284–288
as a modular integration mechanism (*see* modularity, massive, and theory of mind as an integration mechanism)
neural substrates for, 282
and neurodevelopmental disorders, 18, 272, 276–284, 286–288
and nonhuman primates, 242–244, 246
and parent-offspring conflict (*see* parental investment and parent-offspring conflict, and the development of social understanding)
and preverbal infants, 239–240, 242, 244–253, 254–271, 276
problems in establishing presence of in infants and animals, 254, 257–258, 269–271
and the reinterpretation hypothesis, 243–244
and Williams syndrome (WMS), 278–280, 283–284, 286–288
Thornton, R., 179
Tomasello, M., 254, 255–256, 270, 285
Tooby, J., 18 54n1, 77, 114, 120, 292
topographic maps, 29–32, 167
Torguud, 204
totemism, 78
travelling salesman problem, 111n6, 113
Trivers, R., 240, 241
trolley dilemma, 344–346, 347, 351, 359, 360–362. *See also* doctrine of double effect; personal/impersonal distinction
Tsivkin, S., 221, 227–228, 230–232
Turner syndrome, 272
Turing, A., 68, 153

ultimatum game, 348–349
universal grammar, 17, 58, 157, 175–177, 178–181, 183, 356. *See also* language acquisition; universal grammar, overspecified versus underspecified views of
  comparison with cryptography, 172–173
  and human biology, 176–177, 189

principles and parameters approach to, 158
universal grammar, overspecified versus underspecified views of, 17, 156, 157–159
 and the appeal of underdeterminism, 159–161
 and evolutionary concerns, 159–161, 170–174
 and the head directionality parameter (HDP), 161–162, 165–166
 and parsimony, 156, 159–161, 166–169, 173
 and phonological development, 158–159
 and the purpose of language, 170–173
 and the style of mental representation, 166–167, 173
 and the target of agreement parameter (TAP), 163–166
universal moral grammar, 351, 356, 358–364. See also moral psychology, linguistic analogy for
universal quantifier, 186, 193–194, 195–196, 208

vagueness, 224
"verb second" phenomenon, 163–164
vertical drops, innate avoidance of in infants, 57–58
Vezo, 204
visual perception, impossibility of, 40–42
visual system, 6n5, 16, 28, 146, 223n7
 and assumption of single overhead light source, 46–48
 Bayesian models of, 34, 40, 43–50, 51–52
 and coincidence avoidance, 42–43
 development of, 29–33, 50–51, 292
 and face perception, 51
 modularity of, 36, 48, 52, 58
 primate, 59
 subsystems of, 42
 and unconscious inference, 42–43, 44–45

Walk, R., 57–58
Wason selection task, 57n5
Waxman, S., 199–200
Weber's law, 227
Wellman, H., 256, 281n1
Whalen, J., 220
Wiesel, T., 50
Williams, G., 141
Williams syndrome (WMS), 18, 130, 273, 275–276, 277
 causes of, 278
 and language, 278–279, 280, 286–288
 and theory of mind, 278–280, 283–284, 286–288
Wilson, D., 62
Wilson, M., 297–298
Woodward, A., 256–257, 258, 265, 266
word processors, 166–167, 168
World War II., 171
Wynn, K., 79, 227, 229

Xu, F., 219–220, 234

Yanomamo, 301
Yerkes, A., 321
Yerkes, R., 321
Yoruba, 170
Yukatek Maya, 147